W9-CGX-571

INSURANCE
STATISTICS
YEARBOOK
1990-1997

ANNUAIRE
DES STATISTIQUES
D'ASSURANCE

Université d'Ottawa
BIBLIOTHEQUES

LIBRARIES
University of Ottawa

ORGANISATION FOR ECONOMIC CO-OPERATION AND DEVELOPMENT
ORGANISATION DE COOPÉRATION ET DE DÉVELOPPEMENT ÉCONOMIQUES

ORGANISATION FOR ECONOMIC CO-OPERATION AND DEVELOPMENT

Pursuant to Article 1 of the Convention signed in Paris on 14th December 1960, and which came into force on 30th September 1961, the Organisation for Economic Co-operation and Development (OECD) shall promote policies designed:

- to achieve the highest sustainable economic growth and employment and a rising standard of living in Member countries, while maintaining financial stability, and thus to contribute to the development of the world economy;
- to contribute to sound economic expansion in Member as well as non-member countries in the process of economic development; and
- to contribute to the expansion of world trade on a multilateral, non-discriminatory basis in accordance with international obligations.

The original Member countries of the OECD are Austria, Belgium, Canada, Denmark, France, Germany, Greece, Iceland, Ireland, Italy, Luxembourg, the Netherlands, Norway, Portugal, Spain, Sweden, Switzerland, Turkey, the United Kingdom and the United States. The following countries became Members subsequently through accession at the dates indicated hereafter: Japan (28th April 1964), Finland (28th January 1969), Australia (7th June 1971), New Zealand (29th May 1973), Mexico (18th May 1994), the Czech Republic (21st December 1995), Hungary (7th May 1996), Poland (22nd November 1996) and Korea (12th December 1996). The Commission of the European Communities takes part in the work of the OECD (Article 13 of the OECD Convention).

© OECD 1999

Permission to reproduce a portion of this work for non-commercial purposes or classroom use should be obtained through the Centre français d'exploitation du droit de copie (CFC), 20, rue des Grands-Augustins, 75006 Paris, France, Tel. (33-1) 44 07 47 70, Fax (33-1) 46 34 67 19, for every country except the United States. In the United States permission should be obtained through the Copyright Clearance Center, Customer Service, (508)750-8400, 222 Rosewood Drive, Danvers, MA 01923 USA, or CCC Online: http://www.copyright.com/. All other applications for permission to reproduce or translate all or part of this book should be made to OECD Publications, 2, rue André-Pascal, 75775 Paris Cedex 16, France.

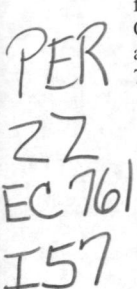

PER
ZZ
EC 761
I57

ORGANISATION DE COOPÉRATION ET DE DÉVELOPPEMENT ÉCONOMIQUES

En vertu de l'article 1er de la Convention signée le 14 décembre 1960, à Paris, et entrée en vigueur le 30 septembre 1961, l'Organisation de Coopération et de Développement Économiques (OCDE) a pour objectif de promouvoir des politiques visant :

- à réaliser la plus forte expansion de l'économie et de l'emploi et une progression du niveau de vie dans les pays Membres, tout en maintenant la stabilité financière, et à contribuer ainsi au développement de l'économie mondiale ;
- à contribuer à une saine expansion économique dans les pays Membres, ainsi que les pays non membres, en voie de développement économique ;
- à contribuer à l'expansion du commerce mondial sur une base multilatérale et non discriminatoire conformément aux obligations internationales.

Les pays Membres originaires de l'OCDE sont : l'Allemagne, l'Autriche, la Belgique, le Canada, le Danemark, l'Espagne, les États-Unis, la France, la Grèce, l'Irlande, l'Islande, l'Italie, le Luxembourg, la Norvège, les Pays-Bas, le Portugal, le Royaume-Uni, la Suède, la Suisse et la Turquie. Les pays suivants sont ultérieurement devenus Membres par adhésion aux dates indiquées ci-après : le Japon (28 avril 1964), la Finlande (28 janvier 1969), l'Australie (7 juin 1971), la Nouvelle-Zélande (29 mai 1973), le Mexique (18 mai 1994), la République tchèque (21 décembre 1995), la Hongrie (7 mai 1996), la Pologne (22 novembre 1996) et la Corée (12 décembre 1996). La Commission des Communautés européennes participe aux travaux de l'OCDE (article 13 de la Convention de l'OCDE).

© OCDE 1999

Les permissions de reproduction partielle à usage non commercial ou destinée à une formation doivent être adressées au Centre français d'exploitation du droit de copie (CFC), 20, rue des Grands-Augustins, 75006 Paris, France, Tél. (33-1) 44 07 47 70, Fax (33-1) 46 34 67 19, pour tous les pays à l'exception des États-Unis. Aux États-Unis, l'autorisation doit être obtenue du Copyright Clearance Center, Service Client, (508)750-8400, 222 Rosewood Drive, Danvers, MA 01923 USA, or CCC Online: http://www.copyright.com/. Toute autre demande d'autorisation de reproduction ou de traduction totale ou partielle de cette publication doit être adressée aux Éditions de l'OCDE, 2, rue André-Pascal, 75775 Paris Cedex 16, France.

FOREWORD

This publication, the eighth in a series which is updated annually, contains time series of insurance statistics. It was compiled as part of the work by the OECD Insurance Committee and, more particularly, its Task Force on Insurance Statistics. It contains data collected from official bodies in OECD Member countries as well as the Slovak Republic which has an observer status at the OECD Insurance Committee, on the number of insurance companies and employees, insurance premiums and investments by insurance companies. Meanwhile, the scope of data collection has been expanded to include gross claims payments, gross operating expenses and commissions. The data, which are also available on diskette, relate to the period 1990-1997 and are broken down under numerous sub-headings.

This compilation has been prepared by the Directorate for Financial, Fiscal and Enterprise Affairs. However, it was made possible only by the close co-operation between the OECD and the various national bodies which collect data on insurance, and the work of the Task Force on Insurance Statistics. This work is published under the responsibility of the Secretary General of the OECD.

AVANT PROPOS

Cette publication, la huitième d'une série qui est mise à jour annuellement, contient des données chronologiques sur les statistiques d'assurance. Elle s'inscrit dans le cadre des travaux du Comité des assurances de l'OCDE, et plus particulièrement de son Groupe de réflexion sur les statistiques d'assurance. Elle contient des données collectées auprès des organismes officiels des pays Membres de l'OCDE ainsi que de la République slovaque qui a le statut d'observateur auprès du Comité des assurances de l'OCDE, sur le nombre de compagnies d'assurance et d'employés, les primes d'assurance et les investissements des compagnies d'assurance. Entre-temps, le champ de la collecte de données a été étendu et couvre les paiements bruts de sinistres, les dépenses brutes d'exploitation et les commissions. Ces données, également disponibles sous forme de disquettes, portent sur la période 1990-1997 et sont détaillées en nombreuses sous-rubriques.

Cette publication a été préparée par la Direction des affaires financières, fiscales et des entreprises. Cependant elle n'a pu être réalisée que grâce à une étroite coopération entre l'OCDE et les diverses administrations nationales chargées de la collecte des données statistiques en matière d'assurance, ainsi que grâce aux travaux du Groupe de réflexion sur les statistiques d'assurance. Elle est publiée sous la responsabilité du Secrétaire Général de l'OCDE.

TABLE OF CONTENTS

TABLE DES MATIÈRES

INTRODUCTION

In November 1982, the OECD Insurance Committee constituted the Working Group on insurance statistics. Since then, the Working Group, which has been transformed in 1999 into the Task Force, has collected and analysed data on various insurance statistics, as well as discussed relevant methodologies.

As the qualitative and quantitative content of the statistical database has improved considerably over time, the Committee decided in November 1992 to issue a publication that would make the considerable body of information already collected available to the public at large. This publication is the eighth in a series which is updated annually.

This publication has the following three characteristics;

1. It covers major official insurance data from 1990 to 1997, obtained from all the governments of OECD countries as well as the Slovak Republic which has an observer status at the OECD Insurance Committee. (Exceptionally, data for the Czech Republic, Hungary, Korea, Mexico and Poland are available respectively since 1993, 1991, 1994, 1992 and 1993 only). The publication contains not only general information on insurance activities (number of companies, number of employees, gross premiums, net premiums etc.) but also data related to major trends of the international insurance industry such as the market share by foreign companies in each country, business written abroad, premiums in terms of risk destination (foreign or domestic risks), foreign and domestic investments. Meanwhile, the scope of data collection has been expanded to include gross claims payments, gross operating expenses and commissions.

2. In order to contribute to a better understanding of the insurance market, important insurance activity indicators (OECD market share, penetration, density, premiums per employee...) are included in the comparative tables. Some of these indicators are also shown in the graphs. With these indicators, the characteristics of insurance market can be more clearly perceived, in particular, in relation to national economic conditions.

3. In the comparative tables, a significant effort has been made to achieve comparability among OECD countries. Definitions, classifications, calculation methods, and units have been standardised as far as possible.

The publication has been prepared by the Directorate for Financial, Fiscal and Enterprises Affairs and is issued under the responsibility of the Secretary General of the Organisation. However, the collaboration with national administrations was essential to its achievement.

THE CONTENTS OF THE PUBLICATION

This publication consists of three main parts; comparative tables by indicators, statistical tables by country and notes and definitions relating to these tables.

Part I: Comparative Tables by Indicators

This part consists of tables by indicators, which reflect the most significant characteristics of the OECD insurance market. In most cases, the tables contain data of all OECD countries as well as aggregated "OECD", "EU15" (the 15 member countries of the European Union in 1995) and "NAFTA" data from 1990 to 1997, for the following categories: life insurance, non-life insurance and total. The premiums amounts are converted from national currencies into US dollar. Exchange rates used are an average for the reference year. Some of these indicators are also shown in the graphs.

1.   Total Gross Premiums

Gross premium, which represents total insurance premium written in the reporting country, is a major indicator of the importance of insurance industry in the economy of each country.

2.   Market Share in the OECD (Direct Gross Premiums Basis)

This indicator measures the importance of national insurance market of each OECD country as compared to the whole OECD insurance market.

3.   Density of Insurance Industry

This indicator is calculated by dividing direct gross premiums by the population and represents the average insurance spending per capita in a given country.

4.   Penetration of Insurance Industry

This is the ratio of direct gross premiums to Gross Domestic Product (GDP), which represents the relative importance of the insurance industry in the domestic economy.

5.   Life Insurance Share

This is the ratio of gross life insurance premium to total gross premium, which measures the relative importance of life insurance as compared to non-life insurance.

6.   Premiums per Employee

This indicator of the relative efficiency of a national insurance industry is calculated by dividing the direct gross premiums by the number of employees in insurance companies.

7.   Retention Ratio

This is the ratio of net written premiums to total gross premiums. This ratio represents the proportion of retained business and thus, indirectly, the importance of reinsurance for domestic insurance companies.

8.   Ratio of Reinsurance Accepted

This is calculated by dividing reinsurance accepted by total gross premiums and provides an indication of the significance of reinsurance accepted in the national insurance market.

9.   Foreign Companies' Market Share in the Domestic Market

This figure describes the importance of foreign companies in the domestic insurance market and is measured through the following indicators :
a) Market share of "foreign-controlled companies" and "branches and agencies of foreign companies" in "total gross premiums".
b) Market share of "branches and agencies of foreign companies" in "total gross premiums".

Part II: Statistical tables by country

In this part, the main insurance statistics are presented through separate tables for each country following the order mentioned in the "complete list of items" reproduced in Part III. The premiums and the investment amounts are described in millions of the national currency unit. Figures refer to the calendar year. If all data concerning one line are not available, the line is deleted. The line is also deleted if all data are equal to "0" and if this is made obvious by reading other lines of the tables.

The tables of each country contain the following six parts;

(A and B)	General information on number of insurance companies and employees within the sector.
(C)	Business written in the reporting country on a gross and net premium basis. It contains a breakdown between domestic companies, foreign-controlled companies and branches and agencies of foreign companies.
(D)	Breakdown of net premiums written in the reporting country in terms of domestic risks and foreign risks, thus providing an indicator of direct cross-border operations of insurance business.
(E)	Premiums written abroad classified by subsidiaries, branches and agencies of domestic companies.
(F)	Outstanding investment by direct insurance companies, classified by investment category, by the companies' nationality and by its destination (domestic or foreign).
(G)	Breakdown of non-life insurance premiums by main non-life classification.
(H-J)	Gross claims payments, gross operating expenses and commissions in the reporting country, containing a breakdown between domestic companies, foreign-controlled companies and branches and agencies of foreign companies.

11

Part III: Definitions and Notes

This part covers the definitions of the main items used in the publication and the explanatory notes relating to the statistical tables.

1.   Common Definitions and Notes

This part includes definitions and notes that are common to all statistical tables.

2.   Complete List of Items Contained in Tables by Country

This list covers all items in tables by country and helps to understand which items are deleted in the tables of each country.

3.   Definitions and Notes by Country

This part is made of definitions and notes related only to the tables by country. After a paragraph on possible "General Remarks" and a paragraph on "Definition of Foreign Controlled Companies" this part follows the order of the sections of tables by country.

4.   Definitions of Classes of Non-life Insurance

This includes definitions of categories of non-life insurance, which detail the content of classes listed in section G "Others: breakdown of non-life premiums" of the tables by country.

DATA SOURCE

All the data in the statistical tables of each country have been reported by the relevant national insurance authorities. Regarding comparative tables of indicators, the data are mainly drawn from the tables by country mentioned above. The economic data on exchange rates and population are from the OECD MAIN ECONOMIC INDICATORS publication. The data on GDP come from NATIONAL ACCOUNTS OF OECD COUNTRIES publication.

ABBREVIATIONS

The following abbreviations are used:

" - - ": not available.

INTRODUCTION

En novembre 1982, le Comité des assurances de l'OCDE a constitué un Groupe de Travail sur les statistiques. Depuis, le Groupe de travail, qui a été transformé en 1999 en groupe de réflexion, s'est consacré à la collecte et à l'analyse de données statistiques sur différents aspects de l'assurance, et à la discussion des méthodologies à adopter.

Face aux considérables améliorations, d'ordre tant qualitatif que quantitatif de la base de données statistiques, le Comité a décidé en novembre 1992 de diffuser une publication qui mettrait les très nombreuses informations déjà rassemblées à la disposition du grand public. Cette publication est la huitième d'une nouvelle série qui sera mise à jour annuellement.

Cette publication possède les trois caractères suivants ;

1. Elle contient des données officielles majeures des assurances de 1990 à 1997, transmises par tous les gouvernements des pays de l'OCDE ainsi que par la République slovaque qui a le statut d'observateur auprès du Comité des assurances de l'OCDE. (Exceptionnellement, les données de la Corée, de la Hongrie, du Mexique, de la Pologne, de la République tchèque ne sont respectivement disponibles que depuis 1994, 1991, 1992, 1993 et 1993). La publication n'inclut pas seulement les informations générales sur les activités des assurances (nombre d'entreprises, effectifs, primes brutes, primes nettes...), mais également des indicateurs des grandes tendances du marché international de l'assurance comme les parts de marché des entreprises étrangères dans chacun des pays de l'OCDE, les opérations à l'étranger, la ventilation des primes en fonction de la destination des risques (risques dans le pays ou risques à l'étranger), les investissements dans le pays et à l'étranger. Entre-temps, le champ de la collecte de données a été étendu et couvre les paiements bruts de sinistres, les dépenses brutes d'exploitation et les commissions.

2. Pour contribuer à une meilleure compréhension du marché de l'assurance, les indicateurs importants des activités d'assurances (parts de marché dans les pays de l'OCDE, pénétration, densité, primes par employé ...) sont inclus dans les tableaux comparatifs. Certains de ces indicateurs sont également représentés par des graphiques. Grâce à ces indicateurs, les caractéristiques du marché de l'assurance peuvent être plus clairement perçues, en particulier par rapport aux conditions économiques nationales.

3. Dans les tableaux comparatifs, un effort important a été réalisé pour assurer la comparabilité des données entre les pays de l'OCDE. Définitions, classifications, modes de calcul et unités ont été standardisés autant que possible.

La publication a été préparée par la Direction des affaires financières, fiscales et des entreprises, et est diffusée sous la responsabilité du Secrétaire général de l'OCDE. Cependant, la collaboration avec les administrations nationales a été essentielle pour la réaliser.

LE CONTENU DE LA PUBLICATION

Cette publication se compose de trois parties principales ; tableaux comparatifs par indicateurs, tableaux statistiques par pays et notes et définitions relatives à ces tableaux.

Partie I : Tableaux comparatifs par indicateurs

Cette partie se compose de tableaux d'indicateurs qui reflètent les caractéristiques les plus significatives du marché de l'assurance de l'OCDE. Le plus souvent, les tableaux contiennent les données de tous les pays de l'OCDE, ainsi que les données "OCDE", "UE15" (les 15 pays membres de l'Union Européenne en 1995) et "ALENA"de 1990 à 1997, pour les catégories suivantes : assurance-vie, assurance non-vie et total des assurances. Les montants des primes sont convertis à partir de la monnaie nationale en dollar US. Les taux de change utilisés sont une moyenne sur l'année à laquelle il est fait référence. Certains de ces indicateurs sont également représentés par des graphiques.

1.   Total des primes brutes

Les primes brutes, qui représentent les primes totales des assurances émises dans le pays déclarant, sont un indicateur essentiel de l'importance de l'industrie de l'assurance dans chaque pays.

2.   Part de marché dans l'OCDE (sur la base des primes brutes directes)

Cet indicateur représente l'importance relative de l'assurance de chacun des pays de l'OCDE par rapport au marché de l'assurance dans l'ensemble de la zone de l'OCDE.

3.   Densité de l'industrie de l'assurance

Cet indicateur est calculé en divisant les primes brutes directes par la population nationale ; il représente les dépenses moyennes d'assurance par tête dans le pays considéré.

4.   Pénétration de l'industrie de l'assurance

C'est le rapport des primes brutes directes d'assurances sur le Produit Intérieur Brut (PIB) ; il représente l'importance de l'industrie de l'assurance dans l'économie nationale.

5.   Parts de l'assurance-vie

C'est le rapport des primes brutes d'assurance-vie sur les primes brutes totales ; il mesure l'importance relative de l'assurance-vie par rapport à l'assurance non-vie et vice-versa.

6.   Primes par employé

Cet indicateur de l'efficacité des effectifs dans l'industrie de l'assurance est calculé en faisant le rapport des primes brutes directes sur le nombre d'employés des entreprises d'assurances.

7.   Taux de rétention

C'est le rapport entre les primes nettes émises et le total des primes brutes. Il représente la proportion des affaires retenues, et donc indirectement, l'importance de la réassurance pour les entreprises d'assurances nationales.

8.   Taux de réassurance acceptée

C'est le rapport des réassurances acceptées sur les primes brutes totales ; il rend compte de l'importance de la réassurance acceptée dans le marché national des assurances.

9.   Part du marché national détenue par les entreprises étrangères.

Elle mesure l'importance des entreprises étrangères dans le marché national des assureurs en fonction des indicateurs suivants :

a) Part de marché des "entreprises sous contrôle étranger" et "succursales et agences d'entreprises étrangères" dans le "total des primes brutes".

b) Part de marché des "succursales et agences d'entreprises étrangères" dans le "total des primes brutes".

Partie II: Tableaux statistiques par pays

Dans cette partie, les principales statistiques d'assurances sont présentées dans des tableaux séparés pour chaque pays suivant l'ordre indiqué dans la "liste complète de points" reproduite dans la partie III. Le montant des primes et des placements est inscrit en millions dans la monnaie nationale. Les chiffres correspondent à l'année civile. Si toutes les données d'une ligne sont "non disponibles", la ligne est supprimée. Elle l'est également si toutes les données sont égales à "0" et que ce résultat apparaît clairement à la lecture d'autres lignes.

Les tableaux par pays contiennent les six parties suivantes :

(A et B)   Informations générales sur le nombre de compagnics d'assurances et le nombre d'employés.

(C)   Chiffres concernant les opérations conclues dans le pays déclarant, sur la base des primes brutes et nettes. On distingue les entreprises nationales, les entreprises sous contrôle étranger et les agences et succursales d'entreprises étrangères.

(D)   Ventilation des primes nettes émises dans le pays déclarant : risques nationaux et étrangers, fournissant un indicateur des opérations transfrontières des compagnies d'assurances.

(E) Primes émises à l'étranger par des filiales, succursales et agences d'entreprises nationales.

(F) Encours des placements des entreprises d'assurances directes dans le pays déclarant, classés par catégorie de placements, par nationalité des entreprises, ainsi que par destination des placements (dans le pays ou à l'étranger).

(G) Ventilation des primes d'assurances non-vie par catégories principales d'assurances non-vie.

(H-J) Paiements bruts des sinistres, dépenses brutes d'exploitation et commissions dans le pays déclarant, avec une ventilation entre les entreprises nationales, les entreprises sous contrôle étranger et les succursales et agences d'entreprises étrangères.

Partie III: Définitions et notes

Cette partie contient les définitions des points principaux utilisés dans la publication et les notes relatives aux tableaux statistiques.

1. Définitions et notes communes

Cette partie inclut les définitions et notes communes à tous les tableaux statistiques.

2. Liste complète des points contenus dans les tableaux par pays

Cette liste couvre tous les points des tableaux par pays et permet d'identifier ceux qui ont été supprimés dans les tableaux de chaque pays.

3. Définitions et notes par pays

Cette partie se compose des définitions qui se rapportent uniquement aux tableaux par pays. Après un paragraphe contenant d'éventuelles "Remarques générales" et un paragraphe relatif à la "Définition d'entreprises sous contrôle étranger", cette partie suit l'ordre des sections des tableaux par pays.

4. Définitions relatives aux branches des assurances non-vie

Cette partie inclut les définitions des catégories d'assurance non-vie qui détaillent le contenu des branches dans la section G : "Autres : ventilation des primes non vie" des tableaux par pays.

SOURCES DES DONNÉES

Toutes les données des tableaux chronologiques statistiques par pays ont été fournies par les autorités d'assurances nationales compétentes.

Concernant les tableaux comparatifs chronologiques d'indicateurs, les données sont, en principe, extraites des tableaux par pays mentionnés ci-dessus. Les données économiques utilisées (taux de change, population) sont extraites de la publication de l'OCDE : PRINCIPAUX INDICATEURS ÉCONOMIQUES. Les données sur le PIB proviennent de la publication de l'OCDE : COMPTES NATIONAUX DES PAYS DE L'OCDE.

ABRÉVIATIONS

L'abréviation suivante a été utilisée :

" - -" : non-disponible.

PART I

PARTIE I

COMPARATIVE TABLES

TABLEAUX COMPARATIFS

Market share in OECD - Total / Part de marché dans l'OCDE - Total

1997

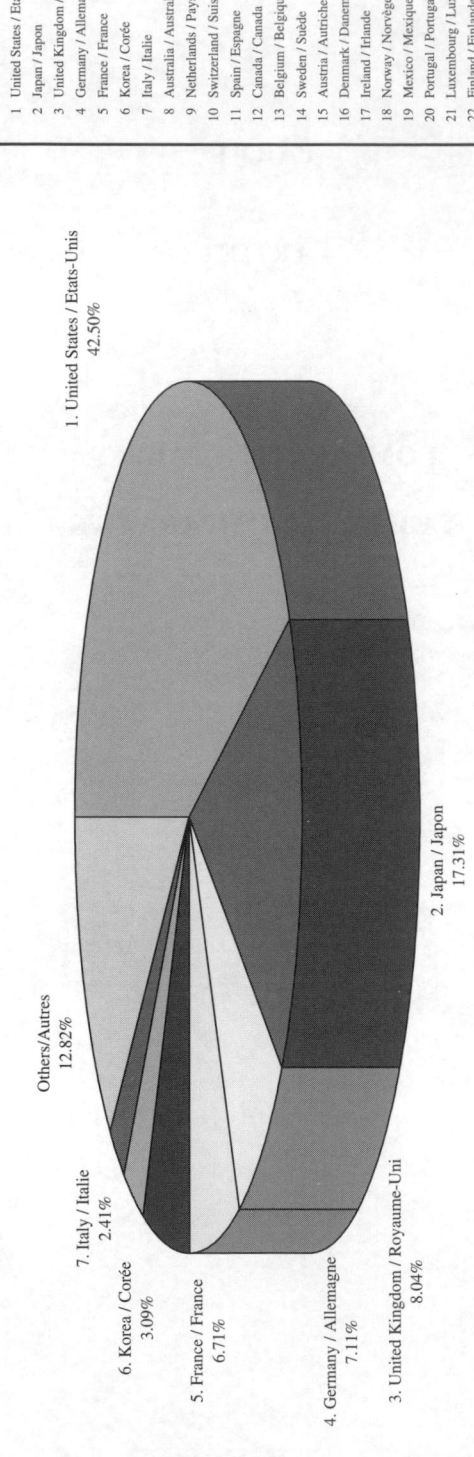

1. United States / Etats-Unis
42.50%

2. Japan / Japon
17.31%

3. United Kingdom / Royaume-Uni
8.04%

4. Germany / Allemagne
7.11%

5. France / France
6.71%

6. Korea / Corée
3.09%

7. Italy / Italie
2.41%

Others/Autres
12.82%

1	United States / Etats-Unis	42.50
2	Japan / Japon	17.31
3	United Kingdom / Royaume-Uni	8.04
4	Germany / Allemagne	7.11
5	France / France	6.71
6	Korea / Corée	3.09
7	Italy / Italie	2.41
8	Australia / Australie	1.84
9	Netherlands / Pays-Bas	1.74
10	Switzerland / Suisse	1.56
11	Spain / Espagne	1.41
12	Canada / Canada	1.34
13	Belgium / Belgique	0.72
14	Sweden / Suède	0.68
15	Austria / Autriche	0.57
16	Denmark / Danemark	0.56
17	Ireland / Irlande	0.39
18	Norway / Norvège	0.37
19	Mexico / Mexique	0.26
20	Portugal / Portugal	0.26
21	Luxembourg / Luxembourg	0.25
22	Finland / Finlande	0.23
23	Poland / Pologne	0.19
24	New Zealand / Nouvelle-Zélande	0.13
25	Greece / Grèce	0.11
26	Turkey / Turquie	0.10
27	Czech Republic / République Tchèque	0.08
28	Hungary / Hongrie	0.05
29	Iceland / Islande	0.01

Market share in OECD - Life / Part de marché dans l'OCDE - Vie

1997

1	United States / États-Unis	31.47
2	Japan / Japon	24.57
3	United Kingdom / Royaume-Uni	9.86
4	France / France	8.72
5	Germany - Allemagne	5.78
6	Korea / Corée	4.33
7	Italy / Italie	2.11
8	Australia / Australie	2.10
9	Switzerland / Suisse	2.09
10	Netherlands / Pays-Bas	1.86
11	Spain / Espagne	1.28
12	Canada / Canada	0.98
13	Sweden / Suède	0.83
14	Belgium / Belgique	0.69
15	Denmark / Danemark	0.65
16	Ireland / Irlande	0.48
17	Luxembourg / Luxembourg	0.43
18	Austria / Autriche	0.41
19	Norway / Norvège	0.35
20	Portugal / Portugal	0.23
21	Finland / Finlande	0.21
22	Mexico / Mexique	0.18
23	Greece / Grèce	0.10
24	Poland / Pologne	0.10
25	New Zealand / Nouvelle-Zélande	0.09
26	Czech Republic / République Tchèque	0.04
27	Hungary / Hongrie	0.03
28	Turkey / Turquie	0.03
29	Iceland / Islande	0.00

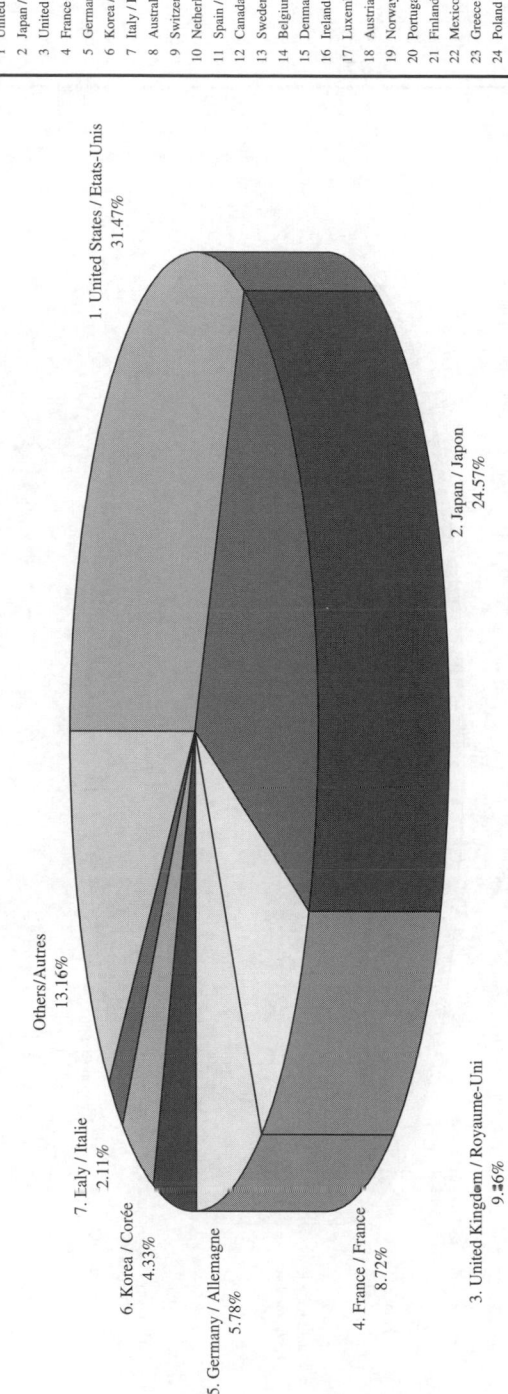

1. United States / États-Unis
31.47%

2. Japan / Japon
24.57%

Others/Autres
13.16%

7. Italy / Italie
2.11%

6. Korea / Corée
4.33%

5. Germany / Allemagne
5.78%

4. France / France
8.72%

3. United Kingdom / Royaume-Uni
9.86%

Market share in OECD - Non-Life / Part de marché dans l'OCDE - Non-Vie

1997

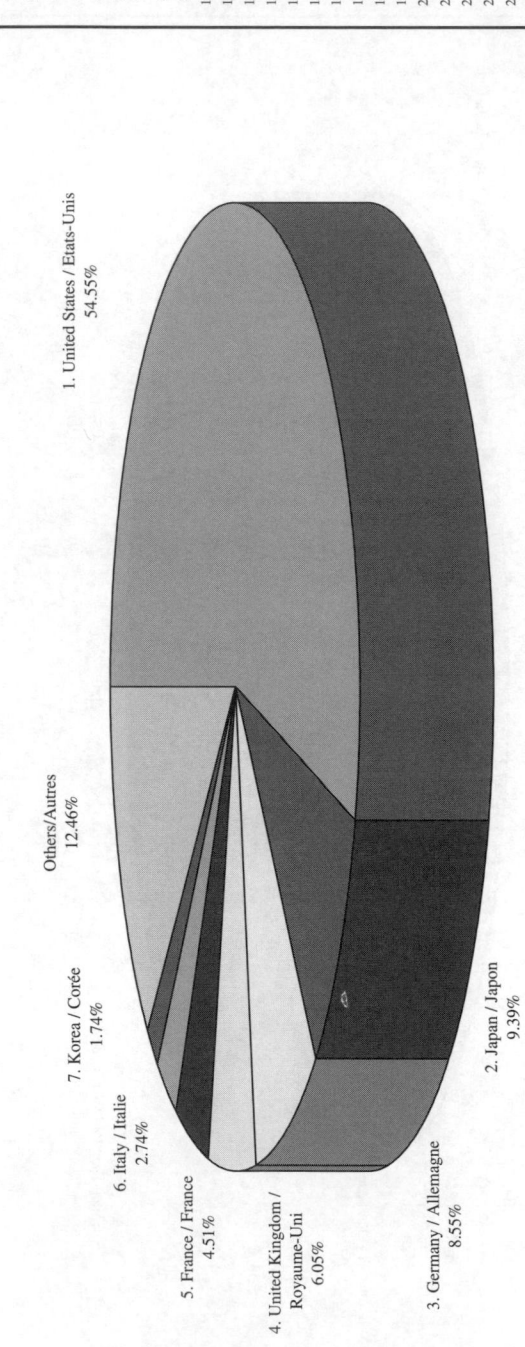

1. United States / Etats-Unis
54.55%

Others/Autres
12.46%

7. Korea / Corée
1.74%

6. Italy / Italie
2.74%

5. France / France
4.51%

4. United Kingdom /
Royaume-Uni
6.05%

3. Germany / Allemagne
8.55%

2. Japan / Japon
9.39%

1	United States / Etats-Unis	54.55
2	Japan / Japon	9.39
3	Germany / Allemagne	8.55
4	United Kingdom / Royaume-Uni	6.05
5	France / France	4.51
6	Italy / Italie	2.74
7	Korea / Corée	1.74
8	Canada / Canada	1.74
9	Netherlands / Pays-Bas	1.60
10	Australia / Australie	1.56
11	Spain / Espagne	1.55
12	Switzerland / Suisse	0.99
13	Belgium / Belgique	0.75
14	Austria / Autriche	0.74
15	Sweden / Suède	0.51
16	Denmark / Danemark	0.46
17	Norway / Norvège	0.39
18	Mexico / Mexique	0.34
19	Ireland / Irlande	0.29
20	Portugal / Portugal	0.29
21	Poland / Pologne	0.29
22	Finland / Finlande	0.24
23	New Zealand / Nouvelle-Zélande	0.18
24	Turkey / Turquie	0.17
25	Czech Republic / République Tchèque	0.12
26	Greece / Grèce	0.11
27	Hungary / Hongrie	0.08
28	Luxembourg / Luxembourg	0.05
29	Iceland / Islande	0.02

Premiums per capita - Total / Primes par tête - Total (1997)

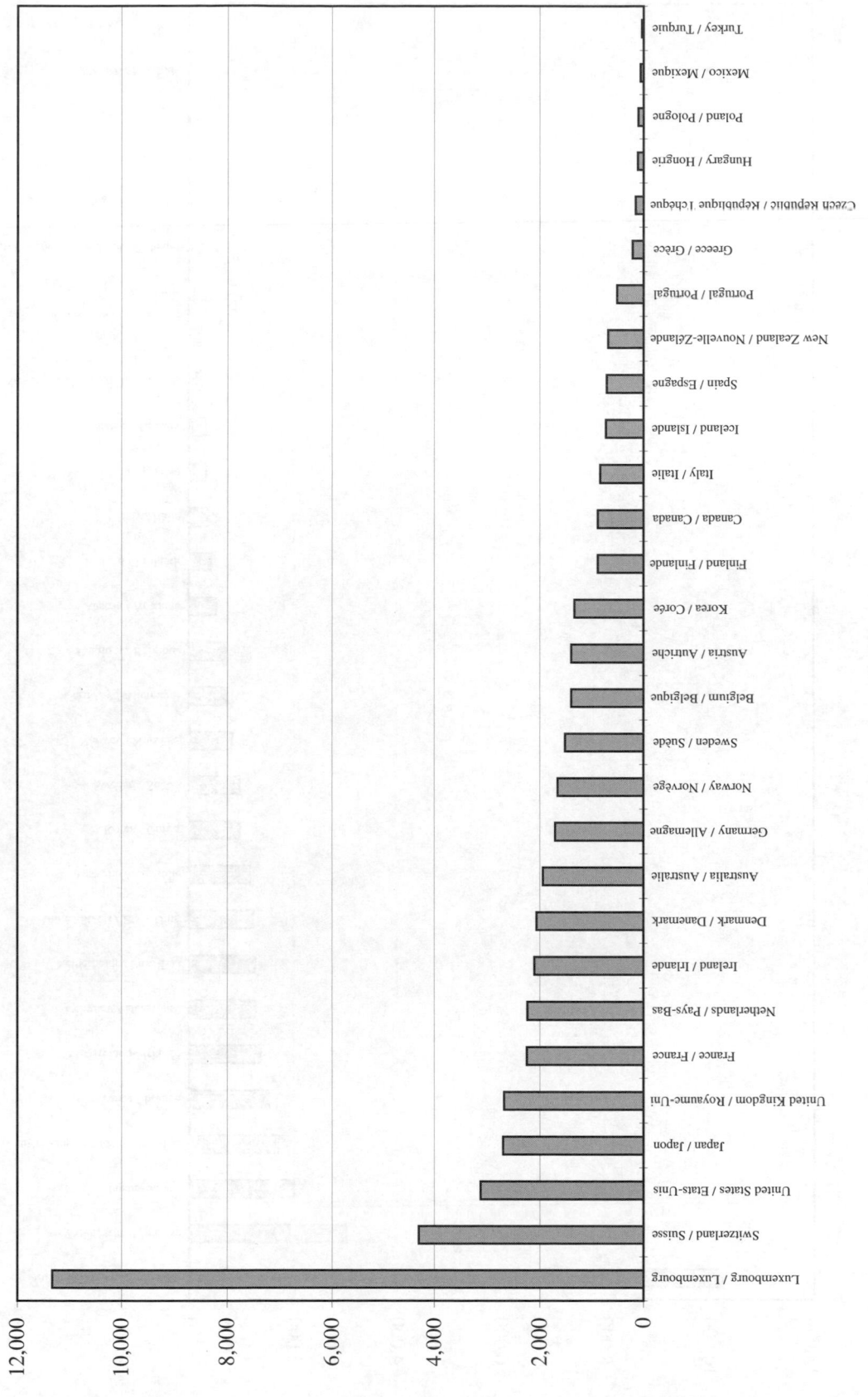

Premiums per capita - Life / Primes par tête - Vie (1997)

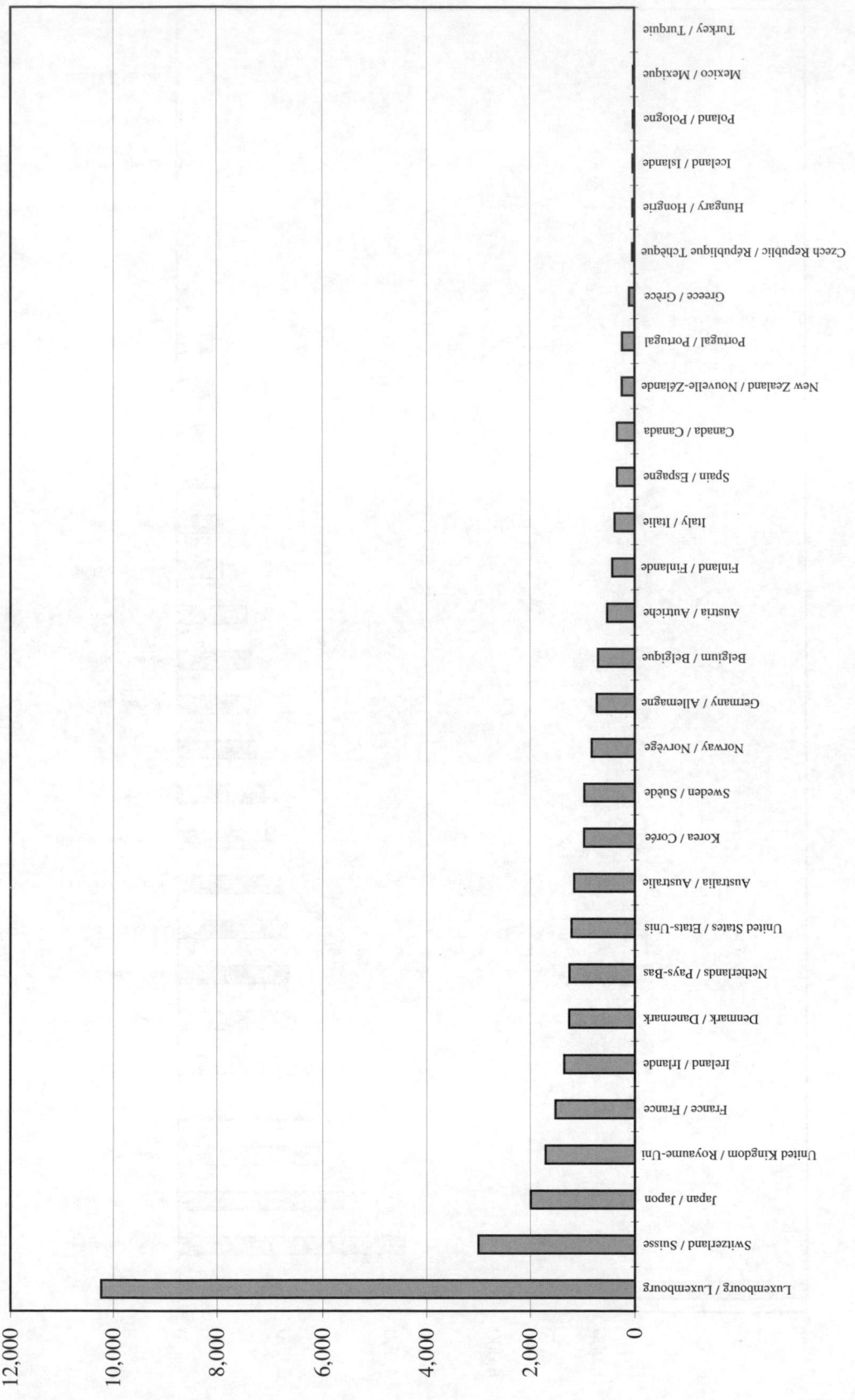

Premiums per capita - Non-Life / Primes par tête - Non-Vie (1997)

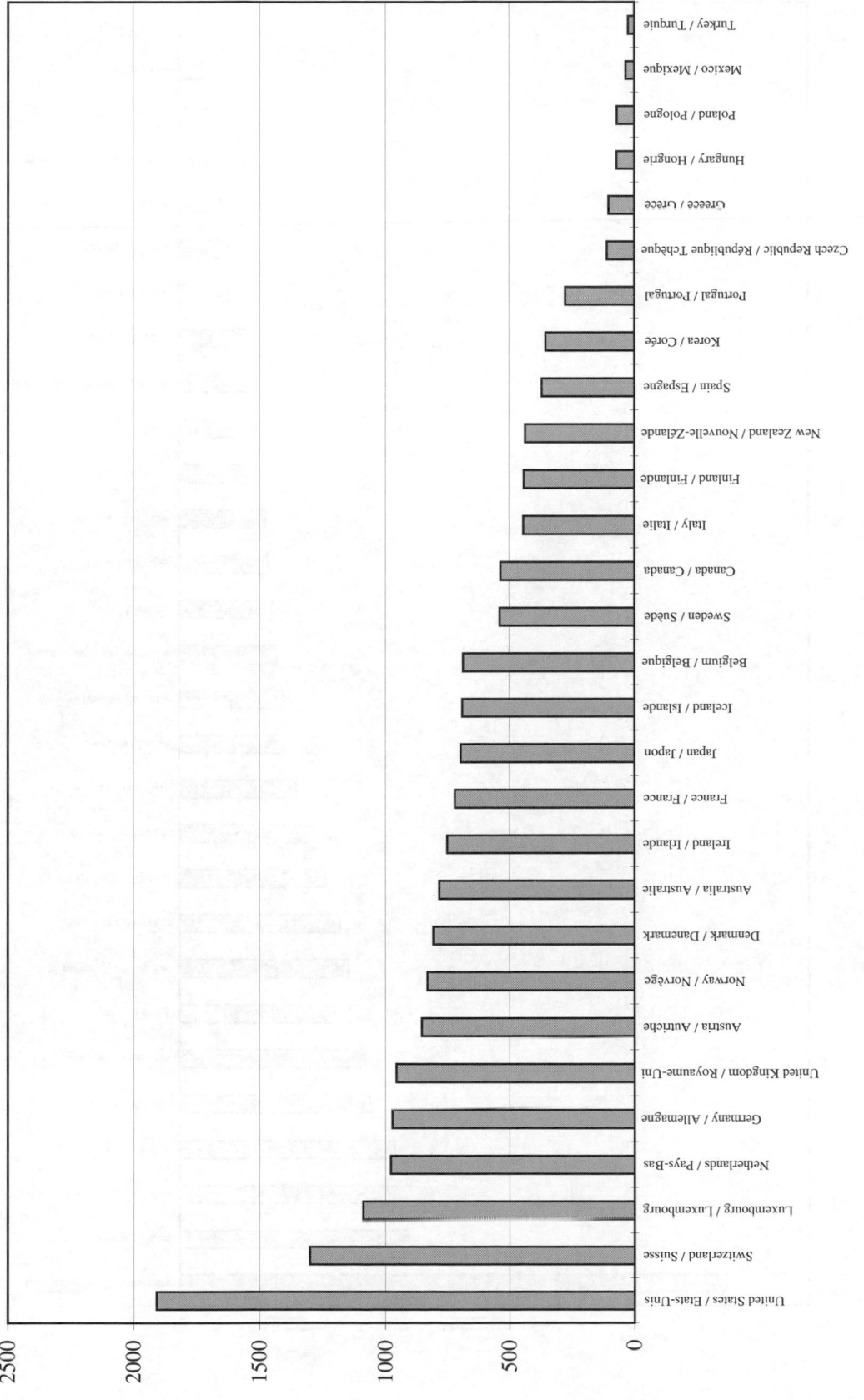

Premiums/GDP - Total / Primes/PIB - Total (1997)

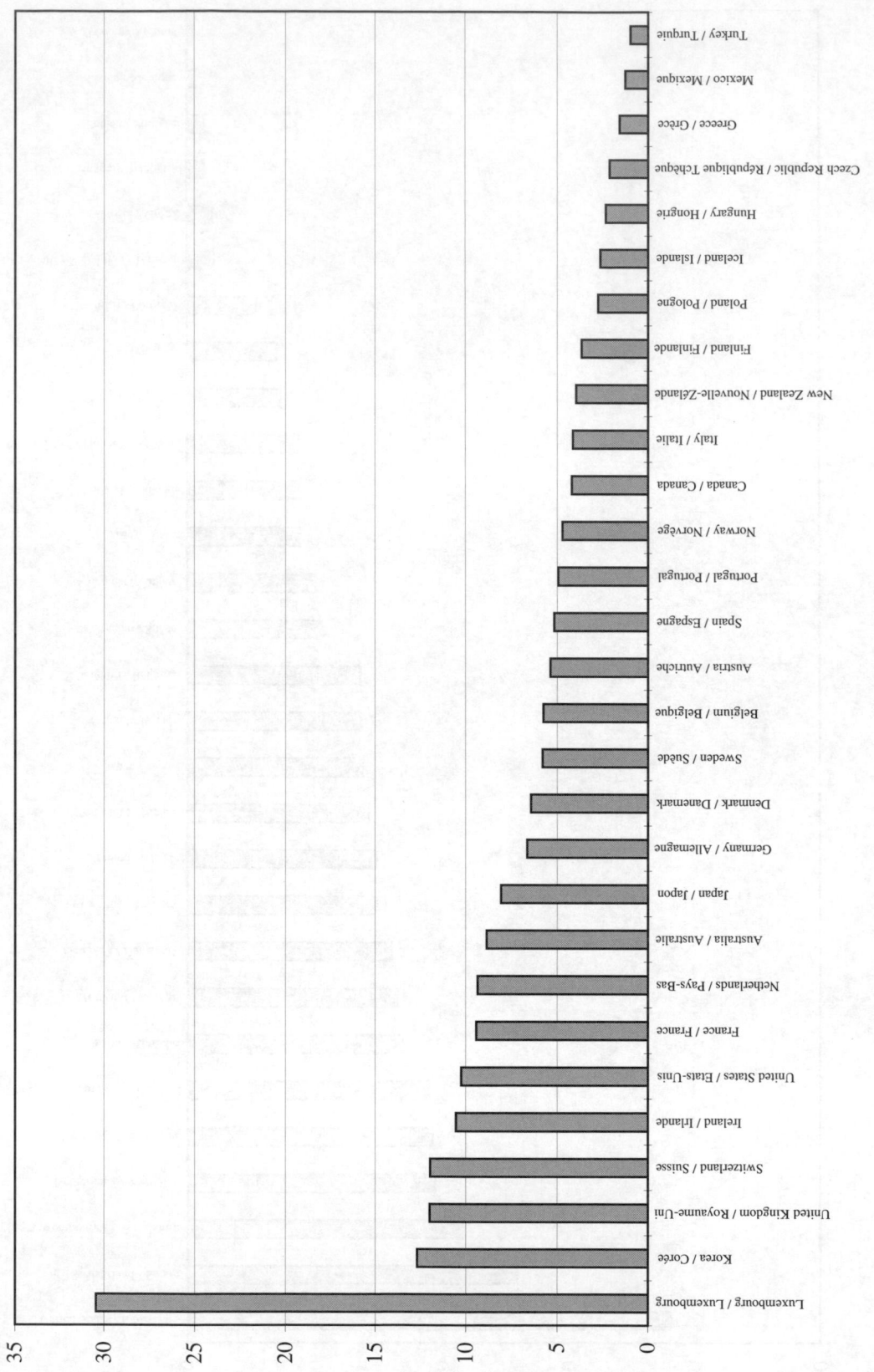

Premiums/GDP - Life / Primes/PIB - Vie (1997)

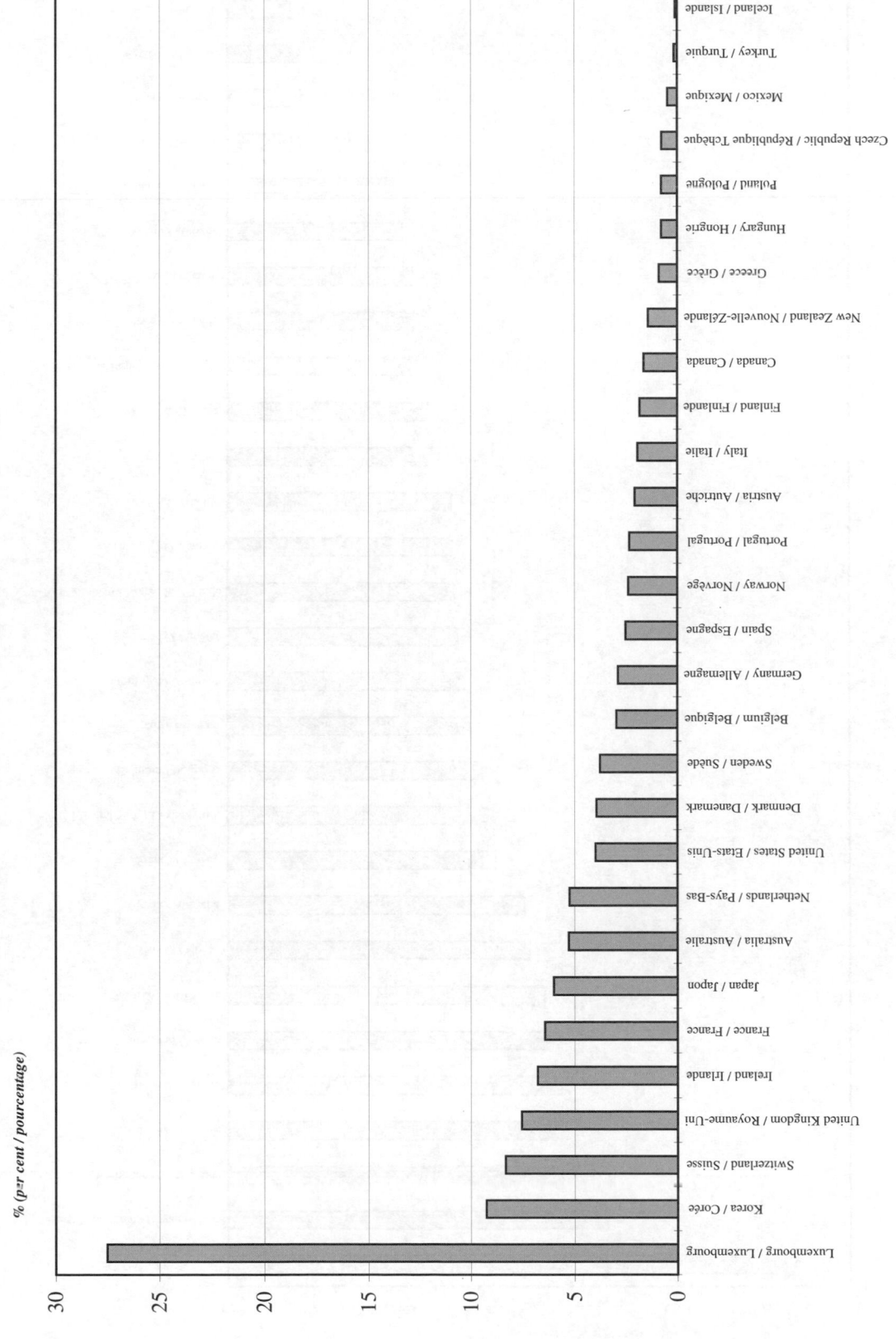

% (per cent / pourcentage)

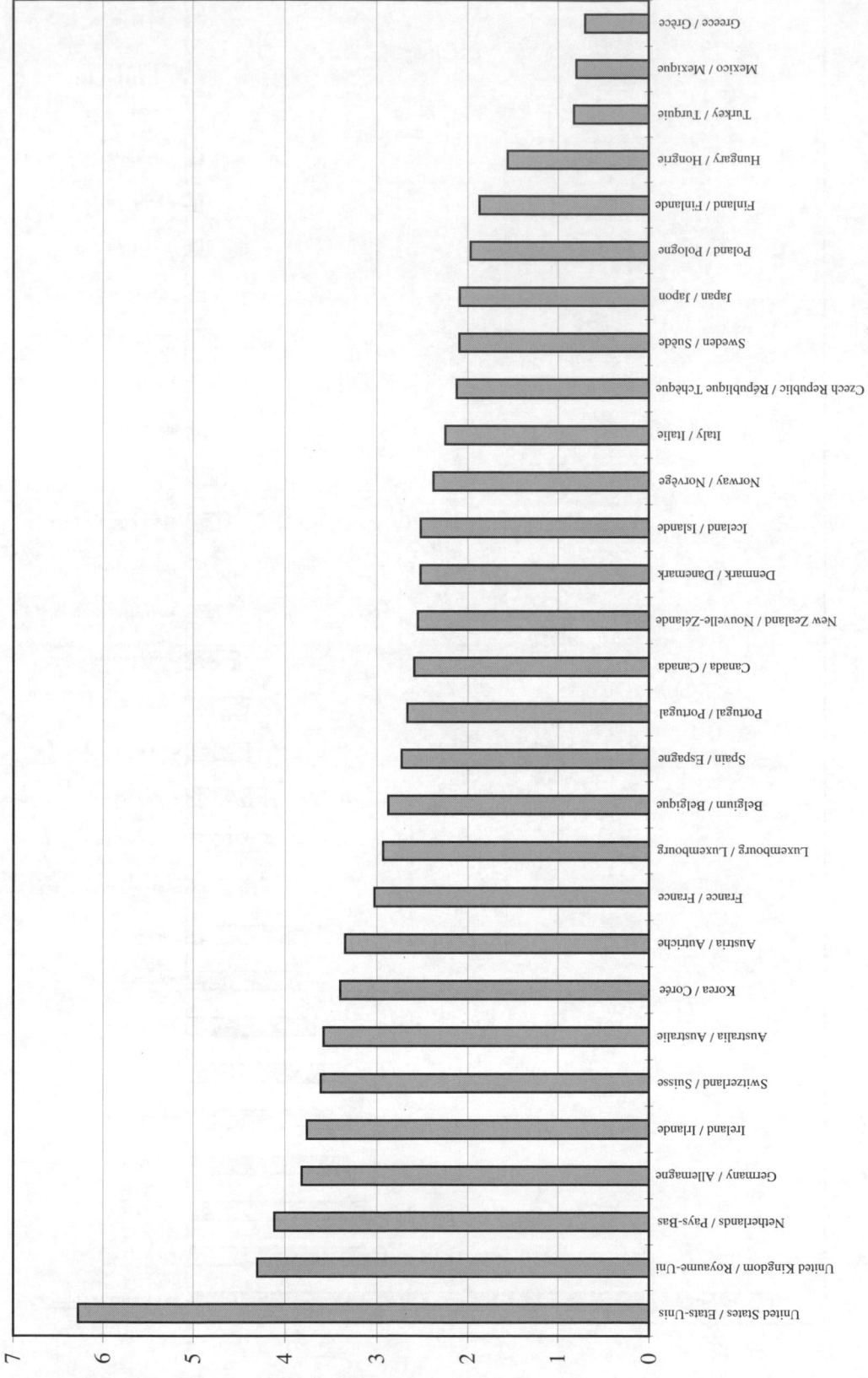

Premiums/GDP - Non-Life / Primes/PIB - Non-Vie (1997)

United States / Etats-Unis	
United Kingdom / Royaume-Uni	
Netherlands / Pays-Bas	
Germany / Allemagne	
Ireland / Irlande	
Switzerland / Suisse	
Australia / Australie	
Korea / Corée	
Austria / Autriche	
France / France	
Luxembourg / Luxembourg	
Belgium / Belgique	
Spain / Espagne	
Portugal / Portugal	
Canada / Canada	
New Zealand / Nouvelle-Zélande	
Denmark / Danemark	
Iceland / Islande	
Norway / Norvège	
Italy / Italie	
Czech Republic / République Tchèque	
Sweden / Suède	
Japan / Japon	
Poland / Pologne	
Finland / Finlande	
Hungary / Hongrie	
Turkey / Turquie	
Mexico / Mexique	
Greece / Grèce	

Life and non-life insurance / Part de l'assurance-vie et non-vie
(1997)

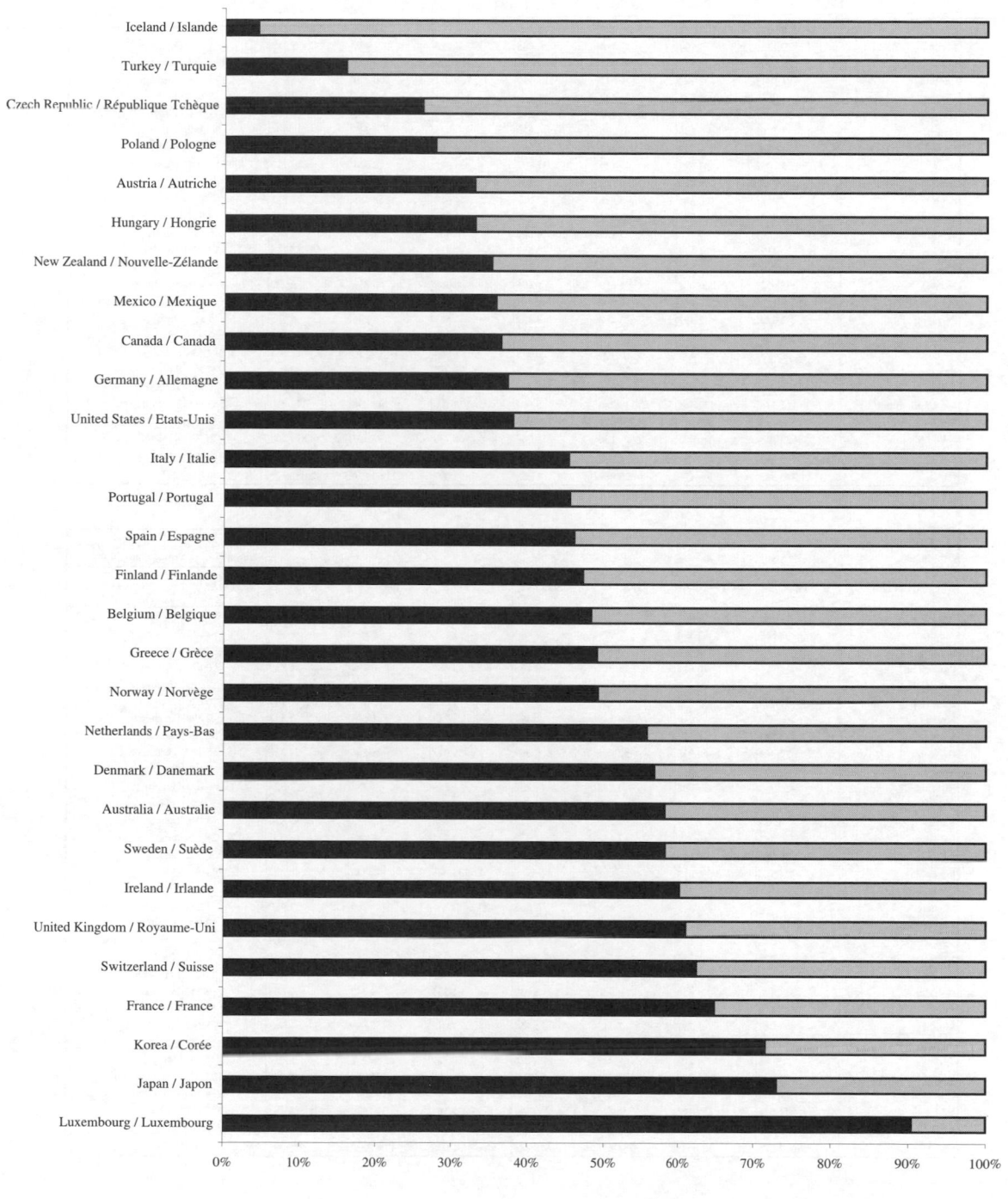

Life/Vie ■ Non-Life/Non-Vie

I. Total gross premiums / Primes brutes totales

I.1 Total /Total

Million U.S. $ / Millions de $ U.S.

COUNTRY	1990	1991	1992	1993	1994	1995	1996	1997	PAYS
Australia[1]	21 272	20 725	19 254	27 187	30 604	29 449	32 659	37 302	Australie[1]
Austria	8 540	8 837	10 341	11 024	12 120	14 240	16 013	12 844	Autriche
Belgium	9 695	10 203	11 594	11 378	12 349	15 458	15 813	14 743	Belgique
Canada	32 443	34 652	31 940	28 033	28 758	30 083	30 232	29 914	Canada
Czech Republic	..	..	..	788	1 031	1 273	1 515	1 513	République Tchèque
Denmark	6 862	7 051	8 317	8 109	9 758	11 376	12 332	11 700	Danemark
Finland	9 433	9 194	7 414	2 665	3 115	4 474	5 319	4 658	Finlande
France	78 390	83 358	99 451	107 304	119 249	142 123	149 294	139 333	France
Germany	91 194	101 783	144 623	151 150	168 412	200 200	196 995	177 621	Allemagne
Greece[2]	1 067	1 175	1 429	1 525	1 655	1 925	2 194	2 143	Grèce[2]
Hungary[3]	..	800	748	812	895	947	1 008	1 066	Hongrie[3]
Iceland	226	258	275	230	228	237	234	217	Islande
Ireland	4 096	4 239	4 741	4 685	4 984	5 680	6 825	8 269	Irlande
Italy	33 108	37 297	43 426	37 097	38 943	42 654	48 245	52 001	Italie
Japan	258 310	286 850	316 151	372 829	406 604	448 384	376 514	344 074	Japon
Korea	..	..	..	..	44 450	58 488	63 815	61 705	Corée
Luxembourg[4]	444	503	562	528	1 582	4 156	3 631	4 811	Luxembourg[4]
Mexico	..	..	5 127	6 027	6 307	3 882	4 217	5 195	Mexique
Netherlands	22 712	22 647	26 789	26 647	29 911	36 502	37 118	34 654	Pays-Bas
New Zealand	1 790	1 573	1 603	1 489	1 688	1 854	2 528	2 570	Nouvelle Zélande
Norway[5]	5 932	6 096	6 659	5 996	6 388	6 850	6 979	7 255	Norvège[5]
Poland	..	..	..	1 707	1 824	2 302	3 038	3 757	Pologne
Portugal	2 079	2 492	3 242	3 322	3 632	4 856	5 585	5 100	Portugal
Spain	18 141	21 691	24 671	21 640	25 703	27 971	30 378	28 527	Espagne
Sweden[6,7]	14 198	15 877	16 404	12 329	13 064	14 386	15 667	14 638	Suède[6,7]
Switzerland	27 315	29 004	32 658	33 723	37 985	45 444	38 963	34 713	Suisse
Turkey	895	1 008	1 216	1 564	1 084	1 394	1 591	1 883	Turquie
United Kingdom[8]	115 274	132 466	148 254	138 604	138 100	140 298	148 610	165 969	Royaume-Uni[8]
United States	606 925	621 413	654 071	705 008	731 673	763 639	795 115	891 694	Etats-Unis
NAFTA[9]	639 368	656 065	691 138	739 067	766 738	797 605	829 564	926 804	ALENA[9]
EU-15[9]	415 233	458 812	551 260	538 006	582 578	666 299	694 017	677 010	UE-15[9]
OECD[9]	1 370 342	1 461 190	1 620 960	1 723 398	1 882 097	2 060 526	2 052 423	2 099 868	OCDE[9]

I.2 Life / Vie

Million U.S. $ / Millions de $ U.S.

COUNTRY	1990	1991	1992	1993	1994	1995	1996	1997	PAYS
Australia[1]	14 754	14 061	13 202	16 063	16 727	15 328	16 087	21 651	Australie[1]
Austria	2 569	2 528	2 879	3 480	3 592	4 655	6 315	4 217	Autriche
Belgium	3 132	3 344	3 809	3 965	4 838	6 250	6 920	7 113	Belgique
Canada	15 189	16 610	14 217	10 776	15 686	16 799	11 239	10 872	Canada
Czech Republic	..	..	..	203	259	352	403	393	République Tchèque
Denmark	2 438	2 733	3 199	3 640	4 629	5 785	6 744	6 620	Danemark
Finland	6 068	5 910	4 539	490	742	1 643	2 587	2 196	Finlande
France	38 385	42 117	51 646	59 246	71 505	86 344	93 229	90 346	France
Germany	37 363	40 936	51 585	53 599	59 918	71 564	72 231	66 137	Allemagne
Greece[2]	446	543	689	706	786	921	1 032	1 050	Grèce[2]
Hungary[3]	..	208	133	172	229	282	321	351	Hongrie[3]
Iceland	6	7	7	7	8	9	8	9	Islande
Ireland	2 389	2 349	2 599	2 651	2 666	2 977	3 850	4 976	Irlande
Italy	8 881	10 391	12 436	11 337	12 995	15 699	18 639	23 526	Italie
Japan	188 684	209 969	233 121	273 375	298 246	327 029	269 751	250 922	Japon
Korea	..	..	..	..	33 436	43 723	46 353	44 146	Corée
Luxembourg[4]	141	173	181	169	1 150	3 649	3 083	4 348	Luxembourg[4]
Mexico	..	..	1 695	1 965	2 137	1 269	1 419	1 854	Mexique
Netherlands	11 772	12 645	14 393	13 754	15 213	19 445	20 040	19 239	Pays-Bas
New Zealand	646	659	628	639	735	659	869	902	Nouvelle Zélande
Norway	1 908	2 336	2 557	2 236	2 729	2 981	3 065	3 565	Norvège
Poland	..	..	..	489	565	634	869	1 040	Pologne
Portugal	487	652	930	1 032	1 251	2 092	2 604	2 317	Portugal
Spain	5 423	7 422	7 976	6 950	10 809	11 080	12 968	13 121	Espagne
Sweden[6]	7 081	7 797	7 713	5 758	7 047	7 899	8 963	8 502	Suède[6]
Switzerland	11 364	12 213	13 328	14 098	16 641	21 981	22 826	21 671	Suisse
Turkey	173	203	229	226	130	178	232	297	Turquie
United Kingdom[8]	60 709	71 288	76 721	74 823	74 527	75 753	86 908	101 279	Royaume-Uni[8]
United States	227 668	222 552	240 904	267 026	277 744	294 353	315 538	338 343	Etats-Unis
NAFTA[9]	242 857	239 162	256 816	279 767	295 567	312 420	328 197	351 069	ALENA[9]
EU-15[9]	187 283	210 828	241 293	241 599	271 667	315 757	346 112	354 986	UE-15[9]
OECD[9]	647 675	689 645	761 315	828 874	936 938	1 041 333	1 035 093	1 051 001	OCDE[9]

I. Total gross premiums / Primes brutes totales

I.3 Non-Life / Non-Vie

Million U.S. $ / Millions de $ U.S.

COUNTRY	1990	1991	1992	1993	1994	1995	1996	1997	PAYS
Australia	6 519	6 664	6 052	11 123	13 877	14 121	16 572	15 651	Australie
Austria	5 971	6 310	7 462	7 544	8 528	9 585	9 698	8 627	Autriche
Belgium	6 563	6 859	7 785	7 413	7 511	9 208	8 893	7 631	Belgique
Canada	17 254	18 042	17 723	17 257	13 072	13 285	18 993	19 042	Canada
Czech Republic	..	..	..	383	772	921	1 112	1 120	République Tchèque
Denmark	4 424	4 317	5 118	4 469	5 128	5 591	5 588	5 080	Danemark
Finland	3 365	3 285	2 875	2 175	2 373	2 832	2 732	2 462	Finlande
France	40 005	41 241	47 805	48 058	47 744	55 778	56 064	48 987	France
Germany	53 831	60 847	93 039	97 550	108 495	128 636	124 764	111 485	Allemagne
Greece[2]	621	632	740	819	870	1 004	1 161	1 093	Grèce[2]
Hungary[3]	..	592	614	640	666	665	687	715	Hongrie[3]
Iceland	220	251	267	223	220	228	225	208	Islande
Ireland	1 707	1 890	2 141	2 034	2 319	2 703	2 974	3 293	Irlande
Italy	24 227	26 906	30 990	25 759	25 948	26 955	29 606	28 475	Italie
Japan	69 626	76 880	83 031	99 454	108 358	121 355	106 763	93 152	Japon
Korea	..	..	..	..	11 014	14 765	17 462	17 560	Corée
Luxembourg[4]	302	330	381	359	432	507	548	463	Luxembourg[4]
Mexico	..	..	3 432	4 061	4 170	2 614	2 797	3 342	Mexique
Netherlands	10 941	10 001	12 396	12 893	14 698	17 057	17 078	15 415	Pays-Bas
New Zealand	1 144	914	975	850	953	1 196	1 659	1 668	Nouvelle Zélande
Norway[5]	4 024	3 759	4 102	3 760	3 659	3 868	3 914	3 690	Norvège[5]
Poland	..	..	..	1 218	1 259	1 668	2 169	2 717	Pologne
Portugal	1 593	1 840	2 313	2 290	2 381	2 764	2 981	2 783	Portugal
Spain	12 717	14 269	16 695	14 690	14 894	16 891	17 410	15 406	Espagne
Sweden[7]	7 117	8 080	8 692	6 571	6 017	6 487	6 704	6 136	Suède[7]
Switzerland	15 951	16 792	19 330	19 625	21 344	23 463	16 137	13 041	Suisse
Turkey	722	805	987	1 338	954	1 216	1 358	1 586	Turquie
United Kingdom	54 565	61 177	71 534	63 782	63 573	64 545	61 702	64 689	Royaume-Uni
United States	379 257	398 861	413 167	437 982	453 929	469 286	479 577	553 351	Etats-Unis
NAFTA[9]	396 511	416 903	434 322	459 300	471 171	485 184	501 367	575 735	ALENA[9]
EU-15[9]	227 949	247 984	309 967	296 407	310 911	350 542	347 905	322 024	UE-15[9]
OECD[9]	722 667	771 545	859 645	894 524	945 159	1 019 193	1 017 330	1 048 867	OCDE[9]

1. Net written premiums basis for life for 1994 and 1995 / Sur la base des primes nettes émises pour l'assurance-vie pour les années 1994 et 1995

2. Net written premiums basis until 1991 / Sur la base des primes nettes émises jusqu'à 1991

3. Direct gross premiums basis for 1991 / Sur la base des primes brutes directes pour 1991

4. Direct gross premiums basis until 1993 / Sur la base des primes brutes directes jusqu'à 1993

5. Without branches of foreign insurers for non-life for 1994 and 1995 / Sans les succursales des assureurs étrangers pour l'assurance non-vie pour les années 1994 et 1995

6. Without branches of foreign insurers for life for 1990 / Sans les succursales des assureurs étrangers pour l'assurance vie pour 1990

7. Without branches of foreign insurers for non-life until 1996 / Sans les succursales des assureurs étrangers pour l'assurance non-vie jusqu'à 1996

8. Net written premiums for life until 1992 / Sur la base des primes nettes émises pour l'assurance vie jusqu'à 1992

9. For available data only / Uniquement pour les données disponibles

II. Market share in O.E.C.D. (Direct gross premiums basis) / Part de marché dans l'O.C.D.E. (Sur la base des primes brutes directes)

II.1 Total / Total

% (per cent / pourcentage)

COUNTRY	1990	1991	1992	1993	1994	1995	1996	1997	PAYS
Australia[1]	1.62	1.46	1.24	1.65	1.64	1.46	1.61	1.84	Australie[1]
Austria	0.62	0.60	0.64	0.64	0.61	0.68	0.75	0.57	Autriche
Belgium	0.72	0.71	0.75	0.70	0.70	0.77	0.79	0.72	Belgique
Canada	2.16	2.29	1.91	1.57	1.46	1.42	1.40	1.34	Canada
Czech Republic	..	..	..	0.05	0.06	0.07	0.08	0.08	République Tchèque
Denmark	0.47	0.44	0.47	0.46	0.49	0.55	0.60	0.56	Danemark
Finland	0.71	0.64	0.48	0.15	0.17	0.22	0.27	0.23	Finlande
France	5.56	5.50	6.00	6.10	6.39	6.99	7.39	6.71	France
Germany	7.02	7.34	7.82	7.65	7.67	8.39	8.24	7.11	Allemagne
Greece[2]	0.08	0.09	0.10	0.09	0.09	0.10	0.11	0.11	Grèce[2]
Hungary	..	0.06	0.05	0.05	0.05	0.05	0.05	0.05	Hongrie
Iceland	0.01	0.02	0.02	0.01	0.01	0.01	0.01	0.01	Islande
Ireland	0.32	0.31	0.29	0.28	0.28	0.29	0.35	0.39	Irlande
Italy	2.25	2.37	2.50	2.04	2.00	2.02	2.29	2.41	Italie
Japan	19.78	20.63	20.95	23.26	23.08	23.26	19.55	17.31	Japon
Korea	..	..	..	..	2.51	3.03	3.29	3.09	Corée
Luxembourg	0.04	0.04	0.04	0.03	0.09	0.22	0.19	0.25	Luxembourg
Mexico	..	..	0.33	0.37	0.35	0.20	0.21	0.26	Mexique
Netherlands[3]	1.71	1.60	1.74	1.59	1.63	1.87	1.91	1.74	Pays-Bas[3]
New Zealand[4,5]	0.14	0.11	0.11	0.09	0.09	0.09	0.13	0.13	Nouvelle Zélande[4,5]
Norway[6,7]	0.41	0.41	0.43	0.36	0.36	0.36	0.37	0.37	Norvège[6,7]
Poland[8,9]	..	..	..	0.08	0.08	0.12	0.16	0.19	Pologne[8,9]
Portugal	0.16	0.18	0.22	0.21	0.21	0.25	0.29	0.26	Portugal
Spain	1.37	1.54	1.61	1.32	1.43	1.43	1.55	1.41	Espagne
Sweden	0.95	1.00	0.93	0.73	0.67	0.67	0.75	0.68	Suède
Switzerland	1.45	1.42	1.42	1.37	1.46	1.69	1.74	1.56	Suisse
Turkey	0.07	0.07	0.08	0.04	0.06	0.07	0.08	0.10	Turquie
United Kingdom[10]	8.23	8.87	9.11	7.92	7.10	6.80	7.36	8.04	Royaume-Uni[10]
United States	44.15	42.31	40.79	41.12	39.26	36.93	38.47	42.50	Etats-Unis
NAFTA[11]	46.31	44.60	43.03	43.05	41.07	38.55	40.09	44.10	ALENA[11]
EU-15[11]	30.21	31.21	32.68	29.92	29.53	31.26	32.84	31.17	UE-15[11]

II.2 Life / Vie

% (per cent / pourcentage)

COUNTRY	1990	1991	1992	1993	1994	1995	1996	1997	PAYS
Australia[1]	2.36	2.10	2.47	2.02	1.85	1.53	1.61	2.10	Australie[1]
Austria	0.40	0.37	0.39	0.44	0.39	0.46	0.63	0.41	Autriche
Belgium	0.49	0.49	0.51	0.50	0.53	0.62	0.69	0.69	Belgique
Canada	2.35	2.39	1.86	1.32	1.64	1.58	1.05	0.98	Canada
Czech Republic	..	..	..	0.03	0.03	0.04	0.04	0.04	République Tchèque
Denmark	0.39	0.41	0.43	0.46	0.51	0.58	0.68	0.65	Danemark
Finland	0.97	0.88	0.62	0.06	0.08	0.16	0.26	0.21	Finlande
France	5.89	6.07	6.77	7.25	7.70	8.39	9.19	8.72	France
Germany	5.94	6.09	6.34	6.12	5.96	6.43	6.51	5.78	Allemagne
Greece[2]	0.07	0.08	0.09	0.09	0.09	0.09	0.10	0.10	Grèce[2]
Hungary	..	0.03	0.02	0.02	0.03	0.03	0.03	0.03	Hongrie
Iceland	0.00	0.00	0.00	0.00	0.00	0.00	0.00	0.00	Islande
Ireland	0.38	0.35	0.30	0.30	0.29	0.30	0.38	0.48	Irlande
Italy	1.16	1.28	1.38	1.22	1.28	1.41	1.68	2.11	Italie
Japan	29.96	31.34	31.66	34.48	32.97	32.61	27.04	24.57	Japon
Korea	..	..	..	..	3.70	4.37	4.65	4.33	Corée
Luxembourg	0.02	0.03	0.02	0.02	0.13	0.36	0.00	0.43	Luxembourg
Mexico	..	..	0.23	0.25	0.23	0.13	0.14	0.18	Mexique
Netherlands[3]	1.80	1.81	1.86	1.57	1.53	1.87	1.98	1.86	Pays-Bas[3]
New Zealand[4]	0.10	0.10	0.09	0.08	0.08	0.07	0.09	0.09	Nouvelle Zélande[4]
Norway[6]	0.30	0.35	0.35	0.28	0.30	0.30	0.31	0.35	Norvège[6]
Poland[8]	..	..	..	0.06	0.06	0.06	0.09	0.10	Pologne[8]
Portugal	0.08	0.10	0.13	0.13	0.14	0.21	0.26	0.23	Portugal
Spain	0.86	1.10	1.08	0.87	1.19	1.10	1.30	1.28	Espagne
Sweden	1.07	1.11	0.98	0.69	0.76	0.76	0.90	0.83	Suède
Switzerland	1.63	1.65	1.64	1.62	1.71	2.04	2.21	2.09	Suisse
Turkey	0.03	0.03	0.03	0.03	0.01	0.02	0.02	0.03	Turquie
United Kingdom[10]	9.69	10.65	10.43	9.01	7.49	7.26	8.66	9.86	Royaume-Uni[10]
United States	34.06	31.18	30.33	31.08	29.31	27.24	29.52	31.47	Etats-Unis
NAFTA[11]	36.41	33.57	32.41	32.65	31.19	28.95	30.71	32.63	ALENA[11]
EU-15[11]	29.21	30.82	31.34	28.73	28.07	30.00	33.21	33.64	UE-15[11]

II. Market share in O.E.C.D. (Direct gross premiums basis) / Part de marché dans l'O.C.D.E. (Sur la base des primes brutes directes)

II.3 Non-Life / Non-Vie

% (per cent / pourcentage)

COUNTRY	1990	1991	1992	1993	1994	1995	1996	1997	PAYS
Australia	0.85	0.84	0.67	1.27	1.41	1.37	1.60	1.56	Australie
Austria	0.79	0.83	0.88	0.85	0.86	0.93	0.89	0.74	Autriche
Belgium	0.88	0.92	0.98	0.91	0.88	0.95	0.91	0.75	Belgique
Canada	1.87	2.18	1.94	1.82	1.26	1.24	1.80	1.74	Canada
Czech Republic	..	..	..	0.08	0.09	0.10	0.12	0.12	République Tchèque
Denmark	0.52	0.47	0.50	0.46	0.47	0.52	0.52	0.46	Danemark
Finland	0.43	0.41	0.34	0.25	0.26	0.29	0.28	0.24	Finlande
France	4.95	4.94	5.20	4.92	4.95	5.40	5.40	4.51	France
Germany	13.12	8.56	9.24	9.21	9.55	10.62	10.19	8.55	Allemagne
Greece[2]	0.09	0.09	0.10	0.10	0.10	0.11	0.12	0.11	Grèce[7]
Hungary	..	0.09	0.08	0.08	0.08	0.07	0.08	0.08	Hongrie
Iceland	0.03	0.03	0.03	0.02	0.02	0.02	0.02	0.02	Islande
Ireland	0.24	0.26	0.28	0.25	0.27	0.28	0.31	0.29	Irlande
Italy	3.14	3.43	3.60	2.89	2.79	2.70	2.97	2.74	Italie
Japan	9.28	10.18	10.17	11.79	12.17	12.63	11.24	9.39	Japon
Korea	..	..	..	..	1.20	1.51	1.79	1.74	Corée
Luxembourg	0.04	0.05	0.05	0.05	0.05	0.06	0.06	0.05	Luxembourg
Mexico	..	..	0.44	0.50	0.48	0.28	0.30	0.34	Mexique
Netherlands	1.54	1.40	1.61	1.61	1.74	1.87	1.85	1.60	Pays-Bas
New Zealand[5]	0.16	0.13	0.13	0.09	0.10	0.11	0.18	0.18	Nouvelle Zélande[5]
Norway[7]	0.49	0.47	0.50	0.45	0.43	0.43	0.43	0.39	Norvège[7]
Poland[9]	..	..	..	0.10	0.09	0.19	0.24	0.29	Pologne[9]
Portugal	0.23	0.26	0.31	0.29	0.29	0.31	0.33	0.29	Portugal
Spain	1.77	1.96	2.12	1.77	1.70	1.80	1.84	1.55	Espagne
Sweden	0.79	0.90	0.86	0.77	0.57	0.58	0.59	0.51	Suède
Switzerland	1.19	1.20	1.19	1.12	1.18	1.29	1.24	0.99	Suisse
Turkey	0.10	0.11	0.13	0.17	0.11	0.14	0.15	0.17	Turquie
United Kingdom	6.42	7.12	7.73	6.81	6.67	6.27	5.93	6.05	Royaume-Uni
United States	51.05	53.18	50.92	51.38	50.24	47.93	48.62	54.55	Etats-Unis
NAFTA[11]	52.93	55.36	53.30	53.70	51.98	49.45	50.71	56.63	ALENA[11]
EU-15[11]	34.96	31.59	33.80	31.14	31.14	32.68	32.19	28.46	UE-15[11]

1. Net written premiums basis for life for 1994 and 1995 / Sur la base des primes nettes émises pour l'assurance vie pour 1994 et 1995
2. Net written premiums basis until 1991 / Sur la base des primes nettes émises jusqu'à 1991
3. Net written premiums basis for life until 1994 / Sur la base des primes nettes émises pour l'assurance vie jusqu'à 1994
4. Total gross premiums basis for life since 1996 / Sur la base des primes brutes totales pour l'assurance vie depuis 1996
5. Net written premiums basis for non-life for 1992-1995 / Sur la base des primes nettes émises pour l'assurance non-vie pour les années 1992 à 1995
6. Net written premiums basis for life for 1992 / Sur la base des primes nettes émises pour l'assurance vie pour 1992
7. Without branches of foreign insurers for non-life for 1994 and 1995 / Sans les succursales des assureurs étrangers pour l'assurance non-vie pour 1994 et 1995
8. Net written premiums basis for life until 1995 / Sur la base des primes nettes émises pour l'assurance vie jusqu'à 1995
9. Net written premiums basis for non-life until 1994 / Sur la base des primes nettes émises pour l'assurance non-vie jusqu'à 1994
10. Net written premiums basis for life until 1995 / Sur la base des primes nettes émises pour l'assurance vie jusqu'à 1995
11. For available data only / Uniquement pour les données disponibles

III. Density (Direct gross premiums/Population) / Densité (Primes brutes directes/Population)

III.1 Total / Total

U.S. $ per inhabitant / $ US par habitant

COUNTRY	1990	1991	1992	1993	1994	1995	1996	1997	PAYS
Australia[1]	1 201	1 145	1 039	1 462	1 584	1 517	1 657	1 937	Australie[1]
Austria	1 020	1 043	1 187	1 257	1 317	1 593	1 762	1 373	Autriche
Belgium	912	957	1 100	1 091	1 186	1 436	1 473	1 376	Belgique
Canada	987	1 101	982	847	859	903	882	865	Canada
Czech Republic	..	..	..	76	100	121	147	145	République Tchèque
Denmark	1 151	1 156	1 327	1 384	1 617	1 980	2 157	2 057	Danemark
Finland	1 801	1 726	1 399	474	570	824	985	866	Finlande
France	1 242	1 305	1 538	1 657	1 902	2 264	2 393	2 236	France
Germany	1 405	1 243	1 427	1 475	1 621	1 935	1 902	1 691	Allemagne
Greece[2]	106	115	138	141	153	180	204	200	Grèce[2]
Hungary	..	77	71	78	87	92	98	104	Hongrie
Iceland	732	842	880	733	737	784	770	717	Islande
Ireland	1 150	1 180	1 203	1 214	1 362	1 508	1 804	2 099	Irlande
Italy	503	565	647	560	601	662	752	819	Italie
Japan	2 027	2 253	2 476	2 919	3 179	3 488	2 936	2 680	Japon
Korea	..	..	..	..	969	1 266	1 368	1 313	Corée
Luxembourg	1 154	1 290	1 422	1 316	3 874	10 060	8 662	11 331	Luxembourg
Mexico	..	..	58	67	68	41	44	53	Mexique
Netherlands[3]	1 450	1 439	1 685	1 629	1 820	2 283	2 334	2 224	Pays-Bas[3]
New Zealand[4,5]	523	455	456	391	431	445	674	677	Nouvelle Zélande[4,5]
Norway[6,7]	1 235	1 311	1 463	1 318	1 438	1 551	1 588	1 643	Norvège[6,7]
Poland[8,9]	..	..	..	32	34	59	78	96	Pologne[8,9]
Portugal	207	249	325	332	363	484	555	504	Portugal
Spain	447	535	605	527	630	686	747	700	Espagne
Sweden	1 400	1 569	1 565	1 304	1 303	1 432	1 606	1 496	Suède
Switzerland	2 729	2 834	3 039	3 098	3 573	4 510	4 665	4 305	Suisse
Turkey	15	17	20	26	18	22	25	29	Turquie
United Kingdom[10]	1 811	2 078	2 308	2 128	2 093	2 184	2 366	2 661	Royaume-Uni
United States	2 237	2 268	2 348	2 494	2 593	2 643	2 739	3 111	Etats-Unis[10]
NAFTA[11]	2 112	2 152	1 715	1 804	1 869	1 895	1 955	2 202	ALENA[11]
EU-15[11]	1 098	1 154	1 306	1 267	1 370	1 582	1 664	1 628	UE-15[11]
OECD[11]	1 252	1 294	1 393	1 471	1 605	1 742	1 737	1 784	OCDE[11]

III.2 Life / Vie

U.S. $ per inhabitant / $ US par habitant

COUNTRY	1990	1991	1992	1993	1994	1995	1996	1997	PAYS
Australia[1]	864	814	755	907	938	848	879	1 154	Australie[1]
Austria	327	320	362	432	444	574	778	517	Autriche
Belgium	311	330	375	389	472	607	671	690	Belgique
Canada	530	570	479	360	507	533	348	330	Canada
Czech Republic	..	..	..	20	25	34	39	38	République Tchèque
Denmark	472	528	616	700	885	1 104	1 278	1 250	Danemark
Finland	1 216	1 174	907	97	146	321	504	423	Finlande
France	651	712	867	996	1 202	1 445	1 569	1 517	France
Germany	588	510	579	597	662	788	792	719	Allemagne
Greece[2]	44	53	67	68	75	88	98	100	Grèce[2]
Hungary	..	20	13	16	22	28	31	34	Hongrie
Iceland	22	26	28	26	26	29	31	28	Islande
Ireland	681	666	622	674	743	823	1 052	1 348	Irlande
Italy	128	150	179	169	202	247	291	374	Italie
Japan	1 518	1 691	1 871	2 188	2 382	2 601	2 140	1 986	Japon
Korea	..	..	..	..	749	970	1 017	960	Corée
Luxembourg	368	443	457	420	2 819	8 834	7 355	10 241	Luxembourg
Mexico	..	..	20	22	24	14	15	19	Mexique
Netherlands[3]	752	803	902	815	897	1 214	1 270	1 244	Pays-Bas[3]
New Zealand[4]	192	193	182	184	208	180	234	240	Nouvelle Zélande[4]
Norway[6]	447	548	596	519	629	686	701	812	Norvège[6]
Poland[8]	..	..	..	13	15	16	22	27	Pologne[8]
Portugal	49	66	94	104	126	211	262	232	Portugal
Spain	138	190	203	177	275	281	329	331	Espagne
Sweden	781	858	830	623	776	856	1 012	958	Suède
Switzerland	1 525	1 627	1 759	1 848	2 198	2 896	3 107	3 004	Suisse
Turkey	3	4	4	4	2	3	4	5	Turquie
United Kingdom[10]	1 055	1 233	1 323	1 224	1 158	1 241	1 467	1 704	Royaume-Uni
United States	854	826	873	954	1 016	1 037	1 107	1 203	Etats-Unis[10]
NAFTA[11]	821	800	646	692	745	757	789	851	ALENA[11]
EU-15[11]	525	563	626	615	683	807	895	918	UE-15[11]
OECD[11]	620	640	692	744	843	927	918	932	OCDE[11]

III. Density (Direct gross premiums/Population) / Densité (Primes brutes directes/Population)

III.3 Non-Life / Non-Vie

U.S. $ per inhabitant / $ US par habitant

COUNTRY	1990	1991	1992	1993	1994	1995	1996	1997	PAYS
Australia	338	332	284	555	646	669	779	783	Australie
Austria	693	723	825	825	873	1 019	984	855	Autriche
Belgium	601	627	724	702	714	829	802	686	Belgique
Canada	457	531	504	487	352	370	534	535	Canada
Czech Republic	..	..		57	78	07	107	107	République Tchèque
Denmark	679	628	711	684	731	876	878	808	Danemark
Finland	585	552	492	377	424	503	481	442	Finlande
France	591	593	671	661	700	818	824	719	France
Germany	817	733	848	878	959	1 147	1 109	972	Allemagne
Greece[2]	62	62	72	73	78	92	105	100	Grèce[2]
Hungary	..	57	58	61	64	64	67	70	Hongrie
Iceland	710	816	853	707	711	754	739	689	Islande
Ireland	470	515	580	540	619	685	752	751	Irlande
Italy	375	414	469	392	399	415	461	445	Italie
Japan	509	562	605	731	796	887	796	695	Japon
Korea	..	..	..	..	220	296	351	353	Corée
Luxembourg	786	847	965	895	1 055	1 226	1 307	1 090	Luxembourg
Mexico	..	..	38	44	45	27	29	34	Mexique
Netherlands	697	636	783	814	923	1 069	1 064	979	Pays-Bas
New Zealand[5]	331	261	273	207	222	265	440	437	Nouvelle Zélande[5]
Norway[7]	788	763	867	799	808	865	887	831	Norvège[7]
Poland[9]	..	..	..	20	20	43	56	69	Pologne[9]
Portugal	157	183	230	227	236	273	293	271	Portugal
Spain	309	346	402	350	356	405	418	369	Espagne
Sweden	619	710	734	681	526	576	593	538	Suède
Switzerland	1 204	1 207	1 279	1 250	1 376	1 614	1 558	1 301	Suisse
Turkey	12	13	16	22	16	19	21	25	Turquie
United Kingdom	756	845	986	904	934	943	899	957	Royaume-Uni
United States	1 384	1 443	1 475	1 541	1 577	1 606	1 632	1 908	Etats-Unis
NAFTA[11]	1 291	1 351	1 069	1 112	1 124	1 138	1 166	1 351	ALENA[11]
EU-15[11]	573	591	680	652	687	774	769	710	UE-15[11]
OECD[11]	633	655	700	726	763	815	818	852	OCDE[11]

1. Net written premiums basis for life for 1994 and 1995 / Sur la base des primes nettes émises pour l'assurance vie pour 1994 et 1995
2. Net written premiums basis until 1991 / Sur la base des primes nettes émises jusqu'à 1991
3. Net written premiums basis for life until 1994 / Sur la base des primes nettes émises pour l'assurance vie jusqu'à 1994
4. Total gross premiums basis for life since 1996 / Sur la base des primes brutes totales pour l'assurance vie depuis 1996
5. Net written premiums basis for non-life for 1992-1995 / Sur la base des primes nettes émises pour l'assurance non-vie pour les années 1992 à 1995
6. Net written premiums basis for life for 1992 / Sur la base des primes nettes émises pour l'assurance vie pour 1992
7. Without branches of foreign insurers for non-life for 1994 and 1995 / Sans les succursales des assureurs étrangers pour l'assurance non-vie pour 1994 et 1995
8. Net written premiums basis for life until 1995 / Sur la base des primes nettes émises pour l'assurance vie jusqu'à 1995
9. Net written premiums basis for non-life until 1994 / Sur la base des primes nettes émises pour l'assurance non-vie jusqu'à 1994
10. Net written premiums basis for life until 1995 / Sur la base des primes nettes émises pour l'assurance vie jusqu'à 1995
11. For available data only / Uniquement pour les données disponibles

IV. Penetration (Direct gross premiums/GDP) / Pénétration (Primes brutes directes/PIB)

IV.1 Total / Total

% (per cent / pourcentage)

COUNTRY	1990	1991	1992	1993	1994	1995	1996	1997	PAYS
Australia[1]	6.71	6.38	5.98	8.72	8.36	7.54	7.45	8.86	Australie[1]
Austria	4.93	4.89	5.00	5.50	5.40	5.55	6.22	5.37	Autriche
Belgium	4.64	4.76	4.91	5.13	5.17	5.33	5.59	5.77	Belgique
Canada	4.72	5.19	4.85	4.36	4.47	4.55	4.35	4.19	Canada
Czech Republic	..	..	..	2.39	1.87	1.81	2.14	2.12	République Tchèque
Denmark	4.44	4.44	4.67	5.17	5.54	5.75	6.18	6.42	Danemark
Finland	6.59	7.05	6.49	2.78	2.90	3.28	3.95	3.66	Finlande
France	5.89	6.20	6.68	7.64	8.27	8.57	9.08	9.41	France
Germany	5.92	5.78	5.83	6.26	6.44	6.58	6.65	6.64	Allemagne
Greece[2]	1.28	1.32	1.45	1.42	1.44	1.43	1.54	1.57	Grèce[2]
Hungary	..	2.37	1.96	2.06	2.12	2.11	2.22	2.32	Hongrie
Iceland	2.99	3.23	3.33	3.18	3.15	3.00	2.86	2.62	Islande
Ireland	8.96	9.16	8.33	9.11	9.28	8.63	9.52	10.52	Irlande
Italy	2.63	2.81	3.04	3.27	3.41	3.52	3.58	4.14	Italie
Japan	8.43	8.20	8.29	8.52	8.48	8.53	8.04	8.06	Japon
Korea	..	..	..	..	10.76	11.67	11.97	12.66	Corée
Luxembourg	4.29	4.61	4.45	4.10	10.81	24.03	21.36	30.45	Luxembourg
Mexico	..	..	1.34	1.43	1.44	1.29	1.22	1.25	Mexique
Netherlands[3]	7.64	7.47	7.95	7.96	8.29	8.86	9.11	9.35	Pays-Bas[3]
New Zealand[4,5]	4.06	3.73	3.97	3.18	3.00	2.74	3.85	3.95	Nouvelle Zélande[4,5]
Norway[6,7]	4.54	4.74	4.97	4.89	5.07	4.60	4.39	4.70	Norvège[6,7]
Poland[8,9]	..	..	..	1.45	1.43	1.92	2.25	2.73	Pologne[8,9]
Portugal	2.95	3.14	3.38	3.91	4.08	4.55	5.06	4.95	Portugal
Spain	3.53	3.94	4.09	4.30	5.10	4.81	5.04	5.17	Espagne
Sweden	5.23	5.66	5.49	6.14	5.79	5.47	5.64	5.81	Suède
Switzerland	8.02	8.28	8.58	9.08	9.59	10.33	11.18	11.94	Suisse
Turkey	0.57	0.64	0.75	0.85	0.82	0.81	0.87	0.98	Turquie
United Kingdom[10]	10.58	11.68	12.58	12.95	11.81	11.38	11.81	11.97	Royaume-Uni
United States	9.73	9.69	9.60	9.82	9.73	9.57	9.49	10.23	Etats-Unis[10]
NAFTA[11]	9.27	9.28	8.80	8.96	8.92	8.91	8.81	9.43	ALENA[11]
EU-15[11]	5.79	6.04	6.29	6.75	6.89	6.97	7.20	7.51	UE-15[11]
OECD[11]	7.44	7.47	7.55	7.91	8.01	8.01	7.97	8.40	OCDE[11]

IV.2 Life / Vie

% (per cent / pourcentage)

COUNTRY	1990	1991	1992	1993	1994	1995	1996	1997	PAYS
Australia[1]	4.83	4.53	4.34	5.41	4.95	4.22	3.95	5.27	Australie[1]
Austria	1.58	1.50	1.52	1.89	1.82	2.00	2.75	2.03	Autriche
Belgium	1.58	1.64	1.68	1.83	2.06	2.25	2.55	2.89	Belgique
Canada	2.53	2.69	2.36	1.85	2.64	2.69	1.71	1.60	Canada
Czech Republic	..	..	..	0.59	0.65	0.69	0.71	0.76	République Tchèque
Denmark	1.82	2.03	2.17	2.61	3.04	3.21	3.66	3.90	Danemark
Finland	4.45	4.79	4.21	0.57	0.74	1.28	2.02	1.79	Finlande
France	3.09	3.38	3.76	4.59	5.23	5.47	5.95	6.39	France
Germany	2.48	2.37	2.37	2.53	2.63	2.68	2.77	2.82	Allemagne
Greece[2]	0.54	0.61	0.70	0.76	0.79	0.79	0.84	0.87	Grèce[2]
Hungary	..	0.62	0.35	0.43	0.55	0.63	0.71	0.77	Hongrie
Iceland	0.09	0.10	0.11	0.11	0.11	0.11	0.11	0.10	Islande
Ireland	5.30	5.17	4.31	5.06	5.06	4.71	5.55	6.76	Irlande
Italy	0.67	0.75	0.84	0.98	1.15	1.31	1.39	1.89	Italie
Japan	6.32	6.16	6.26	6.39	6.35	6.36	5.86	5.97	Japon
Korea	..	..	..	..	8.31	8.94	8.90	9.26	Corée
Luxembourg	1.37	1.58	1.43	1.31	7.86	21.10	18.14	27.52	Luxembourg
Mexico	..	..	0.46	0.48	0.50	0.44	0.42	0.46	Mexique
Netherlands[3]	3.97	4.17	4.26	3.98	4.09	4.71	4.96	5.23	Pays-Bas[3]
New Zealand[4]	1.49	1.59	1.59	1.49	1.45	1.11	1.34	1.40	Nouvelle Zélande[4]
Norway[6]	1.64	1.98	2.02	1.93	2.22	2.03	1.94	2.32	Norvège[6]
Poland[8]	..	..	..	0.57	0.61	0.53	0.65	0.77	Pologne[8]
Portugal	0.70	0.83	0.98	1.23	1.42	1.98	2.39	2.28	Portugal
Spain	1.09	1.40	1.37	1.44	2.22	1.97	2.22	2.45	Espagne
Sweden	2.92	3.10	2.92	2.93	3.45	3.27	3.56	3.72	Suède
Switzerland	4.48	4.75	4.97	5.41	5.90	6.63	7.45	8.33	Suisse
Turkey	0.11	0.13	0.14	0.13	0.10	0.10	0.13	0.16	Turquie
United Kingdom[10]	6.16	6.93	7.21	7.45	6.54	6.47	7.16	7.54	Royaume-Uni
United States	3.74	3.54	3.58	3.76	3.79	3.70	3.84	3.96	Etats-Unis[10]
NAFTA[11]	3.61	3.45	3.32	3.44	3.55	3.56	3.56	3.64	ALENA[11]
EU-15[11]	2.77	2.95	3.02	3.28	3.44	3.56	3.87	4.23	UE-15[11]
OECD[11]	3.68	3.69	3.75	4.00	4.21	4.26	4.22	4.39	OCDE[11]

IV. Penetration (Direct gross premiums/GDP) / Pénétration (Primes brutes directes/PIB)

IV.3 Non-Life / Non-Vie

% (per cent / pourcentage)

COUNTRY	1990	1991	1992	1993	1994	1995	1996	1997	PAYS
Australia	1.89	1.85	1.63	3.31	3.41	3.33	3.50	3.58	Australie
Austria	3.35	3.39	3.48	3.61	3.58	3.55	3.47	3.35	Autriche
Belgium	3.05	3.12	3.24	3.30	3.11	3.08	3.04	2.87	Belgique
Canada	2.18	2.51	2.49	2.51	1.83	1.86	2.63	2.59	Canada
Czech Republic	..	..	..	1.69	1.93	1.77	1.96	2.12	République Tchèque
Denmark	2.62	2.41	2.50	2.56	2.51	2.54	2.52	2.52	Danemark
Finland	2.14	2.25	2.28	2.22	2.16	2.00	1.93	1.87	Finlande
France	2.81	2.82	2.91	3.05	3.04	3.10	3.13	3.03	France
Germany	3.44	3.41	3.47	3.73	3.81	3.90	3.88	3.82	Allemagne
Greece[2]	0.75	0.71	0.75	0.65	0.64	0.63	0.71	0.70	Grèce[2]
Hungary	..	1.75	1.61	1.62	1.58	1.48	1.51	1.56	Hongrie
Iceland	2.90	3.13	3.23	3.07	3.04	2.89	2.74	2.52	Islande
Ireland	3.66	3.99	4.02	4.05	4.22	3.92	3.97	3.76	Irlande
Italy	1.96	2.06	2.20	2.28	2.26	2.21	2.19	2.25	Italie
Japan	2.12	2.05	2.02	2.13	2.12	2.17	2.18	2.09	Japon
Korea	..	..	..	..	2.44	2.73	3.07	3.40	Corée
Luxembourg	2.92	3.03	3.02	2.79	2.94	2.93	3.22	2.93	Luxembourg
Mexico	..	..	0.88	0.95	0.94	0.86	0.80	0.80	Mexique
Netherlands	3.68	3.30	3.69	3.97	4.21	4.15	4.15	4.12	Pays-Bas
New Zealand[5]	2.57	2.14	2.38	1.69	1.55	1.63	2.51	2.55	Nouvelle Zélande[5]
Norway[7]	2.89	2.76	2.94	2.97	2.85	2.57	2.45	2.38	Norvège[7]
Poland[9]	..	..	..	0.88	0.82	1.39	1.60	1.97	Pologne[9]
Portugal	2.24	2.30	2.40	2.68	2.66	2.57	2.67	2.66	Portugal
Spain	2.44	2.55	2.72	2.86	2.88	2.84	2.82	2.73	Espagne
Sweden	2.32	2.56	2.58	3.21	2.34	2.20	2.09	2.09	Suède
Switzerland	3.54	3.53	3.61	3.66	3.69	3.70	3.73	3.61	Suisse
Turkey	0.45	0.51	0.60	0.73	0.72	0.71	0.74	0.82	Turquie
United Kingdom	4.42	4.75	5.37	5.50	5.27	4.91	4.49	4.30	Royaume-Uni
United States	6.02	6.16	6.03	6.06	5.92	5.81	5.66	6.28	Etats-Unis
NAFTA[11]	5.67	5.83	5.48	5.52	5.36	5.35	5.25	5.78	ALENA[11]
EU-15[11]	3.02	3.09	3.27	3.47	3.45	3.41	3.33	3.28	UE-15[11]
OECD[11]	3.76	3.78	3.80	3.91	3.80	3.75	3.76	4.01	OCDE[11]

1. Net written premiums basis for life for 1994 and 1995 / Sur la base des primes nettes émises pour l'assurance vie pour 1994 et 1995
2. Net written premiums basis until 1991 / Sur la base des primes nettes émises jusqu'à 1991
3. Net written premiums basis for life until 1994 / Sur la base des primes nettes émises pour l'assurance vie jusqu'à 1994
4. Total gross premiums basis for life since 1996 / Sur la base des primes brutes totales pour l'assurance vie depuis 1996
5. Net written premiums basis for non-life for 1992-1995 / Sur la base des primes nettes émises pour l'assurance non-vie pour les années 1992 à 1995
6. Net written premiums basis for life for 1992 / Sur la base des primes nettes émises pour l'assurance vie pour 1992
7. Without branches of foreign insurers for non-life for 1994 and 1995 / Sans les succursales des assureurs étrangers pour l'assurance non-vie pour 1994 et 1995
8. Net written premiums basis for life until 1995 / Sur la base des primes nettes émises pour l'assurance vie jusqu'à 1995
9. Net written premiums basis for non-life until 1994 / Sur la base des primes nettes émises pour l'assurance non-vie jusqu'à 1994
10. Net written premiums basis for life until 1995 / Sur la base des primes nettes émises pour l'assurance vie jusqu'à 1995
11. For available data only / Uniquement pour les données disponibles

V. Life Insurance share / Part de l'assurance-vie

									% (per cent / pourcentage)	
COUNTRY	1990	1991	1992	1993	1994	1995	1996	1997	PAYS
Australia[1]	69.36	67.84	68.57	59.09	59.81	56.71	49.26	58.04	Australie[1]
Austria	30.08	28.60	27.84	31.57	29.64	32.69	39.44	32.83	Autriche
Belgium	32.31	32.78	32.85	34.85	39.18	40.43	43.76	48.24	Belgique
Canada	46.82	47.93	44.51	38.44	54.55	55.84	37.18	36.34	Canada
Czech Republic	..	..	..	25.77	25.10	27.64	26.60	25.98	République Tchèque
Denmark	35.53	38.77	38.46	44.89	47.44	50.86	54.69	56.58	Danemark
Finland	64.33	64.27	61.22	18.37	23.82	36.71	48.63	47.15	Finlande
France	48.97	50.53	51.93	55.21	59.96	60.75	62.45	64.84	France
Germany	40.97	40.22	35.67	35.46	35.58	35.75	36.67	37.23	Allemagne
Greece[2]	41.80	46.21	48.19	46.30	47.46	47.85	47.05	48.99	Grèce[2]
Hungary[3]	..	25.99	17.83	21.18	25.59	29.80	31.87	32.91	Hongrie[3]
Iceland	2.59	2.71	2.71	3.05	3.51	3.96	3.55	4.22	Islande
Ireland	58.33	55.42	54.83	56.58	53.48	52.41	56.42	60.17	Irlande
Italy	26.82	27.86	28.64	30.56	33.37	36.81	38.63	45.24	Italie
Japan	73.05	73.20	73.74	73.32	73.35	72.93	71.64	72.93	Japon
Korea	..	..	..	..	75.22	74.76	72.64	71.54	Corée
Luxembourg[4]	31.87	34.33	32.13	31.95	72.70	87.80	84.91	90.38	Luxembourg[4]
Mexico	..	..	33.06	32.61	33.88	32.67	33.66	35.68	Mexique
Netherlands	51.83	55.84	53.73	51.62	50.86	53.27	53.99	55.52	Pays-Bas
New Zealand	36.10	41.88	39.18	42.89	43.54	35.53	34.38	35.11	Nouvelle Zélande
Norway[5]	32.16	38.33	38.40	37.29	42.72	43.53	43.92	49.14	Norvège[5]
Poland	..	..	..	28.65	30.98	27.54	28.60	27.67	Pologne
Portugal	23.40	26.15	28.68	31.06	34.44	43.07	46.62	45.43	Portugal
Spain	29.90	34.22	32.33	32.12	42.05	39.61	42.69	45.99	Espagne
Sweden[6]	49.87	49.11	47.02	46.70	53.94	54.90	57.21	58.08	Suède[6]
Switzerland	41.60	42.11	40.81	41.81	43.81	48.37	58.58	62.43	Suisse
Turkey	19.37	20.18	18.84	14.45	11.97	12.79	14.61	15.75	Turquie
United Kingdom[7]	59.76	61.13	58.14	53.98	53.97	53.99	58.48	61.02	Royaume-Uni[7]
United States	37.51	35.81	36.83	37.88	37.96	38.55	39.68	37.94	Etats-Unis
NAFTA[8]	37.98	36.45	37.16	37.85	38.55	39.17	39.56	37.88	ALENA[8]
EU-15[8]	46.64	47.59	45.10	44.91	46.63	47.39	49.87	52.43	UE-15[8]
OECD[8]	47.74	47.71	47.44	48.10	49.85	50.60	50.43	50.05	OCDE[8]

1. Net written premiums basis for 1994 and 1995 / Sur la base des primes nettes émises pour les années 1994 et 1995
2. Net written premiums basis until 1991 / Sur la base des primes nettes émises jusqu'à 1991
3. Direct gross premiums basis for 1991 / Sur la base des primes brutes directes pour 1991
4. Direct gross premiums basis until 1993 / Sur la base des primes brutes directes jusqu'à 1993
5. Without branches of foreign insurers for non-life for 1994 and 1995 / Sans les succursales des assureurs étrangers pour l'assurance non-vie pour 1994 et 1995
6. Without branches of foreign insurers for life for 1990 and without branches of foreign insurers for non-life until 1996 / Sans les succursales des assureurs étrangers pour l'assurance vie pour 1990 et sans les succursales des assureurs étrangers pour l'assurance non-vie jusqu'à 1996
7. Net written premiums basis until 1992 / Sur la base des primes nettes émises jusqu'à 1992
8. For available data only / Uniquement pour les données disponibles

VI. Direct total gross premiums / Number of employees of the insurance companies
Total des primes brutes directes / Nombre d'employés des entreprises d'assurances

| | | | | | | | | | U.S. $ per employee / $ U.S. par employé | |
COUNTRY	1990	1991	1992	1993	1994	1995	1996	1997	PAYS
Australia	..	..	..	..	..	..	..	..	Australie
Austria	240 102	246 520	285 804	304 575	326 102	396 267	437 246	344 835	Autriche
Belgium	304 849	328 818	395 605	407 221	462 149	571 916	597 558	554 060	Belgique
Canada	244 869	336 533	..	..	..	..	..	269 495	Canada
Czech Republic	..	..	..	70 966	79 111	93 348	99 436	92 315	République Tchèque
Denmark	..	..	..	..	..	719 215	..	714 800	Danemark
Finland	748 172	761 451	575 147	203 407	322 169	454 289	534 190	468 488	Finlande
France	570 920	601 377	712 996	782 934	902 495	1 078 813	1 031 945	984 698	France
Germany	406 551	391 493	450 703	470 660	526 868	673 398	697 723	644 662	Allemagne
Greece	..	..	142 872	172 292	166 745	196 308	..	..	Grèce
Hungary	..	65 034	55 185	51 316	54 277	54 997	38 509	36 192	Hongrie
Iceland	440 083	505 093	529 696	449 906	452 788	476 155	470 086	418 818	Islande
Ireland	435 311	423 669	421 816	429 049	469 078	522 847	639 228	765 918	Irlande
Italy	615 765	676 748	762 896	664 587	733 794	815 784	954 898	1 069 121	Italie
Japan	463 053	417 146	475 468	560 665	631 423	703 861	618 696	620 805	Japon
Korea	..	..	..	..	579 550	713 783	714 123	714 842	Corée
Luxembourg	403 244	433 639	472 082	436 684	1 233 489	3 184 741	2 275 972	2 791 343	Luxembourg
Mexico	..	..	237 579	287 717	297 701	191 130	206 567	244 642	Mexique
Netherlands	..	..	..	..	..	736 747	..	686 241	Pays-Bas
New Zealand	..	..	..	..	..	..	..	..	Nouvelle Zélande
Norway	476 126	465 497	..	488 078	..	..	744 648	790 206	Norvège
Poland	..	..	..	..	..	..	117 413	143 299	Pologne
Portugal	138 508	173 357	214 245	224 721	256 388	341 979	402 571	343 922	Portugal
Spain	405 234	450 107	504 531	462 058	538 337	562 955	607 679	673 923	Espagne
Sweden	242 510	260 650	339 190	285 183	604 393	674 777	767 539	801 410	Suède
Switzerland	511 496	516 423	559 852	577 135	686 973	867 197	..	..	Suisse
Turkey	182 761	187 477	228 406	259 836	190 915	209 424	210 972	230 782	Turquie
United Kingdom	..	..	..	..	..	..	694 089	687 257	Royaume-Uni
United States	382 146	383 454	405 235	423 981	435 884	451 264	..	..	Etats-Unis
NAFTA[1]	372 388	380 734	402 924	422 204	434 095	448 031	206 567	265 159	ALENA[1]
EU-15[1]	432 004	442 032	504 120	507 541	595 925	726 081	748 105	725 441	UE-15[1]
OECD[1]	404 043	401 656	441 552	469 618	511 125	568 428	657 086	627 930	OCDE[1]

1. For available data only / Uniquement pour les données disponibles

VII. Retention ratio (= Net written premiums / Total gross premiums) / Taux de rétention (= Primes nettes émises / Total des primes brutes)

VII.1 Total / Total

% (per cent / pourcentage)

COUNTRY	1990	1991	1992	1993	1994	1995	1996	1997	PAYS
Australia	94.50	93.59	93.39	87.69	..	..	91.67	92.95	Australie
Austria	84.48	84.66	83.37	83.73	78.45	80.79	80.86	78.58	Autriche
Belgium	84.77	84.54	85.00	86.04	87.36	90.06	91.24	92.60	Belgique
Canada	87.86	87.78	86.31	84.66	84.72	85.78	84.45	84.30	Canada
Czech Republic	..	..	..	93.41	91.05	88.12	86.71	85.85	République Tchèque
Denmark	..	..	..	..	..	..	94.07	..	Danemark
Finland	96.24	95.88	95.08	90.38	89.91	92.05	94.17	94.17	Finlande
France	89.50	89.79	90.44	91.52	91.60	91.57	92.50	93.03	France
Germany	83.26	82.78	80.46	80.92	81.65	82.43	82.65	82.98	Allemagne
Greece	..	..	100.00	78.41	78.55	78.90	81.09	84.13	Grèce
Hungary	..	..	84.42	80.99	79.64	78.99	81.48	86.66	Hongrie
Iceland	64.49	66.71	65.39	66.45	66.53	68.47	70.61	71.42	Islande
Ireland	90.88	90.40	82.09	84.36	89.03	87.91	88.82	91.81	Irlande
Italy	80.37	79.99	79.26	81.36	84.95	86.06	86.94	88.28	Italie
Japan	95.00	95.44	95.44	95.78	95.79	95.68	95.68	..	Japon
Korea	..	..	..	..	96.27	96.53	96.69	96.80	Corée
Luxembourg	..	..	..	..	86.54	94.61	86.03	92.16	Luxembourg
Mexico	..	..	80.73	79.80	80.57	77.91	77.50	79.46	Mexique
Netherlands	90.45	90.50	90.66	88.27	88.37	90.28	91.40	91.79	Pays-Bas
New Zealand	95.05	98.02	97.87	91.36	89.96	87.72	..	..	Nouvelle Zélande
Norway	82.62	85.64	85.95	84.46	..	..	90.58	91.04	Norvège
Poland	..	..	..	73.06	72.68	75.22	75.22	75.13	Pologne
Portugal	87.43	88.21	89.40	89.90	91.01	91.61	91.20	90.78	Portugal
Spain	86.13	87.64	87.00	86.90	89.54	90.11	90.73	91.70	Espagne
Sweden	..	..	..	..	..	..	..	90.76	Suède
Switzerland	86.93	87.88	86.95	86.63	..	..	87.15	91.02	Suisse
Turkey	57.53	61.75	61.27	85.78	79.87	80.43	81.36	81.00	Turquie
United Kingdom	..	..	..	87.75	84.95	87.64	89.30	90.33	Royaume-Uni
United States	90.48	90.48	90.02	89.90	90.47	88.95	89.85	92.10	Etats-Unis
NAFTA[1]	90.35	90.34	89.78	89.62	90.17	88.78	89.59	91.78	ALENA[1]
EU-15[1]	86.13	85.97	84.78	85.91	85.77	87.02	88.02	88.78	UE-15[1]
OECD[1]	90.24	90.33	89.57	89.61	90.10	89.90	90.30	90.75	OCDE[1]

VII.2 Life / Vie

% (per cent / pourcentage)

COUNTRY	1990	1991	1992	1993	1994	1995	1996	1997	PAYS
Australia	100.00	100.00	100.00	90.44	..	..	100.00	100.00	Australie
Austria	89.40	89.06	88.82	90.51	89.50	91.67	92.60	91.70	Autriche
Belgium	94.14	94.28	94.29	95.33	96.34	99.93	99.93	99.96	Belgique
Canada	95.42	94.72	94.95	92.56	91.63	91.29	88.88	87.78	Canada
Czech Republic	..	..	..	100.00	100.00	99.02	98.91	98.84	République Tchèque
Denmark	98.59	98.72	98.75	99.41	98.40	98.56	98.60	98.70	Danemark
Finland	99.20	99.45	99.20	95.47	95.28	98.48	99.12	99.01	Finlande
France	96.45	96.68	96.24	96.93	97.16	96.80	97.74	97.58	France
Germany	91.58	91.15	91.18	91.87	92.13	92.31	91.95	92.05	Allemagne
Greece	..	..	100.00	84.06	84.44	85.01	87.70	91.67	Grèce
Hungary	..	..	74.34	62.98	64.25	66.02	67.13	91.40	Hongrie
Iceland	61.29	62.32	64.02	66.03	71.71	72.58	66.18	72.20	Islande
Ireland	95.90	96.93	82.41	86.56	96.98	95.91	95.93	97.38	Irlande
Italy	81.64	81.63	81.46	83.07	89.68	90.68	90.95	92.24	Italie
Japan	99.83	99.86	99.86	99.85	99.84	99.83	99.81	99.50	Japon
Korea	..	..	..	..	99.72	99.73	99.69	99.50	Corée
Luxembourg	..	..	..	..	95.50	98.20	88.00	94.17	Luxembourg
Mexico	..	..	94.43	94.49	93.61	93.28	92.58	92.59	Mexique
Netherlands	95.57	95.69	95.21	90.64	90.67	92.90	94.44	94.37	Pays-Bas
New Zealand	100.00	100.00	100.00	100.00	100.00	100.00	..	..	Nouvelle Zélande
Norway	99.10	99.79	99.91	100.00	100.00	100.00	98.76	98.92	Norvège
Poland	..	..	..	100.00	99.93	99.87	99.70	98.85	Pologne
Portugal	95.15	95.92	97.39	97.66	97.91	97.74	98.11	98.26	Portugal
Spain	96.60	97.41	96.91	96.76	97.86	97.36	97.68	98.25	Espagne
Sweden	..	98.69	99.05	96.92	98.67	97.80	98.98	98.88	Suède
Switzerland	96.29	96.68	96.71	96.74	96.71	97.15	98.14	98.65	Suisse
Turkey	95.66	95.70	96.21	98.58	98.39	97.48	97.52	97.76	Turquie
United Kingdom	..	..	..	95.35	90.76	96.00	96.96	97.70	Royaume-Uni
United States	94.24	94.16	92.88	92.31	94.78	91.27	92.55	95.56	Etats-Unis
NAFTA[1]	94.31	94.20	93.00	92.33	94.61	91.27	92.42	95.30	ALENA[1]
EU-15[1]	93.69	93.95	93.37	94.07	93.50	95.10	95.65	96.06	UE-15[1]
OECD[1]	96.19	96.28	95.66	95.38	96.22	95.70	96.02	96.92	OCDE[1]

VII. Retention ratio (= Net written premiums / Total gross premiums) / Taux de rétention (= Primes nettes émises / Total des primes brutes)

VII.3 Non-Life / Non-Vie

% (per cent / pourcentage)

COUNTRY	1990	1991	1992	1993	1994	1995	1996	1997	PAYS
Australia	82.06	80.07	78.98	83.72	80.99	82.88	83.59	83.19	Australie
Austria	82.36	82.90	81.27	80.60	73.79	75.51	73.22	72.16	Autriche
Belgium	80.30	79.80	80.44	81.08	81.57	83.35	84.48	85.74	Belgique
Canada	81.21	81.39	79.38	79.73	76.44	78.81	81.83	82.32	Canada
Czech Republic	..	..	..	91.13	88.06	83.96	82.29	81.29	République Tchèque
Denmark	..	..	..	..	..	..	88.60	..	Danemark
Finland	90.91	89.46	88.56	89.23	88.23	88.31	89.47	89.85	Finlande
France	82.83	82.75	84.18	84.85	83.28	83.46	83.78	84.65	France
Germany	77.49	77.15	74.51	74.90	75.87	76.94	77.27	77.60	Allemagne
Greece	..	..	100.00	73.53	73.23	73.29	75.22	76.89	Grèce
Hungary	..	..	86.61	85.83	84.94	84.50	88.19	84.33	Hongrie
Iceland	64.58	66.84	65.42	66.46	66.34	68.30	70.78	71.38	Islande
Ireland	83.86	82.28	81.70	81.49	79.90	79.09	79.62	83.40	Irlande
Italy	79.91	79.36	78.38	80.60	82.58	83.36	84.41	85.01	Italie
Japan	76.99	79.05	78.99	80.69	81.17	81.01	81.82	..	Japon
Korea	..	..	..	..	85.78	87.05	88.70	89.99	Corée
Luxembourg	..	..	..	..	62.66	68.79	74.91	73.36	Luxembourg
Mexico	..	..	73.97	72.69	73.89	70.46	69.86	72.18	Mexique
Netherlands	84.93	83.95	85.38	85.74	85.99	87.29	87.84	88.56	Pays-Bas
New Zealand	92.26	96.60	96.50	84.88	82.21	80.95	86.82	87.90	Nouvelle Zélande
Norway	74.82	76.84	77.24	75.21	..	..	84.18	83.42	Norvège
Poland	..	..	..	62.25	60.45	65.86	65.42	66.06	Pologne
Portugal	85.08	85.48	86.19	86.40	87.38	86.98	85.16	84.55	Portugal
Spain	81.67	82.56	82.26	82.23	83.50	85.35	85.55	86.13	Espagne
Sweden	..	..	..	..	..	..	..	79.51	Suède
Switzerland	80.27	81.49	80.22	79.36	..	..	71.59	78.35	Suisse
Turkey	48.37	53.17	53.16	83.62	77.35	77.93	78.60	77.86	Turquie
United Kingdom	74.92	74.10	77.21	78.84	78.15	77.82	78.51	78.79	Royaume-Uni
United States	88.23	88.42	88.36	88.43	87.82	87.50	88.07	89.99	Etats-Unis
NAFTA[1]	87.93	88.12	87.88	87.97	87.38	87.17	87.73	89.63	ALENA[1]
EU-15[1]	79.26	78.72	78.70	79.40	79.27	79.94	80.57	80.84	UE-15[1]
OECD[1]	84.07	84.12	83.58	84.13	83.87	83.87	84.38	86.31	OCDE[1]

1. For available data only / Uniquement pour les données disponibles

VIII. Ratio of reinsurance accepted (= Reinsurance accepted / Total gross premiums) / Taux de réassurance acceptée (= Réassurance acceptée / Total des primes brutes)

VIII.1 Total / Total

% (per cent / pourcentage)

COUNTRY	1990	1991	1992	1993	1994	1995	1996	1997	PAYS
Australia	..	..	..	5.02	..	..	7.08	3.76	Australie
Austria	7.83	7.67	9.50	8.87	12.72	9.99	11.31	13.74	Autriche
Belgium	6.24	6.16	4.74	3.34	2.81	5.65	5.26	5.06	Belgique
Canada	10.21	10.65	12.21	12.55	12.66	11.08	12.57	12.45	Canada
Czech Republic	..	..	..	0.00	0.00	1.60	0.29	1.10	République Tchèque
Denmark	13.77	15.46	17.48	11.46	13.77	9.01	7.98	7.09	Danemark
Finland	4.83	5.59	4.89	9.93	6.91	5.88	5.06	4.48	Finlande
France	10.13	10.69	11.24	10.98	7.67	7.39	6.41	5.93	France
Germany	2.56	2.34	20.49	20.76	21.61	21.07	20.95	21.87	Allemagne
Greece	..	..	..	3.95	3.62	2.11	2.74	1.84	Grèce
Hungary	..	..	1.47	1.22	0.58	0.44	0.33	0.28	Hongrie
Iceland	17.27	15.88	16.25	15.79	14.19	11.67	10.94	10.82	Islande
Ireland	1.61	1.87	9.97	7.64	2.11	4.40	4.17	7.09	Irlande
Italy	13.84	14.08	15.23	13.80	11.76	11.04	10.44	9.31	Italie
Japan	3.02	2.57	2.55	2.30	2.25	2.33	1.85	1.71	Japon
Korea	..	..	..	..	2.69	2.43	2.40	2.17	Corée
Luxembourg	..	..	..	..	0.43	0.08	0.21	0.21	Luxembourg
Mexico	..	..	4.13	4.20	3.95	4.50	3.69	3.29	Mexique
Netherlands	..	..	..	..	..	3.32	2.58	1.98	Pays-Bas
New Zealand	..	..	..	..	..	..	..	..	Nouvelle Zélande
Norway	11.71	8.36	..	5.25	..	..	0.56	0.54	Norvège
Poland	..	..	..	..	..	..	0.44	1.19	Pologne
Portugal	1.90	1.38	1.28	1.30	1.11	1.15	1.41	1.70	Portugal
Spain	4.18	3.94	4.29	4.83	3.97	3.85	3.44	3.49	Espagne
Sweden	..	..	..	..	..	..	..	9.56	Suède
Switzerland	32.94	33.56	36.03	36.27	33.97	30.12	15.33	12.11	Suisse
Turkey	4.72	3.54	2.05	1.47	1.39	1.21	1.15	1.00	Turquie
United Kingdom	..	..	..	..	..	..	6.40	5.38	Royaume-Uni
United States	7.88	7.77	8.31	8.69	7.62	8.92	8.51	6.91	Etats-Unis
NAFTA[1]	8.00	7.92	8.45	8.80	7.78	8.98	8.63	7.07	ALENA[1]
EU-15[1]	6.85	6.60	14.19	14.31	13.22	12.20	10.35	9.83	UE-15[1]
OECD[1]	7.26	7.00	9.19	8.97	7.55	7.99	7.79	6.89	OCDE[1]

VIII.2 Life / Vie

% (per cent / pourcentage)

COUNTRY	1990	1991	1992	1993	1994	1995	1996	1997	PAYS
Australia	..	..	..	0.30	..	..	0.00	1.24	Australie
Austria	1.89	0.96	0.97	0.79	0.71	0.71	0.71	0.98	Autriche
Belgium	1.07	1.37	1.02	1.11	1.24	1.35	1.33	1.28	Belgique
Canada	3.02	3.55	3.93	3.31	5.44	5.95	7.28	8.06	Canada
Czech Republic	..	..	..	0.00	0.00	0.00	0.00	0.00	République Tchèque
Denmark	0.40	0.42	0.38	0.27	0.46	0.25	0.25	0.26	Danemark
Finland	0.10	0.11	-0.73	0.04	0.10	0.08	0.14	0.97	Finlande
France	3.83	3.56	3.64	3.09	2.68	2.67	1.74	1.57	France
Germany	0.45	0.45	9.60	9.54	10.06	10.04	10.17	10.83	Allemagne
Greece	..	..	..	0.14	0.11	0.06	0.16	0.09	Grèce
Hungary	..	..	0.73	1.61	0.00	0.00	0.00	0.00	Hongrie
Iceland	4.11	4.59	2.34	2.11	14.77	16.91	0.36	17.51	Islande
Ireland	0.19	0.13	15.05	9.38	0.18	0.43	0.96	0.82	Irlande
Italy	18.47	17.79	18.36	15.00	11.12	9.85	10.23	8.43	Italie
Japan	0.55	0.11	0.12	0.12	0.13	0.14	0.15	0.15	Japon
Korea	..	..	..	..	0.00	0.01	0.12	0.00	Corée
Luxembourg	..	..	..	..	0.34	0.06	0.20	0.20	Luxembourg
Mexico	..	..	1.00	1.13	1.13	1.14	1.07	1.32	Mexique
Netherlands	..	..	..	..	..	3.48	1.79	1.19	Pays-Bas
New Zealand	..	..	..	..	..	..	..	..	Nouvelle Zélande
Norway	0.63	0.03	..	0.00	0.00	0.00	0.00	0.00	Norvège
Poland	..	..	..	..	..	..	0.00	0.00	Pologne
Portugal	0.03	0.03	0.11	0.08	0.01	0.02	0.15	0.20	Portugal
Spain	1.08	0.57	0.61	0.68	0.44	0.65	0.44	0.68	Espagne
Sweden	..	4.88	6.42	5.39	2.90	4.26	0.13	0.31	Suède
Switzerland	9.94	9.43	9.25	9.07	7.30	7.24	3.75	1.77	Suisse
Turkey	0.04	0.05	0.02	0.02	0.03	0.57	0.54	0.55	Turquie
United Kingdom	..	..	..	..	..	..	0.76	0.71	Royaume-Uni
United States	6.31	6.25	7.40	7.82	4.66	7.31	6.79	5.12	Etats-Unis
NAFTA[1]	6.11	6.06	7.17	7.60	4.67	7.21	6.79	5.19	ALENA[1]
EU-15[1]	3.21	3.21	6.76	6.11	5.37	5.11	3.52	3.34	UE-15[1]
OECD[1]	3.70	3.38	4.60	4.37	3.04	3.88	3.46	2.96	OCDE[1]

VIII. Ratio of reinsurance accepted (= Reinsurance accepted / Total gross premiums) / Taux de réassurance acceptée (= Réassurance acceptée / Total des primes brutes)

VIII.3 Non-Life / Non-Vie

% (per cent / pourcentage)

COUNTRY	1990	1991	1992	1993	1994	1995	1996	1997	PAYS
Australia	11.49	13.98	17.94	11.84	16.97	14.40	13.95	7.25	Australie
Austria	10.39	10.36	12.79	12.60	17.78	14.49	18.21	19.98	Autriche
Belgium	8.71	8.50	6.55	4.53	3.83	8.57	8.32	8.59	Belgique
Canada	16.54	17.19	18.84	18.32	21.33	17.57	15.71	14.95	Canada
Czech Republic	..	..	..	0.00	0.00	2.21	0.40	1.48	République Tchèque
Denmark	21.13	24.99	28.17	20.59	25.79	18.07	17.31	15.99	Danemark
Finland	21.13	24.99	28.17	20.59	25.79	18.07	17.31	15.99	Finlande
France	16.16	17.96	19.46	20.71	15.13	14.70	14.17	13.98	France
Germany	4.02	3.61	26.52	26.92	27.99	27.21	27.19	28.42	Allemagne
Greece	..	..	..	7.23	6.80	3.99	5.03	3.52	Grèce
Hungary	..	..	1.63	1.12	0.77	0.63	0.49	0.42	Hongrie
Iceland	17.62	16.20	16.64	16.22	14.17	11.45	11.33	10.53	Islande
Ireland	3.59	4.04	3.81	5.39	4.33	8.77	8.33	16.55	Irlande
Italy	12.14	12.65	13.97	13.28	12.07	11.73	10.57	10.04	Italie
Japan	9.71	9.27	9.37	8.30	8.10	8.24	6.14	5.92	Japon
Korea	..	..	..	..	10.86	9.62	8.46	7.60	Corée
Luxembourg	..	..	..	..	0.66	0.19	0.21	0.26	Luxembourg
Mexico	..	..	5.68	5.68	5.39	6.14	5.01	4.38	Mexique
Netherlands	4.71	4.13	4.09	3.48	3.35	3.14	3.50	2.96	Pays-Bas
New Zealand	2.57	3.69	..	..	..	..	1.53	1.44	Nouvelle Zélande
Norway	16.97	13.53	9.39	8.37	..	..	1.00	1.06	Norvège
Poland	..	..	..	..	..	0.63	0.61	1.65	Pologne
Portugal	2.47	1.85	1.74	1.85	1.68	1.99	2.52	2.95	Portugal
Spain	5.50	5.69	6.05	6.80	6.53	5.95	5.68	5.88	Espagne
Sweden	..	..	..	..	..	..	..	22.37	Suède
Switzerland	49.33	51.12	54.50	55.80	54.76	51.56	31.72	29.29	Suisse
Turkey	5.84	4.42	2.52	1.71	1.58	1.30	1.25	1.08	Turquie
United Kingdom	20.24	20.19	20.06	17.35	14.17	14.37	14.34	12.70	Royaume-Uni
United States	8.82	8.62	8.83	9.21	9.43	9.94	9.64	8.00	Etats-Unis
NAFTA[1]	9.15	8.99	9.22	9.52	9.73	10.13	9.84	8.21	ALENA[1]
EU-15[1]	11.87	11.74	18.60	19.28	17.98	17.25	17.02	16.90	UE-15[1]
OECD[1]	10.99	10.86	13.60	13.29	12.10	12.34	12.14	10.77	OCDE[1]

1. For available data only / Uniquement pour les données disponibles

IX.1 Foreign companies' market share in the domestic market (Gross premiums basis) / Life
Part du marché national détenue par les entreprises étrangères (Sur la base des primes brutes) / Vie

IX.1.1 Market share of (foreign controlled undertakings) and (branches/agencies of foreign undertakings) in total domestic business (Gross premium basis)

Part du marché des (entreprises sous contrôle étranger) et (succursales et agences d'entreprises étrangères) dans le marché national (Sur la base des primes brutes)   % (per cent \ pourcentage)

COUNTRY	1990	1991	1992	1993	1994	1995	1996	1997	PAYS
Australia	18.86	22.27	26.17	..	..	..	30.32	45.50	Australie
Austria	34.01	36.08	36.49	33.82	37.51	34.74	34.36	35.03	Autriche
Belgium	..							..	Belgique
Canada	35.29	34.09	35.81	28.72	33.17	38.19	37.25	..	Canada
Czech Republic	..	..	..	6.88	14.96	20.85	24.34	28.23	République Tchèque
Denmark	9.06	9.33	9.55	7.65	8.67	7.54	7.48	6.88	Danemark
Finland	0.00	0.00	0.00	..	0.00	..	..	0.00	Finlande
France	8.15	..	6.66	..	..	..	..	..	France
Germany	12.54	12.47	11.43	11.33	9.80	9.14	8.48	8.58	Allemagne
Greece	12.54	12.47	11.43	11.33	9.80	9.14	8.48	8.58	Grèce
Hungary	..	..	99.66	99.78	99.62	98.63	97.07	94.86	Hongrie
Iceland	0.00	0.72	1.64	3.38	4.09	4.76	4.88	0.00	Islande
Ireland	..	..	..	..	..	..	..	..	Irlande
Italy	..	..	..	..	..	..	..	..	Italie
Japan	2.24	2.35	2.48	2.66	3.07	3.40	3.81	3.77	Japon
Korea	..	..	..	..	0.38	0.34	0.36	0.38	Corée
Luxembourg	..	..	..	..	..	..	91.70	82.96	Luxembourg
Mexico	..	..	0.00	0.00	0.00	1.13	2.04	9.85	Mexique
Netherlands	24.90	19.89	23.30	22.85	22.36	22.22	20.77	21.75	Pays-Bas
New Zealand	..	..	..	..	..	..	..	..	Nouvelle Zélande
Norway	0.00	1.73	2.18	1.77	..	2.48	2.80	2.82	Norvège
Poland	..	..	..	1.17	5.28	14.03	23.89	33.07	Pologne
Portugal	30.92	33.28	27.86	28.78	29.35	12.15	12.11	13.16	Portugal
Spain	16.35	17.06	..	27.13	19.43	26.69	21.56	20.41	Espagne
Sweden	..	0.00	0.00	0.00	0.00	0.00	0.00	0.00	Suède
Switzerland	2.92	2.43	2.35	2.78	..	7.35	..	..	Suisse
Turkey	0.57	1.17	..	4.88	5.80	6.60	8.96	6.76	Turquie
United Kingdom	..	..	..	..	..	..	21.50	19.94	Royaume-Uni
United States	9.18	8.19	12.14	15.15	13.41	12.65	14.34	12.97	Etats-Unis

IX.1.2 Market share of (branches/agencies of foreign undertakings) in total domestic business (Gross premium basis)

Part du marché des (succursales et agences d'entreprises étrangères) dans le marché national (Sur la base des primes brutes)   % (per cent \ pourcentage)

COUNTRY	1990	1991	1992	1993	1994	1995	1996	1997	PAYS
Australia	5.41	7.66	8.17	..	..	..	0.09	0.00	Australie
Austria	0.28	0.33	0.37	0.52	0.07	0.12	0.00	0.00	Autriche
Belgium	7.64	7.32	7.09	8.40	8.19	4.16	3.56	3.50	Belgique
Canada	19.88	17.96	19.39	8.73	20.99	21.54	18.57	16.78	Canada
Czech Republic	..	..	..	5.43	9.70	14.09	15.49	17.30	République Tchèque
Denmark	2.35	2.39	2.37	1.70	0.68	0.58	0.48	0.40	Danemark
Finland	0.00	0.00	0.00	..	0.00	..	0.00	0.00	Finlande
France	2.05	2.00	1.94	1.65	1.07	1.00	1.03	0.95	France
Germany	3.31	3.23	2.99	3.00	2.65	2.09	2.10	2.10	Allemagne
Greece	..	..	23.04	23.50	24.16	25.25	25.97	10.20	Grèce
Hungary	..	..	0.00	0.00	0.00	0.00	0.00	0.00	Hongrie
Iceland	0.00	0.00	0.00	0.00	0.00	0.00	0.00	0.00	Islande
Ireland	31.17	32.63	24.75	21.95	23.69	22.43	22.59	19.45	Irlande
Italy	1.49	1.43	1.42	1.57	1.80	2.18	2.49	2.41	Italie
Japan	1.61	1.76	1.94	2.10	2.38	2.31	2.66	2.77	Japon
Korea	..	..	..	..	0.13	0.11	0.10	0.10	Corée
Luxembourg	..	..	..	..	4.05	2.26	2.28	2.82	Luxembourg
Mexico	..	..	0.00	0.00	0.00	0.00	0.00	0.00	Mexique
Netherlands	7.96	6.36	5.82	6.51	5.68	5.64	5.50	5.14	Pays-Bas
New Zealand	29.10	..	..	..	..	..	..	..	Nouvelle Zélande
Norway	0.00	0.00	0.00	0.00	..	0.00	0.02	0.01	Norvège
Poland	..	..	..	0.00	0.00	0.00	0.00	0.00	Pologne
Portugal	22.65	24.90	18.73	12.91	5.89	2.22	1.93	2.33	Portugal
Spain	6.90	5.82	6.30	5.51	7.11	3.67	3.94	3.63	Espagne
Sweden	..	0.00	0.00	0.00	0.00	0.00	0.00	0.00	Suède
Switzerland	0.00	0.00	0.00	0.00	..	0.00	0.00	..	Suisse
Turkey	0.00	0.00	..	0.00	0.00	0.00	0.00	0.00	Turquie
United Kingdom	..	..	..	2.27	2.12	2.68	3.06	2.51	Royaume-Uni
United States	2.37	2.30	2.44	2.15	1.14	1.19	1.04	0.59	Etats-Unis

IX.2 Foreign companies' market share in the domestic market (Gross premiums basis) / Non-Life
Part du marché national détenue par les entreprises étrangères (Sur la base des primes brutes) / Non-Vie

IX.2.1 Market share of (foreign controlled undertakings) and (branches/agencies of foreign undertakings) in total domestic business (Gross premium basis)

Part du marché des (entreprises sous contrôle étranger) et (succursales et agences d'entreprises étrangères) dans le marché national (Sur la base des primes brutes)   % (per cent \ pourcentage)

COUNTRY	1990	1991	1992	1993	1994	1995	1996	1997	PAYS
Australia	43.81	40.70	58.08	38.91	37.05	38.13	36.89	32.87	Australie
Austria	47.44	46.89	48.18	48.78	49.25	47.60	49.34	49.16	Autriche
Belgium	..	..	..	..	..	..	..	..	Belgique
Canada	63.32	62.33	64.37	61.58	70.50	72.06	63.68	..	Canada
Czech Republic	..	..	..	9.64	20.66	25.63	30.03	28.43	République Tchèque
Denmark	27.18	27.06	34.48	36.74	22.15	32.84	30.86	28.64	Danemark
Finland	0.23	0.22	0.23	..	..	..	..	0.13	Finlande
France	12.12	..	18.29	..	..	..	..	..	France
Germany	17.66	13.95	14.26	16.29	7.83	7.30	13.08	12.70	Allemagne
Greece	..	..	..	..	..	..	..	..	Grèce
Hungary	..	..	95.20	95.69	93.96	92.30	91.01	90.93	Hongrie
Iceland	0.00	3.35	3.92	4.11	0.68	3.63	3.57	0.00	Islande
Ireland	..	..	..	..	..	..	..	..	Irlande
Italy	..	..	..	..	..	..	..	..	Italie
Japan	2.86	2.99	3.17	3.16	3.29	3.33	3.33	3.59	Japon
Korea	..	..	..	..	0.24	0.59	0.41	0.36	Corée
Luxembourg	..	..	..	..	..	..	36.03	31.74	Luxembourg
Mexico	..	..	0.00	0.00	0.05	3.87	6.99	10.98	Mexique
Netherlands	27.42	20.08	29.05	25.85	23.51	22.29	20.96	24.02	Pays-Bas
New Zealand	..	..	..	..	..	..	..	..	Nouvelle Zélande
Norway	15.17	17.38	15.72	16.60	..	..	19.25	21.02	Norvège
Poland	..	..	..	1.22	1.05	1.73	3.00	7.89	Pologne
Portugal	13.06	27.30	25.72	12.76	9.12	15.35	14.94	15.03	Portugal
Spain	31.52	39.12	..	41.29	32.10	33.09	29.32	27.29	Espagne
Sweden	..	..	..	..	..	..	..	..	Suède
Switzerland	9.83	9.56	9.79	12.22	10.89	7.81	..	..	Suisse
Turkey	12.54	13.35	12.30	11.47	10.01	9.82	10.18	8.74	Turquie
United Kingdom	..	..	..	..	..	..	..	37.34	Royaume-Uni
United States	7.10	9.43	10.04	10.39	9.81	10.00	10.73	8.75	Etats-Unis

IX.2.2 Market share of (branches/agencies of foreign undertakings) in total domestic business (Gross premium basis)

Part du marché des (succursales et agences d'entreprises étrangères) dans le marché national (Sur la base des primes brutes)   % (per cent \ pourcentage)

COUNTRY	1990	1991	1992	1993	1994	1995	1996	1997	PAYS
Australia	12.76	7.71	6.96	5.86	4.68	5.12	4.88	5.00	Australie
Austria	1.15	0.92	0.89	0.85	0.16	0.17	0.16	0.17	Autriche
Belgium	11.11	10.07	7.25	6.84	2.92	2.34	2.57	2.46	Belgique
Canada	26.61	25.62	25.04	24.59	26.96	26.62	26.80	25.17	Canada
Czech Republic	..	..	..	0.32	0.87	0.68	1.10	1.44	République Tchèque
Denmark	5.19	1.78	5.09	6.24	3.42	2.43	1.80	1.73	Danemark
Finland	0.23	0.22	0.23	0.32	0.44	0.12	0.12	0.13	Finlande
France	3.49	3.06	2.75	2.73	1.35	1.25	1.25	1.24	France
Germany	3.19	3.03	2.27	2.21	1.53	1.11	0.70	0.66	Allemagne
Greece	..	..	13.99	12.32	10.91	10.67	10.13	10.25	Grèce
Hungary	..	..	0.00	0.00	0.00	0.00	0.00	0.00	Hongrie
Iceland	0.00	0.00	0.00	0.00	0.00	0.00	0.00	0.00	Islande
Ireland	37.53	35.30	34.36	27.80	24.86	18.07	19.68	16.05	Irlande
Italy	4.00	3.98	3.74	3.67	2.80	3.67	3.86	4.53	Italie
Japan	2.66	2.73	2.88	2.86	2.96	3.00	2.59	2.74	Japon
Korea	..	..	..	..	0.24	0.59	0.41	0.36	Corée
Luxembourg	..	..	..	..	18.70	15.91	15.78	14.94	Luxembourg
Mexico	..	..	0.00	0.00	0.00	0.00	0.00	0.00	Mexique
Netherlands	6.37	5.94	6.27	5.80	5.11	3.06	2.55	2.50	Pays-Bas
New Zealand	30.90	..	..	..	..	..	..	..	Nouvelle Zélande
Norway	1.30	1.51	1.37	1.45	..	..	1.76	2.84	Norvège
Poland	..	..	..	0.00	0.00	0.00	0.00	0.00	Pologne
Portugal	7.69	7.71	7.37	7.65	3.67	0.70	0.71	0.74	Portugal
Spain	7.77	7.59	7.69	6.32	6.67	3.77	3.19	3.38	Espagne
Sweden	..	..	..	..	..	..	..	..	Suède
Switzerland	1.62	1.20	1.09	1.07	1.07	0.97	1.60	1.81	Suisse
Turkey	0.42	0.67	0.12	0.30	0.20	0.10	0.00	0.00	Turquie
United Kingdom	4.84	4.41	5.24	6.25	6.35	6.25	6.60	7.40	Royaume-Uni
United States	0.91	0.99	0.87	1.00	0.84	1.06	0.95	0.65	Etats-Unis

45

7

PART II

PARTIE II

TABLES BY COUNTRY

TABLEAUX PAR PAYS

AUSTRALIA

Monetary Unit: million Australian dollars

	1990	1991	1992	1993	1994	1995	1996	1997	
A. NUMBER OF COMPANIES IN THE REPORTING COUNTRY									**A. NOMBRE D'ENTREPRISES DANS LE PAYS DECLARANT**
A.1. Life									**A.1. Vie**
A.1.1. Domestic Companies	51	50	46	37	41	42	42	40	A.1.1. Entreprises Nationales
A.1.2. (Foreign Controlled Companies)	24	24	19	13	18	18	19	21	A.1.2. (Entreprises Sous Contrôle Etranger)
A.1.3. Branches & Agencies of Foreign Cies	3	2	2	7	2	1	1	0	A.1.3. Succursales et Agences d'Ent. Etrangères
A.1. All Companies	54	52	48	44	43	43	43	40	A.1. Ensemble des Entreprises
A.2. Non-Life									**A.2. Non-Vie**
A.2.1. Domestic Companies	124	112	108	108	119	124	126	129	A.2.1. Entreprises Nationales
A.2.2. (Foreign Controlled Companies)	52	48	45	44	53	51	45	39	A.2.2. (Entreprises Sous Contrôle Etranger)
A.2.3. Branches & Agencies of Foreign Cies	41	39	21	21	17	17	17	15	A.2.3. Succursales et Agences d'Ent. Etrangères
A.2. All Companies	165	151	129	129	136	141	143	144	A.2. Ensemble des Entreprises
A.3. Composite									**A.3. Mixte**
A.3.1. Domestic Companies	1	1	0	2	0	0	0	0	A.3.1. Entreprises Nationales
A.3.2. (Foreign Controlled Companies)	1	1	0	1	0	0	0	0	A.3.2. (Entreprises Sous Contrôle Etranger)
A.3. All Companies	1	1	0	2	0	0	0	0	A.3. Ensemble des Entreprises
A.4. Reinsurance									**A.4. Réassurance**
A.4.1. Domestic Companies	19	31	17	12	18	18	19	20	A.4.1. Entreprises Nationales
A.4.2. (Foreign Controlled Companies)	17	29	14	9	13	15	15	17	A.4.2. (Entreprises Sous Contrôle Etranger)
A.4.3. Branches & Agencies of Foreign Cies	16	1	15	15	13	14	14	12	A.4.3. Succursales et Agences d'Ent. Etrangères
A.4. All Companies	35	32	32	27	31	32	33	32	A.4. Ensemble des Entreprises
A.5. Total									**A.5. Total**
A.5.1. Domestic Companies	195	194	171	159	178	184	187	189	A.5.1. Entreprises Nationales
A.5.2. (Foreign Controlled Companies)	94	102	78	67	84	84	79	77	A.5.2. (Entreprises Sous Contrôle Etranger)
A.5.3. Branches & Agencies of Foreign Cies	60	42	38	43	32	32	32	27	A.5.3. Succursales et Agences d'Ent. Etrangères
A.5. All Insurance Companies	255	236	209	202	210	216	219	216	A.5. Ensemble des Entreprises d'Assurances
C. BUSINESS WRITTEN IN THE REPORTING COUNTRY									**C. OPERATIONS CONCLUES DANS LE PAYS DECLARANT**
C.1. Life									**C.1. Vie**
C.1.1. Gross Premiums									**C.1.1. Primes Brutes**
C.1.1.1. Direct Business									C.1.1.1. Assurances Directes
C.1.1.1.1. Domestic Companies	17 888	16 672	16 514	23 591	..	..	20 522	28 824	C.1.1.1.1. Entreprises Nationales
C.1.1.1.2. (Foreign Controlled Companies)	2 543	2 638	3 236	6 492	..	..	6 208	12 919	C.1.1.1.2. (Entreprises Sous Contrôle Etranger)
C.1.1.1.3. Branches & Agencies of Foreign Cies	1 023	1 382	1 470		..	..	19	0	C.1.1.1.3. Succursales et Agences d'Ent. Etrangères
C.1.1.1. Total	18 912	18 054	17 985	23 591	..	..	20 541	28 824	C.1.1.1. Total
C.1.1.2. Reinsurance Accepted									C.1.1.2. Réassurance Acceptée
C.1.1.2.1. Domestic Companies	..	..	..	71			0	362	C.1.1.2.1. Entreprises Nationales
C.1.1.2.2. (Foreign Controlled Companies)	..	..	..	68			0	362	C.1.1.2.2. (Entreprises Sous Contrôle Etranger)
C.1.1.2. Total	..	..	..	71			0	362	C.1.1.2. Total
C.1.1.3. Total									C.1.1.3. Total
C.1.1.3.1. Domestic Companies	17 888	16 672	16 514	23 662	..	..	20 522	29 186	C.1.1.3.1. Entreprises Nationales
C.1.1.3.2. (Foreign Controlled Companies)	2 543	2 638	3 236	6 560	..	..	6 208	13 281	C.1.1.3.2. (Entreprises Sous Contrôle Etranger)
C.1.1.3.3. Branches & Agencies of Foreign Cies	1 023	1 382	1 470	19	..	..	19	0	C.1.1.3.3. Succursales et Agences d'Ent. Etrangères
C.1.1.3. Total Gross Premiums	18 912	18 054	17 985	23 662	..	..	20 541	29 186	C.1.1.3. Total des Primes Brutes
C.1.2. Ceded Premiums									**C.1.2. Primes Cédées**
C.1.2.1. Domestic Companies	..	..	..	2 263	..	..	0	..	C.1.2.1. Entreprises Nationales
C.1.2.2. (Foreign Controlled Companies)	..	..	..	621	..	..	0	..	C.1.2.2. (Entreprises Sous Contrôle Etranger)
C.1.2. Total	..	..	..	2 263	..	..	0	..	C.1.2. Total
C.1.3. Net Written Premiums									**C.1.3. Primes Nettes Emises**
C.1.3.1. Domestic Companies	17 888	16 672	16 514	21 399	21 434	20 667	20 522	29 186	C.1.3.1. Entreprises Nationales
C.1.3.2. (Foreign Controlled Companies)	2 543	2 638	3 236	5 939	4 475	5 646	6 208	13 281	C.1.3.2. (Entreprises Sous Contrôle Etranger)
C.1.3.3. Branches & Agencies of Foreign Cies	1 023	1 382	1 470	..	1 466	19	19	0	C.1.3.3. Succursales et Agences d'Ent. Etrangères
C.1.3. Total	18 912	18 054	17 985	21 399	22 900	20 686	20 541	29 186	C.1.3. Total

Monetary Unit: million Australian dollars

C.2. Non-Life / C.2. Non-Vie

Label	1990	1991	1992	1993	1994	1995	1996	1997	Libellé
C.2.1. Gross premiums									C.2.1. Primes Brutes
C.2.1.1. Direct Business									C.2.1.1. Assurances Directes
C.2.1.1.1. Domestic Companies	6 559	6 990	6 525	13 971	15 399	15 874	17 769	19 159	C.2.1.1.1. Entreprises Nationales
C.2.1.1.2. (Foreign Controlled Companies)	1 994	2 142	3 314	4 554	5 328	5 221	5 576	5 200	C.2.1.1.2. « Entreprises Sous Contrôle Etranger)
C.2.1.1.3. Branches & Agencies of Foreign Cies	837	371	240	474	376	438	439	409	C.2.1.1.3. Succursales et Agences d'Ent. Etrangères
C.2.1.1. Total	7 396	7 361	6 765	14 445	15 775	16 312	18 208	19 568	C.2.1.1. Total
C.2.1.2. Reinsurance Accepted									C.2.1.2. Réassurance Acceptée
C.2.1.2.1. Domestic Companies	731	907	926	1 454	2 711	2 207	2 359	884	C.2.1.2.1. Entreprises Nationales
C.2.1.2.2. (Foreign Controlled Companies)	601	681	900	962	822	1 070	1 197	680	C.2.1.2.2. (Entreprises Sous Contrôle Etranger)
C.2.1.2.3. Branches & Agencies of Foreign Cies	229	289	334	486	513	538	594	646	C.2.1.2.3. Succursales et Agences d'Ent. Etrangères
C.2.1.2. Total	960	1 196	1 479	1 940	3 224	2 745	2 953	1 530	C.2.1.2. Total
C.2.1.3. Total									C.2.1.3. Total
C.2.1.3.1. Domestic Companies	7 290	7 897	7 451	15 425	18 110	18 081	20 128	20 043	C.2.1.3.1. Entreprises Nationales
C.2.1.3.2. (Foreign Controlled Companies)	2 595	2 823	4 214	5 416	6 150	6 291	6 773	5 880	C.2.1.3.2. (Entreprises Sous Contrôle Etranger)
C.2.1.3.3. Branches & Agencies of Foreign Cies	1 066	660	574	960	889	976	1 033	1 055	C.2.1.3.3. Succursales et Agences d'Ent. Etrangères
C.2.1.3. Total Gross Premiums	8 356	8 557	8 244	16 385	18 999	19 057	21 161	21 098	C.2.1.3. Total des Primes Brutes
C.2.2. Ceded Premiums									C.2.2. Primes Cédées
C.2.2.1. Domestic Companies	1 309	1 504	1 569	2 342	3 312	3 020	3 266	2 977	C.2.2.1. Entreprises Nationales
C.2.2.2. (Foreign Controlled Companies)	550	669	1 009	1 491	1 362	1 595	1 861	1 835	C.2.2.2. (Entreprises Sous Contrôle Etranger)
C.2.2.3. Branches & Agencies of Foreign Cies	190	201	164	324	300	243	206	569	C.2.2.3. Succursales et Agences d'Ent. Etrangères
C.2.2. Total	1 499	1 705	1 733	2 667	3 612	3 263	3 472	3 546	C.2.2. Total
C.2.3. Net Written Premiums									C.2.3. Primes Nettes Emises
C.2.3.1. Domestic Companies	5 981	6 394	5 918	13 083	14 798	15 061	16 862	17 066	C.2.3.1. Entreprises Nationales
C.2.3.2. (Foreign Controlled Companies)	2 045	2 154	3 205	3 925	4 788	4 696	4 912	4 045	C.2.3.2. (Entreprises Sous Contrôle Etranger)
C.2.3.3. Branches & Agencies of Foreign Cies	876	458	410	636	589	733	827	486	C.2.3.3. Succursales et Agences d'Ent. Etrangères
C.2.3. Total	6 857	6 852	6 511	13 718	15 387	15 794	17 689	17 552	C.2.3. Total

C.3. Total / C.3. Total

Label	1990	1991	1992	1993	1994	1995	1996	1997	Libellé
C.3.1. Gross Premiums									C.3.1. Primes Brutes
C.3.1.1. Direct Business									C.3.1.1. Assurances Directes
C.3.1.1.1. Domestic Companies	24 447	23 662	23 039	37 562	...	...	38 291	47 983	C.3.1.1.1. Entreprises Nationales
C.3.1.1.2. (Foreign Controlled Companies)	4 537	4 780	6 550	11 046	...	...	11 784	18 119	C.3.1.1.2. (Entreprises Sous Contrôle Etranger)
C.3.1.1.3. Branches & Agencies of Foreign Cies	1 860	1 753	1 710		...	...	458	409	C.3.1.1.3. Succursales et Agences d'Ent. Etrangères
C.3.1.1. Total	26 308	25 415	24 750	38 036	...	...	38 749	48 392	C.3.1.1. Total
C.3.1.2. Reinsurance Accepted									C.3.1.2. Réassurance Acceptée
C.3.1.2.1. Domestic Companies	...	...	...	1 525	...	...	2 359	1 246	C.3.1.2.1. Entreprises Nationales
C.3.1.2.2. (Foreign Controlled Companies)	...	...	...	1 030	...	...	1 197	1 042	C.3.1.2.2. (Entreprises Sous Contrôle Etranger)
C.3.1.2.3. Branches & Agencies of Foreign Cies	...	...	...		...	...	594	646	C.3.1.2.3. Succursales et Agences d'Ent. Etrangères
C.3.1.2. Total	...	...	...	2 011	...	...	2 953	1 892	C.3.1.2. Total
C.3.1.3. Total									C.3.1.3. Total
C.3.1.3.1. Domestic Companies	25 178	24 570	23 965	39 087	...	...	40 650	49 229	C.3.1.3.1. Entreprises Nationales
C.3.1.3.2. (Foreign Controlled Companies)	5 138	5 461	7 450	11 976	...	...	12 981	19 161	C.3.1.3.2. (Entreprises Sous Contrôle Etranger)
C.3.1.3.3. Branches & Agencies of Foreign Cies	2 089	2 044	2 044		...	...	1 052	1 055	C.3.1.3.3. Succursales et Agences d'Ent. Etrangères
C.3.1.3. Total Gross Premiums	27 268	26 611	26 229	40 047	...	...	41 702	50 284	C.3.1.3. Total des Primes Brutes
C.3.2. Ceded Premiums									C.3.2. Primes Cédées
C.3.2.1. Domestic Companies	...	...	...	4 605	...	...	3 266	...	C.3.2.1. Entreprises Nationales
C.3.2.2. (Foreign Controlled Companies)	...	...	...	2 112	...	...	1 861	...	C.3.2.2. (Entreprises Sous Contrôle Etranger)
C.3.2.3. Branches & Agencies of Foreign Cies	...	...	...		...	...	206	569	C.3.2.3. Succursales et Agences d'Ent. Etrangères
C.3.2. Total	...	...	...	4 930	...	...	3 472	...	C.3.2. Total
C.3.3. Net Written Premiums									C.3.3. Primes Nettes Emises
C.3.3.1. Domestic Companies	23 869	23 066	22 432	34 482	36 232	35 728	37 384	46 252	C.3.3.1. Entreprises Nationales
C.3.3.2. (Foreign Controlled Companies)	4 588	4 793	6 441	9 864	9 263	10 342	11 120	17 326	C.3.3.2. (Entreprises Sous Contrôle Etranger)
C.3.3.3. Branches & Agencies of Foreign Cies	1 899	1 840	1 880		2 055	752	846	486	C.3.3.3. Succursales et Agences d'Ent. Etrangères
C.3.3. Total	25 769	24 906	24 496	35 117	38 287	36 480	38 230	46 738	C.3.3. Total

AUSTRALIA

Monetary Unit: million Australian dollars — Unité monétaire : million de dollars australiens

D. NET WRITTEN PREMIUMS IN THE REPORTING COUNTRY IN TERMS OF DOMESTIC AND FOREIGN RISKS
D. PRIMES NETTES EMISES DANS LE PAYS DECLARANT EN RISQUES NATIONAUX ET ETRANGERS

	1990	1991	1992	1993	1994	1995	1996	1997
D.1. Life / D.1. Vie								
D.1.1. Domestic Risks / D.1.1. Risques Nationaux								
D.1.1.1. Domestic Companies / Entreprises Nationales	17 888	16 672	:	:	:	:	:	27 899
D.1.1.2. (Foreign Controlled Companies) / (Entreprises Sous Contrôle Etranger)	2 543	2 638	:	:	:	:	:	12 695
D.1.1.3. Branches & Agencies of Foreign Cies / Succursales et Agences d'Ent. Etrangères	1 023	1 382	:	:	:	:	:	0
D.1.1. Total / Total des Primes Nettes Vie	18 912	18 054	:	:	:	:	:	27 899
D.1.2. Foreign Risks / D.1.2. Risques Etrangers								
D.1.2.1. Domestic Companies / Entreprises Nationales	:	:	:	:	:	:	:	1 287
D.1.2.2. (Foreign Controlled Companies) / (Entreprises Sous Contrôle Etranger)	:	:	:	:	:	:	:	586
D.1.2. Total / Total des Primes Nettes Vie	:	:	:	:	:	:	:	1 287
D.1.3. Total								
D.1.3.1. Domestic Companies / Entreprises Nationales	17 888	16 672		21 399	21 434	20 667	20 522	29 186
D.1.3.2. (Foreign Controlled Companies) / (Entreprises Sous Contrôle Etranger)	2 543	2 638		5 939	4 425	5 646	6 208	13 281
D.1.3.3. Branches & Agencies of Foreign Cies / Succursales et Agences d'Ent. Etrangères	1 023	1 382			1 466	19	19	0
D.1.3. Total of Life Net Premiums / Total des Primes Nettes Vie	18 912	18 054			22 900	20 686	20 541	29 186
D.2. Non-Life / D.2. Non-Vie								
D.2.1. Domestic Risks / D.2.1. Risques Nationaux								
D.2.1.1. Domestic Companies / Entreprises Nationales	5 775	6 394	2 713	11 360	13 769	13 927	15 619	15 712
D.2.1.2. (Foreign Controlled Companies) / (Entreprises Sous Contrôle Etranger)	2 045	2 154	3 205	3 790	4 698	4 563	4 760	3 912
D.2.1.3. Branches & Agencies of Foreign Cies / Succursales et Agences d'Ent. Etrangères	876	458	410	623	589	733	826	483
D.2.1. Total / Total des Primes Nettes Vie	6 651	6 852	6 511	11 983	14 358	14 660	16 445	16 195
D.2.2. Foreign Risks / D.2.2. Risques Etrangers								
D.2.2.1. Domestic Companies / Entreprises Nationales	:	137	:	1 723	1 029	1 134	1 243	1 354
D.2.2.2. (Foreign Controlled Companies) / (Entreprises Sous Contrôle Etranger)	:	41	:	135	90	133	152	133
D.2.2.3. Branches & Agencies of Foreign Cies / Succursales et Agences d'Ent. Etrangères	:	0	:	13	0	0	1	3
D.2.2. Total / Total des Primes Nettes Vie	:	137	:	1 736	1 029	1 134	1 244	1 357
D.2.3. Total								
D.2.3.1. Domestic Companies / Entreprises Nationales	5 775	6 530	2 713	13 083	14 798	15 061	16 862	17 066
D.2.3.2. (Foreign Controlled Companies) / (Entreprises Sous Contrôle Etranger)	2 045	2 195	3 205	3 925	4 788	4 696	4 912	4 045
D.2.3.3. Branches & Agencies of Foreign Cies / Succursales et Agences d'Ent. Etrangères	876	458	410	636	589	733	827	486
D.2.3. Total / Total des Primes Nettes Vie	6 651	6 988	6 511	13 719	15 387	15 794	17 689	17 552

E. BUSINESS WRITTEN ABROAD
E. OPERATIONS A L'ETRANGER

	1990	1991	1992	1993	1994	1995	1996	1997
E.1. Life / E.1. Vie								
E.1.1. Gross Premiums / E.1.1. Primes Brutes								
E.1.1.1. Direct Business / Assurance Directe								
E.1.1.1. Total / Total	1 567	1 457	1 378	:	:	:	1 150	:
E.1.1.3. Total / Total								
E.1.1.3. Total Gross Premiums / Total des Primes Brutes	1 567	1 457	1 378	:	:	:	1 150	:
E.1.3. Net Written Premiums / E.1.3. Primes Nettes Emises								
E.1.3. Total / Total	1 567	1 457	1 378	:	1 397	1 189	1 150	:

Monetary Unit: million Australian dollars   Unité monétaire : million de dollars australiens

E.2. Non-Life / E.2. Non-Vie

Item (EN)	Item (FR)	1990	1991	1992	1993	1994	1995	1996	1997
E.2.1. Gross Premiums	E.2.1. Primes Brutes								
E.2.1.1. Direct Business	E.2.1.1. Assurance Directe								
E.2.1.1.1. Branches & Agencies	E.2.1.1.1. Succursales & Agences	79	116	83	..	..	..	..	..
E.2.1.1. Total	E.2.1.1. Total			83			146	245	295
E.2.1.2. Reinsurance Accepted	E.2.1.2. Réassurance Acceptée								
E.2.1.2.1. Branches & Agencies	E.2.1.2.1. Succursales & Agences	51	64	65	..	..	..	..	..
E.2.1.2. Total	E.2.1.2. Total			65			1 194	1 215	1 463
E.2.1.3. Total	E.2.1.3. Total								
E.2.1.3.1. Branches & Agencies	E.2.1.3.1. Succursales & Agences	130	179	148	..	..	..	..	..
E.2.1.3. Total Gross Premiums	E.2.1.3. Total des Primes Brutes			148			1 340	1 460	1 758
E.2.2. Ceded Premiums	E.2.2. Primes Cédées								
E.2.2.1. Branches & Agencies	E.2.2.1. Succursales & Agences	32	43	12	..	..	..	..	..
E.2.2. Total	E.2.2. Total			12			246	216	401
E.2.3. Net Written Premiums	E.2.3. Primes Nettes Emises								
E.2.3.1. Branches & Agencies	E.2.3.1. Succursales & Agences	98	137	136	..	..	..	..	..
E.2.3. Total	E.2.3. Total			136			1 267	1 244	1 357

F. OUTSTANDING INVESTMENT BY DIRECT INSURANCE COMPANIES / F. ENCOURS DES PLACEMENTS DES ENTREPRISES D'ASSURANCES DIRECTES

F.1. Life / F.1. Vie

Item (EN)	Item (FR)	1990	1991	1992	1993	1994	1995	1996	1997
F.1.1. Real Estate	F.1.1. Immobilier								
F.1.1.1. Domestic Companies	F.1.1.1. Entreprises Nationales	10 425	9 329	9 093	8 221	8 363	8 160	8 131	13 745
F.1.1.2. (Foreign Controlled Companies)	F.1.1.2. (Entreprises Sous Contrôle Etranger)	649	395	317	836	989	933	938	5 395
F.1.1.3. Branches & Agencies of Foreign Cies	F.1.1.3. Succursales et Agences d'Ent. Etrangères	879	795	636	..	509	0	0	0
F.1.1.4. Domestic Investment	F.1.1.4. Placement dans le Pays	11 953	10 519	10 046	8 221	..	7 111	7 081	3 519
F.1.1.5. Foreign Investment	F.1.1.5. Placement à l'Etranger	2 357	1 801	1 358	..	..	1 050	1 051	226
F.1.1. Total	F.1.1. Total	14 328	12 320	11 404	..	8 872	8 161	8 131	3 745
F.1.2. Mortgage Loans	F.1.2. Prêts Hypothécaires								
F.1.2.1. Domestic Companies	F.1.2.1. Entreprises Nationales	..	..	..	2 223	..	0	0	0
F.1.2.2. (Foreign Controlled Companies)	F.1.2.2. (Entreprises Sous Contrôle Etranger)				1 217		0	0	0
F.1.2.4. Domestic Investment	F.1.2.4. Placement dans le Pays				2 223		0	0	0
F.1.3. Shares	F.1.3. Actions								
F.1.3.1. Domestic Companies	F.1.3.1. Entreprises Nationales	15 411	19 356	20 943	31 703	28 970	46 578	45 415	57 449
F.1.3.2. (Foreign Controlled Companies)	F.1.3.2. (Entreprises Sous Contrôle Etranger)	1 442	3 111	3 556	6 493	4 512	7 168	7 593	25 508
F.1.3.3. Branches & Agencies of Foreign Cies	F.1.3.3. Succursales et Agences d'Ent. Etrangères	712	1 222	1 280	..	1 589	0	0	0
F.1.3.4. Domestic Investment	F.1.3.4. Placement dans le Pays	17 565	23 688	25 778	31 703	..	31 211	30 285	41 284
F.1.3.5. Foreign Investment	F.1.3.5. Placement à l'Etranger	9 248	11 734	9 796	..	..	15 367	15 130	16 165
F.1.3. Total	F.1.3. Total	26 813	35 423	35 574	..	30 559	46 578	45 415	57 449
F.1.4. Bonds with Fixed Revenue	F.1.4. Obligations								
F.1.4.1. Domestic Companies	F.1.4.1. Entreprises Nationales	8 264	12 102	15 383	31 100	22 734	29 517	29 835	60 303
F.1.4.2. (Foreign Controlled Companies)	F.1.4.2. (Entreprises Sous Contrôle Etranger)	2 618	3 430	3 924	7 703	4 997	6 405	6 900	27 102
F.1.4.3. Branches & Agencies of Foreign Cies	F.1.4.3. Succursales et Agences d'Ent. Etrangères	707	1 071	1 273	..	2 139	4	4	0
F.1.4.4. Domestic Investment	F.1.4.4. Placement dans le Pays	11 588	16 603	20 581	31 100	..	23 742	23 986	56 350
F.1.4.5. Foreign Investment	F.1.4.5. Placement à l'Etranger	3 847	4 854	4 932	..	..	5 779	5 853	3 953
F.1.4. Total	F.1.4. Total	15 435	21 457	25 513	..	24 873	29 521	29 839	60 303
F.1.5. Loans other than Mortgage Loans	F.1.5. Prêts Autres qu'Hypothécaires								
F.1.5.1. Domestic Companies	F.1.5.1. Entreprises Nationales	6 416	3 349	3 062	4 845	5 814	9 270	9 094	9 394
F.1.5.2. (Foreign Controlled Companies)	F.1.5.2. (Entreprises Sous Contrôle Etranger)	1 297	1 154	1 416	1 640	1 911	4 622	4 741	6 185
F.1.5.3. Branches & Agencies of Foreign Cies	F.1.5.3. Succursales et Agences d'Ent. Etrangères	742	943	1 030	..	1 214	1	1	0
F.1.5.4. Domestic Investment	F.1.5.4. Placement dans le Pays	8 455	5 446	5 508	4 845	..	8 647	8 468	8 579
F.1.5.5. Foreign Investment	F.1.5.5. Placement à l'Etranger	1 009	776	520	..	..	624	626	815
F.1.5. Total	F.1.5. Total	9 463	6 221	6 028	..	7 028	9 271	9 094	9 394

AUSTRALIA

Monetary Unit: million Australian dollars

Item (English)	1990	1991	1992	1993	1994	1995	1996	1997	Poste (Français)
F.1.6. Other Investments									**F.1.6. Autres Placements**
F.1.6.1. Domestic Companies	17 876	22 453	22 109	21 878	28 659	41 223	47 291	9 533	F.1.6.1. Entreprises Nationales
F.1.6.2. (Foreign Controlled Companies)	4 508	4 868	5 088	4 649	4 299	8 087	8 846	4 145	F.1.6.2. (Entreprises Sous Contrôle Etranger)
F.1.6.3. Branches & Agencies of Foreign Cies	939	824	777	..	655	2	2	0	F.1.6.3. Succursales et Agences d'Ent. Etrangères
F.1.6.4. Domestic Investment	23 323	28 145	27 974	21 878	..	34 128	39 143	8 138	F.1.6.4. Placement dans le Pays
F.1.6.5. Foreign Investment	4 540	5 855	6 018	..	..	7 097	8 151	1 395	F.1.6.5. Placement à l' Etranger
F.1.6. Total	27 863	34 000	33 992	..	29 314	41 225	47 293	9 533	F.1.6. Total
F.1.7. Total									**F.1.7. Total**
F.1.7.1. Domestic Companies	58 391	66 589	70 590	99 970	94 540	134 748	139 767	150 424	F.1.7.1. Entreprises Nationales
F.1.7.2. (Foreign Controlled Companies)	10 514	12 958	14 301	22 539	16 708	27 215	29 018	68 335	F.1.7.2. (Entreprises Sous Contrôle Etranger)
F.1.7.3. Branches & Agencies of Foreign Cies	3 978	4 855	4 996	..	6 106	7	7	0	F.1.7.3. Succursales et Agences d'Ent. Etrangères
F.1.7.4. Domestic Investment	72 883	84 401	89 888	99 970	..	104 839	108 963	127 870	F.1.7.4. Placement dans le Pays
F.1.7.5. Foreign Investment	21 019	25 020	22 623	16 457	..	29 917	30 811	22 554	F.1.7.5. Placement à l' Etranger
F.1.7. Total of Life Investments	93 902	109 421	112 511	116 647	100 646	134 756	139 774	150 424	F.1.7. Total des Placements Vie
F.2. Non-Life									**F.2. Non-Vie**
F.2.1. Real Estate									**F.2.1. Immobilier**
F.2.1.1. Domestic Companies	..	..	534	1 045	1 038	2 317	1 881	3 497	F.2.1.1. Entreprises Nationales
F.2.1.2. (Foreign Controlled Companies)	..	..	385	362	387	375	345	412	F.2.1.2. (Entreprises Sous Contrôle Etranger)
F.2.1.3. Branches & Agencies of Foreign Cies	..	..	43	36	47	46	2	54	F.2.1.3. Succursales et Agences d'Ent. Etrangères
F.2.1.4. Domestic Investment	..	..	961	1 081	..	2 363	1 929	3 550	F.2.1.4. Placement dans le Pays
F.2.1.5. Foreign Investment	..	..	1	0	..	0	1	..	F.2.1.5. Placement à l' Etranger
F.2.1. Total	1 297	1 141	962	1 081	1 085	2 363	1 930	3 551	F.2.1. Total
F.2.2. Mortgage Loans									**F.2.2. Prêts Hypothécaires**
F.2.2.1. Domestic Companies	..	..	..	710	794	794	895	856	F.2.2.1. Entreprises Nationales
F.2.2.2. (Foreign Controlled Companies)	..	..	..	271	210	155	143	173	F.2.2.2. (Entreprises Sous Contrôle Etranger)
F.2.2.3. Branches & Agencies of Foreign Cies	..	..	..	4	3	3	2	2	F.2.2.3. Succursales et Agences d'Ent. Etrangères
F.2.2.4. Domestic Investment	160	..	..	714	797	797	896	858	F.2.2.4. Placement dans le Pays
F.2.2. Total	..	..	..	714	797	797	896	858	F.2.2. Total
F.2.3. Shares									**F.2.3. Actions**
F.2.3.1. Domestic Companies	..	..	2 637	5 059	5 025	10 663	10 742	11 522	F.2.3.1. Entreprises Nationales
F.2.3.2. (Foreign Controlled Companies)	..	..	1 423	1 792	1 343	1 706	2 124	2 155	F.2.3.2. (Entreprises Sous Contrôle Etranger)
F.2.3.3. Branches & Agencies of Foreign Cies	..	..	234	268	279	385	439	483	F.2.3.3. Succursales et Agences d'Ent. Etrangères
F.2.3.4. Domestic Investment	..	..	4 089	5 327	..	9 728	10 609	11 245	F.2.3.4. Placement dans le Pays
F.2.3.5. Foreign Investment	..	..	205	247	..	1 320	571	760	F.2.3.5. Placement à l' Etranger
F.2.3. Total	3 576	4 163	4 294	5 571	5 304	11 048	11 181	12 005	F.2.3. Total
F.2.4. Bonds with Fixed Revenue									**F.2.4. Obligations**
F.2.4.1. Domestic Companies	..	..	3 598	9 500	10 104	19 063	20 327	22 173	F.2.4.1. Entreprises Nationales
F.2.4.2. (Foreign Controlled Companies)	..	..	3 684	4 588	4 078	4 961	5 472	5 730	F.2.4.2. (Entreprises Sous Contrôle Etranger)
F.2.4.3. Branches & Agencies of Foreign Cies	..	..	1 060	1 414	1 048	1 211	1 381	1 518	F.2.4.3. Succursales et Agences d'Ent. Etrangères
F.2.4.4. Domestic Investment	..	..	7 995	10 914	..	19 147	20 627	22 420	F.2.4.4. Placement dans le Pays
F.2.4.5. Foreign Investment	..	..	347	671	..	1 127	1 081	1 271	F.2.4.5. Placement à l' Etranger
F.2.4. Total	5 133	6 193	8 342	11 585	11 152	20 274	21 708	23 691	F.2.4. Total
F.2.5. Loans other than Mortgage Loans									**F.2.5. Prêts Autres qu'Hypothécaires**
F.2.5.1. Domestic Companies	..	..	1 462	1 108	1 102	1 558	1 480	1 915	F.2.5.1. Entreprises Nationales
F.2.5.2. (Foreign Controlled Companies)	..	..	500	160	185	211	263	312	F.2.5.2. (Entreprises Sous Contrôle Etranger)
F.2.5.3. Branches & Agencies of Foreign Cies	..	..	4	4	2	2	..	..	F.2.5.3. Succursales et Agences d'Ent. Etrangères
F.2.5.4. Domestic Investment	..	..	1 965	1 112	..	1 549	1 469	1 732	F.2.5.4. Placement dans le Pays
F.2.5.5. Foreign Investment	..	..	1	4	..	11	13	184	F.2.5.5. Placement à l' Etranger
F.2.5. Total	4 380	4 172	1 966	1 116	1 104	1 560	1 482	1 916	F.2.5. Total
F.2.6. Other Investments									**F.2.6. Autres Placements**
F.2.6.1. Domestic Companies	..	..	971	10 810	11 992	20 994	24 766	23 526	F.2.6.1. Entreprises Nationales
F.2.6.2. (Foreign Controlled Companies)	..	..	818	5 650	5 987	6 801	8 182	10 251	F.2.6.2. (Entreprises Sous Contrôle Etranger)
F.2.6.3. Branches & Agencies of Foreign Cies	..	..	134	1 265	1 043	1 182	1 224	1 345	F.2.6.3. Succursales et Agences d'Ent. Etrangères
F.2.6.4. Domestic Investment	..	..	1 712	12 075	..	19 721	23 618	23 918	F.2.6.4. Placement dans le Pays
F.2.6.5. Foreign Investment	..	..	211	1 032	..	2 455	2 372	953	F.2.6.5. Placement à l' Etranger
F.2.6. Total	4 484	4 943	1 923	13 107	13 035	22 176	25 990	24 871	F.2.6. Total

Monetary Unit: million Australian dollars — Unité monétaire : million de dollars australiens

	1990	1991	1992	1993	1994	1995	1996	1997	
F.2.7. Total									**F.2.7. Total**
F.2.7.1. Domestic Companies	..	..	9 202	28 232	30 055	55 389	60 091	63 489	F.2.7.1. Entreprises Nationales
F.2.7.2. (Foreign Controlled Companies)	..	..	6 810	12 823	12 190	14 209	16 530	19 033	F.2.7.2. (Entreprises Sous Contrôle Etranger)
F.2.7.3. Branches & Agencies of Foreign Cies	..	..	1 475	2 991	2 422	2 829	3 096	3 403	F.2.7.3. Succursales et Agences d'Ent. Etrangères
F.2.7.4. Domestic Investment	..	..	16 722	31 223	..	53 305	59 148	63 723	F.2.7.4. Placement dans le Pays
F.2.7.5. Foreign Investment	..	..	764	1 954		4 913	4 038	3 169	F.2.7.5. Placement à l'Etranger
F.2.7. Total of Non-Life Investments	19 030	20 612	17 486	33 177	32 477	58 218	63 186	66 892	F.2.7. Total des Placements Non-Vie
G. BREAKDOWN OF NON-LIFE PREMIUMS									**G. VENTILATIONS DES PRIMES NON-VIE**
G.1. Motor vehicle									**G.1. Assurance Automobile**
G.1.1. Direct Business									G.1.1. Assurances Directes
G.1.1.1. Gross Premiums	3 688	3 812	2 991	5 578	5 746	6 238	6 698	7 003	G.1.1.1. Primes Brutes
G.1.1.2. Ceded Premiums	384	477					616	641	G.1.1.2. Primes Cédées
G.1.1.3. Net Written Premiums	3 304	3 335	..				6 082	6 362	G.1.1.3. Primes Nettes Emises
G.1.2. Reinsurance Accepted									G.1.2. Réassurance Acceptée
G.1.2.1. Gross Premiums	91	106	407				..	..	G.1.2.1. Primes Brutes
G.1.2.2. Ceded Premiums	21	26					..	..	G.1.2.2. Primes Cédées
G.1.2.3. Net Written Premiums	70	80					..	..	G.1.2.3. Primes Nettes Emises
G.1.3. Total									G.1.3. Total
G.1.3.1. Gross Premiums	3 779	3 918	3 398				..	..	G.1.3.1. Primes Brutes
G.1.3.2. Ceded Premiums	405	503	472				..	..	G.1.3.2. Primes Cédées
G.1.3.3. Net Written Premiums	3 374	3 415	2 926				..	..	G.1.3.3. Primes Nettes Emises
G.2. Marine, Aviation									**G.2. Marine, Aviation**
G.2.1. Direct Business									G.2.1. Assurances Directes
G.2.1.1. Gross Premiums	298	268	184	178	406	273	244	247	G.2.1.1. Primes Brutes
G.2.1.2. Ceded Premiums	84	81					72	57	G.2.1.2. Primes Cédées
G.2.1.3. Net Written Premiums	214	187	..				172	190	G.2.1.3. Primes Nettes Emises
G.2.2. Reinsurance Accepted									G.2.2. Réassurance Acceptée
G.2.2.1. Gross Premiums	31	35	79				..	..	G.2.2.1. Primes Brutes
G.2.2.2. Ceded Premiums	9	10					..	..	G.2.2.2. Primes Cédées
G.2.2.3. Net Written Premiums	22	25	..				..	..	G.2.2.3. Primes Nettes Emises
G.2.3. Total									G.2.3. Total
G.2.3.1. Gross Premiums	329	303	263				..	..	G.2.3.1. Primes Brutes
G.2.3.2. Ceded Premiums	93	91	73				..	..	G.2.3.2. Primes Cédées
G.2.3.3. Net Written Premiums	236	212	190				..	..	G.2.3.3. Primes Nettes Emises
G.3. Freight									**G.3. Fret**
G.3.1. Direct Business									G.3.1. Assurances Directes
G.3.1.1. Gross Premiums	..	..	165	163	163	180	179	161	G.3.1.1. Primes Brutes
G.3.1.2. Ceded Premiums	..	..					42	37	G.3.1.2. Primes Cédées
G.3.1.3. Net Written Premiums	..	..					137	134	G.3.1.3. Primes Nettes Emises
G.3.2. Reinsurance Accepted									G.3.2. Réassurance Acceptée
G.3.2.1. Gross Premiums	..	..	34				..	..	G.3.2.1. Primes Brutes
G.3.3. Total									G.3.3. Total
G.3.3.1. Gross Premiums	..	..	139				..	..	G.3.3.1. Primes Brutes
G.3.3.2. Ceded Premiums	..	..	35				..	..	G.3.3.2. Primes Cédées
G.3.3.3. Net Written Premiums	..	..	104				..	..	G.3.3.3. Primes Nettes Emises
G.4. Fire, Property Damages									**G.4. Incendie, Dommages aux Biens**
G.4.1. Direct Business									G.4.1. Assurances Directes
G.4.1.1. Gross Premiums	1 729	1 811	1 863	3 076	3 590	3 556	3 735	3 587	G.4.1.1. Primes Brutes
G.4.1.2. Ceded Premiums	449	511					912	833	G.4.1.2. Primes Cédées
G.4.1.3. Net Written Premiums	1 280	1 300					2 823	2 754	G.4.1.3. Primes Nettes Emises
G.4.2. Reinsurance Accepted									G.4.2. Réassurance Acceptée
G.4.2.1. Gross Premiums	300	383	639				..	..	G.4.2.1. Primes Brutes
G.4.2.2. Ceded Premiums	115	146					..	..	G.4.2.2. Primes Cédées
G.4.2.3. Net Written Premiums	185	237	..				..	..	G.4.2.3. Primes Nettes Emises
G.4.3. Total									G.4.3. Total
G.4.3.1. Gross Premiums	2 029	2 194	2 502				..	..	G.4.3.1. Primes Brutes
G.4.3.2. Ceded Premiums	564	657	740				..	..	G.4.3.2. Primes Cédées
G.4.3.3. Net Written Premiums	1 465	1 537	1 762				..	..	G.4.3.3. Primes Nettes Emises

Monetary Unit: million Australian dollars

	1990	1991	1992	1993	1994	1995	1996	1997	
G.5. Pecuniary Losses									G.5. Pertes Pécunières
G.5.1. Direct Business									G.5.1. Assurances Directes
G.5.1.1. Gross Premiums	..	..	192	295	375	326	333	240	G.5.1.1. Primes Brutes
G.5.1.2. Ceded Premiums	..	..	..				49	32	G.5.1.2. Primes Cédées
G.5.1.3. Net Written Premiums	..	..	..				284	208	G.5.1.3. Primes Nettes Emises
G.5.2. Reinsurance Accepted									G.5.2. Réassurance Acceptée
G.5.2.1. Gross Premiums	..	..	29				..	..	G.5.2.1. Primes Brutes
G.5.3. Total									G.5.3. Total
G.5.3.1. Gross Premiums	..	..	221				..	..	G.5.3.1. Primes Brutes
G.5.3.2. Ceded Premiums	..	..	50				..	..	G.5.3.2. Primes Cédées
G.5.3.3. Net Written Premiums	..	..	171				..	..	G.5.3.3. Primes Nettes Emises
G.6. General Liability									G.6. Responsabilité Générale
G.6.1. Direct Business									G.6.1. Assurances Directes
G.6.1.1. Gross Premiums	963	880	902	4 524	4 518	4 606	5 248	6 237	G.6.1.1. Primes Brutes
G.6.1.2. Ceded Premiums	161	169	..				1 238	1 147	G.6.1.2. Primes Cédées
G.6.1.3. Net Written Premiums	802	711	..				4 010	5 090	G.6.1.3. Primes Nettes Emises
G.6.2. Reinsurance Accepted									G.6.2. Réassurance Acceptée
G.6.2.1. Gross Premiums	110	109	167				..	..	G.6.2.1. Primes Brutes
G.6.2.2. Ceded Premiums	32	33	..				..	..	G.6.2.2. Primes Cédées
G.6.2.3. Net Written Premiums	78	76	..				..	..	G.6.2.3. Primes Nettes Emises
G.6.3. Total									G.6.3. Total
G.6.3.1. Gross Premiums	1 073	989	1 069				..	..	G.6.3.1. Primes Brutes
G.6.3.2. Ceded Premiums	193	202	217				..	..	G.6.3.2. Primes Cédées
G.6.3.3. Net Written Premiums	880	787	852				..	..	G.6.3.3. Primes Nettes Emises
G.7. Accident, Health									G.7. Accident, Santé
G.7.1. Direct Business									G.7.1. Assurances Directes
G.7.1.1. Gross Premiums	..	..	173	193	216	233	1 101	1 301	G.7.1.1. Primes Brutes
G.7.1.2. Ceded Premiums	..	..	..				19	36	G.7.1.2. Primes Cédées
G.7.1.3. Net Written Premiums	..	..	..				1 082	1 265	G.7.1.3. Primes Nettes Emises
G.7.2. Reinsurance Accepted									G.7.2. Réassurance Acceptée
G.7.2.1. Gross Premiums	..	..	17				..	..	G.7.2.1. Primes Brutes
G.7.3. Total									G.7.3. Total
G.7.3.1. Gross Premiums	..	..	190				..	..	G.7.3.1. Primes Brutes
G.7.3.2. Ceded Premiums	..	..	25				..	..	G.7.3.2. Primes Cédées
G.7.3.3. Net Written Premiums	..	..	165				..	..	G.7.3.3. Primes Nettes Emises
G.8. Others									G.8. Autres
G.8.1. Direct Business									G.8.1. Assurances Directes
G.8.1.1. Gross Premiums	979	978	355	856	760	900	670	792	G.8.1.1. Primes Brutes
G.8.1.2. Ceded Premiums	159	199	..				152	287	G.8.1.2. Primes Cédées
G.8.1.3. Net Written Premiums	820	779	..				518	505	G.8.1.3. Primes Nettes Emises
G.8.2. Reinsurance Accepted									G.8.2. Réassurance Acceptée
G.8.2.1. Gross Premiums	167	175	106				..	..	G.8.2.1. Primes Brutes
G.8.2.2. Ceded Premiums	85	53	..				..	..	G.8.2.2. Primes Cédées
G.8.2.3. Net Written Premiums	82	122	..				..	..	G.8.2.3. Primes Nettes Emises
G.8.3. Total									G.8.3. Total
G.8.3.1. Gross Premiums	1 146	1 153	461				..	..	G.8.3.1. Primes Brutes
G.8.3.2. Ceded Premiums	244	252	119				..	..	G.8.3.2. Primes Cédées
G.8.3.3. Net Written Premiums	902	901	342				..	..	G.8.3.3. Primes Nettes Emises
G.10. Total									G.10. Total
G.10.1. Direct Business									G.10.1. Assurances Directes
G.10.1.1. Gross Premiums	7 657	7 749	6 765	14 763	15 775	16 312	18 208	19 568	G.10.1.1. Primes Brutes
G.10.1.2. Ceded Premiums	1 237	1 437	..				3 100	3 070	G.10.1.2. Primes Cédées
G.10.1.3. Net Written Premiums	6 420	6 312	..				15 108	16 498	G.10.1.3. Primes Nettes Emises
G.10.2. Reinsurance Accepted									G.10.2. Réassurance Acceptée
G.10.2.1. Gross Premiums	699	808	1 478	2 005	3 224	2 745	2 953	1 530	G.10.2.1. Primes Brutes
G.10.2.2. Ceded Premiums	262	268	..				372	476	G.10.2.2. Primes Cédées
G.10.2.3. Net Written Premiums	437	540	..				2 581	1 054	G.10.2.3. Primes Nettes Emises
G.10.3. Total									G.10.3. Total
G.10.3.1. Gross Premiums	8 356	8 557	8 243	16 768	18 999	19 057	21 161	21 098	G.10.3.1. Primes Brutes
G.10.3.2. Ceded Premiums	1 499	1 705	1 733	..	3 612	3 263	3 472	3 546	G.10.3.2. Primes Cédées
G.10.3.3. Net Written Premiums	6 857	6 852	6 510	..	15 387	15 794	17 689	17 552	G.10.3.3. Primes Nettes Emises

AUSTRALIA

Monetary Unit: million Australian dollars

H. GROSS CLAIMS PAYMENTS — H. PAIEMENTS BRUTS DES SINISTRES

	1990	1991	1992	1993	1994	1995	1996	1997
H.1. Life — H.1. Vie								
H.1.1. Domestic Companies — H.1.1. Entreprises Nationales							3 929	25 166
H.1.2. (Foreign Controlled Companies) — H.1.2. (Entreprises Sous Contrôle Etranger)							867	13 927
H.1.3. Branches & Agencies of Foreign Cies — H.1.3. Succursales et Agences d'Ent. Etrangères							12	0
H.1. Total — H.1. Total							3 941	25 166
H.2. Non-Life — H.2. Non-Vie								
H.2.1. Domestic Companies — H.2.1. Entreprises Nationales							13 867	12 860
H.2.2. (Foreign Controlled Companies) — H.2.2. (Entreprises Sous Contrôle Etranger)							3 786	4 946
H.2.3. Branches & Agencies of Foreign Cies — H.2.3. Succursales et Agences d'Ent. Etrangères							440	714
H.2. Total — H.2. Total							14 307	13 574

I. GROSS OPERATING EXPENSES — I. DEPENSES BRUTES D'EXPLOITATION

	1990	1991	1992	1993	1994	1995	1996	1997
I.1. Life — I.1. Vie								
I.1.1. Domestic Companies — I.1.1. Entreprises Nationales							2 248	3 584
I.1.2. (Foreign Controlled Companies) — I.1.2. (Entreprises Sous Contrôle Etranger)							583	1 912
I.1.3. Branches & Agencies of Foreign Cies — I.1.3. Succursales et Agences d'Ent. Etrangères							2	0
I.1. Total — I.1. Total des Primes Nettes Vie							2 250	3 584
I.2. Non-Life — I.2. Non-Vie								
I.2.1. Domestic Companies — I.2.1. Entreprises Nationales							2 480	3 360
I.2.2. (Foreign Controlled Companies) — I.2.2. (Entreprises Sous Contrôle Etranger)							941	1 357
I.2.3. Branches & Agencies of Foreign Cies — I.2.3. Succursales et Agences d'Ent. Etrangères							118	255
I.2. Total — I.2. Total							2 598	3 615

J. COMMISSIONS — J. COMMISSIONS

	1990	1991	1992	1993	1994	1995	1996	1997
J.1. Life — J.1. Vie								
J.1.1. Direct Business — J.1.1. Assurance directe								
J.1.1.1. Domestic Companies — J.1.1.1. Entreprises Nationales							818	822
J.1.1.2. (Foreign Controlled Companies) — J.1.1.2. (Entreprises Sous Contrôle Etranger)							358	400
J.1.1.3. Branches & Agencies of Foreign Cies — J.1.1.3. Succursales et Agences d'Ent. Etrangères							2	0
J.1.1. Total — J.1.1. Total							820	822
J.1.2. Reinsurance Accepted — J.1.2. Réassurances acceptées								
J.1.2.1. Domestic Companies — J.1.2.1. Entreprises Nationales							0	83
J.1.2.2. (Foreign Controlled Companies) — J.1.2.2. (Entreprises Sous Contrôle Etranger)							0	83
J.1.2. Total — J.1.2. Total							0	83
J.1.3. Total — J.1.3. Total								
J.1.3.1. Domestic Companies — J.1.3.1. Entreprises Nationales							818	905
J.1.3.2. (Foreign Controlled Companies) — J.1.3.2. (Entreprises Sous Contrôle Etranger)							358	483
J.1.3.3. Branches & Agencies of Foreign Cies — J.1.3.3. Succursales et Agences d'Ent. Etrangères							2	0
J.1.3. Total of Life Net Premiums — J.1.3. Total							820	905

55

Monetary Unit: million Australian dollars

J.2. Non-Life

	1990	1991	1992	1993	1994	1995	1996	1997
J.2.1. Direct Business								
J.2.1.1. Domestic Companies							1 175	1 144
J.2.1.2. (Foreign Controlled Companies)							595	584
J.2.1.3.　Branches & Agencies of Foreign Cies							53	52
J.2.1.　Total							1 228	1 196
J.2.2. Reinsurance Accepted								
J.2.2.1. Domestic Companies							181	161
J.2.2.2. (Foreign Controlled Companies)							152	135
J.2.2.3.　Branches & Agencies of Foreign Cies							140	125
J.2.2.　Total							321	286
J.2.3. Total								
J.2.3.1. Domestic Companies							1 356	1 305
J.2.3.2. (Foreign Controlled Companies)							747	719
J.2.3.3.　Branches & Agencies of Foreign Cies							193	177
J.2.3.　Total							1 549	1 482

Unité monétaire : million de dollars australiens

J.2. Non-Vie

J.2.1. Assurance directe
J.2.1.1. Entreprises Nationales
J.2.1.2. (Entreprises Sous Contrôle Etranger)
J.2.1.3. Succursales et Agences d'Ent. Etrangères
J.2.1.　Total des Primes Nettes Vie
J.2.2. Réassurances acceptées
J.2.2.1. Entreprises Nationales
J.2.2.2. (Entreprises Sous Contrôle Etranger)
J.2.2.3. Succursales et Agences d'Ent. Etrangères
J.2.2.　Total
J.2.3. Total
J.2.3.1. Entreprises Nationales
J.2.3.2. (Entreprises Sous Contrôle Etranger)
J.2.3.3. Succursales et Agences d'Ent. Etrangères
J.2.3.　Total

56

Monetary Unit: million schillings — Unité monétaire : million de schillings

	1990	1991	1992	1993	1994	1995	1996	1997	
A. NUMBER OF COMPANIES IN THE REPORTING COUNTRY									**A. NOMBRE D'ENTREPRISES DANS LE PAYS DECLARANT**
A.1. Life									**A.1. Vie**
A.1.1. Domestic Companies	6	6	5	5	5	6	7	7	A.1.1. Entreprises Nationales
A.1.2. (Foreign Controlled Companies)	2	2	2	2	3	3	4	4	A.1.2. (Entreprises Sous Contrôle Etranger)
A.1.3. Branches & Agencies of Foreign Cies	1	1	1	1	1	1	0	0	A.1.3. Succursales et Agences d'Ent. Etrangères
A.1. All Companies	7	7	6	6	6	7	7	7	A.1. Ensemble des Entreprises
A.2. Non-Life									**A.2. Non-Vie**
A.2.1. Domestic Companies	18	18	19	19	19	18	17	16	A.2.1. Entreprises Nationales
A.2.2. (Foreign Controlled Companies)	8	6	6	6	8	7	7	6	A.2.2. (Entreprises Sous Contrôle Etranger)
A.2.3. Branches & Agencies of Foreign Cies	13	11	10	9	3	3	3	2	A.2.3. Succursales et Agences d'Ent. Etrangères
A.2. All Companies	31	29	29	28	22	21	20	18	A.2. Ensemble des Entreprises
A.3. Composite									**A.3. Mixte**
A.3.1. Domestic Companies	32	31	32	32	34	34	35	34	A.3.1. Entreprises Nationales
A.3.2. (Foreign Controlled Companies)	12	13	12	12	12	12	12	11	A.3.2. (Entreprises Sous Contrôle Etranger)
A.3. All Companies	32	31	32	32	34	34	35	34	A.3. Ensemble des Entreprises
A.4. Reinsurance									**A.4. Réassurance**
A.4.1. Domestic Companies	2	3	3	3	4	4	5	5	A.4.1. Entreprises Nationales
A.4.2. (Foreign Controlled Companies)	1	2	2	2	3	3	3	3	A.4.2. (Entreprises Sous Contrôle Etranger)
A.4. All Companies	2	3	3	3	4	4	5	5	A.4. Ensemble des Entreprises
A.5. Total									**A.5. Total**
A.5.1. Domestic Companies	58	58	59	59	62	62	64	62	A.5.1. Entreprises Nationales
A.5.2. (Foreign Controlled Companies)	23	23	22	22	26	25	26	24	A.5.2. (Entreprises Sous Contrôle Etranger)
A.5.3. Branches & Agencies of Foreign Cies	14	12	11	10	4	4	3	2	A.5.3. Succursales et Agences d'Ent. Etrangères
A.5. All Insurance Companies	72	70	70	69	66	66	67	64	A.5. Ensemble des Entreprises d'Assurances
B. NUMBER OF EMPLOYEES									**B. NOMBRE D'EMPLOYES**
B.1. Insurance Companies	32 783	33 100	32 744	32 985	32 440	32 346	32 481	32 128	B.1. Entreprises d'Assurances
C. BUSINESS WRITTEN IN THE REPORTING COUNTRY									**C. OPERATIONS CONCLUES DANS LE PAYS DECLARANT**
C.1. Life									**C.1. Vie**
C.1.1. Gross Premiums									C.1.1. Primes Brutes
C.1.1.1. Direct Business									C.1.1.1. Assurances Directes
C.1.1.1.1. Domestic Companies	28 568	29 119	31 213	39 957	40 703	46 545	66 335	50 930	C.1.1.1.1. Entreprises Nationales
C.1.1.1.2. (Foreign Controlled Companies)	9 805	10 493	11 373	13 426	15 299	16 180	22 889	17 946	C.1.1.1.2. (Entreprises Sous Contrôle Etranger)
C.1.1.1.3. Branches & Agencies of Foreign Cies	82	98	117	209	27	55	0	0	C.1.1.1.3. Succursales et Agences d'Ent. Etrangères
C.1.1.1. Total	28 650	29 217	31 330	40 166	40 730	46 600	66 335	50 930	C.1.1.1. Total
C.1.1.2. Reinsurance Accepted									C.1.1.2. Réassurance Acceptée
C.1.1.2.1. Domestic Companies	552	282	308	320	293	335	472	503	C.1.1.2.1. Entreprises Nationales
C.1.1.2.2. (Foreign Controlled Companies)	45	53	56	58	63	68	67	70	C.1.1.2.2. (Entreprises Sous Contrôle Etranger)
C.1.1.2. Total	552	282	308	320	293	335	472	503	C.1.1.2. Total
C.1.1.3. Total									C.1.1.3. Total
C.1.1.3.1. Domestic Companies	29 120	29 401	31 521	40 277	40 996	46 880	66 807	51 433	C.1.1.3.1. Entreprises Nationales
C.1.1.3.2. (Foreign Controlled Companies)	9 850	10 546	11 429	13 484	15 362	16 248	22 956	18 016	C.1.1.3.2. (Entreprises Sous Contrôle Etranger)
C.1.1.3.3. Branches & Agencies of Foreign Cies	82	98	117	209	27	55	0	0	C.1.1.3.3. Succursales et Agences d'Ent. Etrangères
C.1.1.3. Total Gross Premiums	29 203	29 499	31 638	40 486	41 023	46 935	66 807	51 433	C.1.1.3. Total des Primes Brutes
C.1.2. Ceded Premiums									C.1.2. Primes Cédées
C.1.2.1. Domestic Companies	3 042	3 164	3 480	3 770	4 308	3 912	4 944	4 268	C.1.2.1. Entreprises Nationales
C.1.2.2. (Foreign Controlled Companies)	2 300	2 401	2 634	2 861	3 365	2 901	3 874	3 163	C.1.2.2. (Entreprises Sous Contrôle Etranger)
C.1.2.3. Branches & Agencies of Foreign Cies	54	63	57	72	0	0	0	0	C.1.2.3. Succursales et Agences d'Ent. Etrangères
C.1.2. Total	3 096	3 227	3 537	3 842	4 308	3 912	4 944	4 268	C.1.2. Total
C.1.3. Net Written Premiums									C.1.3. Primes Nettes Emises
C.1.3.1. Domestic Companies	26 078	26 237	28 041	36 507	36 688	42 968	61 863	47 165	C.1.3.1. Entreprises Nationales
C.1.3.2. (Foreign Controlled Companies)	7 550	8 145	8 795	10 623	11 997	13 347	19 082	14 853	C.1.3.2. (Entreprises Sous Contrôle Etranger)
C.1.3.3. Branches & Agencies of Foreign Cies	29	35	60	137	27	55	0	0	C.1.3.3. Succursales et Agences d'Ent. Etrangères
C.1.3. Total	26 107	26 272	28 101	36 644	36 715	43 023	61 863	47 165	C.1.3. Total

Monetary Unit: million schillings

Unité monétaire : million de schillings

C.2. Non-Life / C.2. Non-Vie

	1990	1991	1992	1993	1994	1995	1996	1997
C.2.1. Gross premiums / C.2.1. Primes Brutes								
C.2.1.1. Direct Business / C.2.1.1. Assurances Directes								
C.2.1.1.1. Domestic Companies / Entreprises Nationales	60 109	65 366	70 823	75 976	79 913	82 478	83 746	84 040
C.2.1.1.2. (Foreign Controlled Companies) / (Entreprises Sous Contrôle Etranger)	26 861	29 211	31 678	34 023	35 831	36 806	37 290	37 157
C.2.1.1.3. Branches & Agencies of Foreign Cies / Succursales et Agences d'Ent. Etrangères	731	642	703	726	160	161	161	161
C.2.1.1. Total	60 840	66 008	71 526	76 702	80 073	82 639	83 907	84 201
C.2.1.2. Reinsurance Accepted / Réassurance Acceptée								
C.2.1.2.1. Domestic Companies / Entreprises Nationales	7 003	7 589	10 461	11 029	17 312	14 004	18 675	21 008
C.2.1.2.2. (Foreign Controlled Companies) / (Entreprises Sous Contrôle Etranger)	4 569	4 637	7 108	8 030	11 974	9 039	13 159	14 391
C.2.1.2.3. Branches & Agencies of Foreign Cies / Succursales et Agences d'Ent. Etrangères	48	36	28	24	0	0	6	17
C.2.1.2. Total	7 051	7 625	10 489	11 053	17 312	14 004	18 681	21 025
C.2.1.3. Total								
C.2.1.3.1. Domestic Companies / Entreprises Nationales	67 113	72 955	81 284	87 005	97 225	96 482	102 421	105 048
C.2.1.3.2. (Foreign Controlled Companies) / (Entreprises Sous Contrôle Etranger)	31 429	33 848	38 786	42 053	47 805	45 845	50 449	51 548
C.2.1.3.3. Branches & Agencies of Foreign Cies / Succursales et Agences d'Ent. Etrangères	778	678	731	750	160	161	167	178
C.2.1.3. Total Gross Premiums / Total des Primes Brutes	67 891	73 633	82 015	87 755	97 385	96 643	102 588	105 226
C.2.2. Ceded Premiums / C.2.2. Primes Cédées								
C.2.2.1. Domestic Companies / Entreprises Nationales	11 638	12 262	15 003	16 673	25 507	23 655	27 451	29 282
C.2.2.2. (Foreign Controlled Companies) / (Entreprises Sous Contrôle Etranger)	7 161	6 642	9 107	10 629	15 886	13 605	15 842	16 794
C.2.2.3. Branches & Agencies of Foreign Cies / Succursales et Agences d'Ent. Etrangères	336	329	360	355	16	16	19	9
C.2.2. Total	11 974	12 591	15 363	17 028	25 523	23 671	27 470	29 291
C.2.3. Net Written Premiums / C.2.3. Primes Nettes Emises								
C.2.3.1. Domestic Companies / Entreprises Nationales	55 475	60 693	66 281	70 332	71 718	72 827	74 970	75 766
C.2.3.2. (Foreign Controlled Companies) / (Entreprises Sous Contrôle Etranger)	24 269	27 206	29 679	31 424	31 919	32 240	34 607	34 754
C.2.3.3. Branches & Agencies of Foreign Cies / Succursales et Agences d'Ent. Etrangères	443	349	371	395	144	145	148	169
C.2.3. Total	55 917	61 042	66 652	70 727	71 862	72 972	75 118	75 935

C.3. Total

	1990	1991	1992	1993	1994	1995	1996	1997
C.3.1. Gross Premiums / C.3.1. Primes Brutes								
C.3.1.1. Direct Business / C.3.1.1. Assurances Directes								
C.3.1.1.1. Domestic Companies / Entreprises Nationales	88 677	94 485	102 036	115 933	120 616	129 023	150 081	134 970
C.3.1.1.2. (Foreign Controlled Companies) / (Entreprises Sous Contrôle Etranger)	36 666	39 704	43 051	47 449	51 130	52 986	60 179	55 103
C.3.1.1.3. Branches & Agencies of Foreign Cies / Succursales et Agences d'Ent. Etrangères	813	740	820	935	187	216	161	161
C.3.1.1. Total	89 490	95 225	102 856	116 868	120 803	129 239	150 242	135 131
C.3.1.2. Reinsurance Accepted / Réassurance Acceptée								
C.3.1.2.1. Domestic Companies / Entreprises Nationales	7 556	7 871	10 769	11 349	17 605	14 339	19 147	21 511
C.3.1.2.2. (Foreign Controlled Companies) / (Entreprises Sous Contrôle Etranger)	4 613	4 690	7 164	8 088	12 037	9 107	13 226	14 461
C.3.1.2.3. Branches & Agencies of Foreign Cies / Succursales et Agences d'Ent. Etrangères	48	36	28	24	0	0	6	17
C.3.1.2. Total	7 603	7 907	10 797	11 373	17 605	14 339	19 153	21 528
C.3.1.3. Total								
C.3.1.3.1. Domestic Companies / Entreprises Nationales	96 233	102 356	112 805	127 282	138 221	143 362	169 228	156 481
C.3.1.3.2. (Foreign Controlled Companies) / (Entreprises Sous Contrôle Etranger)	41 279	44 394	50 215	55 537	63 167	62 093	73 405	69 564
C.3.1.3.3. Branches & Agencies of Foreign Cies / Succursales et Agences d'Ent. Etrangères	861	776	848	959	187	216	167	178
C.3.1.3. Total Gross Premiums / Total des Primes Brutes	97 094	103 132	113 653	128 241	138 408	143 578	169 395	156 659
C.3.2. Ceded Premiums / C.3.2. Primes Cédées								
C.3.2.1. Domestic Companies / Entreprises Nationales	14 680	15 426	18 483	20 443	29 815	27 567	32 395	33 550
C.3.2.2. (Foreign Controlled Companies) / (Entreprises Sous Contrôle Etranger)	9 461	9 043	11 741	13 490	19 251	16 506	19 716	19 957
C.3.2.3. Branches & Agencies of Foreign Cies / Succursales et Agences d'Ent. Etrangères	390	392	417	427	16	16	19	9
C.3.2. Total	15 070	15 818	18 900	20 870	29 831	27 583	32 414	33 559
C.3.3. Net Written Premiums / C.3.3. Primes Nettes Emises								
C.3.3.1. Domestic Companies / Entreprises Nationales	81 553	86 930	94 322	106 839	108 406	115 795	136 833	122 931
C.3.3.2. (Foreign Controlled Companies) / (Entreprises Sous Contrôle Etranger)	31 818	35 351	38 474	42 047	43 916	45 587	53 689	49 607
C.3.3.3. Branches & Agencies of Foreign Cies / Succursales et Agences d'Ent. Etrangères	471	384	431	532	171	200	148	169
C.3.3. Total	82 024	87 314	94 753	107 371	108 577	115 995	136 981	123 100

Monetary Unit: million schillings — Unité monétaire : million de schillings

D. NET WRITTEN PREMIUMS IN THE REPORTING COUNTRY IN TERMS OF DOMESTIC AND FOREIGN RISKS
D. PRIMES NETTES EMISES DANS LE PAYS DECLARANT EN RISQUES NATIONAUX ET ETRANGERS

D.1. Life / D.1. Vie

	1990	1991	1992	1993	1994	1995	1996	1997
D.1.1. Domestic Risks / Risques Nationaux								
D.1.1.1. Domestic Companies / Entreprises Nationales	:	:	:	:	:	42 964	:	:
D.1.1.2. (Foreign Controlled Companies) / (Entreprises Sous Contrôle Etranger)	:	:	:	:	:	13 344	:	:
D.1.1.3. Branches & Agencies of Foreign Cies / Succursales et Agences d'Ent. Etrangères	:	:	:	:	:	55	:	:
D.1.1. Total / Total des Primes Nettes Vie	:	:	:	:	:	43 019	:	:
D.1.2. Foreign Risks / Risques Etrangers								
D.1.2.1. Domestic Companies / Entreprises Nationales	:	:	:	:	:	4	:	:
D.1.2.2. (Foreign Controlled Companies) / (Entreprises Sous Contrôle Etranger)	:	:	:	:	:	3	:	:
D.1.2. Total / Total des Primes Nettes Vie	:	:	:	:	:	4	:	:
D.1.3. Total								
D.1.3.1. Domestic Companies / Entreprises Nationales	:	:	:	36 507	:	42 968	61 863	47 165
D.1.3.2. (Foreign Controlled Companies) / (Entreprises Sous Contrôle Etranger)	:	:	:	10 623	:	13 347	19 082	14 853
D.1.3.3. Branches & Agencies of Foreign Cies / Succursales et Agences d'Ent. Etrangères	:	:	:	137	:	55	0	0
D.1.3. Total of Life Net Premiums / Total des Primes Nettes Vie	:	:	:	36 644	:	43 023	61 863	47 165

D.2. Non-Life / D.2. Non-Vie

	1990	1991	1992	1993	1994	1995	1996	1997
D.2.1. Domestic Risks / Risques Nationaux								
D.2.1.1. Domestic Companies / Entreprises Nationales	:	:	:	:	:	72 802	:	:
D.2.1.2. (Foreign Controlled Companies) / (Entreprises Sous Contrôle Etranger)	:	:	:	:	:	32 224	:	:
D.2.1.3. Branches & Agencies of Foreign Cies / Succursales et Agences d'Ent. Etrangères	:	:	:	:	:	145	:	:
D.2.1. Total / Total des Primes Nettes Vie	:	:	:	:	:	72 947	:	:
D.2.2. Foreign Risks / Risques Etrangers								
D.2.2.1. Domestic Companies / Entreprises Nationales	:	:	:	:	:	25	:	:
D.2.2.2. (Foreign Controlled Companies) / (Entreprises Sous Contrôle Etranger)	:	:	:	:	:	16	:	:
D.2.2. Total / Total des Primes Nettes Vie	:	:	:	:	:	25	:	:
D.2.3. Total								
D.2.3.1. Domestic Companies / Entreprises Nationales	:	:	:	70 332	:	72 827	74 970	75 766
D.2.3.2. (Foreign Controlled Companies) / (Entreprises Sous Contrôle Etranger)	:	:	:	31 424	:	32 240	34 607	34 754
D.2.3.3. Branches & Agencies of Foreign Cies / Succursales et Agences d'Ent. Etrangères	:	:	:	395	:	145	148	169
D.2.3. Total / Total des Primes Nettes Vie	:	:	:	70 727	:	72 972	75 118	75 935

E. BUSINESS WRITTEN ABROAD / E. OPERATIONS A L'ETRANGER

E.1. Life / E.1. Vie

	1990	1991	1992	1993	1994	1995	1996	1997
E.1.1. Gross Premiums / Primes Brutes								
E.1.1.1. Direct Business / Assurance Directe								
E.1.1.1. Branches & Agencies / Succursales & Agences	0	0	:	:	1	1	1	1
E.1.1.1. Total	0	:	:	:	1	1	1	1
E.1.1.3. Total								
E.1.1.3. Branches & Agencies / Succursales & Agences	0	0	:	:	1	1	1	1
E.1.1.3. Total Gross Premiums / Total des Primes Brutes	0	:	:	:	:	:	:	:
E.1.2. Ceded Premiums / Primes Cédées								
E.1.2.1. Branches & Agencies / Succursales & Agences	0	0	:	:	1	1	0	0
E.1.2. Total	0	:	:	:	1	:	:	:
E.1.3. Net Written Premiums / Primes Nettes Emises								
E.1.3.1. Branches & Agencies / Succursales & Agences	0	0	:	:	1	0	1	1
E.1.3. Total	0	:	:	:	1	:	:	:

Monetary Unit: million schillings   Unité monétaire : million de schillings

E.2. Non-Life — E.2. Non-Vie

Item (English)	1990	1991	1992	1993	1994	1995	1996	1997	Item (Français)
E.2.1. Gross Premiums									E.2.1. Primes Brutes
E.2.1.1. Direct Business									E.2.1.1. Assurance Directe
E.2.1.1.1. Branches & Agencies	61	74	83	67	21	1	1	1	E.2.1.1.1. Succursales & Agences
E.2.1.1. Total	61	74	83	67	21	1	1	1	E.2.1.1. Total
E.2.1.2. Reinsurance Accepted									E.2.1.2. Réassurance Acceptée
E.2.1.2.1. Branches & Agencies	2 297	2 370	2 235	2 444	0	2 920	:	0	E.2.1.2.1. Succursales & Agences
E.2.1.2. Total	2 297	2 370	2 235	2 444	0	:	:	0	E.2.1.2. Total
E.2.1.3. Total									E.2.1.3. Total
E.2.1.3.1. Branches & Agencies	2 358	2 443	2 317	2 511	21	2 921	1	1	E.2.1.3.1. Succursales & Agences
E.2.1.3. Total Gross Premiums	2 358	2 443	2 317	2 511	21	2 921	1	1	E.2.1.3. Total des Primes Brutes
E.2.2. Ceded Premiums									E.2.2. Primes Cédées
E.2.2.1. Branches & Agencies	1 292	1 381	1 464	1 657	7	1 841	1	1	E.2.2.1. Succursales & Agences
E.2.2. Total	1 292	1 381	1 464	1 657	7	1 841	1	1	E.2.2. Total
E.2.3. Net Written Premiums									E.2.3. Primes Nettes Emises
E.2.3.1. Branches & Agencies	1 066	1 062	853	854	15	1 080	0	0	E.2.3.1. Succursales & Agences
E.2.3. Total	1 066	1 062	853	854	15	1 080	:	0	E.2.3. Total

F. OUTSTANDING INVESTMENT BY DIRECT INSURANCE COMPANIES — F. ENCOURS DES PLACEMENTS DES ENTREPRISES D'ASSURANCES DIRECTES

F.1. Life — F.1. Vie

Item (English)	1990	1991	1992	1993	1994	1995	1996	1997	Item (Français)
F.1.1. Real Estate									F.1.1. Immobilier
F.1.1.1. Domestic Companies	9 112	9 334	6 773	13 521	16 045	17 218	17 683	16 411	F.1.1.1. Entreprises Nationales
F.1.1.2. (Foreign Controlled Companies)	3 983	4 173	4 339	4 997	6 113	5 928	6 130	5 781	F.1.1.2. (Entreprises Sous Controle Etranger)
F.1.1.3. Branches & Agencies of Foreign Cies	124	0	0	0	0	0	0	0	F.1.1.3. Succursales et Agences d'Ent. Etrangères
F.1.1.4. Domestic Investment	9 112	9 334	11 112	:	:	:	:	:	F.1.1.4. Placement dans le Pays
F.1.1.5. Foreign Investment	124	0	0	:	:	:	:	:	F.1.1.5. Placement à l' Etranger
F.1.1. Total	9 236	9 334	11 112	13 521	16 045	:	17 683	:	F.1.1. Total
F.1.2. Mortgage Loans									F.1.2. Prêts Hypothécaires
F.1.2.1. Domestic Companies	3 923	4 517	4 719	5 047	6 084	6 587	6 533	6 611	F.1.2.1. Entreprises Nationales
F.1.2.2. (Foreign Controlled Companies)	134	115	117	113	234	302	337	619	F.1.2.2. (Entreprises Sous Controle Etranger)
F.1.2.3. Branches & Agencies of Foreign Cies	1	1	11	12	0	0	0	0	F.1.2.3. Succursales et Agences d'Ent. Etrangères
F.1.2.4. Domestic Investment	3 923	4 517	4 847	:	:	:	:	:	F.1.2.4. Placement dans le Pays
F.1.2.5. Foreign Investment				:	:	:	:	:	F.1.2.5. Placement à l' Etranger
F.1.2. Total	3 925	4 518	4 847	5 059	6 084	:	6 533	:	F.1.2. Total
F.1.3. Shares									F.1.3. Actions
F.1.3.1. Domestic Companies	2 481	4 162	13 420	25 747	29 117	32 746	39 998	52 032	F.1.3.1. Entreprises Nationales
F.1.3.2. (Foreign Controlled Companies)	638	925	5 576	7 162	9 147	10 061	11 824	15 423	F.1.3.2. (Entreprises Sous Controle Etranger)
F.1.3.3. Branches & Agencies of Foreign Cies		0	8	194	0	0	0	0	F.1.3.3. Succursales et Agences d'Ent. Etrangères
F.1.3.4. Domestic Investment	2 481	4 162	19 004	25 941	29 117	:	:	:	F.1.3.4. Placement dans le Pays
									F.1.3.5. Placement à l' Etranger
F.1.3. Total	2 481	4 162	19 004	25 941	29 117	:	39 998	:	F.1.3. Total
F.1.4. Bonds with Fixed Revenue									F.1.4. Obligations
F.1.4.1. Domestic Companies	63 947	72 087	45 935	75 037	83 387	99 628	118 281	133 613	F.1.4.1. Entreprises Nationales
F.1.4.2. (Foreign Controlled Companies)	24 949	29 687	33 093	25 142	27 744	39 508	47 222	52 762	F.1.4.2. (Entreprises Sous Controle Etranger)
F.1.4.3. Branches & Agencies of Foreign Cies	168	233	300	262	35	30	0	0	F.1.4.3. Succursales et Agences d'Ent. Etrangères
F.1.4.4. Domestic Investment	63 947	72 087	79 329	:	:	:	:	:	F.1.4.4. Placement dans le Pays
F.1.4.5. Foreign Investment	168	233	0	:	:	:	:	:	F.1.4.5. Placement à l' Etranger
F.1.4. Total	64 115	72 320	79 329	75 299	83 422	:	118 281	:	F.1.4. Total
F.1.5. Loans other than Mortgage Loans									F.1.5. Prêts Autres qu'Hypothécaires
F.1.5.1. Domestic Companies	71 751	79 635	57 990	102 151	112 045	131 182	144 883	139 150	F.1.5.1. Entreprises Nationales
F.1.5.2. (Foreign Controlled Companies)	26 831	29 411	33 954	38 207	41 737	50 315	55 762	54 984	F.1.5.2. (Entreprises Sous Controle Etranger)
F.1.5.3. Branches & Agencies of Foreign Cies	11	21	22	21	0	0	0	0	F.1.5.3. Succursales et Agences d'Ent. Etrangères
F.1.5.4. Domestic Investment	71 751	79 635	91 967	102 172	112 045	:	:	:	F.1.5.4. Placement dans le Pays
F.1.5.5. Foreign Investment	11	21	0	:	:	:	:	:	F.1.5.5. Placement à l' Etranger
F.1.5. Total	71 762	79 656	91 967	102 172	112 045	:	144 883	:	F.1.5. Total

Monetary Unit: million schillings   Unité monétaire : million de schillings

Code / Label (EN)	1990	1991	1992	1993	1994	1995	1996	1997	Label (FR)
F.1.6. Other Investments									**F.1.6. Autres Placements**
F.1.6.1. Domestic Companies	16 786	18 410	4 331	23 372	26 814	16 558	19 508	26 801	F.1.6.1. Entreprises Nationales
F.1.6.2. (Foreign Controlled Companies)	5 955	5 699	1 545	12 690	14 008	2 103	3 374	10 223	F.1.6.2. (Entreprises Sous Contrôle Etranger)
F.1.6.3. Branches & Agencies of Foreign Cies	9	4	1	0	0	0	0	0	F.1.6.3. Succursales et Agences d'Ent. Etrangères
F.1.6.4. Domestic Investment	16 786	18 410	5 876	23 372	26 814	:	:	:	F.1.6.4. Placement dans le Pays
F.1.6.5. Foreign Investment	9	4	0	0	:	:	:	:	F.1.6.5. Placement à l'Etranger
F.1.6. Total	16 795	18 414	5 876	23 372	26 814	19 508	19 508	19 508	F.1.6. Total
F.1.7. Total									**F.1.7. Total**
F.1.7.1. Domestic Companies	168 000	188 144	133 168	244 875	273 492	303 919	346 886	374 618	F.1.7.1. Entreprises Nationales
F.1.7.2. (Foreign Controlled Companies)	62 491	70 009	78 624	88 311	98 983	108 217	124 649	139 792	F.1.7.2. (Entreprises Sous Contrôle Etranger)
F.1.7.3. Branches & Agencies of Foreign Cies	313	259	342	489	35	30	0	0	F.1.7.3. Succursales et Agences d'Ent. Etrangères
F.1.7.4. Domestic Investment	168 000	188 144	212 135	:	:	:	:	:	F.1.7.4. Placement dans le Pays
F.1.7.5. Foreign Investment	313	259	0	:	:	:	:	:	F.1.7.5. Placement à l'Etranger
F.1.7. Total of Life Investments	168 313	188 403	212 135	245 364	273 527	:	346 886	:	F.1.7. Total des Placements Vie
F.2. Non-Life									**F.2. Non-Vie**
F.2.1. Real Estate									**F.2.1. Immobilier**
F.2.1.1. Domestic Companies	14 963	17 968	10 984	23 158	22 359	22 699	24 176	26 004	F.2.1.1. Entreprises Nationales
F.2.1.2. (Foreign Controlled Companies)	6 761	7 708	9 835	10 839	9 965	10 311	10 415	10 460	F.2.1.2. (Entreprises Sous Contrôle Etranger)
F.2.1.3. Branches & Agencies of Foreign Cies	0	123	120	117	38	37	36	2	F.2.1.3. Succursales et Agences d'Ent. Etrangères
F.2.1.4. Domestic Investment	14 963	17 968	20 939	23 275	22 397	:	24 212	:	F.2.1.4. Placement dans le Pays
F.2.1.5. Foreign Investment	0	123	0	:	:	:	:	:	F.2.1.5. Placement à l'Etranger
F.2.1. Total	14 963	18 090	20 939	23 275	22 397	:	24 212	:	F.2.1. Total
F.2.2. Mortgage Loans									**F.2.2. Prêts Hypothécaires**
F.2.2.1. Domestic Companies	4 520	3 793	2 457	4 465	5 191	5 384	6 252	6 164	F.2.2.1. Entreprises Nationales
F.2.2.2. (Foreign Controlled Companies)	1 956	1 409	1 804	1 630	1 839	1 962	1 924	1 960	F.2.2.2. (Entreprises Sous Contrôle Etranger)
F.2.2.3. Branches & Agencies of Foreign Cies	0	0	1	1	0	0	0	0	F.2.2.3. Succursales et Agences d'Ent. Etrangères
F.2.2.4. Domestic Investment	4 520	3 793	4 175	4 466	5 191	:	6 252	:	F.2.2.4. Placement dans le Pays
F.2.2.5. Foreign Investment	0	0	86	:	:	:	:	:	F.2.2.5. Placement à l'Etranger
F.2.2. Total	4 520	3 793	4 261	4 466	5 191	6 252	6 252	6 252	F.2.2. Total
F.2.3. Shares									**F.2.3. Actions**
F.2.3.1. Domestic Companies	4 162	4 554	9 144	19 215	20 450	21 943	24 802	27 767	F.2.3.1. Entreprises Nationales
F.2.3.2. (Foreign Controlled Companies)	1 624	1 512	6 363	7 134	6 927	7 629	9 117	11 096	F.2.3.2. (Entreprises Sous Contrôle Etranger)
F.2.3.3. Branches & Agencies of Foreign Cies	1	1	2	2	0	0	0	0	F.2.3.3. Succursales et Agences d'Ent. Etrangères
F.2.3.4. Domestic Investment	4 162	4 555	15 321	19 217	20 450	:	24 802	:	F.2.3.4. Placement dans le Pays
F.2.3.5. Foreign Investment	1	1	190	:	:	:	:	:	F.2.3.5. Placement à l'Etranger
F.2.3. Total	4 163	4 555	15 511	19 217	20 450	:	24 802	:	F.2.3. Total
F.2.4. Bonds with Fixed Revenue									**F.2.4. Obligations**
F.2.4.1. Domestic Companies	24 483	25 259	13 976	28 735	30 414	32 802	34 429	35 539	F.2.4.1. Entreprises Nationales
F.2.4.2. (Foreign Controlled Companies)	11 479	12 667	13 456	14 684	14 258	15 256	15 550	16 251	F.2.4.2. (Entreprises Sous Contrôle Etranger)
F.2.4.3. Branches & Agencies of Foreign Cies	512	463	517	490	197	228	292	262	F.2.4.3. Succursales et Agences d'Ent. Etrangères
F.2.4.4. Domestic Investment	24 483	25 259	27 839	29 225	30 611	:	34 721	:	F.2.4.4. Placement dans le Pays
F.2.4.5. Foreign Investment	512	463	109	:	:	:	:	:	F.2.4.5. Placement à l'Etranger
F.2.4. Total	24 995	25 722	27 948	29 225	30 611	:	34 721	:	F.2.4. Total
F.2.5. Loans other than Mortgage Loans									**F.2.5. Prêts Autres qu'Hypothécaires**
F.2.5.1. Domestic Companies	17 196	20 881	12 950	25 540	27 477	33 612	34 748	33 928	F.2.5.1. Entreprises Nationales
F.2.5.2. (Foreign Controlled Companies)	7 853	8 972	10 623	12 361	13 840	16 117	17 925	16 939	F.2.5.2. (Entreprises Sous Contrôle Etranger)
F.2.5.3. Branches & Agencies of Foreign Cies	99	77	81	88	19	19	25	32	F.2.5.3. Succursales et Agences d'Ent. Etrangères
F.2.5.4. Domestic Investment	17 196	20 881	23 299	25 628	27 496	:	34 773	:	F.2.5.4. Placement dans le Pays
F.2.5.5. Foreign Investment	99	77	355	:	:	:	:	:	F.2.5.5. Placement à l'Etranger
F.2.5. Total	17 296	20 958	23 654	25 628	27 496	:	34 773	:	F.2.5. Total
F.2.6. Other Investments									**F.2.6. Autres Placements**
F.2.6.1. Domestic Companies	21 568	17 368	8 252	36 056	30 308	16 518	18 221	38 176	F.2.6.1. Entreprises Nationales
F.2.6.2. (Foreign Controlled Companies)	9 356	7 904	7 454	21 973	4 167	3 395	2 877	14 333	F.2.6.2. (Entreprises Sous Contrôle Etranger)
F.2.6.3. Branches & Agencies of Foreign Cies	196	199	190	341	55	50	14	61	F.2.6.3. Succursales et Agences d'Ent. Etrangères
F.2.6.4. Domestic Investment	21 568	17 368	14 696	36 397	30 363	:	18 235	:	F.2.6.4. Placement dans le Pays
F.2.6.5. Foreign Investment	196	199	1 199	:	:	:	:	:	F.2.6.5. Placement à l'Etranger
F.2.6. Total	21 764	17 567	15 895	36 397	30 363	:	18 235	:	F.2.6. Total

AUSTRIA

Monetary Unit: million schillings   Unité monétaire : million de schillings

	1990	1991	1992	1993	1994	1995	1996	1997	
F.2.7. Total									**F.2.7. Total**
F.2.7.1. Domestic Companies	86 892	89 824	57 763	137 169	136 199	132 958	142 628	167 578	F.2.7.1. Entreprises Nationales
F.2.7.2. (Foreign Controlled Companies)	39 029	40 173	49 535	68 621	50 996	54 670	57 808	71 039	F.2.7.2. (Entreprises Sous Contrôle Etranger)
F.2.7.3. Branches & Agencies of Foreign Cies	808	862	911	1 039	309	334	367	357	F.2.7.3. Succursales et Agences d'Ent. Etrangères
F.2.7.4. Domestic Investment	86 892	89 824	106 269	..	..	..	..	..	F.2.7.4. Placement dans le Pays
F.2.7.5. Foreign Investment	808	862	1 939	..	..	..	..	..	F.2.7.5. Placement à l' Etranger
F.2.7. Total of Non-Life Investments	87 700	90 686	108 208	138 208	136 508	..	142 995	..	F.2.7. Total des Placements Non-Vie
G. BREAKDOWN OF NON-LIFE PREMIUMS									**G. VENTILATIONS DES PRIMES NON-VIE**
G.1. Motor vehicle									**G.1. Assurance Automobile**
G.1.1. Direct Business									G.1.1. Assurances Directes
G.1.1.1. Gross Premiums	22 438	23 464	26 924	28 411	30 013	30 377	30 360	29 590	G.1.1.1. Primes Brutes
G.1.1.2. Ceded Premiums	3 018	2 629	3 020	3 350	4 568	4 615	4 995	5 238	G.1.1.2. Primes Cédées
G.1.1.3. Net Written Premiums	19 420	20 835	23 904	25 061	25 445	25 762	25 365	24 352	G.1.1.3. Primes Nettes Emises
G.2. Marine, Aviation									**G.2. Marine, Aviation**
G.2.1. Direct Business									G.2.1. Assurances Directes
G.2.1.1. Gross Premiums	91	90	129	160	146	81	83	92	G.2.1.1. Primes Brutes
G.2.1.2. Ceded Premiums	75	73	108	139	134	25	28	34	G.2.1.2. Primes Cédées
G.2.1.3. Net Written Premiums	16	17	21	21	12	56	55	58	G.2.1.3. Primes Nettes Emises
G.3. Freight									**G.3. Fret**
G.3.1. Direct Business									G.3.1. Assurances Directes
G.3.1.1. Gross Premiums	1 020	1 152	1 139	1 174	1 116	1 020	984	1 016	G.3.1.1. Primes Brutes
G.3.1.2. Ceded Premiums	385	463	446	446	449	411	422	421	G.3.1.2. Primes Cédées
G.3.1.3. Net Written Premiums	635	689	693	728	667	609	562	595	G.3.1.3. Primes Nettes Emises
G.3.2. Reinsurance Accepted									G.3.2. Reassurance Acceptée
G.3.2.1. Gross Premiums	238	265	..	..	..	..	..	..	G.3.2.1. Primes Brutes
G.3.2.2. Ceded Premiums	102	110	..	..	..	..	..	..	G.3.2.2. Primes Cédées
G.3.2.3. Net Written Premiums	136	155	..	..	..	..	..	..	G.3.2.3. Primes Nettes Emises
G.3.3. Total									G.3.3. Total
G.3.3.1. Gross Premiums	1 258	1 417	..	..	..	..	..	..	G.3.3.1. Primes Brutes
G.3.3.2. Ceded Premiums	487	573	..	..	..	..	..	..	G.3.3.2. Primes Cédées
G.3.3.3. Net Written Premiums	771	844	..	..	..	..	..	..	G.3.3.3. Primes Nettes Emises
G.4. Fire, Property Damages									**G.4. Incendie, Dommages aux Biens**
G.4.1. Direct Business									G.4.1. Assurances Directes
G.4.1.1. Gross Premiums	14 742	14 840	15 550	17 734	18 486	19 415	20 083	20 444	G.4.1.1. Primes Brutes
G.4.1.2. Ceded Premiums	4 574	4 563	4 692	5 408	6 974	7 425	8 002	7 706	G.4.1.2. Primes Cédées
G.4.1.3. Net Written Premiums	10 168	10 277	10 858	12 326	11 512	11 990	12 081	12 738	G.4.1.3. Primes Nettes Emises
G.5. Pecuniary Losses									**G.5. Pertes Pécunières**
G.5.1. Direct Business									G.5.1. Assurances Directes
G.5.1.1. Gross Premiums	352	425	497	484	537	594	690	763	G.5.1.1. Primes Brutes
G.5.1.2. Ceded Premiums	291	350	407	437	474	519	588	638	G.5.1.2. Primes Cédées
G.5.1.3. Net Written Premiums	61	75	90	47	63	75	102	125	G.5.1.3. Primes Nettes Emises
G.6. General Liability									**G.6. Responsabilité Générale**
G.6.1. Direct Business									G.6.1. Assurances Directes
G.6.1.1. Gross Premiums	3 474	3 693	4 165	4 602	4 736	5 010	5 224	5 421	G.6.1.1. Primes Brutes
G.6.1.2. Ceded Premiums	548	569	677	743	988	1 027	1 094	1 330	G.6.1.2. Primes Cédées
G.6.1.3. Net Written Premiums	2 927	3 124	3 488	3 859	3 748	3 983	4 130	4 091	G.6.1.3. Primes Nettes Emises
G.7. Accident, Health									**G.7. Accident, Santé**
G.7.1. Direct Business									G.7.1. Assurances Directes
G.7.1.1. Gross Premiums	16 108	17 361	18 660	20 621	21 475	22 293	22 339	22 425	G.7.1.1. Primes Brutes
G.7.1.2. Ceded Premiums	728	759	781	983	1 174	1 039	1 089	1 189	G.7.1.2. Primes Cédées
G.7.1.3. Net Written Premiums	15 381	16 602	17 879	19 638	20 301	21 254	21 250	21 236	G.7.1.3. Primes Nettes Emises
G.8. Others									**G.8. Autres**
G.8.1. Direct Business									G.8.1. Assurances Directes
G.8.1.1. Gross Premiums	2 615	2 663	4 106	3 346	3 564	3 849	4 144	4 450	G.8.1.1. Primes Brutes
G.8.1.2. Ceded Premiums	350	386	993	537	680	808	780	882	G.8.1.2. Primes Cédées
G.8.1.3. Net Written Premiums	2 265	2 277	3 113	2 809	2 884	3 041	3 364	3 568	G.8.1.3. Primes Nettes Emises

AUSTRIA / AUTRICHE

Monetary Unit: million schillings — Unité monétaire : million de schillings

	1990	1991	1992	1993	1994	1995	1996	1997
G.10. Total								
G.10.1. Direct Business — Assurances Directes								
G.10.1.1. Gross Premiums — Primes Brutes	60 840	63 688	71 170	76 532	80 073	82 639	83 907	84 201
G.10.1.2. Ceded Premiums — Primes Cédées	9 967	9 792	11 124	12 043	15 441	15 869	16 998	17 438
G.10.1.3. Net Written Premiums — Primes Nettes Emises	50 873	53 896	60 046	64 489	64 632	66 770	66 909	66 763
G.10.2. Reinsurance Accepted — Réassurance Acceptée								
G.10.2.1. Gross Premiums — Primes Brutes	7 051	6 919	10 334	11 139	17 312	14 004	18 681	21 025
G.10.2.2. Ceded Premiums — Primes Cédées	2 007	2 163	4 169	4 967	10 082	7 802	10 472	11 853
G.10.2.3. Net Written Premiums — Primes Nettes Emises	5 045	4 756	6 165	6 172	7 230	6 202	8 209	9 172
G.10.3. Total								
G.10.3.1. Gross Premiums — Primes Brutes	67 891	70 607	81 504	87 671	97 385	96 643	102 588	105 226
G.10.3.2. Ceded Premiums — Primes Cédées	11 974	11 955	15 293	17 010	25 523	23 671	27 470	29 291
G.10.3.3. Net Written Premiums — Primes Nettes Emises	55 917	58 652	66 211	70 661	71 862	72 972	75 118	75 935
H. GROSS CLAIMS PAYMENTS — H. PAIEMENTS BRUTS DES SINISTRES								
H.1. Life — H.1. Vie								
H.1.1. Domestic Companies — Entreprises Nationales							29 930	38 743
H.1.2. (Foreign Controlled Companies) — (Entreprises Sous Contrôle Etranger)							11 218	14 607
H.1. Total — Total							29 930	38 743
H.2. Non-Life — H.2. Non-Vie								
H.2.1. Domestic Companies — Entreprises Nationales							65 520	67 558
H.2.2. (Foreign Controlled Companies) — (Entreprises Sous Contrôle Etranger)							32 616	33 700
H.2.3. Branches & Agencies of Foreign Cies — Succursales at Agences d'Ent. Etrangeres							98	71
H.2. Total — Total							65 618	67 629
I. GROSS OPERATING EXPENSES — I. DEPENSES BRUITES D'EXPLOITATION								
I.1. Life — I.1. Vie								
I.1.1. Domestic Companies — Entreprises Nationales							9 152	9 016
I.1.2. (Foreign Controlled Companies) — (Entreprises Sous Contrôle Etranger)							3 388	3 104
I.1. Total — Total des Primes Nettes Vie							9 152	9 016
I.2. Non-Life — I.2. Non-Vie								
I.2.1. Domestic Companies — Entreprises Nationales							28 656	30 478
I.2.2. (Foreign Controlled Companies) — (Entreprises Sous Contrôle Etranger)							14 927	15 924
I.2.3. Branches & Agencies of Foreign Cies — Succursales et Agences d'Ent. Etrangères							58	55
I.2. Total — Total							28 714	30 533
J. COMMISSIONS — J. COMMISSIONS								
J.1. Life — J.1. Vie								
J.1.1. Direct Business — Assurance directe								
J.1.1.1. Domestic Companies — Entreprises Nationales							3 910	3 483
J.1.1.2. (Foreign Controlled Companies) — (Entreprises Sous Contrôle Etranger)							1 166	923
J.1.1. Total — Total							3 910	3 483
J.1.2. Reinsurance Accepted — Réassurances acceptées								
J.1.2.1. Domestic Companies — Entreprises Nationales							137	105
J.1.2.2. (Foreign Controlled Companies) — (Entreprises Sous Contrôle Etranger)							13	9
J.1.2. Total — Total							137	105
J.1.3. Total								
J.1.3.1. Domestic Companies — Entreprises Nationales							4 047	3 588
J.1.3.2. (Foreign Controlled Companies) — (Entreprises Sous Contrôle Etranger)							1 179	932
J.1.3. Total Of Life Net Premiums — Total							4 047	3 588

Monetary Unit: million schillings

Unité monétaire : million de schillings

J.2. Non-Life

J.2. Non-Vie

	1990	1991	1992	1993	1994	1995	1996	1997	
J.2.1. Direct Business									J.2.1. Assurance directe
J.2.1.1. Domestic Companies							7 250	7 472	J.2.1.1. Entreprises Nationales
J.2.1.2. (Foreign Controlled Companies)							3 768	3 833	J.2.1.2. (Entreprises Sous Contrôle Etranger)
J.2.1.3. Branches & Agencies of Foreign Cies							28	26	J.2.1.3. Succursales et Agences d'Ent. Etrangères
J.2.1. Total							7 278	7 498	J.2.1. Total des Primes Nettes Vie
J.2.2. Reinsurance Accepted									J.2.2. Réassurances acceptées
J.2.2.1. Domestic Companies							2 339	2 760	J.2.2.1. Entreprises Nationales
J.2.2.2. (Foreign Controlled Companies)							900	968	J.2.2.2. (Entreprises Sous Contrôle Etranger)
J.2.2.3. Branches & Agencies of Foreign Cies							1	1	J.2.2.3. Succursales et Agences d'Ent. Etrangères
J.2.2. Total							2 340	2 761	J.2.2. Total
J.2.3. Total									J.2.3. Total
J.2.3.1. Domestic Companies							9 589	10 232	J.2.3.1. Entreprises Nationales
J.2.3.2. (Foreign Controlled Companies)							4 668	4 801	J.2.3.2. (Entreprises Sous Contrôle Etranger)
J.2.3.3. Branches & Agencies of Foreign Cies							29	27	J.2.3.3. Succursales et Agences d'Ent. Etrangères
J.2.3. Total							9 618	10 259	J.2.3. Total

Monetary Unit: million Belgian francs

Unité monétaire : million de francs belges

A. NUMBER OF COMPANIES IN THE REPORTING COUNTRY / A. NOMBRE D'ENTREPRISES DANS LE PAYS DECLARANT

English	1990	1991	1992	1993	1994	1995	1996	1997	Français
A.1. Life									**A.1. Vie**
A.1.1. Domestic Companies	28	31	32	31	30	30	27	27	A.1.1. Entreprises Nationales
A.1.3. Branches & Agencies of Foreign Cies	10	9	11	11	1	0	0	0	A.1.3. Succursales et Agences d'Ent. Etrangères
A.1. All Companies	38	40	43	42	31	30	27	27	A.1. Ensemble des Entreprises
A.2. Non-Life									**A.2. Non-Vie**
A.2.1. Domestic Companies	82	86	86	85	84	82	84	87	A.2.1. Entreprises Nationales
A.2.3. Branches & Agencies of Foreign Cies	94	90	83	78	9	8	8	6	A.2.3. Succursales et Agences d'Ent. Etrangères
A.2. All Companies	176	176	169	163	93	90	92	93	A.2. Ensemble des Entreprises
A.3. Composite									**A.3. Mixte**
A.3.1. Domestic Companies	53	52	51	47	44	41	44	40	A.3.1. Entreprises Nationales
A.3.3. Branches & Agencies of Foreign Cies	5	4	3	3	3	2	2	2	A.3.3. Succursales et Agences d'Ent. Etrangères
A.3. All Companies	58	56	54	50	47	43	46	42	A.3. Ensemble des Entreprises
A.5. Total									**A.5. Total**
A.5.1. Domestic Companies	163	169	169	163	158	153	155	154	A.5.1. Entreprises Nationales
A.5.3. Branches & Agencies of Foreign Cies	109	103	97	92	13	10	10	8	A.5.3. Succursales et Agences d'Ent. Etrangères
A.5. All Insurance Companies	272	272	266	255	171	163	165	162	A.5. Ensemble des Entreprises d'Assurances

B. NUMBER OF EMPLOYEES / B. NOMBRE D'EMPLOYES

English	1990	1991	1992	1993	1994	1995	1996	1997	Français
B.1. Insurance Companies	29 818	29 117	27 920	27 007	25 969	25 501	25 070	25 262	B.1. Entreprises d'Assurances
B.2. Intermediaries	25 000	24 000	24 000	24 000	24 000	28 750	28 085	28 642	B.2. Intermediaires
B. Total	54 818	53 117	51 920	51 007	49 969	54 251	53 155	53 904	B. Total

C. BUSINESS WRITTEN IN THE REPORTING COUNTRY / C. OPERATIONS CONCLUES DANS LE PAYS DECLARANT

C.1. Life / C.1. Vie

English	1990	1991	1992	1993	1994	1995	1996	1997	Français
C.1.1. Gross Premiums									**C.1.1. Primes Brutes**
C.1.1.1. Direct Business									**C.1.1.1. Assurances Directes**
C.1.1.1.1. Domestic Companies	95 594	104 374	112 562	124 087	146 610	174 220	203 871	242 192	C.1.1.1.1. Entreprises Nationales
C.1.1.1.3. Branches & Agencies of Foreign Cies	7 978	8 308	8 638	11 361	13 260	7 661	7 619	8 894	C.1.1.1.3. Succursales et Agences d'Ent. Etrangères
C.1.1.1. Total	103 572	112 682	121 200	135 448	159 870	181 881	211 490	251 086	C.1.1.1. Total
C.1.1.2. Reinsurance Accepted									**C.1.1.2. Réassurance Acceptée**
C.1.1.2.1. Domestic Companies	1 104	1 512	1 203	1 384	2 000	2 482	2 847	3 252	C.1.1.2.1. Entreprises Nationales
C.1.1.2.3. Branches & Agencies of Foreign Cies	16	57	48	140	4	3	3	3	C.1.1.2.3. Succursales et Agences d'Ent. Etrangères
C.1.1.2. Total	1 120	1 570	1 252	1 523	2 004	2 485	2 850	3 254	C.1.1.2. Total
C.1.1.3. Total									**C.1.1.3. Total**
C.1.1.3.1. Domestic Companies	96 699	105 886	113 765	125 470	148 610	176 702	206 718	245 444	C.1.1.3.1. Entreprises Nationales
C.1.1.3.3. Branches & Agencies of Foreign Cies	7 994	8 365	8 686	11 501	13 264	7 664	7 622	8 896	C.1.1.3.3. Succursales et Agences d'Ent. Etrangères
C.1.1.3 Total Gross Premiums	104 692	114 252	122 451	136 971	161 874	184 367	214 340	254 340	C.1.1.3. Total des Primes Brutes
C.1.2. Ceded Premiums									**C.1.2. Primes Cédées**
C.1.2.1. Domestic Companies	5 530	5 822	6 180	5 672	5 790	0	0	0	C.1.2.1. Entreprises Nationales
C.1.2.3. Branches & Agencies of Foreign Cies	607	717	806	718	132	131	160	92	C.1.2.3. Succursales et Agences d'Ent. Etrangères
C.1.2. Total	6 137	6 539	6 986	6 390	5 922	131	160	92	C.1.2. Total
C.1.3. Net Written Premiums									**C.1.3. Primes Nettes Emises**
C.1.3.1. Domestic Companies	91 169	100 065	107 585	119 798	142 820	176 702	206 718	245 444	C.1.3.1. Entreprises Nationales
C.1.3.3. Branches & Agencies of Foreign Cies	7 387	7 648	7 880	10 783	13 132	7 533	7 462	8 804	C.1.3.3. Succursales et Agences d'Ent. Etrangères
C.1.3. Total	98 556	107 713	115 465	130 581	155 952	184 236	214 180	254 248	C.1.3. Total

BELGIUM / BELGIQUE

Monetary Unit: million Belgian francs — Unité monétaire : million de francs belges

C.2. Non-Life / C.2. Non-Vie

Label (EN)	1990	1991	1992	1993	1994	1995	1996	1997	Label (FR)
C.2.1. Gross premiums									**C.2.1. Primes Brutes**
C.2.1.1. Direct Business									C.2.1.1. Assurances Directes
C.2.1.1.1. Domestic Companies	178 169	193 645	217 617	227 735	234 503	242 070	245 673	242 896	C.2.1.1.1. Entreprises Nationales
C.2.1.1.3. Branches & Agencies of Foreign Cies	22 065	20 743	16 247	16 778	7 206	6 249	6 874	6 516	C.2.1.1.3. Succursales et Agences d'Ent. Etrangères
C.2.1.1. Total	200 234	214 388	233 864	244 513	241 709	248 319	252 547	249 412	C.2.1.1. Total
C.2.1.2. Reinsurance Accepted									C.2.1.2. Réassurance Acceptée
C.2.1.2.1. Domestic Companies	16 804	17 059	14 494	10 848	9 496	23 183	22 700	23 255	C.2.1.2.1. Entreprises Nationales
C.2.1.2.3. Branches & Agencies of Foreign Cies	2 301	2 854	1 904	747	126	95	217	188	C.2.1.2.3. Succursales et Agences d'Ent. Etrangères
C.2.1.2. Total	19 105	19 913	16 398	11 595	9 622	23 278	22 917	23 443	C.2.1.2. Total
C.2.1.3. Total									C.2.1.3. Total
C.2.1.3.1. Domestic Companies	194 973	210 704	232 112	238 583	243 999	265 253	268 373	266 152	C.2.1.3.1. Entreprises Nationales
C.2.1.3.3. Branches & Agencies of Foreign Cies	24 366	23 597	18 151	17 526	7 332	6 345	7 091	6 704	C.2.1.3.3. Succursales et Agences d'Ent. Etrangères
C.2.1.3. Total Gross Premiums	219 339	234 301	250 263	256 109	251 331	271 598	275 464	272 856	C.2.1.3. Total des Primes Brutes
C.2.2. Ceded Premiums									**C.2.2. Primes Cédées**
C.2.2.1. Domestic Companies	35 777	40 291	43 336	43 370	45 245	44 403	41 909	38 143	C.2.2.1. Entreprises Nationales
C.2.2.3. Branches & Agencies of Foreign Cies	7 424	7 045	5 602	5 095	1 069	807	855	775	C.2.2.3. Succursales et Agences d'Ent. Etrangères
C.2.2. Total	43 201	47 336	48 938	48 465	46 314	45 210	42 764	38 917	C.2.2. Total
C.2.3. Net Written Premiums									**C.2.3. Primes Nettes Emises**
C.2.3.1. Domestic Companies	159 196	170 413	188 775	195 213	198 754	220 850	226 464	228 009	C.2.3.1. Entreprises Nationales
C.2.3.3. Branches & Agencies of Foreign Cies	16 942	16 552	12 549	12 430	6 263	5 537	6 236	5 929	C.2.3.3. Succursales et Agences d'Ent. Etrangères
C.2.3. Total	176 138	186 965	201 324	207 643	205 017	226 387	232 700	233 938	C.2.3. Total

C.3. Total / C.3. Total

Label (EN)	1990	1991	1992	1993	1994	1995	1996	1997	Label (FR)
C.3.1. Gross Premiums									**C.3.1. Primes Brutes**
C.3.1.1. Direct Business									C.3.1.1. Assurances Directes
C.3.1.1.1. Domestic Companies	273 763	298 019	330 179	351 822	381 113	416 290	449 544	485 088	C.3.1.1.1. Entreprises Nationales
C.3.1.1.3. Branches & Agencies of Foreign Cies	30 043	29 051	24 885	28 139	20 466	13 910	14 493	15 410	C.3.1.1.3. Succursales et Agences d'Ent. Etrangères
C.3.1.1. Total	303 806	327 070	355 064	379 961	401 579	430 200	464 037	500 498	C.3.1.1. Total
C.3.1.2. Reinsurance Accepted									C.3.1.2. Réassurance Acceptée
C.3.1.2.1. Domestic Companies	17 908	18 571	15 697	12 232	11 496	25 665	25 547	26 507	C.3.1.2.1. Entreprises Nationales
C.3.1.2.3. Branches & Agencies of Foreign Cies	2 317	2 911	1 952	887	130	98	220	191	C.3.1.2.3. Succursales et Agences d'Ent. Etrangères
C.3.1.2. Total	20 225	21 483	17 650	13 118	11 626	25 763	25 767	26 697	C.3.1.2. Total
C.3.1.3. Total									C.3.1.3. Total
C.3.1.3.1. Domestic Companies	291 672	316 590	345 877	364 053	392 609	441 955	475 091	511 596	C.3.1.3.1. Entreprises Nationales
C.3.1.3.3. Branches & Agencies of Foreign Cies	32 360	31 962	26 837	29 027	20 596	14 009	14 713	15 600	C.3.1.3.3. Succursales et Agences d'Ent. Etrangères
C.3.1.3. Total Gross Premiums	324 031	348 553	372 714	393 080	413 205	455 965	489 804	527 196	C.3.1.3. Total des Primes Brutes
C.3.2. Ceded Premiums									**C.3.2. Primes Cédées**
C.3.2.1. Domestic Companies	41 307	46 113	49 516	49 042	51 035	44 403	41 909	38 143	C.3.2.1. Entreprises Nationales
C.3.2.3. Branches & Agencies of Foreign Cies	8 031	7 762	6 408	5 813	1 201	938	1 015	867	C.3.2.3. Succursales et Agences d'Ent. Etrangères
C.3.2. Total	49 338	53 875	55 924	54 855	52 236	45 341	42 924	39 009	C.3.2. Total
C.3.3. Net Written Premiums									**C.3.3. Primes Nettes Emises**
C.3.3.1. Domestic Companies	250 365	270 478	296 360	315 011	341 574	397 552	433 182	473 453	C.3.3.1. Entreprises Nationales
C.3.3.3. Branches & Agencies of Foreign Cies	24 329	24 200	20 429	23 213	19 395	13 070	13 698	14 733	C.3.3.3. Succursales et Agences d'Ent. Etrangères
C.3.3. Total	274 694	294 678	316 789	338 224	360 969	410 623	446 880	488 186	C.3.3. Total

E. BUSINESS WRITTEN ABROAD / E. OPERATIONS A L'ETRANGER

E.1. Life / E.1. Vie

Label (EN)	1990	1991	1992	1993	1994	1995	1996	1997	Label (FR)
E.1.1. Gross Premiums									**E.1.1. Primes Brutes**
E.1.1.1. Direct Business									E.1.1.1. Assurance Directe
E.1.1.1.1. Branches & Agencies	..	..	..	..	..	1 194	1 749	2 715	E.1.1.1.1. Succursales & Agences
E.1.1.1. Total							1 749	2 715	E.1.1.1. Total
E.1.1.3. Total	1 460	1 722	3 309	2 648	2 253				E.1.1.3. Total
E.1.1.3.1. Branches & Agencies	..	..	..	..	..	..	..	..	E.1.1.3.1. Succursales & Agences

Monetary Unit: million Belgian francs   Unité monétaire : million de francs belges

	1990	1991	1992	1993	1994	1995	1996	1997
E.1.2. Ceded Premiums / Primes Cédées	225	311	517	637	349	:	:	:
E.1.2.1. Branches & Agencies / Succursales & Agences						:		:
E.1.3. Net Written Premiums / Primes Nettes Emises	1 236	1 411	2 793	2 012	1 904	:	:	:
E.1.3.1. Branches & Agencies / Succursales & Agences						:		:
E.2. Non-Life / E.2. Non-Vie								
E.2.1. Gross Premiums / Primes Brutes								
E.2.1.1. Direct Business / Assurance Directe								
E.2.1.1.1. Branches & Agencies / Succursales & Agences	:	:	:	:	:	38 373	43 296	49 338
E.2.1.1. Total							43 296	49 338
E.2.1.3. Total								
E.2.1.3.1. Branches & Agencies / Succursales & Agences	32 275	39 004	37 368	48 768	49 816	:	:	:
E.2.2. Ceded Premiums / Primes Cédées	13 224	15 697	14 714	18 469	18 031	:	:	:
E.2.2.1. Branches & Agencies / Succursales & Agences						:		:
E.2.3. Net Written Premiums / Primes Nettes Emises	19 051	23 307	22 654	30 298	31 785	:	:	:
E.2.3.1. Branches & Agencies / Succursales & Agences						:		:
F. OUTSTANDING INVESTMENT BY DIRECT INSURANCE COMPANIES / F. ENCOURS DES PLACEMENTS DES ENTREPRISES D'ASSURANCES DIRECTES								
F.1. Life / F.1. Vie								
F.1.1. Real Estate / Immobilier								
F.1.1.1. Domestic Companies / Entreprises Nationales	61 715	67 335	71 183	43 864	49 665	51 214	50 725	57 541
F.1.1.3. Branches & Agencies of Foreign Cies / Succursales et Agences d'Ent. Etrangères	6 518	8 029	8 029	9 266	7 081	7 081	7 081	6 327
F.1.2. Mortgage Loans / Prêts Hypothécaires								
F.1.2.1. Domestic Companies / Entreprises Nationales	181 949	189 156	195 088	197 161	203 194	199 834	189 813	174 906
F.1.2.3. Branches & Agencies of Foreign Cies / Succursales et Agences d'Ent. Etrangères	7 770	7 363	7 445	7 143	2 384	2 347	2 348	2 343
F.1.3. Shares / Actions								
F.1.3.1. Domestic Companies / Entreprises Nationales	109 082	120 607	118 545	136 977	175 551	219 970	258 710	369 108
F.1.3.3. Branches & Agencies of Foreign Cies / Succursales et Agences d'Ent. Etrangères	3 352	3 319	4 356	7 153	3 511	5 460	9 182	11 636
F.1.4. Bonds with Fixed Revenue / Obligations								
F.1.4.1. Domestic Companies / Entreprises Nationales	363 009	411 154	481 363	560 343	624 764	731 850	824 227	952 202
F.1.4.3. Branches & Agencies of Foreign Cies / Succursales et Agences d'Ent. Etrangères	32 768	38 834	44 765	50 426	36 150	41 891	44 250	45 457
F.1.5. Loans other than Mortgage Loans / Prêts Autres qu'Hypothécaires								
F.1.5.1. Domestic Companies / Entreprises Nationales	20 244	21 599	19 815	26 745	20 617	19 467	20 240	19 702
F.1.5.3. Branches & Agencies of Foreign Cies / Succursales et Agences d'Ent. Etrangères	56	49	42	34	11	10	8	6
F.1.6. Other Investments / Autres Placements								
F.1.6.1. Domestic Companies / Entreprises Nationales	58 444	64 425	64 903	70 254	68 132	91 355	110 031	133 904
F.1.6.3. Branches & Agencies of Foreign Cies / Succursales et Agences d'Ent. Etrangères	4 952	5 174	5 765	7 081	4 023	3 790	4 613	6 574
F.1.7. Total								
F.1.7.1. Domestic Companies / Entreprises Nationales	794 443	874 276	950 897	1 035 345	1 141 923	1 313 689	1 453 746	1 707 363
F.1.7.3. Branches & Agencies of Foreign Cies / Succursales et Agences d'Ent. Etrangères	55 416	62 768	70 402	81 104	53 160	60 579	67 482	72 344
F.2. Non-Life / F.2. Non-Vie								
F.2.1. Real Estate / Immobilier								
F.2.1.1. Domestic Companies / Entreprises Nationales	27 182	32 829	35 371	55 809	54 436	51 047	49 266	51 333
F.2.1.3. Branches & Agencies of Foreign Cies / Succursales et Agences d'Ent. Etrangères	6 518	4 104	4 090	4 028	2 564	2 554	2 312	1 966
F.2.2. Mortgage Loans / Prêts Hypothécaires								
F.2.2.1. Domestic Companies / Entreprises Nationales	33 257	34 532	31 936	20 533	22 361	22 224	21 166	18 547
F.2.2.3. Branches & Agencies of Foreign Cies / Succursales et Agences d'Ent. Etrangères	294	43	56	46	0	8	8	8
F.2.3. Shares / Actions								
F.2.3.1. Domestic Companies / Entreprises Nationales	48 835	50 855	54 114	63 082	77 447	89 780	109 371	152 948
F.2.3.3. Branches & Agencies of Foreign Cies / Succursales et Agences d'Ent. Etrangères	1 498	626	690	542	0	997	1 621	2 421
F.2.4. Bonds with Fixed Revenue / Obligations								
F.2.4.1. Domestic Companies / Entreprises Nationales	158 848	182 849	206 941	225 835	258 946	280 475	307 088	308 656
F.2.4.3. Branches & Agencies of Foreign Cies / Succursales et Agences d'Ent. Etrangères	20 097	13 360	11 752	13 309	5 665	6 335	7 505	7 749

Monetary Unit: million Belgian francs

Unité monétaire : million de francs belges

	1990	1991	1992	1993	1994	1995	1996	1997	
F.2.5. Loans other than Mortgage Loans									F.2.5. Prêts Autres qu'Hypothécaires
F.2.5.1. Domestic Companies	1 810	1 913	1 435	1 942	713	712	790	1 121	F.2.5.1. Entreprises Nationales
F.2.5.3. Branches & Agencies of Foreign Cies	281	393	409	81	0	62	57	51	F.2.5.3. Succursales et Agences d'Ent. Etrangères
F.2.6. Other Investments									F.2.6. Autres Placements
F.2.6.1. Domestic Companies	44 477	52 397	56 625	51 557	73 901	111 841	127 149	136 143	F.2.6.1. Entreprises Nationales
F.2.6.3. Branches & Agencies of Foreign Cies	6 611	5 906	5 604	6 147	1 210	655	623	663	F.2.6.3. Succursales et Agences d'Ent. Etrangères
F.2.7. Total									F.2.7. Total
F.2.7.1. Domestic Companies	314 409	355 375	386 422	418 759	487 804	556 079	614 830	668 748	F.2.7.1. Entreprises Nationales
F.2.7.3. Branches & Agencies of Foreign Cies	35 030	24 432	22 601	24 153	9 439	10 611	12 126	12 858	F.2.7.3. Succursales et Agences d'Ent. Etrangères
G. BREAKDOWN OF NON-LIFE PREMIUMS									**G. VENTILATIONS DES PRIMES NON-VIE**
G.1. Motor vehicle									G.1. Assurance Automobile
G.1.1. Direct Business									G.1.1. Assurances Directes
G.1.1.1. Gross Premiums	82 007	87 604	91 899	91 615	92 122	95 987	95 257	94 081	G.1.1.1. Primes Brutes
G.2. Marine, Aviation									G.2. Marine, Aviation
G.2.1. Direct Business									G.2.1. Assurances Directes
G.2.1.1. Gross Premiums	5 380	5 515	6 663	5 629	5 112	5 301	5 402	5 186	G.2.1.1. Primes Brutes
G.4. Fire, Property Damages									G.4. Incendie, Dommages aux Biens
G.4.1. Direct Business									G.4.1. Assurances Directes
G.4.1.1. Gross Premiums	45 184	47 956	50 564	50 499	50 724	53 018	54 552	52 588	G.4.1.1. Primes Brutes
G.5. Pecuniary Losses									G.5. Pertes Pécunières
G.5.1. Direct Business									G.5.1. Assurances Directes
G.5.1.1. Gross Premiums	6 426	7 111	7 568	9 759	10 522	10 241	9 755	9 216	G.5.1.1. Primes Brutes
G.6. General Liability									G.6. Responsabilité Générale
G.6.1. Direct Business									G.6.1. Assurances Directes
G.6.1.1. Gross Premiums	13 934	15 039	16 245	16 280	16 779	17 636	18 402	18 571	G.6.1.1. Primes Brutes
G.7. Accident, Health									G.7. Accident, Santé
G.7.1. Direct Business									G.7.1. Assurances Directes
G.7.1.1. Gross Premiums	38 485	41 950	49 184	52 410	53 854	54 271	58 242	58 238	G.7.1.1. Primes Brutes
G.8. Others									G.8. Autres
G.8.1. Direct Business									G.8.1. Assurances Directes
G.8.1.1. Gross Premiums	7 770	8 116	10 180	16 324	11 356	9 126	10 937	11 532	G.8.1.1. Primes Brutes
G.10. Total									G.10. Total
G.10.1. Direct Business									G.10.1. Assurances Directes
G.10.1.1. Gross Premiums	199 186	213 291	232 304	242 516	240 469	245 580	252 547	249 412	G.10.1.1. Primes Brutes
H. GROSS CLAIMS PAYMENTS									**H. PAIEMENTS BRUTS DES SINISTRES**
H.1. Life									H.1. Vie
H.1.1. Domestic Companies				90 067	92 209	97 986	109 891	124 542	H.1.1. Entreprises Nationales
H.1.3. Branches & Agencies of Foreign Cies				6 558	6 046	7 336	5 481	8 285	H.1.3. Succursales et Agences d'Ent. Etrangères
H.1. Total				96 625	98 255	105 322	115 372	132 827	H.1. Total
H.2. Non-Life									H.2. Non-Vie
H.2.1. Domestic Companies				141 866	144 291	142 553	142 351	146 883	H.2.1. Entreprises Nationales
H.2.3. Branches & Agencies of Foreign Cies				9 712	3 787	3 188	3 722	3 576	H.2.3. Succursales et Agences d'Ent. Etrangères
H.2. Total				151 577	148 078	145 741	146 073	150 459	H.2. Total

Monetary Unit: million Belgian francs — Unité monétaire : million de francs belges

	1990	1991	1992	1993	1994	1995	1996	1997	
I. GROSS OPERATING EXPENSES									**I. DEPENSES BRUITES D'EXPLOITATION**
I.1. Life									**I.1. Vie**
I.1.1. Domestic Companies				24 708	24 768	21 169	21 924	23 218	I.1.1. Entreprises Nationales
I.1.3. Branches & Agencies of Foreign Cies				2 326	1 755	1 304	1 462	1 505	I.1.3. Succursales et Agences d'Ent. Etrangères
I.1.1. Tota				27 034	26 522	22 473	23 386	24 723	I.1. Total des Primes Nettes Vie
I.2. Non-Life									**I.2. Non-Vie**
I.2.1. Domestic Companies				63 655	64 820	58 132	58 371	60 493	I.2.1. Entreprises Nationales
I.2.3. Branches & Agencies of Foreign Cies				3 858	1 683	1 240	1 473	1 441	I.2.3. Succursales et Agences d'Ent. Etrangères
I.2. Total				67 513	66 503	59 372	59 844	61 934	I.2. Total
J. COMMISSIONS									**J. COMMISSIONS**
J.1. Life									**J.1. Vie**
J.1.1. Direct Business									J.1.1. Assurance directe
J.1.1.1. Domestic Companies				6 301	7 609	8 813	9 621	11 119	J.1.1.1. Entreprises Nationales
J.1.1.3. Branches & Agencies of Foreign Cies				590	332	229	230	261	J.1.1.3. Succursales et Agences d'Ent. Etrangères
J.1.1. Tota				6 892	7 942	9 041	9 851	11 379	J.1.1. Total
J.1.2. Reinsurance Accepted									J.1.2. Réassurances acceptées
J.1.2.1. Domestic Companies				0	0	318	469	327	J.1.2.1. Entreprises Nationales
J.1.2. Tota				0	0	318	469	327	J.1.2. Total
J.1.3. Total									J.1.3. Total
J.1.3.1. Domestic Companies				6 301	7 609	9 131	10 090	11 446	J.1.3.1. Entreprises Nationales
J.1.3.3. Branches & Agencies of Foreign Cies				590	332	229	230	261	J.1.3.3. Succursales et Agences d'Ent. Etrangères
J.1.3. Total of Life Net Premiums				6 892	7 942	9 360	10 320	11 707	J.1.3. Total
J.2. Non-Life									**J.2. Non-Vie**
J.2.1. Direct Business									J.2.1. Assurance directe
J.2.1.1. Domestic Companies				32 982	33 246	34 794	35 303	34 813	J.2.1.1. Entreprises Nationales
J.2.1.3. Branches & Agencies of Foreign Cies				2 490	871	841	907	957	J.2.1.3. Succursales et Agences d'Ent. Etrangères
J.2.1. Total				35 472	34 117	35 635	36 210	35 771	J.2.1. Total des Primes Nettes Vie
J.2.2. Reinsurance Accepted									J.2.2. Réassurances acceptées
J.2.2.1. Domestic Companies				169	68	4 558	4 667	4 663	J.2.2.1. Entreprises Nationales
J.2.2.3. Branches & Agencies of Foreign Cies				27	9	13	21	21	J.2.2.3. Succursales et Agences d'Ent. Etrangères
J.2.2. Total				196	77	4 571	4 688	4 684	J.2.2. Total
J.2.3. Total									J.2.3. Total
J.2.3.1. Domestic Companies				33 150	33 314	39 352	39 970	39 476	J.2.3.1. Entreprises Nationales
J.2.3.3. Branches & Agencies of Foreign Cies				2 517	880	854	928	978	J.2.3.3. Succursales et Agences d'Ent. Etrangères
J.2.3. Total				35 667	34 194	40 206	40 898	40 454	J.2.3. Total

CANADA

Monetary Unit: million Ca..dian dollars — Unité monétaire : million de dollars ca..diens

A. NUMBER OF COMPANIES IN THE REPORTING COUNTRY — A. NOMBRE D'ENTREPRISES DANS LE PAYS DECLARANT

	1990	1991	1992	1993	1994	1995	1996	1997
A.1. Life — A.1. Vie								
A.1.1. Domestic Companies — A.1.1. Entreprises Nationales	64	65	63	60	63	70	59	52
A.1.2. (Foreign Controlled Companies) — A.1.2. (Entreprises Sous Contrôle Etranger)	24	26	27	26	22	27	23	..
A.1.3. Branches & Agencies of Foreign Cies — A.1.3. Succursales et Agences d'Ent. Etrangères	86	81	79	74	74	89	65	58
A.1. All Companies — A.1. Ensemble des Entreprises	150	146	142	134	137	159	124	110
A.2. Non-Life — A.2. Non-Vie								
A.2.1. Domestic Companies — A.2.1. Entreprises Nationales	98	97	92	92	89	90	91	90
A.2.2. (Foreign Controlled Companies) — A.2.2. (Entreprises Sous Contrôle Etranger)	46	44	42	38	38	43	45	..
A.2.3. Branches & Agencies of Foreign Cies — A.2.3. Succursales et Agences d'Ent. Etrangères	113	109	103	98	94	100	88	98
A.2. All Companies — A.2. Ensemble des Entreprises	211	206	195	190	183	190	179	188
A.3. Composite — A.3. Mixte								
A.3.1. Domestic Companies — A.3.1. Entreprises Nationales	2	2	1	1	0	0	0	0
A.3.2. (Foreign Controlled Companies) — A.3.2. (Entreprises Sous Contrôle Etranger)	1	1	1	1	0	0	..	0
A.3.3. Branches & Agencies of Foreign Cies — A.3.3. Succursales et Agences d'Ent. Etrangères	8	11	8	6	1	0	0	0
A.3. All Companies — A.3. Ensemble des Entreprises	10	13	9	7	1	0	0	0
A.4. Reinsurance — A.4. Réassurance								
A.4.1. Domestic Companies — A.4.1. Entreprises Nationales	12	9	11	11	10	10	11	9
A.4.2. (Foreign Controlled Companies) — A.4.2. (Entreprises Sous Contrôle Etranger)	10	8	9	9	10	10	9	..
A.4.3. Branches & Agencies of Foreign Cies — A.4.3. Succursales et Agences d'Ent. Etrangères	53	43	42	39	43	44	55	30
A.4. All Companies — A.4. Ensemble des Entreprises	65	52	53	50	53	54	66	39
A.5. Total								
A.5.1. Domestic Companies — A.5.1. Entreprises Nationales	176	173	167	164	162	170	161	151
A.5.2. (Foreign Controlled Companies) — A.5.2. (Entreprises Sous Contrôle Etranger)	83	79	79	74	70	80	77	..
A.5.3. Branches & Agencies of Foreign Cies — A.5.3. Succursales et Agences d'Ent. Etrangères	240	244	232	217	212	233	208	186
A.5. All Insurance Companies — A.5. Ensemble des Entreprises d'Assurances	434	417	399	381	374	403	369	337

B. NUMBER OF EMPLOYEES — B. NOMBRE D'EMPLOYES

	1990	1991	1992	1993	1994	1995	1996	1997
B.1. Insurance Companies — B.1. Entreprises d'Assurances	111 965	92 000	:	:	:	:	:	97 184
B.2. Intermediaries — B.2. Intermédiaires	70 775	90 000	:	:	:	:	:	107 574
B. Total	182 740	182 000	172 520	:	:	:	:	204 758

C. BUSINESS WRITTEN IN THE REPORTING COUNTRY — C. OPERATIONS CONCLUES DANS LE PAYS DECLARANT

C.1. Life — C.1. Vie

	1990	1991	1992	1993	1994	1995	1996	1997
C.1.1. Gross Premiums — C.1.1. Primes Brutes								
C.1.1.1. Direct Business — C.1.1.1. Assurances Directes								
C.1.1.1.1. Domestic Companies — C.1.1.1.1. Entreprises Nationales	14 027	15 331	13 504	12 357	16 410	17 428	11 917	11 880
C.1.1.1.2. (Foreign Controlled Companies) — C.1.1.1.2. (Entreprises Sous Contrôle Etranger)	2 648	2 898	2 558	2 545	2 255	3 433	2 486	..
C.1.1.1.3. Branches & Agencies of Foreign Cies — C.1.1.1.3. Succursales et Agences d'Ent. Etrangères	3 163	3 030	3 007	1 086	3 851	4 257	2 295	1 964
C.1.1.1. Total	17 190	18 361	16 511	13 443	20 261	21 685	14 212	13 845
C.1.1.2. Reinsurance Accepted — C.1.1.2. Réassurance Acceptée								
C.1.1.2.1. Domestic Companies — C.1.1.2.1. Entreprises Nationales	175	287	350	332	519	661	564	651
C.1.1.2.2. (Foreign Controlled Companies) — C.1.1.2.2. (Entreprises Sous Contrôle Etranger)	83	173	264	234	354	405	377	..
C.1.1.2.3. Branches & Agencies of Foreign Cies — C.1.1.2.3. Succursales et Agences d'Ent. Etrangères	361	389	326	128	646	710	552	563
C.1.1.2. Total	536	676	676	460	1 165	1 371	1 116	1 214
C.1.1.3. Total								
C.1.1.3.1. Domestic Companies — C.1.1.3.1. Entreprises Nationales	14 202	15 618	13 854	12 689	16 929	18 089	12 481	12 531
C.1.1.3.2. (Foreign Controlled Companies) — C.1.1.3.2. (Entreprises Sous Contrôle Etranger)	2 731	3 071	2 822	2 779	2 609	3 838	2 863	..
C.1.1.3.3. Branches & Agencies of Foreign Cies — C.1.1.3.3. Succursales et Agences d'Ent. Etrangères	3 524	3 419	3 333	1 214	4 497	4 967	2 847	2 527
C.1.1.3. Total des Primes Brutes	17 726	19 037	17 187	13 903	21 426	23 056	15 328	15 058
C.1.2. Ceded Premiums — C.1.2. Primes Cédées								
C.1.2.1. Domestic Companies — C.1.2.1. Entreprises Nationales	668	855	708	975	1 362	1 555	1 323	1 506
C.1.2.2. (Foreign Controlled Companies) — C.1.2.2. (Entreprises Sous Contrôle Etranger)	301	412	358	427	523	666	582	..
C.1.2.3. Branches & Agencies of Foreign Cies — C.1.2.3. Succursales et Agences d'Ent. Etrangères	144	150	160	59	432	454	382	335
C.1.2. Total	812	1 005	868	1 034	1 794	2 009	1 705	1 841

Monetary Unit: million Ca..dian dollars — Urité monétaire : million de dollars ca..diens

	1990	1991	1992	1993	1994	1995	1996	1997
C.1.3. Net Written Premiums / Primes Nettes Emses								
C.1.3.1. Domestic Companies / Entreprises Nationales	13 534	14 763	13 146	11 714	15 567	16 534	11 158	11 025
C.1.3.2. (Foreign Controlled Companies) / (Entreprises Sous Contrôle Etranger)	2 430	2 659	2 464	2 352	2 086	3 172	2 281	..
C.1.3.3. Branches & Agencies of Foreign Cies / Succursales et Agences d'Ent. Etrangères	3 380	3 269	3 173	1 155	4 065	4 513	2 465	2 193
C.1.3. Total	16 914	18 032	16 319	12 869	19 632	21 047	13 623	13 218
C.2. Non-Life / Non-Vie								
C.2.1. Gross premiums / Primes Brutes								
C.2.1.1. Direct Business / Assurances Directes								
C.2.1.1.1. Domestic Companies / Entreprises Nationales	12 904	13 253	13 779	14 229	10 741	11 584	16 694	17 498
C.2.1.1.2. (Foreign Controlled Companies) / (Entreprises Sous Contrôle Etranger)	5 908	5 969	6 510	6 198	5 715	6 660	7 418	
C.2.1.1.3. Branches & Agencies of Foreign Cies / Succursales et Agences d'Ent. Etrangères	3 903	3 872	3 609	3 957	3 306	3 445	5 140	4 931
C.2.1.1. Total	16 807	17 125	17 388	18 186	14 047	15 029	21 834	22 429
C.2.1.2. Reinsurance Accepted / Réassurance Acceptée								
C.2.1.2.1. Domestic Companies / Entreprises Nationales	1 875	2 129	2 282	2 562	2 301	1 795	2 267	2 237
C.2.1.2.2. (Foreign Controlled Companies) / (Entreprises Sous Contrôle Etranger)	1 485	1 623	1 917	2 039	2 060	1 625	2 135	
C.2.1.2.3. Branches & Agencies of Foreign Cies / Succursales et Agences d'Ent. Etrangères	1 455	1 425	1 755	1 517	1 507	1 409	1 801	1 707
C.2.1.2. Total	3 330	3 554	4 037	4 079	3 808	3 204	4 068	3 944
C.2.1.3. Total								
C.2.1.3.1. Domestic Companies / Entreprises Nationales	14 779	15 382	16 061	16 791	13 042	13 379	18 961	19 735
C.2.1.3.2. (Foreign Controlled Companies) / (Entreprises Sous Contrôle Etranger)	7 393	7 592	8 427	8 237	7 775	8 285	9 553	
C.2.1.3.3. Branches & Agencies of Foreign Cies / Succursales et Agences d'Ent. Etrangères	5 358	5 297	5 364	5 474	4 813	4 854	6 941	6 638
C.2.1.3. Total Gross Premiums / Total des Primes Brutes	20 137	20 679	21 425	22 265	17 855	18 233	25 902	26 373
C.2.2. Ceded Premiums / Primes Cédées								
C.2.2.1. Domestic Companies / Entreprises Nationales	2 824	2 890	3 257	3 426	3 051	2 803	3 410	3 394
C.2.2.2. (Foreign Controlled Companies) / (Entreprises Sous Contrôle Etranger)	1 783	1 906	2 362	2 130	2 050	1 901	2 251	
C.2.2.3. Branches & Agencies of Foreign Cies / Succursales et Agences d'Ent. Etrangères	960	958	1 161	1 088	1 156	1 061	1 297	1 270
C.2.2. Total	3 784	3 848	4 418	4 514	4 207	3 864	4 707	4 663
C.2.3. Net Written Premiums / Primes Nettes Emises								
C.2.3.1. Domestic Companies / Entreprises Nationales	11 955	12 492	12 804	13 365	9 991	10 576	15 551	16 341
C.2.3.2. (Foreign Controlled Companies) / (Entreprises Sous Contrôle Etranger)	5 610	5 686	6 065	6 107	5 725	6 384	7 302	
C.2.3.3. Branches & Agencies of Foreign Cies / Succursales et Agences d'Ent. Etrangères	4 398	4 339	4 203	4 386	3 657	3 793	5 644	5 368
C.2.3. Total	16 353	16 831	17 007	17 751	13 648	14 369	21 195	21 710
C.3. Total								
C.3.1. Gross Premiums / Primes Brutes								
C.3.1.1. Direct Business / Assurances Directes								
C.3.1.1.1. Domestic Companies / Entreprises Nationales	26 931	28 584	27 283	26 586	27 151	29 012	28 611	29 378
C.3.1.1.2. (Foreign Controlled Companies) / (Entreprises Sous Contrôle Etranger)	8 556	8 867	9 068	8 743	7 970	10 093	9 904	6 895
C.3.1.1.3. Branches & Agencies of Foreign Cies / Succursales et Agences d'Ent. Etrangères	7 066	6 902	6 616	5 043	7 157	7 702	7 435	
C.3.1.1. Total	31 997	35 486	33 899	31 629	34 308	36 714	36 046	36 274
C.3.1.2. Reinsurance Accepted / Réassurance Acceptée								
C.3.1.2.1. Domestic Companies / Entreprises Nationales	2 050	2 416	2 632	2 894	2 820	2 456	2 831	2 888
C.3.1.2.2. (Foreign Controlled Companies) / (Entreprises Sous Contrôle Etranger)	1 568	1 796	2 181	2 273	2 414	2 030	2 512	2 270
C.3.1.2.3. Branches & Agences of Foreign Cies / Succursales et Agences d'Ent. Etrangères	1 816	1 814	2 081	1 645	2 153	2 119	2 353	
C.3.1.2. Total	3 866	4 230	4 713	4 539	4 973	4 575	5 184	5 158
C.3.1.3. Total								
C.3.1.3.1. Domestic Companies / Entreprises Nationales	28 981	31 000	29 915	29 480	29 971	31 468	31 442	32 266
C.3.1.3.2. (Foreign Controlled Companies) / (Entreprises Sous Contrôle Etranger)	10 124	10 663	11 249	11 016	10 384	12 123	12 416	
C.3.1.3.3. Branches & Agencies of Foreign Cies / Succursales et Agences d'Ent. Etrangères	8 882	8 716	8 697	6 688	9 310	9 821	9 788	9 165
C.3.1.3. Total Gross Premiums / Total des Primes Brutes	37 863	39 716	38 612	36 168	39 281	41 289	41 230	41 431
C.3.2. Ceded Premiums / Primes Cédées								
C.3.2.1. Domestic Companies / Entreprises Nationales	3 492	3 745	3 965	4 401	4 413	4 358	4 733	4 900
C.3.2.2. (Foreign Controlled Companies) / (Entreprises Sous Contrôle Etranger)	2 084	2 318	2 720	2 557	2 573	2 567	2 833	
C.3.2.3. Branches & Agencies of Foreign Cies / Succursales et Agences d'Ent. Etrangères	1 104	1 108	1 321	1 147	1 588	1 515	1 679	1 605
C.3.2. Total	4 596	4 853	5 286	5 548	6 001	5 873	6 412	6 504

CANADA

Monetary Unit: million Ca..dian dollars

	1990	1991	1992	1993	1994	1995	1996	1997	
C.3.3. Net Written Premiums									**C.3.3. Primes Nettes Emises**
C.3.3.1. Domestic Companies	25 489	27 255	25 950	25 079	25 558	27 110	26 709	27 366	C.3.3.1. Entreprises Nationales
C.3.3.2. (Foreign Controlled Companies)	8 040	8 345	8 529	8 459	7 811	9 556	9 583	..	C.3.3.2. (Entreprises Sous Contrôle Etranger)
C.3.3.3. Branches & Agencies of Foreign Cies	7 778	7 608	7 376	5 541	7 722	8 306	8 109	7 561	C.3.3.3. Succursales et Agences d'Ent. Etrangères
C.3.3. Total	33 267	34 863	33 326	30 620	33 280	35 416	34 818	34 928	C.3.3. Total
D. NET WRITTEN PREMIUMS IN THE REPORTING COUNTRY IN TERMS OF DOMESTIC AND FOREIGN RISKS									**D. PRIMES NETTES EMISES DANS LE PAYS DECLARANT EN RISQUES NATIONAUX ET ETRANGERS**
D.1. Life									**D.1. Vie**
D.1.1. Domestic Risks									D.1.1. Risques Nationaux
D.1.1.1. Domestic Companies	13 534	14 763	13 146	11 714	..	..	..	11 025	D.1.1.1. Entreprises Nationales
D.1.1.2. (Foreign Controlled Companies)	2 430	2 659	2 464	2 352	..	..	..	..	D.1.1.2. (Entreprises Sous Contrôle Etranger)
D.1.1.3. Branches & Agencies of Foreign Cies	3 380	3 269	3 173	1 155	..	..	..	2 193	D.1.1.3. Succursales et Agences d'Ent. Etrangères
D.1.1. Total	16 914	18 032	16 319	12 869	..	..	..	13 218	D.1.1. Total des Primes Nettes Vie
D.1.3. Total									D.1.3. Total
D.1.3.1. Domestic Companies	13 534	14 763	13 146	11 714	15 567	16 534	11 158	11 025	D.1.3.1. Entreprises Nationales
D.1.3.2. (Foreign Controlled Companies)	2 430	2 659	2 464	2 352	2 086	3 172	2 281	..	D.1.3.2. (Entreprises Sous Contrôle Etranger)
D.1.3.3. Branches & Agencies of Foreign Cies	3 380	3 269	3 173	1 155	4 065	4 513	2 465	2 193	D.1.3.3. Succursales et Agences d'Ent. Etrangères
D.1.3. Total of Life Net Premiums	16 914	18 032	16 319	12 869	19 632	21 047	13 623	13 218	D.1.3. Total des Primes Nettes Vie
D.2. Non-Life									**D.2. Non-Vie**
D.2.1. Domestic Risks									D.2.1. Risques Nationaux
D.2.1.1. Domestic Companies	11 955	12 492	12 804	13 365	..	..	..	16 341	D.2.1.1. Entreprises Nationales
D.2.1.2. (Foreign Controlled Companies)	5 610	5 686	6 065	6 107	..	..	..	..	D.2.1.2. (Entreprises Sous Contrôle Etranger)
D.2.1.3. Branches & Agencies of Foreign Cies	4 398	4 339	4 203	4 386	..	..	..	5 368	D.2.1.3. Succursales et Agences d'Ent. Etrangères
D.2.1. Total	16 353	16 831	17 007	17 751	..	..	..	21 710	D.2.1. Total des Primes Nettes Vie
D.2.3. Total									D.2.3. Total
D.2.3.1. Domestic Companies	11 955	12 492	12 804	13 365	9 991	10 576	15 551	16 341	D.2.3.1. Entreprises Nationales
D.2.3.2. (Foreign Controlled Companies)	5 610	5 686	6 065	6 107	5 725	6 384	7 302	..	D.2.3.2. (Entreprises Sous Contrôle Etranger)
D.2.3.3. Branches & Agencies of Foreign Cies	4 398	4 339	4 203	4 386	3 657	3 793	5 644	5 368	D.2.3.3. Succursales et Agences d'Ent. Etrangères
D.2.3. Total	16 353	16 831	17 007	17 751	13 648	14 369	21 195	21 710	D.2.3. Total des Primes Nettes Vie
E. BUSINESS WRITTEN ABROAD									**E. OPERATIONS A L'ETRANGER**
E.1. Life									**E.1. Vie**
E.1.1. Gross Premiums									E.1.1. Primes Brutes
E.1.1.1. Direct Business									E.1.1.1. Assurance Directe
E.1.1.1.1. Branches & Agencies	10 067	9 719	8 222	8 176	9 771	10 829	10 022	..	E.1.1.1.1. Succursales & Agences
E.1.1.1. Total	10 067	9 719	8 222	8 176	..	..	..	4 389	E.1.1.1. Total
E.1.1.2. Reinsurance Accepted									E.1.1.2. Réassurance Acceptée
E.1.1.2.1. Branches & Agencies	578	770	843	493	1 654	1 857	779	..	E.1.1.2.1. Succursales & Agences
E.1.1.2. Total	578	770	843	493	..	..	..	450	E.1.1.2. Total
E.1.1.3. Total									E.1.1.3. Total
E.1.1.3.1. Branches & Agencies	10 645	10 489	9 065	8 669	11 425	12 686	10 801	..	E.1.1.3.1. Succursales & Agences
E.1.1.3. Total Gross Premiums	10 645	10 489	9 065	8 669	..	..	..	4 839	E.1.1.3. Total des Primes Brutes
E.1.2. Ceded Premiums									E.1.2. Primes Cédées
E.1.2.1. Branches & Agencies	515	565	880	835	1 805	1 198	894	..	E.1.2.1. Succursales & Agences
E.1.2. Total	515	565	880	835	..	..	..	681	E.1.2. Total
E.1.3. Net Written Premiums									E.1.3. Primes Nettes Emises
E.1.3.1. Branches & Agencies	10 130	9 924	8 185	7 834	9 620	11 488	9 907	..	E.1.3.1. Succursales & Agences
E.1.3. Total	10 130	9 924	8 185	7 834	..	..	..	4 159	E.1.3. Total

CANADA

Monetary Unit: million Ca..dian dollars

Unité monétaire : million de dollars ca..diens

E.2. Non-Life

	1990	1991	1992	1993	1994	1995	1996	1997
E.2.1. Gross Premiums								
E.2.1.1. Direct Business								
E.2.1.1.1. Branches & Agencies	818	911	763	1 194	279	334	..	..
E.2.1.1. Total	818	911	763	1 194	..	..	877	883
E.2.1.2. Reinsurance Accepted								
E.2.1.2.1. Branches & Agencies	662	879	1 272	1 006	244	231	..	..
E.2.1.2. Total	662	879	1 272	1 006	..	..	1 413	1 099
E.2.1.3. Total								
E.2.1.3.1. Branches & Agencies	1 480	1 790	2 035	2 200	523	565	..	..
E.2.1.3. Total Gross Premiums	1 480	1 790	2 035	2 200	..	..	2 290	1 982
E.2.2. Ceded Premiums								
E.2.2.1. Branches & Agencies	291	535	377	540	172	224	..	..
E.2.2. Total	291	535	377	540	..	..	628	499
E.2.3. Net Written Premiums								
E.2.3.1. Branches & Agencies	1 189	1 255	1 658	1 660	351	341	..	..
E.2.3. Total	1 189	1 255	1 658	1 660	..	..	1 662	1 483

F. OUTSTANDING INVESTMENT BY DIRECT INSURANCE COMPANIES

F.1. Life

	1990	1991	1992	1993	1994	1995	1996	1997
F.1.1. Real Estate								
F.1.1.1. Domestic Companies	6 364	7 181	9 819	9 455	8 956	7 881	7 701	6 308
F.1.1.2. (Foreign Controlled Companies)	121	133	260	236	283	251	235	..
F.1.1.3. Branches & Agencies of Foreign Cies	834	1 112	1 237	1 345	1 704	839	1 787	1 503
F.1.1.4. Domestic Investment	..	5 945	..	..	..	..	..	6 208
F.1.1.5. Foreign Investment	..	2 481	..	..	..	..	..	1 603
F.1.1. Total	7 197	8 426	..	..	10 660	..	..	7 810
F.1.2. Mortgage Loans								
F.1.2.1. Domestic Companies	45 344	43 259	46 668	43 613	41 474	41 000	7 099	39 044
F.1.2.2. (Foreign Controlled Companies)	4 389	4 606	5 016	4 418	3 522	3 656	335	..
F.1.2.3. Branches & Agencies of Foreign Cies	5 584	6 388	7 204	8 014	9 606	3 710	7 314	6 719
F.1.2.4. Domestic Investment	..	40 643	..	..	..	..	..	40 566
F.1.2.5. Foreign Investment	..	13 610	..	..	..	..	..	5 197
F.1.2. Total	50 928	54 252	..	..	51 080	..	..	45 763
F.1.3. Shares								
F.1.3.1. Domestic Companies	10 393	11 309	11 152	10 185	11 950	10 590	11 827	10 535
F.1.3.2. (Foreign Controlled Companies)	401	425	2 217	549	673	677	589	..
F.1.3.3. Branches & Agencies of Foreign Cies	1 146	978	1 201	701	882	747	585	560
F.1.3.4. Domestic Investment	..	7 742	..	..	..	..	..	5 929
F.1.3.5. Foreign Investment	..	4 971	..	..	..	..	..	5 166
F.1.3. Total	11 539	12 712	..	..	12 832	..	..	11 096
F.1.4. Bonds with Fixed Revenue								
F.1.4.1. Domestic Companies	44 188	45 720	54 569	52 607	62 981	70 640	74 621	76 188
F.1.4.2. (Foreign Controlled Companies)	4 331	5 521	12 619	7 554	7 301	9 158	8 605	..
F.1.4.3. Branches & Agencies of Foreign Cies	6 754	7 436	14 661	9 663	12 718	12 802	11 603	12 708
F.1.4.4. Domestic Investment	..	40 149	..	..	..	..	..	73 812
F.1.4.5. Foreign Investment	..	18 529	..	..	..	..	..	15 084
F.1.4. Total	50 942	58 678	..	..	75 699	..	..	88 895
F.1.5. Loans other than Mortgage Loans								
F.1.5.1. Domestic Companies	5 081	5 381	9 435	5 702	5 633	6 090	37 757	4 750
F.1.5.2. (Foreign Controlled Companies)	129	131	175	168	150	351	3 485	..
F.1.5.3. Branches & Agencies of Foreign Cies	423	430	810	460	622	672	345	409
F.1.5.4. Domestic Investment	..	2 715	..	..	..	..	..	3 814
F.1.5.5. Foreign Investment	..	3 227	..	..	..	..	..	1 346
F.1.5. Total	5 503	5 942	..	..	6 255	..	..	5 160

French row labels (right-hand margin):

E.2. Non-Vie
- E.2.1. Primes Brutes
  - E.2.1.1. Assurance Directe
    - E.2.1.1.1. Succursales & Agences
    - E.2.1.1. Total
  - E.2.1.2. Réassurance Acceptée
    - E.2.1.2.1. Succursales & Agences
    - E.2.1.2. Total
  - E.2.1.3. Total
    - E.2.1.3.1. Succursales & Agences
    - E.2.1.3. Total des Primes Brutes
- E.2.2. Primes Cédées
  - E.2.2.1. Succursales & Agences
  - E.2.2. Total
- E.2.3. Primes Nettes Emises
  - E.2.3.1. Succursales & Agences
  - E.2.3. Total

F. ENCOURS DES PLACEMENTS DES ENTREPRISES D'ASSURANCES DIRECTES

F.1. Vie
- F.1.1. Immobilier
  - F.1.1.1. Entreprises Nationales
  - F.1.1.2. (Entreprises Sous Contrôle Etranger)
  - F.1.1.3. Succursales et Agences d'Ent. Etrangères
  - F.1.1.4. Placement dans le Pays
  - F.1.1.5. Placement à l'Etranger
  - F.1.1. Total
- F.1.2. Prêts Hypothécaires
  - F.1.2.1. Entreprises Nationales
  - F.1.2.2. (Entreprises Sous Contrôle Etranger)
  - F.1.2.3. Succursales et Agences d'Ent. Etrangères
  - F.1.2.4. Placement dans le Pays
  - F.1.2.5. Placement à l'Etranger
  - F.1.2. Total
- F.1.3. Actions
  - F.1.3.1. Entreprises Nationales
  - F.1.3.2. (Entreprises Sous Contrôle Etranger)
  - F.1.3.3. Succursales et Agences d'Ent. Etrangères
  - F.1.3.4. Placement dans le Pays
  - F.1.3.5. Placement à l'Etranger
  - F.1.3. Total
- F.1.4. Obligations
  - F.1.4.1. Entreprises Nationales
  - F.1.4.2. (Entreprises Sous Contrôle Etranger)
  - F.1.4.3. Succursales et Agences d'Ent. Etrangères
  - F.1.4.4. Placement dans le Pays
  - F.1.4.5. Placement à l'Etranger
  - F.1.4. Total
- F.1.5. Prêts Autres qu'Hypothécaires
  - F.1.5.1. Entreprises Nationales
  - F.1.5.2. (Entreprises Sous Contrôle Etranger)
  - F.1.5.3. Succursales et Agences d'Ent. Etrangères
  - F.1.5.4. Placement dans le Pays
  - F.1.5.5. Placement à l'Etranger
  - F.1.5. Total

CANADA

Monetary Unit: million Ca..dian dollars

Unité monétaire : million de dollars ca..diens

	1990	1991	1992	1993	1994	1995	1996	1997
F.1.6. Other Investments / Autres Placements								
F.1.6.1. Domestic Companies / Entreprises Nationales	1 168	1 165	8 158	8 737	8 534	16 006	6 089	6 024
F.1.6.2. (Foreign Controlled Companies) / (Entreprises Sous Contrôle Etranger)	10	9	117	62	194	883	495	624
F.1.6.3. Branches & Agencies of Foreign Cies / Succursales et Agences d'Ent. Etrangères	..	..	489	306	685	1 550	1 819	..
F.1.6.4. Domestic Investment / Placement dans le Pays	..	614	..	..	..	..	..	5 282
F.1.6.5. Foreign Investment / Placement à l' Etranger	..	560	..	..	..	..	..	1 366
F.1.6. Total	1 168	1 174	..	..	9 219	..	..	6 648
F.1.7. Total								
F.1.7.1. Domestic Companies / Entreprises Nationales	112 537	114 015	139 801	130 299	139 528	152 207	145 094	142 848
F.1.7.2. (Foreign Controlled Companies) / (Entreprises Sous Contrôle Etranger)	9 381	10 825	20 403	12 987	12 123	14 976	13 744	22 523
F.1.7.3. Branches & Agencies of Foreign Cies / Succursales et Agences d'Ent. Etrangères	14 740	16 344	25 602	20 488	26 217	20 320	23 453	..
F.1.7.4. Domestic Investment / Placement dans le Pays	..	97 808	..	..	..	..	..	135 610
F.1.7.5. Foreign Investment / Placement à l' Etranger	..	43 377	..	..	..	..	..	29 761
F.1.7. Total of Life Investments / Total des Placements Vie	127 277	141 275	..	..	165 745	..	..	165 371
F.2. Non-Life / F.2. Non-Vie								
F.2.1. Real Estate / Immobilier								
F.2.1.1. Domestic Companies / Entreprises Nationales	240	211	175	180	239	226	218	186
F.2.1.2. (Foreign Controlled Companies) / (Entreprises Sous Contrôle Etranger)	42	44	37	34	76	81	71	29
F.2.1.3. Branches & Agencies of Foreign Cies / Succursales et Agences d'Ent. Etrangères	31	30	24	24	29	30	52	..
F.2.1.4. Domestic Investment / Placement dans le Pays	..	285	..	..	..	..	..	214
F.2.1.5. Foreign Investment / Placement à l' Etranger	..	1	..	..	..	..	..	..
F.2.1. Total	270	286	..	..	268	..	..	214
F.2.2. Mortgage Loans / Prêts Hypothécaires								
F.2.2.1. Domestic Companies / Entreprises Nationales	2 819	2 605	283	212	529	367	352	334
F.2.2.2. (Foreign Controlled Companies) / (Entreprises Sous Contrôle Etranger)	364	362	212	191	306	226	212	42
F.2.2.3. Branches & Agencies of Foreign Cies / Succursales et Agences d'Ent. Etrangères	128	176	55	52	52	49	46	..
F.2.2.4. Domestic Investment / Placement dans le Pays	..	2 757	..	..	..	..	..	374
F.2.2.5. Foreign Investment / Placement à l' Etranger	..	386	..	..	..	..	..	3
F.2.2. Total	2 947	3 143	..	..	581	..	..	376
F.2.3. Shares / Actions								
F.2.3.1. Domestic Companies / Entreprises Nationales	3 296	2 015	1 779	1 977	3 705	4 065	4 414	5 427
F.2.3.2. (Foreign Controlled Companies) / (Entreprises Sous Contrôle Etranger)	1 664	1 706	1 664	1 700	1 844	2 328	2 178	868
F.2.3.3. Branches & Agencies of Foreign Cies / Succursales et Agences d'Ent. Etrangères	486	396	448	457	557	758	771	..
F.2.3.4. Domestic Investment / Placement dans le Pays	..	4 076	..	..	..	..	..	6 295
F.2.3.5. Foreign Investment / Placement à l' Etranger	..	41	..	..	..	..	..	..
F.2.3. Total	3 783	4 117	..	..	4 262	..	..	6 295
F.2.4. Bonds with Fixed Revenue / Obligations								
F.2.4.1. Domestic Companies / Entreprises Nationales	11 015	6 886	3 545	3 888	10 049	11 727	12 975	13 460
F.2.4.2. (Foreign Controlled Companies) / (Entreprises Sous Contrôle Etranger)	4 703	5 193	5 271	5 129	5 974	7 661	8 400	9 138
F.2.4.3. Branches & Agencies of Foreign Cies / Succursales et Agences d'Ent. Etrangères	7 083	7 289	5 309	5 598	7 544	7 430	8 451	..
F.2.4.4. Domestic Investment / Placement dans le Pays	..	18 631	..	..	..	..	..	22 308
F.2.4.5. Foreign Investment / Placement à l' Etranger	..	737	..	..	..	..	..	290
F.2.4. Total	18 098	19 368	..	..	17 593	..	..	22 598
F.2.6. Other Investments / Autres Placements								
F.2.6.1. Domestic Companies / Entreprises Nationales	151	78	47	22	537	643	664	163
F.2.6.2. (Foreign Controlled Companies) / (Entreprises Sous Contrôle Etranger)	52	2	20	17	358	309	278	28
F.2.6.3. Branches & Agencies of Foreign Cies / Succursales et Agences d'Ent. Etrangères	52	1	..	4	4	357	0	..
F.2.6.4. Domestic Investment / Placement dans le Pays	..	68	..	..	..	..	..	154
F.2.6.5. Foreign Investment / Placement à l' Etranger	..	13	..	..	..	..	..	37
F.2.6. Total	202	81	..	..	541	..	..	191
F.2.7. Total								
F.2.7.1. Domestic Companies / Entreprises Nationales	17 520	11 795	5 830	6 275	15 059	17 028	18 623	19 570
F.2.7.2. (Foreign Controlled Companies) / (Entreprises Sous Contrôle Etranger)	6 824	7 306	7 204	7 071	8 558	10 605	11 139	10 104
F.2.7.3. Branches & Agencies of Foreign Cies / Succursales et Agences d'Ent. Etrangères	7 780	7 893	5 835	6 134	8 186	8 624	9 320	29 345
F.2.7.4. Domestic Investment / Placement dans le Pays	..	25 817	..	..	..	..	..	29 345
F.2.7.5. Foreign Investment / Placement à l' Etranger	..	1 177	..	..	..	..	..	330
F.2.7. Total of Non-Life Investments / Total des Placements Non-Vie	25 299	26 994	..	..	23 245	..	..	29 674

74

Monetary Unit: million Canadian dollars   Unité monétaire : million de dollars canadiens

G. BREAKDOWN OF NON-LIFE PREMIUMS / G. VENTILATIONS DES PRIMES NON-VIE

	1990	1991	1992	1993	1994	1995	1996	1997
G.1. Motor vehicle / Assurance Automobile								
G.1.1. Direct Business / Assurances Directes								
G.1.1.1. Gross Premiums / Primes Brutes	6 460	6 590	6 575	6 642	6 988	7 489	7 721	7 859
G.1.1.2. Ceded Premiums / Primes Cédées	1 157	1 218	1 525	1 398	1 435	1 282	1 334	:
G.1.1.3. Net Written Premiums / Primes Nettes Emises	5 303	5 372	5 050	5 244	5 553	6 207	6 387	:
G.1.2. Reinsurance Accepted / Réassurance Acceptée								
G.1.2.1. Gross Premiums / Primes Brutes	1 100	1 233	1 497	1 415	1 405	1 111	1 248	1 238
G.1.2.3. Net Written Premiums / Primes Nettes Emises	1 100	1 233	1 497	1 415	1 405	1 111	1 248	:
G.1.3. Total / Total								
G.1.3.1. Gross Premiums / Primes Brutes	7 560	7 823	8 072	8 057	8 393	8 600	8 969	9 097
G.1.3.2. Ceded Premiums / Primes Cédées	1 157	1 218	1 525	1 398	1 435	1 282	1 334	1 381
G.1.3.3. Net Written Premiums / Primes Nettes Emises	6 403	6 605	6 547	6 659	6 958	7 318	7 635	7 716
G.2. Marine, Aviation / Marine, Aviation								
G.2.1. Direct Business / Assurances Directes								
G.2.1.1. Gross Premiums / Primes Brutes	173	168	215	252	270	218	308	325
G.2.1.2. Ceded Premiums / Primes Cédées	123	127	179	210	228	152	195	:
G.2.1.3. Net Written Premiums / Primes Nettes Emises	50	41	36	42	42	66	113	:
G.2.2. Reinsurance Accepted / Réassurance Acceptée								
G.2.2.1. Gross Premiums / Primes Brutes	81	88	116	132	173	84	112	87
G.2.2.3. Net Written Premiums / Primes Nettes Emises	81	88	116	132	173	84	112	:
G.2.3. Total / Total								
G.2.3.1. Gross Premiums / Primes Brutes	254	256	331	384	443	302	420	412
G.2.3.2. Ceded Premiums / Primes Cédées	123	127	179	210	228	152	195	154
G.2.3.3. Net Written Premiums / Primes Nettes Emises	131	129	152	174	215	150	225	258
G.4. Fire, Property Damages / Incendie, Dommages aux Biens								
G.4.1. Direct Business / Assurances Directes								
G.4.1.1. Gross Premiums / Primes Brutes	4 009	4 044	4 197	4 420	4 850	5 065	5 290	5 132
G.4.1.2. Ceded Premiums / Primes Cédées	1 489	1 486	1 712	1 748	1 845	1 874	1 951	:
G.4.1.3. Net Written Premiums / Primes Nettes Emises	2 520	2 558	2 485	2 672	3 005	3 191	3 339	:
G.4.2. Reinsurance Accepted / Réassurance Acceptée								
G.4.2.1. Gross Premiums / Primes Brutes	1 340	1 398	1 572	1 608	1 663	1 517	1 690	1 473
G.4.2.3. Net Written Premiums / Primes Nettes Emises	1 340	1 398	1 572	1 608	1 663	1 517	1 690	:
G.4.3. Total / Total								
G.4.3.1. Gross Premiums / Primes Brutes	5 349	5 442	5 769	6 028	6 513	6 582	6 980	6 605
G.4.3.2. Ceded Premiums / Primes Cédées	1 489	1 486	1 712	1 748	1 845	1 874	1 951	1 699
G.4.3.3. Net Written Premiums / Primes Nettes Emises	3 860	3 956	4 057	4 280	4 668	4 708	5 029	4 906
G.5. Pecuniary Losses / Pertes Pécuniaires								
G.5.1. Direct Business / Assurances Directes								
G.5.1.1. Gross Premiums / Primes Brutes	221	232	219	225	233	209	270	234
G.5.1.2. Ceded Premiums / Primes Cédées	112	117	121	110	114	91	102	:
G.5.1.3. Net Written Premiums / Primes Nettes Emises	109	115	98	115	119	118	168	:
G.5.2. Reinsurance Accepted / Réassurance Acceptée								
G.5.2.1. Gross Premiums / Primes Brutes	78	82	89	77	73	66	67	90
G.5.2.3. Net Written Premiums / Primes Nettes Emises	78	82	89	77	73	66	67	:
G.5.3. Total / Total								
G.5.3.1. Gross Premiums / Primes Brutes	299	314	308	302	306	275	337	324
G.5.3.2. Ceded Premiums / Primes Cédées	112	117	121	110	114	91	102	94
G.5.3.3. Net Written Premiums / Primes Nettes Emises	187	197	187	192	192	184	235	230

CANADA

Monetary Unit: million Ca..dian dollars / Unité monétaire : million de dollars ca..diens

	1990	1991	1992	1993	1994	1995	1996	1997
G.6. General Liability / G.6. Responsabilité Générale								
G.6.1. Direct Business / G.6.1. Assurances Directes								
G.6.1.1. Gross Premiums / G.6.1.1. Primes Brutes	1 237	1 192	1 172	225	1 359	1 438	1 604	1 640
G.6.1.2. Ceded Premiums / G.6.1.2. Primes Cédées	435	453	454	110	510	407	493	..
G.6.1.3. Net Written Premiums / G.6.1.3. Primes Nettes Emises	1 672	739	718	115	849	1 031	1 111	..
G.6.2. Reinsurance Accepted / G.6.2. Réassurance Acceptée								
G.6.2.1. Gross Premiums / G.6.2.1. Primes Brutes	373	402	403	77	424	356	428	401
G.6.2.3. Net Written Premiums / G.6.2.3. Primes Nettes Emises	373	402	403	77	424	356	428	
G.6.3. Total								
G.6.3.1. Gross Premiums / G.6.3.1. Primes Brutes	1 610	1 594	1 575	302	1 783	1 794	2 032	2 041
G.6.3.2. Ceded Premiums / G.6.3.2. Primes Cédées	435	453	454	110	510	407	493	488
G.6.3.3. Net Written Premiums / G.6.3.3. Primes Nettes Emises	1 175	1 141	1 121	192	1 273	1 387	1 539	1 553
G.7. Accident, Health / G.7. Accident, Santé								
G.7.1. Direct Business / G.7.1. Assurances Directes								
G.7.1.1. Gross Premiums / G.7.1.1. Primes Brutes	4 542	4 730	4 833	1 226	346	606	6 634	6 911
G.7.1.2. Ceded Premiums / G.7.1.2. Primes Cédées	411	390	360	470	75	57	632	..
G.7.1.3. Net Written Premiums / G.7.1.3. Primes Nettes Emises	4 953	4 340	4 473	756	271	549	6 002	..
G.7.2. Reinsurance Accepted / G.7.2. Réassurance Acceptée								
G.7.2.1. Gross Premiums / G.7.2.1. Primes Brutes	312	301	304	390	70	70	523	575
G.7.2.3. Net Written Premiums / G.7.2.3. Primes Nettes Emises	312	301	304	390	70	70	523	
G.7.3. Total								
G.7.3.1. Gross Premiums / G.7.3.1. Primes Brutes	4 854	5 031	5 137	1 616	416	676	7 157	7 486
G.7.3.2. Ceded Premiums / G.7.3.2. Primes Cédées	411	390	360	470	75	57	632	715
G.7.3.3. Net Written Premiums / G.7.3.3. Primes Nettes Emises	4 443	4 641	4 777	1 146	341	619	6 525	6 772
G.8. Others / G.8. Autres								
G.8.1. Direct Business / G.8.1. Assurances Directes								
G.8.1.1. Gross Premiums / G.8.1.1. Primes Brutes	165	168	178	5 273	1	4	7	329
G.8.1.2. Ceded Premiums / G.8.1.2. Primes Cédées	57	57	68	501	0	0	0	..
G.8.1.3. Net Written Premiums / G.8.1.3. Primes Nettes Emises	222	111	110	4 773	1	4	7	..
G.8.2. Reinsurance Accepted / G.8.2. Réassurance Acceptée								
G.8.2.1. Gross Premiums / G.8.2.1. Primes Brutes	46	50	55	399	0	0	0	79
G.8.2.3. Net Written Premiums / G.8.2.3. Primes Nettes Emises	46	50	55	399	0	0	0	
G.8.3. Total								
G.8.3.1. Gross Premiums / G.8.3.1. Primes Brutes	211	281	233	5 672	1	4	7	408
G.8.3.2. Ceded Premiums / G.8.3.2. Primes Cédées	57	57	68	501	0	0	0	133
G.8.3.3. Net Written Premiums / G.8.3.3. Primes Nettes Emises	154	161	165	5 171	1	4	7	275
G.10. Total								
G.10.1. Direct Business / G.10.1. Assurances Directes								
G.10.1.1. Gross Premiums / G.10.1.1. Primes Brutes	16 807	17 124	17 389	18 185	14 047	15 029	21 834	22 429
G.10.1.2. Ceded Premiums / G.10.1.2. Primes Cédées	3 784	3 848	4 419	4 514	4 207	3 863	4 707	..
G.10.1.3. Net Written Premiums / G.10.1.3. Primes Nettes Emises	20 591	13 276	12 970	13 671	9 840	11 166	17 127	..
G.10.2. Reinsurance Accepted / G.10.2. Réassurance Acceptée								
G.10.2.1. Gross Premiums / G.10.2.1. Primes Brutes	3 330	3 554	4 036	4 079	3 808	3 204	4 068	3 944
G.10.2.3. Net Written Premiums / G.10.2.3. Primes Nettes Emises	3 330	3 554	4 036	4 079	3 808	3 204	4 068	
G.10.3. Total								
G.10.3.1. Gross Premiums / G.10.3.1. Primes Brutes	20 137	20 678	21 425	22 264	17 855	18 233	25 902	26 373
G.10.3.2. Ceded Premiums / G.10.3.2. Primes Cédées	3 784	3 848	4 419	4 514	4 207	3 863	4 707	4 663
G.10.3.3. Net Written Premiums / G.10.3.3. Primes Nettes Emises	16 353	16 830	17 006	17 750	13 648	14 370	21 195	21 710

H. GROSS CLAIMS PAYMENTS / H. PAIEMENTS BRUTS DES SINISTRES

H.1. Life / H.1. Vie

	1990	1991	1992	1993	1994	1995	1996	1997
H.1.1. Domestic Companies / H.1.1. Entreprises Nationales							14 255	15 051
H.1.2. (Foreign Controlled Companies) / H.1.2. (Entreprises Sous Contrôle Etranger)							2 555	
H.1.3. Branches & Agencies of Foreign Cies / H.1.3. Succursales et Agences d'Ent. Etrangères							2 942	2 546
H.1. Total							17 197	17 597

CANADA

Monetary Unit: million Ca..dian dollars · Unité monétaire : million de dollars ca..diens

H.2. Non-Life / H.2. Non-Vie

	1990	1991	1992	1993	1994	1995	1996	1997
H.2.1. Domestic Companies / Entreprises Nationales							16 888	14 296
H.2.2. (Foreign Controlled Companies) / (Entreprises Sous Contrôle Etranger)							6 832	..
H.2.3. Branches & Agencies of Foreign Cies / Succursales et Agences d'Ent. Etrangères							5 552	4 671
H.2. Total							22 440	18 966

I. GROSS OPERATING EXPENSES / I. DEPENSES BRUTES D'EXPLOITATION

I.1. Life / I.1. Vie

	1990	1991	1992	1993	1994	1995	1996	1997
I.1.1. Domestic Companies / Entreprises Nationales							3 309	5 220
I.1.2. (Foreign Controlled Companies) / (Entreprises Sous Contrôle Etranger)							543	..
I.1.3. Branches & Agencies of Foreign Cies / Succursales et Agences d'Ent. Etrangères							666	952
I.1. Total / Total des Primes Nettes Vie							3 975	6 172

I.2. Non-Life / I.2. Non-Vie

	1990	1991	1992	1993	1994	1995	1996	1997
I.2.1. Domestic Companies / Entreprises Nationales							782	3 677
I.2.2. (Foreign Controlled Companies) / (Entreprises Sous Contrôle Etranger)							407	..
I.2.3. Branches & Agencies of Foreign Cies / Succursales et Agences d'Ent. Etrangères							321	1 288
I.2. Total							1 103	4 965

J. COMMISSIONS / J. COMMISSIONS

J.1. Life / J.1. Vie

	1990	1991	1992	1993	1994	1995	1996	1997
J.1.1. Direct Business / Assurance directe								
J.1.1.1. Domestic Companies / Entreprises Nationales							1 038	1 164
J.1.1.2. (Foreign Controlled Companies) / (Entreprises Sous Contrôle Etranger)							214	..
J.1.1.3. Branches & Agencies of Foreign Cies / Succursales et Agences d'Ent. Etrangères							159	138
J.1.1. Total							1 197	1 302
J.1.2. Reinsurance accepted / Réassurances acceptées								
J.1.2.1. Domestic Companies / Entreprises Nationales							74	148
J.1.2.2. (Foreign Controlled Companies) / (Entreprises Sous Contrôle Etranger)							61	..
J.1.2.3. Branches & Agencies of Foreign Cies / Succursales et Agences d'Ent. Etrangères							93	171
J.1.2. Total							167	319
J.1.3. Total								
J.1.3.1. Domestic Companies / Entreprises Nationales							1 112	1 313
J.1.3.2. (Foreign Controlled Companies) / (Entreprises Sous Contrôle Etranger)							275	..
J.1.3.3. Branches & Agencies of Foreign Cies / Succursales et Agences d'Ent. Etrangères							252	309
J.1.3. Total of Life Net Premiums							1 364	1 622

J.2. Non-Life / J.2. Non-Vie

	1990	1991	1992	1993	1994	1995	1996	1997
J.2.1. Direct Business / Assurance directe								
J.2.1.1. Domestic Companies / Entreprises Nationales							1 744	1 787
J.2.1.2. (Foreign Controlled Companies) / (Entreprises Sous Contrôle Etranger)							1 012	..
J.2.1.3. Branches & Agencies of Foreign Cies / Succursales et Agences d'Ent. Etrangères							431	431
J.2.1. Total							2 175	2 218
J.2.2. Reinsurance Accepted / Réassurances acceptées								
J.2.2.1. Domestic Companies / Entreprises Nationales							445	469
J.2.2.2. (Foreign Controlled Companies) / (Entreprises Sous Contrôle Etranger)							404	..
J.2.2.3. Branches & Agencies of Foreign Cies / Succursales et Agences d'Ent. Etrangères							309	287
J.2.2. Total							754	756
J.2.3. Total								
J.2.3.1. Domestic Companies / Entreprises Nationales							2 189	2 256
J.2.3.2. (Foreign Controlled Companies) / (Entreprises Sous Contrôle Etranger)							1 416	..
J.2.3.3. Branches & Agencies of Foreign Cies / Succursales et Agences d'Ent. Etrangères							740	718
J.2.3. Total							2 929	2 974

Monetary Unit: million Czech koruna

Unité monétaire : million de couronnes tchèques

	1990	1991	1992	1993	1994	1995	1996	1997
A. NUMBER OF COMPANIES IN THE REPORTING COUNTRY / **A. NOMBRE D'ENTREPRISES DANS LE PAYS DECLARANT**								
A.1. Life / **A.1. Vie**								
A.1.1. Domestic Companies / A.1.1. Entreprises Nationales			..	1	1	2	0	2
A.1.2. (Foreign Controlled Companies) / A.1.2. (Entreprises Sous Contrôle Etranger)			..	0	1	0	0	2
A.1.3. Branches & Agencies of Foreign Cies / A.1.3. Succursales et Agences d'Ent. Etrangères			..	4	3	3	2	2
A.1. All Companies / A.1. Ensemble des Entreprises			..	5	4	5	2	4
A.2. Non-Life / **A.2. Non-Vie**								
A.2.1. Domestic Companies / A.2.1. Entreprises Nationales			..	6	7	11	10	14
A.2.2. (Foreign Controlled Companies) / A.2.2. (Entreprises Sous Contrôle Etranger)			..	2	2	3	3	3
A.2.3. Branches & Agencies of Foreign Cies / A.2.3. Succursales et Agences d'Ent. Etrangères			..	1	3	4	4	4
A.2. All Companies / A.2. Ensemble des Entreprises			..	7	10	15	14	18
A.3. Composite / **A.3. Mixte**								
A.3.1. Domestic Companies / A.3.1. Entreprises Nationales			..	7	12	14	17	17
A.3.2. (Foreign Controlled Companies) / A.3.2. (Entreprises Sous Contrôle Etranger)			..	6	7	9	9	8
A.3.3. Branches & Agencies of Foreign Cies / A.3.3. Succursales et Agences d'Ent. Etrangères			..	1	1	1	2	1
A.3. All Companies / A.3. Ensemble des Entreprises			..	8	13	15	19	18
A.5. Total								
A.5.1. Domestic Companies / A.5.1. Entreprises Nationales			..	14	20	27	27	33
A.5.2. (Foreign Controlled Companies) / A.5.2. (Entreprises Sous Contrôle Etranger)			..	8	10	12	12	13
A.5.3. Branches & Agencies of Foreign Cies / A.5.3. Succursales et Agences d'Ent. Etrangères			..	6	7	8	8	7
A.5. All Insurance Companies / A.5. Ensemble des Entreprises d'Assurances			..	20	27	35	35	40
B. NUMBER OF EMPLOYEES / **B. NOMBRE D'EMPLOYES**								
B.1. Insurance Companies / B.1. Entreprises d'Assurances			..	11 097	13 029	13 423	15 189	16 215
B.2. Intermediaries / B.2. Intermediaires			..	2 000	3 000	35 000	35 000	35 500
B. Total			..	13 097	16 029	48 423	50 189	51 715
C. BUSINESS WRITTEN IN THE REPORTING COUNTRY / **C. OPERATIONS CONCLUES DANS LE PAYS DECLARANT**								
C.1. Life / **C.1. Vie**								
C.1.1. Gross Premiums / C.1.1. Primes Brutes								
C.1.1.1. Direct Business / C.1.1.1. Assurances Directes								
C.1.1.1.1. Domestic Companies / C.1.1.1.1. Entreprises Nationales			..	5 596	6 725	8 026	9 243	10 310
C.1.1.1.2. (Foreign Controlled Companies) / C.1.1.1.2. (Entreprises Sous Contrôle Etranger)			..	86	392	632	968	1 363
C.1.1.1.3. Branches & Agencies of Foreign Cies / C.1.1.1.3. Succursales et Agences d'Ent. Etrangères			..	321	722	1 316	1 694	2 157
C.1.1.1. Total / C.1.1.1. Total			..	5 917	7 447	9 342	10 937	12 467
C.1.1.2. Reinsurance Accepted / C.1.1.2. Réassurance Acceptée								
C.1.1.3. Total / C.1.1.3. Total								
C.1.1.3.1. Domestic Companies / C.1.1.3.1. Entreprises Nationales			..	5 596	6 725	8 026	9 243	10 310
C.1.1.3.2. (Foreign Controlled Companies) / C.1.1.3.2. (Entreprises Sous Contrôle Etranger)			..	86	392	632	968	1 363
C.1.1.3.3. Branches & Agencies of Foreign Cies / C.1.1.3.3. Succursales et Agences d'Ent. Etrangères			..	321	722	1 316	1 694	2 157
C.1.1.3. Total Gross Premiums / C.1.1.3. Total des Primes Brutes			..	5 917	7 447	9 342	10 937	12 467
C.1.2. Ceded Premiums / C.1.2. Primes Cédées								
C.1.2.1. Domestic Companies / C.1.2.1. Entreprises Nationales			..	0	0	90	116	139
C.1.2.2. (Foreign Controlled Companies) / C.1.2.2. (Entreprises Sous Contrôle Etranger)			..	0	0	89	114	135
C.1.2.3. Branches & Agencies of Foreign Cies / C.1.2.3. Succursales et Agences d'Ent. Etrangères			..	0	0	2	2	6
C.1.2. Total / C.1.2. Total			..	0	0	92	119	145
C.1.3. Net Written Premiums / C.1.3. Primes Nettes Emises								
C.1.3.1. Domestic Companies / C.1.3.1. Entreprises Nationales			..	5 596	6 725	7 936	9 127	10 171
C.1.3.2. (Foreign Controlled Companies) / C.1.3.2. (Entreprises Sous Contrôle Etranger)			..	86	392	543	854	1 228
C.1.3.3. Branches & Agencies of Foreign Cies / C.1.3.3. Succursales et Agences d'Ent. Etrangères			..	321	722	1 314	1 691	2 151
C.1.3. Total / C.1.3. Total			..	5 917	7 447	9 250	10 818	12 322

Monetary Unit: million Czech koruna

Unité monétaire : million de couronnes tchèques

C.2. Non-Life / C.2. Non-Vie

	French	1990	1991	1992	1993	1994	1995	1996	1997
C.2.1. Gross premiums	**C.2.1. Primes Brutes**								
C.2.1.1. Direct Business	C.2.1.1. Assurances Directes								
C.2.1.1.1. Domestic Companies	C.2.1.1.1. Entreprises Nationales	..	..	..	16 988	22 030	23 746	29 734	34 478
C.2.1.1.2. (Foreign Controlled Companies)	C.2.1.1.2. (Entreprises Sous Contrôle Etranger)	..	..	..	1 589	4 398	6 101	8 731	9 586
C.2.1.1.3. Branches & Agencies of Foreign Cies	C.2.1.1.3. Succursales et Agences d'Ent. Etrangères	..	..	..	54	193	167	333	513
C.2.1.1. Total	C.2.1.1. Total	..	..	..	17 042	22 223	23 913	30 067	34 991
C.2.1.2. Reinsurance Accepted	C.2.1.2. Réassurance Acceptée								
C.2.1.2.1. Domestic Companies	C.2.1.2.1. Ent reprises Nationales	..	..	..	0	0	541	120	526
C.2.1.2. Total	C.2.1.2. Total	..	..	..	0	0	541	120	526
C.2.1.3. Total	C.2.1.3. Total								
C.2.1.3.1. Domestic Companies	C.2.1.3.1. Entreprises Nationales	..	..	..	16 988	22 030	24 287	29 854	35 004
C.2.1.3.2. (Foreign Controlled Companies)	C.2.1.3.2. (Entreprises Sous Contrôle Etranger)	..	..	..	1 589	4 398	6 101	8 731	9 586
C.2.1.3.3. Branches & Agencies of Foreign Cies	C.2.1.3.3. Succursales et Agences d'Ent. Etrangères	..	..	..	54	193	167	333	513
C.2.1.3. Total Gross Premiums	C.2.1.3. Total des Primes Brutes	..	..	..	17 042	22 223	24 454	30 187	35 517
C.2.2. Ceded Premiums	**C.2.2. Primes Cédées**								
C.2.2.1. Domestic Companies	C.2.2.1. Entreprises Nationales	..	..	..	1 478	2 542	3 819	5 219	6 404
C.2.2.2. (Foreign Controlled Companies)	C.2.2.2. (Entreprises Sous Contrôle Etranger)	..	..	..	716	2 430	2 264	3 043	3 519
C.2.2.3. Branches & Agencies of Foreign Cies	C.2.2.3. Succursales et Agences d'Ent. Etrangères	..	..	..	34	112	104	128	241
C.2.2. Total	C.2.2. Total	..	..	..	1 512	2 654	3 923	5 347	6 645
C.2.3. Net Written Premiums	**C.2.3. Primes Nettes Emises**								
C.2.3.1. Domestic Companies	C.2.3.1. Entreprises Nationales	..	..	..	15 510	19 488	20 468	24 635	28 600
C.2.3.2. (Foreign Controlled Companies)	C.2.3.2. (Entreprises Sous Contrôle Etranger)	..	..	..	873	1 968	3 837	5 688	6 067
C.2.3.3. Branches & Agencies of Foreign Cies	C.2.3.3. Succursales et Agences d'Ent. Etrangères	..	..	..	20	81	63	205	272
C.2.3. Total	C.2.3. Total	..	..	..	15 530	19 569	20 531	24 840	28 872

C.3. Total / C.3. Total

	French	1990	1991	1992	1993	1994	1995	1996	1997
C.3.1. Gross Premiums	**C.3.1. Primes Brutes**								
C.3.1.1. Direct Business	C.3.1.1. Assurances Directes								
C.3.1.1.1. Domestic Companies	C.3.1.1.1. Entreprises Nationales	..	..	..	22 584	28 755	31 772	38 977	44 788
C.3.1.1.2. (Foreign Controlled Companies)	C.3.1.1.2. (Entreprises Sous Contrôle Etranger)	..	..	..	1 675	4 790	6 733	9 699	10 949
C.3.1.1.3. Branches & Agencies of Foreign Cies	C.3.1.1.3. Succursales et Agences d'Ent. Etrangères	..	..	..	375	915	1 483	2 027	2 670
C.3.1.1. Total	C.3.1.1. Total	..	..	..	22 959	29 670	33 255	41 004	47 458
C.3.1.2. Reinsurance Accepted	C.3.1.2. Réassurance Acceptée								
C.3.1.2.1. Domestic Companies	C.3.1.2.1. Entreprises Nationales	..	..	..	0	0	541	120	526
C.3.1.2. Total	C.3.1.2. Total	..	..	..	0	0	541	120	526
C.3.1.3. Total	C.3.1.3. Total								
C.3.1.3.1. Domestic Companies	C.3.1.3.1. Entreprises Nationales	..	..	..	22 584	28 755	32 313	39 097	45 314
C.3.1.3.2. (Foreign Controlled Companies)	C.3.1.3.2. (Entreprises Sous Contrôle Etranger)	..	..	..	1 675	4 790	6 733	9 699	10 949
C.3.1.3.3. Branches & Agencies of Foreign Cies	C.3.1.3.3. Succursales et Agences d'Ent. Etrangères	..	..	..	375	915	1 483	2 027	2 670
C.3.1.3. Total Gross Premiums	C.3.1.3. Total des Primes Brutes	..	..	..	22 959	29 670	33 796	41 124	47 984
C.3.2. Ceded Premiums	**C.3.2. Primes Cédées**								
C.3.2.1. Domestic Companies	C.3.2.1. Entreprises Nationales	..	..	..	1 478	2 542	3 909	5 335	6 543
C.3.2.2. (Foreign Controlled Companies)	C.3.2.2. (Entreprises Sous Contrôle Etranger)	..	..	..	716	2 430	2 353	3 157	3 654
C.3.2.3. Branches & Agencies of Foreign Cies	C.3.2.3. Succursales et Agences d'Ent. Etrangères	..	..	..	34	112	106	131	247
C.3.2. Total	C.3.2. Total	..	..	..	1 512	2 654	4 015	5 466	6 790
C.3.3. Net Written Premiums	**C.3.3. Primes Nettes Emises**								
C.3.3.1. Domestic Companies	C.3.3.1. Entreprises Nationales	..	..	..	21 106	26 213	28 404	33 762	38 771
C.3.3.2. (Foreign Controlled Companies)	C.3.3.2. (Entreprises Sous Contrôle Etranger)	..	..	..	959	2 360	4 380	6 542	7 295
C.3.3.3. Branches & Agencies of Foreign Cies	C.3.3.3. Succursales et Agences d'Ent. Etrangères	..	..	..	341	803	1 377	1 896	2 423
C.3.3. Total	C.3.3. Total	..	..	..	21 447	27 016	29 781	35 658	41 194

Monetary Unit: million Czech koruna / Unité monétaire : million de couronnes tchèques

D. NET WRITTEN PREMIUMS IN THE REPORTING COUNTRY IN TERMS OF DOMESTIC AND FOREIGN RISKS
D. PRIMES NETTES EMISES DANS LE PAYS DECLARANT EN RISQUES NATIONAUX ET ETRANGERS

Item	1990	1991	1992	1993	1994	1995	1996	1997	(Français)
D.1. Life									**D.1. Vie**
D.1.1. Domestic Risks									D.1.1. Risques Nationaux
D.1.1.1. Domestic Companies	..	..	..	5 596	6 725	7 936	9 127	10 171	D.1.1.1. Entreprises Nationales
D.1.1.2. (Foreign Controlled Companies)	..	..	..	86	392	543	854	1 228	D.1.1.2. (Entreprises Sous Contrôle Etranger)
D.1.1.3. Branches & Agencies of Foreign Cies	..	..	..	321	722	1 314	1 691	2 151	D.1.1.3. Succursales et Agences d'Ent. Etrangères
D.1.1. Total	..	..	..	5 917	7 447	9 250	10 818	12 322	D.1.1. Total des Primes Nettes Vie
D.1.3. Total									D.1.3. Total
D.1.3.1. Domestic Companies	..	..	..	5 596	6 725	7 936	9 127	10 171	D.1.3.1. Entreprises Nationales
D.1.3.2. (Foreign Controlled Companies)	..	..	..	86	392	543	854	1 228	D.1.3.2. (Entreprises Sous Contrôle Etranger)
D.1.3.3. Branches & Agencies of Foreign Cies	..	..	..	321	722	1 314	1 691	2 151	D.1.3.3. Succursales et Agences d'Ent. Etrangères
D.1.3. Total of Life Net Premiums	..	..	..	5 917	7 447	9 250	10 818	12 322	D.1.3. Total des Primes Nettes Vie
D.2. Non-Life									**D.2. Non-Vie**
D.2.1. Domestic Risks									D.2.1. Risques Nationaux
D.2.1.1. Domestic Companies	..	..	..	14 543	18 511	20 096	24 202	28 176	D.2.1.1. Entreprises Nationales
D.2.1.2. (Foreign Controlled Companies)	..	..	..	873	1 968	3 775	5 538	5 900	D.2.1.2. (Entreprises Sous Contrôle Etranger)
D.2.1.3. Branches & Agencies of Foreign Cies	..	..	..	20	81	63	205	272	D.2.1.3. Succursales et Agences d'Ent. Etrangères
D.2.1. Total	..	..	..	14 563	18 592	20 159	24 407	28 448	D.2.1. Total des Primes Nettes Vie
D.2.2. Foreign Risks									D.2.2. Risques Etrangers
D.2.2.1. Domestic Companies	..	..	..	967	977	372	433	424	D.2.2.1. Entreprises Nationales
D.2.2.2. (Foreign Controlled Companies)	..	..	..	..	..	62	150	167	D.2.2.2. (Entreprises Sous Contrôle Etranger)
D.2.2. Total	..	..	..	967	977	372	433	424	D.2.2. Total des Primes Nettes Vie
D.2.3. Total									D.2.3. Total
D.2.3.1. Domestic Companies	..	..	..	15 510	19 488	20 468	24 635	28 600	D.2.3.1. Entreprises Nationales
D.2.3.2. (Foreign Controlled Companies)	..	..	..	873	1 968	3 837	5 688	6 067	D.2.3.2. (Entreprises Sous Contrôle Etranger)
D.2.3.3. Branches & Agencies of Foreign Cies	..	..	..	20	81	63	205	272	D.2.3.3. Succursales et Agences d'Ent. Etrangères
D.2.3. Total	..	..	..	15 530	19 569	20 531	24 840	28 872	D.2.3. Total des Primes Nettes Vie

F. OUTSTANDING INVESTMENT BY DIRECT INSURANCE COMPANIES
F. ENCOURS DES PLACEMENTS DES ENTREPRISES D'ASSURANCES DIRECTES

Item	1990	1991	1992	1993	1994	1995	1996	1997	(Français)
F.1. Life									**F.1. Vie**
F.1.1. Real Estate									F.1.1. Immobilier
F.1.1.1. Domestic Companies				2 175	3 420	4 603	4 995	5 922	F.1.1.1. Entreprises Nationales
F.1.1.2. (Foreign Controlled Companies)				0	4	4	13	36	F.1.1.2. (Entreprises Sous Contrôle Etranger)
F.1.1.4. Domestic Investment				2 175	3 420	4 603	4 995	5 922	F.1.1.4. Placement dans le Pays
F.1.1.5. Foreign Investment				0	4	0	0	0	F.1.1.5. Placement à l' Etranger
F.1.1. Total				2 175	3 420	4 603	4 995	5 922	F.1.1. Total
F.1.3. Shares									F.1.3. Actions
F.1.3.1. Domestic Companies				5 806	8 816	7 801	11 810	12 032	F.1.3.1. Entreprises Nationales
F.1.3.2. (Foreign Controlled Companies)				0	0	2	3	7	F.1.3.2. (Entreprises Sous Contrôle Etranger)
F.1.3.3. Branches & Agencies of Foreign Cies				..	1	0	0	18	F.1.3.3. Succursales et Agences d'Ent. Etrangères
F.1.3.4. Domestic Investment				5 806	8 816	7 801	11 810	12 050	F.1.3.4. Placement dans le Pays
F.1.3.5. Foreign Investment				0	0	0	0	0	F.1.3.5. Placement à l' Etranger
F.1.3. Total				5 806	8 816	7 801	11 810	12 050	F.1.3. Total
F.1.4. Bonds with Fixed Revenue				36 938	1 738	7 889	15 862	20 309	F.1.4. Obligations
F.1.4.1. Domestic Companies				65	7	411	545	819	F.1.4.1. Entreprises Nationales
F.1.4.2. (Foreign Controlled Companies)				266	234	1 128	1 790	2 700	F.1.4.2. (Entreprises Sous Contrôle Etranger)
F.1.4.3. Branches & Agencies of Foreign Cies				37 204	1 972	9 017	17 652	23 009	F.1.4.3. Succursales et Agences d'Ent. Etrangères
F.1.4.4. Domestic Investment				331	7	0	0	0	F.1.4.4. Placement dans le Pays
F.1.4.5. Foreign Investment				37 204	1 972	9 017	17 652	23 009	F.1.4.5. Placement à l' Etranger
F.1.4. Total									F.1.4. Total

CZECH REPUBLIC

Monetary Unit: million Czech koruna

REPUBLIQUE TCHEQUE

Unité monétaire : million de couronnes tchèques

	1990	1991	1992	1993	1994	1995	1996	1997
F.1.5. Loans other than Mortgage Loans — F.1.5. Prêts Autres qu'Hypothécaires								
F.1.5.1. Domestic Companies — F.1.5.1. Entreprises Nationales				899	1 753	1 694	5 753	5 411
F.1.5.3. Branches & Agencies of Foreign Cies — F.1.5.3. Succursales et Agences d'Ent. Etrangères				..	0	0	246	0
F.1.5.4. Domestic Investment — F.1.5.4. Placement dans le Pays				899	1 753	1 694	5 999	5 411
F.1.5. Total — F.1.5. Total				899	1 753	1 694	5 999	5 411
F.1.6. Other Investments — F.1.6. Autres Placements								
F.1.6.1. Domestic Companies — F.1.6.1. Entreprises Nationales				..	3 357	31 733	16 869	13 388
F.1.6.2. (Foreign Controlled Companies) — F.1.6.2. (Entreprises Sous Contrôle Etranger)				..	13	59	375	583
F.1.6.3. Branches & Agencies of Foreign Cies — F.1.6.3. Succursales et Agences d'Ent. Etrangères				..	80	0	677	728
F.1.6.4. Domestic Investment — F.1.6.4. Placement dans le Pays				..	3 437	31 733	17 546	14 116
F.1.6.5. Foreign Investment — F.1.6.5. Placement à l'Etranger				..	13	0	0	0
F.1.6. Total — F.1.6. Total				..	3 437	31 733	17 546	14 116
F.1.7. Total — F.1.7. Total								
F.1.7.1. Domestic Companies — F.1.7.1. Entreprises Nationales				45 818	19 084	53 720	55 289	57 062
F.1.7.2. (Foreign Controlled Companies) — F.1.7.2. (Entreprises Sous Contrôle Etranger)				65	25	476	936	1 445
F.1.7.3. Branches & Agencies of Foreign Cies — F.1.7.3. Succursales et Agences d'Ent. Etrangères				266	314	1 128	2 713	3 446
F.1.7.4. Domestic Investment — F.1.7.4. Placement dans le Pays				46 084	19 398	54 848	58 002	60 508
F.1.7.5. Foreign Investment — F.1.7.5. Placement à l'Etranger				331	25	0	0	0
F.1.7. Total of Life Investments — F.1.7. Total des Placements Vie				46 084	19 398	54 848	58 002	60 508
F.2. Non-Life — F.2. Non-Vie								
F.2.1. Real Estate — F.2.1. Immobilier								
F.2.1.1. Domestic Companies — F.2.1.1. Entreprises Nationales				66	406	592	652	873
F.2.1.2. (Foreign Controlled Companies) — F.2.1.2. (Entreprises Sous Contrôle Etranger)				40	368	534	597	740
F.2.1.3. Branches & Agencies of Foreign Cies — F.2.1.3. Succursales et Agences d'Ent. Etrangères				..	2	0	0	0
F.2.1.4. Domestic Investment — F.2.1.4. Placement dans le Pays				66	408	592	652	873
F.2.1.5. Foreign Investment — F.2.1.5. Placement à l'Etranger				40	408	0	0	0
F.2.1. Total — F.2.1. Total				66	774	592	652	873
F.2.2. Mortgage Loans — F.2.2. Prêts Hypothécaires								
F.2.2.1. Domestic Companies — F.2.2.1. Entreprises Nationales				0	0	0	0	0
F.2.2.2. (Foreign Controlled Companies) — F.2.2.2. (Entreprises Sous Contrôle Etranger)				0	0	1	1	0
F.2.2.4. Domestic Investment — F.2.2.4. Placement dans le Pays				..	0	1	1	0
F.2.2. Total — F.2.2. Total				..	0	1	1	0
F.2.3. Shares — F.2.3. Actions								
F.2.3.1. Domestic Companies — F.2.3.1. Entreprises Nationales				39	245	200	4 312	2 887
F.2.3.2. (Foreign Controlled Companies) — F.2.3.2. (Entreprises Sous Contrôle Etranger)				29	82	200	238	163
F.2.3.3. Branches & Agencies of Foreign Cies — F.2.3.3. Succursales et Agences d'Ent. Etrangères				..	2	0	0	3
F.2.3.4. Domestic Investment — F.2.3.4. Placement dans le Pays				39	245	200	4 312	2 890
F.2.3.5. Foreign Investment — F.2.3.5. Placement à l'Etranger				29	82	0	0	0
F.2.3. Total — F.2.3. Total				39	245	200	4 312	2 890
F.2.4. Bonds with Fixed Revenue — F.2.4. Obligations								
F.2.4.1. Domestic Companies — F.2.4.1. Entreprises Nationales				1 341	465	322	7 011	5 066
F.2.4.2. (Foreign Controlled Companies) — F.2.4.2. (Entreprises Sous Contrôle Etranger)				627	262	147	822	1 445
F.2.4.3. Branches & Agencies of Foreign Cies — F.2.4.3. Succursales et Agences d'Ent. Etrangères				21	0	0	0	508
F.2.4.4. Domestic Investment — F.2.4.4. Placement dans le Pays				1 989	465	322	7 011	5 574
F.2.4.5. Foreign Investment — F.2.4.5. Placement à l'Etranger				648	262	0	0	0
F.2.4. Total — F.2.4. Total				1 989	465	322	7 011	5 574
F.2.5. Loans other than Mortgage Loans — F.2.5. Prêts Autres qu'Hypothécaires								
F.2.5.1. Domestic Companies — F.2.5.1. Entreprises Nationales				35	146	51	3 533	4 906
F.2.5.2. (Foreign Controlled Companies) — F.2.5.2. (Entreprises Sous Contrôle Etranger)				35	146	51	840	13
F.2.5.4. Domestic Investment — F.2.5.4. Placement dans le Pays				35	146	51	3 533	4 906
F.2.5.5. Foreign Investment — F.2.5.5. Placement à l'Etranger				35	146	0	0	0
F.2.5. Total — F.2.5. Total				35	146	51	3 533	4 906
F.2.6. Other Investments — F.2.6. Autres Placements								
F.2.6.1. Domestic Companies — F.2.6.1. Entreprises Nationales				..	649	12 160	12 123	17 739
F.2.6.2. (Foreign Controlled Companies) — F.2.6.2. (Entreprises Sous Contrôle Etranger)				..	422	577	2 345	2 222
F.2.6.3. Branches & Agencies of Foreign Cies — F.2.6.3. Succursales et Agences d'Ent. Etrangères				..	0	57	85	265
F.2.6.4. Domestic Investment — F.2.6.4. Placement dans le Pays				..	649	12 217	12 208	18 004
F.2.6.5. Foreign Investment — F.2.6.5. Placement à l'Etranger				..	422	0	0	0
F.2.6. Total — F.2.6. Total				..	649	12 217	12 208	18 004

Monetary Unit: million Czech koruna — Unité monétaire : million de couronnes tchèques

Label (EN)	1990	1991	1992	1993	1994	1995	1996	1997	Label (FR)
F.2.7. Total									F.2.7. Total
F.2.7.1. Domestic Companies				2 108	1 911	13 326	27 632	31 471	F.2.7.1. Entreprises Nationales
F.2.7.2. (Foreign Controlled Companies)				731	1 280	1 510	4 843	4 583	F.2.7.2. (Entreprises Sous Contrôle Etranger)
F.2.7.3. Branches & Agencies of Foreign Cies				21	2	57	85	776	F.2.7.3. Succursales et Agences d'Ent. Etrangères
F.2.7.4. Domestic Investment				2 129	1 913	13 383	27 717	32 247	F.2.7.4. Placement dans le Pays
F.2.7.5. Foreign Investment				752	1 280		0	0	F.2.7.5. Placement à l'Etranger
F.2.7. Total of Non-Life Investments				2 129	1 913	13 383	27 717	32 247	F.2.7. Total des Placements Non-Vie
G. BREAKDOWN OF NON-LIFE PREMIUMS									**G. VENTILATIONS DES PRIMES NON-VIE**
G.1. Motor vehicle									G.1. Assurance Automobile
G.1.1. Direct Business									G.1.1. Assurances Directes
G.1.1.1. Gross Premiums				4 886	4 519	5 057	8 620	15 355	G.1.1.1. Primes Brutes
G.1.1.2. Ceded Premiums				::	::	::	::	1 528	G.1.1.2. Primes Cédées
G.1.1.3. Net Written Premiums				::	::	::	::	13 827	G.1.1.3. Primes Nettes Emises
G.1.3. Total									G.1.3. Total
G.1.3.1. Gross Premiums				4 886	4 519	5 057	8 620	15 355	G.1.3.1. Primes Brutes
G.1.3.2. Ceded Premiums				::	0	::	::	1 528	G.1.3.2. Primes Cédées
G.1.3.3. Net Written Premiums				::	0	::	::	13 827	G.1.3.3. Primes Nettes Emises
G.2. Marine, Aviation									G.2. Marine, Aviation
G.2.1. Direct Business									G.2.1. Assurances Directes
G.2.1.1. Gross Premiums				686	1 029	972	1 014	239	G.2.1.1. Primes Brutes
G.2.1.2. Ceded Premiums				::	::	::	::	175	G.2.1.2. Primes Cédées
G.2.1.3. Net Written Premiums				::	::	::	::	64	G.2.1.3. Primes Nettes Emises
G.2.2. Reinsurance Accepted									G.2.2. Réassurance Acceptée
G.2.2.1. Gross Premiums				::	::	170	120	0	G.2.2.1. Primes Brutes
G.2.3. Total									G.2.3. Total
G.2.3.1. Gross Premiums				686	1 029	1 142	1 134	239	G.2.3.1. Primes Brutes
G.2.3.2. Ceded Premiums				::	::	::	::	175	G.2.3.2. Primes Cédées
G.2.3.3. Net Written Premiums				::	::	::	::	64	G.2.3.3. Primes Nettes Emises
G.3. Freight									G.3. Fret
G.3.1. Direct Business									G.3.1. Assurances Directes
G.3.1.1. Gross Premiums				284	426	268	268	278	G.3.1.1. Primes Brutes
G.3.1.2. Ceded Premiums				::	::	::	::	167	G.3.1.2. Primes Cédées
G.3.1.3. Net Written Premiums				::	::	::	::	111	G.3.1.3. Primes Nettes Emises
G.3.2. Reinsurance Accepted									G.3.2. Réassurance Acceptée
G.3.2.1. Gross Premiums				::	::	170	0	0	G.3.2.1. Primes Brutes
G.3.3. Total									G.3.3. Total
G.3.3.1. Gross Premiums				284	426	438	268	278	G.3.3.1. Primes Brutes
G.3.3.2. Ceded Premiums				::	::	::	::	167	G.3.3.2. Primes Cédées
G.3.3.3. Net Written Premiums				::	::	::	::	111	G.3.3.3. Primes Nettes Emises
G.4. Fire, Property Damages									G.4. Incendie, Dommages aux Biens
G.4.1. Direct Business									G.4.1. Assurances Directes
G.4.1.1. Gross Premiums				2 302	5 844	7 261	7 420	7 869	G.4.1.1. Primes Brutes
G.4.1.2. Ceded Premiums				::	::	::	::	2 604	G.4.1.2. Primes Cédées
G.4.1.3. Net Written Premiums				::	::	::	::	5 265	G.4.1.3. Primes Nettes Emises
G.4.2. Reinsurance Accepted									G.4.2. Réassurance Acceptée
G.4.2.1. Gross Premiums				::	::	190	0	526	G.4.2.1. Primes Brutes
G.4.2.3. Net Written Premiums				::	::	::	::	526	G.4.2.3. Primes Nettes Emises
G.4.3. Total									G.4.3. Total
G.4.3.1. Gross Premiums				2 302	5 844	7 451	7 420	8 395	G.4.3.1. Primes Brutes
G.4.3.2. Ceded Premiums				::	::	::	::	2 604	G.4.3.2. Primes Cédées
G.4.3.3. Net Written Premiums				::	::	::	::	5 791	G.4.3.3. Primes Nettes Emises

CZECH REPUBLIC

Monetary Unit: million Czech koruna
Unité monétaire : million de couronnes tchèques

	1990	1991	1992	1993	1994	1995	1996	1997	
G.5. Pecuniary Losses									G.5. Pertes Pécunières
G.5.1. Direct Business									G.5.1. Assurances Directes
G.5.1.1. Gross Premiums				200	625	650	720	49	G.5.1.1. Primes Brutes
G.5.1.2. Ceded Premiums				::	::	::	::	34	G.5.1.2. Primes Cédées
G.5.1.3. Net Written Premiums				::	::	::	::	15	G.5.1.3. Primes Nettes Emises
G.5.3. Total									G.5.3. Total
G.5.3.1. Gross Premiums				200	625	650	720	49	G.5.3.1. Primes Brutes
G.5.3.2. Ceded Premiums				::	::	::	::	34	G.5.3.2. Primes Cédées
G.5.3.3. Net Written Premiums				::	::	::	::	15	G.5.3.3. Primes Nettes Emises
G.6. General Liability									G.6. Responsabilité Générale
G.6.1. Direct Business									G.6.1. Assurances Directes
G.6.1.1. Gross Premiums				3 198	3 872	4 299	6 220	1 809	G.6.1.1. Primes Brutes
G.6.1.2. Ceded Premiums				::	::	::	::	500	G.6.1.2. Primes Cédées
G.6.1.3. Net Written Premiums				::	::	::	::	1 309	G.6.1.3. Primes Nettes Emises
G.6.2. Reinsurance Accepted									G.6.2. Réassurance Acceptée
G.6.2.1. Gross Premiums				::	::	11	0	0	G.6.2.1. Primes Brutes
G.6.3. Total									G.6.3. Total
G.6.3.1. Gross Premiums				3 198	3 872	4 310	6 220	1 809	G.6.3.1. Primes Brutes
G.6.3.2. Ceded Premiums				::	::	::	::	500	G.6.3.2. Primes Cédées
G.6.3.3. Net Written Premiums				::	::	::	::	1 309	G.6.3.3. Primes Nettes Emises
G.7. Accident, Health									G.7. Accident, Santé
G.7.1. Direct Business									G.7.1. Assurances Directes
G.7.1.1. Gross Premiums				1 499	1 730	1 981	2 254	3 714	G.7.1.1. Primes Brutes
G.7.1.2. Ceded Premiums				::	::	::	::	805	G.7.1.2. Primes Cédées
G.7.1.3. Net Written Premiums				::	::	::	::	2 909	G.7.1.3. Primes Nettes Emises
G.7.3. Total									G.7.3. Total
G.7.3.1. Gross Premiums				1 499	1 730	1 981	2 254	3 714	G.7.3.1. Primes Brutes
G.7.3.2. Ceded Premiums				::	::	::	::	805	G.7.3.2. Primes Cédées
G.7.3.3. Net Written Premiums				::	::	::	::	2 909	G.7.3.3. Primes Nettes Emises
G.8. Others									G.8. Autres
G.8.1. Direct Business									G.8.1. Assurances Directes
G.8.1.1. Gross Premiums				3 987	4 178	3 425	3 551	5 678	G.8.1.1. Primes Brutes
G.8.1.2. Ceded Premiums				::	::	::	::	832	G.8.1.2. Primes Cédées
G.8.1.3. Net Written Premiums				::	::	::	::	4 846	G.8.1.3. Primes Nettes Emises
G.8.3. Total									G.8.3. Total
G.8.3.1. Gross Premiums				3 987	4 178	3 425	3 551	5 678	G.8.3.1. Primes Brutes
G.8.3.2. Ceded Premiums				::	0	::	::	832	G.8.3.2. Primes Cédées
G.8.3.3. Net Written Premiums				::	0	::	::	4 846	G.8.3.3. Primes Nettes Emises
G.10. Total									G.10. Total
G.10.1. Direct Business									G.10.1. Assurances Directes
G.10.1.1. Gross Premiums				17 042	22 223	23 913	30 067	34 991	G.10.1.1. Primes Brutes
G.10.1.2. Ceded Premiums				1 512	2 654	::	::	6 645	G.10.1.2. Primes Cédées
G.10.1.3. Net Written Premiums				15 530	19 569	::	::	28 346	G.10.1.3. Primes Nettes Emises
G.10.2. Reinsurance Accepted									G.10.2. Réassurance Acceptée
G.10.2.1. Gross Premiums				::	::	541	120	526	G.10.2.1. Primes Brutes
G.10.2.3. Net Written Premiums				::	::	::	::	526	G.10.2.3. Primes Nettes Emises
G.10.3. Total									G.10.3. Total
G.10.3.1. Gross Premiums				17 042	22 223	24 454	30 187	35 517	G.10.3.1. Primes Brutes
G.10.3.2. Ceded Premiums				1 512	2 654	3 923	5 347	6 645	G.10.3.2. Primes Cédées
G.10.3.3. Net Written Premiums				15 530	19 569	20 531	24 840	28 872	G.10.3.3. Primes Nettes Emises

CZECH REPUBLIC

Monetary Unit: million Czech koruna — Unité monétaire : million de couronnes tchèques

H. GROSS CLAIMS PAYMENTS — H. PAIEMENTS BRUTS DES SINISTRES

	1997	1996	1995	1994	1993	1992	1991	1990
H.1. Life — H.1. Vie								
H.1.1. Domestic Companies — H.1.1. Entreprises Nationales	7 976	6 901						
H.1.2. (Foreign Controlled Companies) — H.1.2. (Entreprises Sous Contrôle Etranger)	75	41						
H.1.3. Branches & Agencies of Foreign Cies — H.1.3. Succursales & Agences d'Ent. Etrangères	184	90						
H.1. Total	8 160	6 991						
H.2. Non-Life — H.2. Non-Vie								
H.2.1. Domestic Companies — H.2.1. Entreprises Nationales	24 790	14 659						
H.2.2. (Foreign Controlled Companies) — H.2.2. (Entreprises Sous Contrôle Etranger)	5 865	3 207						
H.2.3. Branches & Agencies of Foreign Cies — H.2.3. Succursales et Agences d'Ent. Etrangères	72	43						
H.2. Total	24 862	14 702						

I. GROSS OPERATING EXPENSES — I. DEPENSES BRUTES D'EXPLOITATION

	1997	1996	1995	1994	1993	1992	1991	1990
I.1. Life — I.1. Vie								
I.1.1. Domestic Companies — I.1.1. Entreprises Nationales	2 735	2 117						
I.1.2. (Foreign Controlled Companies) — I.1.2. (Entreprises Sous Contrôle Etranger)	804	625						
I.1.3. Branches & Agencies of Foreign Cies — I.1.3. Succursales et Agences d'Ent. Etrangères	449	361						
I.1. Total — I.1. Total des Primes Nettes Vie	3 184	2 478						
I.2. Non-Life — I.2. Non-Vie								
I.2.1. Domestic Companies — I.2.1. Entreprises Nationales	7 959	6 157						
I.2.2. (Foreign Controlled Companies) — I.2.2. (Entreprises Sous Contrôle Etranger)	2 645	1 916						
I.2.3. Branches & Agencies of Foreign Cies — I.2.3. Succursales et Agences d'Ent. Etrangères	136	120						
I.2. Total	8 095	6 277						

J. COMMISSIONS — J. COMMISSIONS

	1997	1996	1995	1994	1993	1992	1991	1990
J.1. Life — J.1. Vie								
J.1.1. Direct Business — J.1.1. Assurance directe								
J.1.1.1. Domestic Companies — J.1.1.1. Entreprises Nationales	75	373						
J.1.1.2. (Foreign Controlled Companies) — J.1.1.2. (Entreprises Sous Contrôle Etranger)	75	156						
J.1.1. Total	75	373						
J.1.3. Total								
J.1.3.1. Domestic Companies — J.1.3.1. Entreprises Nationales	75	373						
J.1.3.2. (Foreign Controlled Companies) — J.1.3.2. (Entreprises Sous Contrôle Etranger)	75	156						
J.1.3. Total of Life Net Premiums — J.1.3. Total	75	373						
J.2. Non-Life — J.2. Non-Vie								
J.2.1. Direct Business — J.2.1. Assurance directe								
J.2.1.1. Domestic Companies — J.2.1.1. Entreprises Nationales	1 940	2 873						
J.2.1.2. (Foreign Controlled Companies) — J.2.1.2. (Entreprises Sous Contrôle Etranger)	1 193	1 106						
J.2.1.3. Branches & Agencies of Foreign Cies — J.2.1.3. Succursales et Agences d'Ent. Etrangères	54	33						
J.2.1. Total — J.2.1. Total des Primes Nettes Vie	1 994	2 906						
J.2.2. Reinsurance Accepted — J.2.2. Réassurances acceptées								
J.2.3. Total								
J.2.3.1. Domestic Companies — J.2.3.1. Entreprises Nationales	1 940	2 873						
J.2.3.2. (Foreign Controlled Companies) — J.2.3.2. (Entreprises Sous Contrôle Etranger)	1 193	1 106						
J.2.3.3. Branches & Agencies of Foreign Cies — J.2.3.3. Succursales et Agences d'Ent. Etrangères	54	33						
J.2.3. Total	1 994	2 906						

DENMARK

Monetary Unit: million Danish kroner

	1990	1991	1992	1993	1994	1995	1996	1997	
A. NUMBER OF COMPANIES IN THE REPORTING COUNTRY									**A. NOMBRE D'ENTREPRISES DANS LE PAYS DECLARANT**
A.1. Life									**A.1. Vie**
A.1.1. Domestic Companies	30	35	39	48	84	83	88	85	A.1.1. Entreprises Nationales
A.1.2. (Foreign Controlled Companies)	4	4	6	6	8	7	7	10	A.1.2. (Entreprises Sous Contrôle Etranger)
A.1.3. Branches & Agencies of Foreign Cies	2	2	2	2	1	1	1	1	A.1.3. Succursales et Agences d'Ent. Etrangères
A.1. All Companies	32	37	41	50	85	84	89	86	A.1. Ensemble des Entreprises
A.2. Non-Life									**A.2. Non-Vie**
A.2.1. Domestic Companies	149	147	148	156	151	149	156	139	A.2.1. Entreprises Nationales
A.2.2. (Foreign Controlled Companies)	16	16	15	15	11	12	12	11	A.2.2. (Entreprises Sous Contrôle Etranger)
A.2.3. Branches & Agencies of Foreign Cies	27	27	27	33	8	3	5	2	A.2.3. Succursales et Agences d'Ent. Etrangères
A.2. All Companies	176	174	175	189	159	152	161	141	A.2. Ensemble des Entreprises
A.4. Reinsurance									**A.4. Réassurance**
A.4.1. Domestic Companies	9	9	9	4	8	5	5	9	A.4.1. Entreprises Nationales
A.4.2. (Foreign Controlled Companies)	1	1	1	1	2	2	2	3	A.4.2. (Entreprises Sous Contrôle Etranger)
A.4.3. Branches & Agencies of Foreign Cies	21	19	20	15	4	0	0	0	A.4.3. Succursales et Agences d'Ent. Etrangères
A.4. All Companies	30	28	29	19	12	5	5	9	A.4. Ensemble des Entreprises
A.5. Total									**A.5. Total**
A.5.1. Domestic Companies	188	191	196	208	243	237	249	233	A.5.1. Entreprises Nationales
A.5.2. (Foreign Controlled Companies)	21	21	22	22	21	21	21	24	A.5.2. (Entreprises Sous Contrôle Etranger)
A.5.3. Branches & Agencies of Foreign Cies	50	48	49	50	13	4	6	3	A.5.3. Succursales et Agences d'Ent. Etrangères
A.5. All Insurance Companies	238	239	245	258	256	241	255	236	A.5. Ensemble des Entreprises d'Assurances
B. NUMBER OF EMPLOYEES									**B. NOMBRE D'EMPLOYES**
B.1. Insurance Companies	13 800	14 300	14 300	14 662	15 000	14 393	15 512	15 207	B.1. Entreprises d'Assurances
B. Total	..	..	..	..	..	..	..	..	B. Total
C. BUSINESS WRITTEN IN THE REPORTING COUNTRY									**C. OPERATIONS CONCLUES DANS LE PAYS DECLARANT**
C.1. Life									**C.1. Vie**
C.1.1. Gross Premiums									**C.1.1. Primes Brutes**
C.1.1.1. Direct Business									**C.1.1.1. Assurances Directes**
C.1.1.1.1 Domestic Companies	14 666	16 983	18 784	23 132	29 109	32 151	38 817	43 428	C.1.1.1.1. Entreprises Nationales
C.1.1.1.2. (Foreign Controlled Companies)	1 013	1 214	1 386	1 403	2 337	2 242	2 723	2 816	C.1.1.1.2. (Entreprises Sous Contrôle Etranger)
C.1.1.1.3 Branches & Agencies of Foreign Cies	354	417	458	402	201	189	189	176	C.1.1.1.3. Succursales et Agences d'Ent. Etrangères
C.1.1.1. Total	15 020	17 400	19 242	23 534	29 310	32 340	39 006	43 604	C.1.1.1. Total
C.1.1.2. Reinsurance Accepted									**C.1.1.2. Réassurance Acceptée**
C.1.1.2.1. Domestic Companies	61	73	74	63	134	80	97	115	C.1.1.2.1. Entreprises Nationales
C.1.1.2.2. (Foreign Controlled Companies)	0	0	0	0	13	13	13	14	C.1.1.2.2. (Entreprises Sous Contrôle Etranger)
C.1.1.2. Total	61	73	74	63	134	80	97	115	C.1.1.2. Total
C.1.1.3. Total									**C.1.1.3. Total**
C.1.1.3.1. Domestic Companies	14 727	17 056	18 858	23 195	29 243	32 231	38 914	43 543	C.1.1.3.1. Entreprises Nationales
C.1.1.3.2. (Foreign Controlled Companies)	1 013	1 214	1 386	1 403	2 351	2 255	2 736	2 830	C.1.1.3.2. (Entreprises Sous Contrôle Etranger)
C.1.1.3.3. Branches & Agencies of Foreign Cies	354	417	458	402	201	189	189	176	C.1.1.3.3. Succursales et Agences d'Ent. Etrangères
C.1.1.3. Total Gross Premiums	15 081	17 473	19 316	23 597	29 444	32 420	39 103	43 719	C.1.1.3. Total des Primes Brutes
C.1.2. Ceded Premiums									**C.1.2. Primes Cédées**
C.1.2.1. Domestic Companies	188	204	222	205	471	465	547	569	C.1.2.1. Entreprises Nationales
C.1.2.2. (Foreign Controlled Companies)	34	38	40	47	50	48	71	54	C.1.2.2. (Entreprises Sous Contrôle Etranger)
C.1.2.3. Branches & Agencies of Foreign Cies	25	20	20	- 65	1	1	1	1	C.1.2.3. Succursales et Agences d'Ent. Etrangères
C.1.2. Total	213	224	242	140	472	466	548	570	C.1.2. Total
C.1.3. Net Written Premiums									**C.1.3. Primes Nettes Emises**
C.1.3.1. Domestic Companies	14 539	16 852	18 636	22 990	28 772	31 766	38 367	42 974	C.1.3.1. Entreprises Nationales
C.1.3.2. (Foreign Controlled Companies)	979	1 174	1 346	1 356	2 301	2 207	2 665	2 776	C.1.3.2. (Entreprises Sous Contrôle Etranger)
C.1.3.3. Branches & Agencies of Foreign Cies	329	397	438	467	200	188	188	175	C.1.3.3. Succursales et Agences d'Ent. Etrangères
C.1.3. Total	14 868	17 249	19 074	23 457	28 972	31 954	38 555	43 149	C.1.3. Total

C.2. Non-Life — C.2. Non-Vie

	1990	1991	1992	1993	1994	1995	1996	1997
C.2.1. Gross premiums — C.2.1. Primes Brutes								
C.2.1.1. Direct Business — C.2.1.1. Assurances Directes								
C.2.1.1.1. Domestic Companies — C.2.1.1.1. Entreprises Nationales	20 371	20 295	20 789	21 403	23 314	25 142	26 416	27 842
C.2.1.1.2. (Foreign Controlled Companies) — C.2.1.1.2. (Entreprises Sous Contrôle Etranger)	2 996	3 034	3 172	5 397	5 560	5 847	5 911	6 231
C.2.1.1.3. Branches & Agencies of Foreign Cies — C.2.1.1.3. Succursales et Agences d'Ent. Etrangères	1 215	408	1 411	1 600	892	526	375	340
C.2.1.1. Total	21 586	20 703	22 200	23 003	24 206	25 668	26 791	28 182
C.2.1.2. Reinsurance Accepted — C.2.1.2. Réassurance Acceptée								
C.2.1.2.1. Domestic Companies — C.2.1.2.1. Entreprises Nationales	5 577	6 814	8 544	5 756	8 189	5 427	5 402	5 123
C.2.1.2.2. (Foreign Controlled Companies) — C.2.1.2.2. (Entreprises Sous Contrôle Etranger)	3 021	3 944	5 911	3 438	550	3 682	3 506	2 797
C.2.1.2.3. Branches & Agencies of Foreign Cies — C.2.1.2.3. Succursales et Agences d'Ent. Etrangères	206	83	161	207	223	234	208	241
C.2.1.2. Total	5 783	6 897	8 705	5 963	8 412	5 661	5 610	5 364
C.2.1.3. Total								
C.2.1.3.1. Domestic Companies — C.2.1.3.1. Entreprises Nationales	25 948	27 109	29 333	27 159	31 503	30 569	31 818	32 965
C.2.1.3.2. (Foreign Controlled Companies) — C.2.1.3.2. (Entreprises Sous Contrôle Etranger)	6 017	6 978	9 083	8 835	6 110	9 529	9 417	9 028
C.2.1.3.3. Branches & Agencies of Foreign Cies — C.2.1.3.3. Succursales et Agences d'Ent. Etrangères	1 421	491	1 572	1 807	1 115	760	583	581
C.2.1.3. Total Gross Premiums — C.2.1.3. Total des Primes Brutes	27 369	27 600	30 905	28 966	32 618	31 329	32 401	33 546
C.2.2. Ceded Premiums — C.2.2. Primes Cédées								
C.2.2.1. Domestic Companies — C.2.2.1. Entreprises Nationales	4 646	4 820	4 517	4 389	4 372	4 235	3 693	3 865
C.2.2.2. (Foreign Controlled Companies) — C.2.2.2. (Entreprises Sous Contrôle Etranger)	1 281	1 241	1 170	1 730	1 381	1 598	1 313	1 534
C.2.2. Total							3 693	:
C.2.3. Net Written Premiums — C.2.3. Primes Nettes Emises								
C.2.3.1. Domestic Companies — C.2.3.1. Entreprises Nationales	21 302	22 289	24 816	22 770	27 131	26 334	28 125	29 100
C.2.3.2. (Foreign Controlled Companies) — C.2.3.2. (Entreprises Sous Contrôle Etranger)	4 736	5 737	7 913	7 105	4 729	7 931	8 104	7 494
C.2.3.3. Branches & Agencies of Foreign Cies — C.2.3.3. Succursales et Agences d'Ent. Etrangères	:	:	:	:	:	:	583	:
C.2.3. Total	:	:	:	:	:	:	28 708	:

C.3. Total

	1990	1991	1992	1993	1994	1995	1996	1997
C.3.1. Gross Premiums — C.3.1. Primes Brutes								
C.3.1.1. Direct Business — C.3.1.1. Assurances Directes								
C.3.1.1.1. Domestic Companies — C.3.1.1.1. Entreprises Nationales	35 037	37 278	39 573	44 535	52 423	57 293	65 233	71 270
C.3.1.1.2. (Foreign Controlled Companies) — C.3.1.1.2. (Entreprises Sous Contrôle Etranger)	4 009	4 248	4 558	6 800	7 897	8 089	8 634	9 047
C.3.1.1.3. Branches & Agencies of Foreign Cies — C.3.1.1.3. Succursales et Agences d'Ent. Etrangères	1 569	825	1 869	2 002	1 093	715	564	516
C.3.1.1. Total	36 606	38 103	41 442	46 537	53 516	58 008	65 797	71 786
C.3.1.2. Reinsurance Accepted — C.3.1.2. Réassurance Acceptée								
C.3.1.2.1. Domestic Companies — C.3.1.2.1. Entreprises Nationales	5 638	6 887	8 618	5 819	8 323	5 507	5 499	5 238
C.3.1.2.2. (Foreign Controlled Companies) — C.3.1.2.2. (Entreprises Sous Contrôle Etranger)	3 021	3 944	5 911	3 438	563	3 695	3 519	2 811
C.3.1.2.3. Branches & Agencies of Foreign Cies — C.3.1.2.3. Succursales et Agences d'Ent. Etrangères	206	83	161	207	223	234	208	241
C.3.1.2. Total	5 844	6 970	8 779	6 026	8 546	5 741	5 707	5 479
C.3.1.3. Total								
C.3.1.3.1. Domestic Companies — C.3.1.3.1. Entreprises Nationales	40 675	44 165	48 191	50 354	60 746	62 800	70 732	76 508
C.3.1.3.2. (Foreign Controlled Companies) — C.3.1.3.2. (Entreprises Sous Contrôle Etranger)	7 030	8 192	10 469	10 238	8 461	11 784	12 153	11 858
C.3.1.3.3. Branches & Agencies of Foreign Cies — C.3.1.3.3. Succursales et Agences d'Ent. Etrangères	1 775	908	2 030	2 209	1 316	949	772	757
C.3.1.3. Total Gross Premiums — C.3.1.3. Total des Primes Brutes	42 450	45 073	50 221	52 563	62 062	63 749	71 504	77 265
C.3.2. Ceded Premiums — C.3.2. Primes Cédées								
C.3.2.1. Domestic Companies — C.3.2.1. Entreprises Nationales	4 834	5 024	4 739	4 594	4 843	4 700	4 240	4 434
C.3.2.2. (Foreign Controlled Companies) — C.3.2.2. (Entreprises Sous Contrôle Etranger)	1 315	1 279	1 210	1 777	1 431	1 646	1 384	1 588
C.3.2. Total	:	:	:	:	:	:	4 241	:
C.3.3. Net Written Premiums — C.3.3. Primes Nettes Emises								
C.3.3.1. Domestic Companies — C.3.3.1. Entreprises Nationales	35 841	39 141	43 452	45 760	55 903	58 100	66 492	72 074
C.3.3.2. (Foreign Controlled Companies) — C.3.3.2. (Entreprises Sous Contrôle Etranger)	5 715	6 911	9 259	8 461	7 030	10 138	10 769	10 270
C.3.3.3. Branches & Agencies of Foreign Cies — C.3.3.3. Succursales et Agences d'Ent. Etrangères	:	:	:	:	:	:	771	:
C.3.3. Total	:	:	:	:	:	:	67 263	:

Monetary Unit: million Danish kroner — Unité monétaire : million de couronnes danoises

D. NET WRITTEN PREMIUMS IN THE REPORTING COUNTRY IN TERMS OF DOMESTIC AND FOREIGN RISKS
D. PRIMES NETTES EMISES DANS LE PAYS DECLARANT EN RISQUES NATIONAUX ET ETRANGERS

	1990	1991	1992	1993	1994	1995	1996	1997
D.2. Non-Life / D.2. Non-Vie								
D.2.1. Domestic Risks / Risques Nationaux								
D.2.1.1. Domestic Companies / Entreprises Nationales	17 809	17 436	17 871	23 926	20 391	22 658	22 206	24 863
D.2.1.2. (Foreign Controlled Companies) / (Entreprises Sous Contrôle Etranger)	2 740	2 893	3 009	4 927	4 537	5 587	7 039	5 381
D.2.2. Foreign Risks / Risques Etrangers								
D.2.2.1. Domestic Companies / Entreprises Nationales	1 994	2 286	3 668	4 452	6 740	3 676	4 217	4 237
D.2.2.2. (Foreign Controlled Companies) / (Entreprises Sous Contrôle Etranger)	469	509	1 831	2 033	192	2 344	2 649	2 113
D.2.3. Total / Total								
D.2.3.1. Domestic Companies / Entreprises Nationales	19 803	19 722	21 540	28 378	27 131	26 334	26 423	29 100
D.2.3.2. (Foreign Controlled Companies) / (Entreprises Sous Contrôle Etranger)	3 209	3 402	4 840	6 960	4 729	7 931	9 688	7 494
E. BUSINESS WRITTEN ABROAD / E. OPERATIONS A L'ETRANGER								
E.1. Life / E.1. Vie								
E.1.1. Gross Premiums / Primes Brutes								
E.1.1.1. Direct Business / Assurance Directe								
E.1.1.1.1. Branches & Agencies / Succursales & Agences	0	0	0	0	0	119	..	0
E.2. Non-Life / E.2. Non-Vie								
E.2.1. Gross Premiums / Primes Brutes								
E.2.1.1. Direct Business / Assurance Directe								
E.2.1.1.1. Branches & Agencies / Succursales & Agences	323	383	349	361	375	399	75	85
E.2.1.2. Reinsurance Accepted / Réassurance Acceptée	4 087	5 057	6 980	4 654	7 118	3 655	1 790	859
E.2.1.2.1. Branches & Agencies / Succursales & Agences								
E.2.1.3. Total / Total								
E.2.1.3.1. Branches & Agencies / Succursales & Agences	4 410	5 440	7 329	5 015	7 493	4 054	1 865	944
E.2.2. Ceded Premiums / Primes Cédées								
E.2.2.1. Branches & Agencies / Succursales & Agences	..	..	..	..	..	..	84	11
E.2.3. Net Written Premiums / Primes Nettes Emises								
E.2.3.1. Branches & Agencies / Succursales & Agences	..	..	..	..	..	..	1 781	933
F. OUTSTANDING INVESTMENT BY DIRECT INSURANCE COMPANIES / F. ENCOURS DES PLACEMENTS DES ENTREPRISES D'ASSURANCES DIRECTES								
F.1. Life / F.1. Vie								
F.1.1. Real Estate / Immobilier								
F.1.1.1. Domestic Companies / Entreprises Nationales	7 244	7 947	7 315	5 370	12 760	14 270	14 794	15 353
F.1.1.2. (Foreign Controlled Companies) / (Entreprises Sous Contrôle Etranger)	237	234	264	278	311	282	292	854
F.1.1.3. Branches & Agencies of Foreign Cies / Succursales et Agences d'Ent. Etrangères	..	..	2	0	0	0		
F.1.1. Total / Total	..	7 949	7 317	5 372	12 760	14 270	14 794	15 353
F.1.2. Mortgage Loans / Prêts Hypothécaires								
F.1.2.1. Domestic Companies / Entreprises Nationales	3 953	3 959	4 105	4 357	5 833	5 026	4 230	3 506
F.1.2.2. (Foreign Controlled Companies) / (Entreprises Sous Contrôle Etranger)	11	9	6	5	3	1	0	1
F.1.2.3. Branches & Agencies of Foreign Cies / Succursales et Agences d'Ent. Etrangères	..	..	70	70	0	0	0	
F.1.2. Total / Total	..	4 029	4 175	4 427	5 833	5 026	4 230	3 506
F.1.3. Shares / Actions								
F.1.3.1. Domestic Companies / Entreprises Nationales	30 859	44 068	61 522	79 516	116 166	132 716	166 320	221 277
F.1.3.2. (Foreign Controlled Companies) / (Entreprises Sous Contrôle Etranger)	624	1 312	1 892	2 398	4 409	5 377	7 361	15 808
F.1.3.3. Branches & Agencies of Foreign Cies / Succursales et Agences d'Ent. Etrangères	..	157	120	171	154	170	219	
F.1.3.4. Domestic Investment / Placement dans le Pays	..	37 621	51 873	66 387	93 899	105 410	127 376	162 109
F.1.3.5. Foreign Investment / Placement à l'Etranger	..	6 604	9 769	13 067	22 421	27 476	39 163	59 168
F.1.3. Total / Total	..	44 225	61 642	79 454	116 320	132 886	166 539	221 277

Monetary Unit: million Danish kroner — Unité monétaire : million de couronnes danoises

	1990	1991	1992	1993	1994	1995	1996	1997
F.1.4. Bonds with Fixed Revenue — F.1.4. Obligations								
F.1.4.1. Domestic Companies — F.1.4.1. Entreprises Nationales	165 336	168 649	169 669	195 410	298 231	320 575	352 732	378 721
F.1.4.2. (Foreign Controlled Companies) — F.1.4.2. (Entreprises Sous Contrôle Etranger)	9 261	9 691	10 572	11 873	17 686	16 127	17 219	34 477
F.1.4.3. Branches & Agencies of Foreign Cies — F.1.4.3. Succursales et Agences d'Ent. Etrangères	..	1 607	1 904	2 277	1 036	1 127	1 223	..
F.1.4.4. Domestic Investment — F.1.4.4. Placement dans le Pays	..	169 714	170 933	197 386	297 477	318 994	350 299	372 830
F.1.4.5. Foreign Investment — F.1.4.5. Placement à l'Etranger	..	542	640	301	1 790	2 708	3 656	5 891
F.1.4. Total — F.1.4. Total	..	170 256	171 573	197 687	299 267	321 702	353 955	378 721
F.1.5. Loans other than Mortgage Loans — F.1.5. Prêts Autres qu'Hypothécaires								
F.1.5.1. Domestic Companies — F.1.5.1. Entreprises Nationales	3 717	3 273	3 120	3 009	2 896	2 370	2 227	1 814
F.1.5.2. (Foreign Controlled Companies) — F.1.5.2. (Entreprises Sous Contrôle Etranger)	74	68	65	60	54	43	39	71
F.1.5.3. Branches & Agencies of Foreign Cies — F.1.5.3. Succursales et Agences d'Ent. Etrangères	..	4	5	4	3	3	2	..
F.1.5. Total — F.1.5. Total	..	3 277	3 125	3 013	2 899	2 373	2 229	1 814
F.1.6. Other Investments — F.1.6. Autres Placements								
F.1.6.1. Domestic Companies — F.1.6.1. Entreprises Nationales	10 356	15 861	16 479	17 205	25 254	2 609	2 310	2 285
F.1.6.2. (Foreign Controlled Companies) — F.1.6.2. (Entreprises Sous Contrôle Etranger)	531	645	1 089	862	912	28	506	404
F.1.6.3. Branches & Agencies of Foreign Cies — F.1.6.3. Succursales et Agences d'Ent. Etrangères	..	293	320	327	127	39	58	..
F.1.6. Total — F.1.6. Total	..	16 154	16 799	17 532	25 381	2 648	2 368	2 285
F.1.7. Total — F.1.7. Total								
F.1.7.1. Domestic Companies — F.1.7.1. Entreprises Nationales	221 465	243 757	262 210	304 867	461 140	477 566	542 613	622 956
F.1.7.2. (Foreign Controlled Companies) — F.1.7.2. (Entreprises Sous Contrôle Etranger)	10 738	11 959	13 888	15 476	23 375	21 858	25 417	51 615
F.1.7.3. Branches & Agencies of Foreign Cies — F.1.7.3. Succursales et Agences d'Ent. Etrangères	..	2 133	2 421	2 851	1 320	1 339	1 502	..
F.1.7.4. Domestic Investment — F.1.7.4. Placement dans le Pays	..	..	..	66 387	..	..	..	..
F.1.7.5. Foreign Investment — F.1.7.5. Placement à l'Etranger	..	..	..	13 067	..	..	..	..
F.1.7. Total of Life Investments — F.1.7. Total des Placements Vie	..	245 890	264 631	307 485	462 460	478 905	544 115	622 956
F.2. Non-Life — F.2. Non-Vie								
F.2.1. Real Estate — F.2.1. Immobilier								
F.2.1.1. Domestic Companies — F.2.1.1. Entreprises Nationales	2 793	3 368	3 354	3 480	3 301	2 848	2 940	3 121
F.2.1.2. (Foreign Controlled Companies) — F.2.1.2. (Entreprises Sous Contrôle Etranger)	1 081	1 205	1 327	1 298	1 306	1 223	1 366	1 491
F.2.1. Total — F.2.1. Total	..	3 368	3 354	3 480	3 301	2 848	2 940	3 121
F.2.2. Mortgage Loans — F.2.2. Prêts Hypothécaires								
F.2.2.1. Domestic Companies — F.2.2.1. Entreprises Nationales	1 932	2 051	2 036	1 758	1 345	1 087	852	612
F.2.2.2. (Foreign Controlled Companies) — F.2.2.2. (Entreprises Sous Contrôle Etranger)	226	187	229	416	137	74	37	24
F.2.2. Total — F.2.2. Total	..	2 051	2 036	1 758	1 345	1 087	852	612
F.2.3. Shares — F.2.3. Actions								
F.2.3.1. Domestic Companies — F.2.3.1. Entreprises Nationales	27 204	30 049	21 529	22 707	23 922	23 331	28 311	32 748
F.2.3.2. (Foreign Controlled Companies) — F.2.3.2. (Entreprises Sous Contrôle Etranger)	3 048	3 082	2 698	6 197	6 803	5 393	6 129	8 563
F.2.3.4. Domestic Investment — F.2.3.4. Placement dans le Pays	..	28 527	20 428	21 515	..	..	26 183	29 994
F.2.3.5. Foreign Investment — F.2.3.5. Placement à l'Etranger	..	1 522	1 101	1 193	..	..	2 128	2 754
F.2.3. Total — F.2.3. Total	..	30 049	21 529	22 709	23 922	23 331	28 311	32 748
F.2.4. Bonds with Fixed Revenue — F.2.4. Obligations								
F.2.4.1. Domestic Companies — F.2.4.1. Entreprises Nationales	33 896	36 577	37 208	39 254	43 010	39 449	51 956	49 274
F.2.4.2. (Foreign Controlled Companies) — F.2.4.2. (Entreprises Sous Contrôle Etranger)	7 330	8 542	8 192	8 139	4 475	5 088	13 205	11 212
F.2.4.4. Domestic Investment — F.2.4.4. Placement dans le Pays	..	32 307	32 059	34 439	..	..	43 419	43 165
F.2.4.5. Foreign Investment — F.2.4.5. Placement à l'Etranger	..	4 270	5 149	4 816	..	..	8 537	6 109
F.2.4. Total — F.2.4. Total	..	36 577	37 208	39 255	43 010	39 449	51 956	49 274
F.2.5. Loans other than Mortgage Loans — F.2.5. Prêts Autres qu'Hypothécaires								
F.2.5.1. Domestic Companies — F.2.5.1. Entreprises Nationales	943	1 361	3 159	2 344	1 461	563	428	177
F.2.5.2. (Foreign Controlled Companies) — F.2.5.2. (Entreprises Sous Contrôle Etranger)	349	930	700	682	204	707	109	70
F.2.5. Total — F.2.5. Total	..	1 361	3 159	2 344	1 461	563	428	177
F.2.6. Other Investments — F.2.6. Autres Placements								
F.2.6.1. Domestic Companies — F.2.6.1. Entreprises Nationales	17 306	17 870	18 024	17 451	15 509	3 762	3 246	3 519
F.2.6.2. (Foreign Controlled Companies) — F.2.6.2. (Entreprises Sous Contrôle Etranger)	3 850	4 975	7 943	8 348	2 029	267	1 432	1 262
F.2.6. Total — F.2.6. Total	..	17 870	18 024	17 451	15 509	3 762	3 246	3 519
F.2.7. Total — F.2.7. Total								
F.2.7.1. Domestic Companies — F.2.7.1. Entreprises Nationales	84 074	91 276	85 310	86 996	88 548	71 040	87 733	89 451
F.2.7.2. (Foreign Controlled Companies) — F.2.7.2. (Entreprises Sous Contrôle Etranger)	15 584	18 921	21 089	25 080	14 954	12 752	22 278	22 622
F.2.7.4. Domestic Investment — F.2.7.4. Placement dans le Pays	..	..	..	21 515	..	..	..	..
F.2.7.5. Foreign Investment — F.2.7.5. Placement à l'Etranger	..	..	..	1 193	..	..	..	..
F.2.7. Total of Non-Life Investments — F.2.7. Total des Placements Non-Vie	..	91 276	85 310	86 997	88 548	71 040	87 733	89 451

Monetary Unit: million Danish kroner — Unité monétaire : million de couronnes danoises

G. BREAKDOWN OF NON-LIFE PREMIUMS — G. VENTILATIONS DES PRIMES NON-VIE

Code / Label (EN)	1990	1991	1992	1993	1994	1995	1996	1997	Label (FR)
G.1. Motor vehicle									G.1. Assurance Automobile
G.1.1. Direct Business									G.1.1. Assurances Directes
G.1.1.1. Gross Premiums	6 025	5 838	5 774	5 881	6 339	7 016	7 390	8 162	G.1.1.1. Primes Brutes
G.2. Marine, Aviation									G.2. Marine, Aviation
G.2.1. Direct Business									G.2.1. Assurances Directes
G.2.1.1. Gross Premiums	1 218	1 328	1 364	1 297	1 295	987	1 010	944	G.2.1.1. Primes Brutes
G.4. Fire, Property Damages									G.4. Incendie, Dommages aux Biens
G.4.1. Direct Business									G.4.1. Assurances Directes
G.4.1.1. Gross Premiums	8 560	8 569	8 764	8 862	9 191	9 510	9 874	11 380	G.4.1.1. Primes Brutes
G.5. Pecuniary Losses									G.5. Pertes Pécuniaires
G.5.1. Direct Business									G.5.1. Assurances Directes
G.5.1.1. Gross Premiums	275	322	474	484	466	492	483	303	G.5.1.1. Primes Brutes
G.6. General Liability									G.6. Responsabilité Générale
G.6.1. Direct Business									G.6.1. Assurances Directes
G.6.1.1. Gross Premiums	720	724	770	867	815	885	930	960	G.6.1.1. Primes Brutes
G.7. Accident, Health									G.7. Accident, Santé
G.7.1. Direct Business									G.7.1. Assurances Directes
G.7.1.1. Gross Premiums	3 638	3 539	3 788	4 253	4 679	5 621	5 960	6 432	G.7.1.1. Primes Brutes
G.8. Others									G.8. Autres
G.8.1. Direct Business									G.8.1. Assurances Directes
G.8.1.1. Gross Premiums	828	878	915	997	1 046	1 156	1 144	1	G.8.1.1. Primes Brutes
G.9. Treaty Reinsurance									G.9. Réassurance Obligatoire
G.9.1. Direct Business									G.9.1. Assurances Directes
G.9.1.1. Gross Premiums					375	0	0	0	G.9.1.1. Primes Brutes
G.10. Total									G.10. Total
G.10.1. Direct Business									G.10.1. Assurances Directes
G.10.1.1. Gross Premiums	21 264	21 198	21 849	22 641	24 206	25 667	26 791	28 182	G.10.1.1. Primes Brutes
G.10.2. Reinsurance Accepted									G.10.2. Réassurance Acceptée
G.10.2.1. Gross Premiums	5 783	6 996	8 705	5 963	8 412	5 662	5 610	5 364	G.10.2.1. Primes Brutes
G.10.3. Total									G.10.3. Total
G.10.3.1. Gross Premiums	27 369	28 576	30 905	28 966	32 618	31 329	32 401	33 546	G.10.3.1. Primes Brutes
G.10.3.2. Ceded Premiums	..	..	..	..	..	..	3 693	..	G.10.3.2. Primes Cédées
G.10.3.3. Net Written Premiums	..	..	..	..	..	..	28 708	..	G.10.3.3. Primes Nettes Emises

H. GROSS CLAIMS PAYMENTS — H. PAIEMENTS BRUTS DES SINISTRES

Code / Label (EN)	1996	1997	Label (FR)
H.1. Life			H.1. Vie
H.1.1. Domestic Companies	24 797	25 808	H.1.1. Entreprises Nationales
H.1.2. (Foreign Controlled Companies)	1 275	3 146	H.1.2. (Entreprises Sous Contrôle Etranger)
H.1.3. Branches & Agencies of Foreign Cies	112	139	H.1.3. Succursales et Agences d'Ent. Etrangères
H.1. Total	24 909	25 947	H.1. Total
H.2. Non-Life			H.2. Non-Vie
H.2.1. Domestic Companies	25 755	20 294	H.2.1. Entreprises Nationales
H.2.2. (Foreign Controlled Companies)	9 476	9 639	H.2.2. (Entreprises Sous Contrôle Etranger)
H.2.3. Branches & Agencies of Foreign Cies	532	463	H.2.3. Succursales et Agences d'Ent. Etrangères
H.2. Total	26 287	20 757	H.2. Total

I. GROSS OPERATING EXPENSES — I. DEPENSES BRUTES D'EXPLOITATION

Code / Label (EN)	1996	1997	Label (FR)
I.1. Life			I.1. Vie
I.1.1. Domestic Companies	2 064	2 867	I.1.1. Entreprises Nationales
I.1.2. (Foreign Controlled Companies)	123	330	I.1.2. (Entreprises Sous Contrôle Etranger)
I.1.3. Branches & Agencies of Foreign Cies	17	22	I.1.3. Succursales et Agences d'Ent. Etrangères
I.1. Total	2 081	2 889	I.1. Total des Primes Nettes Vie

Monetary Unit: million Danish kroner   Unité monétaire : million de couronnes danoises

		1990	1991	1992	1993	1994	1995	1996	1997
I.2. Non-Life	**I.2. Non-Vie**								
I.2.1. Domestic Companies	I.2.1. Entreprises Nationales							4 862	8 355
I.2.2. (Foreign Controlled Companies)	I.2.2. (Entreprises Sous Contrôle Etranger)							1 382	2 736
I.2. Total	I.2. Total							4 862	..
J. COMMISSIONS	**J. COMMISSIONS**								
J.1. Life	**J.1. Vie**								
J.1.3. Total	J.1.3. Total							305	382
J.1.3.1. Domestic Companies	J.1.3.1. Entreprises Nationales							69	76
J.1.3.2. (Foreign Controlled Companies)	J.1.3.2. (Entreprises Sous Contrôle Etranger)							2	3
J.1.3.3. Branches & Agencies of Foreign Cies	J.1.3.3. Succursales et Agences d'Ent. Etrangères								
J.1.3. Total of Life Net Premiums	J.1.3. Total							307	385
J.2. Non-Life	**J.2. Non-Vie**								
J.2.3. Total	J.2.3. Total							2 220	2 387
J.2.3.1. Domestic Companies	J.2.3.1. Entreprises Nationales							1 235	1 244
J.2.3.2. (Foreign Controlled Companies)	J.2.3.2. (Entreprises Sous Contrôle Etranger)							2 220	..
J.2.3. Total	J.2.3. Total								

FINLAND — FINLANDE

Monetary Unit: million markka — Unité monétaire : million de markkas

	1990	1991	1992	1993	1994	1995	1996	1997
A. NUMBER OF COMPANIES IN THE REPORTING COUNTRY / **A. NOMBRE D'ENTREPRISES DANS LE PAYS DECLARANT**								
A.1. Life / **A.1. Vie**								
A.1.1. Domestic Companies / A.1.1. Entreprises Nationales	17	17	17	12	12	11	14	14
A.1. All Companies / A.1. Ensemble des Entreprises	17	17	17	12	12	11	14	14
A.2. Non-Life / **A.2. Non-Vie**								
A.2.1. Domestic Companies / A.2.1. Entreprises Nationales	29	29	29	28	146	145	145	147
A.2.3. Branches & Agencies of Foreign Cies / A.2.3. Succursales et Agences d'Ent. Etrangères	2	2	2	2	2	2	2	2
A.2. All Companies / A.2. Ensemble des Entreprises	31	31	31	30	148	147	147	149
A.4. Reinsurance / **A.4. Réassurance**								
A.4.1. Domestic Companies / A.4.1. Entreprises Nationales	9	9	9	11	12	9	8	6
A.4. All Companies / A.4. Ensemble des Entreprises	9	9	9	11	12	9	8	6
A.5. Total / **A.5. Total**								
A.5.1. Domestic Companies / A.5.1. Entreprises Nationales	55	55	55	51	170	165	167	167
A.5.3. Branches & Agencies of Foreign Cies / A.5.3. Succursales et Agences d'Ent. Etrangères	2	2	2	2	2	2	2	2
A.5. All Insurance Companies / A.5. Ensemble des Entreprises d'Assurances	57	57	57	53	172	167	169	169
B. NUMBER OF EMPLOYEES / **B. NOMBRE D'EMPLOYES**								
B.1. Insurance Companies / B.1. Entreprises d'Assurances	12 000	11 400	12 260	11 800	9 000	9 270	9 454	9 497
B.2. Intermediaries / B.2. Intermediaires	53 000	30 000	..	..	..	100	93	119
B. Total / B. Total	65 000	41 400	..	..	..	9 370	9 547	..
C. BUSINESS WRITTEN IN THE REPORTING COUNTRY / **C. OPERATIONS CONCLUES DANS LE PAYS DECLARANT**								
C.1. Life / **C.1. Vie**								
C.1.1. Gross Premiums / C.1.1. Primes Brutes								
C.1.1.1. Direct Business / C.1.1.1. Assurances Directes								
C.1.1.1.1. Domestic Companies / C.1.1.1.1. Entreprises Nationales	23 171	23 868	20 509	2 800	3 871	7 168	11 862	11 281
C.1.1.1. Total / C.1.1.1. Total	23 171	23 868	20 509	2 800	3 871	7 168	11 862	11 281
C.1.1.2. Reinsurance Accepted / C.1.1.2. Réassurance Acceptée								
C.1.1.2.1. Domestic Companies / C.1.1.2.1. Entreprises Nationales	24	26	- 148	1	4	6	17	111
C.1.1.2. Total / C.1.1.2. Total	24	26	- 148	1	4	6	17	111
C.1.1.3. Total / C.1.1.3. Total								
C.1.1.3. Domestic Companies / C.1.1.3.1. Entreprises Nationales	23 195	23 894	20 361	2 801	3 875	7 174	11 879	11 392
C.1.1.3. Total Gross Premiums / C.1.1.3. Total des Primes Brutes	23 195	23 894	20 361	2 801	3 875	7 174	11 879	11 392
C.1.2. Ceded Premiums / C.1.2. Primes Cédées								
C.1.2.1. Domestic Companies / C.1.2.1. Entreprises Nationales	186	132	162	127	183	109	104	113
C.1.2. Total / C.1.2. Total	186	132	162	127	183	109	104	113
C.1.3. Net Written Premiums / C.1.3. Primes Nettes Emises								
C.1.3.1. Domestic Companies / C.1.3.1. Entreprises Nationales	23 009	23 762	20 199	2 674	3 692	7 065	11 775	11 279
C.1.3. Total / C.1.3. Total	23 009	23 762	20 199	2 674	3 692	7 065	11 775	11 279
C.2. Non-Life / **C.2. Non-Vie**								
C.2.1. Gross premiums / C.2.1. Primes Brutes								
C.2.1.1. Direct Business / C.2.1.1. Assurances Directes								
C.2.1.1.1. Domestic Companies / C.2.1.1.1. Entreprises Nationales	11 135	11 218	11 111	10 911	11 249	11 212	11 319	11 786
C.2.1.1.3. Branches & Agencies of Foreign Cies / C.2.1.1.3. Succursales et Agences d'Ent. Etrangères	13	11	11	20	24	11	11	12
C.2.1.1. Total / C.2.1.1. Total	11 148	11 229	11 122	10 931	11 273	11 223	11 330	11 798
C.2.1.2. Reinsurance Accepted / C.2.1.2. Réassurance Acceptée								
C.2.1.2.1. Domestic Companies / C.2.1.2.1. Entreprises Nationales	1 700	2 034	1 756	1 492	1 089	1 139	1 214	968
C.2.1.2.3. Branches & Agencies of Foreign Cies / C.2.1.2.3. Succursales et Agences d'Ent. Etrangères	16	18	19	20	31	4	4	4
C.2.1.2. Total / C.2.1.2. Total	1 716	2 052	1 775	1 512	1 120	1 143	1 218	972
C.2.1.3. Total / C.2.1.3. Total								
C.2.1.3.1. Domestic Companies / C.2.1.3.1. Entreprises Nationales	12 835	13 252	12 867	12 403	12 338	12 351	12 533	12 754
C.2.1.3.3. Branches & Agencies of Foreign Cies / C.2.1.3.3. Succursales et Agences d'Ent. Etrangères	29	29	30	40	55	15	15	16
C.2.1.3. Total Gross Premiums / C.2.1.3. Total des Primes Brutes	12 864	13 281	12 897	12 443	12 393	12 366	12 548	12 770

Monetary Unit: million markka   Unité monétaire : million de markkas

	1990	1991	1992	1993	1994	1995	1996	1997
C.2.2. Ceded Premiums — Primes Cédées								
C.2.2.1. Domestic Companies — Entreprises Nationales	1 150	1 378	1 456	1 315	1 423	1 435	1 314	1 292
C.2.2.3. Branches & Agencies of Foreign Cies — Succursales et Agences d'Ent. Etrangères	19	22	19	25	37	10	7	4
C.2.2. Total	1 169	1 400	1 475	1 340	1 460	1 445	1 321	1 296
C.2.3. Net Written Premiums — Primes Nettes Emises								
C.2.3.1. Domestic Companies — Entreprises Nationales	11 685	11 874	11 411	11 088	10 915	10 916	11 219	11 462
C.2.3.3. Branches & Agencies of Foreign Cies — Succursales et Agences d'Ent. Etrangères	10	7	11	15	19	5	8	12
C.2.3. Total	11 695	11 881	11 422	11 103	10 934	10 921	11 227	11 474
C.3. Total								
C.3.1. Gross Premiums — Primes Brutes								
C.3.1.1. Direct Business — Assurances Directes								
C.3.1.1.1. Domestic Companies — Entreprises Nationales	34 306	35 086	31 620	13 711	15 120	18 380	23 181	23 067
C.3.1.1.3. Branches & Agencies of Foreign Cies — Succursales et Agences d'Ent. Etrangères	13	11	11	...	24	11	11	12
C.3.1.1. Total	34 319	35 097	31 631	13 731	15 144	18 391	23 192	23 079
C.3.1.2. Reinsurance Accepted — Réassurance Acceptée								
C.3.1.2.1. Domestic Companies — Entreprises Nationales	1 724	2 060	1 608	1 493	1 093	1 145	1 231	1 079
C.3.1.2.3. Branches & Agencies of Foreign Cies — Succursales et Agences d'Ent. Etrangères	16	18	19	20	31	4	4	4
C.3.1.2. Total	1 740	2 078	1 627	1 513	1 124	1 149	1 235	1 083
C.3.1.3. Total								
C.3.1.3.1. Domestic Companies — Entreprises Nationales	36 030	37 146	33 228	15 204	16 213	19 525	24 412	24 146
C.3.1.3.3. Branches & Agencies of Foreign Cies — Succursales et Agences d'Ent. Etrangères	29	29	30	...	55	15	15	16
C.3.1.3. Total Gross Premiums — Total des Primes Brutes	36 059	37 175	33 258	15 244	16 268	19 540	24 427	24 162
C.3.2. Ceded Premiums — Primes Cédées								
C.3.2.1. Domestic Companies — Entreprises Nationales	1 336	1 510	1 618	1 442	1 606	1 544	1 418	1 405
C.3.2.3. Branches & Agencies of Foreign Cies — Succursales et Agences d'Ent. Etrangères	19	22	19	25	37	10	7	4
C.3.2. Total	1 355	1 532	1 637	1 467	1 643	1 554	1 425	1 409
C.3.3. Net Written Premiums — Primes Nettes Emises								
C.3.3.1. Domestic Companies — Entreprises Nationales	34 694	35 636	31 610	13 762	14 607	17 981	22 994	22 741
C.3.3.3. Branches & Agencies of Foreign Cies — Succursales et Agences d'Ent. Etrangères	10	7	11	...	19	5	8	12
C.3.3. Total	34 704	35 643	31 621	13 777	14 626	17 986	23 002	22 753
D. NET WRITTEN PREMIUMS IN THE REPORTING COUNTRY IN TERMS OF DOMESTIC AND FOREIGN RISKS — D. PRIMES NETTES EMISES DANS LE PAYS DECLARANT EN RISQUES NATIONAUX ET ETRANGERS								
D.1. Life — D.1. Vie								
D.1.1. Domestic Risks — Risques Nationaux								
D.1.1.1. Domestic Companies — Entreprises Nationales	23 009	23 762	20 199	2 674	...	7 064	11 775	11 279
D.1.1. Total — Total des Primes Nettes Vie	23 009	23 762	20 199	2 674	...	7 064	11 775	11 279
D.1.2. Foreign Risks — Risques Etrangers								
D.1.2.1. Domestic Companies — Entreprises Nationales	0	0	0	...	...	1	0	0
D.1.2. Total — Total des Primes Nettes Vie	0	0	0	...	...	1	0	0
D.1.3. Total								
D.1.3.1. Domestic Companies — Entreprises Nationales	23 009	23 762	20 199	2 674	3 692	7 065	11 775	11 279
D.1.3. Total of Life Net Premiums — Total des Primes Nettes Vie	23 009	23 762	20 199	2 674	3 692	7 065	11 775	11 279

Monetary Unit: million markka — Unité monétaire : million de markkas

D.2. Non-Life / D.2. Non-Vie

Code	English	French	1990	1991	1992	1993	1994	1995	1996	1997
D.2.1.	Domestic Risks	Risques Nationaux								
D.2.1.1.	Domestic Companies	Entreprises Nationales	11 355	10 581	10 384	11 088		10 791	11 187	11 428
D.2.1.3.	Branches & Agencies of Foreign Cies	Succursales et Agences d'Ent. Etrangères	11	4	11	15	19	5	8	12
D.2.1.	Total	Total des Primes Nettes Vie	11 366	10 585	10 395	11 103	..	10 796	11 195	11 440
D.2.2.	Foreign Risks	Risques Etrangers								
D.2.2.1.	Domestic Companies	Entreprises Nationales	1 071	1 294	1 027	..	..	125	32	34
D.2.2.3.	Branches & Agencies of Foreign Cies	Succursales et Agences d'Ent. Etrangères	3	2	0	..	..	0	0	0
D.2.2.	Total	Total des Primes Nettes Vie	1 074	1 296	1 027	..	..	125	32	34
D.2.3.	Total	Total								
D.2.3.1.	Domestic Companies	Entreprises Nationales	12 426	11 581	11 411	11 088	10 915	10 916	11 219	11 462
D.2.3.3.	Branches & Agencies of Foreign Cies	Succursales et Agences d'Ent. Etrangères	14	6	11	15	..	5	8	12
D.2.3.	Total	Total des Primes Nettes Vie	12 440	11 587	11 422	11 103	10 934	10 921	11 227	11 474

E. BUSINESS WRITTEN ABROAD / E. OPERATIONS A L'ETRANGER

E.1. Life / E.1. Vie

Code	English	French	1990	1991	1992	1993	1994	1995	1996	1997
E.1.1.	Gross Premiums	Primes Brutes								
E.1.1.1.	Direct Business	Assurance Directe								
E.1.1.1.	Total	Total	0	0	0	..	44	..	..	0

E.2. Non-Life / E.2. Non-Vie

Code	English	French	1990	1991	1992	1993	1994	1995	1996	1997
E.2.1.	Gross Premiums	Primes Brutes								
E.2.1.1.	Direct Business	Assurance Directe								
E.2.1.1.	Branches & Agencies	Succursales & Agences	77	201	0	167	44	- 2	41	14
E.2.1.1.	Total	Total	77	201	0	167	44	- 2	..	14
E.2.1.2.	Reinsurance Accepted	Réassurance Acceptée								
E.2.1.3.	Branches & Agencies	Succursales & Agences	..	..	0	..	44	- 2	..	0
E.2.1.3.	Total Gross Premiums	Total des Primes Brutes	..	..	0	..	0	- 2	..	0

F. OUTSTANDING INVESTMENT BY DIRECT INSURANCE COMPANIES / F. ENCOURS DES PLACEMENTS DES ENTREPRISES D'ASSURANCES DIRECTES

F.1. Life / F.1. Vie

Code	English	French	1990	1991	1992	1993	1994	1995	1996	1997
F.1.1.	Real Estate	Immobilier								
F.1.1.1.	Domestic Companies	Entreprises Nationales	7 716	10 478	13 087	4 975	3 366	7 609	7 589	7 535
F.1.1.4.	Domestic Investment	Placement dans le Pays	7 716	10 478	..	4 975	3 366	7 609	7 589	7 535
F.1.1.	Total	Total	7 716	10 478	13 087	4 975	3 366	7 609	7 589	7 535
F.1.2.	Mortgage Loans	Prêts Hypothécaires								
F.1.2.1.	Domestic Companies	Entreprises Nationales	0	0	0	..	0	1 737	1 416	1 325
F.1.2.4.	Domestic Investment	Placement dans le Pays	0	0	0	..	..	1 737	1 416	1 325
F.1.2.	Total	Total	0	0	0	..	..	1 737	1 416	1 325
F.1.3.	Shares	Actions								
F.1.3.1.	Domestic Companies	Entreprises Nationales	3 869	3 419	3 608	1 934	2 438	4 209	6 924	10 942
F.1.3.4.	Domestic Investment	Placement dans le Pays	3 869	3 419	..	1 934	2 438	4 209	6 924	10 942
F.1.3.	Total	Total	3 869	3 419	3 608	1 934	2 438	4 209	6 924	10 942
F.1.4.	Bonds with Fixed Revenue	Obligations								
F.1.4.1.	Domestic Companies	Entreprises Nationales	5 631	7 589	10 023	6 006	..	..	..	..
F.1.4.4.	Domestic Investment	Placement dans le Pays	5 631	7 589	..	6 006	..	..	..	..
F.1.4.	Total	Total	5 631	7 589	10 023	6 006	..	..	..	..
F.1.5.	Loans other than Mortgage Loans	Prêts Autres qu'Hypothécaires								
F.1.5.1.	Domestic Companies	Entreprises Nationales	63 891	72 440	77 535	3 584	14 266	17 987	23 960	32 015
F.1.5.4.	Domestic Investment	Placement dans le Pays	63 891	72 440	..	3 584	14 266	17 987	23 960	32 015
F.1.5.	Total	Total	63 891	72 440	77 535	3 584	14 266	17 987	23 960	32 015

Monetary Unit: million markka

Unité monétaire : million de markkas

	1990	1991	1992	1993	1994	1995	1996	1997	
F.1.6. Other Investments									**F.1.6. Autres Placements**
F.1.6.1. Domestic Companies	3 772	3 100	4 504	1 255	1 952	5	2 558	3 158	F.1.6.1. Entreprises Nationales
F.1.6.4. Domestic Investment	3 772	3 100	4 504	1 255	1 952	5	2 558	3 158	F.1.6.4. Placement dans le Pays
F.1.6. Total	3 772	3 100	4 504	1 255	1 952	5	2 558	3 158	F.1.6. Total
F.1.7. Total									**F.1.7. Total**
F.1.7.1. Domestic Companies	84 879	97 026	108 757	17 754	22 022	31 547	42 447	54 975	F.1.7.1. Entreprises Nationales
F.1.7.4. Domestic Investment	84 879	97 026	108 757	17 754	22 022	31 547	42 447	54 975	F.1.7.4. Placement dans le Pays
F.1.7. Total of Life Investments	84 879	97 026	108 757	17 754	22 022	31 547	42 447	54 975	F.1.7. Total des Placements Vie
F.2. Non-Life									**F.2. Non-Vie**
F.2.1. Real Estate									**F.2.1. Immobilier**
F.2.1.1. Domestic Companies	5 006	6 130	5 997	6 376	4 517	8 299	7 214	8 103	F.2.1.1. Entreprises Nationales
F.2.1.3. Branches & Agencies of Foreign Cies	13	17	17	17	17	17	231	30	F.2.1.3. Succursales et Agences d'Ent. Etrangères
F.2.1.4. Domestic Investment	5 006	6 147	..	6 376	4 534	8 316	7 445	8 133	F.2.1.4. Placement dans le Pays
F.2.1.5. Foreign Investment	..	..	..	17	..	..	..	..	F.2.1.5. Placement à l'Etranger
F.2.1. Total	5 019	6 147	6 014	6 393	4 534	8 316	7 445	8 133	F.2.1. Total
F.2.2. Mortgage Loans									**F.2.2. Prêts Hypothécaires**
F.2.2.1. Domestic Companies	0	0	0	..	0	1 221	1 019	983	F.2.2.1. Entreprises Nationales
F.2.2.3. Branches & Agencies of Foreign Cies	0	0	0	..	0	..	13	0	F.2.2.3. Succursales et Agences d'Ent. Etrangères
F.2.2.4. Domestic Investment	0	0	0	..	0	1 221	1 032	983	F.2.2.4. Placement dans le Pays
F.2.2. Total	0	0	0	..	0	1 221	1 032	983	F.2.2. Total
F.2.3. Shares									**F.2.3. Actions**
F.2.3.1. Domestic Companies	4 586	3 687	3 396	4 401	5 506	8 177	9 460	13 201	F.2.3.1. Entreprises Nationales
F.2.3.3. Branches & Agencies of Foreign Cies	0	0	..	0	0	4	48	..	F.2.3.3. Succursales et Agences d'Ent. Etrangères
F.2.3.4. Domestic Investment	4 586	3 687	3 396	4 401	5 506	8 181	9 508	13 201	F.2.3.4. Placement dans le Pays
F.2.3. Total	4 586	3 687	3 396	4 401	5 506	8 181	9 508	13 201	F.2.3. Total
F.2.4. Bonds with Fixed Revenue									**F.2.4. Obligations**
F.2.4.1. Domestic Companies	3 017	3 586	3 870	5 696	..	..	0	..	F.2.4.1. Entreprises Nationales
F.2.4.4. Domestic Investment	3 017	3 586	3 870	5 696	..	..	0	..	F.2.4.4. Placement dans le Pays
F.2.4. Total	3 017	3 586	3 870	5 696	..	..	0	..	F.2.4. Total
F.2.5. Loans other than Mortgage Loans									**F.2.5. Prêts Autres qu'Hypothécaires**
F.2.5.1. Domestic Companies	7 151	7 675	7 847	6 072	14 890	13 663	11 293	13 757	F.2.5.1. Entreprises Nationales
F.2.5.3. Branches & Agencies of Foreign Cies	0	28	28	32	32	28	12	0	F.2.5.3. Succursales et Agences d'Ent. Etrangères
F.2.5.4. Domestic Investment	7 151	7 703	..	6 072	14 960	13 691	11 305	13 757	F.2.5.4. Placement dans le Pays
F.2.5.5. Foreign Investment	..	..	..	32	..	..	..	..	F.2.5.5. Placement à l'Etranger
F.2.5. Total	7 151	7 703	7 875	6 104	14 922	13 691	11 305	13 757	F.2.5. Total
F.2.6. Other Investments									**F.2.6. Autres Placements**
F.2.6.1. Domestic Companies	1 194	738	1 713	1 298	1 204	338	6 420	1 580	F.2.6.1. Entreprises Nationales
F.2.6.3. Branches & Agencies of Foreign Cies	17	0	0	1	0	1	285	73	F.2.6.3. Succursales et Agences d'Ent. Etrangères
F.2.6.4. Domestic Investment	1 194	738	..	1 298	1 204	339	6 705	1 653	F.2.6.4. Placement dans le Pays
F.2.6.5. Foreign Investment	..	..	1 713	1	..	..	..	..	F.2.6.5. Placement à l'Etranger
F.2.6. Total	1 211	738	1 713	1 299	1 204	339	6 705	1 653	F.2.6. Total
F.2.7. Total									**F.2.7. Total**
F.2.7.1. Domestic Companies	20 954	21 816	22 823	23 843	26 117	31 698	35 406	37 624	F.2.7.1. Entreprises Nationales
F.2.7.3. Branches & Agencies of Foreign Cies	30	45	45	50	49	50	589	103	F.2.7.3. Succursales et Agences d'Ent. Etrangères
F.2.7.4. Domestic Investment	20 954	21 861	..	23 843	26 166	31 748	35 995	37 727	F.2.7.4. Placement dans le Pays
F.2.7.5. Foreign Investment	..	..	..	50	0	..	..	..	F.2.7.5. Placement à l'Etranger
F.2.7. Total of Non-Life Investments	20 984	21 861	22 868	23 893	26 166	31 748	35 995	37 727	F.2.7. Total des Placements Non-Vie
G. BREAKDOWN OF NON-LIFE PREMIUMS									**G. VENTILATIONS DES PRIMES NON-VIE**
G.1. Motor vehicle									**G.1. Assurance Automobile**
G.1.1. Direct Business									**G.1.1. Assurances Directes**
G.1.1.1. Gross Premiums	4 150	4 158	3 888	3 527	3 124	3 208	3 403	3 715	G.1.1.1. Primes Brutes
G.1.1.2. Ceded Premiums	..	..	..	..	0	56	60	65	G.1.1.2. Primes Cédées
G.1.1.3. Net Written Premiums	..	..	3 888	..	0	3 152	3 343	3 650	G.1.1.3. Primes Nettes Emises
G.1.3. Total									**G.1.3. Total**
G.1.3.1. Gross Premiums	..	..	3 888	..	0	..	3 403	..	G.1.3.1. Primes Brutes
G.1.3.2. Ceded Premiums	..	..	..	..	0	..	60	..	G.1.3.2. Primes Cédées
G.1.3.3. Net Written Premiums	..	..	3 888	..	0	..	3 343	..	G.1.3.3. Primes Nettes Emises

FINLAND

Monetary Unit: million markka

	1990	1991	1992	1993	1994	1995	1996	1997
G.2. Marine, Aviation								
G.2.1. Direct Business								
G.2.1.1. Gross Premiums	206	236	278	707	702	308	259	235
G.2.1.2. Ceded Premiums	:	:	:	:	:	109	172	126
G.2.1.3. Net Written Premiums	:	:	:	:	:	199	87	109
G.2.3. Total								
G.2.3.1. Gross Premiums	:	:	278	:	:	:	259	:
G.2.3.2. Ceded Premiums	:	:	:	:	:	:	172	:
G.2.3.3. Net Written Premiums	:	:	:	:	:	:	87	:
G.3. Freight								
G.3.1. Direct Business								
G.3.1.1. Gross Premiums	384	342	323	:	:	372	355	365
G.3.1.2. Ceded Premiums	:	:	:	:	:	132	24	23
G.3.1.3. Net Written Premiums	:	:	:	:	:	240	331	342
G.3.3. Total								
G.3.3.1. Gross Premiums	:	:	323	:	:	:	355	:
G.3.3.2. Ceded Premiums	:	:	:	:	:	:	24	:
G.3.3.3. Net Written Premiums	:	:	:	:	:	:	331	:
G.4. Fire, Property Damages								
G.4.1. Direct Business								
G.4.1.1. Gross Premiums	2 598	2 722	2 698	3 025	2 959	2 968	2 902	2 943
G.4.1.2. Ceded Premiums	:	:	:	:	:	450	438	461
G.4.1.3. Net Written Premiums	:	:	:	:	:	2 518	2 464	2 482
G.4.3. Total								
G.4.3.1. Gross Premiums	:	:	2 698	:	:	:	2 902	:
G.4.3.2. Ceded Premiums	:	:	:	:	:	:	438	:
G.4.3.3. Net Written Premiums	:	:	:	:	:	:	2 464	:
G.5. Pecuniary Losses								
G.5.1. Direct Business								
G.5.1.1. Gross Premiums	216	176	161	:	1 072	747	577	367
G.5.1.2. Ceded Premiums	:	:	:	:	:	54	44	41
G.5.1.3. Net Written Premiums	:	:	:	:	:	693	533	326
G.5.3. Total								
G.5.3.1. Gross Premiums	:	:	161	:	:	:	577	:
G.5.3.2. Ceded Premiums	:	:	:	:	:	:	44	:
G.5.3.3. Net Written Premiums	:	:	:	:	:	:	533	:
G.6. General Liability								
G.6.1. Direct Business								
G.6.1.1. Gross Premiums	313	327	294	288	296	468	512	536
G.6.1.2. Ceded Premiums	:	:	:	:	:	93	89	98
G.6.1.3. Net Written Premiums	:	:	:	:	:	375	423	438
G.6.3. Total								
G.6.3.1. Gross Premiums	:	:	294	:	:	:	512	:
G.6.3.2. Ceded Premiums	:	:	:	:	:	:	89	:
G.6.3.3. Net Written Premiums	:	:	:	:	:	:	423	:
G.7. Accident, Health								
G.7.1. Direct Business								
G.7.1.1. Gross Premiums	2 870	2 741	2 535	2 526	2 693	2 778	2 910	3 238
G.7.1.2. Ceded Premiums	:	:	:	:	:	101	98	85
G.7.1.3. Net Written Premiums	:	:	:	:	:	2 677	2 812	3 153
G.7.3. Total								
G.7.3.1. Gross Premiums	:	:	2 535	:	:	:	2 910	:
G.7.3.2. Ceded Premiums	:	:	:	:	:	:	98	:
G.7.3.3. Net Written Premiums	:	:	:	:	:	:	2 812	:

G.2. Marine, Aviation — G.2.1. Assurances Directes — G.2.1.1. Primes Brutes — G.2.1.2. Primes Cédées — G.2.1.3. Primes Nettes Emises — G.2.3. Total — G.2.3.1. Primes Brutes — G.2.3.2. Primes Cédées — G.2.3.3. Primes Nettes Emises — G.3. Fret — G.3.1. Assurances Directes — G.3.1.1. Primes Brutes — G.3.1.2. Primes Cédées — G.3.1.3. Primes Nettes Emises — G.3.3. Total — G.3.3.1. Primes Brutes — G.3.3.2. Primes Cédées — G.3.3.3. Primes Nettes Emises — G.4. Incendie, Dommages aux Biens — G.4.1. Assurances Directes — G.4.1.1. Primes Brutes — G.4.1.2. Primes Cédées — G.4.1.3. Primes Nettes Emises — G.4.3. Total — G.4.3.1. Primes Brutes — G.4.3.2. Primes Cédées — G.4.3.3. Primes Nettes Emises — G.5. Pertes Pécunières — G.5.1. Assurances Directes — G.5.1.1. Primes Brutes — G.5.1.2. Primes Cédées — G.5.1.3. Primes Nettes Emises — G.5.3. Total — G.5.3.1. Primes Brutes — G.5.3.2. Primes Cédées — G.5.3.3. Primes Nettes Emises — G.6. Responsabilité Générale — G.6.1. Assurances Directes — G.6.1.1. Primes Brutes — G.6.1.2. Primes Cédées — G.6.1.3. Primes Nettes Emises — G.6.3. Total — G.6.3.1. Primes Brutes — G.6.3.2. Primes Cédées — G.6.3.3. Primes Nettes Emises — G.7. Accident, Santé — G.7.1. Assurances Directes — G.7.1.1. Primes Brutes — G.7.1.2. Primes Cédées — G.7.1.3. Primes Nettes Emises — G.7.3. Total — G.7.3.1. Primes Brutes — G.7.3.2. Primes Cédées — G.7.3.3. Primes Nettes Emises

Monetary Unit: million markka   Unité monétaire : million de markkas

	1990	1991	1992	1993	1994	1995	1996	1997	
G.8. Others									**G.8. Autres**
G.8.1. Direct Business									G.8.1. Assurances Directes
G.8.1.1. Gross Premiums	411	527	766	1 385	427	374	412	395	G.8.1.1. Primes Brutes
G.8.1.2. Ceded Premiums	:	:	:	:	:	176	165	145	G.8.1.2. Primes Cédées
G.8.1.3. Net Written Premiums	:	:	:	:	:	198	247	250	G.8.1.3. Primes Nettes Emises
G.8.3. Total									G.8.3. Total
G.8.3.1. Gross Premiums	:	:	766	:	:	:	412	395	G.8.3.1. Primes Brutes
G.8.3.2. Ceded Premiums	:	:	:	:	:	:	165	145	G.8.3.2. Primes Cédées
G.8.3.3. Net Written Premiums	:	:	:	:	:	:	247	250	G.8.3.3. Primes Nettes Emises
G.9. Treaty Reinsurance									**G.9. Réassurance Obligatoire**
G.9.1. Direct Business									G.9.1. Assurances Directes
G.9.1.1. Gross Premiums	:	:	179	:	:	:	0	:	G.9.1.1. Primes Brutes
G.9.2. Reinsurance Accepted									G.9.2. Réassurance Acceptée
G.9.2.1. Gross Premiums	:	:	1 775	:	:	:	1 216	971	G.9.2.1. Primes Brutes
G.9.2.2. Ceded Premiums	:	:	:	:	:	:	229	218	G.9.2.2. Primes Cédées
G.9.2.3. Net Written Premiums	:	:	:	:	:	:	987	753	G.9.2.3. Primes Nettes Emises
G.9.3. Total									G.9.3. Total
G.9.3.1. Gross Premiums	:	:	1 954	:	:	:	1 216	:	G.9.3.1. Primes Brutes
G.9.3.2. Ceded Premiums	:	:	:	:	:	:	229	:	G.9.3.2. Primes Cédées
G.9.3.3. Net Written Premiums	:	:	:	:	:	:	987	:	G.9.3.3. Primes Nettes Emises
G.10. Total									**G.10. Total**
G.10.1. Direct Business									G.10.1. Assurances Directes
G.10.1.1. Gross Premiums	11 148	11 229	11 122	11 458	11 273	11 223	11 330	11 794	G.10.1.1. Primes Brutes
G.10.1.2. Ceded Premiums	:	:	:	:	:	1 171	1 090	1 044	G.10.1.2. Primes Cédées
G.10.1.3. Net Written Premiums	:	:	:	:	:	10 052	10 240	10 750	G.10.1.3. Primes Nettes Emises
G.10.2. Reinsurance Accepted									G.10.2. Réassurance Acceptée
G.10.2.1. Gross Premiums	:	:	1 775	:	:	:	1 216	:	G.10.2.1. Primes Brutes
G.10.2.2. Ceded Premiums	:	:	:	:	:	:	229	:	G.10.2.2. Primes Cédées
G.10.2.3. Net Written Premiums	:	:	:	:	:	:	987	:	G.10.2.3. Primes Nettes Emises
G.10.3. Total									G.10.3. Total
G.10.3.1. Gross Premiums	:	:	12 897	:	:	:	12 546	:	G.10.3.1. Primes Brutes
G.10.3.2. Ceded Premiums	:	:	1 475	:	:	:	1 319	:	G.10.3.2. Primes Cédées
G.10.3.3. Net Written Premiums	:	:	11 422	:	:	:	11 227	:	G.10.3.3. Primes Nettes Emises
H. GROSS CLAIMS PAYMENTS									**H. PAIEMENTS BRUTS DES SINISTRES**
H.1. Life									**H.1. Vie**
H.1.1. Domestic Companies							2 661	3 260	H.1.1. Entreprises Nationales
H.1. Total							2 661	3 260	H.1. Total
H.2. Non-Life									**H.2. Non-Vie**
H.2.1. Domestic Companies							10 260	10 828	H.2.1. Entreprises Nationales
H.2.3. Branches & Agencies of Foreign Cies							18	7	H.2.3. Succursales et Agences d'Ent. Etrangères
H.2. Total							10 278	10 835	H.2. Total
I. GROSS OPERATING EXPENSES									**I. DEPENSES BRUITES D'EXPLOITATION**
I.1. Life									**I.1. Vie**
I.1.1. Domestic Companies							766	844	I.1.1. Entreprises Nationales
I.1. Total							766	844	I.1. Total des Primes Nettes Vie
I.2. Non-Life									**I.2. Non-Vie**
I.2.1. Domestic Companies							2 310	2 326	I.2.1. Entreprises Nationales
I.2.3. Branches & Agencies of Foreign Cies							4	6	I.2.3. Succursales et Agences d'Ent. Etrangères
I.2. Total							2 314	2 332	I.2. Total

Monetary Unit: million markka   Unité monétaire : million de markkas

J. COMMISSIONS / J. COMMISSIONS

J.1. Life / J.1. Vie

	1990	1991	1992	1993	1994	1995	1996	1997
J.1.1. Direct Business — J.1.1. Assurance directe								
J.1.1.1. Domestic Companies — J.1.1.1. Entreprises Nationales							158	177
J.1.1. Total — J.1.1. Total							158	177
J.1.2. Reinsurance Accepted — J.1.2. Réassurances acceptées								
J.1.2.1. Domestic Companies — J.1.2.1. Entreprises Nationales							1	20
J.1.2. Total — J.1.2. Total							1	20
J.1.3. Total — J.1.3. Total								
J.1.3.1. Domestic Companies — J.1.3.1. Entreprises Nationales							159	197
J.1.3. Total of Life Net Premiums — J.1.3. Total							159	197

J.2. Non-Life / J.2. Non-Vie

	1990	1991	1992	1993	1994	1995	1996	1997
J.2.1. Direct Business — J.2.1. Assurance directe								
J.2.1.1. Domestic Companies — J.2.1.1. Entreprises Nationales							170	111
J.2.1.3. Branches & Agencies of Foreign Cies — J.2.1.3. Succursales et Agences d'Ent. Etrangères							0	1
J.2.1. Total — J.2.1. Total des Primes Nettes Vie							170	112
J.2.2. Reinsurance Accepted — J.2.2. Réassurances acceptées								
J.2.2.1. Domestic Companies — J.2.2.1. Entreprises Nationales							243	189
J.2.2.3. Branches & Agencies of Foreign Cies — J.2.2.3. Succursales et Agences d'Ent. Etrangères							1	1
J.2.2. Total — J.2.2. Total							244	190
J.2.3. Total — J.2.3. Total								
J.2.3.1. Domestic Companies — J.2.3.1. Entreprises Nationales							413	300
J.2.3.3. Branches & Agencies of Foreign Cies — J.2.3.3. Succursales et Agences d'Ent. Etrangères							1	2
J.2.3. Total — J.2.3. Total							414	302

FRANCE

Monetary Unit: million French francs

Unité monétaire : million de francs français

	1990	1991	1992	1993	1994	1995	1996	1997
A. NUMBER OF COMPANIES IN THE REPORTING COUNTRY / **A. NOMBRE D'ENTREPRISES DANS LE PAYS DECLARANT**								
A.1. Life / **A.1. Vie**								
A.1.1. Domestic Companies / A.1.1. Entreprises Nationales	127	134	136	133	132	132	123	111
A.1.3. Branches & Agencies of Foreign Cies / A.1.3. Succursales et Agences d'Ent. Etrangères	14	14	11	10	6	5	5	5
A.1. All Companies / A.1. Ensemble des Entreprises	141	148	147	143	138	137	128	116
A.2. Non-Life / **A.2. Non-Vie**								
A.2.1. Domestic Companies / A.2.1. Entreprises Nationales	327	349	333	352	333	329	327	298
A.2.3. Branches & Agencies of Foreign Cies / A.2.3. Succursales et Agences d'Ent. Etrangères	136	140	134	114	23	16	16	14
A.2. All Companies / A.2. Ensemble des Entreprises	463	489	467	466	356	345	343	312
A.3. Composite / **A.3. Mixte**								
A.3.1. Domestic Companies / A.3.1. Entreprises Nationales	..	0	..	0	0	1	14	22
A.3. All Companies / A.3. Ensemble des Entreprises	..	0	..	..	0	1	14	22
A.4. Reinsurance / **A.4. Réassurance**								
A.4.1. Domestic Companies / A.4.1. Entreprises Nationales	20	20	20	21	20	21	22	26
A.4. All Companies / A.4. Ensemble des Entreprises	20	20	20	21	20	21	22	26
A.5. Total / **A.5. Total**								
A.5.1. Domestic Companies / A.5.1. Entreprises Nationales	474	503	489	506	485	483	486	457
A.5.3. Branches & Agencies of Foreign Cies / A.5.3. Succursales et Agences d'Ent. Etrangères	150	154	145	124	29	21	21	19
A.5. All Insurance Companies / A.5. Ensemble des Entreprises d'Assurances	624	657	634	630	514	504	507	476
B. NUMBER OF EMPLOYEES / **B. NOMBRE D'EMPLOYES**								
B.1. Insurance Companies / B.1. Entreprises d'Assurances	123 400	123 800	123 800	122 000	122 000	122 000	135 400	133 100
B.2. Intermediaries / B.2. Intermediaires	95 500	93 400	89 800	89 100	75 200	75 200	74 900	74 700
B. Total / B. Total	218 900	217 200	213 600	211 100	197 200	197 200	210 300	207 800
C. BUSINESS WRITTEN IN THE REPORTING COUNTRY / **C. OPERATIONS CONCLUES DANS LE PAYS DECLARANT**								
C.1. Life / **C.1. Vie**								
C.1.1. Gross Premiums / C.1.1. Primes Brutes								
C.1.1.1. Direct Business / C.1.1. Assurances Directes								
C.1.1.1.1. Domestic Companies / C.1.1.1.1. Entreprises Nationales	196 739	224 349	258 148	319 769	382 305	415 105	463 734	514 104
C.1.1.1.2. (Foreign Controlled Companies) / C.1.1.1.2. (Entreprises Sous Contrôle Etranger)	11 600	..	..	..	..	..	..	..
C.1.1.1.3. Branches & Agencies of Foreign Cies / C.1.1.1.3. Succursales et Agences d'Ent. Etrangères	4 288	4 757	5 303	5 328	4 037	4 311	4 902	4 991
C.1.1.1. Total / C.1.1.1. Total	201 027	229 106	263 451	325 097	386 342	419 416	468 636	519 095
C.1.1.2. Reinsurance Accepted / C.1.1.2. Réassurance Acceptée								
C.1.1.2.1. Domestic Companies / C.1.1.2.1. Entreprises Nationales	8 013	8 467	9 940	10 175	10 445	11 513	8 290	8 239
C.1.1.2.2. (Foreign Controlled Companies) / C.1.1.2.2. (Entreprises Sous Contrôle Etranger)	1 150	..	..	..	..	..	..	..
C.1.1.2.3. Branches & Agencies of Foreign Cies / C.1.1.2.3. Succursales et Agences d'Ent. Etrangères	1	1	9	197	211	0	16	42
C.1.1.2. Total / C.1.1.2. Total	8 014	8 468	9 949	10 372	10 656	11 513	8 306	8 281
C.1.1.3. Total / C.1.1.3. Total								
C.1.1.3.1. Domestic Companies / C.1.1.3.1. Entreprises Nationales	204 752	232 816	268 088	329 944	392 750	426 618	472 024	522 343
C.1.1.3.2. (Foreign Controlled Companies) / C.1.1.3.2. (Entreprises Sous Contrôle Etranger)	12 750	..	12 890	..	..	..	..	..
C.1.1.3.3. Branches & Agencies of Foreign Cies / C.1.1.3.3. Succursales et Agences d'Ent. Etrangères	4 289	4 758	5 312	5 525	4 248	4 311	4 918	5 033
C.1.1.3. Total Gross Premiums / C.1.1.3. Total des Primes Brutes	209 041	237 574	273 400	335 469	396 998	430 929	476 942	527 376
C.1.2. Ceded Premiums / C.1.2. Primes Cédées								
C.1.2.1. Domestic Companies / C.1.2.1. Entreprises Nationales	7 212	7 661	9 993	9 922	10 957	13 387	10 353	12 378
C.1.2.2. (Foreign Controlled Companies) / C.1.2.2. (Entreprises Sous Contrôle Etranger)	2 900	..	..	..	..	..	..	..
C.1.2.3. Branches & Agencies of Foreign Cies / C.1.2.3. Succursales et Agences d'Ent. Etrangères	207	216	295	389	327	388	406	392
C.1.2. Total / C.1.2. Total	7 419	7 877	10 288	10 311	11 284	13 775	10 759	12 770
C.1.3. Net Written Premiums / C.1.3. Primes Nettes Emises								
C.1.3.1. Domestic Companies / C.1.3.1. Entreprises Nationales	197 540	225 155	258 095	320 022	381 793	413 231	461 671	509 965
C.1.3.2. (Foreign Controlled Companies) / C.1.3.2. (Entreprises Sous Contrôle Etranger)	9 850	..	..	..	..	..	..	..
C.1.3.3. Branches & Agencies of Foreign Cies / C.1.3.3. Succursales et Agences d'Ent. Etrangères	4 082	4 542	5 017	5 136	3 921	3 923	4 512	4 641
C.1.3. Total / C.1.3. Total	201 622	229 697	263 112	325 158	385 714	417 154	466 183	514 606

FRANCE

Monetary Unit: million French francs

C.2. Non-Life

Label	1990	1991	1992	1993	1994	1995	1996	1997	(Non-Vie)
C.2.1. Gross premiums									**C.2.1. Primes Brutes**
C.2.1.1. Direct Business									C.2.1.1. Assurances Directes
C.2.1.1.1. Domestic Companies	175 347	184 070	197 163	208 698	221 450	234 048	242 630	242 440	C.2.1.1.1. Entreprises Nationales
C.2.1.1.2. (Foreign Controlled Companies)	23 300								C.2.1.1.2. (Entreprises Sous Contrôle Etranger)
C.2.1.1.3. Branches & Agencies of Foreign Cies	7 301	6 788	6 656	7 059	3 514	3 404	3 541	3 521	C.2.1.1.3. Succursales et Agences d'Ent. Etrangères
C.2.1.1. Total	182 648	190 858	203 819	215 757	224 964	237 452	246 171	245 961	C.2.1.1. Total
C.2.1.2. Reinsurance Accepted									C.2.1.2. Réassurance Acceptée
C.2.1.2.1. Domestic Companies	34 909	41 443	48 950	56 000	40 045	40 850	40 589	39 960	C.2.1.2.1. Entreprises Nationales
C.2.1.2.2. (Foreign Controlled Companies)	4 500								C.2.1.2.2. (Entreprises Sous Contrôle Etranger)
C.2.1.2.3. Branches & Agencies of Foreign Cies	308	335	298	365	70	77	54	29	C.2.1.2.3. Succursales et Agences d'Ent. Etrangères
C.2.1.2. Total	35 217	41 778	49 248	56 365	40 115	40 927	40 643	39 989	C.2.1.2. Total
C.2.1.3. Tota									C.2.1.3. Total
C.2.1.3.1. Domestic Companies	210 256	225 513	246 113	264 698	261 495	274 898	283 219	282 400	C.2.1.3.1. Entreprises Nationales
C.2.1.3.2. (Foreign Controlled Companies)	18 800								C.2.1.3.2. (Entreprises Sous Contrôle Etranger)
C.2.1.3.3. Branches & Agencies of Foreign Cies	7 609	7 123	6 954	7 424	3 584	3 481	3 595	3 550	C.2.1.3.3. Succursales et Agences d'Ent. Etrangères
C.2.1.3. Total Gross Premiums	217 865	232 636	253 067	272 122	265 079	278 379	286 814	285 950	C.2.1.3. Tota des Primes Brutes
C.2.2. Ceded Premiums									**C.2.2. Primes Cédées**
C.2.2.1. Domestic Companies	35 314	38 214	38 050	38 910	43 683	45 600	46 036	43 392	C.2.2.1. Entreprises Nationales
C.2.2.2. (Foreign Controlled Companies)	7 700								C.2.2.2. (Entreprises Sous Contrôle Etranger)
C.2.2.3. Branches & Agencies of Foreign Cies	2 091	1 924	1 984	2 315	645	451	489	513	C.2.2.3. Succursales et Agences d'Ent. Etrangères
C.2.2. Total	37 405	40 138	40 034	41 225	44 328	46 051	46 525	43 905	C.2.2. Total
C.2.3. Net Written Premiums									**C.2.3. Primes Nettes Emises**
C.2.3.1. Domestic Companies	174 942	187 299	208 063	225 788	217 812	229 298	237 183	239 008	C.2.3.1. Entreprises Nationales
C.2.3.2. (Foreign Controlled Companies)	11 100								C.2.3.2. (Entreprises Sous Contrôle Etranger)
C.2.3.3. Branches & Agencies of Foreign Cies	5 518	5 199	4 970	5 109	2 939	3 030	3 106	3 037	C.2.3.3. Succursales et Agences d'Ent. Etrangères
C.2.3. Total	180 460	192 498	213 033	230 897	220 751	232 328	240 289	242 045	C.2.3. Total

C.3. Total

Label	1990	1991	1992	1993	1994	1995	1996	1997	(Total)
C.3.1. Gross Premiums									**C.3.1. Primes Brutes**
C.3.1.1. Direct Business									C.3.1.1. Assurances Directes
C.3.1.1.1. Domestic Companies	372 086	408 419	455 311	528 467	603 755	649 153	706 364	756 544	C.3.1.1.1. Entreprises Nationales
C.3.1.1.2. (Foreign Controlled Companies)	34 900								C.3.1.1.2. (Entreprises Sous Contrôle Etranger)
C.3.1.1.3. Branches & Agencies of Foreign Cies	11 589	11 545	11 959	12 387	7 551	7 715	8 443	8 512	C.3.1.1.3. Succursales et Agences d'Ent. Etrangères
C.3.1.1. Total	383 675	419 964	467 270	540 854	611 306	656 868	714 807	765 056	C.3.1.1. Total
C.3.1.2. Reinsurance Accepted									C.3.1.2. Réassurance Acceptée
C.3.1.2.1. Domestic Companies	42 922	49 910	58 890	66 175	50 490	52 363	48 879	48 199	C.3.1.2.1. Entreprises Nationales
C.3.1.2.2. (Foreign Controlled Companies)	5 650								C.3.1.2.2. (Entreprises Sous Contrôle Etranger)
C.3.1.2.3. Branches & Agencies of Foreign Cies	309	336	307	562	281	77	70	71	C.3.1.2.3. Succursales et Agences d'Ent. Etrangères
C.3.1.2. Total	43 231	50 246	59 197	66 737	50 771	52 440	48 949	48 270	C.3.1.2. Total
C.3.1.3. Total									C.3.1.3. Total
C.3.1.3.1 Domestic Companies	415 008	458 329	514 201	594 642	654 245	701 516	755 243	804 743	C.3.1.3.1. Entreprises Nationales
C.3.1.3.2. (Foreign Controlled Companies)	31 550		52 210						C.3.1.3.2. (Entreprises Sous Contrôle Etranger)
C.3.1.3.3 Branches & Agencies of Foreign Cies	11 898	11 881	12 266	12 949	7 832	7 792	8 513	8 583	C.3.1.3.3. Succursales et Agences d'Ent. Etrangères
C.3.1.3. Total Gross Premiums	426 906	470 210	526 467	607 591	662 077	709 308	763 756	813 326	C.3.1.3. Total des Primes Brutes
C.3.2. Ceded Premiums									**C.3.2. Primes Cédées**
C.3.2.1. Domestic Companies	42 526	45 875	48 043	48 832	54 640	58 987	56 389	55 770	C.3.2.1. Entreprises Nationales
C.3.2.2. (Foreign Controlled Companies)	10 600								C.3.2.2. (Entreprises Sous Contrôle Etranger)
C.3.2.3. Branches & Agencies of Foreign Cies	2 298	2 140	2 279	2 704	972	839	895	905	C.3.2.3. Succursales et Agences d'Ent. Etrangères
C.3.2. Total	44 824	48 015	50 322	51 536	55 612	59 826	57 284	56 675	C.3.2. Total
C.3.3. Net Written Premiums									**C.3.3. Primes Nettes Emises**
C.3.3.1. Domestic Companies	372 482	412 454	466 158	545 810	599 605	642 529	698 854	748 973	C.3.3.1. Entreprises Nationales
C.3.3.2. (Foreign Controlled Companies)	20 950								C.3.3.2. (Entreprises Sous Contrôle Etranger)
C.3.3.3. Branches & Agencies of Foreign Cies	9 600	9 741	9 987	10 245	6 860	6 953	7 618	7 678	C.3.3.3. Succursales et Agences d'Ent. Etrangères
C.3.3. Total	382 082	422 195	476 145	556 055	606 465	649 482	706 472	756 651	C.3.3. Total

FRANCE

Monetary Unit: million French francs

Unité monétaire : million de francs français

E. BUSINESS WRITTEN ABROAD / E. OPERATIONS A L'ETRANGER

E.1. Life / E.1. Vie

Code	Item	1990	1991	1992	1993	1994	1995	1996	1997
E.1.1.	Gross Premiums / Primes Brutes								
E.1.1.1.	Direct Business / Assurance Directe								
E.1.1.1.1.	Branches & Agencies / Succursales & Agences	652	955	636	484	563	1 117	618	446
E.1.1.1.2.	Subsidiaries / Filliales	31 150	35 216	70 719	104 976	102 556	:	:	:
E.1.1.1.	Total / Total	31 802	36 171	71 355	105 460	103 119	:	:	:
E.1.1.2.	Reinsurance Accepted / Réassurance Acceptée								
E.1.1.2.1.	Branches & Agencies / Succursales & Agences	8	5	4	191	154	7	:	2
E.1.1.3.	Total / Total								
E.1.1.3.1.	Branches & Agencies / Succursales & Agences	660	960	640	675	717	1 124	620	448
E.1.2.	Ceded Premiums / Primes Cédées								
E.1.2.1.	Branches & Agencies / Succursales & Agences	52	49	56	46	32	37	43	12
E.1.3.	Net Written Premiums / Primes Nettes Emises								
E.1.3.1.	Branches & Agencies / Succursales & Agences	608	911	584	629	685	1 087	577	436

E.2. Non-Life / E.2. Non-Vie

Code	Item	1990	1991	1992	1993	1994	1995	1996	1997
E.2.1.	Gross Premiums / Primes Brutes								
E.2.1.1.	Direct Business / Assurance Directe								
E.2.1.1.1.	Branches & Agencies / Succursales & Agences	4 376	6 032	6 009	7 107	6 476	6 679	6 023	5 880
E.2.1.1.2.	Subsidiaries / Filliales	90 429	65 024	71 572	76 305	74 732	:	:	:
E.2.1.1.	Total / Total	94 805	71 056	77 581	83 412	81 208	:	:	:
E.2.1.2.	Reinsurance Accepted / Réassurance Acceptée								
E.2.1.2.1.	Branches & Agencies / Succursales & Agences	801	931	1 773	1 848	1 781	428	894	865
E.2.1.2.2.	Subsidiaries / Filliales	11 293	18 520	18 917	25 990	11 817	:	:	:
E.2.1.2.	Total / Total	12 094	19 451	20 690	27 838	13 598	:	:	:
E.2.1.3.	Total								
E.2.1.3.1.	Branches & Agencies / Succursales & Agences	5 177	6 963	7 782	8 955	8 257	7 107	6 917	6 745
E.2.1.3.2.	Subsidiaries / Filliales	101 722	83 544	90 489	102 295	86 549	:	:	:
E.2.1.3.	Total Gross Premiums / Total des Primes Brutes	106 899	90 507	98 271	111 250	94 806	:	:	:
E.2.2.	Ceded Premiums / Primes Cédées								
E.2.2.1.	Branches & Agencies / Succursales & Agences	2 706	3 154	3 428	3 782	3 596	3 527	3 653	3 777
E.2.3.	Net Written Premiums / Primes Nettes Emises								
E.2.3.1.	Branches & Agencies / Succursales & Agences	2 471	3 809	4 354	5 173	4 661	3 580	3 264	2 968

F. OUTSTANDING INVESTMENT BY DIRECT INSURANCE COMPANIES / F. ENCOURS DES PLACEMENTS DES ENTREPRISES D'ASSURANCES DIRECTES

F.1. Life / F.1. Vie

Code	Item	1990	1991	1992	1993	1994	1995	1996	1997
F.1.1.	Real Estate / Immobilier								
F.1.1.1.	Domestic Companies / Entreprises Nationales	102 898	130 423	137 324	150 215	151 878	:	:	:
F.1.1.3.	Branches & Agencies of Foreign Cies / Succursales et Agences d'Ent. Etrangères	2 662	3 582	3 930	4 081	2 332	:	:	:
F.1.1.4.	Domestic Investment / Placement dans le Pays	105 279	134 005	141 254	154 296	154 210	:	:	:
F.1.1.5.	Foreign Investment / Placement à l'Etranger	281	307	276	279	269	:	:	:
F.1.1.	Total / Total	105 560	134 312	141 530	154 575	154 479	142 933	142 338	128 580
F.1.2.	Mortgage Loans / Prêts Hypothécaires								
F.1.2.	Total / Total	:	:	:	:	:	4 310	3 967	1 898
F.1.3.	Shares / Actions								
F.1.3.1.	Domestic Companies / Entreprises Nationales	177 785	235 714	264 585	307 198	366 170	:	:	:
F.1.3.3.	Branches & Agencies of Foreign Cies / Succursales et Agences d'Ent. Etrangères	4 148	4 599	5 995	6 863	4 603	:	:	:
F.1.3.4.	Domestic Investment / Placement dans le Pays	181 327	240 313	270 580	314 061	370 773	:	:	:
F.1.3.5.	Foreign Investment / Placement à l'Etranger	606	699	668	933	1 718	:	:	:
F.1.3.	Total / Total	181 933	241 012	271 248	314 994	372 491	300 294	355 194	487 259

Monetary Unit: million French francs

Code	Description (EN)	Description (FR)	1990	1991	1992	1993	1994	1995	1996	1997
F.1.4.	Bonds with Fixed Revenue	Obligations								
F.1.4.1.	Domestic Companies	Entreprises Nationales	560 601	710 420	854 319	1 064 655	1 310 595	:	:	:
F.1.4.3.	Branches & Agencies of Foreign Cies	Succursales et Agences d'Ent. Etrangères	12 238	13 939	15 774	17 619	16 695	:	:	:
F.1.4.4.	Domestic Investment	Placement dans le Pays	570 843	724 359	870 093	1 082 274	1 327 290	:	:	:
F.1.4.5.	Foreign Investment	Placement à l'Etranger	1 996	1 443	1 616	3 195	6 486	:	:	:
F.1.4.	Total	Total	572 839	725 802	871 709	1 085 469	1 333 776	1 681 078	2 107 976	2 469 365
F.1.5.	Loans other than Mortgage Loans	Prêts Autres qu'Hypothécaires								
F.1.5.1.	Domestic Companies	Entreprises Nationales	70 457	32 714	44 206	58 506	56 544	:	:	:
F.1.5.3.	Branches & Agencies of Foreign Cies	Succursales et Agences d'Ent. Etrangères	1 010	555	689	629	331	:	:	:
F.1.5.4.	Domestic Investment	Placement dans le Pays	71 323	33 269	44 895	59 135	56 875	:	:	:
F.1.5.5.	Foreign Investment	Placement à l'Etranger	144	227	180	73	47	:	:	:
F.1.5.	Total	Total	71 467	33 496	45 075	59 208	56 922	44 153	57 472	63 552
F.1.6.	Other Investments	Autres Placements								
F.1.6.1.	Domestic Companies	Entreprises Nationales	42 160	56 653	62 027	78 316	82 456	:	:	:
F.1.6.3.	Branches & Agencies of Foreign Cies	Succursales et Agences d'Ent. Etrangères	655	1 055	1 156	918	1 097	:	:	:
F.1.6.4.	Domestic Investment	Placement dans le Pays	42 509	57 708	63 183	79 234	83 553	:	:	:
F.1.6.5.	Foreign Investment	Placement à l'Etranger	306	441	1 785	1 849	988	:	:	:
F.1.6.	Total	Total	42 815	58 149	64 968	81 083	84 541	52 305	55 935	54 582
F.1.7.	Total	Total								
F.1.7.1.	Domestic Companies	Entreprises Nationales	953 901	1 165 924	1 362 461	1 658 890	1 967 643	:	:	:
F.1.7.3.	Branches & Agencies of Foreign Cies	Succursales et Agences d'Ent. Etrangères	20 713	23 730	27 544	30 110	25 058	:	:	:
F.1.7.4.	Domestic Investment	Placement dans le Pays	971 281	1 189 654	1 390 005	1 689 000	1 992 700	:	:	:
F.1.7.5.	Foreign Investment	Placement à l'Etranger	3 333	3 117	4 525	6 329	9 508	:	:	:
F.1.7.	Total of Life Investments	Total des Placements Vie	974 614	1 192 771	1 394 530	1 695 329	2 002 208	2 225 073	2 722 882	3 206 236
F.2.	Non-Life	Non-Vie								
F.2.1.	Real Estate	Immobilier								
F.2.1.1.	Domestic Companies	Entreprises Nationales	54 542	58 782	68 189	71 553	79 663	:	:	:
F.2.1.3.	Branches & Agencies of Foreign Cies	Succursales et Agences d'Ent. Etrangères	1 487	1 738	1 772	1 811	1 348	:	:	:
F.2.1.4.	Domestic Investment	Placement dans le Pays	55 412	60 520	69 961	73 364	81 011	:	:	:
F.2.1.5.	Foreign Investment	Placement à l'Etranger	617	844	709	689	528	:	:	:
F.2.1.	Total	Total	56 029	61 364	70 670	74 053	81 539	66 133	65 221	64 317
F.2.2.	Mortgage Loans	Prêts Hypothécaires								
F.2.2.	Total	Total	:	:	:	:	:	1 014	886	593
F.2.3.	Shares	Actions								
F.2.3.1.	Domestic Companies	Entreprises Nationales	113 354	115 492	128 681	137 029	147 578	:	:	:
F.2.3.3.	Branches & Agencies of Foreign Cies	Succursales et Agences d'Ent. Etrangères	3 117	2 657	3 243	3 349	2 249	:	:	:
F.2.3.4.	Domestic Investment	Placement dans le Pays	113 558	118 149	131 924	140 378	149 827	:	:	:
F.2.3.5.	Foreign Investment	Placement à l'Etranger	2 913	2 652	3 285	4 252	3 980	:	:	:
F.2.3.	Total	Total	116 471	120 801	135 209	144 630	153 807	133 965	136 668	147 013
F.2.4.	Bonds with Fixed Revenue	Obligations								
F.2.4.1.	Domestic Companies	Entreprises Nationales	137 770	146 093	160 138	167 786	184 873	:	:	:
F.2.4.3.	Branches & Agencies of Foreign Cies	Succursales et Agences d'Ent. Etrangères	6 765	6 854	5 843	6 385	3 144	:	:	:
F.2.4.4.	Domestic Investment	Placement dans le Pays	141 846	152 947	165 981	174 171	188 017	:	:	:
F.2.4.5.	Foreign Investment	Placement à l'Etranger	2 689	3 126	3 373	3 908	3 934	:	:	:
F.2.4.	Total	Total	144 535	156 073	169 354	178 079	191 951	198 125	230 279	267 595
F.2.5.	Loans other than Mortgage Loans	Prêts Autres qu'Hypothécaires								
F.2.5.1.	Domestic Companies	Entreprises Nationales	15 034	9 804	13 509	12 522	10 462	:	:	:
F.2.5.3.	Branches & Agencies of Foreign Cies	Succursales et Agences d'Ent. Etrangères	336	467	356	291	100	:	:	:
F.2.5.4.	Domestic Investment	Placement dans le Pays	15 127	10 271	13 865	12 813	10 562	:	:	:
F.2.5.5.	Foreign Investment	Placement à l'Etranger	243	286	335	334	303	:	:	:
F.2.5.	Total	Total	15 370	10 557	14 200	13 147	10 865	9 671	11 418	12 486
F.2.6.	Other Investments	Autres Placements								
F.2.6.1.	Domestic Companies	Entreprises Nationales	36 583	40 320	44 778	50 476	51 088	:	:	:
F.2.6.3.	Branches & Agencies of Foreign Cies	Succursales et Agences d'Ent. Etrangères	631	648	550	686	391	:	:	:
F.2.6.4.	Domestic Investment	Placement dans le Pays	33 812	40 968	45 328	51 162	51 479	:	:	:
F.2.6.5.	Foreign Investment	Placement à l'Etranger	3 402	3 791	3 920	4 126	4 243	:	:	:
F.2.6.	Total	Total	37 214	44 677	49 246	55 288	55 722	29 407	35 203	30 234

FRANCE

Monetary Unit: million French francs

	1990	1991	1992	1993	1994	1995	1996	1997	
F.2.7. Total									**F.2.7. Total**
F.2.7.1. Domestic Companies	357 283	370 491	415 295	439 366	473 664	:	:	:	F.2.7.1. Entreprises Nationales
F.2.7.3. Branches & Agencies of Foreign Cies	12 336	12 364	11 764	12 522	7 232	:	:	:	F.2.7.3. Succursales et Agences d'Ent. Etrangères
F.2.7.4. Domestic Investment	359 755	382 855	427 057	451 888	480 896	:	:	:	F.2.7.4. Placement dans le Pays
F.2.7.5. Foreign Investment	9 864	10 699	11 622	13 309	12 988				F.2.7.5. Placement à l' Etranger
F.2.7. Total of Non-Life Investments	369 619	393 474	438 679	465 197	493 884	438 315	479 675	522 238	F.2.7. Total des Placements Non-Vie
G. BREAKDOWN OF NON-LIFE PREMIUMS									**G. VENTILATIONS DES PRIMES NON-VIE**
G.1. Motor vehicle									**G.1. Assurance Automobile**
G.1.1. Direct Business									G.1.1. Assurances Directes
G.1.1.1. Gross Premiums	69 436	71 508	73 489	77 714	82 494	89 212	92 340	92 444	G.1.1.1. Primes Brutes
G.1.1.2. Ceded Premiums	3 671	4 070	4 110	4 522	5 021	7 220	7 444	7 018	G.1.1.2. Primes Cédées
G.1.1.3. Net Written Premiums	65 765	67 438	69 379	73 192	77 473	81 992	84 896	85 426	G.1.1.3. Primes Nettes Emises
G.2. Marine, Aviation									**G.2. Marine, Aviation**
G.2.1. Direct Business									G.2.1. Assurances Directes
G.2.1.1. Gross Premiums	6 578	7 124	8 215	5 089	9 257	9 838	9 205	6 601	G.2.1.1. Primes Brutes
G.2.1.2. Ceded Premiums	3 261	3 530	4 152	4 353	4 538	4 926	4 628	3 499	G.2.1.2. Primes Cédées
G.2.1.3. Net Written Premiums	3 317	3 594	4 063	1 736	4 719	4 912	4 577	3 102	G.2.1.3. Primes Nettes Emises
G.3. Freight									**G.3. Fret**
G.3.1. Direct Business									G.3.1. Assurances Directes
G.3.1.1. Gross Premiums			3 119	3 142		:	:	2 227	G.3.1.1. Primes Brutes
G.3.1.2. Ceded Premiums						:	:	1 180	G.3.1.2. Primes Cédées
G.3.1.3. Net Written Premiums				3 142		:	:	1 047	G.3.1.3. Primes Nettes Emises
G.4. Fire, Property Damages									**G.4. Incendie, Dommages aux Biens**
G.4.1. Direct Business									G.4.1. Assurances Directes
G.4.1.1. Gross Premiums	45 218	46 277	53 076	56 480	57 568	61 995	65 040	65 337	G.4.1.1. Primes Brutes
G.4.1.2. Ceded Premiums	10 197	10 198	12 575	13 539	13 538	15 321	15 900	14 117	G.4.1.2. Primes Cédées
G.4.1.3. Net Written Premiums	35 021	36 079	40 501	42 941	44 030	46 674	49 140	51 220	G.4.1.3. Primes Nettes Emises
G.5. Pecuniary Losses									**G.5. Pertes Pécuniaires**
G.5.1. Direct Business									G.5.1. Assurances Directes
G.5.1.1. Gross Premiums	2 519	2 833		3 446		:	:	4 000	G.5.1.1. Primes Brutes
G.5.1.2. Ceded Premiums						:	:	1 836	G.5.1.2. Primes Cédées
G.5.1.3. Net Written Premiums				3 446		:	:	2 164	G.5.1.3. Primes Nettes Emises
G.6. General Liability									**G.6. Responsabilité Générale**
G.6.1. Direct Business									G.6.1. Assurances Directes
G.6.1.1. Gross Premiums	8 537	8 782	11 830	11 840	11 756	12 827	14 022	14 700	G.6.1.1. Primes Brutes
G.6.1.2. Ceded Premiums	1 276	1 278	1 657	1 947	1 795	2 137	2 409	2 586	G.6.1.2. Primes Cédées
G.6.1.3. Net Written Premiums	7 261	7 504	10 173	9 893	9 961	10 690	11 613	12 114	G.6.1.3. Primes Nettes Emises
G.7. Accident, Health									**G.7. Accident, Santé**
G.7.1. Direct Business									G.7.1. Assurances Directes
G.7.1.1. Gross Premiums	34 499	37 784	43 581	45 776	48 051	49 900	51 601	54 287	G.7.1.1. Primes Brutes
G.7.1.2. Ceded Premiums	4 185	4 891	4 877	5 416	6 092	7 120	7 362	7 155	G.7.1.2. Primes Cédées
G.7.1.3. Net Written Premiums	30 314	32 893	38 704	40 360	41 959	42 780	44 239	47 132	G.7.1.3. Primes Nettes Emises
G.8. Others									**G.8. Autres**
G.8.1. Direct Business									G.8.1. Assurances Directes
G.8.1.1. Gross Premiums	18 380	19 383	13 628	11 270	15 838	13 680	13 963	6 365	G.8.1.1. Primes Brutes
G.8.1.2. Ceded Premiums	4 415	4 913	3 210	3 179	3 204	2 735	2 541	924	G.8.1.2. Primes Cédées
G.8.1.3. Net Written Premiums	14 453	14 470	10 418	8 091	12 634	10 945	11 422	5 441	G.8.1.3. Primes Nettes Emises
G.9. Treaty Reinsurance									**G.9. Réassurance Obligatoire**
G.9.1. Direct Business									G.9.1. Assurances Directes
G.9.1.1. Gross Premiums	14 014	0	0	0	0	0	0	0	G.9.1.1. Primes Brutes
G.9.1.2. Ceded Premiums	2 840	0	0	0	0	0	0	0	G.9.1.2. Primes Cédées
G.9.1.3. Net Written Premiums	11 174	0	0	0	0	0	0	0	G.9.1.3. Primes Nettes Emises

FRANCE

Monetary Unit: million French francs — Unité monétaire : million de francs français

Code / Label (EN / FR)	1990	1991	1992	1993	1994	1995	1996	1997
G.10. Total								
G.10.1. Direct Business / Assurances Directes								
G.10.1.1. Gross Premiums / Primes Brutes	182 648	190 858	203 819	215 757	224 964	237 452	246 171	245 961
G.10.1.2. Ceded Premiums / Primes Cédées	27 005	28 881	30 581	32 956	34 188	39 459	40 284	38 315
G.10.1.3. Net Written Premiums / Primes Nettes Emises	155 643	161 977	173 238	182 801	190 776	197 993	205 887	207 646
G.10.2. Reinsurance Accepted / Réassurance Acceptée								
G.10.2.1. Gross Premiums / Primes Brutes	35 217	41 778	49 248	56 365	40 115	40 927	40 643	39 989
G.10.2.2. Ceded Premiums / Primes Cédées	10 400	11 257	9 453	8 269	10 140	6 592	6 241	5 590
G.10.2.3. Net Written Premiums / Primes Nettes Emises	24 817	30 521	39 795	48 096	29 975	34 335	34 402	34 399
G.10.3. Total								
G.10.3.1. Gross Premiums / Primes Brutes	217 865	232 636	253 067	272 122	265 079	278 379	286 814	385 950
G.10.3.2. Ceded Premiums / Primes Cédées	37 405	40 138	40 034	41 225	44 328	46 051	46 525	43 905
G.10.3.3. Net Written Premiums / Primes Nettes Emises	180 460	192 498	213 033	230 897	220 751	232 328	240 289	242 045
H. GROSS CLAIMS PAYMENTS / H. PAIEMENTS BRUTS DES SINISTRES								
H.1. Life / H.1. Vie								
H.1.1. Domestic Companies / Entreprises Nationales				137 381	162 694	191 744	193 424	206 066
H.1.3. Branches & Agencies of Foreign Cies / Succursales et Agences d'Ent. Etrangères				2 631	2 951	3 347	3 322	3 225
H.1. Total				140 012	165 645	195 091	196 746	209 291
H.2. Non-Life / H.2. Non-Vie								
H.2.1. Domestic Companies / Entreprises Nationales				184 368	187 835	193 781	196 692	206 832
H.2.3. Branches & Agencies of Foreign Cies / Succursales et Agences d'Ent. Etrangères				2 995	2 566	2 523	2 395	2 429
H.2. Total				187 363	190 401	196 304	199 087	209 261
I. GROSS OPERATING EXPENSES / I. DEPENSES BRUTES D'EXPLOITATION								
I.1. Life / I.1. Vie								
I.1.1. Domestic Companies / Entreprises Nationales				21 317	21 834	10 590	11 257	12 134
I.1.3. Branches & Agencies of Foreign Cies / Succursales et Agences d'Ent. Etrangères				560	464	254	254	255
I.1. Total / Total des Primes Nettes Vie				21 877	22 298	10 844	11 511	12 389
I.2. Non-Life / I.2. Non-Vie								
I.2.1. Domestic Companies / Entreprises Nationales				38 179	41 033	23 619	24 209	24 347
I.2.3. Branches & Agencies of Foreign Cies / Succursales et Agences d'Ent. Etrangères				927	817	362	372	285
I.2. Total				39 106	41 850	23 981	24 581	24 632
J. COMMISSIONS								
J.1. Life / J.1. Vie								
J.1.1. Direct Business / Assurance directe								
J.1.1.1. Domestic Companies / Entreprises Nationales				10 429	12 134	23 336	24 526	25 972
J.1.1.3. Branches & Agencies of Foreign Cies / Succursales et Agences d'Ent. Etrangères				119	264	358	340	363
J.1.1. Total				10 548	12 398	23 694	24 866	26 335
J.1.2. Reinsurance Accepted / Réassurances acceptées								
J.1.2.1. Domestic Companies / Entreprises Nationales				508	565	354	330	279
J.1.2.3. Branches & Agencies of Foreign Cies / Succursales e Agences d'Ent. Etrangères				35	32	..	..	..
J.1.2. Total				543	597	354	330	279
J.1.3. Total								
J.1.3.1. Domestic Companies / Entreprises Nationales				10 937	12 699	23 690	24 856	26 251
J.1.3.3. Branches & Agencies of Foreign Cies / Succursales e Agences d'Ent. Etrangères				154	296	358	340	363
J.1.3. Total of Life Net Premiums / Total				11 091	12 995	24 048	25 196	26 614

103

FRANCE

Monetary Unit: million French francs

Unité monétaire : million de francs français

J.2. Non-Life

J.2. Non-Vie

	1990	1991	1992	1993	1994	1995	1996	1997	
									J.2.1. Assurance directe
J.2.1. Direct Business									
J.2.1.1. Domestic Companies				25 506	26 395	29 441	31 180	32 559	J.2.1.1. Entreprises Nationales
J.2.1.3. Branches & Agencies of Foreign Cies				638	641	621	710	777	J.2.1.3. Succursales et Agences d'Ent. Etrangères
J.2.1. Total				26 144	27 036	30 062	31 890	33 336	J.2.1. Total des Primes Nettes Vie
J.2.2. Reinsurance Accepted									J.2.2. Réassurances acceptées
J.2.2.1. Domestic Companies				4 453	4 934	4 074	4 385	4 121	J.2.2.1. Entreprises Nationales
J.2.2.3. Branches & Agencies of Foreign Cies				7	19	3	5	3	J.2.2.3. Succursales et Agences d'Ent. Etrangères
J.2.2. Total				4 460	4 953	4 077	4 390	4 124	J.2.2. Total
J.2.3. Total									J.2.3. Total
J.2.3.1. Domestic Companies				29 959	31 329	33 515	35 565	36 680	J.2.3.1. Entreprises Nationales
J.2.3.3. Branches & Agencies of Foreign Cies				645	660	624	715	780	J.2.3.3. Succursales et Agences d'Ent. Etrangères
J.2.3. Total				30 604	31 989	34 139	36 280	37 460	J.2.3. Total

Monetary Unit: million deutschmarks — Unité monétaire : million de deutschemarks

A. NUMBER OF COMPANIES IN THE REPORTING COUNTRY — A. NOMBRE D'ENTREPRISES DANS LE PAYS DECLARANT

	1990	1991	1992	1993	1994	1995	1996	1997
A.1. Life — A.1. Vie								
A.1.1. Domestic Companies — A.1.1. Entreprises Nationales	332	336	321	321	315	319	316	315
A.1.2. (Foreign Controlled Companies) — A.1.2. (Entreprises Sous Contrôle Etranger)	20	20	20	19	16	16	16	16
A.1.3. Branches & Agencies of Foreign Cies — A.1.3. Succursales et Agences d'Ent. Etrangères	6	6	5	6	4	4	4	4
A.1. All Companies — A.1. Ensemble des Entreprises	338	342	326	327	319	323	320	319
A.2. Non-Life — A.2. Non-Vie								
A.2.1. Domestic Companies — A.2.1. Entreprises Nationales	322	331	333	332	324	327	325	323
A.2.2. (Foreign Controlled Companies) — A.2.2. (Entreprises Sous Contrôle Etranger)	38	38	38	39	29	29	29	29
A.2.3. Branches & Agencies of Foreign Cies — A.2.3. Succursales et Agences d'Ent. Etrangères	77	76	77	71	10	10	9	8
A.2. All Companies — A.2. Ensemble des Entreprises	399	407	410	403	334	337	334	331
A.4. Reinsurance — A.4. Réassurance								
A.4.1. Domestic Companies — A.4.1. Entreprises Nationales	29	28	31	32	32	36	36	36
A.4.2. (Foreign Controlled Companies) — A.4.2. (Entreprises Sous Contrôle Etranger)	6	5	5	5	5	7	8	8
A.4. All Companies — A.4. Ensemble des Entreprises	29	28	31	32	32	36	36	36
A.5. Total								
A.5.1. Domestic Companies — A.5.1. Entreprises Nationales	683	695	685	685	671	682	677	674
A.5.2. (Foreign Controlled Companies) — A.5.2. (Entreprises Sous Contrôle Etranger)	64	63	63	63	50	52	53	53
A.5.3. Branches & Agencies of Foreign Cies — A.5.3. Succursales et Agences d'Ent. Etrangères	83	82	82	77	14	14	13	12
A.5. All Insurance Companies — A.5. Ensemble des Entreprises d'Assurances	766	777	767	762	685	696	690	686

B. NUMBER OF EMPLOYEES — B. NOMBRE D'EMPLOYES

	1990	1991	1992	1993	1994	1995	1996	1997
B.1. Insurance Companies — B.1. Entreprises d'Assurances	218 573	253 905	255 149	254 484	250 561	234 653	223 199	215 273

C. BUSINESS WRITTEN IN THE REPORTING COUNTRY — C. OPERATIONS CONCLUES DANS LE PAYS DECLARANT

	1990	1991	1992	1993	1994	1995	1996	1997
C.1. Life — C.1. Vie								
C.1.1. Gross Premiums — C.1.1. Primes Brutes								
C.1.1.1. Direct Business — C.1.1.1. Assurances Directes								
C.1.1.1.1. Domestic Companies — C.1.1.1.1. Entreprises Nationales	58 106	65 413	70 429	77 499	84 882	90 106	95 344	99 864
C.1.1.1.2. (Foreign Controlled Companies) — C.1.1.1.2. (Entreprises Sous Contrôle Etranger)	5 572	6 279	..	..	..	..	..	..
C.1.1.1.3. Branches & Agencies of Foreign Cies — C.1.1.1.3. Succursales et Agences d'Ent. Etrangères	1 999	2 190	2 413	2 661	2 576	2 148	2 286	2 408
C.1.1.1. Total — C.1.1.1. Total	60 105	67 603	72 842	80 160	87 458	92 255	97 630	102 272
C.1.1.2. Reinsurance Accepted — C.1.1.2. Réassurance Acceptée								
C.1.1.2.1. Domestic Companies — C.1.1.2.1. Entreprises Nationales	267	303	7 731	8 456	9 784	10 297	11 054	12 418
C.1.1.2.2. (Foreign Controlled Companies) — C.1.1.2.2. (Entreprises Sous Contrôle Etranger)	2	0	0	0	0	0	0	0
C.1.1.2. Total — C.1.1.2. Total	269	303	7 731	8 456	9 784	10 297	11 054	12 418
C.1.1.3.1. Domestic Companies — C.1.1.3.1. Entreprises Nationales	58 373	65 716	78 160	85 955	94 666	100 403	106 398	112 283
C.1.1.3.2. (Foreign Controlled Companies) — C.1.1.3.2. (Entreprises Sous Contrôle Etranger)	5 572	6 279	6 794	7 383	6 957	7 227	6 931	7 428
C.1.1.3.3. Branches & Agencies of Foreign Cies — C.1.1.3.3. Succursales et Agences d'Ent. Etrangères	2 001	2 190	2 413	2 661	2 576	2 148	2 286	2 408
C.1.1.3. Total Gross Premiums — C.1.1.3. Total des Primes Brutes	60 374	67 906	80 573	88 616	97 242	102 552	108 684	114 690
C.1.2. Ceded Premiums — C.1.2. Primes Cédées								
C.1.2.1. Domestic Companies — C.1.2.1. Entreprises Nationales	5 058	5 980	7 074	7 167	7 611	7 720	8 563	8 930
C.1.2.2. (Foreign Controlled Companies) — C.1.2.2. (Entreprises Sous Contrôle Etranger)	..	..	..	..	..	556	558	591
C.1.2.3. Branches & Agencies of Foreign Cies — C.1.2.3. Succursales et Agences d'Ent. Etrangères	27	29	30	36	45	165	184	192
C.1.2. Total — C.1.2. Total	5 084	6 009	7 104	7 203	7 656	7 885	8 747	9 122
C.1.3. Net Written Premiums — C.1.3. Primes Nettes Emises								
C.1.3.1. Domestic Companies — C.1.3.1. Entreprises Nationales	53 315	59 736	71 086	78 788	87 055	92 683	97 835	103 352
C.1.3.2. (Foreign Controlled Companies) — C.1.3.2. (Entreprises Sous Contrôle Etranger)	5 572	6 279	..	..	..	6 672	6 373	6 837
C.1.3.3. Branches & Agencies of Foreign Cies — C.1.3.3. Succursales et Agences d'Ent. Etrangères	1 974	2 161	2 383	2 625	2 531	1 983	2 102	2 216
C.1.3. Total — C.1.3. Total	55 290	61 897	73 469	81 413	89 586	94 667	99 937	105 568

GERMANY

Monetary Unit: million deutschmarks

C.2. Non-Life / C.2. Non-Vie

C.2.1. Gross premiums / C.2.1. Primes Brutes

Item	1990	1991	1992	1993	1994	1995	1996	1997
C.2.1.1. Direct Business / Assurances Directes								
C.2.1.1.1. Domestic Companies / Entreprises Nationales	80 962	94 513	103 788	114 621	124 272	132 137	135 373	137 106
C.2.1.1.2. (Foreign Controlled Companies) / (Entreprises Sous Contrôle Etranger)	12 594	11 028						
C.2.1.1.3. Branches & Agencies of Foreign Cies / Succursales et Agences d'Ent. Etrangères	2 521	2 775	2 990	3 245	2 517	2 045	1 321	1 284
C.2.1.1. Total	83 483	97 288	106 778	117 866	126 789	134 182	136 694	138 389
C.2.1.2. Reinsurance Accepted / Réassurance Acceptée								
C.2.1.2.1. Domestic Companies / Entreprises Nationales	3 251	3 366	38 241	43 094	49 113	50 154	51 035	54 941
C.2.1.2.3. Branches & Agencies of Foreign Cies / Succursales et Agences d'Ent. Etrangères	250	280	304	321	177	0	0	0
C.2.1.2. Total	3 501	3 646	38 545	43 415	49 290	50 154	51 035	54 941
C.2.1.3. Total								
C.2.1.3.1. Domestic Companies / Entreprises Nationales	84 213	97 879	142 029	157 715	173 385	182 291	186 408	192 046
C.2.1.3.2. (Foreign Controlled Companies) / (Entreprises Sous Contrôle Etranger)	12 594	11 028		22 701	11 087	11 418	23 235	23 276
C.2.1.3.3. Branches & Agencies of Foreign Cies / Succursales et Agences d'Ent. Etrangères	2 771	3 055	3 294	3 566	2 694	2 045	1 321	1 284
C.2.1.3. Total Gross Premiums / Total des Primes Brutes	86 984	100 934	145 323	161 281	176 079	184 336	187 729	193 330
C.2.2. Ceded Premiums / Primes Cédées								
C.2.2.1. Domestic Companies / Entreprises Nationales	18 998	22 448	36 239	39 664	42 212	42 040	42 377	43 022
C.2.2.2. (Foreign Controlled Companies) / (Entreprises Sous Contrôle Etranger)						2 633	5 282	5 214
C.2.2.3. Branches & Agencies of Foreign Cies / Succursales et Agences d'Ent. Etrangères	586	619	804	824	273	472	300	288
C.2.2. Total	19 584	23 067	37 043	40 488	42 485	42 512	42 677	43 310
C.2.3. Net Written Premiums / Primes Nettes Emises								
C.2.3.1. Domestic Companies / Entreprises Nationales	65 215	75 431	105 790	118 051	131 173	140 251	144 031	149 024
C.2.3.2. (Foreign Controlled Companies) / (Entreprises Sous Contrôle Etranger)	12 594	11 028				8 785	17 953	18 061
C.2.3.3. Branches & Agencies of Foreign Cies / Succursales et Agences d'Ent. Etrangères	2 185	2 436	2 490	2 742	2 421	1 574	1 020	996
C.2.3. Total	67 400	77 867	108 280	120 793	133 594	141 824	145 052	150 020

C.3. Total / C.3. Total

C.3.1. Gross Premiums / C.3.1. Primes Brutes

Item	1990	1991	1992	1993	1994	1995	1996	1997
C.3.1.1. Direct Business / Assurances Directes								
C.3.1.1.1. Domestic Companies / Entreprises Nationales	139 068	159 926	174 217	192 120	209 154	222 243	230 717	236 970
C.3.1.1.2. (Foreign Controlled Companies) / (Entreprises Sous Contrôle Etranger)	18 166	17 307						
C.3.1.1.3. Branches & Agencies of Foreign Cies / Succursales et Agences d'Ent. Etrangères	4 520	4 965	5 403	5 906	5 093	4 193	3 607	3 692
C.3.1.1. Total	143 588	164 891	179 620	198 026	214 247	226 437	234 324	240 661
C.3.1.2. Reinsurance Accepted / Réassurance Acceptée								
C.3.1.2.1. Domestic Companies / Entreprises Nationales	3 518	3 669	45 972	51 550	58 897	60 451	62 089	67 359
C.3.1.2.3. Branches & Agencies of Foreign Cies / Succursales et Agences d'Ent. Etrangères	252	280	304	321	177	0	0	0
C.3.1.2. Total	3 770	3 949	46 276	51 871	59 074	60 451	62 089	67 359
C.3.1.3. Total								
C.3.1.3.1. Domestic Companies / Entreprises Nationales	142 586	163 595	220 189	243 670	268 051	282 694	292 806	304 329
C.3.1.3.2. (Foreign Controlled Companies) / (Entreprises Sous Contrôle Etranger)	18 166	17 307	24 225	30 084	18 044	18 645	30 166	30 704
C.3.1.3.3. Branches & Agencies of Foreign Cies / Succursales et Agences d'Ent. Etrangères	4 772	5 245	5 707	6 227	5 270	4 193	3 607	3 692
C.3.1.3. Total Gross Premiums / Total des Primes Brutes	147 358	168 840	225 896	249 897	273 321	286 888	296 413	308 020
C.3.2. Ceded Premiums / Primes Cédées								
C.3.2.1. Domestic Companies / Entreprises Nationales	24 056	28 428	43 313	46 831	49 823	49 760	50 940	51 952
C.3.2.2. (Foreign Controlled Companies) / (Entreprises Sous Contrôle Etranger)						3 189	5 840	5 805
C.3.2.3. Branches & Agencies of Foreign Cies / Succursales et Agences d'Ent. Etrangères	613	648	834	860	318	637	484	480
C.3.2. Total	24 668	29 076	44 147	47 691	50 141	50 397	51 424	52 432
C.3.3. Net Written Premiums / Primes Nettes Emises								
C.3.3.1. Domestic Companies / Entreprises Nationales	118 530	135 167	176 876	196 839	218 228	232 934	241 866	252 376
C.3.3.2. (Foreign Controlled Companies) / (Entreprises Sous Contrôle Etranger)	18 166	17 307				15 457	24 326	24 898
C.3.3.3. Branches & Agencies of Foreign Cies / Succursales et Agences d'Ent. Etrangères	4 159	4 597	4 873	5 367	4 952	3 557	3 122	3 212
C.3.3. Total	122 690	139 764	181 749	202 206	223 180	236 491	244 989	255 588

Monetary Unit: million deutschmarks — Unité monétaire : million de deutschemarks

D. NET WRITTEN PREMIUMS IN THE REPORTING COUNTRY IN TERMS OF DOMESTIC AND FOREIGN RISKS
D. PRIMES NETTES EMISES DANS LE PAYS DECLARANT EN RISQUES NATIONAUX ET ETRANGERS

D.1. Life — D.1. Vie

	1990	1991	1992	1993	1994	1995	1996	1997
D.1.1. Domestic Risks — D.1.1. Risques Nationaux								
D.1.1.1. Domestic Companies — D.1.1.1. Entreprises Nationales	..	..				90 038	94 585	99 037
D.1.1.2. (Foreign Controlled Companies) — D.1.1.2. (Entreprises Sous Contrôle Etranger)	..	..				6 481	6 161	6 552
D.1.1.3. Branches & Agencies of Foreign Cies — D.1.1.3. Succursales et Agences d'Ent. Etrangères	..	..				1 983	2 102	2 216
D.1.1. Total — D.1.1. Total des Primes Nettes Vie	55 232	61 818				92 021	96 687	101 254
D.1.2. Foreign Risks — D.1.2. Risques Etrangers								
D.1.2.1. Domestic Companies — D.1.2.1. Entreprises Nationales	..	..				2 645	3 251	4 315
D.1.2.2. (Foreign Controlled Companies) — D.1.2.2. (Entreprises Sous Contrôle Etranger)	..	..				190	212	285
D.1.2. Total — D.1.2. Total des Primes Nettes Vie	58	79				2 645	3 251	4 315
D.1.3. Total								
D.1.3.1. Domestic Companies — D.1.3.1. Entreprises Nationales				78 788		92 683	97 835	103 352
D.1.3.2. (Foreign Controlled Companies) — D.1.3.2. (Entreprises Sous Contrôle Etranger)						6 672	6 373	6 837
D.1.3.3. Branches & Agencies of Foreign Cies — D.1.3.3. Succursales et Agences d'Ent. Etrangères				2 625	2 531	1 983	2 102	2 216
D.1.3. Total of Life Net Premiums — D.1.3. Total des Primes Nettes Vie	55 290	61 897		81 413	89 586	94 667	99 937	105 568

D.2. Non-Life — D.2. Non-Vie

	1990	1991	1992	1993	1994	1995	1996	1997
D.2.1. Domestic Risks — D.2.1. Risques Nationaux								
D.2.1.1. Domestic Companies — D.2.1.1. Entreprises Nationales	..	..				126 235	129 647	131 553
D.2.1.2. (Foreign Controlled Companies) — D.2.1.2. (Entreprises Sous Contrôle Etranger)	..	..				7 907	16 160	15 944
D.2.1.3. Branches & Agencies of Foreign Cies — D.2.1.3. Succursales at Agences d'Ent. Etrangères	..	..				1 574	1 020	996
D.2.1. Total — D.2.1. Total des Primes Nettes Vie	66 389	76 906				127 808	130 667	132 550
D.2.2. Foreign Risks — D.2.2. Risques Etrangers								
D.2.2.1. Domestic Companies — D.2.2.1. Entreprises Nationales	..	..				14 016	14 384	17 470
D.2.2.2. (Foreign Controlled Companies) — D.2.2.2. (Entreprises Sous Contrôle Etranger)	..	..				878	1 793	2 117
D.2.2. Total — D.2.2. Total des Primes Nettes Vie	1 011	961				14 016	14 384	17 470
D.2.3. Total								
D.2.3.1. Domestic Companies — D.2.3.1. Entreprises Nationales				118 051	131 173	140 251	144 031	149 024
D.2.3.2. (Foreign Controlled Companies) — D.2.3.2. (Entreprises Sous Contrôle Etranger)						8 785	17 953	18 061
D.2.3.3. Branches & Agencies of Foreign Cies — D.2.3.3. Succursales et Agences d'Ent. Etrangères				2 742	2 421	1 574	1 020	996
D.2.3. Total — D.2.3. Total des Primes Nettes Vie	67 400	77 867		120 793	133 594	141 824	145 052	150 020

E. BUSINESS WRITTEN ABROAD — E. OPERATIONS A L'ETRANGER

E.1. Life — E.1. Vie

	1990	1991	1992	1993	1994	1995	1996	1997
E.1.1. Gross Premiums — E.1.1. Primes Brutes								
E.1.1.1. Direct Business — E.1.1.1. Assurance Directe								
E.1.1.1.1 Branches & Agencies — E.1.1.1.1. Succursales & Agences	58	79	97	105	1	1	4	10
E.1.1.1. Total — E.1.1.1. Total	..	..	..	..	..	..	..	..
E.1.1.3. Total — E.1.1.3. Total	58	79	97	105	1	1	4	10
E.1.1.3.1. Branches & Agencies — E.1.1.3.1. Succursales & Agences	..	..	..	..	..	..	..	..
E.1.1.3. Total Gross Premiums — E.1.1.3. Total ces Primes Brutes	..	..	..	..	..	..	..	..
E.1.2. Ceded Premiums — E.1.2. Primes Cédées								
E.1.2.1. Branches & Agencies — E.1.2.1. Succursales & Agences	..	..				0	0	1
E.1.3. Net Written Premiums — E.1.3. Primes Nettes Emises								
E.1.3.1. Branches & Agencies — E.1.3.1. Succursales & Agences	58	79				1	4	9
E.1.3. Total — E.1.3. Total	..	..	..	..	..	..	..	..

Monetary Unit: million deutschmarks — Unité monétaire : million de deutschemarks

E.2. Non-Life / E.2. Non-Vie

(EN)	1990	1991	1992	1993	1994	1995	1996	1997	(FR)
E.2.1. Gross Premiums									**E.2.1. Primes Brutes**
E.2.1.1. Direct Business									E.2.1.1. Assurance Directe
E.2.1.1.1. Branches & Agencies	:	:	:	:	:	:	:	:	E.2.1.1.1. Succursales & Agences
E.2.1.1. Total	1 011	961	894	1 022	1 148	1 042	1 168	1 367	E.2.1.1. Total
E.2.1.2. Reinsurance Accepted									E.2.1.2. Réassurance Acceptée
E.2.1.2.1. Branches & Agencies	:	:	14 994	17 815	21 954	0	0	0	E.2.1.2.1. Succursales & Agences
E.2.1.3. Total									E.2.1.3. Total
E.2.1.3.1. Branches & Agencies	:	:	15 888	18 837	23 102	:	:	:	E.2.1.3.1. Succursales & Agences
E.2.1.3. Total Gross Premiums	1 011	961				1 042	1 168	1 367	E.2.1.3. Total des Primes Brutes
E.2.2. Ceded Premiums									**E.2.2. Primes Cédées**
E.2.2.1. Branches & Agencies	:	:	:	:	:	240	266	306	E.2.2.1. Succursales & Agences
E.2.3. Net Written Premiums									**E.2.3. Primes Nettes Emises**
E.2.3.1. Branches & Agencies	:	:	:	:	:	:	:	:	E.2.3.1. Succursales & Agences
E.2.3. Total	1 011	961				802	903	1 061	E.2.3. Total

F. OUTSTANDING INVESTMENT BY DIRECT INSURANCE COMPANIES / F. ENCOURS DES PLACEMENTS DES ENTREPRISES D'ASSURANCES DIRECTES

F.1. Life / F.1. Vie

(EN)	1990	1991	1992	1993	1994	1995	1996	1997	(FR)
F.1.1. Real Estate									**F.1.1. Immobilier**
F.1.1.1. Domestic Companies	31 166	32 867	34 501	36 743	38 081	:	:	:	F.1.1.1. Entreprises Nationales
F.1.1.3. Branches & Agencies of Foreign Cies	672	728	789	808	795	:	:	:	F.1.1.3. Succursales et Agences d'Ent. Etrangères
F.1.1. Total	31 838	33 595	35 290	37 551	38 876	38 792	37 476	37 773	F.1.1. Total
F.1.2. Mortgage Loans									**F.1.2. Prêts Hypothécaires**
F.1.2.1. Domestic Companies	78 790	84 933	91 541	97 093	105 809	:	:	:	F.1.2.1. Entreprises Nationales
F.1.2.3. Branches & Agencies of Foreign Cies	1 640	1 744	1 830	1 874	1 985	:	:	:	F.1.2.3. Succursales et Agences d'Ent. Etrangères
F.1.2. Total	80 430	86 677	93 371	98 967	107 794	112 686	116 470	120 077	F.1.2. Total
F.1.3. Shares									**F.1.3. Actions**
F.1.3.1. Domestic Companies	19 748	23 005	27 123	29 399	33 832	:	:	:	F.1.3.1. Entreprises Nationales
F.1.3.3. Branches & Agencies of Foreign Cies	277	190	269	347	410	:	:	:	F.1.3.3. Succursales et Agences d'Ent. Etrangères
F.1.3. Total	20 026	23 196	27 392	29 746	34 242	37 193	43 409	54 934	F.1.3. Total
F.1.4. Bonds with Fixed Revenue									**F.1.4. Obligations**
F.1.4.1. Domestic Companies	69 733	82 650	91 562	102 739	103 263	:	:	:	F.1.4.1. Entreprises Nationales
F.1.4.3. Branches & Agencies of Foreign Cies	2 315	2 638	3 114	3 436	2 839	:	:	:	F.1.4.3. Succursales et Agences d'Ent. Etrangères
F.1.4. Total	72 048	85 288	94 676	106 175	106 102	112 074	112 540	114 141	F.1.4. Total
F.1.5. Loans other than Mortgage Loans									**F.1.5. Prêts Autres qu'Hypothécaires**
F.1.5.1. Domestic Companies	249 869	268 634	273 762	298 943	335 264	:	:	:	F.1.5.1. Entreprises Nationales
F.1.5.3. Branches & Agencies of Foreign Cies	7 597	8 186	8 701	9 706	10 938	:	:	:	F.1.5.3. Succursales et Agences d'Ent. Etrangères
F.1.5. Total	257 466	276 820	282 463	308 649	346 202	399 001	441 220	464 652	F.1.5. Total
F.1.6. Other Investments									**F.1.6. Autres Placements**
F.1.6.1. Domestic Companies	67 277	76 479	84 131	96 277	103 036	:	:	:	F.1.6.1. Entreprises Nationales
F.1.6.3. Branches & Agencies of Foreign Cies	1 652	2 109	2 397	2 745	3 328	:	:	:	F.1.6.3. Succursales et Agences d'Ent. Etrangères
F.1.6. Total	68 929	78 588	86 528	99 022	106 364	102 263	124 222	157 141	F.1.6. Total
F.1.7. Total									**F.1.7. Total**
F.1.7.1. Domestic Companies	516 582	568 569	602 620	661 794	719 285	:	:	:	F.1.7.1. Entreprises Nationales
F.1.7.3. Branches & Agencies of Foreign Cies	14 155	15 595	17 100	18 916	20 295	:	:	:	F.1.7.3. Succursales et Agences d'Ent. Etrangères
F.1.7. Total of Life Investments	530 737	584 164	619 720	680 100	739 580	802 009	875 337	948 718	F.1.7. Total des Placements Vie

Monetary Unit: million deutschmarks

Unité monétaire : million de deutschemarks

F.2. Non-Life / F.2. Non-Vie

Item	1990	1991	1992	1993	1994	1995	1996	1997	Intitulé
F.2.1. Real Estate									**F.2.1. Immobilier**
F.2.1.1. Domestic Companies	9 542	10 508	11 230	11 509	11 893	..	..	..	F.2.1.1. Entreprises Nationales
F.2.1.3. Branches & Agencies of Foreign Cies	411	497	550	539	553	..	..	..	F.2.1.3. Succursales et Agences d'Ent. Etrangères
F.2.1. Total	9 952	11 005	11 780	12 048	12 446	12 325	12 462	12 838	F.2.1. Total
F.2.2. Mortgage Loans									**F.2.2. Prêts Hypothécaires**
F.2.2.1. Domestic Companies	4 227	4 723	5 115	5 508	5 915	..	..	..	F.2.2.1. Entreprises Nationales
F.2.2.3. Branches & Agencies of Foreign Cies	52	63	82	80	77	..	..	..	F.2.2.3. Succursales et Agences d'Ent. Etrangères
F.2.2. Total	4 281	4 786	5 197	5 588	5 992	6 328	6 412	6 623	F.2.2. Total
F.2.3. Shares									**F.2.3. Actions**
F.2.3.1. Domestic Companies	12 371	14 106	15 790	17 219	20 256	..	..	..	F.2.3.1. Entreprises Nationales
F.2.3.3. Branches & Agencies of Foreign Cies	327	311	339	381	361	..	..	..	F.2.3.3. Succursales et Agences d'Ent. Etrangères
F.2.3. Total	12 697	14 417	16 129	17 600	20 617	25 633	30 282	34 170	F.2.3. Total
F.2.4. Bonds with Fixed Revenue									**F.2.4. Obligations**
F.2.4.1. Domestic Companies	24 511	27 132	31 690	34 874	38 006	..	..	..	F.2.4.1. Entreprises Nationales
F.2.4.3. Branches & Agencies of Foreign Cies	1 056	1 099	1 210	1 375	884	..	..	..	F.2.4.3. Succursales et Agences d'Ent. Etrangères
F.2.4. Total	25 567	28 231	32 900	36 249	38 890	41 084	41 690	41 546	F.2.4. Total
F.2.5. Loans other than Mortgage Loans									**F.2.5. Prêts Autres qu'Hypthécaires**
F.2.5.1. Domestic Companies	55 340	59 215	61 364	68 328	79 267	..	..	..	F.2.5.1. Entreprises Nationales
F.2.5.3. Branches & Agencies of Foreign Cies	1 100	1 108	1 180	1 165	1 366	..	..	..	F.2.5.3. Succursales et Agences d'Ent. Etrangères
F.2.5. Total	56 439	60 323	62 544	69 493	80 633	96 456	110 619	120 330	F.2.5. Total
F.2.6. Other Investments									**F.2.6. Autres Placements**
F.2.6.1. Domestic Companies	18 024	21 837	24 325	28 110	31 534	..	..	..	F.2.6.1. Entreprises Nationales
F.2.6.3. Branches & Agencies of Foreign Cies	396	466	585	672	570	..	..	..	F.2.6.3. Succursales et Agences d'Ent. Etrangères
F.2.6. Total	18 420	22 302	24 910	28 782	32 104	34 537	40 890	50 383	F.2.6. Total
F.2.7. Total									**F.2.7. Total**
F.2.7.1. Domestic Companies	124 015	137 521	149 514	165 548	186 871	..	..	..	F.2.7.1. Entreprises Nationales
F.2.7.3. Branches & Agencies of Foreign Cies	3 342	3 543	3 946	4 212	3 811	..	..	..	F.2.7.3. Succursales et Agences d'Ent. Etrangères
F.2.7. Total of Non-Life Investments	127 357	141 064	153 460	169 760	190 682	216 363	242 355	265 890	F.2.7. Total des Placements Non-Vie

G. BREAKDOWN OF NON-LIFE PREMIUMS / G. VENTILATIONS DES PRIMES NON-VIE

Item	1990	1991	1992	1993	1994	1995	1996	1997	Intitulé
G.1. Motor vehicle									**G.1. Assurance Automobile**
G.1.1. Direct Business									**G.1.1. Assurances Directes**
G.1.1.1. Gross Premiums	27 111	31 929	35 446	38 766	43 186	44 378	42 782	40 908	G.1.1.1. Primes Brutes
G.1.1.2. Ceded Premiums	7 234	8 475	9 468	10 468	11 289	11 503	10 909	10 247	G.1.1.2. Primes Cédées
G.1.1.3. Net Written Premiums	19 877	23 454	25 978	28 298	31 897	32 875	31 873	30 661	G.1.1.3. Primes Nettes Emises
G.1.2. Reinsurance Accepted									**G.1.2. Réassurance Acceptée**
G.1.2.1. Gross Premiums	969	1 055	11 108	12 365	13 934	14 190	13 791	13 978	G.1.2.1. Primes Brutes
G.1.2.2. Ceded Premiums	251	355	3 337	3 536	3 904	3 818	4 024	4 050	G.1.2.2. Primes Cédées
G.1.2.3. Net Written Premiums	718	700	7 771	8 829	10 030	10 372	9 767	9 928	G.1.2.3. Primes Nettes Emises
G.1.3. Total									**G.1.3. Total**
G.1.3.1. Gross Premiums	28 080	32 984	46 554	51 131	57 120	58 568	56 574	54 885	G.1.3.1. Primes Brutes
G.1.3.2. Ceded Premiums	7 485	8 830	12 805	14 004	15 193	15 321	14 934	14 297	G.1.3.2. Primes Cédées
G.1.3.3. Net Written Premiums	20 595	24 154	33 749	37 127	41 927	43 246	41 640	40 589	G.1.3.3. Primes Nettes Emises

GERMANY

Monetary Unit: million deutschmarks — Unité monétaire : million de deutschemarks

	1990	1991	1992	1993	1994	1995	1996	1997
G.2. Marine, Aviation								
G.2.1. Direct Business								
G.2.1.1. Gross Premiums	2 034	2 413	2 734	2 984	2 882	2 827	2 904	2 980
G.2.1.2. Ceded Premiums	865	1 057	1 213	1 345	1 279	1 227	1 219	1 209
G.2.1.3. Net Written Premiums	1 169	1 356	1 521	1 639	1 603	1 599	1 685	1 771
G.2.2. Reinsurance Accepted								
G.2.2.1. Gross Premiums	242	218	2 140	2 971	3 612	3 674	3 767	4 643
G.2.2.2. Ceded Premiums	85	72	657	852	873	768	784	1 130
G.2.2.3. Net Written Premiums	157	146	1 483	2 119	2 739	2 905	2 983	3 514
G.2.3. Total								
G.2.3.1. Gross Premiums	2 276	2 631	4 874	5 955	6 494	6 500	6 672	7 623
G.2.3.2. Ceded Premiums	950	1 129	1 870	2 197	2 152	1 996	2 004	2 339
G.2.3.3. Net Written Premiums	1 326	1 502	3 004	3 758	4 342	4 505	4 668	5 284
G.4. Fire, Property Damages								
G.4.1. Direct Business								
G.4.1.1. Gross Premiums	18 036	21 720	23 745	26 579	27 486	26 479	27 155	27 519
G.4.1.2. Ceded Premiums	6 212	7 612	8 211	9 014	9 260	8 420	8 460	8 199
G.4.1.3. Net Written Premiums	11 824	14 108	15 534	17 565	18 226	18 059	18 695	19 320
G.4.2. Reinsurance Accepted								
G.4.2.1. Gross Premiums	1 659	1 704	16 116	18 107	20 798	19 381	20 167	21 322
G.4.2.2. Ceded Premiums	653	595	5 649	6 085	6 428	5 750	5 789	6 170
G.4.2.3. Net Written Premiums	1 006	1 109	10 467	12 022	14 370	13 631	14 378	15 152
G.4.3. Total								
G.4.3.1. Gross Premiums	19 695	23 424	39 861	44 686	48 284	45 860	47 323	48 841
G.4.3.2. Ceded Premiums	6 865	8 207	13 859	15 099	15 688	14 170	14 249	14 369
G.4.3.3. Net Written Premiums	12 830	15 217	26 002	29 587	32 596	31 690	33 073	34 472
G.5. Pecuniary Losses								
G.5.1. Direct Business								
G.5.1.1. Gross Premiums	1 217	1 202	1 211	1 306	1 322	2 854	2 934	2 972
G.5.1.2. Ceded Premiums	812	820	865	939	968	2 116	2 148	2 168
G.5.1.3. Net Written Premiums	405	382	346	367	354	738	787	805
G.5.2. Reinsurance Accepted								
G.5.2.1. Gross Premiums	96	99	1 230	1 380	1 505	2 760	2 895	3 196
G.5.2.2. Ceded Premiums	17	13	162	181	202	618	587	699
G.5.2.3. Net Written Premiums	79	86	1 068	1 199	1 303	2 143	2 308	2 497
G.5.3. Total								
G.5.3.1. Gross Premiums	1 313	1 301	2 441	2 686	2 827	5 615	5 830	6 168
G.5.3.2. Ceded Premiums	829	833	1 027	1 120	1 170	2 734	2 735	2 866
G.5.3.3. Net Written Premiums	484	468	1 414	1 566	1 657	2 881	3 095	3 302
G.6. General Liability								
G.6.1. Direct Business								
G.6.1.1. Gross Premiums	7 067	8 517	9 221	10 124	10 901	11 416	11 862	12 280
G.6.1.2. Ceded Premiums	2 238	2 649	2 928	3 230	3 350	3 410	3 406	3 508
G.6.1.3. Net Written Premiums	4 829	5 868	6 293	6 894	7 551	8 006	8 456	8 772
G.6.2. Reinsurance Accepted								
G.6.2.1. Gross Premiums	257	272	4 557	4 954	5 550	5 845	5 642	6 039
G.6.2.2. Ceded Premiums	81	81	1 229	1 286	1 325	1 166	1 345	1 438
G.6.2.3. Net Written Premiums	176	191	3 328	3 668	4 225	4 678	4 296	4 601
G.6.3. Total								
G.6.3.1. Gross Premiums	7 324	8 789	13 778	15 078	16 451	17 260	17 504	18 319
G.6.3.2. Ceded Premiums	2 319	2 730	4 157	4 516	4 675	4 576	4 751	4 947
G.6.3.3. Net Written Premiums	5 005	6 059	9 621	10 562	11 776	12 684	12 752	13 372

French row labels (right margin):

- G.2. Marine, Aviation
  - G.2.1. Assurances Directes
    - G.2.1.1. Primes Brutes
    - G.2.1.2. Primes Cédées
    - G.2.1.3. Primes Nettes Emises
  - G.2.2. Réassurance Acceptée
    - G.2.2.1. Primes Brutes
    - G.2.2.2. Primes Cédées
    - G.2.2.3. Primes Nettes Emises
  - G.2.3. Total
    - G.2.3.1. Primes Brutes
    - G.2.3.2. Primes Cédées
    - G.2.3.3. Primes Nettes Emises
- G.4. Incendie, Dommages aux Biens
  - G.4.1. Assurances Directes
    - G.4.1.1. Primes Brutes
    - G.4.1.2. Primes Cédées
    - G.4.1.3. Primes Nettes Emises
  - G.4.2. Réassurance Acceptée
    - G.4.2.1. Primes Brutes
    - G.4.2.2. Primes Cédées
    - G.4.2.3. Primes Nettes Emises
  - G.4.3. Total
    - G.4.3.1. Primes Brutes
    - G.4.3.2. Primes Cédées
    - G.4.3.3. Primes Nettes Emises
- G.5. Pertes Pécuniaires
  - G.5.1. Assurances Directes
    - G.5.1.1. Primes Brutes
    - G.5.1.2. Primes Cédées
    - G.5.1.3. Primes Nettes Emises
  - G.5.2. Réassurance Acceptée
    - G.5.2.1. Primes Brutes
    - G.5.2.2. Primes Cédées
    - G.5.2.3. Primes Nettes Emises
  - G.5.3. Total
    - G.5.3.1. Primes Brutes
    - G.5.3.2. Primes Cédées
    - G.5.3.3. Primes Nettes Emises
- G.6. Responsabilité Générale
  - G.6.1. Assurances Directes
    - G.6.1.1. Primes Brutes
    - G.6.1.2. Primes Cédées
    - G.6.1.3. Primes Nettes Emises
  - G.6.2. Réassurance Acceptée
    - G.6.2.1. Primes Brutes
    - G.6.2.2. Primes Cédées
    - G.6.2.3. Primes Nettes Emises
  - G.6.3. Total
    - G.6.3.1. Primes Brutes
    - G.6.3.2. Primes Cédées
    - G.6.3.3. Primes Nettes Emises

GERMANY

Monetary Unit: million deutschmarks — Unité monétaire : million de deutschemarks

	1990	1991	1992	1993	1994	1995	1996	1997	
G.7. Accident, Health									G.7. Accident, Santé
G.7.1. Direct Business									G.7.1. Assurances Directes
G.7.1.1 Gross Premiums	24 738	27 933	30 594	34 039	36 759	41 287	43 833	46 223	G.7.1.1. Primes Brutes
G.7.1.2 Ceded Premiums	1 787	1 990	2 141	2 293	2 335	2 370	2 535	2 681	G.7.1.2. Primes Cédées
G.7.1.3 Net Written Premiums	22 951	25 943	28 453	31 746	34 424	38 917	41 298	43 542	G.7.1.3. Primes Nettes Emises
G.7.2. Reinsurance Accepted									G.7.2. Réassurance Acceptée
G.7.2.1 Gross Premiums	108	136	2 842	3 067	3 287	3 546	3 954	4 863	G.7.2.1. Primes Brutes
G.7.2.2 Ceded Premiums	11	20	618	675	677	619	676	930	G.7.2.2. Primes Cédées
G.7.2.3 Net Written Premiums	97	116	2 224	2 392	2 610	2 927	3 278	3 933	G.7.2.3. Primes Nettes Emises
G.7.3. Total									G.7.3. Total
G.7.3.1 Gross Premiums	24 846	28 069	33 436	37 106	40 046	44 833	47 787	51 086	G.7.3.1. Primes Brutes
G.7.3.2 Ceded Premiums	1 798	2 010	2 759	2 968	3 012	2 989	3 211	3 611	G.7.3.2. Primes Cédées
G.7.3.3 Net Written Premiums	23 048	26 059	30 677	34 138	37 034	41 844	44 576	47 475	G.7.3.3. Primes Nettes Emises
G.8. Others									G.8. Autres
G.8.1. Direct Business									G.8.1. Assurances Directes
G.8.1.1 Gross Premiums	3 281	3 575	3 827	4 067	4 253	4 942	5 223	5 508	G.8.1.1. Primes Brutes
G.8.1.2 Ceded Premiums	436	465	499	519	525	623	657	688	G.8.1.2. Primes Cédées
G.8.1.3 Net Written Premiums	2 845	3 110	3 328	3 550	3 728	4 319	4 566	4 819	G.8.1.3. Primes Nettes Emises
G.8.2. Reinsurance Accepted									G.8.2. Réassurance Acceptée
G.8.2.1 Gross Premiums	170	162	552	570	604	758	818	900	G.8.2.1. Primes Brutes
G.8.2.2 Ceded Premiums	9	10	65	65	71	102	136	193	G.8.2.2. Primes Cédées
G.8.2.3 Net Written Premiums	161	152	487	505	533	657	681	707	G.8.2.3. Primes Nettes Emises
G.8.3. Total									G.8.3. Total
G.8.3.1 Gross Premiums	3 451	3 737	4 379	4 637	4 857	5 700	6 041	6 408	G.8.3.1. Primes Brutes
G.8.3.2 Ceded Premiums	445	475	564	584	596	725	793	881	G.8.3.2. Primes Cédées
G.8.3.3 Net Written Premiums	3 006	3 262	3 815	4 055	4 261	4 975	5 247	5 526	G.8.3.3. Primes Nettes Emises
G.10. Total									G.10. Total
G.10.1. Direct Business									G.10.1. Assurances Directes
G.10.1.1 Gross Premiums	83 483	97 288	106 778	117 866	126 789	134 182	136 694	138 389	G.10.1.1. Primes Brutes
G.10.1.2 Ceded Premiums	19 585	23 067	25 325	27 808	29 006	29 670	29 335	28 700	G.10.1.2. Primes Cédées
G.10.1.3 Net Written Premiums	63 898	74 222	81 453	90 059	97 783	104 512	107 359	109 689	G.10.1.3. Primes Nettes Emises
G.10.2. Reinsurance Accepted									G.10.2. Réassurance Acceptée
G.10.2.1 Gross Premiums	3 501	3 646	38 545	43 415	49 290	50 154	51 035	54 941	G.10.2.1. Primes Brutes
G.10.2.2 Ceded Premiums	1 107	1 147	11 717	12 680	13 480	12 842	13 343	14 610	G.10.2.2. Primes Cédées
G.10.2.3 Net Written Premiums	2 394	2 499	26 828	30 734	35 810	37 312	37 692	40 331	G.10.2.3. Primes Nettes Emises
G.10.3. Total									G.10.3. Total
G.10.3.1 Gross Premiums	86 984	100 934	145 323	161 281	176 079	184 336	187 729	193 330	G.10.3.1. Primes Brutes
G.10.3.2 Ceded Premiums	20 692	24 214	37 043	40 488	42 485	42 512	42 677	43 310	G.10.3.2. Primes Cédées
G.10.3.3 Net Written Premiums	66 292	76 720	108 281	120 793	133 594	141 824	145 052	150 020	G.10.3.3. Primes Nettes Emises
H. GROSS CLAIMS PAYMENTS									**H. PAIEMENTS BRUTS DES SINISTRES**
H.1. Life									**H.1. Vie**
H.1.1. Domestic Companies				45 594	51 553	57 514	62 220	69 157	H.1.1. Entreprises Nationales
H.1.2. (Foreign Controlled Companies)				3 916	3 789	4 140	4 053	4 575	H.1.2. (Entreprises Sous Contrôle Etranger)
H.1.3. Branches & Agencies of Foreign Cies				1 412	1 403	1 230	1 337	1 483	H.1.3. Succursales et Agences d'Ent. Etrangères
H.1. Total				47 006	52 956	58 744	63 557	70 640	H.1. Total
H.2. Non-Life									**H.2. Non-Vie**
H.2.1. Domestic Companies				121 109	124 121	125 594	131 883	136 338	H.2.1. Entreprises Nationales
H.2.2. (Foreign Controlled Companies)				17 432	7 937	7 867	16 439	16 524	H.2.2. (Entreprises Sous Contrôle Etranger)
H.2.3. Branches & Agencies of Foreign Cies				2 738	1 929	1 409	934	911	H.2.3. Succursales et Agences d'Ent. Etrangères
H.2. Total				123 848	126 050	127 003	132 817	137 249	H.2. Total

Monetary Unit: million deutschmarks   Unité monétaire : million de deutschemarks

I. GROSS OPERATING EXPENSES / I. DEPENSES BRUTES D'EXPLOITATION

	1990	1991	1992	1993	1994	1995	1996	1997
I.1. Life / I.1. Vie								
I.1.1. Domestic Companies / Entreprises Nationales				17 139	17 876	17 041	17 831	18 535
I.1.2. (Foreign Controlled Companies) / (Entreprises Sous Contrôle Etranger)				1 472	1 314	1 227	1 162	1 226
I.1.3. Branches & Agencies of Foreign Cies / Succursales et Agences d'Ent. Etrangères				531	486	365	383	397
I.1. Total / Total des Primes Nettes Vie				17 670	18 363	17 405	18 214	18 933
I.2. Non-Life / I.2. Non-Vie								
I.2.1. Domestic Companies / Entreprises Nationales				37 158	38 340	41 440	42 723	45 317
I.2.2. (Foreign Controlled Companies) / (Entreprises Sous Contrôle Etranger)				5 348	2 452	2 596	5 325	5 492
I.2.3. Branches & Agencies of Foreign Cies / Succursales et Agences d'Ent. Etrangères				840	596	465	303	303
I.2. Total				37 998	38 936	41 905	43 026	45 620

J. COMMISSIONS

	1990	1991	1992	1993	1994	1995	1996	1997
J.1. Life / J.1. Vie								
J.1.1. Direct Business / Assurance directe								
J.1.1.1. Domestic Companies / Entreprises Nationales				6 810	7 216	6 561	7 125	7 160
J.1.1.3. Branches & Agencies of Foreign Cies / Succursales et Agences d'Ent. Etrangères				234	219	225	171	173
J.1.1. Total				7 044	7 435	6 786	7 296	7 333
J.1.2. Reinsurance Accepted / Réassurances acceptées								
J.1.2.1. Domestic Companies / Entreprises Nationales				2 673	2 940	2 390	2 634	3 257
J.1.2. Total				2 673	2 940	2 390	2 634	3 257
J.1.3. Total								
J.1.3.1. Domestic Companies / Entreprises Nationales				9 483	10 155	8 951	9 759	10 417
J.1.3.2. (Foreign Controlled Companies) / (Entreprises Sous Contrôle Etranger)				810	742	647	633	686
J.1.3.3. Branches & Agencies of Foreign Cies / Succursales et Agences d'Ent. Etrangères				234	219	225	171	173
J.1.3. Total of Life Net Premiums				9 717	10 374	9 176	9 930	10 590
J.2. Non-Life / J.2. Non-Vie								
J.2.1. Direct Business / Assurance directe								
J.2.1.1. Domestic Companies / Entreprises Nationales				12 179	12 889	12 867	13 410	13 950
J.2.1.3. Branches & Agencies of Foreign Cies / Succursales et Agences d'Ent. Etrangères				345	261	364	131	131
J.2.1. Total / Total des Primes Nettes Vie				12 523	13 150	13 231	13 541	14 080
J.2.2. Reinsurance Accepted / Réassurances acceptées								
J.2.2.1. Domestic Companies / Entreprises Nationales				11 923	11 974	11 431	11 943	13 145
J.2.2.3. Branches & Agencies of Foreign Cies / Succursales et Agences d'Ent. Etrangères				89	43	85	0	0
J.2.2. Total				12 012	12 017	11 516	11 943	13 145
J.2.3. Total								
J.2.3.1. Domestic Companies / Entreprises Nationales				24 102	24 863	24 297	25 353	27 094
J.2.3.2. (Foreign Controlled Companies) / (Entreprises Sous Contrôle Etranger)				3 453	1 585	1 533	3 154	3 278
J.2.3.3. Branches & Agencies of Foreign Cies / Succursales et Agences d'Ent. Etrangères				434	304	449	131	131
J.2.3. Total				24 536	25 167	24 747	25 484	27 225

Monetary Unit: million drachmas | Unité monétaire : million de drachmes

English Label	1990	1991	1992	1993	1994	1995	1996	1997	French Label
A. NUMBER OF COMPANIES IN THE REPORTING COUNTRY									**A. NOMBRE D'ENTREPRISES DANS LE PAYS DECLARANT**
A.1. Life									**A.1. Vie**
A.1.1. Domestic Companies	8	29	21	23	18	25	24	22	A.1.1. Entreprises Nationales
A.1.3. Branches & Agencies of Foreign Cies	3	5	4	1	2	2	3	2	A.1.3. Succursales et Agences d'Ent. Etrangères
A.1. All Companies	11	34	25	24	20	27	27	24	A.1. Ensemble des Entreprises
A.2. Non-Life									**A.2. Non-Vie**
A.2.1. Domestic Companies	39	59	60	59	57	67	64	58	A.2.1. Entreprises Nationales
A.2.3. Branches & Agencies of Foreign Cies	65	68	61	51	45	49	45	42	A.2.3. Succursales et Agences d'Ent. Etrangères
A.2. All Companies	104	125	121	110	102	116	109	100	A.2. Ensemble des Entreprises
A.3. Composite									**A.3. Mixte**
A.3.1. Domestic Companies	34	18	31	20	25	13	15	16	A.3.1. Entreprises Nationales
A.3.2. (Foreign Controlled Companies)	10	1	1	:	:	:	:	:	A.3.2. (Entreprises Sous Contrôle Etranger)
A.3.3. Branches & Agencies of Foreign Cies	1	1	1	1	1	1	1	1	A.3.3. Succursales et Agences d'Ent. Etrangères
A.3. All Companies	45	19	32	21	26	14	16	17	A.3. Ensemble des Entreprises
A.4. Reinsurance									**A.4. Réassurance**
A.4.1. Domestic Companies	1	:	:	0	0	0	0	0	A.4.1. Entreprises Nationales
A.4.3. Branches & Agencies of Foreign Cies	0	:	:	1	1	0	0	0	A.4.3. Succursales et Agences d'Ent. Etrangères
A.4. All Companies	1	:	:	1	1	0	0	0	A.4. Ensemble des Entreprises
A.5. Total									**A.5. Total**
A.5.1. Domestic Companies	82	106	112	102	100	105	103	96	A.5.1. Entreprises Nationales
A.5.2. (Foreign Controlled Companies)	10								A.5.2. (Entreprises Sous Contrôle Etranger)
A.5.3. Branches & Agencies of Foreign Cies	69	74	66	54	49	52	49	45	A.5.3. Succursales et Agences d'Ent. Etrangères
A.5. All Insurance Companies	161	180	178	156	149	157	152	141	A.5. Ensemble des Entreprises d'Assurances
B. NUMBER OF EMPLOYEES									**B. NOMBRE D'EMPLOYES**
B.1. Insurance Companies	9 500	9 300	10 000	8 500	9 596	9 600	:	:	B.1. Entreprises d'Assurances
B.2. Intermediaries	28 000	29 000	30 000	:	:	:	:	:	B.2. Intermediaires
B. Total	37 500	38 300	40 000	:	:	:	:	:	B. Total
C. BUSINESS WRITTEN IN THE REPORTING COUNTRY									**C. OPERATIONS CONCLUES DANS LE PAYS DECLARANT**
C.1. Life									**C.1. Vie**
C.1.1. Gross Premiums									C.1.1. Primes Brutes
C.1.1.1. Direct Business									C.1.1.1. Assurances Directes
C.1.1.1.1 Domestic Companies	:	:	100 927	123 494	144 111	159 337	183 692	257 025	C.1.1.1.1. Entreprises Nationales
C.1.1.1.3 Branches & Agencies of Foreign Cies	:	:	30 220	37 996	45 967	53 854	64 318	29 230	C.1.1.1.3. Succursales et Agences d'Ent. Etrangères
C.1.1.1. Total	:	:	131 147	161 490	190 078	213 192	248 010	286 255	C.1.1.1. Total
C.1.1.2. Reinsurance Accepted									C.1.1.2. Réassurance Acceptée
C.1.1.2.1 Domestic Companies	:	:	:	229	209	132	205	269	C.1.1.2.1. Entreprises Nationales
C.1.1.2.3 Branches & Agencies of Foreign Cies	:	:	:	0	0	:	200	:	C.1.1.2.3. Succursales et Agences d'Ent. Etrangères
C.1.1.2. Total	:	:	:	229	209	132	405	269	C.1.1.2. Total
C.1.1.3.1. Domestic Companies	:	:	100 927	123 723	144 320	159 470	183 897	257 294	C.1.1.3.1. Entreprises Nationales
C.1.1.3.3. Branches & Agencies of Foreign Cies	:	:	30 220	37 996	45 967	53 854	64 518	29 230	C.1.1.3.3. Succursales et Agences d'Ent. Etrangères
C.1.1.3. Total Gross Premiums	:	:	131 147	161 719	190 287	213 325	248 415	286 524	C.1.1.3. Total des Primes Brutes
C.1.2. Ceded Premiums									C.1.2. Primes Cédées
C.1.2.1. Domestic Companies	:	:	:	25 264	29 168	31 407	29 763	23 070	C.1.2.1. Entreprises Nationales
C.1.2.3. Branches & Agencies of Foreign Cies	:	:	:	515	435	565	786	795	C.1.2.3. Succursales et Agences d'Ent. Etrangères
C.1.2. Total	:	:	:	25 779	29 603	31 972	30 549	23 865	C.1.2. Total
C.1.3. Net Written Premiums									C.1.3. Primes Nettes Emises
C.1.3.1. Domestic Companies	:	:	100 927	98 459	115 152	128 063	154 134	234 224	C.1.3.1. Entreprises Nationales
C.1.3.3. Branches & Agencies of Foreign Cies	:	:	30 220	37 481	45 532	53 289	63 732	28 435	C.1.3.3. Succursales et Agences d'Ent. Etrangères
C.1.3. Total	70 559	98 847	131 147	135 940	160 684	181 353	217 866	262 659	C.1.3. Total

Monetary Unit: million drachmas

C.2. Non-Life / C.2. Non-Vie

Code / Label (EN)	1990	1991	1992	1993	1994	1995	1996	1997	Label (FR)
C.2.1. Gross premiums									**C.2.1. Primes Brutes**
C.2.1.1. Direct Business									C.2.1.1. Assurances Directes
C.2.1.1.1. Domestic Companies	..	..	121 249	153 159	175 235	200 772	239 409	261 174	C.2.1.1.1. Entreprises Nationales
C.2.1.1.3. Branches & Agencies of Foreign Cies	..	..	19 729	20 820	21 134	22 459	26 035	26 677	C.2.1.1.3. Succursales et Agences d'Ent. Etrangères
C.2.1.1. Total	..	..	140 978	173 979	196 369	223 231	265 444	287 851	C.2.1.1. Total
C.2.1.2. Reinsurance Accepted									C.2.1.2. Réassurance Acceptée
C.2.1.2.1. Domestic Companies	..	..	..	11 270	12 471	6 923	11 782	6 608	C.2.1.2.1. Entreprises Nationales
C.2.1.2.3. Branches & Agencies of Foreign Cies	..	..	..	2 284	1 854	2 359	2 288	3 891	C.2.1.2.3. Succursales et Agences d'Ent. Etrangères
C.2.1.2. Total	..	..	..	13 554	14 325	9 283	14 070	10 499	C.2.1.2. Total
C.2.1.3. Total									C.2.1.3. Total
C.2.1.3.1. Domestic Companies	..	..	121 249	164 429	187 706	207 695	251 191	267 782	C.2.1.3.1. Entreprises Nationales
C.2.1.3.3. Branches & Agencies of Foreign Cies	..	..	19 729	23 104	22 988	24 819	28 323	30 568	C.2.1.3.3. Succursales et Agences d'Ent. Etrangères
C.2.1.3. Total Gross Premiums	..	..	140 978	187 533	210 694	232 515	279 514	298 350	C.2.1.3. Total des Primes Brutes
C.2.2. Ceded Premiums									**C.2.2. Primes Cédées**
C.2.2.1. Domestic Companies	..	..	..	42 378	49 259	56 522	61 326	59 973	C.2.2.1. Entreprises Nationales
C.2.2.3. Branches & Agencies of Foreign Cies	..	..	..	7 254	7 143	5 584	7 931	8 979	C.2.2.3. Succursales et Agences d'Ent. Etrangères
C.2.2. Total	..	..	..	49 632	56 402	62 106	69 257	68 952	C.2.2. Total
C.2.3. Net Written Premiums									**C.2.3. Primes Nettes Emises**
C.2.3.1. Domestic Companies	..	..	..	122 051	138 447	151 173	189 865	207 809	C.2.3.1. Entreprises Nationales
C.2.3.3. Branches & Agencies of Foreign Cies	..	..	..	15 850	15 845	19 235	20 392	21 589	C.2.3.3. Succursales et Agences d'Ent. Etrangères
C.2.3. Total	98 248	115 079	140 978	137 901	154 292	170 409	210 257	229 398	C.2.3. Total

C.3. Total

Code / Label (EN)	1990	1991	1992	1993	1994	1995	1996	1997	Label (FR)
C.3.1. Gross Premiums									**C.3.1. Primes Brutes**
C.3.1.1. Direct Business									C.3.1.1. Assurances Directes
C.3.1.1.1. Domestic Companies	..	..	222 177	276 653	319 346	360 109	423 101	518 199	C.3.1.1.1. Entreprises Nationales
C.3.1.1.3. Branches & Agencies of Foreign Cies	..	..	49 948	58 816	67 101	76 313	90 353	55 907	C.3.1.1.3. Succursales et Agences d'Ent. Etrangères
C.3.1.1. Total	..	..	272 125	335 469	386 447	436 423	513 454	574 106	C.3.1.1. Total
C.3.1.2. Reinsurance Accepted									C.3.1.2. Réassurance Acceptée
C.3.1.2.1. Domestic Companies	..	..	..	11 499	12 680	7 055	11 987	6 877	C.3.1.2.1. Entreprises Nationales
C.3.1.2.3. Branches & Agencies of Foreign Cies	..	..	..	2 284	1 854	2 360	2 488	3 891	C.3.1.2.3. Succursales et Agences d'Ent. Etrangères
C.3.1.2. Total	..	..	..	13 783	14 534	9 415	14 475	10 768	C.3.1.2. Total
C.3.1.3. Total									C.3.1.3. Total
C.3.1.3.1. Domestic Companies	..	..	222 177	288 152	332 026	367 165	435 088	525 076	C.3.1.3.1. Entreprises Nationales
C.3.1.3.3. Branches & Agencies of Foreign Cies	..	..	49 948	61 100	68 955	78 673	92 841	59 798	C.3.1.3.3. Succursales et Agences d'Ent. Etrangères
C.3.1.3. Total Gross Premiums	..	..	272 125	349 252	400 981	445 840	527 929	584 874	C.3.1.3. Total des Primes Brutes
C.3.2. Ceded Premiums									**C.3.2. Primes Cédées**
C.3.2.1. Domestic Companies	..	..	..	67 642	78 427	87 929	91 089	83 043	C.3.2.1. Entreprises Nationales
C.3.2.3. Branches & Agencies of Foreign Cies	..	..	..	7 769	7 578	6 149	8 717	9 774	C.3.2.3. Succursales et Agences d'Ent. Etrangères
C.3.2. Total	..	..	..	75 411	86 005	94 078	99 806	92 817	C.3.2. Total
C.3.3. Net Written Premiums									**C.3.3. Primes Nettes Emises**
C.3.3.1. Domestic Companies	..	..	222 177	220 510	253 599	279 236	343 999	442 033	C.3.3.1. Entreprises Nationales
C.3.3.3. Branches & Agencies of Foreign Cies	..	..	49 948	53 331	61 377	72 524	84 124	50 024	C.3.3.3. Succursales et Agences d'Ent. Etrangères
C.3.3. Total	168 807	213 926	272 125	273 841	314 976	351 762	428 123	492 057	C.3.3. Total

D. NET WRITTEN PREMIUMS IN THE REPORTING COUNTRY IN TERMS OF DOMESTIC AND FOREIGN RISKS / D. PRIMES NETTES EMISES DANS LE PAYS DECLARANT EN RISQUES NATIONAUX ET ETRANGERS

D.1. Life / D.1. Vie

Code / Label (EN)	1990	1991	1992	1993	1994	1995	1996	1997	Label (FR)
D.1.1. Domestic Risks									D.1.1. Risques Nationaux
D.1.1.1. Domestic Companies	53 998	74 860	..	..	..	..	154 134	154 134	D.1.1.1. Entreprises Nationales
D.1.1.3. Branches & Agencies of Foreign Cies	16 561	23 987	..	..	..	..	63 732	63 732	D.1.1.3. Succursales et Agences d'Ent. Etrangères
D.1.1. Total	70 559	98 847	..	..	..	..	217 866	217 866	D.1.1. Total des Primes Nettes Vie
D.1.3. Total									D.1.3. Total
D.1.3.1. Domestic Companies	53 998	74 860	..	98 459	115 152	128 063	154 134	154 134	D.1.3.1. Entreprises Nationales
D.1.3.3. Branches & Agencies of Foreign Cies	16 561	23 987	..	37 481	45 532	53 289	63 732	63 732	D.1.3.3. Succursales et Agences d'Ent. Etrangères
D.1.3. Total of Life Net Premiums	70 559	98 847	..	135 940	160 684	181 353	217 866	217 866	D.1.3. Total des Primes Nettes Vie

Monetary Unit: million drachmas　　　　　　　　　　　　　　Unité monétaire : million de drachmes

D.2. Non-Life — D.2. Non-Vie

	1990	1991	1992	1993	1994	1995	1996	1997
D.2.1. Domestic Risks — D.2.1. Risques Nationaux								
D.2.1.1. Domestic Companies — D.2.1.1. Entreprises Nationales	81 779	93 338	:	:	:	:	189 865	
D.2.1.3. Branches & Agencies of Foreign Cies — D.2.1.3. Succursales et Agences d'Ent. Etrangères	16 469	21 740	:	:	:	:	20 392	
D.2.1. Tota — D.2.1. Total des Primes Nettes Vie	98 248	115 079	:	:	:	:	210 257	
D.2.3. Total								
D.2.3.1. Domestic Companies — D.2.3.1. Entreprises Nationales	81 779	93 338	:	122 051	138 447	151 173	189 865	
D.2.3.3. Branches & Agencies of Foreign Cies — D.2.3.3. Succursales et Agences d'Ent. Etrangères	16 469	21 740	:	15 850	15 845	19 235	20 392	
D.2.3. Total — D.2.3. Total des Primes Nettes Vie	98 248	115 079	:	137 901	154 292	170 409	210 257	

F. OUTSTANDING INVESTMENT BY DIRECT INSURANCE COMPANIES — F. ENCOURS DES PLACEMENTS DES ENTREPRISES D'ASSURANCES DIRECTES

F.1. Life — F.1. Vie

	1990	1991	1992	1993	1994	1995	1996	1997
F.1.1. Real Estate — F.1.1. Immobilier								
F.1.1.1. Domestic Companies — F.1.1.1. Entreprises Nationales	11 259	:	:	:	:	:	:	
F.1.1.3. Branches & Agencies of Foreign Cies — F.1.1.3. Succursales et Agences d'Ent. Etrangères	641	:	:	:	:	:	:	
F.1.1. Total	:	:	:	:	:	:	:	38 275
F.1.2. Mortgage Loans — F.1.2. Prêts Hypothécaires								
F.1.2.1. Domestic Companies — F.1.2.1. Entreprises Nationales	266	:	:	:	:	:	:	
F.1.2.3. Branches & Agencies of Foreign Cies — F.1.2.3. Succursales at Agences d'Ent. Etrangères	461	:	:	:	:	:	:	
F.1.2. Total	:	:	:	:	:	:	:	1 120
F.1.3. Shares — F.1.3. Actions								
F.1.3.1. Domestic Companies — F.1.3.1. Entreprises Nationales	4 630	:	:	:	:	:	:	
F.1.3.3. Branches & Agencies of Foreign Cies — F.1.3.3. Succursales at Agences d'Ent. Etrangères	26	:	:	:	:	:	:	
F.1.3. Total	:	:	:	:	:	:	:	104 832
F.1.4. Bonds with Fixed Revenue — F.1.4. Obligations								
F.1.4.1. Domestic Companies — F.1.4.1. Entreprises Nationales	20 839	:	:	:	:	:	:	
F.1.4.3. Branches & Agencies of Foreign Cies — F.1.4.3. Succursales et Agences d'Ent. Etrangères	30	:	:	:	:	:	:	
F.1.4. Total	:	:	:	:	:	:	:	261 280
F.1.5. Loans other than Mortgage Loans — F.1.5. Prêts Autres qu'Hypothécaires								
F.1.5.1. Domestic Companies — F.1.5.1. Entreprises Nationales	861	:	:	:	:	:	:	
F.1.5.3. Branches & Agencies of Foreign Cies — F.1.5.3. Succursales et Agences d'Ent. Etrangères	384	:	:	:	:	:	:	
F.1.5. Total	:	:	:	:	:	:	:	10 447
F.1.6. Other Investments — F.1.6. Autres Placements								
F.1.6. Total	:	:	:	:	:	:	:	32 960
F.1.7. Total								
F.1.7.1. Domestic Companies — F.1.7.1. Entreprises Nationales	37 855	:	:	:	:	:	:	
F.1.7.3. Branches & Agencies of Foreign Cies — F.1.7.3. Succursales et Agences d'Ent. Etrangères	1 542	:	:	:	:	:	:	
F.1.7. Total of Life Investments — F.1.7. Total des Placements Vie	:	:	:	:	:	:	:	448 914

F.2. Non-Life — F.2. Non-Vie

	1990	1991	1992	1993	1994	1995	1996	1997
F.2.1. Real Estate — F.2.1. Immobilier								
F.2.1.1. Domestic Companies — F.2.1.1. Entreprises Nationales	1 996	:	:	:	:	:	:	
F.2.1.3. Branches & Agencies of Foreign Cies — F.2.1.3. Succursales et Agences d'Ent. Etrangères	422	:	:	:	:	:	:	
F.2.1. Total	:	:	:	:	:	:	:	59 188
F.2.2. Mortgage Loans — F.2.2. Prêts Hypothécaires								
F.2.2.1. Domestic Companies — F.2.2.1. Entreprises Nationales	218	:	:	:	:	:	:	
F.2.2. Total	:	:	:	:	:	:	:	4 916
F.2.3. Shares — F.2.3. Actions								
F.2.3.1. Domestic Companies — F.2.3.1. Entreprises Nationales	369	:	:	:	:	:	:	
F.2.3.3. Branches & Agencies of Foreign Cies — F.2.3.3. Succursales et Agences d'Ent. Etrangères	90	:	:	:	:	:	:	
F.2.3. Total	:	:	:	:	:	:	:	108 928
F.2.4. Bonds with Fixed Revenue — F.2.4. Obligations								
F.2.4.1. Domestic Companies — F.2.4.1. Entreprises Nationales	6 411	:	:	:	:	:	:	
F.2.4.3. Branches & Agencies of Foreign Cies — F.2.4.3. Succursales et Agences d'Ent. Etrangères	70	:	:	:	:	:	:	
F.2.4. Total	:	:	:	:	:	:	:	340 580

Monetary Unit: million drachmas

Unité monétaire : million de drachmes

	1990	1991	1992	1993	1994	1995	1996	1997
F.2.5. Loans other than Mortgage Loans / F.2.5. Prêts Autres qu'Hypothécaires								
F.2.5. Total / F.2.5. Total	..	..	..	..	..	..	..	5 379
F.2.6. Other Investments / F.2.6. Autres Placements								
F.2.6. Total / F.2.6. Total	..	..	..	..	..	..	..	37 050
F.2.7. Total / F.2.7. Total								
F.2.7.1. Domestic Companies / F.2.7.1. Entreprises Nationales	8 995	..	..	..	..	..	..	..
F.2.7.3. Branches & Agencies of Foreign Cies / F.2.7.3. Succursales et Agences d'Ent. Etrangères	582	..	..	..	..	..	..	..
F.2.7. Total of Non-Life Investments / F.2.7. Total des Placements Non-Vie	..	..	..	..	..	..	..	556 041
G. BREAKDOWN OF NON-LIFE PREMIUMS / G. VENTILATIONS DES PRIMES NON-VIE								
G.1. Motor vehicle / G.1. Assurance Automobile								
G.1.1. Direct Business / G.1.1. Assurances Directes								
G.1.1.1. Gross Premiums / G.1.1.1. Primes Brutes	53 713	..	76 845	104 464	118 227	134 936	164 239	186 128
G.1.1.3. Net Written Premiums / G.1.1.3. Primes Nettes Emises	..	60 774						
G.1.2. Reinsurance Accepted / G.1.2. Réassurance Acceptée								
G.1.2.1. Gross Premiums / G.1.2.1. Primes Brutes	..	..	..	1 517	1 365	1 065	1 092	635
G.1.3. Total / G.1.3. Total								
G.1.3.1. Gross Premiums / G.1.3.1. Primes Brutes	53 713	..	..	105 981	119 592	136 001	165 331	186 763
G.1.3.3. Net Written Premiums / G.1.3.3. Primes Nettes Emises	..	60 774						
G.2. Marine, Aviation / G.2. Marine, Aviation								
G.2.1. Direct Business / G.2.1. Assurances Directes								
G.2.1.1. Gross Premiums / G.2.1.1. Primes Brutes	8 342	8 857	10 788	12 470	5 784	6 468	4 767	16 517
G.2.1.3. Net Written Premiums / G.2.1.3. Primes Nettes Emises								
G.2.2. Reinsurance Accepted / G.2.2. Réassurance Acceptée								
G.2.2.1. Gross Premiums / G.2.2.1. Primes Brutes	..	..	..	1 089	684	674	424	619
G.2.3. Total / G.2.3. Total								
G.2.3.1. Gross Premiums / G.2.3.1. Primes Brutes	8 342	8 857	..	13 559	6 468	7 142	5 191	17 136
G.2.3.3. Net Written Premiums / G.2.3.3. Primes Nettes Emises								
G.3. Freight / G.3. Fret								
G.3.1. Direct Business / G.3.1. Assurances Directes								
G.3.1.1. Gross Premiums / G.3.1.1. Primes Brutes			773	..	8 859	10 118	9 705	9 893
G.3.2. Reinsurance Accepted / G.3.2. Réassurance Acceptée								
G.3.2.1. Gross Premiums / G.3.2.1. Primes Brutes				..	535	603	480	687
G.3.3. Total / G.3.3. Total								
G.3.3.1. Gross Premiums / G.3.3.1. Primes Brutes				..	9 394	10 721	10 185	10 580
G.4. Fire, Property Damages / G.4. Incendie, Dommages aux Biens								
G.4.1. Direct Business / G.4.1. Assurances Directes								
G.4.1.1. Gross Premiums / G.4.1.1. Primes Brutes	29 928	34 984	32 122	33 570	36 268	38 190	53 066	41 482
G.4.1.3. Net Written Premiums / G.4.1.3. Primes Nettes Emises								
G.4.2. Reinsurance Accepted / G.4.2. Réassurance Acceptée								
G.4.2.1. Gross Premiums / G.4.2.1. Primes Brutes	..	..	..	3 332	4 070	3 063	3 828	3 836
G.4.3. Total / G.4.3. Total								
G.4.3.1. Gross Premiums / G.4.3.1. Primes Brutes	29 928	34 984	..	36 902	40 338	41 253	56 894	45 318
G.4.3.3. Net Written Premiums / G.4.3.3. Primes Nettes Emises								
G.5. Pecuniary Losses / G.5. Pertes Pécuniaires								
G.5.1. Direct Business / G.5.1. Assurances Directes								
G.5.1.1. Gross Premiums / G.5.1.1. Primes Brutes			72	..	..	..	1 980	1 475
G.5.2. Reinsurance Accepted / G.5.2. Réassurance Acceptée								
G.5.2.1. Gross Premiums / G.5.2.1. Primes Brutes				..	..	..	207	163
G.5.3. Total / G.5.3. Total								
G.5.3.1. Gross Premiums / G.5.3.1. Primes Brutes				..	..	..	2 187	1 638
G.6. General Liability / G.6. Responsabilité Générale								
G.6.1. Direct Business / G.6.1. Assurances Directes								
G.6.1.1. Gross Premiums / G.6.1.1. Primes Brutes	..	..	1 837	2 291	2 980	3 453	3 853	5 111
G.6.2. Reinsurance Accepted / G.6.2. Réassurance Acceptée								
G.6.2.1. Gross Premiums / G.6.2.1. Primes Brutes	..	..	..	126	177	134	218	313
G.6.3. Total / G.6.3. Total								
G.6.3.1. Gross Premiums / G.6.3.1. Primes Brutes	..	..	..	2 417	3 157	3 587	4 071	5 424

116

Monetary Unit: million drachmas Unité monétaire : million de drachmes

	1990	1991	1992	1993	1994	1995	1996	1997
G.7. Accident, Santé								
G.7.1. Assurances Directes								
G.7.1.1. Primes Brutes	6 265	12 442	7 032	8 653	9 932	11 245	11 962	13 439
G.7.1.3 Net Written Premiums / Primes Nettes Emises	::	::	::	::	::	::	::	::
G.7.2. Réassurance Acceptée								
G.7.2.1. Primes Brutes	::	::	::	2 381	2 514	2 664	2 538	3 704
G.7.3. Total								
G.7.3.1. Primes Brutes	6 265	12 442	::	11 034	12 446	13 909	14 500	17 143
G.7.3.3. Primes Nettes Emises	::	::	::	::	::	::	::	::
G.8. Autres								
G.8.1. Assurances Directes								
G.8.1.1. Primes Brutes	::	::	::	12 531	14 319	18 821	15 872	13 806
G.8.2. Réassurance Acceptée								
G.8.2.1. Primes Brutes	::	::	::	5 109	4 980	1 080	5 283	542
G.8.3. Total								
G.8.3.1. Primes Brutes	::	::	::	17 640	19 299	19 901	21 155	14 348
G.10. Total								
G.10.1. Assurances Directes								
G.10.1.1. Primes Brutes	98 248	117 057	129 469	173 979	196 369	223 231	265 444	287 851
G.10.1.3. Primes Nettes Emises	::	::	::	::	::	::	::	::
G.10.2. Réassurance Acceptée								
G.10.2.1. Primes Brutes	::	4 770	::	13 554	14 325	9 283	14 070	10 499
G.10.2.3 Primes Nettes Emises	::	::	::	::	::	::	::	::
G.10.3. Total								
G.10.3.1 Primes Brutes	::	::	::	187 533	210 694	232 514	279 514	298 350
G.10.3.2 Primes Cédées	::	::	::	49 632	56 402	::	::	::
G.10.3.3 Primes Nettes Emises	98 248	::	::	137 901	154 292	::	::	::
H. PAIEMENTS BRUTS DES SINISTRES								
H.1. Vie								
H.1.1. Entreprises Nationales							69 784	101 852
H.1.3. Succursales et Agences d'Ent. Etrangères							20 982	17 310
H.1. Total							90 766	119 162
H.2. Non-Vie								
H.2.1. Entreprises Nationales							148 109	160 246
H.2.3. Succursales et Agences d'Ent. Etrangères							13 667	16 240
H.2. Total							161 776	176 486
I. DEPENSES BRUTES D'EXPLOITATION								
I.1. Vie								
I.1.1. Entreprises Nationales							225 201	80 381
I.1.3. Succursales et Agences d'Ent. Etrangères							80 433	3 019
I.1. Total des Primes Nettes Vie							305 634	83 400
I.2. Non-Vie								
I.2.1. Entreprises Nationales							288 296	85 186
I.2.3. Succursales et Agences d'Ent. Etrangères							32 391	6 325
I.2. Total							320 687	91 511

English row labels:

- G.7. Accident, Health
  - G.7.1. Direct Business
    - G.7.1.1 Gross Premiums
    - G.7.1.3 Net Written Premiums
  - G.7.2. Reinsurance Accepted
    - G.7.2.1 Gross Premiums
  - G.7.3. Total
    - G.7.3.1 Gross Premiums
    - G.7.3.3 Net Written Premiums
- G.8. Others
  - G.8.1. Direct Business
    - G.8.1.1. Gross Premiums
  - G.8.2. Reinsurance Accepted
    - G.8.2.1.Gross Premiums
  - G.8.3. Total
    - G.8.3.1.Gross Premiums
- G.10. Total
  - G.10.1. Direct Business
    - G.10.1.1 Gross Premiums
    - G.10.1.3 Net Written Premiums
  - G.10.2. Reinsurance Accepted
    - G.10.2.1 Gross Premiums
    - G.10.2.3 Net Written Premiums
  - G.10.3. Total
    - G.10.3.1 Gross Premiums
    - G.10.3.2 Ceded Premiums
    - G.10.3.3 Net Written Premiums

H. GROSS CLAIMS PAYMENTS

H.1. Life
- H.1.1. Domestic Companies
- H.1.3. Branches & Agencies of Foreign Cies
- H.1. Total

H.2. Non-Life
- H.2.1. Domestic Companies
- H.2.3. Branches & Agencies of Foreign Cies
- H.2. Total

I. GROSS OPERATING EXPENSES

I.1. Life
- I.1.1. Domestic Companies
- I.1.3. Branches & Agencies of Foreign Cies
- I.1. Total

I.2. Non-Life
- I.2.1. Domestic Companies
- I.2.3. Branches & Agencies of Foreign Cies
- I.2. Total

GREECE

Monetary Unit: million drachmas

Unité monétaire : million de drachmes

J. COMMISSIONS

J.1. Life / J.1. Vie

	1990	1991	1992	1993	1994	1995	1996	1997	
J.1.1. Direct Business									J.1.1. Assurance directe
J.1.1.1. Domestic Companies							28 520	40 302	J.1.1.1. Entreprises Nationales
J.1.1.3. Branches & Agencies of Foreign Cies							7 550	2 073	J.1.1.3. Succursales et Agences d'Ent. Etrangères
J.1.1. Total							36 070	42 375	J.1.1. Total
J.1.2. Reinsurance Accepted									J.1.2. Réassurances acceptées
J.1.2.1. Domestic Companies							14	..	J.1.2.1. Entreprises Nationales
J.1.2. Total							14	..	J.1.2. Total
J.1.3. Total									J.1.3. Total
J.1.3.1. Domestic Companies							28 534	40 302	J.1.3.1. Entreprises Nationales
J.1.3.3. Branches & Agencies of Foreign Cies							7 550	2 073	J.1.3.3. Succursales et Agences d'Ent. Etrangères
J.1.3. Total of Life Net Premiums							36 084	42 375	J.1.3. Total

J.2. Non-Life / J.2. Non-Vie

	1990	1991	1992	1993	1994	1995	1996	1997	
J.2.1. Direct Business									J.2.1. Assurance directe
J.2.1.1. Domestic Companies							34 995	39 065	J.2.1.1. Entreprises Nationales
J.2.1.3. Branches & Agencies of Foreign Cies							5 590	5 905	J.2.1.3. Succursales et Agences d'Ent. Etrangères
J.2.1. Total							40 585	44 970	J.2.1. Total des Primes Nettes Vie
J.2.2. Reinsurance Accepted									J.2.2. Réassurances acceptées
J.2.2.1. Domestic Companies							3 106	..	J.2.2.1. Entreprises Nationales
J.2.2.3. Branches & Agencies of Foreign Cies							731	..	J.2.2.3. Succursales et Agences d'Ent. Etrangères
J.2.2. Total							3 837	..	J.2.2. Total
J.2.3. Total									J.2.3. Total
J.2.3.1. Domestic Companies							38 101	39 065	J.2.3.1. Entreprises Nationales
J.2.3.3. Branches & Agencies of Foreign Cies							6 321	5 905	J.2.3.3. Succursales et Agences d'Ent. Etrangères
J.2.3. Total							44 422	44 970	J.2.3. Total

Monetary Unit: million forints

A. NUMBER OF COMPANIES IN THE REPORTING COUNTRY
A. NOMBRE D'ENTREPRISES DANS LE PAYS DECLARANT

	1990	1991	1992	1993	1994	1995	1996	1997	
A.1. Life									**A.1. Vie**
A.1.1. Domestic Companies	..	0	0	0	0	0	4	5	A.1.1. Entreprises Nationales
A.1.2. (Foreign Controlled Companies)		0	0	0	0	0	1	1	A.1.2. (Entreprises Sous Contrôle Etranger)
A.1. All Companies		0	0	0	0	0	4	5	A.1. Ensemble des Entreprises
A.2. Non-Life									**A.2. Non-Vie**
A.2.1. Domestic Companies		..	0	..	1	1	25	29	A.2.1. Entreprises Nationales
A.2.2. (Foreign Controlled Companies)		..	0	0	1	0	2	3	A.2.2. (Entreprises Sous Contrôle Etranger)
A.2. All Companies		..	..	..	1	1	25	29	A.2. Ensemble des Entreprises
A.3. Composite									**A.3. Mixte**
A.3.1. Domestic Companies		11	13	14	13	14	14	14	A.3.1. Entreprises Nationales
A.3.2. (Foreign Controlled Companies)		9	10	11	11	11	12	12	A.3.2. (Entreprises Sous Contrôle Etranger)
A.3. All Companies		11	13	14	13	14	14	14	A.3. Ensemble des Entreprises
A.5. Total									**A.5. Total**
A.5.1. Domestic Companies		11	13	14	14	15	43	48	A.5.1. Entreprises Nationales
A.5.2. (Foreign Controlled Companies)		9	10	11	11	11	15	16	A.5.2. (Entreprises Sous Contrôle Etranger)
A.5. All Insurance Companies		11	13	14	14	15	43	48	A.5. Ensemble des Entreprises d'Assurances

B. NUMBER OF EMPLOYEES
B. NOMBRE D'EMPLOYES

	1990	1991	1992	1993	1994	1995	1996	1997	
B.1. Insurance Companies	..	12 294	13 349	15 636	16 388	17 138	26 100	29 365	B.1. Entreprises d'Assurances
B.2. Intermediaries	..	..	..	755	642	..	..	..	B.2. Intermediaires
B. Total			..	16 391	17 030				B. Total

C. BUSINESS WRITTEN IN THE REPORTING COUNTRY
C. OPERATIONS CONCLUES DANS LE PAYS DECLARANT

C.1. Life / C.1. Vie

	1990	1991	1992	1993	1994	1995	1996	1997	
C.1.1. Gross Premiums									**C.1.1. Primes Brutes**
C.1.1.1. Direct Business									**C.1.1.1. Assurances Directes**
C.1.1.1.1. Domestic Companies	..	15 538	10 455	15 559	24 070	35 469	49 040	65 451	C.1.1.1.1. Entreprises Nationales
C.1.1.1.2. (Foreign Controlled Companies)		15 529	10 419	15 524	23 978	34 983	47 602	62 086	C.1.1.1.2. (Entreprises Sous Contrôle Etranger)
C.1.1.1. Total		15 538	10 455	15 559	24 070	35 469	49 040	65 451	C.1.1.1. Total
C.1.1.2. Reinsurance Accepted									**C.1.1.2. Réassurance Acceptée**
C.1.1.2.1. Domestic Companies		..	77	255	0	0	0	0	C.1.1.2.1. Entreprises Nationales
C.1.1.2.2. (Foreign Controlled Companies)		..	77	255	0	0	0	0	C.1.1.2.2. (Entreprises Sous Contrôle Etranger)
C.1.1.2. Total		..	77	255	0	0	0	0	C.1.1.2. Total
C.1.1.3. Total									**C.1.1.3. Total**
C.1.1.3.1. Domestic Companies		..	10 532	15 814	24 070	35 469	49 040	65 451	C.1.1.3.1. Entreprises Nationales
C.1.1.3.2. (Foreign Controlled Companies)		..	10 496	15 779	23 978	34 983	47 602	62 086	C.1.1.3.2. (Entreprises Sous Contrôle Etranger)
C.1.1.3. Total Gross Premiums		..	10 532	15 814	24 070	35 469	49 040	65 451	C.1.1.3. Total des Primes Brutes
C.1.2. Ceded Premiums									**C.1.2. Primes Cédées**
C.1.2.1. Domestic Companies		..	2 703	5 855	8 606	12 053	16 121	5 629	C.1.2.1. Entreprises Nationales
C.1.2.2. (Foreign Controlled Companies)		..	2 703	5 854	8 604	12 048	16 118	5 587	C.1.2.2. (Entreprises Sous Contrôle Etranger)
C.1.2. Total		..	2 703	5 855	8 606	12 053	16 121	5 629	C.1.2. Total
C.1.3. Net Written Premiums									**C.1.3. Primes Nettes Emises**
C.1.3.1. Domestic Companies		..	7 829	9 959	15 464	23 416	32 919	59 322	C.1.3.1. Entreprises Nationales
C.1.3.2. (Foreign Controlled Companies)		..	7 793	9 925	15 373	22 935	31 484	56 499	C.1.3.2. (Entreprises Sous Contrôle Etranger)
C.1.3. Total		..	7 829	9 959	15 464	23 416	32 919	59 322	C.1.3. Total

Monetary Unit: million forints

Unité monétaire : million de forints

C.2. Non-Life / C.2. Non-Vie

	1990	1991	1992	1993	1994	1995	1996	1997	
C.2.1. Gross premiums									**C.2.1. Primes Brutes**
C.2.1.1. Direct Business									C.2.1.1. Assurances Directes
C.2.1.1.1. Domestic Companies	..	44 242	47 734	58 187	69 435	83 026	104 346	132 895	C.2.1.1.1. Entreprises Nationales
C.2.1.1.2. (Foreign Controlled Companies)	..	42 855	45 404	55 827	65 226	76 651	95 018	120 977	C.2.1.1.2. (Entreprises Sous Contrôle Etranger)
C.2.1.1. Total	..	44 242	47 734	58 187	69 435	83 026	104 346	132 895	C.2.1.1. Total
C.2.1.2. Reinsurance Accepted									C.2.1.2. Réassurance Acceptée
C.2.1.2.1. Domestic Companies	..	..	789	658	542	527	513	560	C.2.1.2.1. Entreprises Nationales
C.2.1.2.2. (Foreign Controlled Companies)	..	..	789	483	522	469	416	374	C.2.1.2.2. (Entreprises Sous Contrôle Etranger)
C.2.1.2. Total	..	..	789	658	542	527	513	560	C.2.1.2. Total
C.2.1.3. Total									C.2.1.3. Total
C.2.1.3.1. Domestic Companies	..	..	48 523	58 845	69 978	83 553	104 859	133 455	C.2.1.3.1. Entreprises Nationales
C.2.1.3.2. (Foreign Controlled Companies)	..	..	46 193	56 310	65 748	77 120	95 434	121 351	C.2.1.3.2. (Entreprises Sous Contrôle Etranger)
C.2.1.3. Total Gross Premiums	..	..	48 523	58 845	69 978	83 553	104 859	133 455	C.2.1.3. Total des Primes Brutes
C.2.2. Ceded Premiums									C.2.2. Primes Cédées
C.2.2.1. Domestic Companies	..	..	6 496	8 341	10 541	12 953	12 384	20 907	C.2.2.1. Entreprises Nationales
C.2.2.2. (Foreign Controlled Companies)	..	..	6 374	8 075	10 185	12 293	11 978	20 304	C.2.2.2. (Entreprises Sous Contrôle Etranger)
C.2.2. Total	..	..	6 496	8 341	10 541	12 953	12 384	20 907	C.2.2. Total
C.2.3. Net Written Premiums									C.2.3. Primes Nettes Emises
C.2.3.1. Domestic Companies	..	..	42 027	50 504	59 437	70 600	92 475	112 548	C.2.3.1. Entreprises Nationales
C.2.3.2. (Foreign Controlled Companies)	..	..	39 819	48 235	55 562	64 827	83 456	101 047	C.2.3.2. (Entreprises Sous Contrôle Etranger)
C.2.3. Total	..	..	42 027	50 504	59 437	70 600	92 475	112 548	C.2.3. Total

C.3. Total

	1990	1991	1992	1993	1994	1995	1996	1997	
C.3.1. Gross Premiums									**C.3.1. Primes Brutes**
C.3.1.1. Direct Business									C.3.1.1. Assurances Directes
C.3.1.1.1. Domestic Companies	..	59 780	58 189	73 746	93 505	118 495	153 386	198 346	C.3.1.1.1. Entreprises Nationales
C.3.1.1.2. (Foreign Controlled Companies)	..	58 384	55 823	71 351	89 204	111 634	142 620	183 063	C.3.1.1.2. (Entreprises Sous Contrôle Etranger)
C.3.1.1. Total	..	59 780	58 189	73 746	93 505	118 495	153 386	198 346	C.3.1.1. Total
C.3.1.2. Reinsurance Accepted									C.3.1.2. Réassurance Acceptée
C.3.1.2.1. Domestic Companies	..	..	866	913	542	527	513	560	C.3.1.2.1. Entreprises Nationales
C.3.1.2.2. (Foreign Controlled Companies)	..	..	866	738	522	469	416	374	C.3.1.2.2. (Entreprises Sous Contrôle Etranger)
C.3.1.2. Total	..	..	866	913	542	527	513	560	C.3.1.2. Total
C.3.1.3. Total									C.3.1.3. Total
C.3.1.3.1. Domestic Companies	..	..	59 055	74 659	94 048	119 022	153 899	198 906	C.3.1.3.1. Entreprises Nationales
C.3.1.3.2. (Foreign Controlled Companies)	..	..	56 689	72 089	89 726	112 103	143 036	183 437	C.3.1.3.2. (Entreprises Sous Contrôle Etranger)
C.3.1.3. Total Gross Premiums	..	..	59 055	74 659	94 048	119 022	153 899	198 906	C.3.1.3. Total des Primes Brutes
C.3.2. Ceded Premiums									C.3.2. Primes Cédées
C.3.2.1. Domestic Companies	..	..	9 199	14 196	19 147	25 006	28 505	26 536	C.3.2.1. Entreprises Nationales
C.3.2.2. (Foreign Controlled Companies)	..	..	9 077	13 929	18 789	24 341	28 096	25 891	C.3.2.2. (Entreprises Sous Contrôle Etranger)
C.3.2. Total	..	..	9 199	14 196	19 147	25 006	28 505	26 536	C.3.2. Total
C.3.3. Net Written Premiums									C.3.3. Primes Nettes Emises
C.3.3.1. Domestic Companies	..	..	49 856	60 463	74 901	94 016	125 394	172 370	C.3.3.1. Entreprises Nationales
C.3.3.2. (Foreign Controlled Companies)	..	..	47 612	58 160	70 935	87 762	114 940	157 546	C.3.3.2. (Entreprises Sous Contrôle Etranger)
C.3.3. Total	..	..	49 856	60 463	74 901	94 016	125 394	172 370	C.3.3. Total

Monetary Unit: million forints

Unité monétaire : million de forints

D. NET WRITTEN PREMIUMS IN THE REPORTING COUNTRY IN TERMS OF DOMESTIC AND FOREIGN RISKS
D. PRIMES NETTES EMISES DANS LE PAYS DECLARANT EN RISQUES NATIONAUX ET ETRANGERS

D.1. Life / D.1. Vie

	1990	1991	1992	1993	1994	1995	1996	1997
D.1.1. Domestic Risks / D.1.1. Risques Nationaux								
D.1.1.1. Domestic Companies / D.1.1.1. Entreprises Nationales		..	..	..	12 281	23 416	32 919	..
D.1.1.2. (Foreign Controlled Companies) / D.1.1.2. (Entreprises Sous Contrôle Etranger)		..	..	..	12 191	22 935	31 484	..
D.1.1. Total / D.1.1. Total des Primes Nettes Vie		..	..	..	12 281	23 416	32 919	..
D.1.2. Foreign Risks / D.1.2. Risques Etrangers								
D.1.2.1. Domestic Companies / D.1.2.1. Entreprises Nationales		..	..	..	3 182	0	..	..
D.1.2.2. (Foreign Controlled Companies) / D.1.2.2. (Entreprises Sous Contrôle Etranger)		..	..	..	3 182	0	..	..
D.1.2. Total / D.1.2. Total des Primes Nettes Vie		..	..	..	3 182	0	..	..
D.1.3. Total								
D.1.3.1. Domestic Companies / D.1.3.1. Entreprises Nationales		..	..	9 959	15 464	23 416	32 919	59 822
D.1.3.2. (Foreign Controlled Companies) / D.1.3.2. (Entreprises Sous Contrôle Etranger)		..	..	9 925	15 373	22 935	31 484	56 499
D.1.3. Total of Life Net Premiums / D.1.3. Total des Primes Nettes Vie		..	..	9 959	15 464	23 416	32 919	59 822

D.2. Non-Life / D.2. Non-Vie

	1990	1991	1992	1993	1994	1995	1996	1997
D.2.1. Domestic Risks / D.2.1. Risques Nationaux								
D.2.1.1. Domestic Companies / D.2.1.1. Entreprises Nationales		..	..	..	57 308	69 721	..	..
D.2.1.2. (Foreign Controlled Companies) / D.2.1.2. (Entreprises Sous Contrôle Etranger)		..	..	..	54 216	64 754	..	..
D.2.1. Total / D.2.1. Total des Primes Nettes Vie		..	..	..	57 308	69 721	..	..
D.2.2. Foreign Risks / D.2.2. Risques Etrangers								
D.2.2.1. Domestic Companies / D.2.2.1. Entreprises Nationales		..	..	..	2 129	879	..	..
D.2.2.2. (Foreign Controlled Companies) / D.2.2.2. (Entreprises Sous Contrôle Etranger)		..	..	..	1 346	73	..	..
D.2.2. Total / D.2.2. Total des Primes Nettes Vie		..	..	..	2 129	879	..	..
D.2.3. Total								
D.2.3.1. Domestic Companies / D.2.3.1. Entreprises Nationales		..	..	50 504	59 437	70 600	92 475	112 548
D.2.3.2. (Foreign Controlled Companies) / D.2.3.2. (Entreprises Sous Contrôle Etranger)		..	..	48 235	55 562	64 827	83 456	101 047
D.2.3. Total / D.2.3. Total des Primes Nettes Vie		..	..	50 504	59 437	70 600	92 475	112 548

F. OUTSTANDING INVESTMENT BY DIRECT INSURANCE COMPANIES
F. ENCOURS DES PLACEMENTS DES ENTREPRISES D'ASSURANCES DIRECTES

F.1. Life / F.1. Vie

	1990	1991	1992	1993	1994	1995	1996	1997
F.1.1. Real Estate / F.1.1. Immobilier								
F.1.1.1. Domestic Companies / F.1.1.1. Entreprises Nationales		3 604	3 872	4 105	3 270	2 156	2 141	375
F.1.1.2. (Foreign Controlled Companies) / F.1.1.2. (Entreprises Sous Contrôle Etranger)		3 604	3 872	4 105	3 270	2 010	2 062	124
F.1.1. Total / F.1.1. Total		3 604	3 872	4 105	3 270	..	..	..
F.1.3. Shares / F.1.3. Actions								
F.1.3.1. Domestic Companies / F.1.3.1. Entreprises Nationales		6 522	3 343	2 820	3 570	3 481	774	5 735
F.1.3.2. (Foreign Controlled Companies) / F.1.3.2. (Entreprises Sous Contrôle Etranger)		6 522	3 343	2 820	3 570	3 481	728	5 565
F.1.3. Total / F.1.3. Total		6 522	3 343	2 820	..	..	..	..
F.1.4. Bonds with Fixed Revenue / F.1.4. Obligations								
F.1.4.1. Domestic Companies / F.1.4.1. Entreprises Nationales		13 126	24 533	37 803	44 997	57 711	110 394	114 871
F.1.4.2. (Foreign Controlled Companies) / F.1.4.2. (Entreprises Sous Contrôle Etranger)		12 914	24 323	37 590	44 755	57 501	107 638	114 228
F.1.4. Total / F.1.4. Total		13 126	24 533	37 803	..	..	..	..
F.1.5. Loans other than Mortgage Loans / F.1.5. Prêts Autres qu'Hypothécaires								
F.1.5.1. Domestic Companies / F.1.5.1. Entreprises Nationales		0	3 909	3 692	3 678	3 986	2 434	1 805
F.1.5.2. (Foreign Controlled Companies) / F.1.5.2. (Entreprises Sous Contrôle Etranger)		0	3 909	3 692	3 678	3 986	2 334	1 760
F.1.5. Total / F.1.5. Total		0	3 909	3 692	..	..	..	..
F.1.6. Other Investments / F.1.6. Autres Placements								
F.1.6.1. Domestic Companies / F.1.6.1. Entreprises Nationales		14 532	6 027	4 486	1 949	1 514	1 182	2 437
F.1.6.2. (Foreign Controlled Companies) / F.1.6.2. (Entreprises Sous Contrôle Etranger)		14 232	5 917	4 486	1 937	1 348	1 058	1 726
F.1.6. Total / F.1.6. Total		14 532	6 027	4 486	..	..	..	..

Monetary Unit: million forints   Unité monétaire : million de forints

Label (EN)	Label (FR)	1990	1991	1992	1993	1994	1995	1996	1997
F.1.7. Total	**F.1.7. Total**								
F.1.7.1. Domestic Companies	F.1.7.1. Entreprises Nationales		37 784	41 684	52 906	57 464	68 848	116 925	125 223
F.1.7.2. (Foreign Controlled Companies)	F.1.7.2. (Entreprises Sous Controle Etranger)		37 272	41 364	52 693	57 210	68 326	113 820	123 403
F.1.7. Total of Life Investments	F.1.7. Total des Placements Vie		37 784	41 684	52 906	:	:	:	:
F.2. Non-Life	**F.2. Non-Vie**								
F.2.1. Real Estate	**F.2.1. Immobilier**								
F.2.1.1. Domestic Companies	F.2.1.1. Entreprises Nationales		869	1 384	2 143	2 328	2 668	2 476	5 055
F.2.1.2. (Foreign Controlled Companies)	F.2.1.2. (Entreprises Sous Controle Etranger)		869	1 384	2 143	2 328	2 175	2 428	3 938
F.2.1. Total	F.2.1. Total		869	1 384	2 143	:	:	:	:
F.2.3. Shares	**F.2.3. Actions**								
F.2.3.1. Domestic Companies	F.2.3.1. Entreprises Nationales		1 252	694	1 228	1 124	6 913	10 043	6 230
F.2.3.2. (Foreign Controlled Companies)	F.2.3.2. (Entreprises Sous Controle Etranger)		1 252	694	1 228	1 124	6 913	9 880	5 956
F.2.3. Total	F.2.3. Total		1 252	694	1 228	:	:	:	:
F.2.4. Bonds with Fixed Revenue	**F.2.4. Obligations**								
F.2.4.1. Domestic Companies	F.2.4.1. Entreprises Nationales		2 388	2 574	18 246	26 984	47 127	56 884	71 903
F.2.4.2. (Foreign Controlled Companies)	F.2.4.2. (Entreprises Sous Controle Etranger)		2 245	2 281	17 269	25 545	46 074	55 680	70 433
F.2.4. Total	F.2.4. Total		2 388	2 574	18 246	:	:	:	:
F.2.6. Other Investments	**F.2.6. Autres Placements**								
F.2.6.1. Domestic Companies	F.2.6.1. Entreprises Nationales		2 642	6 528	2 529	11 205	3 570	5 130	8 046
F.2.6.2. (Foreign Controlled Companies)	F.2.6.2. (Entreprises Sous Controle Etranger)		2 617	6 528	2 504	11 143	2 972	2 943	6 787
F.2.6. Total	F.2.6. Total		2 642	6 528	2 529	:	:	:	:
F.2.7. Total	**F.2.7. Total**								
F.2.7.1. Domestic Companies	F.2.7.1. Entreprises Nationales		7 151	11 180	24 146	41 641	60 278	74 533	91 234
F.2.7.2. (Foreign Controlled Companies)	F.2.7.2. (Entreprises Sous Controle Etranger)		6 983	10 887	23 144	40 139	58 134	70 931	87 114
F.2.7. Total of Non-Life Investments	F.2.7. Total des Placements Non-Vie		7 151	11 180	24 146	:	:	:	:
G. BREAKDOWN OF NON-LIFE PREMIUMS	**G. VENTILATIONS DES PRIMES NON-VIE**								
G.1. Motor vehicle	**G.1. Assurance Automobile**								
G.1.1. Direct Business	G.1.1. Assurances Directes								
G.1.1.1. Gross Premiums	G.1.1.1. Primes Brutes		24 905	25 698	32 441	41 541	49 216	63 375	78 514
G.1.2. Reinsurance Accepted	G.1.2. Réassurance Acceptée								
G.1.2.1. Gross Premiums	G.1.2.1. Primes Brutes		:	:	:	269	428	416	454
G.1.3. Total	G.1.3. Total								
G.1.3.1. Gross Premiums	G.1.3.1. Primes Brutes		:	:	:	41 810	49 644	63 791	78 968
G.1.3.2. Ceded Premiums	G.1.3.2. Primes Cédées		:	:	:	:	3 841	4 199	6 647
G.1.3.3. Net Written Premiums	G.1.3.3. Primes Nettes Emises		:	:	:	:	45 803	59 592	72 321
G.3. Freight	**G.3. Fret**								
G.3.1. Direct Business	G.3.1. Assurances Directes								
G.3.1.1. Gross Premiums	G.3.1.1. Primes Brutes		1 759	954	596	845	1 215	1 480	2 026
G.3.2. Reinsurance Accepted	G.3.2. Réassurance Acceptée								
G.3.2.1. Gross Premiums	G.3.2.1. Primes Brutes		:	:	:	2		0	0
G.3.3. Total	G.3.3. Total								
G.3.3.1. Gross Premiums	G.3.3.1. Primes Brutes		:	:	:	847	1 215	1 480	2 026
G.3.3.2. Ceded Premiums	G.3.3.2. Primes Cédées		:	:	:	:	692	560	1 066
G.3.3.3. Net Written Premiums	G.3.3.3. Primes Nettes Emises		:	:	:	:	523	920	960
G.4. Fire, Property Damages	**G.4. Incendie, Dommages aux Biens**								
G.4.1. Direct Business	G.4.1. Assurances Directes								
G.4.1.1. Gross Premiums	G.4.1.1. Primes Brutes		13 683	16 117	17 331	18 747	8 724	14 013	11 632
G.4.2. Reinsurance Accepted	G.4.2. Réassurance Acceptée								
G.4.2.1. Gross Premiums	G.4.2.1. Primes Brutes		:	:	:	185	5	5	7
G.4.3. Total	G.4.3. Total								
G.4.3.1. Gross Premiums	G.4.3.1. Primes Brutes		:	:	:	18 933	8 729	14 018	11 639
G.4.3.2. Ceded Premiums	G.4.3.2. Primes Cédées		:	:	:	:	5 202	5 380	6 117
G.4.3.3. Net Written Premiums	G.4.3.3. Primes Nettes Emises		:	:	:	:	3 527	8 638	5 522

Monetary Unit: million forints | Unité monétaire : million de forints

	1990	1991	1992	1993	1994	1995	1996	1997
G.5. Pecuniary Losses / G.5. Pertes Pécuniaires								
G.5.1. Direct Business / Assurances Directes								
G.5.1.1. Gross Premiums / Primes Brutes		37	232	489	79	239	644	901
G.5.2. Reinsurance Accepted / Réassurance Acceptée								
G.5.2.1. Gross Premiums / Primes Brutes			..	..	2	1	0	0
G.5.3. Total								
G.5.3.1. Gross Premiums / Primes Brutes		..	..	..	81	240	644	901
G.5.3.2. Ceded Premiums / Primes Cédées		..	..	..	..	1	232	508
G.5.3.3. Net Written Premiums / Primes Nettes Emises		..	..	..	..	239	412	393
G.6. General Liability / Responsabilité Générale								
G.6.1. Direct Business / Assurances Directes								
G.6.1.1. Gross Premiums / Primes Brutes		381	940	1 667	1 855	2 732	4 108	5 125
G.6.2. Reinsurance Accepted / Réassurance Acceptée								
G.6.3. Total								
G.6.3.1. Gross Premiums / Primes Brutes		..	..	..	1 855	2 732	4 108	5 125
G.6.3.2. Ceded Premiums / Primes Cédées		..	..	..	..	643	700	1 906
G.6.3.3. Net Written Premiums / Primes Nettes Emises		..	..	..	..	2 089	3 408	3 219
G.7. Accident, Health / Accident, Santé								
G.7.1. Direct Business / Assurances Directes								
G.7.1.1. Gross Premiums / Primes Brutes		3 170	3 246	3 330	1 981	2 652	2 928	5 248
G.7.2. Reinsurance Accepted / Réassurance Acceptée								
G.7.2.1. Gross Premiums / Primes Brutes		..	..	..	20	58	56	62
G.7.3. Total								
G.7.3.1. Gross Premiums / Primes Brutes		..	..	..	2 001	2 710	2 984	5 310
G.7.3.2. Ceded Premiums / Primes Cédées		..	..	..	..	126	120	258
G.7.3.3. Net Written Premiums / Primes Nettes Emises		..	..	..	..	2 584	2 864	5 052
G.8. Others / Autres								
G.8.1. Direct Business / Assurances Directes								
G.8.1.1. Gross Premiums / Primes Brutes		298	547	2 333	4 387	18 248	17 798	28 449
G.8.2. Reinsurance Accepted / Réassurance Acceptée								
G.8.2.1. Gross Premiums / Primes Brutes		..	..	..	64	35	36	37
G.8.3. Total								
G.8.3.1. Gross Premiums / Primes Brutes		..	..	..	4 451	18 283	17 834	29 486
G.8.3.2. Ceded Premiums / Primes Cédées		..	..	..	..	2 448	1 193	4 405
G.8.3.3. Net Written Premiums / Primes Nettes Emises		..	..	..	..	15 835	16 641	25 081
G.9.2. Reinsurance Accepted / Réassurance Acceptée								
G.9.2.1. Gross Premiums / Primes Brutes		..	789	658	0	0	0	0
G.10. Total								
G.10.1. Direct Business / Assurances Directes								
G.10.1.1. Gross Premiums / Primes Brutes		44 242	47 734	58 187	69 435	83 026	104 346	132 895
G.10.2. Reinsurance Accepted / Réassurance Acceptée								
G.10.2.1. Gross Premiums / Primes Brutes		..	789	658	542	527	513	560
G.10.3. Total								
G.10.3.1. Gross Premiums / Primes Brutes		..	48 523	58 845	69 978	83 553	104 859	133 455
G.10.3.2. Ceded Premiums / Primes Cédées		..	6 496	8 341	..	12 953	12 384	20 907
G.10.3.3. Net Written Premiums / Primes Nettes Emises		..	42 027	50 504	..	70 600	92 475	112 548
H. GROSS CLAIMS PAYMENTS / H. PAIEMENTS BRUTS DES SINISTRES								
H.1. Life / H.1. Vie								
H.1.1 Domestic Companies / Entreprises Nationales							16 519	16 326
H.1.2. (Foreign Controlled Companies) / (Entreprises Sous Contrôle Etranger)							16 179	16 343
H.1. Total / H.1. Total							16 519	16 326
H.2. Non-Life / H.2. Non-Vie								
H.2.1. Domestic Companies / Entreprises Nationales							61 090	68 161
H.2.2. (Foreign Controlled Companies) / (Entreprises Sous Contrôle Etranger)							55 766	62 487
H.2. Total / H.2. Total							61 090	68 161

Monetary Unit: million forints | Unité monétaire : million de forints

	1990	1991	1992	1993	1994	1995	1996	1997
I. GROSS OPERATING EXPENSES / **I. DEPENSES BRUTES D'EXPLOITATION**								
I.1. Life / **I.1. Vie**								
I.1.1. Domestic Companies / I.1.1. Entreprises Nationales							9 426	10 836
I.1.2. (Foreign Controlled Companies) / I.1.2. (Entreprises Sous Contrôle Etranger)							9 077	9 924
I.1. Total / I.1. Total des Primes Nettes Vie							9 426	10 836
I.2. Non-Life / **I.2. Non-Vie**								
I.2.1. Domestic Companies / I.2.1. Entreprises Nationales							18 451	22 930
I.2.2. (Foreign Controlled Companies) / I.2.2. (Entreprises Sous Contrôle Etranger)							15 583	22 213
I.2. Total / I.2. Total							18 451	22 930
J. COMMISSIONS / **J. COMMISSIONS**								
J.1. Life / **J.1. Vie**								
J.1.3. Total / J.1.3. Total								
J.1.3.1. Domestic Companies / J.1.3.1. Entreprises Nationales							9 448	13 533
J.1.3.2. (Foreign Controlled Companies) / J.1.3.2. (Entreprises Sous Contrôle Etranger)							9 204	12 995
J.1.3. Total of Life Net Premiums / J.1.3. Total							9 448	13 533
J.2. Non-Life / **J.2. Non-Vie**								
J.2.3. Total / J.2.3. Total								
J.2.3.1. Domestic Companies / J.2.3.1. Entreprises Nationales							8 550	12 356
J.2.3.2. (Foreign Controlled Companies) / J.2.3.2. (Entreprises Sous Contrôle Etranger)							7 598	11 728
J.2.3. Total / J.2.3. Total							8 550	12 356

ICELAND

Monetary Unit: million Icelandic kronur

	1990	1991	1992	1993	1994	1995	1996	1997	
A. NUMBER OF COMPANIES IN THE REPORTING COUNTRY									**A. NOMBRE D'ENTREPRISES DANS LE PAYS DECLARANT**
A.1. Life									**A.1. Vie**
A.1.1. Domestic Companies	..	5	5	5	5	4	4	3	A.1.1. Entreprises Nationales
A.1.2. (Foreign Controlled Companies)	..	1	1	1	1	1	1	0	A.1.2. (Entreprises Sous Contrôle Etranger)
A.1. All Companies	..	5	5	5	5	4	4	3	A.1. Ensemble des Entreprises
A.2. Non-Life									**A.2. Non-Vie**
A.2.1. Domestic Companies	19	19	19	19	17	14	13	10	A.2.1. Entreprises Nationales
A.2.2. (Foreign Controlled Companies)	0	2	2	2	1	1	1	0	A.2.2. (Entreprises Sous Contrôle Etranger)
A.2. All Companies	19	19	19	19	17	14	13	10	A.2. Ensemble des Entreprises
A.4. Reinsurance									**A.4. Réassurance**
A.4.1. Domestic Companies	1	2	2	2	1	1	1	1	A.4.1. Entreprises Nationales
A.4.2. (Foreign Controlled Companies)	0	1	1	1	0	0	0	0	A.4.2. (Entreprises Sous Contrôle Etranger)
A.4. All Companies	1	2	2	2	1	1	1	1	A.4. Ensemble des Entreprises
A.5. Total									**A.5. Total**
A.5.1. Domestic Companies	27	26	26	26	23	19	18	14	A.5.1. Entreprises Nationales
A.5.2. (Foreign Controlled Companies)	0	4	4	4	2	2	2	0	A.5.2. (Entreprises Sous Contrôle Etranger)
A.5. All Insurance Companies	27	26	26	26	23	19	18	14	A.5. Ensemble des Entreprises d'Assurances
B. NUMBER OF EMPLOYEES									**B. NOMBRE D'EMPLOYES**
B.1. Insurance Companies	424	430	434	430	433	440	443	463	B.1. Entreprises d'Assurances
C. BUSINESS WRITTEN IN THE REPORTING COUNTRY									**C. OPERATIONS CONCLUES DANS LE PAYS DECLARANT**
C.1. Life									**C.1. Vie**
C.1.1. Gross Premiums									C.1.1. Primes Brutes
C.1.1.1. Direct Business									C.1.1.1. Assurances Directes
C.1.1.1.1. Domestic Companies	327	395	418	464	479	506	551	537	C.1.1.1.1. Entreprises Nationales
C.1.1.1.2. (Foreign Controlled Companies)	0	3	7	16	23	29	27	0	C.1.1.1.2. (Entreprises Sous Contrôle Etranger)
C.1.1.1. Total	327	395	418	464	479	506	551	537	C.1.1.1. Total
C.1.1.2. Reinsurance Accepted									C.1.1.2. Réassurance Acceptée
C.1.1.2.1. Domestic Companies	14	19	10	10	83	103	2	114	C.1.1.2.1. Entreprises Nationales
C.1.1.2. Total	14	19	10	10	83	103	2	114	C.1.1.2. Total
C.1.1.3. Total									C.1.1.3. Total
C.1.1.3.1. Domestic Companies	341	414	428	474	562	609	553	651	C.1.1.3.1. Entreprises Nationales
C.1.1.3.2. (Foreign Controlled Companies)	0	3	7	16	23	29	27	0	C.1.1.3.2. (Entreprises Sous Contrôle Etranger)
C.1.1.3. Total Gross Premiums	341	414	428	474	562	609	553	651	C.1.1.3. Total des Primes Brutes
C.1.2. Ceded Premiums									C.1.2. Primes Cédées
C.1.2.1. Domestic Companies	132	156	154	161	159	167	186	182	C.1.2.1. Entreprises Nationales
C.1.2.2. (Foreign Controlled Companies)	0	1	3	8	15	22	14	0	C.1.2.2. (Entreprises Sous Contrôle Etranger)
C.1.2. Total	132	156	154	161	159	167	186	182	C.1.2. Total
C.1.3. Net Written Premiums									C.1.3. Primes Nettes Emises
C.1.3.1. Domestic Companies	209	258	274	313	403	442	366	470	C.1.3.1. Entreprises Nationales
C.1.3.2. (Foreign Controlled Companies)	0	2	4	8	8	7	13	0	C.1.3.2. (Entreprises Sous Contrôle Etranger)
C.1.3. Total	209	258	274	313	403	442	366	470	C.1.3. Total

ICELAND
Monetary Unit: million Icelandic kronur

C.2. Non-Life / C.2. Non-Vie

	1990	1991	1992	1993	1994	1995	1996	1997
C.2.1. Gross premiums / C.2.1. Primes Brutes								
C.2.1.1. Direct Business / C.2.1.1. Assurances Directes								
C.2.1.1.1. Domestic Companies / Entreprises Nationales	10 566	12 440	12 828	12 622	13 243	13 063	13 322	13 210
C.2.1.1.2. (Foreign Controlled Companies) / (Entreprises Sous Contrôle Etranger)	0	484	604	619	370	535	536	0
C.2.1.1. Total	10 566	12 440	12 828	12 622	13 243	13 063	13 322	13 210
C.2.1.2. Reinsurance Accepted / C.2.1.2. Réassurance Acceptée								
C.2.1.2.1. Domestic Companies / Entreprises Nationales	2 260	2 404	2 561	2 443	2 187	1 689	1 703	1 554
C.2.1.2.2. (Foreign Controlled Companies) / (Entreprises Sous Contrôle Etranger)	0	13	0	0	0	0	0	0
C.2.1.2. Total	2 260	2 404	2 561	2 443	2 187	1 689	1 703	1 554
C.2.1.3. Total								
C.2.1.3.1. Domestic Companies / Entreprises Nationales	12 826	14 844	15 389	15 065	15 430	14 752	15 025	14 764
C.2.1.3.2. (Foreign Controlled Companies) / (Entreprises Sous Contrôle Etranger)	0	497	604	619	105	535	536	0
C.2.1.3. Total Gross Premiums / Total des Primes Brutes	12 826	14 844	15 389	15 065	15 430	14 752	15 025	14 764
C.2.2. Ceded Premiums / C.2.2. Primes Cédées								
C.2.2.1. Domestic Companies / Entreprises Nationales	4 543	4 923	5 321	5 053	5 193	4 677	4 391	4 225
C.2.2.2. (Foreign Controlled Companies) / (Entreprises Sous Contrôle Etranger)	0	117	206	206	185	270	268	0
C.2.2. Total	4 543	4 923	5 321	5 053	5 193	4 677	4 391	4 225
C.2.3. Net Written Premiums / C.2.3. Primes Nettes Emises								
C.2.3.1. Domestic Companies / Entreprises Nationales	8 283	9 921	10 068	10 012	10 237	10 075	10 634	10 539
C.2.3.2. (Foreign Controlled Companies) / (Entreprises Sous Contrôle Etranger)	0	380	398	413	185	265	268	0
C.2.3. Total	8 283	9 921	10 068	10 012	10 237	10 075	10 634	10 539
C.3. Total								
C.3.1. Gross Premiums / C.3.1. Primes Brutes								
C.3.1.1. Direct Business / C.3.1.1. Assurances Directes								
C.3.1.1.1. Domestic Companies / Entreprises Nationales	10 893	12 835	13 246	13 086	13 722	13 569	13 873	13 747
C.3.1.1.2. (Foreign Controlled Companies) / (Entreprises Sous Contrôle Etranger)	0	487	611	635	393	564	563	0
C.3.1.1. Total	10 893	12 835	13 246	13 086	13 722	13 569	13 873	13 747
C.3.1.2. Reinsurance Accepted / C.3.1.2. Réassurance Acceptée								
C.3.1.2.1. Domestic Companies / Entreprises Nationales	2 274	2 423	2 571	2 453	2 270	1 792	1 705	1 668
C.3.1.2.2. (Foreign Controlled Companies) / (Entreprises Sous Contrôle Etranger)	0	13	0	0	0	0	0	0
C.3.1.2. Total	2 274	2 423	2 571	2 453	2 270	1 792	1 705	1 668
C.3.1.3. Total								
C.3.1.3.1. Domestic Companies / Entreprises Nationales	13 167	15 258	15 817	15 539	15 992	15 361	15 578	15 415
C.3.1.3.2. (Foreign Controlled Companies) / (Entreprises Sous Contrôle Etranger)	0	500	611	635	128	564	563	0
C.3.1.3. Total Gross Premiums / Total des Primes Brutes	13 167	15 258	15 817	15 539	15 992	15 361	15 578	15 415
C.3.2. Ceded Premiums / C.3.2. Primes Cédées								
C.3.2.1. Domestic Companies / Entreprises Nationales	4 675	5 079	5 475	5 214	5 352	4 844	4 577	4 407
C.3.2.2. (Foreign Controlled Companies) / (Entreprises Sous Contrôle Etranger)	0	118	209	214	200	292	282	0
C.3.2. Total	4 675	5 079	5 475	5 214	5 352	4 844	4 577	4 407
C.3.3. Net Written Premiums / C.3.3. Primes Nettes Emises								
C.3.3.1. Domestic Companies / Entreprises Nationales	8 492	10 179	10 342	10 325	10 640	10 517	11 000	11 009
C.3.3.2. (Foreign Controlled Companies) / (Entreprises Sous Contrôle Etranger)	0	382	402	421	193	272	281	0
C.3.3. Total	8 492	10 179	10 342	10 325	10 640	10 517	11 000	11 009
D. NET WRITTEN PREMIUMS IN THE REPORTING COUNTRY IN TERMS OF DOMESTIC AND FOREIGN RISKS / D. PRIMES NETTES EMISES DANS LE PAYS DECLARANT EN RISQUES NATIONAUX ET ETRANGERS								
D.1. Life / D.1. Vie								
D.1.1. Domestic Risks / D.1.1. Risques Nationaux								
D.1.1.1. Domestic Companies / Entreprises Nationales	209	258	274	475	403	:	366	470
D.1.1.2. (Foreign Controlled Companies) / (Entreprises Sous Contrôle Etranger)	0	2	4	16	8	:	13	0
D.1.1. Total	209	258	274	475	403	:	366	470
D.1.3. Total								
D.1.3.1. Domestic Companies / Entreprises Nationales	209	258	274	475	403	:	366	470
D.1.3.2. (Foreign Controlled Companies) / (Entreprises Sous Contrôle Etranger)	0	2	4	16	8	:	13	0
D.1.3. Total of Life Net Premiums / Total des Primes Nettes Vie	209	258	274	475	403	:	366	470

Monetary Unit: million Icelandic kronur — Unité monétaire : million de couronnes islandaises

D.2. Non-Life — D.2. Non-Vie

English	French	1990	1991	1992	1993	1994	1995	1996	1997
D.2.1. Domestic Risks	D.2.1. Risques Nationaux								
D.2.1.1. Domestic Companies	D.2.1.1. Entreprises Nationales	8 264	9 905	10 061	15 065	10 237	..	10 614	10 494
D.2.1.2. (Foreign Controlled Companies)	D.2.1.2. (Entreprises Sous Contrôle Etranger)	0	380	398	619	185	..	268	0
D.2.1. Total	D.2.1. Total	8 264	9 905	10 061	15 065	10 237	..	10 614	10 494
D.2.2. Foreign Risks	D.2.2. Risques Etrangers								
D.2.2.1. Domestic Companies	D.2.2.1. Entreprises Nationales	19	16	7	- 1	0	..	20	45
D.2.2. Total	D.2.2. Total des Primes Nettes Vie	19	16	7	- 1	0	..	20	45
D.2.3. Total	D.2.3. Total								
D.2.3.1. Domestic Companies	D.2.3.1. Entreprises Nationales	8 283	9 921	10 068	15 064	10 237	..	10 634	10 539
D.2.3.2. (Foreign Controlled Companies)	D.2.3.2. (Entreprises Sous Contrôle Etranger)	0	380	398	619	185	..	268	0
D.2.3. Total	D.2.3. Total des Primes Nettes Vie	8 283	9 921	10 068	15 064	10 237	..	10 634	10 539

F. OUTSTANDING INVESTMENT BY DIRECT INSURANCE COMPANIES — F. ENCOURS DES PLACEMENTS DES ENTREPRISES D'ASSURANCES DIRECTES

F.1. Life — F.1. Vie

English	French	1990	1991	1992	1993	1994	1995	1996	1997
F.1.1. Real Estate	F.1.1. Immobilier								
F.1.1.1. Domestic Companies	F.1.1.1. Entreprises Nationales	11	11	13	15	..	..	..	52
F.1.1.4. Domestic Investment	F.1.1.4. Placement cans le Pays	11	11	13	15	..	..	..	..
F.1.1. Total	F.1.1. Total	11	11	13	15	..	..	..	..
F.1.2. Mortgage Loans	F.1.2. Prêts Hypothécaires								
F.1.2.1. Domestic Companies	F.1.2.1. Entreprises Nationales	128	16	0	214	..	..	..	41
F.1.2.2. (Foreign Controlled Companies)	F.1.2.2. (Entreprises Sous Contrôle Etranger)	0	0	2	1	..	..	..	..
F.1.2.4. Domestic Investment	F.1.2.4. Placement dans le Pays	128	16	32	214	..	..	..	..
F.1.2. Total	F.1.2. Total	128	16	32	214	..	..	..	..
F.1.3. Shares	F.1.3. Actions								
F.1.3.1. Domestic Companies	F.1.3.1. Entreprises Nationales	13	108	117	126	..	..	..	268
F.1.3.4. Domestic Investment	F.1.3.4. Placement dans le Pays	13	108	117	126	..	..	..	..
F.1.3. Total	F.1.3. Total	13	108	117	126	..	..	..	..
F.1.4. Bonds with Fixed Revenue	F.1.4. Obligations								
F.1.4.1. Domestic Companies	F.1.4.1. Entreprises Nationales	264	286	353	461	..	..	..	1 096
F.1.4.2. (Foreign Controlled Companies)	F.1.4.2. (Entreprises Sous Contrôle Etranger)	0	3	1	1	..	..	..	..
F.1.4.4. Domestic Investment	F.1.4.4. Placement dans le Pays	264	286	353	461	..	..	..	..
F.1.4. Total	F.1.4. Total	264	286	353	461	..	..	..	..
F.1.5. Loans other than Mortgage Loans	F.1.5. Prêts Autres qu'Hypothécaires								
F.1.5.1. Domestic Companies	F.1.5.1. Entreprises Nationales	49	228	250	155	..	..	..	..
F.1.5.2. (Foreign Controlled Companies)	F.1.5.2. (Entreprises Sous Contrôle Etranger)	0	2	1	0	..	..	..	..
F.1.5.4. Domestic Investment	F.1.5.4. Placement dans le Pays	49	228	250	155	..	..	..	..
F.1.5. Total	F.1.5. Total	49	228	250	155	..	..	..	..
F.1.6. Other Investments	F.1.6. Autres Placements								
F.1.6.1. Domestic Companies	F.1.6.1. Entreprises Nationales	14	12	8	5	..	..	..	..
F.1.6.4. Domestic Investment	F.1.6.4. Placement dans le Pays	14	12	8	5	..	..	..	..
F.1.6. Total	F.1.6. Total	14	12	8	5	..	..	..	..
F.1.7. Total	F.1.7. Total								
F.1.7.1. Domestic Companies	F.1.7.1. Entreprises Nationales	479	660	773	976	..	..	1 325	1 456
F.1.7.2. (Foreign Controlled Companies)	F.1.7.2. (Entreprises Sous Contrôle Etranger)	0	5	2	2	..	..	..	..
F.1.7.4. Domestic Investment	F.1.7.4. Placement dans le Pays	479	660	773	976	..	..	..	..
F.1.7. Total of Life Investments	F.1.7. Total des Placements Vie	479	660	773	976	..	..	..	..

F.2. Non-Life — F.2. Non-Vie

English	French	1990	1991	1992	1993	1994	1995	1996	1997
F.2.1. Real Estate	F.2.1. Immobilier								
F.2.1.1. Domestic Companies	F.2.1.1. Entreprises Nationales	1 549	1 669	1 689	1 710	..	..	..	1 567
F.2.1.2. (Foreign Controlled Companies)	F.2.1.2. (Entreprises Sous Contrôle Etranger)	0	23	22	22	..	..	..	..
F.2.1.4. Domestic Investment	F.2.1.4. Placement dans le Pays	1 549	1 669	1 689	1 710	..	..	..	..
F.2.1. Total	F.2.1. Total	1 549	1 669	1 689	1 710	..	..	..	..

Monetary Unit: million Icelandic kronur

	1990	1991	1992	1993	1994	1995	1996	1997	
F.2.2. Mortgage Loans									**F.2.2. Prêts Hypothécaires**
F.2.2.1. Domestic Companies	2 285	296	575	3 733	...	...	...	10 919	F.2.2.1. Entreprises Nationales
F.2.2.2. (Foreign Controlled Companies)	0	8	12	70	:	:	:	:	F.2.2.2. (Entreprises Sous Contrôle Etranger)
F.2.2.4. Domestic Investment	2 285	296	575	3 733	...	...	...	:	F.2.2.4. Placement dans le Pays
F.2.2. Total	2 285	296	575	3 733	...	...	...	:	F.2.2. Total
F.2.3. Shares									**F.2.3. Actions**
F.2.3.1. Domestic Companies	1 603	1 985	2 694	3 151	...	...	...	6 996	F.2.3.1. Entreprises Nationales
F.2.3.2. (Foreign Controlled Companies)	0	19	21	24	:	:	:	:	F.2.3.2. (Entreprises Sous Contrôle Etranger)
F.2.3.4. Domestic Investment	1 603	1 985	2 694	3 151	...	...	...	:	F.2.3.4. Placement dans le Pays
F.2.3. Total	1 603	1 985	2 694	3 151	...	...	...	:	F.2.3. Total
F.2.4. Bonds with Fixed Revenue									**F.2.4. Obligations**
F.2.4.1. Domestic Companies	4 727	5 338	6 452	8 042	...	...	...	10 542	F.2.4.1. Entreprises Nationales
F.2.4.2. (Foreign Controlled Companies)	0	139	126	152	:	:	:	:	F.2.4.2. (Entreprises Sous Contrôle Etranger)
F.2.4.4. Domestic Investment	4 727	5 338	6 452	8 052	...	...	...	:	F.2.4.4. Placement dans le Pays
F.2.4. Total	4 727	5 338	6 452	8 052	...	...	...	:	F.2.4. Total
F.2.5. Loans other than Mortgage Loans									**F.2.5. Prêts Autres qu'Hypothécaires**
F.2.5.1. Domestic Companies	935	4 259	4 494	2 586	...	...	...	1 985	F.2.5.1. Entreprises Nationales
F.2.5.2. (Foreign Controlled Companies)	0	111	87	49	:	:	:	:	F.2.5.2. (Entreprises Sous Contrôle Etranger)
F.2.5.4. Domestic Investment	935	4 259	4 494	2 586	...	...	...	:	F.2.5.4. Placement dans le Pays
F.2.5. Total	935	4 259	4 494	2 586	...	...	...	:	F.2.5. Total
F.2.6. Other Investments									**F.2.6. Autres Placements**
F.2.6.1. Domestic Companies	425	435	375	315	...	...	...	97	F.2.6.1. Entreprises Nationales
F.2.6.2. (Foreign Controlled Companies)	0	49	38	37	:	:	:	:	F.2.6.2. (Entreprises Sous Contrôle Etranger)
F.2.6.4. Domestic Investment	425	435	0	315	...	...	...	:	F.2.6.4. Placement dans le Pays
F.2.6. Total	425	435	0	315	...	...	...	:	F.2.6. Total
F.2.7. Total									**F.2.7. Total**
F.2.7.1. Domestic Companies	11 525	13 982	16 279	19 537	...	...	31 932	32 205	F.2.7.1. Entreprises Nationales
F.2.7.2. (Foreign Controlled Companies)	0	349	306	354	:	:	:	:	F.2.7.2. (Entreprises Sous Contrôle Etranger)
F.2.7.4. Domestic Investment	11 525	13 982	16 279	19 537	...	...	...	:	F.2.7.4. Placement dans le Pays
F.2.7. Total of Non-Life Investments	11 525	13 982	16 279	19 537	...	...	...	:	F.2.7. Total des Placements Non-Vie
G. BREAKDOWN OF NON-LIFE PREMIUMS									**G. VENTILATIONS DES PRIMES NON-VIE**
G.1. Motor vehicle									**G.1. Assurance Automobile**
G.1.1. Direct Business									G.1.1. Assurances Directes
G.1.1.1. Gross Premiums	4 549	5 722	5 554	5 309	5 658	5 562	5 685	5 098	G.1.1.1. Primes Brutes
G.1.1.2. Ceded Premiums	110	123	220	223	292	330	328	83	G.1.1.2. Primes Cédées
G.1.1.3. Net Written Premiums	4 439	5 599	5 334	5 086	5 366	5 232	5 357	5 015	G.1.1.3. Primes Nettes Emises
G.1.2. Reinsurance Accepted									G.1.2. Réassurance Acceptée
G.1.2.1. Gross Premiums	22	28	19	32	35	36	46	23	G.1.2.1. Primes Brutes
G.1.2.2. Ceded Premiums	8	20	7	7	11	11	22	11	G.1.2.2. Primes Cédées
G.1.2.3. Net Written Premiums	14	8	12	25	24	25	24	12	G.1.2.3. Primes Nettes Emises
G.1.3. Total									G.1.3. Total
G.1.3.1. Gross Premiums	4 571	5 750	5 573	5 341	5 693	5 598	5 731	5 121	G.1.3.1. Primes Brutes
G.1.3.2. Ceded Premiums	118	143	227	230	303	341	350	94	G.1.3.2. Primes Cédées
G.1.3.3. Net Written Premiums	4 453	5 607	5 346	5 111	5 390	5 257	5 381	5 027	G.1.3.3. Primes Nettes Emises
G.2. Marine, Aviation									**G.2. Marine, Aviation**
G.2.1. Direct Business									G.2.1. Assurances Directes
G.2.1.1. Gross Premiums	1 790	1 859	1 912	1 913	1 918	1 780	1 695	1 757	G.2.1.1. Primes Brutes
G.2.1.2. Ceded Premiums	1 139	1 163	1 187	1 163	1 186	1 086	957	929	G.2.1.2. Primes Cédées
G.2.1.3. Net Written Premiums	651	696	725	750	732	694	738	829	G.2.1.3. Primes Nettes Emises
G.2.2. Reinsurance Accepted									G.2.2. Réassurance Acceptée
G.2.2.1. Gross Premiums	1 174	1 122	1 177	1 155	1 182	995	934	886	G.2.2.1. Primes Brutes
G.2.2.2. Ceded Premiums	735	638	684	648	713	629	563	510	G.2.2.2. Primes Cédées
G.2.2.3. Net Written Premiums	439	484	493	507	469	366	371	376	G.2.2.3. Primes Nettes Emises
G.2.3. Total									G.2.3. Total
G.2.3.1. Gross Premiums	2 964	2 981	3 089	3 068	3 100	2 775	2 629	2 643	G.2.3.1. Primes Brutes
G.2.3.2. Ceded Premiums	1 874	1 801	1 871	1 811	1 898	1 715	1 520	1 439	G.2.3.2. Primes Cédées
G.2.3.3. Net Written Premiums	1 090	1 180	1 218	1 257	1 202	1 060	1 109	1 204	G.2.3.3. Primes Nettes Emises

Monetary Unit: million Icelandic kronur   Unité monétaire : million de couronnes islandaises

		1990	1991	1992	1993	1994	1995	1996	1997
G.3. Freight	**G.3. Fret**								
G.3.1. Direct Business	G.3.1. Assurances Directes								
G.3.1.1. Gross Premiums	G.3.1.1. Primes Brutes	430	440	407	374	365	374	434	458
G.3.1.2. Ceded Premiums	G.3.1.2. Primes Cédées	202	211	178	167	153	145	101	117
G.3.1.3. Net Written Premiums	G.3.1.3. Primes Nettes Emises	228	229	229	207	212	229	333	341
G.3.2. Reinsurance Accepted	G.3.2. Réassurance Acceptée								
G.3.2.1. Gross Premiums	G.3.2.1. Primes Brutes	21	30	20	21	12	10	0	0
G.3.2.2. Ceded Premiums	G.3.2.2. Primes Cédées	16	22	15	16	3	1	0	0
G.3.2.3. Net Written Premiums	G.3.2.3. Primes Nettes Emises	5	8	5	5	9	9	0	0
G.3.3. Total	G.3.3. Total								
G.3.3.1. Gross Premiums	G.3.3.1. Primes Brutes	451	470	427	395	377	384	434	458
G.3.3.2. Ceded Premiums	G.3.3.2. Primes Cédées	218	233	193	183	156	146	101	117
G.3.3.3. Net Written Premiums	G.3.3.3. Primes Nettes Emises	233	237	234	212	221	238	333	341
G.4. Fire, Property Damages	**G.4. Incendie, Dommages aux Biens**								
G.4.1. Direct Business	G.4.1. Assurances Directes								
G.4.1.1. Gross Premiums	G.4.1.1. Primes Brutes	2 444	2 882	3 150	3 236	3 373	3 400	3 549	3 766
G.4.1.2. Ceded Premiums	G.4.1.2. Primes Cédées	1 226	1 451	1 541	1 469	1 601	1 553	1 554	1 652
G.4.1.3. Net Written Premiums	G.4.1.3. Primes Nettes Emises	1 218	1 431	1 609	1 767	1 771	1 847	1 995	2 115
G.4.2. Reinsurance Accepted	G.4.2. Réassurance Acceptée								
G.4.2.1. Gross Premiums	G.4.2.1. Primes Brutes	460	584	686	576	327	112	127	99
G.4.2.2. Ceded Premiums	G.4.2.2. Primes Cédées	359	463	585	471	274	49	59	21
G.4.2.3. Net Written Premiums	G.4.2.3. Primes Nettes Emises	101	121	101	105	52	63	68	78
G.4.3. Total	G.4.3. Total								
G.4.3.1. Gross Premiums	G.4.3.1. Primes Brutes	2 940	3 466	3 836	3 812	3 699	3 512	3 676	3 865
G.4.3.2. Ceded Premiums	G.4.3.2. Primes Cédées	1 585	1 914	2 126	1 940	1 876	1 602	1 613	1 672
G.4.3.3. Net Written Premiums	G.4.3.3. Primes Nettes Emises	1 319	1 552	1 710	1 872	1 823	1 910	2 063	2 193
G.5. Pecuniary Losses	**G.5. Pertes Pécuniaires**								
G.5.1. Direct Business	G.5.1. Assurances Directes								
G.5.1.1. Gross Premiums	G.5.1.1. Primes Brutes	0	19	20	13	14	12	25	35
G.5.1.2. Ceded Premiums	G.5.1.2. Primes Cédées	0	15	16	9	9	8	18	27
G.5.1.3. Net Written Premiums	G.5.1.3. Primes Nettes Emises	0	4	4	4	4	4	7	9
G.5.3. Total	G.5.3. Total								
G.5.3.1 Gross Premiums	G.5.3.1. Primes Brutes	0	19	19	13	14	12	25	35
G.5.3.2 Ceded Premiums	G.5.3.2. Primes Cédées	0	15	16	9	9	8	18	27
G.5.3.3 Net Written Premiums	G.5.3.3. Primes Nettes Emises	0	4	3	4	4	4	7	9
G.6. General Liability	**G.6. Responsabilité Générale**								
G.6.1. Direct Business	G.6.1. Assurances Directes								
G.6.1.1. Gross Premiums	G.6.1.1. Primes Brutes	536	570	635	632	690	701	743	836
G.6.1.2. Ceded Premiums	G.6.1.2. Primes Cédées	179	196	213	203	214	190	196	222
G.6.1.3. Net Written Premiums	G.6.1.3. Primes Nettes Emises	357	374	422	429	476	511	547	614
G.6.2. Reinsurance Accepted	G.6.2. Réassurance Acceptée								
G.6.2.1. Gross Premiums	G.6.2.1. Primes Brutes	205	226	244	236	240	190	192	221
G.6.2.2. Ceded Premiums	G.6.2.2. Primes Cédées	95	103	109	104	103	79	73	79
G.6.2.3. Net Written Premiums	G.6.2.3. Primes Nettes Emises	110	123	135	132	137	111	119	142
G.6.3. Total	G.6.3. Total								
G.6.3.1. Gross Premiums	G.6.3.1. Primes Brutes	741	796	879	868	930	891	935	1 057
G.6.3.2. Ceded Premiums	G.6.3.2. Primes Cédées	274	299	322	307	317	269	269	302
G.6.3.3. Net Written Premiums	G.6.3.3. Primes Nettes Emises	467	497	557	561	613	622	666	755

Monetary Unit: million Icelandic kronur — Unité monétaire : million de couronnes islandaises

English	1990	1991	1992	1993	1994	1995	1996	1997	Français
G.7. Accident, Health									**G.7. Accident, Santé**
G.7.1. Direct Business									G.7.1. Assurances Directes
G.7.1.1. Gross Premiums	814	948	1 150	1 145	1 225	1 235	1 215	1 259	G.7.1.1. Primes Brutes
G.7.1.2. Ceded Premiums	339	374	425	431	478	458	421	460	G.7.1.2. Primes Cédées
G.7.1.3. Net Written Premiums	475	574	725	814	747	777	794	799	G.7.1.3. Primes Nettes Emises
G.7.2. Reinsurance Accepted									G.7.2. Réassurance Acceptée
G.7.2.1. Gross Premiums	292	325	339	350	389	345	312	325	G.7.2.1. Primes Brutes
G.7.2.2. Ceded Premiums	121	131	140	141	156	134	111	115	G.7.2.2. Primes Cédées
G.7.2.3. Net Written Premiums	171	194	199	209	233	211	201	210	G.7.2.3. Primes Nettes Emises
G.7.3. Total									G.7.3. Total
G.7.3.1. Gross Premiums	1 106	1 273	1 489	1 495	1 614	1 580	1 527	1 584	G.7.3.1. Primes Brutes
G.7.3.2. Ceded Premiums	460	505	565	572	634	592	532	575	G.7.3.2. Primes Cédées
G.7.3.3. Net Written Premiums	646	768	924	923	980	988	995	1 009	G.7.3.3. Primes Nettes Emises
G.8. Others									**G.8. Autres**
G.8.1. Direct Business									G.8.1. Assurances Directes
G.8.1.1. Gross Premiums	3	0	0	0	0	0	0	0	G.8.1.1. Primes Brutes
G.8.1.2. Ceded Premiums	2	0	0	0	0	0	0	0	G.8.1.2. Primes Cédées
G.8.1.3. Net Written Premiums	1	0	0	0	0	0	0	0	G.8.1.3. Primes Nettes Emises
G.8.2. Reinsurance Accepted									G.8.2. Réassurance Acceptée
G.8.2.1. Gross Premiums	86	89	76	73	3	0	0	0	G.8.2.1. Primes Brutes
G.8.2.2. Ceded Premiums	12	13	1	1	0	0	0	0	G.8.2.2. Primes Cédées
G.8.2.3. Net Written Premiums	74	76	75	72	3	0	0	0	G.8.2.3. Primes Nettes Emises
G.8.3. Total									G.8.3. Total
G.8.3.1. Gross Premiums	89	89	76	73	3	0	0	0	G.8.3.1. Primes Brutes
G.8.3.2. Ceded Premiums	14	13	1	1	0	0	0	0	G.8.3.2. Primes Cédées
G.8.3.3. Net Written Premiums	75	76	75	72	3	0	0	0	G.8.3.3. Primes Nettes Emises
G.9. Treaty Reinsurance									**G.9. Réassurance Obligatoire**
G.9.2. Reinsurance Accepted									G.9.2. Réassurance Acceptée
G.9.2.1. Gross Premiums	0	0	0	0	:	103	0	0	G.9.2.1. Primes Brutes
G.9.2.3. Net Written Premiums	0	0	0	0	:	103	0	0	G.9.2.3. Primes Nettes Emises
G.10. Total									**G.10. Total**
G.10.1. Direct Business									G.10.1. Assurances Directes
G.10.1.1. Gross Premiums	10 566	12 440	12 828	12 622	:	13 064	13 346	13 210	G.10.1.1. Primes Brutes
G.10.1.2. Ceded Premiums	3 197	3 533	3 780	3 665	:	3 770	3 575	3 490	G.10.1.2. Primes Cédées
G.10.1.3. Net Written Premiums	7 369	8 907	9 048	8 957	:	9 294	9 771	9 720	G.10.1.3. Primes Nettes Emises
G.10.2. Reinsurance Accepted									G.10.2. Réassurance Acceptée
G.10.2.1. Gross Premiums	2 260	2 404	2 561	2 443	:	1 791	1 611	1 554	G.10.2.1. Primes Brutes
G.10.2.2. Ceded Premiums	1 346	1 390	1 541	1 388	:	903	828	735	G.10.2.2. Primes Cédées
G.10.2.3. Net Written Premiums	914	1 014	1 020	1 055	:	888	783	819	G.10.2.3. Primes Nettes Emises
G.10.3. Total									G.10.3. Total
G.10.3.1. Gross Premiums	12 826	14 844	15 389	15 065	:	14 752	14 957	14 764	G.10.3.1. Primes Brutes
G.10.3.2. Ceded Premiums	4 543	4 923	5 321	5 053	:	4 673	4 403	4 225	G.10.3.2. Primes Cédées
G.10.3.3. Net Written Premiums	8 283	9 921	10 068	10 012	:	10 079	10 554	10 539	G.10.3.3. Primes Nettes Emises

H. GROSS CLAIMS PAYMENTS — **H. PAIEMENTS BRUTS DES SINISTRES**

H.1. Life — **H.1. Vie**

English	1990	1991	1992	1993	1994	1995	1996	1997	Français
H.1.1. Domestic Companies							172	208	H.1.1. Entreprises Nationales
H.1. Total							172	208	H.1. Total

H.2. Non-Life — **H.2. Non-Vie**

English	1990	1991	1992	1993	1994	1995	1996	1997	Français
H.2.1. Domestic Companies							10 267	10 296	H.2.1. Entreprises Nationales
H.2.2. (Foreign Controlled Companies)							244	0	H.2.2. (Entreprises Sous Contrôle Etranger)
H.2. Total							10 267	10 296	H.2. Total

ICELAND

ISLANDE

Monetary Unit: million Icelandic kronur — Unité monétaire : million de couronnes islandaises

	1990	1991	1992	1993	1994	1995	1996	1997
I. GROSS OPERATING EXPENSES — **I. DEPENSES BRUITES D'EXPLOITATION**								
I.1. Life — **I.1. Vie**								
I.1.1. Domestic Companies — I.1.1. Entreprises Nationales							217	255
I.1.2. (Foreign Controlled Companies) — I.1.2. (Entreprises Sous Contrôle Etranger)							15	0
I.1. Total — I.1. Total des Primes Nettes Vie							217	255
I.2. Non-Life — **I.2. Non-Vie**								
I.2.1. Domestic Companies — I.2.1. Entreprises Nationales							3 030	3 122
I.2.2. (Foreign Controlled Companies) — I.2.2. (Entreprises Sous Contrôle Etranger)							173	0
I.2. Total — I.2. Total							3 030	3 122
J. COMMISSIONS — **J. COMMISSIONS**								
J.1. Life — **J.1. Vie**								
J.1.3. Total								
J.1.3.1. Domestic Companies — J.1.3.1. Entreprises Nationales							..	37
J.1.3. Total of Life Net Premiums — J.1.3. Total							..	37
J.2. Non-Life — **J.2. Non-Vie**								
J.2.3. Total								
J.2.3.1. Domestic Companies — J.2.3.1. Entreprises Nationales							..	597
J.2.3. Total — J.2.3. Total							..	597

Monetary Unit: million Irish pounds — Unité monétaire : million de livres irlandaises

A. NUMBER OF COMPANIES IN THE REPORTING COUNTRY — A. NOMBRE D'ENTREPRISES DANS LE PAYS DECLARANT

	1990	1991	1992	1993	1994	1995	1996	1997
A.1. Life — A.1. Vie								
A.1.1. Domestic Companies — Entreprises Nationales	..	17	17	17	19	20	22	30
A.1.3. Branches & Agencies of Foreign Cies — Succursales et Agences d'Ent. Etrangères	..	14	14	14	14	13	14	14
A.1. All Companies — Ensemble des Entreprises	..	31	31	33	34	35	40	44
A.2. Non-Life — A.2. Non-Vie								
A.2.1. Domestic Companies — Entreprises Nationales	24	30	34	44	52	61	72	83
A.2.3. Branches & Agencies of Foreign Cies — Succursales et Agences d'Ent. Etrangères	28	30	31	30	30	29	27	23
A.2. All Companies — Ensemble des Entreprises	52	60	65	74	82	90	99	106
A.5. Total — A.5. Total								
A.5.1. Domestic Companies — Entreprises Nationales	38	47	51	63	72	83	98	113
A.5.3. Branches & Agencies of Foreign Cies — Succursales et Agences d'Ent. Etrangères	43	44	45	44	44	42	41	37
A.5. All Insurance Companies — Ensemble des Entreprises d'Assurances	81	91	96	107	116	125	139	150

B. NUMBER OF EMPLOYEES — B. NOMBRE D'EMPLOYES

	1990	1991	1992	1993	1994	1995	1996	1997
B.1. Insurance Companies — Entreprises d'Assurances	9 258	9 818	10 118	10 085	10 402	10 386	10 231	10 031

C. BUSINESS WRITTEN IN THE REPORTING COUNTRY — C. OPERATIONS CONCLUES DANS LE PAYS DECLARANT

C.1. Life — C.1. Vie

	1990	1991	1992	1993	1994	1995	1996	1997
C.1.1. Gross Premiums — Primes Brutes								
C.1.1.1. Direct Business — Assurances Directes								
C.1.1.1.1. Domestic Companies — Entreprises Nationales	992	982	920	1 244	1 359	1 438	1 846	2 626
C.1.1.1.3. Branches & Agencies of Foreign Cies — Succursales et Agences d'Ent. Etrangères	450	477	378	397	423	413	539	633
C.1.1.1. Total	1 442	1 459	1 298	1 641	1 782	1 851	2 385	3 259
C.1.1.2. Reinsurance Accepted — Réassurance Acceptée								
C.1.1.2.1. Domestic Companies — Entreprises Nationales	3	2	230	170	3	4	18	21
C.1.1.2.3. Branches & Agencies of Foreign Cies — Succursales et Agences d'Ent. Etrangères	0	0	0	0	0	4	5	6
C.1.1.2. Total	3	2	230	170	3	8	23	27
C.1.1.3. Total								
C.1.1.3.1. Domestic Companies — Entreprises Nationales	994	984	1 150	1 414	1 362	1 442	1 864	2 647
C.1.1.3.3. Branches & Agencies of Foreign Cies — Succursales et Agences d'Ent. Etrangères	450	477	378	398	423	417	544	639
C.1.1.3. Total Gross Premiums — Total des Primes Brutes	1 445	1 460	1 528	1 811	1 785	1 859	2 408	3 286
C.1.2. Ceded Premiums — Primes Cédées								
C.1.2.1. Domestic Companies — Entreprises Nationales	45	36	257	231	40	62	82	77
C.1.2.3. Branches & Agencies of Foreign Cies — Succursales et Agences d'Ent. Etrangères	15	9	12	13	14	14	16	9
C.1.2. Total	59	45	269	243	54	76	98	86
C.1.3. Net Written Premiums — Primes Nettes Emises								
C.1.3.1. Domestic Companies — Entreprises Nationales	950	948	893	1 183	1 322	1 380	1 782	2 570
C.1.3.3. Branches & Agencies of Foreign Cies — Succursales et Agences d'Ent. Etrangères	436	467	367	385	409	403	528	630
C.1.3. Total	1 385	1 416	1 259	1 568	1 731	1 783	2 310	3 200

C.2. Non-Life — C.2. Non-Vie

	1990	1991	1992	1993	1994	1995	1996	1997
C.2.1. Gross premiums — Primes Brutes								
C.2.1.1. Direct Business — Assurances Directes								
C.2.1.1.1. Domestic Companies — Entreprises Nationales	608	714	779	932	1 102	1 235	1 339	1 467
C.2.1.1.3. Branches & Agencies of Foreign Cies — Succursales et Agences d'Ent. Etrangères	387	414	432	384	384	305	366	348
C.2.1.1. Total	995	1 127	1 211	1 315	1 486	1 540	1 705	1 815
C.2.1.2. Reinsurance Accepted — Réassurance Acceptée								
C.2.1.2.1. Domestic Companies — Entreprises Nationales	37	46	47	72	65	148	155	359
C.2.1.2.3. Branches & Agencies of Foreign Cies — Succursales et Agences d'Ent. Etrangères	0	1	1	3	2	0	0	1
C.2.1.2. Total	37	48	48	75	67	148	155	360

Monetary Unit: million Irish pounds   Unité monétaire : million de livres irlandaises

	1990	1991	1992	1993	1994	1995	1996	1997
C.2.1.3. Total								
C.2.1.3.1. Domestic Companies / Entreprises Nationales	645	760	826	1 004	1 167	1 383	1 494	1 826
C.2.1.3.3. Branches & Agencies of Foreign Cies / Succursales et Agences d'Ent. Etrangères	387	415	433	387	386	305	366	349
C.2.1.3. Total Gross Premiums / Total des Primes Brutes	1 032	1 175	1 259	1 390	1 553	1 688	1 860	2 175
C.2.2. Ceded Premiums / Primes Cédées								
C.2.2.1. Domestic Companies / Entreprises Nationales	109	151	167	202	242	313	324	315
C.2.2.3. Branches & Agencies of Foreign Cies / Succursales et Agences d'Ent. Etrangères	57	57	64	56	71	40	55	46
C.2.2. Total / Total	167	208	230	257	312	353	379	361
C.2.3. Net Written Premiums / Primes Nettes Emises								
C.2.3.1. Domestic Companies / Entreprises Nationales	535	609	659	802	925	1 070	1 170	1 511
C.2.3.3. Branches & Agencies of Foreign Cies / Succursales et Agences d'Ent. Etrangères	330	358	369	331	316	265	311	303
C.2.3. Total / Total	865	967	1 028	1 133	1 241	1 335	1 481	1 814
C.3. Total								
C.3.1. Gross Premiums / Primes Brutes								
C.3.1.1. Direct Business / Assurances Directes								
C.3.1.1.1. Domestic Companies / Entreprises Nationales	1 599	1 696	1 699	2 176	2 461	2 673	3 185	4 093
C.3.1.1.3. Branches & Agencies of Foreign Cies / Succursales et Agences d'Ent. Etrangères	838	890	810	781	807	718	905	981
C.3.1.1. Total / Total	2 437	2 586	2 508	2 957	3 268	3 391	4 090	5 074
C.3.1.2. Reinsurance Accepted / Réassurance Acceptée								
C.3.1.2.1. Domestic Companies / Entreprises Nationales	40	48	277	242	68	152	173	380
C.3.1.2.3. Branches & Agencies of Foreign Cies / Succursales et Agences d'Ent. Etrangères	0	1	1	3	2	4	5	7
C.3.1.2. Total / Total	40	49	278	245	70	156	178	387
C.3.1.3. Total / Total								
C.3.1.3.1. Domestic Companies / Entreprises Nationales	1 639	1 744	1 976	2 417	2 529	2 825	3 358	4 473
C.3.1.3.3. Branches & Agencies of Foreign Cies / Succursales et Agences d'Ent. Etrangères	838	891	811	784	809	722	910	988
C.3.1.3. Total Gross Premiums / Total des Primes Brutes	2 477	2 635	2 786	3 201	3 338	3 547	4 268	5 461
C.3.2. Ceded Premiums / Primes Cédées								
C.3.2.1. Domestic Companies / Entreprises Nationales	154	187	424	432	282	375	406	392
C.3.2.3. Branches & Agencies of Foreign Cies / Succursales et Agences d'Ent. Etrangères	72	66	75	68	84	54	71	55
C.3.2. Total / Total	226	253	499	501	366	429	477	447
C.3.3. Net Written Premiums / Primes Nettes Emises								
C.3.3.1. Domestic Companies / Entreprises Nationales	1 485	1 557	1 552	1 985	2 247	2 450	2 952	4 081
C.3.3.3. Branches & Agencies of Foreign Cies / Succursales et Agences d'Ent. Etrangères	766	825	735	716	725	668	839	933
C.3.3. Total / Total	2 251	2 382	2 287	2 701	2 972	3 118	3 791	5 014

D. NET WRITTEN PREMIUMS IN THE REPORTING COUNTRY IN TERMS OF DOMESTIC AND FOREIGN RISKS
D. PRIMES NETTES EMISES DANS LE PAYS DECLARANT EN RISQUES NATIONAUX ET ETRANGERS

	1990	1991	1992	1993	1994	1995	1996	1997
D.1. Life / D.1. Vie								
D.1.1. Domestic Risks / Risques Nationaux								
D.1.1.1. Domestic Companies / Entreprises Nationales	950	948	893	1 129	1 240	1 219	1 470	1 890
D.1.1.3. Branches & Agencies of Foreign Cies / Succursales et Agences d'Ent. Etrangères	436	467	367	385	409	403	528	630
D.1.1. Total / Total des Primes Nettes Vie	1 386	1 416	1 259	1 514	1 649	1 622	1 998	2 520
D.1.2. Foreign Risks / Risques Etrangers								
D.1.2.1. Domestic Companies / Entreprises Nationales	:	:	:	54	82	161	312	680
D.1.2. Total / Total des Primes Nettes Vie	:	:	:	54	82	161	312	680
D.1.3. Total / Total								
D.1.3.1. Domestic Companies / Entreprises Nationales	950	948	893	1 183	1 322	1 380	1 782	2 570
D.1.3.3. Branches & Agencies of Foreign Cies / Succursales et Agences d'Ent. Etrangères	436	467	367	385	409	403	528	630
D.1.3. Total of Life Net Premiums / Total des Primes Nettes Vie	1 385	1 416	1 259	1 568	1 731	1 783	2 310	3 200
D.2. Non-Life / D.2. Non-Vie								
D.2.1. Domestic Risks / Risques Nationaux								
D.2.1.1. Domestic Companies / Entreprises Nationales	506	561	596	697	818	854	910	997
D.2.1.3. Branches & Agencies of Foreign Cies / Succursales et Agences d'Ent. Etrangères	330	358	368	327	302	264	310	302
D.2.1. Total / Total des Primes Nettes Vie	836	919	964	1 024	1 120	1 118	1 220	1 299

Monetary Unit: million Irish pounds — Unité monétaire : million de livres irlandaises

Item	1990	1991	1992	1993	1994	1995	1996	1997	(Français)
D.2.2. Foreign Risks									D.2.2. Risques Etrangers
D.2.2.1. Domestic Companies	29	48	63	105	107	216	260	514	D.2.2.1. Entreprises Nationales
D.2.2.3. Branches & Agencies of Foreign Cies	0	0	1	4	14	1	1	1	D.2.2.3. Succursales et Agences d'Ent. Etrangères
D.2.2. Total	29	48	65	108	121	217	261	515	D.2.2. Total des Primes Nettes Vie
D.2.3. Total									D.2.3. Total
D.2.3.1. Domestic Companies	535	609	659	802	925	1 070	1 170	1 511	D.2.3.1. Entreprises Nationales
D.2.3.3. Branches & Agencies of Foreign Cies	330	358	369	331	316	265	311	303	D.2.3.3. Succursales et Agences d'Ent. Etrangères
D.2.3. Total	865	967	1 028	1 133	1 241	1 335	1 481	1 814	D.2.3. Total des Primes Nettes Vie
E. BUSINESS WRITTEN ABROAD									**E. OPERATIONS A L'ETRANGER**
E.1. Life									**E.1. Vie**
E.1.1. Gross Premiums									E.1.1. Primes Brutes
E.1.1.1. Direct Business									E.1.1.1. Assurance Directe
E.1.1.1.1. Branches & Agencies	87	109	104	136	114	89	70	10	E.1.1.1.1. Succursales & Agences
E.1.1.1. Total	87	109	104	136	114	89	70	10	E.1.1.1. Total
E.1.1.2. Reinsurance Accepted									E.1.1.2. Reassurance Acceptée
E.1.1.2.1. Branches & Agencies	0	0	0	0	0	0	0	- 1	E.1.1.2.1. Succursales & Agences
E.1.1.2. Total	0	0	0	0	0	0	0	- 1	E.1.1.2. Total
E.1.1.3. Total									E.1.1.3. Total
E.1.1.3.1. Branches & Agencies	87	109	104	136	114	89	70	9	E.1.1.3.1. Succursales & Agences
E.1.1.3. Total Gross Premiums	87	109	104	136	114	89	70	9	E.1.1.3. Total des Primes Brutes
E.1.2. Ceded Premiums									E.1.2. Primes Cédées
E.1.2.1. Branches & Agencies	2	1	1	1	1	63	1	0	E.1.2.1. Succursales & Agences
E.1.2. Total	2	1	1	1	1	63	1	0	E.1.2. Total
E.1.3. Net Written Premiums									E.1.3. Primes Nettes Emises
E.1.3.1. Branches & Agencies	85	108	103	135	112	26	69	9	E.1.3.1. Succursales & Agences
E.1.3. Total	85	108	103	135	112	26	69	9	E.1.3. Total
E.2. Non-Life									**E.2. Non-Vie**
E.2.1. Gross Premiums									E.2.1. Primes Brutes
E.2.1.1. Direct Business									E.2.1.1. Assurance Directe
E.2.1.1.1. Branches & Agencies	31	40	50	68	65	63	114	129	E.2.1.1.1. Succursales & Agences
E.2.1.1. Total	31	40	50	68	65	63	114	129	E.2.1.1. Total
E.2.1.2. Reinsurance Accepted									E.2.1.2. Réassurance Acceptée
E.2.1.2.1. Branches & Agencies	5	1	6	1	1	0	0	0	E.2.1.2.1. Succursales & Agences
E.2.1.2. Total	5	1	6	1	1	0	0	0	E.2.1.2. Total
E.2.1.3. Total									E.2.1.3. Total
E.2.1.3.1. Branches & Agencies	36	41	56	67	66	63	114	129	E.2.1.3.1. Succursales & Agences
E.2.1.3. Total Gross Premiums	36	41	56	67	66	63	114	129	E.2.1.3. Total des Primes Brutes
E.2.2. Ceded Premiums									E.2.2. Primes Cédées
E.2.2.1. Branches & Agencies	11	8	11	13	12	11	42	58	E.2.2.1. Succursales & Agences
E.2.2. Total	11	8	11	13	12	11	42	58	E.2.2. Total
E.2.3. Net Written Premiums									E.2.3. Primes Nettes Emises
E.2.3.1. Branches & Agencies	25	34	45	54	54	52	72	71	E.2.3.1. Succursales & Agences
E.2.3. Total	25	34	45	54	54	52	72	71	E.2.3. Total
F. OUTSTANDING INVESTMENT BY DIRECT INSURANCE COMPANIES									**F. ENCOURS DES PLACEMENTS DES ENTREPRISES D'ASSURANCES DIRECTES**
F.1. Life									**F.1. Vie**
F.1.1. Real Estate									F.1.1. Immobilier
F.1.1.1. Domestic Companies	647	672	571	586	631	625	631	785	F.1.1.1. Entreprises Nationales
F.1.1.3. Branches & Agencies of Foreign Cies	244	172	159	159	20	20	21	17	F.1.1.3. Succursales et Agences d'Ent. Etrangères
F.1.1.4. Domestic Investment	858	819	715	730	629	..	..	..	F.1.1.4. Placement dans le Pays
F.1.1.5. Foreign Investment	33	25	15	16	21	..	..	..	F.1.1.5. Placement à l' Etranger
F.1.1. Total	891	844	730	745	651	653	653	..	F.1.1. Total

Monetary Unit: million Irish pounds   Unité monétaire : million de livres irlandaises

Code (EN)	Label (FR)	1990	1991	1992	1993	1994	1995	1996	1997
F.1.2. Mortgage Loans	**F.1.2. Prêts Hypothécaires**								
F.1.2.1. Domestic Companies	F.1.2.1. Entreprises Nationales	3	..	..	..	0	0	0	0
F.1.2.3. Branches & Agencies of Foreign Cies	F.1.2.3. Succursales at Agences d'Ent. Etrangères	1	..	..	..	0	0	0	0
F.1.2.4. Domestic Investment	F.1.2.4. Placement dans le Pays	4	..	..	..	..	..	..	..
F.1.2. Total	F.1.2. Total	4	..	..	..	0	0	0	0
F.1.3. Shares	**F.1.3. Actions**								
F.1.3.1. Domestic Companies	F.1.3.1. Entreprises Nationales	422	552	444	707	658	3 657	4 200	6 533
F.1.3.3. Branches & Agencies of Foreign Cies	F.1.3.3. Succursales at Agences d'Ent. Etrangères	697	729	709	1 140	72	78	145	225
F.1.3.4. Domestic Investment	F.1.3.4. Placement dans le Pays	898	1 015	946	1 553	482	..	..	..
F.1.3.5. Foreign Investment	F.1.3.5. Placement à l'Etranger	221	267	207	293	248	..	..	..
F.1.3. Total	F.1.3. Total	1 119	1 282	1 153	1 847	730	..	4 346	..
F.1.4. Bonds with Fixed Revenue	**F.1.4. Obligations**								
F.1.4.1. Domestic Companies	F.1.4.1. Entreprises Nationales	2 096	2 299	2 160	2 854	2 650	3 085	3 542	5 224
F.1.4.3. Branches & Agencies of Foreign Cies	F.1.4.3. Succursales at Agences d'Ent. Etrangères	1 009	1 167	1 314	1 682	130	125	165	208
F.1.4.4. Domestic Investment	F.1.4.4. Placement dans le Pays	3 077	3 300	3 321	4 362	2 733	..	..	..
F.1.4.5. Foreign Investment	F.1.4.5. Placement à l'Etranger	28	166	153	174	48	..	..	..
F.1.4. Total	F.1.4. Total	3 105	3 466	3 473	4 536	2 781	..	3 708	..
F.1.5. Loans other than Mortgage Loans	**F.1.5. Prêts Autres qu'Hypothécaires**								
F.1.5.1. Domestic Companies	F.1.5.1. Entreprises Nationales	288	154	233	219	400	456	665	64
F.1.5.3. Branches & Agencies of Foreign Cies	F.1.5.3. Succursales at Agences d'Ent. Etrangères	53	23	31	24	5	1	5	8
F.1.5.4. Domestic Investment	F.1.5.4. Placement dans le Pays	332	177	263	243	405	..	..	..
F.1.5.5. Foreign Investment	F.1.5.5. Placement à l'Etranger	..	..	0	..	0	..	..	..
F.1.5. Total	F.1.5. Total	332	177	264	243	405	..	670	..
F.1.6. Other Investments	**F.1.6. Autres Placements**								
F.1.6.1. Domestic Companies	F.1.6.1. Entreprises Nationales	2 388	3 054	2 641	3 628	3 430	2 404	1 502	3 590
F.1.6.3. Branches & Agencies of Foreign Cies	F.1.6.3. Succursales et Agences d'Ent. Etrangères	620	621	479	694	87	26	40	37
F.1.6.4. Domestic Investment	F.1.6.4. Placement dans le Pays	2 605	3 226	2 950	4 188	3 480	..	..	..
F.1.6.5. Foreign Investment	F.1.6.5. Placement à l'Etranger	403	122	170	134	37	..	..	..
F.1.6. Total	F.1.6. Total	3 008	3 675	3 120	4 323	3 518	..	1 542	..
F.1.7. Total	**F.1.7. Total**								
F.1.7.1. Domestic Companies	F.1.7.1. Entreprises Nationales	5 834	6 732	6 047	7 995	7 769	10 227	10 540	16 196
F.1.7.3. Branches & Agencies of Foreign Cies	F.1.7.3. Succursales et Agences d'Ent. Etrangères	2 625	2 712	2 692	3 699	314	250	376	495
F.1.7.4. Domestic Investment	F.1.7.4. Placement dans le Pays	7 774	8 863	8 195	11 077	7 730	..	..	..
F.1.7.5. Foreign Investment	F.1.7.5. Placement à l'Etranger	685	581	545	617	354	..	..	..
F.1.7. Total of Life Investments	F.1.7. Total des Placements Vie	8 459	9 444	8 740	11 694	8 083	..	10 916	..
F.2. Non-Life	**F.2. Non-Vie**								
F.2.1. Real Estate	**F.2.1. Immobilier**								
F.2.1.1. Domestic Companies	F.2.1.1. Entreprises Nationales	61	47	46	41	54	89	90	64
F.2.1.3. Branches & Agencies of Foreign Cies	F.2.1.3. Succursales et Agences d'Ent. Etrangères	9	11	10	10	0	0	0	0
F.2.1.4. Domestic Investment	F.2.1.4. Placement dans le Pays	69	57	46	41	54	..	..	62
F.2.1.5. Foreign Investment	F.2.1.5. Placement à l'Etranger	1	1	10	10	0	..	..	2
F.2.1. Total	F.2.1. Total	70	58	56	50	54	90	90	64
F.2.3. Shares	**F.2.3. Actions**								
F.2.3.1. Domestic Companies	F.2.3.1. Entreprises Nationales	169	264	180	323	336	433	460	764
F.2.3.3. Branches & Agencies of Foreign Cies	F.2.3.3. Succursales et Agences d'Ent. Etrangères	63	85	52	56	0	0	0	0
F.2.3.4. Domestic Investment	F.2.3.4. Placement dans le Pays	180	243	180	323	336	..	..	555
F.2.3.5. Foreign Investment	F.2.3.5. Placement à l'Etranger	53	105	52	56	0	..	..	209
F.2.3. Total	F.2.3. Total	232	348	231	380	337	..	460	764
F.2.4. Bonds with Fixed Revenue	**F.2.4. Obligations**								
F.2.4.1. Domestic Companies	F.2.4.1. Entreprises Nationales	509	721	845	1 178	1 308	1 689	1 993	0
F.2.4.3. Branches & Agencies of Foreign Cies	F.2.4.3. Succursales et Agences d'Ent. Etrangères	494	567	588	595	4	0	0	0
F.2.4.4. Domestic Investment	F.2.4.4. Placement dans le Pays	966	1 257	845	1 178	1 308	..	..	..
F.2.4.5. Foreign Investment	F.2.4.5. Placement à l'Etranger	37	31	588	595	4	..	..	..
F.2.4. Total	F.2.4. Total	1 003	1 288	1 433	1 773	1 312	..	1 993	..

Monetary Unit: million Irish pounds — Unité monétaire : million de livres irlandaises

	1990	1991	1992	1993	1994	1995	1996	1997
F.2.6. Other Investments / Autres Placements								
F.2.6.1. Domestic Companies / Entreprises Nationales	546	494	457	478	503	982	1 000	3 565
F.2.6.3. Branches & Agencies of Foreign Cies / Succursales et Agences d'Ent. Etrangères	136	73	55	42	1	9	7	5
F.2.6.4. Domestic Investment / Placement dans le Pays	655	564	457	478	503	:	:	2 673
F.2.6.5. Foreign Investment / Placement à l' Etranger	27	4	55	42	1	:	:	897
F.2.6. Total / Total	682	567	512	521	504	:	1 007	3 570
F.2.7. Total / Total								
F.2.7.1. Domestic Companies / Entreprises Nationales	1 285	1 526	1 528	2 020	2 201	3 193	3 543	4 393
F.2.7.3. Branches & Agencies of Foreign Cies / Succursales et Agences d'Ent. Etrangères	702	735	705	703	5	9	7	5
F.2.7.4. Domestic Investment / Placement dans le Pays	1 869	2 063	1 528	2 020	2 201	:	:	3 290
F.2.7.5. Foreign Investment / Placement à l' Etranger	118	198	705	703	5	:	:	1 108
F.2.7. Total of Non-Life Investments / Total des Placements Non-Vie	1 987	2 261	2 233	2 724	2 206	:	3 550	4 398
G. BREAKDOWN OF NON-LIFE PREMIUMS / G. VENTILATIONS DES PRIMES NON-VIE								
G.1. Motor vehicle / G.1. Assurance Automobile								
G.1.1. Direct Business / G.1.1. Assurances Directes								
G.1.1.1. Gross Premiums / Primes Brutes	484	548	582	607	646	692	757	781
G.1.1.2. Ceded Premiums / Primes Cédées	31	33	49	48	44	73	79	59
G.1.1.3. Net Written Premiums / Primes Nettes Emises	453	515	533	559	602	619	678	722
G.1.3. Total / Total								
G.1.3.1. Gross Premiums / Primes Brutes	484	:	:	:	:	:	:	:
G.1.3.2. Ceded Premiums / Primes Cédées	31	:	:	:	:	:	:	:
G.1.3.3. Net Written Premiums / Primes Nettes Emises	453	:	:	:	:	:	:	:
G.2. Marine, Aviation / G.2. Marine, Aviation								
G.2.1. Direct Business / G.2.1. Assurances Directes								
G.2.1.1. Gross Premiums / Primes Brutes	5	7	7	19	29	29	31	38
G.2.1.2. Ceded Premiums / Primes Cédées	2	2	3	7	16	12	13	16
G.2.1.3. Net Written Premiums / Primes Nettes Emises	4	4	5	11	13	17	19	22
G.2.3. Total / Total								
G.2.3.1. Gross Premiums / Primes Brutes	5	:	:	:	:	:	:	:
G.2.3.2. Ceded Premiums / Primes Cédées	2	:	:	:	:	:	:	:
G.2.3.3. Net Written Premiums / Primes Nettes Emises	4	:	:	:	:	:	:	:
G.4. Fire, Property Damages / Incendie, Dommages aux Biens								
G.4.1. Direct Business / G.4.1. Assurances Directes								
G.4.1.1. Gross Premiums / Primes Brutes	241	262	277	303	359	372	420	460
G.4.1.2. Ceded Premiums / Primes Cédées	63	74	80	87	114	123	141	147
G.4.1.3. Net Written Premiums / Primes Nettes Emises	178	189	198	216	246	249	279	313
G.4.3. Total / Total								
G.4.3.1. Gross Premiums / Primes Brutes	241	:	:	:	:	:	:	:
G.4.3.2. Ceded Premiums / Primes Cédées	63	:	:	:	:	:	:	:
G.4.3.3. Net Written Premiums / Primes Nettes Emises	178	:	:	:	:	:	:	:
G.5. Pecuniary Losses / Pertes Pécunières								
G.5.1. Direct Business / G.5.1. Assurances Directes								
G.5.1.1. Gross Premiums / Primes Brutes	29	33	42	47	55	19	:	:
G.5.1.2. Ceded Premiums / Primes Cédées	14	16	19	23	30	7	:	:
G.5.1.3. Net Written Premiums / Primes Nettes Emises	15	17	24	24	25	12	:	:
G.5.3. Total / Total								
G.5.3.1. Gross Premiums / Primes Brutes	29	:	:	:	:	:	:	:
G.5.3.2. Ceded Premiums / Primes Cédées	14	:	:	:	:	:	:	:
G.5.3.3. Net Written Premiums / Primes Nettes Emises	15	:	:	:	:	:	:	:
G.6. General Liability / Responsabilité Générale								
G.6.1. Direct Business / G.6.1. Assurances Directes								
G.6.1.1. Gross Premiums / Primes Brutes	204	242	263	295	347	327	352	350
G.6.1.2. Ceded Premiums / Primes Cédées	35	62	67	73	91	88	99	89
G.6.1.3. Net Written Premiums / Primes Nettes Emises	168	180	197	222	256	239	253	261
G.6.3. Total / Total								
G.6.3.1. Gross Premiums / Primes Brutes	204	:	:	:	:	:	:	:
G.6.3.2. Ceded Premiums / Primes Cédées	35	:	:	:	:	:	:	:
G.6.3.3. Net Written Premiums / Primes Nettes Emises	168	:	:	:	:	:	:	:

IRELAND

Monetary Unit: million Irish pounds

IRLANDE

Unité monétaire : million de livres irlandaises

		1990	1991	1992	1993	1994	1995	1996	1997
G.7. Accident, Health	**G.7. Accident, Santé**								
G.7.1. Direct Business	G.7.1. Assurances Directes								
G.7.1.1. Gross Premiums	G.7.1.1. Primes Brutes	32	34	39	45	50	56	73	101
G.7.1.2. Ceded Premiums	G.7.1.2. Primes Cédées	7	5	6	8	9	7	4	7
G.7.1.3. Net Written Premiums	G.7.1.3. Primes Nettes Emises	25	29	33	37	41	49	69	94
G.7.3. Total	G.7.3. Total								
G.7.3.1. Gross Premiums	G.7.3.1. Primes Brutes	32	..	..	..	..	..	..	..
G.7.3.2. Ceded Premiums	G.7.3.2. Primes Cédées	7	..	..	..	..	..	..	..
G.7.3.3. Net Written Premiums	G.7.3.3. Primes Nettes Emises	25	..	..	..	..	..	..	..
G.8. Others	**G.8. Autres**								
G.8.1. Direct Business	G.8.1. Assurances Directes								
G.8.1.1. Gross Premiums	G.8.1.1. Primes Brutes	..	..	..	..	..	45	72	85
G.8.1.2. Ceded Premiums	G.8.1.2. Primes Cédées	..	..	..	..	..	29	32	26
G.8.1.3. Net Written Premiums	G.8.1.3. Primes Nettes Emises	..	..	..	..	..	16	40	59
G.9. Treaty Reinsurance	**G.9. Réassurance Obligatoire**								
G.9.2. Reinsurance Accepted	G.9.2. Réassurance Acceptée								
G.9.2.1. Gross Premiums	G.9.2.1. Primes Brutes	37	48	48	75	..	148	155	360
G.9.2.2. Ceded Premiums	G.9.2.2. Primes Cédées	15	15	8	10	..	14	11	17
G.9.2.3. Net Written Premiums	G.9.2.3. Primes Nettes Emises	22	33	40	65	..	134	144	343
G.9.3. Total	G.9.3. Total								
G.9.3.1. Gross Premiums	G.9.3.1. Primes Brutes	37	..	..	..	..	..	..	..
G.9.3.2. Ceded Premiums	G.9.3.2. Primes Cédées	15	..	..	..	..	..	..	..
G.9.3.3. Net Written Premiums	G.9.3.3. Primes Nettes Emises	22	..	..	..	..	..	..	..
G.10. Total	**G.10. Total**								
G.10.1. Direct Business	G.10.1. Assurances Directes								
G.10.1.1. Gross Premiums	G.10.1.1. Primes Brutes	995	1 127	1 211	1 315	1 486	1 540	1 705	1 815
G.10.1.2. Ceded Premiums	G.10.1.2. Primes Cédées	115	193	223	247	303	339	368	344
G.10.1.3. Net Written Premiums	G.10.1.3. Primes Nettes Emises	844	934	988	1 868	1 183	1 201	1 337	1 471
G.10.2. Reinsurance Accepted	G.10.2. Réassurance Acceptée								
G.10.2.1. Gross Premiums	G.10.2.1. Primes Brutes	37	..	..	75	67	148	155	360
G.10.2.2. Ceded Premiums	G.10.2.2. Primes Cédées	15	..	..	10	10	14	11	17
G.10.2.3. Net Written Premiums	G.10.2.3. Primes Nettes Emises	22	..	..	65	58	134	144	343
G.10.3. Total	G.10.3. Total								
G.10.3.1. Gross Premiums	G.10.3.1. Primes Brutes	1 032	1 175	1 259	1 390	1 553	1 688	1 860	2 175
G.10.3.2. Ceded Premiums	G.10.3.2. Primes Cédées	167	208	230	257	312	353	379	361
G.10.3.3. Net Written Premiums	G.10.3.3. Primes Nettes Emises	865	967	1 028	1 133	1 241	1 335	1 481	1 814
H. GROSS CLAIMS PAYMENTS	**H. PAIEMENTS BRUTS DES SINISTRES**								
H.1. Life	**H.1. Vie**								
H.1.1. Domestic Companies	H.1.1. Entreprises Nationales				1 143	1 553	1 127	1 124	1 363
H.1.3. Branches & Agencies of Foreign Cies	H.1.3. Succursales et Agences d'Ent. Etrangères				297	27	301	286	300
H.1. Total	H.1. Total				1 441	1 580	1 428	1 410	1 663
H.2. Non-Life	**H.2. Non-Vie**								
H.2.1. Domestic Companies	H.2.1. Entreprises Nationales				683	679	750	929	1 149
H.2.3. Branches & Agencies of Foreign Cies	H.2.3. Succursales et Agences d'Ent. Etrangères				178	180	177	235	226
H.2. Total	H.2. Total				861	859	927	1 164	1 375
I. GROSS OPERATING EXPENSES	**I. DEPENSES BRUTES D'EXPLOITATION**								
I.1. Life	**I.1. Vie**								
I.1.1. Domestic Companies	I.1.1. Entreprises Nationales				194	188	207	222	280
I.1.3. Branches & Agencies of Foreign Cies	I.1.3. Succursales et Agences d'Ent. Etrangères				73	8	74	83	78
I.1. Total	I.1. Total des Primes Nettes Vie				267	196	281	305	358

Monetary Unit: million Irish pounds   Unité monétaire : million de livres irlandaises

	1990	1991	1992	1993	1994	1995	1996	1997	
I.2. Non-Life									**I.2. Non-Vie**
I.2.1. Domestic Companies				138	147	146	155	139	I.2.1. Entreprises Nationales
I.2.3. Branches & Agencies of Foreign Cies				35	33	37	41	40	I.2.3. Succursales et Agences d'Ent. Etrangères
I.2. Total				173	180	183	196	179	I.2. Total
J. COMMISSIONS									**J. COMMISSIONS**
J.1. Life									**J.1. Vie**
J.1.1. Direct Business									J.1.1. Assurance directe
J.1.1.1. Domestic Companies				84	88	97	120	177	J.1.1.1. Entreprises Nationales
J.1.1.3. Branches & Agencies of Foreign Cies				24	0	23	29	24	J.1.1.3. Succursales et Agences d'Ent. Etrangères
J.1.1. Total				108	88	120	149	201	J.1.1. Total
J.1.3. Total									J.1.3. Total
J.1.3.1. Domestic Companies				84	88	97	120	177	J.1.3.1. Entreprises Nationales
J.1.3.3. Branches & Agencies of Foreign Cies				24	0	23	29	24	J.1.3.3. Succursales et Agences d'Ent. Etrangères
J.1.3. Total of Life Net Premiums				108	88	120	149	201	J.1.3. Total
J.2. Non-Life									**J.2. Non-Vie**
J.2.1. Direct Business									J.2.1. Assurance directe
J.2.1.1. Domestic Companies				65	71	78	94	219	J.2.1.1. Entreprises Nationales
J.2.1.3. Branches & Agencies of Foreign Cies				31	34	36	44	44	J.2.1.3. Succursales et Agences d'Ent. Etrangères
J.2.1. Total				96	105	114	138	263	J.2.1. Total des Primes Nettes Vie
J.2.2. Reinsurance Accepted									J.2.2. Réassurances acceptées
J.2.2.1. Domestic Companies				12	16	36	38	108	J.2.2.1. Entreprises Nationales
J.2.2. Total				12	16	36	38	108	J.2.2. Total
J.2.3. Total									J.2.3. Total
J.2.3.1. Domestic Companies				77	87	114	132	327	J.2.3.1. Entreprises Nationales
J.2.3.3. Branches & Agencies of Foreign Cies				31	34	36	44	44	J.2.3.3. Succursales et Agences d'Ent. Etrangères
J.2.3. Total				108	121	150	176	371	J.2.3. Total

ITALIE

Monetary Unit: million lire   Unité monétaire : million de lire

	1990	1991	1992	1993	1994	1995	1996	1997
A. NUMBER OF COMPANIES IN THE REPORTING COUNTRY								
A.1. Life								
A.1.1. Domestic Companies	..	56	65	67	70	71	74	77
A.1.2. (Foreign Controlled Companies)	..	..	..	..	..	..	..	29
A.1.3. Branches & Agencies of Foreign Cies	..	6	6	7	6	6	9	10
A.1. All Companies	..	62	71	74	76	77	83	87
A.2. Non-Life								
A.2.1. Domestic Companies	119	119	119	124	122	122	122	111
A.2.2. (Foreign Controlled Companies)	..	..	..	..	..	..	..	43
A.2.3. Branches & Agencies of Foreign Cies	45	47	43	42	33	32	34	32
A.2. All Companies	164	166	162	166	155	154	156	143
A.3. Composite								
A.3.1. Domestic Companies	27	27	26	25	24	22	22	21
A.3.2. (Foreign Controlled Companies)	..	..	..	..	..	..	..	7
A.3. All Companies	27	27	26	25	24	22	22	21
A.4. Reinsurance								
A.4.1. Domestic Companies	7	8	8	8	8	6	6	6
A.4.2. (Foreign Controlled Companies)	..	..	..	..	..	..	..	5
A.4.3. Branches & Agencies of Foreign Cies	1	1	1	1	2	2	4	4
A.4. All Companies	8	9	9	9	10	8	10	10
A.5. Total								
A.5.1. Domestic Companies	200	210	218	224	224	221	224	215
A.5.2. (Foreign Controlled Companies)	..	..	..	..	..	..	..	84
A.5.3. Branches & Agencies of Foreign Cies	52	54	50	50	41	40	47	46
A.5. All Insurance Companies	252	264	268	274	265	261	271	261
B. NUMBER OF EMPLOYEES								
B.1. Insurance Companies	46 328	47 350	48 253	48 112	46 832	46 516	45 250	44 110
B.2. Intermediaries	84 500	85 000	90 000	90 000	90 200	90 200	90 200	90 200
B. Total	130 828	132 350	138 253	138 112	137 032	136 716	135 450	..
C. BUSINESS WRITTEN IN THE REPORTING COUNTRY								
C.1. Life								
C.1.1. Gross Premiums								
C.1.1.1. Direct Business								
C.1.1.1.1 Domestic Companies	8 518 800	10 414 100	12 291 500	14 884 400	18 251 100	22 501 200	25 208 200	35 899 700
C.1.1.1.2. (Foreign Controlled Companies)								7 164 500
C.1.1.1.3 Branches & Agencies of Foreign Cies	158 300	183 500	216 800	278 800	374 300	554 000	609 100	782 500
C.1.1.1. Total	8 677 100	10 597 600	12 508 300	15 143 000	18 625 400	23 055 200	25 817 700	36 682 200
C.1.1.2. Reinsurance Accepted								
C.1.1.2.1 Domestic Companies	1 965 400	2 293 300	2 813 100	2 671 700	2 328 900	2 514 800	2 836 000	3 195 400
C.1.1.2.3 Branches & Agencies of Foreign Cies	300	400	200	1 600	2 000	4 500	106 700	182 200
C.1.1.2. Total	1 965 700	2 293 700	2 813 300	2 673 300	2 330 900	2 519 300	2 942 700	3 377 600
C.1.1.3. Total								
C.1.1.3.1 Domestic Companies	10 484 200	12 707 400	15 104 600	17 536 100	20 580 000	25 016 000	28 044 600	39 095 100
C.1.1.3.3 Branches & Agencies of Foreign Cies	158 600	183 900	217 000	280 200	376 300	558 500	715 800	964 700
C.1.1.3. Total Gross Premiums	10 342 800	12 891 300	15 321 600	17 818 300	20 956 300	25 574 500	28 760 400	40 059 800
C.1.2. Ceded Premiums								
C.1.2.1. Domestic Companies	1 313 900	2 324 300	2 840 200	2 870 300	2 157 700	2 379 100	2 591 500	3 081 900
C.1.2.3. Branches & Agencies of Foreign Cies	40 100	44 200	100	44 300	4 600	3 300	10 100	25 900
C.1.2. Total	1 954 000	2 368 500	2 840 300	3 014 600	2 162 300	2 382 400	2 601 600	3 107 800
C.1.3. Net Written Premiums								
C.1.3.1. Domestic Companies	8 570 300	10 383 100	12 264 400	14 565 800	18 422 300	22 636 900	25 453 100	36 013 200
C.1.3.3. Branches & Agencies of Foreign Cies	118 500	139 700	216 900	235 900	371 700	555 200	705 700	938 800
C.1.3. Total	8 688 800	10 522 800	12 481 300	14 801 700	18 794 000	23 192 100	26 158 800	36 952 000

French row labels (right margin):

A. NOMBRE D'ENTREPRISES DANS LE PAYS DECLARANT

A.1. Vie
A.1.1. Entreprises Nationales
A.1.2. (Entreprises Sous Contrôle Etranger)
A.1.3. Succursales et Agences d'Ent. Etrangères
A.1. Ensemble des Entreprises

A.2. Non-Vie
A.2.1. Entreprises Nationales
A.2.2. (Entreprises Sous Contrôle Etranger)
A.2.3. Succursales et Agences d'Ent. Etrangères
A.2. Ensemble des Entreprises

A.3. Mixte
A.3.1. Entreprises Nationales
A.3.2. (Entreprises Sous Contrôle Etranger)
A.3. Ensemble des Entreprises

A.4. Réassurance
A.4.1. Entreprises Nationales
A.4.2. (Entreprises Sous Contrôle Etranger)
A.4.3. Succursales et Agences d'Ent. Etrangères
A.4. Ensemble des Entreprises

A.5. Total
A.5.1. Entreprises Nationales
A.5.2. (Entreprises Sous Contrôle Etranger)
A.5.3. Succursales et Agences d'Ent. Etrangères
A.5. Ensemble des Entreprises d'Assurances

B. NOMBRE D'EMPLOYES
B.1. Entreprises d'Assurances
B.2. Intermediaires
B. Total

C. OPERATIONS CONCLUES DANS LE PAYS DECLARANT
C.1. Vie
C.1.1. Primes Brutes
C.1.1.1. Assurances Directes
C.1.1.1.1. Entreprises Nationales
C.1.1.1.2. (Entreprises Sous Contrôle Etranger)
C.1.1.1.3. Succursales et Agences d'Ent. Etrangères
C.1.1.1. Total
C.1.1.2. Réassurance Acceptée
C.1.1.2.1. Entreprises Nationales
C.1.1.2.3. Succursales et Agences d'Ent. Etrangères
C.1.1.2. Total
C.1.1.3. Total
C.1.1.3.1. Entreprises Nationales
C.1.1.3.3. Succursales et Agences d'Ent. Etrangères
C.1.1.3. Total ces Primes Brutes
C.1.2. Primes Cédées
C.1.2.1. Entreprises Nationales
C.1.2.3. Succursales et Agences d'Ent. Etrangères
C.1.2. Total
C.1.3. Primes Nettes Emises
C.1.3.1. Entreprises Nationales
C.1.3.3. Succursales et Agences d'Ent. Etrangères
C.1.3. Total

Monetary Unit: million lire   Unité monétaire : million de lires

C.2. Non-Life — C.2. Non-Vie

Label (English)	1990	1991	1992	1993	1994	1995	1996	1997	Label (Français)
C.2.1. Gross premiums									**C.2.1. Primes Brutes**
C.2.1.1. Direct Business									C.2.1.1. Assurances Directes
C.2.1.1.1. Domestic Companies	24 365 700	27 849 900	31 430 700	33 637 000	35 634 900	37 249 900	39 296 000	41 697 100	C.2.1.1.1. Entreprises Nationales
C.2.1.1.2. (Foreign Controlled Companies)	..	..	..	..	..	..	..	13 182 000	C.2.1.1.2. (Entreprises Sous Contrôle Etranger)
C.2.1.1.3. Branches & Agencies of Foreign Cies	1 143 600	1 307 900	1 414 500	473 200	1 158 800	1 511 700	1 559 700	1 921 000	C.2.1.1.3. Succursales et Agences d'Ent. Etrangères
C.2.1.1. Total	25 509 300	29 157 800	32 845 200	35 110 200	36 793 700	38 761 600	40 855 700	43 618 100	C.2.1.1. Total
C.2.1.2. Reinsurance Accepted									C.2.1.2. Réassurance Acceptée
C.2.1.2.1. Domestic Companies	3 506 700	4 203 700	5 320 100	5 361 100	5 038 500	5 047 800	4 624 100	4 593 600	C.2.1.2.1. Entreprises Nationales
C.2.1.2.3. Branches & Agencies of Foreign Cies	16 900	19 800	14 900	13 800	13 100	101 500	203 300	274 200	C.2.1.2.3. Succursales et Agences d'Ent. Etrangères
C.2.1.2. Total	3 523 600	4 223 500	5 335 000	5 374 900	5 051 600	5 149 300	4 827 400	4 867 800	C.2.1.2. Total
C.2.1.3. Total									C.2.1.3. Total
C.2.1.3.1. Domestic Companies	27 872 400	32 053 600	36 750 800	38 998 100	40 673 400	42 297 700	43 920 100	46 290 700	C.2.1.3.1. Entreprises Nationales
C.2.1.3.3. Branches & Agencies of Foreign Cies	1 160 500	1 327 700	1 429 400	1 487 000	1 171 900	1 613 200	1 763 000	2 195 200	C.2.1.3.3. Succursales et Agences d'Ent. Etrangères
C.2.1.3. Total Gross Premiums	29 032 900	33 381 300	38 180 200	40 485 100	41 845 300	43 910 900	45 683 100	48 485 900	C.2.1.3. Total des Primes Brutes
C.2.2. Ceded Premiums									**C.2.2. Primes Cédées**
C.2.2.1. Domestic Companies	5 588 100	6 632 200	8 016 700	7 619 300	7 103 900	7 013 100	6 796 200	6 944 700	C.2.2.1. Entreprises Nationales
C.2.2.3. Branches & Agencies of Foreign Cies	245 500	256 700	237 100	234 600	187 000	293 200	323 600	325 000	C.2.2.3. Succursales et Agences d'Ent. Etrangères
C.2.2. Total	5 833 600	6 888 900	8 253 800	7 853 900	7 290 900	7 306 300	7 119 800	7 269 700	C.2.2. Total
C.2.3. Net Written Premiums									**C.2.3. Primes Nettes Emises**
C.2.3.1. Domestic Companies	22 284 300	25 421 400	28 734 100	31 378 800	33 569 500	35 284 600	37 123 900	39 346 000	C.2.3.1. Entreprises Nationales
C.2.3.3. Branches & Agencies of Foreign Cies	915 000	1 071 000	1 192 300	1 252 400	984 900	1 320 000	1 439 400	1 870 200	C.2.3.3. Succursales et Agences d'Ent. Etrangères
C.2.3. Total	23 199 300	26 492 400	29 926 400	32 631 200	34 554 400	36 604 600	38 563 300	41 216 200	C.2.3. Total

C.3. Total — C.3. Total

Label (English)	1990	1991	1992	1993	1994	1995	1996	1997	Label (Français)
C.3.1. Gross Premiums									**C.3.1. Primes Brutes**
C.3.1.1. Direct Business									C.3.1.1. Assurances Directes
C.3.1.1.1. Domestic Companies	32 884 500	38 264 000	43 722 200	48 521 400	53 886 000	59 751 100	64 504 600	77 596 800	C.3.1.1.1. Entreprises Nationales
C.3.1.1.2. (Foreign Controlled Companies)	..	..	..	..	..	..	..	20 346 500	C.3.1.1.2. (Entreprises Sous Contrôle Etranger)
C.3.1.1.3. Branches & Agencies of Foreign Cies	1 301 900	1 491 400	1 631 300	752 000	1 533 100	2 065 700	2 168 800	2 703 500	C.3.1.1.3. Succursales et Agences d'Ent. Etrangères
C.3.1.1. Total	34 186 400	39 755 400	45 353 500	50 253 200	55 419 100	61 816 800	66 673 400	80 300 300	C.3.1.1. Total
C.3.1.2. Reinsurance Accepted									C.3.1.2. Réassurance Acceptée
C.3.1.2.1. Domestic Companies	5 472 100	6 497 000	8 133 200	8 032 800	7 367 400	7 562 600	7 460 100	7 789 000	C.3.1.2.1. Entreprises Nationales
C.3.1.2.3. Branches & Agencies of Foreign Cies	17 200	20 200	15 100	15 400	15 100	106 000	310 000	456 400	C.3.1.2.3. Succursales et Agences d'Ent. Etrangères
C.3.1.2. Total	5 489 300	6 517 200	8 148 300	8 048 200	7 382 500	7 668 600	7 770 100	8 245 400	C.3.1.2. Total
C.3.1.3. Total									C.3.1.3. Total
C.3.1.3.1. Domestic Companies	38 356 600	44 761 000	51 855 400	56 534 200	61 253 400	67 313 700	71 964 700	85 385 800	C.3.1.3.1. Entreprises Nationales
C.3.1.3.3. Branches & Agencies of Foreign Cies	1 319 100	1 511 600	1 646 400	1 767 200	1 548 200	2 171 700	2 478 800	3 159 900	C.3.1.3.3. Succursales et Agences d'Ent. Etrangères
C.3.1.3. Total Gross Premiums	39 675 700	46 272 600	53 501 800	58 303 400	62 801 600	69 485 400	74 443 500	88 545 700	C.3.1.3. Total des Primes Brutes
C.3.2. Ceded Premiums									**C.3.2. Primes Cédées**
C.3.2.1. Domestic Companies	7 502 000	8 956 500	10 856 900	10 489 600	9 261 600	9 392 200	9 387 700	10 026 600	C.3.2.1. Entreprises Nationales
C.3.2.3. Branches & Agencies of Foreign Cies	285 600	300 900	237 200	278 900	191 600	296 500	333 700	350 900	C.3.2.3. Succursales et Agences d'Ent. Etrangères
C.3.2. Total	7 787 600	9 257 400	11 094 100	10 868 500	9 453 200	9 688 700	9 721 400	10 377 500	C.3.2. Total
C.3.3. Net Written Premiums									**C.3.3. Primes Nettes Emises**
C.3.3.1. Domestic Companies	30 854 600	35 804 500	40 998 500	45 944 600	51 991 800	57 921 500	62 577 000	75 359 200	C.3.3.1. Entreprises Nationales
C.3.3.3. Branches & Agencies of Foreign Cies	1 033 500	1 210 700	1 409 200	1 488 300	1 356 600	1 875 200	2 145 100	2 809 000	C.3.3.3. Succursales et Agences d'Ent. Etrangères
C.3.3. Total	31 888 100	37 015 200	42 407 700	47 432 900	53 348 400	59 796 700	64 722 100	78 168 200	C.3.3. Total

Monetary Unit: million lire

Unité monétaire : million de lires

D. NET WRITTEN PREMIUMS IN THE REPORTING COUNTRY IN TERMS OF DOMESTIC AND FOREIGN RISKS

D. PRIMES NETTES EMISES DANS LE PAYS DECLARANT EN RISQUES NATIONAUX ET ETRANGERS

D.1. Life — D.1. Vie

	1990	1991	1992	1993	1994	1995	1996	1997
D.1.1. Domestic Risks — D.1.1. Risques Nationaux								
D.1.1.1. Domestic Companies — Entreprises Nationales	3 177 400	9 989 700	11 752 100	13 945 900	17 649 000	21 782 000	24 456 800	34 965 500
D.1.1.3. Branches & Agencies of Foreign Cies — Succursales et Agences d'Ent. Etrangères	118 500	139 700	216 900	235 900	371 700	555 200	705 700	938 800
D.1.1. Total — Total des Primes Nettes Vie	3 295 900	10 129 400	11 969 000	14 181 800	18 020 700	22 337 200	25 162 500	35 904 300
D.1.2. Foreign Risks — D.1.2. Risques Etrangers								
D.1.2.1. Domestic Companies — Entreprises Nationales	392 900	393 400	512 300	619 900	773 300	854 900	996 300	1 047 700
D.1.2. Total — Total des Primes Nettes Vie	392 900	393 400	512 300	619 900	773 300	854 900	996 300	1 047 700
D.1.3. Total								
D.1.3.1. Domestic Companies — Entreprises Nationales	8 570 300	10 383 100	12 264 400	14 565 800	18 422 300	22 636 900	25 453 100	36 013 200
D.1.3.3. Branches & Agencies of Foreign Cies — Succursales et Agences d'Ent. Etrangères	118 500	139 700	216 900	235 900	371 700	555 200	705 700	938 800
D.1.3. Total of Life Net Premiums — Total des Primes Nettes Vie	8 688 800	10 522 800	12 481 300	14 801 700	18 794 000	23 192 100	26 158 800	36 952 000

D.2. Non-Life — D.2. Non-Vie

	1990	1991	1992	1993	1994	1995	1996	1997
D.2.1. Domestic Risks — D.2.1. Risques Nationaux								
D.2.1.1. Domestic Companies — Entreprises Nationales	21 569 900	24 633 500	27 650 200	29 801 300	31 739 300	33 082 700	35 226 800	37 774 900
D.2.1.3. Branches & Agencies of Foreign Cies — Succursales et Agences d'Ent. Etrangères	915 000	1 012 100	1 192 300	1 252 400	984 900	1 320 000	1 439 400	1 870 200
D.2.1. Total — Total des Primes Nettes Vie	22 484 900	25 645 600	28 842 500	31 053 700	32 724 200	34 402 700	36 666 200	39 645 100
D.2.2. Foreign Risks — D.2.2. Risques Etrangers								
D.2.2.1. Domestic Companies — Entreprises Nationales	714 400	787 900	1 173 900	1 577 500	1 830 200	2 201 900	1 897 100	1 571 100
D.2.2. Total — Total des Primes Nettes Vie	714 400	846 800	1 173 900	1 577 900	1 830 200	2 201 900	1 897 100	1 571 100
D.2.3. Total								
D.2.3.1. Domestic Companies — Entreprises Nationales	22 284 300	25 421 400	28 734 100	31 378 800	33 569 500	35 284 600	37 123 900	39 346 000
D.2.3.3. Branches & Agencies of Foreign Cies — Succursales et Agences d'Ent. Etrangères	915 000	1 071 000	1 192 300	1 252 400	984 900	1 320 000	1 439 400	1 870 200
D.2.3. Total — D.2.5. Total des Primes Nettes Vie	23 199 300	26 492 400	29 926 400	32 631 200	34 554 400	36 604 600	38 563 300	41 216 200

E. BUSINESS WRITTEN ABROAD — E. OPERATIONS A L'ETRANGER

E.1. Life — E.1. Vie

	1990	1991	1992	1993	1994	1995	1996	1997
E.1.1. Gross Premiums — E.1.1. Primes Brutes								
E.1.1.1. Direct Business — E.1.1.1. Assurance Directe								
E.1.1.1.1 Branches & Agencies — Succursales & Agences	324 400	356 500	423 700	330 000	156 400	191 500	269 100	329 300
E.1.1.1.2 Subsidiaries — Filiales	2 534 300	3 178 300	5 672 400	6 140 300	8 154 600	12 638 800	13 402 600	15 243 100
E.1.1.1. Total	2 858 700	3 534 800	6 096 100	6 470 300	8 311 000	12 830 300	13 671 700	15 572 400
E.1.1.2. Reinsurance Accepted — E.1.1.2. Réassurance Acceptée								
E.1.1.2.1 Branches & Agencies — Succursales & Agences	249 200	332 100	422 600	590 800	652 400	759 000	897 300	1 050 700
E.1.1.2.2. Subsidiaries — Filiales	151 000	149 800	184 000	184 100	321 300	421 600	796 500	906 800
E.1.1.2. Total	400 200	481 900	606 600	774 900	973 700	1 180 600	1 693 800	1 957 500
E.1.1.3. Total								
E.1.1.3.1. Branches & Agencies — Succursales & Agences	573 600	688 600	846 300	920 800	808 800	950 500	1 166 400	1 380 000
E.1.1.3.2. Subsidiaries — Filiales	2 385 300	3 328 100	5 856 400	6 324 400	8 475 900	13 060 400	14 199 100	16 149 900
E.1.1.3. Total Gross Premiums — Total ces Primes Brutes	3 258 900	4 016 700	6 702 700	7 245 200	9 284 700	14 010 900	15 365 500	17 529 900
E.1.2. Ceded Premiums — E.1.2. Primes Cédées								
E.1.2.1. Branches & Agencies — Succursales & Agences	16 700	15 800	26 700	17 200	24 800	35 700	61 200	75 700
E.1.2.2. Subsidiaries — Filiales	668 400	782 300	1 031 600	1 336 600	1 906 500	1 836 500	2 287 400	2 543 800
E.1.2. Total	685 100	798 100	1 058 300	1 353 800	1 931 300	1 872 200	2 348 600	2 619 500
E.1.3. Net Written Premiums — E.1.3. Primes Nettes Emises								
E.1.3.1. Branches & Agencies — Succursales & Agences	556 900	672 800	819 600	903 600	784 000	914 800	1 105 200	1 304 300
E.1.3.2. Subsidiaries — Filiales	2 016 900	2 545 800	4 824 800	4 987 800	6 569 400	11 223 900	11 911 700	13 606 100
E.1.3. Total	2 573 800	3 218 600	5 644 400	5 891 400	7 353 400	12 138 700	13 016 900	14 910 400

Monetary Unit: million lire — Unité monétaire : million de lires

	1990	1991	1992	1993	1994	1995	1996	1997	
E.2. Non-Life									**E.2. Non-Vie**
E.2.1. Gross Premiums									E.2.1. Primes Brutes
E.2.1.1. Direct Business									E.2.1.1. Assurance Directe
E.2.1.1.1. Branches & Agencies	809 000	990 800	1 422 600	1 637 800	1 531 900	1 161 900	1 119 100	1 212 400	E.2.1.1.1. Succursales & Agences
E.2.1.1.2. Subsidiaries	6 629 300	7 311 500	10 357 000	12 223 900	13 051 000	17 087 400	15 524 100	16 053 900	E.2.1.1.2. Filliales
E.2.1.1. Total	7 438 300	8 302 300	11 779 800	13 861 700	14 582 900	18 249 300	16 643 200	17 266 300	E.2.1.1. Total
E.2.1.2. Reinsurance Accepted									E.2.1.2. Réassurance Acceptée
E.2.1.2.1. Branches & Agencies	370 000	464 500	773 100	760 000	860 800	1 021 000	795 200	801 600	E.2.1.2.1. Succursales & Agences
E.2.1.2.2. Subsidiaries	1 396 700	1 398 700	2 073 400	2 500 900	2 878 400	722 800	2 679 800	2 895 400	E.2.1.2.2. Filliales
E.2.1.2. Total	1 766 700	1 863 200	2 846 500	3 260 900	3 739 200	1 743 800	3 475 000	3 697 000	E.2.1.2. Total
E.2.1.3. Total									E.2.1.3. Total
E.2.1.3.1. Branches & Agencies	1 179 000	1 455 300	2 195 700	2 397 800	2 392 700	2 182 900	1 914 300	2 014 000	E.2.1.3.1. Succursales & Agences
E.2.1.3.2. Subsidiaries	8 026 000	8 710 200	12 430 400	14 724 800	15 929 400	17 810 200	18 203 900	18 949 300	E.2.1.3.2. Filliales
E.2.1.3. Total Gross Premiums	9 205 000	10 165 500	14 626 100	17 122 600	18 322 100	19 993 100	20 118 200	20 963 300	E.2.1.3. Total des Primes Brutes
E.2.2. Ceded Premiums									E.2.2. Primes Cédées
E.2.2.1. Branches & Agencies	274 900	278 900	345 300	509 300	479 600	374 900	365 200	418 800	E.2.2.1. Succursales & Agences
E.2.2.2. Subsidiaries	2 240 700	2 373 100	3 595 000	4 390 400	6 152 900	5 719 400	4 623 600	4 962 000	E.2.2.2. Filliales
E.2.2. Total	2 707 300	2 652 000	3 940 300	4 899 700	6 632 500	6 094 300	4 988 800	5 380 800	E.2.2. Total
E.2.3. Net Written Premiums									E.2.3. Primes Nettes Emises
E.2.3.1. Branches & Agencies	904 100	1 176 400	1 850 400	1 888 500	1 913 100	1 808 000	1 549 100	1 595 200	E.2.3.1. Succursales & Agences
E.2.3.2. Subsidiaries	5 785 300	6 337 100	8 835 400	10 334 400	9 776 500	12 090 800	13 580 300	13 987 300	E.2.3.2. Filliales
E.2.3. Total	6 497 700	7 513 500	10 685 800	12 222 900	11 689 600	13 898 800	15 129 400	15 582 500	E.2.3. Total
F. OUTSTANDING INVESTMENT BY DIRECT INSURANCE COMPANIES									**F. ENCOURS DES PLACEMENTS DES ENTREPRISES D'ASSURANCES DIRECTES**
F.1. Life									**F.1. Vie**
F.1.1. Real Estate									F.1.1. Immobilier
F.1.1.1. Domestic Companies	5 181 300	9 179 100	9 404 200	12 810 300	12 368 700	12 209 600	10 311 700	10 175 400	F.1.1.1. Entreprises Nationales
F.1.1.2. (Foreign Controlled Companies)	..	..	..	..	..	..	..	794 200	F.1.1.2. (Entreprises Sous Contrôle Etranger)
F.1.1.3. Branches & Agencies of Foreign Cies	2 700	2 800	2 900	8 900	7 200	7 200	7 300	1 200	F.1.1.3. Succursales et Agences d'Ent. Etrangères
F.1.1. Total	5 184 000	9 181 900	9 407 100	12 819 200	12 375 900	12 216 800	10 319 000	10 176 600	F.1.1. Total
F.1.2. Mortgage Loans									F.1.2. Prêts Hypothécaires
F.1.2.1. Domestic Companies	2 723 800	3 361 200	2 808 600	1 941 500	1 728 000	2 024 800	2 330 200	..	F.1.2.1. Entreprises Nationales
F.1.2.3. Branches & Agencies of Foreign Cies	2 000	3 400	6 300	11 100	14 500	17 400	20 100	..	F.1.2.3. Succursales et Agences d'Ent. Etrangères
F.1.2. Total	2 725 800	3 364 600	2 814 900	1 952 600	1 742 500	2 042 200	2 350 300	..	F.1.2. Total
F.1.3. Shares									F.1.3. Actions
F.1.3.1. Domestic Companies	5 536 100	5 835 900	6 436 300	10 484 500	12 643 700	14 787 200	16 964 100	24 004 200	F.1.3.1. Entreprises Nationales
F.1.3.2. (Foreign Controlled Companies)	..	..	..	..	..	..	..	3 700 600	F.1.3.2. (Entreprises Sous Contrôle Etranger)
F.1.3.3. Branches & Agencies of Foreign Cies	8 700	17 500	39 800	65 500	95 100	123 700	159 000	242 500	F.1.3.3. Succursales et Agences d'Ent. Etrangères
F.1.3.4. Domestic Investment	2 848 300	326 100	3 338 800	5 898 300	7 591 000	8 780 400	10 513 800	15 588 300	F.1.3.4. Placement dans le Pays
F.1.3.5. Foreign Investment	2 696 500	2 592 400	3 137 300	4 651 700	5 147 800	6 130 500	6 609 300	8 658 400	F.1.3.5. Placement à l' Etranger
F.1.3. Total	5 544 800	5 853 400	6 476 100	10 550 000	12 738 800	14 910 900	17 123 100	24 246 700	F.1.3. Total
F.1.4. Bonds with Fixed Revenue									F.1.4. Obligations
F.1.4.1. Domestic Companies	30 683 400	40 150 600	51 271 600	63 869 700	77 410 700	95 057 800	118 083 200	145 001 300	F.1.4.1. Entreprises Nationales
F.1.4.2. (Foreign Controlled Companies)	..	..	..	..	..	..	..	26 677 600	F.1.4.2. (Entreprises Sous Contrôle Etranger)
F.1.4.3. Branches & Agencies of Foreign Cies	373 500	512 200	651 200	888 100	1 110 400	1 557 800	2 114 300	1 690 200	F.1.4.3. Succursales et Agences d'Ent. Etrangères
F.1.4.4. Domestic Investment	29 765 000	3 862 400	48 743 500	60 560 800	73 593 800	89 939 400	106 737 000	124 911 800	F.1.4.4. Placement dans le Pays
F.1.4.5. Foreign Investment	1 291 900	2 038 800	3 179 300	4 197 000	4 927 300	6 676 200	13 460 500	21 779 700	F.1.4.5. Placement à l' Etranger
F.1.4. Total	31 056 900	40 662 800	51 922 800	64 757 800	78 521 100	96 615 600	120 197 500	146 691 500	F.1.4. Total
F.1.5. Loans other than Mortgage Loans									F.1.5. Prêts Autres qu'Hypothécaires
F.1.5.1. Domestic Companies	..	..	..	..	..	..	..	2 152 300	F.1.5.1. Entreprises Nationales
F.1.5.2. (Foreign Controlled Companies)	..	..	..	..	..	..	..	177 100	F.1.5.2. (Entreprises Sous Contrôle Etranger)
F.1.5.3. Branches & Agencies of Foreign Cies	..	..	..	..	..	..	..	16 400	F.1.5.3. Succursales et Agences d'Ent. Etrangères
F.1.5. Total	..	..	..	..	..	..	..	2 168 700	F.1.5. Total

ITALY / ITALIE

Monetary Unit: million lire — Unité monétaire : million de lires

Code	Label (English)	Libellé (Français)	1990	1991	1992	1993	1994	1995	1996	1997
F.1.6.	Other Investments	Autres Placements								
F.1.6.1.	Domestic Companies	Entreprises Nationales	1 178 400	1 622 800	2 031 200	1 833 300	2 371 300	2 673 200	1 956 300	2 807 800
F.1.6.2.	(Foreign Controlled Companies)	(Entreprises Sous Contrôle Etranger)								641 200
F.1.6.3.	Branches & Agencies of Foreign Cies	Succursales et Agences d'Ent. Etrangères	20 600	24 000	18 800	35 500	50 300	60 900	55 500	39 400
F.1.6.	Total	Total	1 199 000	1 646 800	2 050 000	1 868 800	2 421 600	2 734 100	2 011 800	2 847 200
F.1.7.	Total	Total								
F.1.7.1.	Domestic Companies	Entreprises Nationales	45 303 000	60 149 600	71 951 900	90 939 300	106 522 400	126 752 600	149 645 500	184 141 000
F.1.7.2.	(Foreign Controlled Companies)	(Entreprises Sous Contrôle Etranger)								31 990 700
F.1.7.3.	Branches & Agencies of Foreign Cies	Succursales et Agences d'Ent. Etrangères	407 500	559 900	719 000	1 009 100	1 277 500	1 767 000	2 356 200	1 989 700
F.1.7.	Total of Life Investments	Total des Placements Vie	45 710 500	60 709 500	72 670 900	91 948 400	107 799 900	128 519 600	152 001 700	186 130 700
F.2.	**Non-Life**	**Non-Vie**								
F.2.1.	Real Estate	Immobilier								
F.2.1.1.	Domestic Companies	Entreprises Nationales	7 216 800	10 018 500	10 549 200	10 544 800	11 390 800	11 968 500	12 821 900	12 856 700
F.2.1.2.	(Foreign Controlled Companies)	(Entreprises Sous Contrôle Etranger)								2 677 000
F.2.1.3.	Branches & Agencies of Foreign Cies	Succursales et Agences d'Ent. Etrangères	238 200	278 300	272 800	259 300	221 000	241 200	241 200	212 000
F.2.1.	Total	Total	7 454 800	10 296 800	10 822 000	10 804 100	11 611 800	12 209 700	13 063 100	13 068 700
F.2.2.	Mortgage Loans	Prêts Hypothécaires								
F.2.2.1.	Domestic Companies	Entreprises Nationales	1 096 900	834 400	1 810 000	2 095 300	1 756 400	1 615 800	1 654 800	:
F.2.2.3.	Branches & Agencies of Foreign Cies	Succursales et Agences d'Ent. Etrangères	62 000	77 500	90 800	116 200	46 400	59 100	62 700	:
F.2.2.	Total	Total	1 158 900	911 900	1 900 800	2 211 500	1 802 800	1 674 800	1 717 500	
F.2.3.	Shares	Actions								
F.2.3.1.	Domestic Companies	Entreprises Nationales	9 114 600	10 635 300	12 198 900	11 456 500	13 902 600	15 710 200	17 982 000	18 044 600
F.2.3.2.	(Foreign Controlled Companies)	(Entreprises Sous Contrôle Etranger)								5 407 800
F.2.3.3.	Branches & Agencies of Foreign Cies	Succursales et Agences d'Ent. Etrangères	71 500	99 500	127 500	147 300	251 200	290 200	307 300	456 800
F.2.3.4.	Domestic Investment	Placement dans le Pays	7 350 500	8 273 300	8 984 600	8 768 300	10 157 900	9 883 100	10 928 300	11 451 900
F.2.3.5.	Foreign Investment	Placement à l'Etranger	1 835 600	2 461 500	3 341 800	2 835 500	3 995 100	6 117 300	7 361 000	7 049 500
F.2.3.	Total	Total	9 186 100	10 734 800	12 326 400	11 603 800	14 153 800	16 000 400	18 289 300	18 501 400
F.2.4.	Bonds with Fixed Revenue	Obligations								
F.2.4.1.	Domestic Companies	Entreprises Nationales	21 338 900	24 629 300	28 122 100	34 243 600	36 887 400	40 850 800	43 140 200	43 798 900
F.2.4.2.	(Foreign Controlled Companies)	(Entreprises Sous Contrôle Etranger)								14 894 100
F.2.4.3.	Branches & Agencies of Foreign Cies	Succursales et Agences d'Ent. Etrangères	754 400	903 200	1 050 900	1 103 100	878 500	1 009 100	1 160 400	1 359 700
F.2.4.4.	Domestic Investment	Placement dans le Pays	20 010 500	22 783 200	25 137 800	29 092 900	31 772 800	36 158 500	37 700 200	38 672 400
F.2.4.5.	Foreign Investment	Placement à " Etranger	2 082 800	2 749 300	4 035 200	6 253 800	5 993 100	5 701 400	6 600 400	6 486 200
F.2.4.	Total	Total	22 093 300	25 532 500	29 173 000	35 346 700	37 765 900	41 859 900	44 300 600	45 158 600
F.2.5.	Loans other than Mortgage Loans	Prêts Autres qu'Hypothécaires								
F.2.5.1.	Domestic Companies	Entreprises Nationales	:	:	:	:	:	:	:	1 703 700
F.2.5.2.	(Foreign Controlled Companies)	(Entreprises Sous Contrôle Etranger)	:	:	:	:	:	:	:	298 300
F.2.5.3.	Branches & Agencies of Foreign Cies	Succursales et Agences d'Ent. Etrangères	:	:	:	:	:	:	:	43 900
F.2.5.	Total	Total	:	:	:	:	:	:	:	1 747 600
F.2.6.	Other Investments	Autres Placements								
F.2.6.1.	Domestic Companies	Entreprises Nationales	2 228 200	2 361 800	2 219 500	2 174 900	2 963 200	2 911 000	2 935 200	2 690 700
F.2.6.2.	(Foreign Controlled Companies)	(Entreprises Sous Contrôle Etranger)								584 200
F.2.6.3.	Branches & Agencies of Foreign Cies	Succursales et Agences d'Ent. Etrangères	96 100	96 700	104 200	118 800	102 700	136 200	109 500	90 900
F.2.6.	Total	Total	2 324 300	2 458 500	2 323 700	2 293 700	3 065 900	3 047 200	3 044 700	2 781 600
F.2.7.	Total	Total								
F.2.7.1.	Domestic Companies	Entreprises Nationales	40 995 200	48 479 300	54 899 700	60 515 100	66 900 400	73 056 300	78 534 100	79 094 600
F.2.7.2.	(Foreign Controlled Companies)	(Entreprises Sous Contrôle Etranger)								23 861 400
F.2.7.3.	Branches & Agencies of Foreign Cies	Succursales et Agences d'Ent. Etrangères	1 222 200	1 455 200	1 646 200	1 744 700	1 499 800	1 735 700	1 881 100	2 163 300
F.2.7.	Total o Non-Life Investments	Total des Placements Non-Vie	42 217 400	49 934 500	56 545 900	62 259 800	68 400 200	74 792 000	80 415 200	81 257 900

Monetary Unit: million lire
Unité monétaire : million de lires

G. BREAKDOWN OF NON-LIFE PREMIUMS
G. VENTILATIONS DES PRIMES NON-VIE

Code / Label	French	1990	1991	1992	1993	1994	1995	1996	1997
G.1. Motor vehicle	G.1. Assurance Automobile								
G.1.1. Direct Business	G.1.1. Assurances Directes								
G.1.1.1. Gross Premiums	G.1.1.1. Primes Brutes	14 341 700	16 616 400	18 805 800	20 072 000	20 924 400	22 118 000	23 197 500	25 206 200
G.1.1.2. Ceded Premiums	G.1.1.2. Primes Cédées	677 200	861 400	990 800	762 300	638 300	737 300	711 200	816 100
G.1.1.3. Net Written Premiums	G.1.1.3. Primes Nettes Emises	13 664 500	15 755 000	17 815 000	19 309 700	20 286 100	21 380 700	22 486 300	24 390 100
G.1.2. Reinsurance Accepted	G.1.2. Réassurance Acceptée								
G.1.2.1. Gross Premiums	G.1.2.1. Primes Brutes	297 300	390 900	464 200	315 700	215 900	268 900	296 000	293 300
G.1.2.2. Ceded Premiums	G.1.2.2. Primes Cédées	25 900	38 500	69 900	57 500	49 100	50 300	55 900	56 400
G.1.2.3. Net Written Premiums	G.1.2.3. Primes Nettes Emises	271 400	352 400	394 300	258 200	166 800	218 600	240 100	236 900
G.1.3. Total	G.1.3. Total								
G.1.3.1. Gross Premiums	G.1.3.1. Primes Brutes	14 639 000	17 007 300	19 270 000	20 387 700	21 140 300	22 386 900	23 493 500	25 499 500
G.1.3.2. Ceded Premiums	G.1.3.2. Primes Cédées	703 100	899 900	1 060 700	819 800	687 400	787 600	767 100	872 500
G.1.3.3. Net Written Premiums	G.1.3.3. Primes Nettes Emises	13 935 900	16 107 400	18 209 300	19 567 900	20 452 900	21 599 300	22 726 400	24 627 000
G.2. Marine, Aviation	G.2. Marine, Aviation								
G.2.1. Direct Business	G.2.1. Assurances Directes								
G.2.1.1. Gross Premiums	G.2.1.1. Primes Brutes	155 000	154 200	150 300	202 800	200 800	228 500	243 200	1 486 200
G.2.1.2. Ceded Premiums	G.2.1.2. Primes Cédées	145 300	132 800	134 900	184 300	180 100	211 000	227 400	904 300
G.2.1.3. Net Written Premiums	G.2.1.3. Primes Nettes Emises	9 700	21 400	15 400	18 500	20 700	17 500	15 800	581 900
G.2.2. Reinsurance Accepted	G.2.2. Réassurance Acceptée								
G.2.2.1. Gross Premiums	G.2.2.1. Primes Brutes	146 600	148 900	176 500	197 900	189 400	194 200	198 700	430 700
G.2.2.2. Ceded Premiums	G.2.2.2. Primes Cédées	92 000	95 600	116 800	135 700	129 400	136 000	140 200	268 100
G.2.2.3. Net Written Premiums	G.2.2.3. Primes Nettes Emises	54 600	53 300	59 700	62 200	60 000	58 200	58 500	162 600
G.2.3. Total	G.2.3. Total								
G.2.3.1. Gross Premiums	G.2.3.1. Primes Brutes	301 600	303 100	326 800	400 700	390 200	422 700	441 900	1 916 900
G.2.3.2. Ceded Premiums	G.2.3.2. Primes Cédées	237 300	228 400	251 700	320 000	309 500	347 000	367 600	1 172 400
G.2.3.3. Net Written Premiums	G.2.3.3. Primes Nettes Emises	64 300	74 700	75 100	80 700	80 700	75 700	74 300	744 500
G.3. Freight	G.3. Fret								
G.3.1. Direct Business	G.3.1. Assurances Directes								
G.3.1.1. Gross Premiums	G.3.1.1. Primes Brutes	854 700	1 018 400	1 267 700	1 447 100	1 505 800	1 283 200	1 281 300	:
G.3.1.2. Ceded Premiums	G.3.1.2. Primes Cédées	535 800	652 800	813 200	900 800	934 800	737 100	737 000	:
G.3.1.3. Net Written Premiums	G.3.1.3. Primes Nettes Emises	318 900	365 600	454 500	546 300	571 000	546 100	544 300	:
G.3.2. Reinsurance Accepted	G.3.2. Réassurance Acceptée								
G.3.2.1. Gross Premiums	G.3.2.1. Primes Brutes	227 900	283 900	320 700	314 800	302 400	289 000	263 100	:
G.3.2.2. Ceded Premiums	G.3.2.2. Primes Cédées	134 400	172 900	205 300	212 300	214 400	185 600	166 900	:
G.3.2.3. Net Written Premiums	G.3.2.3. Primes Nettes Emises	93 500	111 000	115 400	102 500	88 000	103 400	96 200	:
G.3.3. Total	G.3.3. Total								
G.3.3.1. Gross Premiums	G.3.3.1. Primes Brutes	1 082 600	1 302 300	1 588 400	1 761 900	1 808 200	1 572 200	1 544 400	:
G.3.3.2. Ceded Premiums	G.3.3.2. Primes Cédées	670 200	825 700	1 018 500	1 113 100	1 149 200	922 700	903 900	:
G.3.3.3. Net Written Premiums	G.3.3.3. Primes Nettes Emises	412 400	476 600	569 900	648 800	659 000	649 500	640 500	:
G.4. Fire, Property, Damages	G.4. Incendie, Dommages aux Biens								
G.4.1. Direct Business	G.4.1. Assurances Directes								
G.4.1.1. Gross Premiums	G.4.1.1. Primes Brutes	3 819 600	4 145 300	4 539 100	4 662 400	4 865 400	5 159 100	5 482 000	5 984 900
G.4.1.2. Ceded Premiums	G.4.1.2. Primes Cédées	1 665 000	1 886 600	2 122 100	1 969 100	1 861 700	2 039 600	1 878 300	2 049 000
G.4.1.3. Net Written Premiums	G.4.1.3. Primes Nettes Emises	2 154 600	2 258 700	2 417 000	2 693 300	3 003 700	3 119 500	3 603 700	3 935 900
G.4.2. Reinsurance Accepted	G.4.2. Réassurance Acceptée								
G.4.2.1. Gross Premiums	G.4.2.1. Primes Brutes	1 156 700	1 258 400	1 559 500	1 314 800	1 185 700	1 186 200	1 032 600	1 165 000
G.4.2.2. Ceded Premiums	G.4.2.2. Primes Cédées	518 700	559 900	813 800	678 900	574 400	643 900	496 500	561 800
G.4.2.3. Net Written Premiums	G.4.2.3. Primes Nettes Emises	638 000	698 500	745 700	637 900	611 300	542 300	536 100	603 200
G.4.3. Total	G.4.3. Total								
G.4.3.1. Gross Premiums	G.4.3.1. Primes Brutes	4 976 300	5 403 700	6 098 600	5 977 200	6 051 100	6 345 300	6 514 600	7 149 900
G.4.3.2. Ceded Premiums	G.4.3.2. Primes Cédées	2 183 700	2 446 500	2 935 900	2 646 000	2 436 100	2 683 500	2 374 800	2 610 800
G.4.3.3. Net Written Premiums	G.4.3.3. Primes Nettes Emises	2 792 600	2 957 200	3 162 700	3 331 200	3 615 000	3 661 800	4 139 800	4 539 100

Monetary Unit: million lire — Unité monétaire : million de lires

	1990	1991	1992	1993	1994	1995	1996	1997
G.5. Pecuniary Losses — G.5. Pertes Pécuniaires								
G.5.1. Direct Business — G.5.1. Assurances Directes								
G.5.1.1. Gross Premiums — Primes Brutes	735 500	792 700	830 800	819 600	939 400	1 019 800	1 137 800	1 300 500
G.5.1.2. Ceded Premiums — Primes Cédées	359 900	390 200	398 800	380 800	445 200	535 300	611 400	685 500
G.5.1.3. Net Written Premiums — Primes Nettes Emises	375 600	402 500	432 000	438 800	494 200	484 500	526 400	615 000
G.5.2. Reinsurance Accepted — G.5.2. Réassurance Acceptée								
G.5.2.1. Gross Premiums — Primes Brutes	150 500	170 600	196 700	192 800	188 600	216 400	240 600	268 500
G.5.2.2. Ceded Premiums — Primes Cédées	69 100	79 600	99 400	92 000	86 300	94 300	102 100	121 900
G.5.2.3. Net Written Premiums — Primes Nettes Emises	81 400	91 000	97 300	100 800	102 300	122 100	138 500	146 600
G.5.3. Total								
G.5.3.1. Gross Premiums — Primes Brutes	886 000	963 300	1 027 500	1 012 400	1 128 000	1 236 200	1 378 400	1 569 000
G.5.3.2. Ceded Premiums — Primes Cédées	429 000	469 800	498 200	472 800	531 500	629 600	713 500	807 400
G.5.3.3. Net Written Premiums — Primes Nettes Emises	457 000	493 500	529 300	539 600	596 500	606 600	664 900	761 600
G.6. General Liability — G.6. Responsabilité Générale								
G.6.1. Direct Business — G.6.1. Assurances Directes								
G.6.1.1. Gross Premiums — Primes Brutes	1 655 300	1 874 200	2 121 200	2 329 300	2 405 000	2 590 900	2 845 600	3 060 300
G.6.1.2. Ceded Premiums — Primes Cédées	281 100	374 100	340 900	303 400	281 200	295 900	328 600	313 800
G.6.1.3. Net Written Premiums — Primes Nettes Emises	1 374 200	1 500 100	1 780 300	2 025 900	2 123 800	2 295 000	2 517 000	2 746 500
G.6.2. Reinsurance Accepted — G.6.2. Réassurance Acceptée								
G.6.2.1. Gross Premiums — Primes Brutes	94 400	208 300	189 800	149 100	126 100	130 100	130 600	143 800
G.6.2.2. Ceded Premiums — Primes Cédées	29 800	27 900	58 600	56 700	43 700	44 400	41 700	45 900
G.6.2.3. Net Written Premiums — Primes Nettes Emises	64 600	180 400	131 200	92 400	82 400	85 700	88 900	97 900
G.6.3. Total								
G.6.3.1. Gross Premiums — Primes Brutes	1 749 700	2 082 500	2 311 000	2 478 400	2 531 100	2 721 000	2 976 200	3 204 100
G.6.3.2. Ceded Premiums — Primes Cédées	310 900	402 000	399 500	360 100	324 900	340 300	370 300	359 700
G.6.3.3. Net Written Premiums — Primes Nettes Emises	1 438 800	1 680 500	1 911 500	2 118 300	2 206 200	2 380 700	2 605 900	2 844 400
G.7. Accident, Health — G.7. Accident, Santé								
G.7.1. Direct Business — G.7.1. Assurances Directes								
G.7.1.1. Gross Premiums — Primes Brutes	3 633 300	4 155 500	4 620 200	4 996 700	5 252 700	5 542 500	5 762 100	6 108 600
G.7.1.2. Ceded Premiums — Primes Cédées	608 500	775 900	934 900	807 400	714 700	733 000	696 200	731 200
G.7.1.3. Net Written Premiums — Primes Nettes Emises	3 024 800	3 379 600	3 685 300	4 189 300	4 538 000	4 809 500	5 065 900	5 377 400
G.7.2. Reinsurance Accepted — G.7.2. Réassurance Acceptée								
G.7.2.1. Gross Premiums — Primes Brutes	291 400	401 200	588 000	514 000	436 800	417 700	420 700	506 400
G.7.2.2. Ceded Premiums — Primes Cédées	65 200	114 100	276 100	271 500	218 300	191 700	168 000	231 000
G.7.2.3. Net Written Premiums — Primes Nettes Emises	226 200	287 100	311 900	242 500	218 500	226 000	252 700	275 400
G.7.3. Total								
G.7.3.1. Gross Premiums — Primes Brutes	3 924 700	4 556 700	5 208 200	5 510 700	5 689 500	5 960 200	6 182 800	6 615 000
G.7.3.2. Ceded Premiums — Primes Cédées	673 700	890 000	1 211 000	1 078 900	933 000	924 700	864 200	962 200
G.7.3.3. Net Written Premiums — Primes Nettes Emises	3 251 000	3 666 700	3 997 200	4 431 800	4 756 500	5 035 500	5 318 600	5 652 800
G.8. Others — G.8. Autres								
G.8.1. Direct Business — G.8.1. Assurances Directes								
G.8.1.1. Gross Premiums — Primes Brutes	314 200	401 100	510 100	580 300	700 200	819 600	906 200	471 400
G.8.1.2. Ceded Premiums — Primes Cédées	143 800	192 500	243 700	246 500	292 900	355 000	370 800	142 200
G.8.1.3. Net Written Premiums — Primes Nettes Emises	170 400	208 600	266 400	333 800	407 300	464 600	535 400	329 200
G.8.2. Reinsurance Accepted — G.8.2. Réassurance Acceptée								
G.8.2.1. Gross Premiums — Primes Brutes	45 300	66 500	164 000	184 400	230 100	248 100	283 000	148 500
G.8.2.2. Ceded Premiums — Primes Cédées	17 900	26 900	79 500	88 700	74 700	69 600	86 300	10 200
G.8.2.3. Net Written Premiums — Primes Nettes Emises	27 400	39 600	84 500	95 700	155 400	178 500	196 700	138 300
G.8.3. Total								
G.8.3.1. Gross Premiums — Primes Brutes	359 500	467 600	674 100	764 700	930 300	1 067 700	1 189 200	619 900
G.8.3.2. Ceded Premiums — Primes Cédées	161 700	219 400	323 200	335 200	367 600	424 600	457 100	152 400
G.8.3.3. Net Written Premiums — Primes Nettes Emises	197 800	248 200	350 900	429 500	562 700	643 100	732 100	467 500
G.9. Treaty Reinsurance — G.9. Réassurance Obligatoire								
G.9.2. Reinsurance Accepted — G.9.2. Réassurance Acceptée								
G.9.2.1. Gross Premiums — Primes Brutes	1 113 500	1 294 800	1 675 600	2 191 400	2 176 600	2 198 700	1 962 100	1 911 600
G.9.2.2. Ceded Premiums — Primes Cédées	464 000	507 200	555 100	708 000	551 700	246 300	301 300	332 300
G.9.2.3. Net Written Premiums — Primes Nettes Emises	649 500	787 600	1 120 500	1 483 400	1 624 900	1 952 400	1 660 800	1 579 300
G.9.3. Total								
G.9.3.1. Gross Premiums — Primes Brutes	1 113 500	1 294 800	1 675 600	2 191 400	2 176 600	2 198 700	1 962 100	1 911 600
G.9.3.2. Ceded Premiums — Primes Cédées	464 000	507 200	555 100	708 000	551 700	246 300	301 300	332 300
G.9.3.3. Net Written Premiums — Primes Nettes Emises	649 500	787 600	1 120 500	1 483 400	1 624 900	1 952 400	1 660 800	1 579 300

Code	Label (EN)	Label (FR)	1990	1991	1992	1993	1994	1995	1996	1997
G.10.	Total	G.10. Total								
G.10.1.	Direct Business	G.10.1. Assurances Directes								
G.10.1.1.	Gross Premiums	G.10.1.1. Primes Brutes	25 509 300	29 157 800	32 845 200	35 110 200	36 793 700	38 761 600	40 855 700	43 618 100
G.10.1.2.	Ceded Premiums	G.10.1.2. Primes Cédées	4 416 600	5 266 300	5 979 300	5 554 600	5 348 900	5 644 200	5 560 900	5 642 100
G.10.1.3.	Net Written Premiums	G.10.1.3. Primes Nettes Emises	21 092 700	23 891 500	26 865 900	29 555 600	31 444 800	33 117 400	35 294 800	37 976 000
G.10.2.	Reinsurance Accepted	G.10.2. Réassurance Acceptée								
G.10.2.1.	Gross Premiums	G.10.2.1. Primes Brutes	3 523 600	4 223 500	5 335 000	5 374 900	5 051 600	5 149 300	4 827 400	4 867 800
G.10.2.2.	Ceded Premiums	G.10.2.2. Primes Cédées	1 417 000	1 622 600	2 274 500	2 299 300	1 942 000	1 662 100	1 558 900	1 627 600
G.10.2.3.	Net Written Premiums	G.10.2.3. Primes Nettes Emises	2 106 600	2 600 900	3 060 500	3 075 600	3 109 600	3 487 200	3 268 500	3 240 200
G.10.3.	Total	G.10.3. Total								
G.10.3.1.	Gross Premiums	G.10.3.1. Primes Brutes	29 032 900	33 381 300	38 180 200	40 485 100	41 845 300	43 910 900	45 683 100	48 485 900
G.10.3.2.	Ceded Premiums	G.10.3.2. Primes Cédées	5 833 600	6 888 900	8 253 800	7 853 900	7 290 900	7 306 300	7 119 800	7 269 700
G.10.3.3.	Net Written Premiums	G.10.3.3. Primes Nettes Emises	23 199 300	26 492 400	29 926 400	32 631 200	34 554 400	36 604 600	38 563 300	41 216 200
H. GROSS CLAIMS PAYMENTS		**H. PAIEMENTS BRUTS DES SINISTRES**								
H.1. Life		**H.1. Vie**								
H.1.1.	Domestic Companies	H.1.1. Entreprises Nationales				4 428 000	5 583 000	6 832 000	8 967 000	11 204 000
H.1.2.	(Foreign Controlled Companies)	H.1.2. (Entreprises Sous Contrôle Etranger)								2 044 000
H.1.3.	Branches & Agencies of Foreign Cies	H.1.3. Succursales et Agences d'Ent. Etrangères				53 000	76 000	114 000	145 000	164 000
H.1.	Total	H.1. Total				4 481 000	5 659 000	6 946 000	9 112 000	11 368 000
H.2. Non-Life		**H.2. Non-Vie**								
H.2.1.	Domestic Companies	H.2.1. Entreprises Nationales				22 305 000	22 547 000	25 275 000	27 856 000	30 180 000
H.2.2.	(Foreign Controlled Companies)	H.2.2. (Entreprises Sous Contrôle Etranger)								9 568 000
H.2.3.	Branches & Agencies of Foreign Cies	H.2.3. Succursales et Agences d'Ent. Etrangères				953 000	703 000	777 000	922 000	1 090 000
H.2.	Total	H.2. Total				23 258 000	23 250 000	26 052 000	28 778 000	31 270 000
I. GROSS OPERATING EXPENSES		**I. DEPENSES BRUTES D'EXPLOITATION**								
I.1. Life		**I.1. Vie**								
I.1.1.	Domestic Companies	I.1.1. Entreprises Nationales				863 000	927 000	973 000	1 061 000	1 181 000
I.1.2.	(Foreign Controlled Companies)	I.1.2. (Entreprises Sous Contrôle Etranger)								331 000
I.1.3.	Branches & Agencies of Foreign Cies	I.1.3. Succursales et Agences d'Ent. Etrangères				26 000	30 000	33 000	37 000	31 000
I.1.	Total	I.1. Total des Primes Nettes Vie				889 000	957 000	1 006 000	1 098 000	1 212 000
I.2. Non-Life		**I.2. Non-Vie**								
I.2.1.	Domestic Companies	I.2.1. Entreprises Nationales				2 415 000	2 519 000	2 627 000	2 785 000	2 772 000
I.2.2.	(Foreign Controlled Companies)	I.2.2. (Entreprises Sous Contrôle Etranger)								1 013 000
I.2.3.	Branches & Agencies of Foreign Cies	I.2.3. Succursales et Agences d'Ent. Etrangères				141 000	107 000	133 000	140 000	159 000
I.2.	Total	I.2. Total				2 556 000	2 626 000	2 760 000	2 925 000	2 931 000
J. COMMISSIONS		**J. COMMISSIONS**								
J.1. Life		**J.1. Vie**								
J.1.1.	Direct Business	J.1.1. Assurance directe								
J.1.1.1.	Domestic Companies	J.1.1.1. Entreprises Nationales				2 083 000	2 333 000	2 581 000	2 817 000	3 307 000
J.1.1.2.	(Foreign Controlled Companies)	J.1.1.2. (Entreprises Sous Contrôle Etranger)								824 000
J.1.1.3.	Branches & Agencies of Foreign Cies	J.1.1.3. Succursales et Agences d'Ent. Etrangères				36 000	45 000	58 000	64 000	58 000
J.1.1.	Total	J.1.1. Total				2 119 000	2 378 000	2 639 000	2 881 000	3 365 000
J.1.2.	Reinsurance Accepted	J.1.2. Réassurances acceptées								
J.1.2.1.	Domestic Companies	J.1.2.1. Entreprises Nationales				507 000	441 000	502 000	535 000	553 000
J.1.2.2.	(Foreign Controlled Companies)	J.1.2.2. (Entreprises Sous Contrôle Etranger)								170 000
J.1.2.3.	Branches & Agencies of Foreign Cies	J.1.2.3. Succursales et Agences d'Ent. Etrangères				0	0	2 000	45 000	87 000
J.1.2.	Total	J.1.2. Total				507 000	441 000	504 000	580 000	640 000

ITALIE

Unité monétaire : million de lires

	1990	1991	1992	1993	1994	1995	1996	1997	
J.1.3. Total									J.1.3. Total
J.1.3.1. Domestic Companies				2 590 000	2 774 000	3 083 000	3 352 000	3 860 000	J.1.3.1. Entreprises Nationales
J.1.3.2. (Foreign Controlled Companies)				..	..	..	..	994 000	J.1.3.2. (Entreprises Sous Contrôle Etranger)
J.1.3.3. Branches & Agencies of Foreign Cies				36 000	45 000	60 000	109 000	145 000	J.1.3.3. Succursales et Agences d'Ent. Etrangères
J.1.3. Total of Life Net Premiums				2 626 000	2 819 000	3 143 000	3 461 000	4 005 000	J.1.3. Total
J.2. Non-Life									**J.2. Non-Vie**
J.2.1. Direct Business									J.2.1. Assurance directe
J.2.1.1. Domestic Companies				6 062 000	6 219 000	6 982 000	7 519 000	7 810 000	J.2.1.1. Entreprises Nationales
J.2.1.2. (Foreign Controlled Companies)				..	..	..	..	2 474 000	J.2.1.2. (Entreprises Sous Contrôle Etranger)
J.2.1.3. Branches & Agencies of Foreign Cies				311 000	252 000	301 000	309 000	359 000	J.2.1.3. Succursales et Agences d'Ent. Etrangères
J.2.1. Total				6 373 000	6 471 000	7 283 000	7 828 000	8 169 000	J.2.1. Total des Primes Nettes Vie
J.2.2. Reinsurance Accepted									J.2.2. Réassurances acceptées
J.2.2.1. Domestic Companies				804 000	717 000	732 000	707 000	728 000	J.2.2.1. Entreprises Nationales
J.2.2.2. (Foreign Controlled Companies)				..	..	..	..	367 000	J.2.2.2. (Entreprises Sous Contrôle Etranger)
J.2.2.3. Branches & Agencies of Foreign Cies				2 000	2 000	44 000	56 000	75 000	J.2.2.3. Succursales et Agences d'Ent. Etrangères
J.2.2. Total				806 000	719 000	776 000	763 000	803 000	J.2.2. Total
J.2.3. Total									J.2.3. Total
J.2.3.1. Domestic Companies				6 866 000	2 774 000	7 714 000	8 226 000	8 538 000	J.2.3.1. Entreprises Nationales
J.2.3.2. (Foreign Controlled Companies)				..	..	..	..	2 841 000	J.2.3.2. (Entreprises Sous Contrôle Etranger)
J.2.3.3. Branches & Agencies of Foreign Cies				313 000	45 000	345 000	365 000	434 000	J.2.3.3. Succursales et Agences d'Ent. Etrangères
J.2.3. Total				7 179 000	2 819 000	8 059 000	8 591 000	8 972 000	J.2.3. Total

147

Monetary Unit: million Japanese yen   Unité monétaire : million de yen japonais

Code / English label	1990	1991	1992	1993	1994	1995	1996	1997	French label
A. NUMBER OF COMPANIES IN THE REPORTING COUNTRY									**A. NOMBRE D'ENTREPRISES DANS LE PAYS DECLARANT**
A.1. Life									**A.1. Vie**
A.1.1. Domestic Companies	:	27	27	27	27	29	41	41	A.1.1. Entreprises Nationales
A.1.2. (Foreign Controlled Companies)	:	5	3	3	3	5	6	5	A.1.2. (Entreprises Sous Contrôle Etranger)
A.1.3. Branches & Agencies of Foreign Cies	:	14	13	13	12	12	13	13	A.1.3. Succursales et Agences d'Ent. Etrangères
A.1. Total	:	41	40	40	39	41	54	54	A.1. Ensemble des Entreprises
A.2. Non-Life									**A.2. Non-Vie**
A.2.1. Domestic Companies	22	23	23	23	24	24	31	31	A.2.1. Entreprises Nationales
A.2.2. (Foreign Controlled Companies)	2	3	3	3	4	4	5	5	A.2.2. (Entreprises Sous Contrôle Etranger)
A.2.3. Branches & Agencies of Foreign Cies	35	34	33	27	27	28	27	28	A.2.3. Succursales et Agences d'Ent. Etrangères
A.2. All Companies	57	57	56	50	51	52	58	59	A.2. Ensemble des Entreprises
A.4. Reinsurance									**A.4. Réassurance**
A.4.1. Domestic Companies	2	2	2	2	2	2	2	2	A.4.1. Entreprises Nationales
A.4.3. Branches & Agencies of Foreign Cies	1	1	1	3	3	3	3	3	A.4.3. Succursales et Agences d'Ent. Etrangères
A.4. All Companies	3	3	3	5	5	5	5	5	A.4. Ensemble des Entreprises
A.5. Total									**A.5. Total**
A.5.1. Domestic Companies	50	52	52	52	53	55	74	74	A.5.1. Entreprises Nationales
A.5.2. (Foreign Controlled Companies)	7	8	6	6	7	9	11	10	A.5.2. (Entreprises Sous Contrôle Etranger)
A.5.3. Branches & Agencies of Foreign Cies	51	48	47	43	42	43	43	44	A.5.3. Succursales et Agences d'Ent. Etrangères
A.5. All Insurance Companies	101	101	99	95	95	98	117	118	A.5. Ensemble des Entreprises d'Assurances
B. NUMBER OF EMPLOYEES									**B. NOMBRE D'EMPLOYES**
B.1. Insurance Companies	541 000	670 000	648 000	649 653	629 432	622 200	597 305	544 756	B.1. Entreprises d'Assurances
B.2. Intermediaries	1 056 000	1 118 000	1 127 000	1 162 380	: :	: :	1 548 232	1 870 521	B.2. Intermediaires
B. Total	1 597 000	1 788 000	1 775 000	1 812 033	: :	: :	2 145 537	2 415 277	B. Total
C. BUSINESS WRITTEN IN THE REPORTING COUNTRY									**C. OPERATIONS CONCLUES DANS LE PAYS DECLARANT**
C.1. Life									**C.1. Vie**
C.1.1. Gross Premiums									C.1.1. Primes Brutes
C.1.1.1. Direct Business									C.1.1.1. Assurances Directes
C.1.1.1.1. Domestic Companies	26 731 284	27 711 270	28 924 314	29 715 907	29 723 454	30 010 633	28 528 700	29 473 151	C.1.1.1.1. Entreprises Nationales
C.1.1.1.2. (Foreign Controlled Companies)	173 707	166 098	159 506	169 839	208 121	335 228	337 788	301 470	C.1.1.1.2. (Entreprises Sous Contrôle Etranger)
C.1.1.1.3. Branches & Agencies of Foreign Cies	439 273	497 651	571 820	639 134	726 581	709 374	780 866	842 418	C.1.1.1.3. Succursales et Agences d'Ent. Etrangères
C.1.1.1. Total	27 170 557	28 208 921	29 496 134	30 355 041	30 450 036	30 720 007	29 309 566	30 315 569	C.1.1.1. Total
C.1.1.2. Reinsurance Accepted									C.1.1.2. Réassurance Acceptée
C.1.1.2.1. Domestic Companies	150 155	31 098	33 982	37 645	39 364	42 060	43 905	45 241	C.1.1.2.1. Entreprises Nationales
C.1.1.2.2. (Foreign Controlled Companies)	5	4	6			4	5		C.1.1.2.2. (Entreprises Sous Contrôle Etranger)
C.1.1.2.3. Branches & Agencies of Foreign Cies	0	1	2	2	3	5	7	0	C.1.1.2.3. Succursales et Agences d'Ent. Etrangères
C.1.1.2. Total	150 155	31 099	33 984	37 647	39 367	42 065	43 912	45 242	C.1.1.2. Total
C.1.1.3. Total									C.1.1.3. Total
C.1.1.3.1. Domestic Companies	26 881 439	27 742 368	28 958 296	29 753 552	29 762 818	30 052 693	28 572 605	29 518 393	C.1.1.3.1. Entreprises Nationales
C.1.1.3.2. (Foreign Controlled Companies)	173 712	166 102	159 512	169 845	208 130	335 232	337 793	301 470	C.1.1.3.2. (Entreprises Sous Contrôle Etranger)
C.1.1.3.3. Branches & Agencies of Foreign Cies	439 273	497 652	571 822	639 136	726 584	709 379	780 873	842 418	C.1.1.3.3. Succursales et Agences d'Ent. Etrangères
C.1.1.3. Total Gross Premiums	27 320 712	28 240 020	29 530 118	30 392 688	30 489 403	30 762 072	29 353 478	30 360 812	C.1.1.3. Total des Primes Brutes
C.1.2. Ceded Premiums									C.1.2. Primes Cédées
C.1.2.1. Domestic Companies	28 017	30 055	31 555	34 239	37 233	42 993	45 853	143 176	C.1.2.1. Entreprises Nationales
C.1.2.2. (Foreign Controlled Companies)	3 371	4 271	3 856	5 055	6 528	11 267	13 484	14 108	C.1.2.2. (Entreprises Sous Contrôle Etranger)
C.1.2.3. Branches & Agencies of Foreign Cies	17 823	10 706	10 119	12 819	11 038	8 506	8 496	8 753	C.1.2.3. Succursales et Agences d'Ent. Etrangères
C.1.2. Total	45 840	40 761	41 674	47 058	48 271	51 499	54 349	151 929	C.1.2. Total
C.1.3. Net Written Premiums									C.1.3. Primes Nettes Emises
C.1.3.1. Domestic Companies	26 853 422	27 712 313	28 926 741	29 719 313	29 725 585	30 009 700	28 526 752	29 375 217	C.1.3.1. Entreprises Nationales
C.1.3.2. (Foreign Controlled Companies)	170 341	161 831	155 656	164 790	201 602	323 965	324 309	287 362	C.1.3.2. (Entreprises Sous Contrôle Etranger)
C.1.3.3. Branches & Agencies of Foreign Cies	421 450	486 946	561 703	626 317	715 546	700 873	772 377	833 665	C.1.3.3. Succursales et Agences d'Ent. Etrangères
C.1.3. Total	27 274 872	28 199 259	29 488 444	30 345 630	30 441 132	30 710 573	29 299 129	30 208 883	C.1.3. Total

Monetary Unit: million Japanese yen

Unité monétaire : million de yen japonais

C.2. Non-Life / C.2. Non-Vie

	1990	1991	1992	1993	1994	1995	1996	1997
C.2.1. Gross premiums / C.2.1. Primes Brutes								
C.2.1.1. Direct Business / C.2.1.1. Assurances Directes								
C.2.1.1.1. Domestic Companies / C.2.1.1.1. Entreprises Nationales	8 854 816	9 120 729	9 252 957	9 846 737	9 873 603	10 155 157	10 621 978	10 313 718
C.2.1.1.2. (Foreign Controlled Companies) / C.2.1.1.2. (Entreprises Sous Contrôle Etranger)	18 466	23 655	26 522	28 841	31 922	33 492	78 727	89 793
C.2.1.1.3. Branches & Agencies of Foreign Cies / C.2.1.1.3. Succursales et Agences d'Ent. Etrangères	247 678	260 353	279 286	292 685	306 023	320 052	281 771	290 372
C.2.1.1. Total / C.2.1.1. Total	9 102 494	9 381 082	9 532 243	10 139 422	10 179 626	10 475 209	10 903 749	10 604 090
C.2.1.2. Reinsurance Accepted / C.2.1.2. Réassurance Acceptée								
C.2.1.2.1. Domestic Companies / C.2.1.2.1. Entreprises Nationales	958 778	936 986	962 123	893 771	875 667	918 124	694 410	648 403
C.2.1.2.2. (Foreign Controlled Companies) / C.2.1.2.2. (Entreprises Sous Contrôle Etranger)	2 347	3 418	4 418	4 355	4 331	4 580	7 065	6 355
C.2.1.2.3. Branches & Agencies of Foreign Cies / C.2.1.2.3. Succursales et Agences d'Ent. Etrangères	20 329	22 023	23 374	23 760	22 072	21 988	19 486	18 583
C.2.1.2. Total / C.2.1.2. Total	979 107	959 009	985 497	917 531	897 739	940 112	713 896	666 986
C.2.1.3. Total / C.2.1.3. Total								
C.2.1.3.1. Domestic Companies / C.2.1.3.1. Entreprises Nationales	9 813 594	10 057 715	10 215 080	10 740 508	10 749 270	11 073 281	11 316 388	10 962 121
C.2.1.3.2. (Foreign Controlled Companies) / C.2.1.3.2. (Entreprises Sous Contrôle Etranger)	20 813	27 073	30 940	33 196	36 253	38 072	85 792	96 148
C.2.1.3.3. Branches & Agencies of Foreign Cies / C.2.1.3.3. Succursales et Agences d'Ent. Etrangères	268 007	282 376	302 660	316 445	328 095	342 040	301 257	308 955
C.2.1.3. Total Gross Premiums / C.2.1.3. Total des Primes Brutes	10 081 601	10 340 091	10 517 740	11 056 953	11 077 365	11 415 321	11 617 645	11 271 076
C.2.2. Ceded Premiums / C.2.2. Primes Cédées								
C.2.2.1. Domestic Companies / C.2.2.1. Entreprises Nationales	1 527 169	1 424 356	1 490 300	1 402 215	1 404 968	1 459 484	1 400 400	1 309 117
C.2.2.2. (Foreign Controlled Companies) / C.2.2.2. (Entreprises Sous Contrôle Etranger)	3 580	4 445	5 091	4 946	4 393	3 312	10 218	32 660
C.2.2.3. Branches & Agencies of Foreign Cies / C.2.2.3. Succursales et Agences d'Ent. Etrangères	160 732	169 779	178 265	180 457	183 680	192 601	191 106	195 541
C.2.2. Total / C.2.2. Total	1 687 901	1 594 135	1 668 565	1 582 672	1 588 648	1 652 085	1 591 506	1 504 658
C.2.3. Net Written Premiums / C.2.3. Primes Nettes Emises								
C.2.3.1. Domestic Companies / C.2.3.1. Entreprises Nationales	5 548 737	5 909 825	6 161 607	6 491 229	6 717 616	6 911 568	7 069 580	7 059 164
C.2.3.2. (Foreign Controlled Companies) / C.2.3.2. (Entreprises Sous Contrôle Etranger)	15 207	19 570	22 571	24 797	28 438	31 173	70 309	57 868
C.2.3.3. Branches & Agencies of Foreign Cies / C.2.3.3. Succursales et Agences d'Ent. Etrangères	97 730	106 350	113 175	121 713	129 279	134 230	94 966	98 365
C.2.3. Total / C.2.3. Total	5 646 467	6 016 175	6 274 782	6 612 942	6 846 895	7 045 798	7 164 546	7 157 529

C.3. Total / C.3. Total

	1990	1991	1992	1993	1994	1995	1996	1997
C.3.1. Gross Premiums / C.3.1. Primes Brutes								
C.3.1.1. Direct Business / C.3.1.1. Assurances Directes								
C.3.1.1.1. Domestic Companies / C.3.1.1.1. Entreprises Nationales	35 586 100	36 831 999	38 177 271	39 562 644	39 597 057	40 165 790	39 150 678	39 786 869
C.3.1.1.2. (Foreign Controlled Companies) / C.3.1.1.2. (Entreprises Sous Contrôle Etranger)	192 173	189 753	186 028	198 680	240 043	368 720	416 515	391 263
C.3.1.1.3. Branches & Agencies of Foreign Cies / C.3.1.1.3. Succursales et Agences d'Ent. Etrangères	686 951	758 004	851 106	931 819	1 032 604	1 029 426	1 062 637	1 132 790
C.3.1.1. Total / C.3.1.1. Total	36 273 051	37 590 003	39 028 377	40 494 463	40 629 662	41 195 216	40 213 315	40 919 659
C.3.1.2. Reinsurance Accepted / C.3.1.2. Réassurance Acceptée								
C.3.1.2.1. Domestic Companies / C.3.1.2.1. Entreprises Nationales	1 108 933	968 084	996 105	931 416	915 031	960 184	738 315	693 644
C.3.1.2.2. (Foreign Controlled Companies) / C.3.1.2.2. (Entreprises Sous Contrôle Etranger)	2 352	3 422	4 424	4 361	4 340	4 584	7 070	6 355
C.3.1.2.3. Branches & Agencies of Foreign Cies / C.3.1.2.3. Succursales et Agences d'Ent. Etrangères	20 329	22 024	23 376	23 762	22 075	21 993	19 493	18 583
C.3.1.2. Total / C.3.1.2. Total	1 129 262	990 108	1 019 481	955 178	937 106	982 177	757 808	712 228
C.3.1.3. Total / C.3.1.3. Total								
C.3.1.3.1. Domestic Companies / C.3.1.3.1. Entreprises Nationales	36 695 033	37 800 083	39 173 376	40 494 060	40 512 088	41 125 974	39 888 993	40 480 514
C.3.1.3.2. (Foreign Controlled Companies) / C.3.1.3.2. (Entreprises Sous Contrôle Etranger)	194 525	193 175	190 452	203 041	244 383	373 304	423 585	397 618
C.3.1.3.3. Branches & Agencies of Foreign Cies / C.3.1.3.3. Succursales et Agences d'Ent. Etrangères	707 280	780 028	874 482	955 581	1 054 679	1 051 419	1 082 130	1 151 373
C.3.1.3. Total Gross Premiums / C.3.1.3. Total des Primes Brutes	37 402 313	38 580 111	40 047 858	41 449 641	41 566 768	42 177 393	40 971 123	41 631 888
C.3.2. Ceded Premiums / C.3.2. Primes Cédées								
C.3.2.1. Domestic Companies / C.3.2.1. Entreprises Nationales	1 555 186	1 454 411	1 521 855	1 436 454	1 442 201	1 502 477	1 446 253	1 452 293
C.3.2.2. (Foreign Controlled Companies) / C.3.2.2. (Entreprises Sous Contrôle Etranger)	6 951	8 716	8 847	10 001	10 921	14 579	23 702	46 768
C.3.2.3. Branches & Agencies of Foreign Cies / C.3.2.3. Succursales et Agences d'Ent. Etrangères	178 555	180 485	188 384	193 276	194 718	201 107	199 602	204 294
C.3.2. Total / C.3.2. Total	1 733 741	1 634 896	1 710 239	1 629 730	1 636 919	1 703 584	1 645 855	1 656 587
C.3.3. Net Written Premiums / C.3.3. Primes Nettes Emises								
C.3.3.1. Domestic Companies / C.3.3.1. Entreprises Nationales	32 402 159	33 622 138	35 088 348	36 210 542	36 443 201	36 921 268	35 596 332	36 434 381
C.3.3.2. (Foreign Controlled Companies) / C.3.3.2. (Entreprises Sous Contrôle Etranger)	185 548	181 401	178 227	189 587	230 040	355 138	394 618	345 230
C.3.3.3. Branches & Agencies of Foreign Cies / C.3.3.3. Succursales et Agences d'Ent. Etrangères	519 180	593 296	674 878	748 030	844 825	835 103	867 343	932 030
C.3.3. Total / C.3.3. Total	32 921 339	34 215 434	35 763 226	36 958 572	37 288 027	37 756 371	36 463 675	37 366 412

Monetary Unit: million Japanese yen / Unité monétaire : million de yen japonais

D. NET WRITTEN PREMIUMS IN THE REPORTING COUNTRY IN TERMS OF DOMESTIC AND FOREIGN RISKS
D. PRIMES NETTES EMISES DANS LE PAYS DECLARANT EN RISQUES NATIONAUX ET ETRANGERS

D.1. Life / D.1. Vie

	1990	1991	1992	1993	1994	1995	1996	1997
D.1.1. Domestic Risks / D.1.1. Risques Nationaux								
D.1.1.1. Domestic Companies / D.1.1.1. Entreprises Nationales	..	..	..	..	..	30 009 700	28 526 752	29 395 217
D.1.1.2. (Foreign Controlled Companies) / D.1.1.2. (Entreprises Sous Contrôle Etranger)	..	..	..	..	..	323 965	324 309	287 362
D.1.1.3. Branches & Agencies of Foreign Cies / D.1.1.3. Succursales et Agences d'Ent. Etrangères	..	..	..	..	..	700 873	772 377	833 665
D.1.1. Total / D.1.1. Total des Primes Nettes Vie	..	..	..	..	..	30 710 573	29 299 129	30 208 883
D.1.3. Total / D.1.3. Total								
D.1.3.1. Domestic Companies / D.1.3.1. Entreprises Nationales	26 853 422	27 712 313	28 926 741	29 719 313	29 725 585	30 009 700	28 526 752	29 395 217
D.1.3.2. (Foreign Controlled Companies) / D.1.3.2. (Entreprises Sous Contrôle Etranger)	170 341	161 831	155 656	164 790	201 602	323 965	324 309	287 362
D.1.3.3. Branches & Agencies of Foreign Cies / D.1.3.3. Succursales et Agences d'Ent. Etrangères	421 450	486 946	561 703	626 317	715 546	700 873	772 377	833 665
D.1.3. Total of Life Net Premiums / D.1.3. Total des Primes Nettes Vie	27 274 872	28 199 259	29 488 444	30 345 630	30 441 132	30 710 573	29 299 129	30 208 883

E. BUSINESS WRITTEN ABROAD / E. OPERATIONS A L'ETRANGER

E.1. Life / E.1. Vie

	1990	1991	1992	1993	1994	1995	1996	1997
E.1.1. Gross Premiums / E.1.1. Primes Brutes								
E.1.1.1. Direct Business / E.1.1.1. Assurance Directe								
E.1.1.1.2. Subsidiaries / E.1.1.1.2. Filiales	4 884	..	..	..	..	10 015	..	..
E.1.1.1. Total / E.1.1.1. Total	4 884	..	..	..	..	10 015	..	..
E.1.1.2. Reinsurance Accepted / E.1.1.2. Réassurance Acceptée								
E.1.1.2.2. Subsidiaries / E.1.1.2.2. Filiales	343	..	..	..	..	117	..	..
E.1.1.2. Total / E.1.1.2. Total	343	..	..	..	..	117	..	..
E.1.1.3. Total								
E.1.1.3.2. Subsidiaries / E.1.1.3.2. Filiales	5 227	..	..	..	..	10 132	..	..
E.1.1.3. Total Gross Premiums / E.1.1.3. Total des Primes Brutes	5 227	..	..	..	..	10 132	..	..
E.1.2. Ceded Premiums / E.1.2. Primes Cédées								
E.1.2.2. Subsidiaries / E.1.2.2. Filiales	1 066	..	..	..	..	2 586	..	..
E.1.2. Total / E.1.2. Total	1 066	..	..	..	..	2 586	..	..
E.1.3. Net Written Premiums / E.1.3. Primes Nettes Emises								
E.1.3.2. Subsidiaries / E.1.3.2. Filiales	4 161	..	..	..	..	7 546	..	..
E.1.3. Total / E.1.3. Total	4 161	..	..	..	..	7 546	..	..

E.2. Non-Life / E.2. Non-Vie

	1990	1991	1992	1993	1994	1995	1996	1997
E.2.1. Gross Premiums / E.2.1. Primes Brutes								
E.2.1.1. Direct Business / E.2.1.1. Assurance Directe								
E.2.1.1.1. Branches & Agencies / E.2.1.1.1. Succursales & Agences	69 450	65 594	69 920	60 505	54 561	56 575	65 202	77 873
E.2.1.2. Reinsurance Accepted / E.2.1.2. Réassurance Acceptée								
E.2.1.2.1. Branches & Agencies / E.2.1.2.1. Succursales & Agences	20 438	38 487	3 275	5 216	5 683	10 436	32 787	28 031
E.2.1.3. Total								
E.2.1.3.1. Branches & Agencies / E.2.1.3.1. Succursales & Agences	89 889	104 081	73 195	65 720	60 244	67 011	97 991	105 904
E.2.1.3.2. Subsidiaries / E.2.1.3.2. Filiales	160 927	175 849	167 745	138 941	123 500	140 491	166 038	186 927
E.2.1.3. Total Gross Premiums / E.2.1.3. Total des Primes Brutes	250 816	279 930	240 940	204 661	183 744	207 502	264 029	292 831
E.2.2. Ceded Premiums / E.2.2. Primes Cédées								
E.2.2.1. Branches & Agencies / E.2.2.1. Succursales & Agences	9 938	22 203	5 761	5 363	12 562	19 273	49 268	38 342
E.2.2.2. Subsidiaries / E.2.2.2. Filiales	98 660	103 358	98 155	77 443	63 460	71 156	83 339	104 704
E.2.2. Total / E.2.2. Total	108 598	125 561	103 916	82 806	76 022	90 429	132 607	143 046
E.2.3. Net Written Premiums / E.2.3. Primes Nettes Emises								
E.2.3.1. Branches & Agencies / E.2.3.1. Succursales & Agences	79 951	81 878	67 434	60 358	47 682	47 738	48 724	67 562
E.2.3.2. Subsidiaries / E.2.3.2. Filiales	62 268	72 492	69 590	61 498	60 040	69 335	82 697	82 222
E.2.3. Total / E.2.3. Total	142 219	154 370	137 024	121 856	107 722	117 073	131 421	149 784

Monetary Unit: million Japanese yen — Unité monétaire : million de yen japonais

	1990	1991	1992	1993	1994	1995	1996	1997	
F. OUTSTANDING INVESTMENT BY DIRECT INSURANCE COMPANIES									**F. ENCOURS DES PLACEMENTS DES ENTREPRISES D'ASSURANCES DIRECTES**
F.1. Life									**F.1. Vie**
F.1.1. Real Estate									F.1.1. Immobilier
F.1.1.1. Domestic Companies	7 181 695	7 753 492	8 364 646	8 958 853	9 442 685	9 734 839	9 698 235	9 832 165	F.1.1.1. Entreprises Nationales
F.1.1.2. (Foreign Controlled Companies)	6 057	8 094	9 045	8 688	8 690	8 899	9 193	1 100	F.1.1.2. (Entreprises Sous Contrôle Etranger)
F.1.1.3. Branches & Agencies of Foreign Cies	4 720	14 949	25 259	25 538	32 383	30 284	28 789	27 358	F.1.1.3. Succursales et Agences d'Ent. Etrangères
F.1.1. Total	..	..	8 398 950	8 993 079	9 475 068	9 765 123	9 727 024	9 859 523	F.1.1. Total
F.1.2. Mortgage Loans									F.1.2. Prêts Hypothécaires
F.1.2.1. Domestic Companies	3 829 187	4 231 430	4 680 784	7 342 258	7 249 375	7 251 368	..	..	F.1.2.1. Entreprises Nationales
F.1.2.2. (Foreign Controlled Companies)	960	2 298	3 398	33 217	40 897	44 733	..	..	F.1.2.2. (Entreprises Sous Contrôle Etranger)
F.1.2.3. Branches & Agencies of Foreign Cies	0	6 294	4 115	1 272	1 556	1 625	..	..	F.1.2.3. Succursales et Agences d'Ent. Etrangères
F.1.2. Total	..	..	4 688 297	7 376 747	7 250 931	7 252 993	..	..	F.1.2. Total
F.1.3. Shares									F.1.3. Actions
F.1.3.1. Domestic Companies	28 766 729	30 692 363	35 354 398	36 803 814	46 695 106	46 948 933	35 518 308	33 731 496	F.1.3.1. Entreprises Nationales
F.1.3.2. (Foreign Controlled Companies)	73 616	71 610	34 568	42 428	180 515	241 753	52 510	28 857	F.1.3.2. (Entreprises Sous Contrôle Etranger)
F.1.3.3. Branches & Agencies of Foreign Cies	150 229	133 054	177 732	182 793	635 030	738 907	128 052	108 128	F.1.3.3. Succursales et Agences d'Ent. Etrangères
F.1.3.4. Domestic Investment	..	..	31 506 834	33 070 784	41 434 636	42 250 550	31 896 190	29 913 175	F.1.3.4. Placement dans le Pays
F.1.3.5. Foreign Investment	..	..	4 059 864	3 958 251	5 895 500	5 437 290	3 750 171	3 927 449	F.1.3.5. Placement à l' Etranger
F.1.3. Total	..	..	35 566 698	37 029 035	47 330 136	47 687 840	35 646 361	33 840 624	F.1.3. Total
F.1.4. Bonds with Fixed Revenue									F.1.4. Obligations
F.1.4.1. Domestic Companies	10 222 229	12 220 354	28 116 446	31 822 130	30 696 666	40 454 441	53 703 298	54 930 528	F.1.4.1. Entreprises Nationales
F.1.4.2. (Foreign Controlled Companies)	153 674	192 418	292 558	340 555	265 294	460 993	789 174	642 328	F.1.4.2. (Entreprises Sous Contrôle Etranger)
F.1.4.3. Branches & Agencies of Foreign Cies	777 522	909 989	1 306 793	1 519 899	1 374 582	1 498 751	2 343 168	2 639 225	F.1.4.3. Succursales et Agences d'Ent. Etrangères
F.1.4.4. Domestic Investment	..	..	19 332 480	25 832 185	7 164 759	33 535 970	44 116 584	44 585 995	F.1.4.4. Placement dans le Pays
F.1.4.5. Foreign Investment	..	..	10 383 317	7 842 899	24 906 489	8 417 222	11 929 886	12 983 755	F.1.4.5. Placement à l' Etranger
F.1.4. Total	..	..	29 715 797	33 682 084	32 071 248	41 953 192	56 046 470	57 569 751	F.1.4. Total
F.1.5. Loans other than Mortgage Loans									F.1.5. Prêts Autres qu'Hypothécaires
F.1.5.1. Domestic Companies	46 040 397	52 012 079	56 275 657	56 561 705	59 602 542	59 919 564	65 092 898	63 299 798	F.1.5.1. Entreprises Nationales
F.1.5.2. (Foreign Controlled Companies)	96 473	117 125	118 615	111 502	140 751	156 705	206 355	21 558	F.1.5.2. (Entreprises Sous Contrôle Etranger)
F.1.5.3. Branches & Agencies of Foreign Cies	25 968	37 342	65 367	117 121	131 009	162 354	202 507	216 963	F.1.5.3. Succursales et Agences d'Ent. Etrangères
F.1.5.4. Domestic Investment	..	..	50 551 854	50 759 241	52 729 976	52 886 372	..	..	F.1.5.4. Placement dans le Pays
F.1.5.5. Foreign Investment	..	..	5 907 785	6 031 087	7 003 575	7 195 546	..	..	F.1.5.5. Placement à l' Etranger
F.1.5. Total	..	..	56 459 639	56 790 328	59 733 551	60 081 918	65 295 405	63 516 761	F.1.5. Total
F.1.6. Other Investments									F.1.6. Autres Placements
F.1.6.1. Domestic Companies	34 211 083	34 791 291	20 900 645	24 973 418	21 969 815	20 666 939	21 819 596	25 203 711	F.1.6.1. Entreprises Nationales
F.1.6.2. (Foreign Controlled Companies)	188 829	218 969	84 935	33 102	78 618	136 352	139 379	104 886	F.1.6.2. (Entreprises Sous Contrôle Etranger)
F.1.6.3. Branches & Agencies of Foreign Cies	409 085	431 461	196 133	189 337	134 730	84 486	124 109	120 619	F.1.6.3. Succursales et Agences d'Ent. Etrangères
F.1.6. Total	..	..	21 181 713	25 250 857	22 104 545	20 751 425	21 943 700	25 324 329	F.1.6. Total
F.1.7. Total									F.1.7. Total
F.1.7.1. Domestic Companies	130 251 320	141 701 009	153 692 576	166 462 178	175 656 189	184 976 084	185 832 335	186 997 695	F.1.7.1. Entreprises Nationales
F.1.7.2. (Foreign Controlled Companies)	519 609	610 514	543 119	624 492	714 765	1 049 435	1 196 611	798 729	F.1.7.2. (Entreprises Sous Contrôle Etranger)
F.1.7.3. Branches & Agencies of Foreign Cies	1 367 524	1 533 089	1 775 399	2 035 460	2 309 290	2 516 407	2 826 625	3 113 293	F.1.7.3. Succursales et Agences d'Ent. Etrangères
F.1.7.4. Domestic Investment	..	..	133 211 321	151 289 893	..	..	..	..	F.1.7.4. Placement dans le Pays
F.1.7.5. Foreign Investment	..	..	22 799 773	17 832 237	..	..	..	..	F.1.7.5. Placement à l' Etranger
F.1.7. Total of Life Investments	..	..	156 011 094	169 122 130	177 965 479	187 492 491	188 658 960	190 110 988	F.1.7. Total des Placements Vie
F.2. Non-Life									**F.2. Non-Vie**
F.2.1. Real Estate									F.2.1. Immobilier
F.2.1.1. Domestic Companies	1 249 379	1 397 745	1 562 915	1 625 669	1 815 981	1 811 907	1 837 566	1 814 999	F.2.1.1. Entreprises Nationales
F.2.1.2. (Foreign Controlled Companies)	111	120	146	141	159	146	839	822	F.2.1.2. (Entreprises Sous Contrôle Etranger)
F.2.1.3. Branches & Agencies of Foreign Cies	654	641	..	..	644	641	397	436	F.2.1.3. Succursales et Agences d'Ent. Etrangères
F.2.1.4. Domestic Investment	..	..	1 563 061	1 625 810	..	..	..	..	F.2.1.4. Placement dans le Pays
F.2.1. Total	..	..	..	..	1 816 625	1 812 548	1 837 963	1 815 435	F.2.1. Total
F.2.2. Mortgage Loans									F.2.2. Prêts Hypothécaires
F.2.2.1. Domestic Companies	448 533	528 264	558 069	577 286	594 299	594 384	..	..	F.2.2.1. Entreprises Nationales
F.2.2.4. Domestic Investment	..	..	558 069	577 246	..	..	..	..	F.2.2.4. Placement dans le Pays
F.2.2. Total	..	..	..	..	594 299	594 384	..	..	F.2.2. Total

JAPAN — JAPON

Monetary Unit: million Japanese yen — Unité monétaire : million de yen japonais

	1990	1991	1992	1993	1994	1995	1996	1997
F.2.3. Shares / Actions								
F.2.3.1. Domestic Companies / Entreprises Nationales	4 294 250	4 534 189	4 735 973	4 929 577	5 241 857	5 338 027	5 889 262	5 793 385
F.2.3.2. (Foreign Controlled Companies) / (Entreprises Sous Contrôle Etranger)	219	260	285	191	310	1 147	1 147	6 167
F.2.3.3. Branches & Agencies of Foreign Cies / Succursales et Agences d'Ent. Etrangères	15 546	14 822	:	:	23 451	28 492	25 903	19 157
F.2.3.4. Domestic Investment / Placement dans le Pays	:	:	:	:	:	:	:	5 391 456
F.2.3.5. Foreign Investment / Placement à l'Etranger	:	:	:	:	:	:	:	421 086
F.2.3. Total	:	:	4 736 258	4 929 768	5 265 308	5 366 519	5 915 165	5 812 542
F.2.4. Bonds with Fixed Revenue / Obligations								
F.2.4.1. Domestic Companies / Entreprises Nationales	6 172 189	6 159 384	7 085 551	7 377 112	8 230 846	8 957 926	8 226 935	8 816 265
F.2.4.2. (Foreign Controlled Companies) / (Entreprises Sous Contrôle Etranger)	21 475	23 868	26 764	31 559	36 247	38 953	81 695	70 038
F.2.4.3. Branches & Agencies of Foreign Cies / Succursales et Agences d'Ent. Etrangères	115 103	115 636	:	:	110 865	322 671	186 940	145 933
F.2.4.4. Domestic Investment / Placement dans le Pays	:	:	:	:	:	:	:	5 519 590
F.2.4.5. Foreign Investment / Placement à l'Etranger	:	:	:	:	:	:	:	3 442 608
F.2.4. Total	:	:	7 112 315	7 408 621	8 341 711	9 280 597	8 413 875	8 962 198
F.2.5. Loans other than Mortgage Loans / Prêts Autres qu'Hypothécaires								
F.2.5.1. Domestic Companies / Entreprises Nationales	7 155 011	7 007 510	6 641 347	6 143 748	5 967 958	5 944 453	6 547 114	6 651 665
F.2.5.2. (Foreign Controlled Companies) / (Entreprises Sous Contrôle Etranger)	1 158	1 232	2 996	1 883	1 323	1 264	1 491	1 474
F.2.5.3. Branches & Agencies of Foreign Cies / Succursales et Agences d'Ent. Etrangères	44 659	16 691	:	:	10 251	9 234	8 532	4 854
F.2.5.4. Domestic Investment / Placement dans le Pays	:	:	:	:	:	:	:	:
F.2.5. Total	:	:	6 644 343	6 145 631	5 978 209	5 953 687	6 555 646	6 656 519
F.2.6. Other Investments / Autres Placements								
F.2.6.1. Domestic Companies / Entreprises Nationales	4 113 103	4 035 977	3 962 072	4 043 040	3 806 328	4 016 581	4 930 403	7 291 713
F.2.6.2. (Foreign Controlled Companies) / (Entreprises Sous Contrôle Etranger)	6 256	9 290	8 627	6 942	7 701	7 103	15 174	44 047
F.2.6.3. Branches & Agencies of Foreign Cies / Succursales et Agences d'Ent. Etrangères	101 285	83 379	:	:	52 060	35 499	36 360	39 593
F.2.6.4. Domestic Investment / Placement dans le Pays	:	:	:	:	:	:	:	:
F.2.6. Total	:	:	3 970 699	4 054 982	3 858 388	4 052 080	4 966 763	7 331 306
F.2.7. Total								
F.2.7.1. Domestic Companies / Entreprises Nationales	23 432 465	23 663 069	24 545 927	24 701 392	25 657 269	26 663 278	27 431 280	30 368 027
F.2.7.2. (Foreign Controlled Companies) / (Entreprises Sous Contrôle Etranger)	29 219	34 770	38 818	40 716	45 740	48 613	104 971	122 548
F.2.7.3. Branches & Agencies of Foreign Cies / Succursales et Agences d'Ent. Etrangères	277 247	231 169	:	:	197 271	396 537	258 132	209 973
F.2.7.4. Domestic Investment / Placement dans le Pays	:	:	:	:	:	:	:	:
F.2.7. Total of Non-Life Investments / Total des Placements Non-Vie	:	:	24 584 745	24 742 108	25 854 540	27 059 815	27 689 412	30 578 000
G. BREAKDOWN OF NON-LIFE PREMIUMS / VENTILATIONS DES PRIMES NON-VIE								
G.1. Motor vehicle / Assurance Automobile								
G.1.1. Direct Business / Assurances Directes								
G.1.1.1. Gross Premiums / Primes Brutes	3 735 305	3 848 556	4 160 318	4 379 638	4 537 409	4 658 804	4 792 901	4 742 745
G.1.2. Reinsurance Accepted / Réassurance Acceptée								
G.1.2.1. Gross Premiums / Primes Brutes	481 203	420 801	437 627	396 614	382 980	397 242	347 311	326 806
G.1.3. Total								
G.1.3.1. Gross Premiums / Primes Brutes	4 216 508	4 269 357	4 597 945	4 776 252	4 920 389	5 056 046	5 140 212	5 069 551
G.1.3.2. Ceded Premiums / Primes Cédées	1 097 156	888 449	937 462	841 095	843 301	870 157	888 349	810 622
G.1.3.3. Net Written Premiums / Primes Nettes Emises	3 119 352	3 380 908	3 660 483	3 935 157	4 077 088	4 185 889	4 251 863	4 258 929
G.2. Marine, Aviation								
G.2.1. Direct Business / Assurances Directes								
G.2.1.1. Gross Premiums / Primes Brutes	254 272	256 716	260 037	251 394	254 829	255 125	278 771	268 497
G.2.2. Reinsurance Accepted / Réassurance Accepté								
G.2.2.1. Gross Premiums / Primes Brutes	129 967	138 157	148 985	143 894	146 914	162 370	120 650	108 093
G.2.3. Total								
G.2.3.1. Gross Premiums / Primes Brutes	384 239	394 873	409 022	395 288	401 743	417 495	399 421	376 590
G.2.3.2. Ceded Premiums / Primes Cédées	146 551	159 304	176 800	176 739	177 740	194 926	161 870	144 448
G.2.3.3. Net Written Premiums / Primes Nettes Emises	237 688	235 569	232 222	218 549	224 003	222 569	237 551	232 142

Monetary Unit: million Japanese yen   Unité monétaire : million de yen japonais

	1990	1991	1992	1993	1994	1995	1996	1997
G.3. Freight / G.3. Fret								
G.3.1. Direct Business / Assurances Directes								
G.3.1.1. Gross Premiums / Primes Brutes	65 517	69 223	68 256	66 448	66 897	68 497	70 212	70 667
G.3.2. Reinsurance Accepted / Réassurance Acceptée								
G.3.2.1. Gross Premiums / Primes Brutes	17 655	17 757	17 508	16 632	15 765	16 105	8 681	7 452
G.3.3. Total / Total								
G.3.3.1. Gross Premiums / Primes Brutes	83 172	86 980	85 764	83 080	82 662	84 602	78 893	78 119
G.3.3.2. Ceded Premiums / Primes Cédées	23 452	23 824	24 519	23 574	22 307	22 255	16 632	15 614
G.3.3.3. Net Written Premiums / Primes Nettes Emises	59 720	63 156	61 245	59 506	60 355	62 347	62 261	62 505
G.4. Fire, Property Damages / G.4. Incendie, Dommages aux Biens								
G.4.1. Direct Business / Assurances Directes								
G.4.1.1. Gross Premiums / Primes Brutes	1 852 764	1 736 866	1 808 733	1 955 794	1 994 506	2 004 317	2 065 268	2 067 156
G.4.2. Reinsurance Accepted / Réassurance Accep-ée								
G.4.2.1. Gross Premiums / Primes Brutes	247 941	249 538	258 221	245 244	240 491	258 823	158 319	160 523
G.4.3. Total / Total								
G.4.3.1. Gross Premiums / Primes Brutes	2 100 705	1 986 404	2 066 954	2 201 038	2 234 997	2 263 140	2 223 587	2 227 719
G.4.3.2. Ceded Premiums / Primes Cédées	234 444	255 765	304 403	316 923	324 012	343 963	305 431	324 756
G.4.3.3. Net Written Premiums / Primes Nettes Emises	1 046 124	1 060 934	1 080 928	1 109 737	1 177 744	1 216 085	1 220 011	1 234 662
G.5. Pecuniary Losses / G.5. Pertes Pécuniéres								
G.5.1. Direct Business / Assurances Directes								
G.5.1.1. Gross Premiums / Primes Brutes	118 558	125 363	114 641	80 878	76 920	75 940	99 962	76 249
G.5.2. Reinsurance Accepted / Réassurance Acceptée								
G.5.2.1. Gross Premiums / Primes Brutes	409	545	833	745	752	619	3 984	4 479
G.5.3. Total / Total								
G.5.3.1. Gross Premiums / Primes Brutes	118 967	125 908	115 474	81 623	77 672	76 559	103 946	80 728
G.5.3.2. Ceded Premiums / Primes Cédées	1 312	1 381	1 566	1 896	1 917	2 229	6 520	7 206
G.5.3.3. Net Written Premiums / Primes Nettes Emises	106 960	95 768	81 630	58 802	56 269	53 206	77 050	59 272
G.6. General Liability / G.6. Responsabilité Générale								
G.6.1. Direct Business / Assurances Directes								
G.6.1.1. Gross Premiums / Primes Brutes	202 018	217 872	234 247	242 830	256 320	285 090	312 436	327 888
G.6.2. Reinsurance Accepted / Réassurance Acceptée								
G.6.2.1. Gross Premiums / Primes Brutes	24 834	23 807	25 560	24 029	24 041	23 761	14 950	14 713
G.6.3. Total / Total								
G.6.3.1. Gross Premiums / Primes Brutes	226 852	241 679	259 807	266 859	280 361	308 851	327 386	342 601
G.6.3.2. Ceded Premiums / Primes Cédées	33 830	31 374	36 351	36 535	38 357	40 061	38 937	38 763
G.6.3.3. Net Written Premiums / Primes Nettes Emises	193 022	210 305	223 456	230 324	242 004	268 790	288 449	303 841
G.7. Accident, Health / G.7. Accident, Santé								
G.7.1. Direct Business / Assurances Directes								
G.7.1.1. Gross Premiums / Primes Brutes	2 594 858	2 786 485	2 664 135	2 921 896	2 754 119	2 871 398	3 153 041	2 919 457
G.7.2. Reinsurance Accepted / Réassurance Acceptée								
G.7.2.1. Gross Premiums / Primes Brutes	18 046	16 152	16 862	16 628	17 971	15 929	16 280	13 550
G.7.3. Total / Total								
G.7.3.1. Gross Premiums / Primes Brutes	2 612 904	2 802 637	2 680 997	2 938 524	2 772 090	2 887 327	3 169 321	2 933 007
G.7.3.2. Ceded Premiums / Primes Cédées	88 539	91 986	97 804	96 150	97 059	98 091	104 853	110 401
G.7.3.3. Net Written Premiums / Primes Nettes Emises	694 227	725 313	736 267	797 494	806 741	832 461	921 394	896 223
G.8. Others / G.8. Autres								
G.8.1. Direct Business / Assurances Directes								
G.8.1.1. Gross Premiums / Primes Brutes	279 202	340 001	221 876	240 544	238 626	256 038	131 155	131 387
G.8.2. Reinsurance Accepted / Réassurance Acceptée								
G.8.2.1. Gross Premiums / Primes Brutes	59 052	92 252	79 901	73 745	68 825	65 263	43 717	31 367
G.8.3. Total / Total								
G.8.3.1. Gross Premiums / Primes Brutes	338 254	432 253	301 777	314 289	307 451	321 301	174 872	162 754
G.8.3.2. Ceded Premiums / Primes Cédées	62 617	142 052	89 660	89 760	83 955	80 403	68 911	52 808
G.8.3.3. Net Written Premiums / Primes Nettes Emises	189 374	244 222	198 551	203 373	202 691	204 451	105 961	109 946
G.10. Total / G.10. Total								
G.10.1. Direct Business / Assurances Directes								
G.10.1.1. Gross Premiums / Primes Brutes	9 102 494	9 381 082	9 532 243	10 139 422	10 179 626	10 475 209	10 903 749	10 604 090
G.10.2. Reinsurance Accepted / Réassurance Acceptée								
G.10.2.1. Gross Premiums / Primes Brutes	979 107	959 009	985 497	917 531	897 739	940 112	713 896	666 986
G.10.3. Total / Total								
G.10.3.1. Gross Premiums / Primes Brutes	10 081 601	10 340 091	10 517 740	11 056 953	11 077 365	11 415 321	11 617 645	11 271 076
G.10.3.2. Ceded Premiums / Primes Cédées	1 687 901	1 594 135	1 668 565	1 582 672	1 588 648	1 652 085	1 591 506	1 504 658
G.10.3.3. Net Written Premiums / Primes Nettes Emises	5 646 467	6 016 175	6 274 782	6 612 942	6 846 895	7 045 798	7 164 546	9 157 529

KOREA

Monetary Unit: million won

Unité monétaire : million de won

	1990	1991	1992	1993	1994	1995	1996	1997
A. NUMBER OF COMPANIES IN THE REPORTING COUNTRY / **A. NOMBRE D'ENTREPRISES DANS LE PAYS DECLARANT**								
A.1. Life / **A.1. Vie**								
A.1.1. Domestic Companies / A.1.1. Entreprises Nationales		:	:	:	31	31	31	31
A.1.2. (Foreign Controlled Companies) / A.1.2. (Entreprises Sous Contrôle Etranger)		:	:	:	3	3	3	3
A.1.3. Branches & Agencies of Foreign Cies / A.1.3. Succursales et Agences d'Ent. Etrangères		:	:	:	2	2	2	2
A.1. All Companies / A.1. Ensemble des Entreprises		:	:	:	33	33	33	33
A.2. Non-Life / **A.2. Non-Vie**								
A.2.1. Domestic Companies / A.2.1. Entreprises Nationales		:	:	:	13	13	13	13
A.2.3. Branches & Agencies of Foreign Cies / A.2.3. Succursales et Agences d'Ent. Etrangères		:	:	:	3	3	3	3
A.2. All Companies / A.2. Ensemble des Entreprises		:	:	:	16	16	16	16
A.4. Reinsurance / **A.4. Réassurance**								
A.4.1. Domestic Companies / A.4.1. Entreprises Nationales		:	:	:	1	1	1	1
A.4. All Companies / A.4. Ensemble des Entreprises		:	:	:	1	1	1	1
A.5. Total / **A.5. Total**								
A.5.1. Domestic Companies / A.5.1. Entreprises Nationales		:	:	:	45	45	45	45
A.5.2. (Foreign Controlled Companies) / A.5.2. (Entreprises Sous Contrôle Etranger)		:	:	:	3	3	3	3
A.5.3. Branches & Agencies of Foreign Cies / A.5.3. Succursales et Agences d'Ent. Etrangères		:	:	:	5	5	5	5
A.5. All Insurance Companies / A.5. Ensemble des Entreprises d'Assurances		:	:	:	50	50	50	50
B. NUMBER OF EMPLOYEES / **B. NOMBRE D'EMPLOYES**								
B.1. Insurance Companies / B.1. Entreprises d'Assurances		:	:	:	74 632	79 948	87 218	84 451
B.2. Intermediaries / B.2. Intermediaires		:	:	:	43 782	46 186	46 385	74 801
B. Total / B. Total		:	:	:	118 414	126 134	133 603	159 252
C. BUSINESS WRITTEN IN THE REPORTING COUNTRY / **C. OPERATIONS CONCLUES DANS LE PAYS DECLARANT**								
C.1. Life / **C.1. Vie**								
C.1.1. Gross Premiums / C.1.1. Primes Brutes								
C.1.1.1. Direct Business / C.1.1.1. Assurances Directes								
C.1.1.1.1. Domestic Companies / C.1.1.1.1. Entreprises Nationales		:	:	:	26 855 269	33 689 944	37 206 444	41 916 538
C.1.1.1.2. (Foreign Controlled Companies) / C.1.1.1.2. (Entreprises Sous Contrôle Etranger)		:	:	:	67 883	79 878	97 090	118 226
C.1.1.1.3. Branches & Agencies of Foreign Cies / C.1.1.1.3. Succursales et Agences d'Ent. Etrangères		:	:	:	35 304	36 098	37 596	42 816
C.1.1.1. Total / C.1.1.1. Total		:	:	:	26 890 573	33 726 042	37 244 040	41 959 354
C.1.1.2. Reinsurance Accepted / C.1.1.2. Réassurance Acceptée								
C.1.1.2.1. Domestic Companies / C.1.1.2.1. Entreprises Nationales		:	:	:	876	1 890	43 164	1 370
C.1.1.2. Total / C.1.1.2. Total		:	:	:	876	1 890	43 164	1 370
C.1.1.3. Total / C.1.1.3. Total								
C.1.1.3.1. Domestic Companies / C.1.1.3.1. Entreprises Nationales		:	:	:	26 856 145	33 691 834	37 249 608	41 917 908
C.1.1.3.2. (Foreign Controlled Companies) / C.1.1.3.2. (Entreprises Sous Contrôle Etranger)		:	:	:	67 883	79 878	97 090	118 226
C.1.1.3.3. Branches & Agencies of Foreign Cies / C.1.1.3.3. Succursales et Agences d'Ent. Etrangères		:	:	:	35 304	36 098	37 596	42 816
C.1.1.3. Total Gross Premiums / C.1.1.3. Total des Primes Brutes		:	:	:	26 891 449	33 727 932	37 287 204	41 960 724
C.1.2. Ceded Premiums / C.1.2. Primes Cédées								
C.1.2.1. Domestic Companies / C.1.2.1. Entreprises Nationales		:	:	:	73 703	90 941	112 644	207 905
C.1.2.2. (Foreign Controlled Companies) / C.1.2.2. (Entreprises Sous Contrôle Etranger)		:	:	:	973	2 616	3 241	4 857
C.1.2.3. Branches & Agencies of Foreign Cies / C.1.2.3. Succursales et Agences d'Ent. Etrangères		:	:	:	1 145	519	1 907	1 226
C.1.2. Total / C.1.2. Total		:	:	:	74 848	91 460	114 551	209 132
C.1.3. Net Written Premiums / C.1.3. Primes Nettes Emises								
C.1.3.1. Domestic Companies / C.1.3.1. Entreprises Nationales		:	:	:	26 782 442	33 600 893	37 136 964	41 710 003
C.1.3.2. (Foreign Controlled Companies) / C.1.3.2. (Entreprises Sous Contrôle Etranger)		:	:	:	66 910	77 262	93 850	113 369
C.1.3.3. Branches & Agencies of Foreign Cies / C.1.3.3. Succursales et Agences d'Ent. Etrangères		:	:	:	34 159	35 579	35 689	41 590
C.1.3. Total / C.1.3. Total		:	:	:	26 816 601	33 636 472	37 172 653	41 751 592

154

Monetary Unit: million won | Unité monétaire : million de won

C.2. Non-Life | C.2. Non-Vie

	1990	1991	1992	1993	1994	1995	1996	1997
C.2.1. Gross premiems / C.2.1. Primes Brutes								
C.2.1.1. Direct Business / C.2.1.1. Assurances Directes								
C.2.1.1.1. Domestic Companies / C.2.1.1.1. Entreprises Nationales	..	..			7 881 422	10 240 861	12 814 382	15 374 350
C.2.1.1.3. Branches & Agencies of Foreign Cies / C.2.1.1.3. Succursales et Agences d'Ent. Etrangères	..	..			14 988	53 328	44 383	47 596
C.2.1.1. Total / C.2.1.1. Tota	..	..			7 896 410	10 294 189	12 858 765	15 421 946
C.2.1.2. Reinsurance Accepted / C.2.1.2. Réassurance Acceptée								
C.2.1.2.1. Domestic Companies / C.2.1.2.1. Entreprises Nationales	..	..			955 857	1 081 115	1 174 816	1 255 636
C.2.1.2.3. Branches & Agencies of Foreign Cies / C.2.1.2.3. Succursales et Agences d'Ent. Etrangères	..	..			5 911	14 310	13 463	13 018
C.2.1.2. Total / C.2.1.2. Tota	..	..			961 768	1 095 425	1 188 279	1 268 654
C.2.1.3. Total / C.2.1.3. Total								
C.2.1.3.1. Domestic Companies / C.2.1.3.1. Entreprises Nationales	..	..			8 837 279	11 321 976	13 989 199	16 629 986
C.2.1.3.3. Branches & Agencies of Foreign Cies / C.2.1.3.3. Succursales et Agences d'Ent. Etrangères	..	..			20 899	67 638	57 846	60 614
C.2.1.3. Total Gross Premiums / C.2.1.3. Tota des Primes Brutes	..	..			8 858 178	11 389 614	14 047 045	16 690 600
C.2.2. Ceded Premiums / C.2.2. Primes Cédées								
C.2.2.1. Domestic Companies / C.2.2.1. Entreprises Nationales	..	..			1 256 508	1 462 248	1 574 205	1 657 733
C.2.2.3. Branches & Agencies of Foreign Cies / C.2.2.3. Succursales et Agences d'Ent. Etrangères	..	..			3 366	12 521	12 793	12 474
C.2.2. Total / C.2.2. Total	..	..			1 259 874	1 474 769	1 586 998	1 670 207
C.2.3. Net Written Premiums / C.2.3. Primes Nettes Emises								
C.2.3.1. Domestic Companies / C.2.3.1. Entreprises Nationales	..	..			7 580 771	9 859 728	12 414 993	14 972 253
C.2.3.3. Branches & Agencies of Foreign Cies / C.2.3.3. Succursales et Agences d'Ent. Etrangères	..	..			17 533	55 117	45 054	48 140
C.2.3. Total / C.2.3. Total	..	..			7 598 304	9 914 845	12 460 047	15 020 393

C.3. Total | C.3. Total

	1990	1991	1992	1993	1994	1995	1996	1997
C.3.1. Gross Premiums / C.3.1. Primes Brutes								
C.3.1.1. Direc Business / C.3.1.1. Assurances Directes								
C.3.1.1.1. Domestic Companies / C.3.1.1.1. Entreprises Nationales	..	..			34 736 691	43 930 805	50 020 826	57 290 888
C.3.1.1.2. (Foreign Controlled Companies) / C.3.1.1.2. (Entreprises Sous Contrôle Etranger)	..	..			67 883	79 878	97 090	118 226
C.3.1.1.3. Branches & Agencies of Foreign Cies / C.3.1.1.3. Succursales et Agences d'Ent. Etrangères	..	..			50 292	89 426	81 979	90 412
C.3.1.1. Total / C.3.1.1. Total	..	..			34 786 983	44 020 231	50 102 805	57 381 300
C.3.1.2. Reinsurance Accepted / C.3.1.2. Réassurance Acceptée								
C.3.1.2.1. Domestic Companies / C.3.1.2.1. Entreprises Nationales	..	..			956 733	1 083 005	1 217 980	1 257 006
C.3.1.2.3. Branches & Agencies of Foreign Cies / C.3.1.2.3. Succursales et Agences d'Ent. Etrangères	..	..			5 911	14 310	13 463	13 018
C.3.1.2. Total / C.3.1.2. Total	..	..			962 644	1 097 315	1 231 443	1 270 024
C.3.1.3. Total / C.3.1.3. Total								
C.3.1.3.1. Domestic Companies / C.3.1.3.1. Entreprises Nationales	..	..			35 693 424	45 013 810	51 238 807	58 547 894
C.3.1.3.2. (Foreign Controlled Companies) / C.3.1.3.2. (Entreprises Sous Contrôle Etranger)	..	..			67 883	79 878	97 090	118 226
C.3.1.3.3. Branches & Agencies of Foreign Cies / C.3.1.3.3. Succursales et Agences d'Ent. Etrangères	..	..			56 203	103 736	95 442	103 430
C.3.1.3. Total Gross Premiums / C.3.1.3. Total des Primes Brutes	..	..			35 749 627	45 117 546	51 334 249	58 651 324
C.3.2. Ceded Premiums / C.3.2. Primes Cédées								
C.3.2.1. Domestic Companies / C.3.2.1. Entreprises Nationales	..	..			1 330 211	1 553 189	1 686 849	1 865 638
C.3.2.2. (Foreign Controlled Companies) / C.3.2.2. (Entreprises Sous Contrôle Etranger)	..	..			973	2 616	3 241	4 857
C.3.2.3. Branches & Agencies of Foreign Cies / C.3.2.3. Succursales et Agences d'Ent. Etrangères	..	..			4 511	13 040	14 700	13 700
C.3.2. Total / C.3.2. Total	..	..			1 334 722	1 566 229	1 701 549	1 879 339
C.3.3. Net Written Premiums / C.3.3. Primes Nettes Emises								
C.3.3.1. Dome-tic Companies / C.3.3.1. Entreprises Nationales	..	..			34 363 213	43 460 621	49 551 957	56 682 256
C.3.3.2. (Foreign Controlled Companies) / C.3.3.2. (Entreprises Sous Contrôle Etranger)	..	..			66 910	77 262	93 850	113 369
C.3.3.3. Branches & Agencies of Foreign Cies / C.3.3.3. Succursales et Agences d'Ent. Etrangères	..	..			51 692	90 696	80 743	89 730
C.3.3. Total / C.3.3. Total	..	..			34 414 905	43 551 317	49 632 700	56 771 985

D. NET WRITTEN PREMIUMS IN THE REPORTING COUNTRY IN TERMS OF DOMESTIC AND FOREIGN RISKS

D. PRIMES NETTES EMISES DANS LE PAYS DECLARANT EN RISQUES NATIONAUX ET ETRANGERS

D.1. Life / D.1. Vie

English label	1990	1991	1992	1993	1994	1995	1996	1997	French label
D.1.1. Domestic Risks									D.1.1. Risques Nationaux
D.1.1.1. Domestic Companies	..	..	..	..	26 781 566	33 599 003	37 093 800	41 708 633	D.1.1.1. Entreprises Nationales
D.1.1.2. (Foreign Controlled Companies)	..	..	..	..	66 910	77 262	93 850	113 369	D.1.1.2. (Entreprises Sous Contrôle Etranger)
D.1.1.3. Branches & Agencies of Foreign Cies	..	..	..	..	34 159	35 579	35 689	41 590	D.1.1.3. Succursales et Agences d'Ent. Etrangères
D.1.1. Total	..	..	..	..	26 815 725	33 634 582	37 129 489	41 750 222	D.1.1. Total des Primes Nettes Vie
D.1.2. Foreign Risks									D.1.2. Risques Etrangers
D.1.2.1. Domestic Companies	..	..	..	..	876	1 890	43 164	1 370	D.1.2.1. Entreprises Nationales
D.1.2. Total	..	..	..	..	876	1 890	43 164	1 370	D.1.2. Total des Primes Nettes Vie
D.1.3. Total									D.1.3. Total
D.1.3.1. Domestic Companies	..	..	..	..	26 782 442	33 600 893	37 136 964	41 710 003	D.1.3.1. Entreprises Nationales
D.1.3.2. (Foreign Controlled Companies)	..	..	..	..	66 910	77 262	93 850	113 369	D.1.3.2. (Entreprises Sous Contrôle Etranger)
D.1.3.3. Branches & Agencies of Foreign Cies	..	..	..	..	34 159	35 579	35 689	41 590	D.1.3.3. Succursales et Agences d'Ent. Etrangères
D.1.3. Total of Life Net Premiums	..	..	..	..	26 816 601	33 636 472	37 172 653	41 751 592	D.1.3. Total des Primes Nettes Vie

D.2. Non-Life / D.2. Non-Vie

English label	1990	1991	1992	1993	1994	1995	1996	1997	French label
D.2.1. Domestic Risks									D.2.1. Risques Nationaux
D.2.1.1. Domestic Companies	..	..	..	..	7 508 382	9 829 164	12 377 730	14 921 240	D.2.1.1. Entreprises Nationales
D.2.1.3. Branches & Agencies of Foreign Cies	..	..	..	..	17 421	53 089	44 736	43 700	D.2.1.3. Succursales et Agences d'Ent. Etrangères
D.2.1. Total	..	..	..	..	7 525 803	9 882 253	12 422 466	14 964 940	D.2.1. Total des Primes Nettes Vie
D.2.2. Foreign Risks									D.2.2. Risques Etrangers
D.2.2.1. Domestic Companies	..	..	..	..	72 389	30 564	37 263	51 013	D.2.2.1. Entreprises Nationales
D.2.2.3. Branches & Agencies of Foreign Cies	..	..	..	..	112	2 028	318	4 440	D.2.2.3. Succursales et Agences d'Ent. Etrangères
D.2.2. Total	..	..	..	..	72 501	32 592	37 581	55 453	D.2.2. Total des Primes Nettes Vie
D.2.3. Total									D.2.3. Total
D.2.3.1. Domestic Companies	..	..	..	..	7 580 771	9 859 728	12 414 993	14 972 253	D.2.3.1. Entreprises Nationales
D.2.3.3. Branches & Agencies of Foreign Cies	..	..	..	..	17 533	55 117	45 054	48 140	D.2.3.3. Succursales et Agences d'Ent. Etrangères
D.2.3. Total	..	..	..	..	7 598 304	9 914 845	12 460 047	15 020 393	D.2.3. Total des Primes Nettes Vie

E. BUSINESS WRITTEN ABROAD / E. OPERATIONS A L'ETRANGER

E.2. Non-Life / E.2. Non-Vie

English label	1990	1991	1992	1993	1994	1995	1996	1997	French label
E.2.1. Gross Premiums									E.2.1. Primes Brutes
E.2.1.1. Direct Business									E.2.1.1. Assurance Directe
E.2.1.1.1. Branches & Agencies	..	..	..	..	38 497	29 588	41 699	56 555	E.2.1.1.1. Succursales & Agences
E.2.1.1.2. Subsidiaries	..	..	..	..	996	896	1 182	13 718	E.2.1.1.2. Filliales
E.2.1.1. Total	..	..	..	..	39 493	30 484	42 881	70 273	E.2.1.1. Total
E.2.1.2. Reinsurance Accepted									E.2.1.2. Réassurance Acceptée
E.2.1.2.1. Branches & Agencies	..	..	..	..	6 223	5 588	7 357	8 235	E.2.1.2.1. Succursales & Agences
E.2.1.2.2. Subsidiaries	..	..	..	..	0	5	4	1	E.2.1.2.2. Filliales
E.2.1.2. Total	..	..	..	..	6 223	5 593	7 361	8 236	E.2.1.2. Total
E.2.1.3.1. Branches & Agencies	..	..	..	..	44 720	35 176	49 056	64 790	E.2.1.3.1. Succursales & Agences
E.2.1.3.2. Subsidiaries	..	..	..	..	996	901	1 186	13 719	E.2.1.3.2. Filliales
E.2.1.3. Total Gross Premiums	..	..	..	..	45 716	36 077	50 242	78 509	E.2.1.3. Total des Primes Brutes
E.2.2. Ceded Premiums									E.2.2. Primes Cédées
E.2.2.1. Branches & Agencies	..	..	..	..	19 487	17 352	22 650	30 188	E.2.2.1. Succursales & Agences
E.2.2.2. Subsidiaries	..	..	..	..	501	358	334	10 186	E.2.2.2. Filliales
E.2.2. Total	..	..	..	..	19 988	17 710	22 984	40 374	E.2.2. Total
E.2.3. Net Written Premiums									E.2.3. Primes Nettes Emises
E.2.3.1. Branches & Agencies	..	..	..	..	25 233	17 824	26 406	34 602	E.2.3.1. Succursales & Agences
E.2.3.2. Subsidiaries	..	..	..	..	495	543	852	3 533	E.2.3.2. Filliales
E.2.3. Total	..	..	..	..	25 728	18 367	27 258	38 135	E.2.3. Total

F. OUTSTANDING INVESTMENT BY DIRECT INSURANCE COMPANIES
F. ENCOURS DES PLACEMENTS DES ENTREPRISES D'ASSURANCES DIRECTES

F.1. Life — F.1. Vie

		1990	1991	1992	1993	1994	1995	1996	1997
F.1.1. Real Estate	F.1.1. Immobilier								
F.1.1.1. Domestic Companies	F.1.1.1. Entreprises Nationales					4 229 015	4 763 520	5 788 271	6 984 429
F.1.1.4. Domestic Investment	F.1.1.4. Placement dans le Pays					4 229 015	4 763 520	5 788 271	6 984 429
F.1.1. Total	F.1.1. Total					4 229 015	..	5 788 271	6 984 429
F.1.2. Mortgage Loans	F.1.2. Prêts Hypothécaires								
F.1.2.1. Domestic Companies	F.1.2.1. Entreprises Nationales					180 555	199 709	195 860	207 600
F.1.2.4. Domestic Investment	F.1.2.4. Placement dans le Pays					180 555	..	195 860	207 600
F.1.2. Total	F.1.2. Total					180 555	..	195 860	207 600
F.1.3. Shares	F.1.3. Actions								
F.1.3.1. Domestic Companies	F.1.3.1. Entreprises Nationales					7 157 134	8 492 186	9 720 103	10 278 321
F.1.3.2. (Foreign Controlled Companies)	F.1.3.2. (Entreprises Sous Contrôle Etranger)					951	1 270	2 674	3 755
F.1.3.3. Branches & Agencies of Foreign Cies	F.1.3.3. Succursales et Agences d'Ent. Etrangères						299	829	1 025
F.1.3.4. Domestic Investment	F.1.3.4. Placement dans le Pays					7 100 399	..	9 578 354	10 069 080
F.1.3.5. Foreign Investment	F.1.3.5. Placement à l'Etranger					56 735	..	142 578	210 266
F.1.3. Total	F.1.3. Total					7 157 134	..	9 720 932	10 279 346
F.1.4. Bonds with Fixed Revenue	F.1.4. Obligations								
F.1.4.1. Domestic Companies	F.1.4.1. Entreprises Nationales					7 880 393	7 766 041	10 000 073	12 696 700
F.1.4.2. (Foreign Controlled Companies)	F.1.4.2. (Entreprises Sous Contrôle Etranger)					56 273	50 263	75 729	105 689
F.1.4.3. Branches & Agencies of Foreign Cies	F.1.4.3. Succursales et Agences d'Ent. Etrangères					31 903	36 536	44 525	50 928
F.1.4.4. Domestic Investment	F.1.4.4. Placement dans le Pays					7 885 890	..	9 976 779	12 592 556
F.1.4.5. Foreign Investment	F.1.4.5. Placement à l'Etranger					26 406	..	67 819	155 072
F.1.4. Total	F.1.4. Total					7 912 296	..	10 044 598	12 747 628
F.1.5. Loans other than Mortgage Loans	F.1.5. Prêts Autres qu'Hypothécaires								
F.1.5.1. Domestic Companies	F.1.5.1. Entreprises Nationales					27 364 435	30 431 824	36 388 349	43 277 907
F.1.5.2. (Foreign Controlled Companies)	F.1.5.2. (Entreprises Sous Contrôle Etranger)					7 692	9 927	11 715	14 134
F.1.5.3. Branches & Agencies of Foreign Cies	F.1.5.3. Succursales et Agences d'Ent. Etrangères					5 522	5 695	6 637	7 477
F.1.5.4. Domestic Investment	F.1.5.4. Placement dans le Pays					27 369 957	..	36 394 986	43 285 384
F.1.5. Total	F.1.5. Total					27 369 957	..	36 394 986	43 285 384
F.1.6. Other Investments	F.1.6. Autres Placements								
F.1.6.1. Domestic Companies	F.1.6.1. Entreprises Nationales					9 037 516	10 757 511	13 422 664	18 851 574
F.1.6.2. (Foreign Controlled Companies)	F.1.6.2. (Entreprises Sous Contrôle Etranger)					54 784	45 559	47 986	88 284
F.1.6.3. Branches & Agencies of Foreign Cies	F.1.6.3. Succursales et Agences d'Ent. Etrangères					23 668	15 651	9 733	31 047
F.1.6.4. Domestic Investment	F.1.6.4. Placement dans le Pays					9 061 184	..	13 432 397	18 882 621
F.1.6. Total	F.1.6. Total					9 061 184	..	13 432 397	18 882 621
F.1.7. Total	F.1.7. Total								
F.1.7.1. Domestic Companies	F.1.7.1. Entreprises Nationales					55 849 048	62 410 791	75 515 320	92 296 531
F.1.7.2. (Foreign Controlled Companies)	F.1.7.2. (Entreprises Sous Contrôle Etranger)					119 700	107 019	138 104	211 861
F.1.7.3. Branches & Agencies of Foreign Cies	F.1.7.3. Succursales et Agences d'Ent. Etrangères					61 093	58 181	61 724	90 477
F.1.7.4. Domestic Investment	F.1.7.4. Placement dans le Pays					55 827 000	..	..	..
F.1.7.5. Foreign Investment	F.1.7.5. Placement à l'Etranger					83 141	..	..	..
F.1.7. Total of Life Investments	F.1.7. Total des Placements Vie					55 910 141	..	75 577 044	92 387 008

F.2. Non-Life — F.2. Non-Vie

		1990	1991	1992	1993	1994	1995	1996	1997
F.2.1. Real Estate	F.2.1. Immobilier								
F.2.1.1. Domestic Companies	F.2.1.1. Entreprises Nationales					887 925	1 049 975	1 228 719	1 509 759
F.2.1.4. Domestic Investment	F.2.1.4. Placement dans le Pays					887 925	..	1 228 719	1 509 759
F.2.1. Total	F.2.1. Total					887 925	..	1 228 719	1 509 759
F.2.3. Shares	F.2.3. Actions								
F.2.3.1. Domestic Companies	F.2.3.1. Entreprises Nationales					1 687 103	1 985 240	2 060 126	2 372 230
F.2.3.3. Branches & Agencies of Foreign Cies	F.2.3.3. Succursales et Agences d'Ent. Etrangères					3 010	2 815	2 616	619
F.2.3.4. Domestic Investment	F.2.3.4. Placement dans le Pays					1 681 900	..	2 053 513	2 369 818
F.2.3.5. Foreign Investment	F.2.3.5. Placement à l'Etranger					8 213	..	9 229	3 031
F.2.3. Total	F.2.3. Total					1 690 113	..	2 062 742	2 372 849

Monetary Unit: million won   Unité monétaire : million de won

Label (EN)	Label (FR)	1990	1991	1992	1993	1994	1995	1996	1997
F.2.4. Bonds with Fixed Revenue	F.2.4. Obligations								
F.2.4.1. Domestic Companies	F.2.4.1. Entreprises Nationales					1 268 593	1 676 319	2 257 999	2 926 245
F.2.4.3. Branches & Agencies of Foreign Cies	F.2.4.3. Succursales et Agences d'Ent. Etrangères					14 959	17 260	16 352	16 668
F.2.4.4. Domestic Investment	F.2.4.4. Placement dans le Pays					1 254 584	..	2 263 803	2 865 304
F.2.4.5. Foreign Investment	F.2.4.5. Placement à l' Etranger					28 968	..	10 548	77 609
F.2.4. Total	F.2.4. Total					1 283 552	..	2 274 351	2 942 913
F.2.5. Loans other than Mortgage Loans	F.2.5. Prêts Autres qu'Hypothécaires								
F.2.5.1. Domestic Companies	F.2.5.1. Entreprises Nationales					1 881 036	2 589 958	3 390 687	4 533 109
F.2.5.3. Branches & Agencies of Foreign Cies	F.2.5.3. Succursales et Agences d'Ent. Etrangères					2 703	2 959	3 585	3 849
F.2.5.4. Domestic Investment	F.2.5.4. Placement dans le Pays					1 883 739	..	..	..
F.2.5. Total	F.2.5. Total					1 883 739	..	3 394 272	4 536 958
F.2.6. Other Investments	F.2.6. Autres Placements								
F.2.6.1. Domestic Companies	F.2.6.1. Entreprises Nationales					3 287 273	2 521 097	2 950 892	6 897 707
F.2.6.3. Branches & Agencies of Foreign Cies	F.2.6.3. Succursales et Agences d'Ent. Etrangères					30 305	17 996	22 586	46 282
F.2.6.4. Domestic Investment	F.2.6.4. Placement dans le Pays					3 317 578	..	..	..
F.2.6. Total	F.2.6. Total					3 317 578	..	2 973 478	6 943 989
F.2.7. Total	F.2.7. Total								
F.2.7.1. Domestic Companies	F.2.7.1. Entreprises Nationales					9 011 930	9 822 589	11 888 423	18 239 050
F.2.7.3. Branches & Agencies of Foreign Cies	F.2.7.3. Succursales et Agences d'Ent. Etrangères					50 977	41 030	45 139	67 418
F.2.7.4. Domestic Investment	F.2.7.4. Placement dans le Pays					9 025 726	..	..	..
F.2.7.5. Foreign Investment	F.2.7.5. Placement à l' Etranger					37 181	..	..	..
F.2.7. Total of Non-Life Investments	F.2.7. Total des Placements Non-Vie					9 062 907	..	11 933 562	18 306 468
G. BREAKDOWN OF NON-LIFE PREMIUMS	**G. VENTILATIONS DES PRIMES NON-VIE**								
G.1. Motor vehicle	G.1. Assurance Automobile								
G.1.1. Direct Business	G.1.1. Assurances Directes								
G.1.1.1. Gross Premiums	G.1.1.1. Primes Brutes					3 861 280	4 724 527	5 958 147	6 283 431
G.1.2. Reinsurance Accepted	G.1.2. Réassurance Acceptée								
G.1.2.1. Gross Premiums	G.1.2.1. Primes Brutes					50 157	56 484	66 168	88 664
G.1.3. Total	G.1.3. Total								
G.1.3.1. Gross Premiums	G.1.3.1. Primes Brutes					3 911 436	4 781 011	6 024 315	6 372 095
G.1.3.2. Ceded Premiums	G.1.3.2. Primes Cédées					58 583	64 382	75 723	97 963
G.1.3.3. Net Written Premiums	G.1.3.3. Primes Nettes Emises					3 852 853	4 716 629	5 948 591	6 274 132
G.2. Marine, Aviation	G.2. Marine, Aviation								
G.2.1. Direct Business	G.2.1. Assurances Directes								
G.2.1.1. Gross Premiums	G.2.1.1. Primes Brutes					186 285	233 001	210 750	191 549
G.2.2. Reinsurance Accepted	G.2.2. Réassurance Acceptée								
G.2.2.1. Gross Premiums	G.2.2.1. Primes Brutes					96 903	105 450	88 731	63 630
G.2.3. Total	G.2.3. Total								
G.2.3.1. Gross Premiums	G.2.3.1. Primes Brutes					283 188	338 451	299 481	255 179
G.2.3.2. Ceded Premiums	G.2.3.2. Primes Cédées					223 761	264 859	225 871	192 518
G.2.3.3. Net Written Premiums	G.2.3.3. Primes Nettes Emises					59 426	73 592	73 610	62 661
G.3. Freight	G.3. Fret								
G.3.1. Direct Business	G.3.1. Assurances Directes								
G.3.1.1. Gross Premiums	G.3.1.1. Primes Brutes					225 646	234 608	212 648	183 290
G.3.2. Reinsurance Accepted	G.3.2. Réassurance Acceptée								
G.3.2.1. Gross Premiums	G.3.2.1. Primes Brutes					44 351	45 492	41 504	33 385
G.3.3. Total	G.3.3. Total								
G.3.3.1. Gross Premiums	G.3.3.1. Primes Brutes					269 997	280 100	254 153	216 675
G.3.3.2. Ceded Premiums	G.3.3.2. Primes Cédées					56 061	59 395	53 694	45 381
G.3.3.3. Net Written Premiums	G.3.3.3. Primes Nettes Emises					213 936	220 705	200 458	171 295
G.4. Fire, Property Damages	G.4. Incendie, Dommages aux Biens								
G.4.1. Direct Business	G.4.1. Assurances Directes								
G.4.1.1. Gross Premiums	G.4.1.1. Primes Brutes					620 938	424 546	399 130	519 873
G.4.2. Reinsurance Accepted	G.4.2. Réassurance Acceptée								
G.4.2.1. Gross Premiums	G.4.2.1. Primes Brutes					347 254	258 201	240 925	467 067
G.4.3. Total	G.4.3. Total								
G.4.3.1. Gross Premiums	G.4.3.1. Primes Brutes					968 191	682 747	640 055	986 940
G.4.3.2. Ceded Premiums	G.4.3.2. Primes Cédées					539 647	357 401	326 032	478 725
G.4.3.3. Net Written Premiums	G.4.3.3. Primes Nettes Emises					428 544	325 346	314 023	508 215

Monetary Unit: million won   Unité monétaire : million de won

	1990	1991	1992	1993	1994	1995	1996	1997
G.5. Pecuniary Losses / Pertes Pécunières								
G.5.1. Direct Business / Assurances Directes								
G.5.1.1. Gross Premiums / Primes Brutes					709 268	680 005	667 306	841 639
G.5.2. Reinsurance Accepted / Réassurance Acceptée								
G.5.2.1. Gross Premiums / Primes Brutes					220 051	204 973	192 520	141 662
G.5.3. Total								
G.5.3.1. Gross Premiums / Primes Brutes					929 318	884 978	859 826	983 301
G.5.3.2. Ceded Premiums / Primes Cédées					234 345	218 586	208 468	165 821
G.5.3.3. Net Written Premiums / Primes Nettes Emises					694 973	666 392	651 359	817 480
G.6. General Liability / Responsabilité Générale								
G.6.1. Direct Business / Assurances Directes								
G.6.1.1. Gross Premiums / Primes Brutes					58 616	178 276	187 963	199 815
G.6.2. Reinsurance Accepted / Réassurance Acceptée								
G.6.2.1. Gross Premiums / Primes Brutes					33 773	73 294	82 926	89 769
G.6.3. Total								
G.6.3.1. Gross Premiums / Primes Brutes					92 389	251 570	270 889	289 584
G.6.3.2. Ceded Premiums / Primes Cédées					48 934	92 931	100 576	112 008
G.6.3.3. Net Written Premiums / Primes Nettes Emises					43 455	158 639	170 312	177 576
G.7. Accident, Health / Accident, Santé								
G.7.1. Direct Business / Assurances Directes								
G.7.1.1. Gross Premiums / Primes Brutes					1 348 959	2 082 951	2 869 366	3 823 836
G.7.2. Reinsurance Accepted / Réassurance Acceptée								
G.7.2.1. Gross Premiums / Primes Brutes					42 900	47 818	63 859	230 928
G.7.3. Total								
G.7.3.1. Gross Premiums / Primes Brutes					1 391 859	2 130 769	2 933 225	4 054 764
G.7.3.2. Ceded Premiums / Primes Cédées					46 296	51 888	71 393	439 706
G.7.3.3. Net Written Premiums / Primes Nettes Emises					1 345 563	2 078 881	2 861 832	3 615 058
G.8. Others / Autres								
G.8.1. Direct Business / Assurances Directes								
G.8.1.1. Gross Premiums / Primes Brutes					885 420	1 736 275	2 353 455	3 378 513
G.8.2. Reinsurance Accepted / Réassurance Acceptée								
G.8.2.1. Gross Premiums / Primes Brutes					92 481	303 713	411 646	153 549
G.8.3. Total								
G.8.3.1. Gross Premiums / Primes Brutes					977 901	2 039 988	2 765 102	3 532 062
G.8.3.2. Ceded Premiums / Primes Cédées					52 144	365 327	525 240	138 085
G.8.3.3. Net Written Premiums / Primes Nettes Emises					925 757	1 674 661	2 239 862	3 393 976
G.9. Treaty Reinsurance / Réassurance Obligatoire								
G.9.2. Reinsurance Accepted / Réassurance Acceptée								
G.9.2.1. Gross Premiums / Primes Brutes					33 899	..	0	0
G.9.3. Total								
G.9.3.1. Gross Premiums / Primes Brutes					33 899	..	0	0
G.9.3.2. Ceded Premiums / Primes Cédées					103	..	0	0
G.9.3.3. Net Written Premiums / Primes Nettes Emises					33 796	..	0	0
G.10. Total								
G.10.1. Direct Business / Assurances Directes								
G.10.1.1. Gross Premiums / Primes Brutes					7 896 410	10 294 189	12 858 765	15 421 946
G.10.2. Reinsurance Accepted / Réassurance Acceptée								
G.10.2.1. Gross Premiums / Primes Brutes					961 768	1 095 425	1 188 279	1 268 654
G.10.3. Total								
G.10.3.1. Gross Premiums / Primes Brutes					8 858 178	11 389 614	14 047 046	16 690 600
G.10.3.2. Ceded Premiums / Primes Cédées					1 259 874	1 474 769	1 586 997	1 670 207
G.10.3.3. Net Written Premiums / Primes Nettes Emises					7 598 304	9 914 845	12 460 047	15 020 393
H. GROSS CLAIMS PAYMENTS / PAIEMENTS BRUTS DES SINISTRES								
H.1. Life / Vie								
H.1.1. Domestic Companies / Entreprises Nationales							23 772 421	30 102 052
H.1.2. (Foreign Controlled Companies) / (Entreprises Sous Contrôle Etranger)							41 623	52 216
H.1.3. Branches & Agencies of Foreign Cies / Succursales et Agences d'Ent. Etrangères							20 450	22 799
H.1. Total							23 792 871	30 124 851

159

H.2. Non-Life / H.2. Non-Vie

Code	Description (EN)	Description (FR)	1990	1991	1992	1993	1994	1995	1996	1997
H.2.1.	Domestic Companies	Entreprises Nationales							6 226 401	7 122 791
H.2.3.	Branches & Agencies of Foreign Cies	Succursales et Agences d'Ent. Etrangères							14 680	21 868
H.2.	Total	Total							6 241 081	7 144 659

I. GROSS OPERATING EXPENSES / I. DEPENSES BRUTES D'EXPLOITATION

I.1. Life / I.1. Vie

Code	Description (EN)	Description (FR)	1990	1991	1992	1993	1994	1995	1996	1997
I.1.1.	Domestic Companies	Entreprises Nationales							6 822 858	7 589 381
I.1.2.	(Foreign Controlled Companies)	(Entreprises Sous Contrôle Etranger)							35 583	58 374
I.1.3.	Branches & Agencies of Foreign Cies	Succursales et Agences d'Ent. Etrangères							18 213	23 880
I.1.	Total	Total des Primes Nettes Vie							6 841 071	7 613 261

I.2. Non-Life / I.2. Non-Vie

Code	Description (EN)	Description (FR)	1990	1991	1992	1993	1994	1995	1996	1997
I.2.1.	Domestic Companies	Entreprises Nationales							2 637 812	3 121 658
I.2.3.	Branches & Agencies of Foreign Cies	Succursales et Agences d'Ent. Etrangères							13 380	15 950
I.2.	Total	Total							2 651 192	3 137 608

J. COMMISSIONS / J. COMMISSIONS

J.1. Life / J.1. Vie

Code	Description (EN)	Description (FR)	1990	1991	1992	1993	1994	1995	1996	1997
J.1.1.	Direct Business	Assurance directe								
J.1.1.1.	Domestic Companies	Entreprises Nationales							3 811 943	4 635 956
J.1.1.2.	(Foreign Controlled Companies)	(Entreprises Sous Contrôle Etranger)							19 322	34 402
J.1.1.3.	Branches & Agencies of Foreign Cies	Succursales et Agences d'Ent. Etrangères							5 824	12 462
J.1.1.	Total	Total							3 817 767	4 648 418
J.1.2.	Reinsurance Accepted	Réassurances acceptées								
J.1.2.1.	Domestic Companies	Entreprises Nationales							144	12 376
J.1.2.3.	Branches & Agencies of Foreign Cies	Succursales et Agences d'Ent. Etrangères							0	1
J.1.2.	Total	Total							144	12 377
J.1.3.	Total	Total								
J.1.3.1.	Domestic Companies	Entreprises Nationales							3 812 088	4 648 332
J.1.3.2.	(Foreign Controlled Companies)	(Entreprises Sous Contrôle Etranger)							19 322	34 402
J.1.3.3.	Branches & Agencies of Foreign Cies	Succursales et Agences d'Ent. Etrangères							5 824	12 463
J.1.3.	Total of Life Net Premiums	Total							3 817 911	4 660 795

J.2. Non-Life / J.2. Non-Vie

Code	Description (EN)	Description (FR)	1990	1991	1992	1993	1994	1995	1996	1997
J.2.1.	Direct Business	Assurance directe								
J.2.1.1.	Domestic Companies	Entreprises Nationales							1 323 980	1 323 980
J.2.1.3.	Branches & Agencies of Foreign Cies	Succursales et Agences d'Ent. Etrangères							10 022	10 022
J.2.1.	Total	Total des Primes Nettes Vie							1 334 002	1 334 002
J.2.2.	Reinsurance Accepted	Réassurances acceptées								
J.2.2.1.	Domestic Companies	Entreprises Nationales							271 113	271 113
J.2.2.3.	Branches & Agencies of Foreign Cies	Succursales et Agences d'Ent. Etrangères							4 885	4 885
J.2.2.	Total	Total							275 998	275 998
J.2.3.	Total	Total								
J.2.3.1.	Domestic Companies	Entreprises Nationales							1 595 093	1 595 093
J.2.3.3.	Branches & Agencies of Foreign Cies	Succursales et Agences d'Ent. Etrangères							14 907	14 907
J.2.3.	Total	Total							1 610 000	1 610 000

160

Monetary Unit: million Luxembourg francs   Unité monétaire : million de Francs luxembourgeois

	1990	1991	1992	1993	1994	1995	1996	1997
A. NUMBER OF COMPANIES IN THE REPORTING COUNTRY / **A. NOMBRE D'ENTREPRISES DANS LE PAYS DECLARANT**								
A.1. Life / **A.1. Vie**								
A.1.1. Domestic Companies / A.1.1. Entreprises Nationales	..	23	27	30	34	39	50	51
A.1.2. (Foreign Controlled Companies) / A.1.2. (Entreprises Sous Contrôle Etranger)	..	..	7	6	5	2	38	37
A.1.3. Branches & Agencies of Foreign Cies / A.1.3. Succursales et Agences d'Ent. Etrangères	..	7	7	6	5	6	4	4
A.1. All Companies / A.1. Ensemble des Entreprises	..	30	34	36	39	45	54	55
A.2. Non-Life / **A.2. Non-Vie**								
A.2.1. Domestic Companies / A.2.1. Entreprises Nationales	15	16	16	20	20	21	21	21
A.2.2. (Foreign Controlled Companies) / A.2.2. (Entreprises Sous Contrôle Etranger)	..	..	16	..	..	2	15	13
A.2.3. Branches & Agencies of Foreign Cies / A.2.3. Succursales et Agences d'Ent. Etrangères	18	18	16	15	14	12	12	11
A.2. All Companies / A.2. Ensemble des Entreprises	33	34	32	35	34	33	33	32
A.3. Composite / **A.3. Mixte**								
A.3.1. Domestic Companies / A.3.1. Entreprises Nationales	1	1	1	1	1	1	0	0
A.3.3. Branches & Agencies of Foreign Cies / A.3.3. Succursales et Agences d'Ent. Etrangères	1	1	1	1	2	2	3	4
A.3. All Companies / A.3. Ensemble des Entreprises	2	2	2	2	3	3	3	4
A.4. Reinsurance / **A.4. Réassurance**								
A.4.1. Domestic Companies / A.4.1. Entreprises Nationales	134	157	173	184	213	234	244	255
A.4.2. (Foreign Controlled Companies) / A.4.2. (Entreprises Sous Contrôle Etranger)	..	..	..	..	..	206	0	217
A.4. All Companies / A.4. Ensemble des Entreprises	134	157	173	184	213	234	244	255
A.5. Total / **A.5. Total**								
A.5.1. Domestic Companies / A.5.1. Entreprises Nationales	170	197	217	235	268	295	315	327
A.5.2. (Foreign Controlled Companies) / A.5.2. (Entreprises Sous Contrôle Etranger)	..	..	..	..	..	210	53	267
A.5.3. Branches & Agencies of Foreign Cies / A.5.3. Succursales et Agences d'Ent. Etrangères	22	26	24	22	21	20	19	19
A.5. All Insurance Companies / A.5. Ensemble des Entreprises d'Assurances	192	223	241	257	289	315	334	346
B. NUMBER OF EMPLOYEES / **B. NOMBRE D'EMPLOYES**								
B.1. Insurance Companies / B.1. Entreprises d'Assurances	1 100	1 160	1 190	1 208	1 277	1 304	1 592	1 720
B.2. Intermediaries / B.2. Intermediaires	350	6 023	6 000	6 200	6 620	6 800	6 985	7 157
B. Total / B. Total	1 450	7 183	7 190	7 408	7 897	8 104	8 577	8 877
C. BUSINESS WRITTEN IN THE REPORTING COUNTRY / **C. OPERATIONS CONCLUES DANS LE PAYS DECLARANT**								
C.1. Life / **C.1. Vie**								
C.1.1. Gross Premiums / C.1.1. Primes Brutes								
C.1.1.1. Direct Business / C.1.1. Assurances Directes								
C.1.1.1.1. Domestic Companies / C.1.1.1. Entreprises Nationales	4 120	4 797	3 971	5 259	36 791	105 136	93 123	150 374
C.1.1.1.2. (Foreign Controlled Companies) / C.1.1.1.2. (Entreprises Sous Contrôle Etranger)	..	..	..	0	..	0	85 383	124 594
C.1.1.1.3. Branches & Agencies of Foreign Cies / C.1.1.1.3. Succursales et Agences d'Ent. Etrangères	604	1 102	1 831	564	1 559	2 430	2 182	4 292
C.1.1.1. Total / C.1.1.1. Total	4 724	5 899	5 803	5 823	38 350	107 566	95 305	155 166
C.1.1.2. Reinsurance Accepted / C.1.1.2. Réassurance Acceptée								
C.1.1.2.1. Domestic Companies / C.1.1.2.1. Entreprises Nationales	..	..	..	..	132	67	195	213
C.1.1.2.2. (Foreign Controlled Companies) / C.1.1.2.2. (Entreprises Sous Contrôle Etranger)	..	..	..	..	..	..	6	5
C.1.1.2.3. Branches & Agencies of Foreign Cies / C.1.1.2.3. Succursales et Agences d'Ent. Etrangères	..	..	..	..	0	0	0	99
C.1.1.2. Total / C.1.1.2. Total	..	..	..	..	132	67	195	312
C.1.1.3.1. Domestic Companies / C.1.1.3.1. Entreprises Nationales	..	..	..	..	36 923	105 203	93 318	151 087
C.1.1.3.2. (Foreign Controlled Companies) / C.1.1.3.2. (Entreprises Sous Contrôle Etranger)	..	..	..	..	..	0	85 389	124 599
C.1.1.3.3. Branches & Agencies of Foreign Cies / C.1.1.3.3. Succursales et Agences d'Ent. Etrangères	..	..	..	..	1 559	2 430	2 182	4 591
C.1.1.3. Total Gross Premiums / C.1.1.3. Total des Primes Brutes	..	..	..	..	38 482	107 633	95 500	155 478

Monetary Unit: million Luxembourg francs

English label	1990	1991	1992	1993	1994	1995	1996	1997	French label
C.1.2. Ceded Premiums									**C.1.2. Primes Cédées**
C.1.2.1. Domestic Companies	:	:	:	:	1 713	1 923	11 441	9 054	C.1.2.1. Entreprises Nationales
C.1.2.2. (Foreign Controlled Companies)	:	:	:	0	:	:	10 879	6 602	C.1.2.2. (Entreprises Sous Contrôle Etranger)
C.1.2.3. Branches & Agencies of Foreign Cies	:	:	:	:	18	18	18	17	C.1.2.3. Succursales et Agences d'Ent. Etrangères
C.1.2. Total	:	:	:	:	1 731	1 941	11 459	9 071	C.1.2. Total
C.1.3. Net Written Premiums									**C.1.3. Primes Nettes Emises**
C.1.3.1. Domestic Companies	:	:	:	:	35 210	103 280	81 877	142 033	C.1.3.1. Entreprises Nationales
C.1.3.2. (Foreign Controlled Companies)	:	:	:	0	:	:	74 510	117 997	C.1.3.2. (Entreprises Sous Contrôle Etranger)
C.1.3.3. Branches & Agencies of Foreign Cies	:	:	:	:	1 541	2 412	2 164	4 374	C.1.3.3. Succursales et Agences d'Ent. Etrangères
C.1.3. Total	:	:	:	:	36 751	105 692	84 041	146 407	C.1.3. Total
C.2. Non-Life									**C.2. Non-Vie**
C.2.1. Gross premiums									**C.2.1. Primes Brutes**
C.2.1.1. Direct Business									C.2.1.1. Assurances Directes
C.2.1.1.1. Domestic Companies	7 777	8 889	9 543	9 899	11 653	12 553	14 252	14 050	C.2.1.1.1. Entreprises Nationales
C.2.1.1.2. (Foreign Controlled Companies)	:	:	:	0	:	:	3 430	2 782	C.2.1.1.2. (Entreprises Sous Contrôle Etranger)
C.2.1.1.3. Branches & Agencies of Foreign Cies	2 324	2 395	2 713	2 502	2 703	2 380	2 678	2 464	C.2.1.1.3. Succursales et Agences d'Ent. Etrangères
C.2.1.1. Total	10 101	11 285	12 256	12 402	14 356	14 933	16 930	16 514	C.2.1.1. Total
C.2.1.2. Reinsurance Accepted									C.2.1.2. Réassurance Acceptée
C.2.1.2.1. Domestic Companies	:	:	:	:	95	28	36	34	C.2.1.2.1. Entreprises Nationales
C.2.1.2.2. (Foreign Controlled Companies)	:	:	:	0	0	0	5	:	C.2.1.2.2. (Entreprises Sous Contrôle Etranger)
C.2.1.2.3. Branches & Agencies of Foreign Cies	:	:	:	:	0	0	0	9	C.2.1.2.3. Succursales et Agences d'Ent. Etrangères
C.2.1.2. Total	:	:	:	:	95	28	36	43	C.2.1.2. Total
C.2.1.3. Total									C.2.1.3. Total
C.2.1.3.1. Domestic Companies	:	:	:	:	11 748	12 582	14 288	14 084	C.2.1.3.1. Entreprises Nationales
C.2.1.3.2. (Foreign Controlled Companies)	:	:	:	0	:	:	3 435	2 782	C.2.1.3.2. (Entreprises Sous Contrôle Etranger)
C.2.1.3.3. Branches & Agencies of Foreign Cies	:	:	:	:	2 703	2 380	2 678	2 473	C.2.1.3.3. Succursales et Agences d'Ent. Etrangères
C.2.1.3. Total Gross Premiums	:	:	:	:	14 451	14 962	16 966	16 557	C.2.1.3. Total des Primes Brutes
C.2.2. Ceded Premiums									**C.2.2. Primes Cédées**
C.2.2.1. Domestic Companies	:	:	:	:	4 379	4 070	3 499	3 513	C.2.2.1. Entreprises Nationales
C.2.2.2. (Foreign Controlled Companies)	:	:	:	0	:	:	1 064	804	C.2.2.2. (Entreprises Sous Contrôle Etranger)
C.2.2.3. Branches & Agencies of Foreign Cies	:	:	:	:	1 017	600	758	898	C.2.2.3. Succursales et Agences d'Ent. Etrangères
C.2.2. Total	:	:	:	:	5 396	4 670	4 257	4 411	C.2.2. Total
C.2.3. Net Written Premiums									**C.2.3. Primes Nettes Emises**
C.2.3.1. Domestic Companies	:	:	:	:	7 369	8 512	10 789	10 571	C.2.3.1. Entreprises Nationales
C.2.3.2. (Foreign Controlled Companies)	:	:	:	0	:	:	2 371	1 978	C.2.3.2. (Entreprises Sous Contrôle Etranger)
C.2.3.3. Branches & Agencies of Foreign Cies	:	:	:	:	1 686	1 780	1 920	1 575	C.2.3.3. Succursales et Agences d'Ent. Etrangères
C.2.3. Total	:	:	:	:	9 055	10 292	12 709	12 146	C.2.3. Total
C.3. Total									**C.3. Total**
C.3.1. Gross Premiums									**C.3.1. Primes Brutes**
C.3.1.1. Direct Business									C.3.1.1. Assurances Directes
C.3.1.1.1. Domestic Companies	11 897	13 686	13 514	15 158	48 444	117 689	107 375	164 924	C.3.1.1.1. Entreprises Nationales
C.3.1.1.2. (Foreign Controlled Companies)	:	:	:	0	:	:	88 813	127 376	C.3.1.1.2. (Entreprises Sous Contrôle Etranger)
C.3.1.1.3. Branches & Agencies of Foreign Cies	2 928	3 497	4 544	3 066	4 262	4 810	4 860	6 756	C.3.1.1.3. Succursales et Agences d'Ent. Etrangères
C.3.1.1. Total	14 825	17 184	18 059	18 225	52 706	122 499	112 235	171 680	C.3.1.1. Total
C.3.1.2. Reinsurance Accepted									C.3.1.2. Réassurance Acceptée
C.3.1.2.1. Domestic Companies	:	:	:	:	227	95	231	247	C.3.1.2.1. Entreprises Nationales
C.3.1.2.2. (Foreign Controlled Companies)	:	:	:	0	0	0	11	:	C.3.1.2.2. (Entreprises Sous Contrôle Etranger)
C.3.1.2.3. Branches & Agencies of Foreign Cies	:	:	:	:	0	0	0	108	C.3.1.2.3. Succursales et Agences d'Ent. Etrangères
C.3.1.2. Total	:	:	:	:	227	95	231	355	C.3.1.2. Total
C.3.1.3. Total									C.3.1.3. Total
C.3.1.3.1. Domestic Companies	:	:	:	:	48 671	117 785	107 606	165 171	C.3.1.3.1. Entreprises Nationales
C.3.1.3.2. (Foreign Controlled Companies)	:	:	:	0	:	:	88 824	127 381	C.3.1.3.2. (Entreprises Sous Contrôle Etranger)
C.3.1.3.3. Branches & Agencies of Foreign Cies	:	:	:	:	4 262	4 810	4 860	6 864	C.3.1.3.3. Succursales et Agences d'Ent. Etrangères
C.3.1.3. Total Gross Premiums	:	:	:	:	52 933	122 595	112 466	172 035	C.3.1.3. Total des Primes Brutes

Monetary Unit: million Luxembourg francs
Unité monétaire : million de Francs luxembourgeois

English Label	1990	1991	1992	1993	1994	1995	1996	1997	French Label
C.3.2. Ceded Premiums									C.3.2. Primes Cédées
C.3.2.1. Domestic Companies	:	:	:	:	6 092	5 993	14 940	12 567	C.3.2.1. Entreprises Nationales
C.3.2.2. (Foreign Controlled Companies)	:	:	:	:	0	:	11 943	7 406	C.3.2.2. (Entreprises Sous Contrôle Etranger)
C.3.2.3. Branches & Agencies of Foreign Cies	:	:	:	:	1 035	618	776	915	C.3.2.3. Succursales at Agences d'Ent. Etrangères
C.3.2. Total	:	:	:	:	7 127	6 611	15 716	13 482	C.3.2. Total
C.3.3. Net Written Premiums									C.3.3. Primes Nettes Emises
C.3.3.1. Domestic Companies	:	:	:	:	42 579	111 792	92 666	152 604	C.3.3.1. Entreprises Nationales
C.3.3.2. (Foreign Controlled Companies)	:	:	:	:	0	:	76 881	119 975	C.3.3.2. (Entreprises Sous Contrôle Etranger)
C.3.3.3. Branches & Agencies of Fcreign Cies	:	:	:	:	3 227	4 192	4 084	5 949	C.3.3.3. Succursales at Agences d'Ent. Etrangères
C.3.3. Total	:	:	:	:	45 806	115 984	96 750	158 553	C.3.3. Total

E. BUSINESS WRITTEN ABROAD — E. OPERATIONS A L'ETRANGER

E.2. Non-Life — E.2. Non-Vie

English Label	1990	1991	1992	1993	1994	1995	1996	1997	French Label
E.2.1. Gross Premiums									E.2.1. Primes Brutes
E.2.1.1. Direct Business									E.2.1.1. Assurance Directe
E.2.1.1.1 Branches & Agencies	:	:	:	:	:	7 580	8 934	10 613	E.2.1.1.1. Succursales & Agences
E.2.1.1. Total	:	:	:	:	:	7 580	8 934	10 613	E.2.1.1. Total
E.2.1.2. Reinsurance Accepted									E.2.1.2. Réassurance Acceptée
E.2.1.2.1 Branches & Agencies	:	:	:	:	:	27	0	0	E.2.1.2.1. Succursales & Agences
E.2.1.2. Total	:	:	:	:	:	27	0	0	E.2.1.2. Total
E.2.1.3. Total									E.2.1.3. Total
E.2.1.3.1. Branches & Agencies	:	:	:	:	:	7 607	8 934	10 613	E.2.1.3.1. Succursales & Agences
E.2.1.3. Total Gross Premiums	:	:	:	:	:	7 607	8 934	10 613	E.2.1.3. Total ces Primes Brutes
E.2.2. Ceded Premiums									E.2.2. Primes Cédées
E.2.2.1. Branches & Agencies	:	:	:	:	:	2 224	2 317	2 774	E.2.2.1. Succursales & Agences
E.2.2. Total	:	:	:	:	:	2 224	2 317	2 774	E.2.2. Total
E.2.3. Net Written Premiums									E.2.3. Primes Nettes Emises
E.2.3.1. Branches & Agencies	:	:	:	:	:	5 383	6 617	7 839	E.2.3.1. Succursales & Agences
E.2.3. Total	:	:	:	:	:	5 383	6 617	7 839	E.2.3. Total

F. OUTSTANDING INVESTMENT BY DIRECT INSURANCE COMPANIES — F. ENCOURS DES PLACEMENTS DES ENTREPRISES D'ASSURANCES DIRECTES

F.1. Life — F.1. Vie

English Label	1990	1991	1992	1993	1994	1995	1996	1997	French Label
F.1.1. Real Estate									F.1.1. Immobilier
F.1.1.1. Domestic Companies	:	942	:	:	941	1 109	781	1 316	F.1.1.1. Entreprises Nationales
F.1.1.2. (Foreign Controlled Companies)	:	:	:	:	:	:	328	845	F.1.1.2. (Entreprises Sous Contrôle Etranger)
F.1.1.3. Branches & Agencies of Foreign Cies	:	142	:	:	:	:	:	:	F.1.1.3. Succursales et Agences d'Ent. Etrangères
F.1.1.4. Domestic Investment	:	1 084	905	1 020	:	1 109	781	:	F.1.1.4. Placement dans le Pays
F.1.1. Total	:	1 084	:	:	:	1 109	781	:	F.1.1. Total
F.1.2. Mortgage Loans									F.1.2. Prêts Hypothécaires
F.1.2.1. Domestic Companies	:	0	:	:	:	8	15	14	F.1.2.1. Entreprises Nationales
F.1.2.2. (Foreign Controlled Companies)	:	:	:	:	:	:	15	14	F.1.2.2. (Entreprises Sous Contrôle Etranger)
F.1.2.4. Domestic Investment	:	0	:	:	:	8	15	:	F.1.2.4. Placement dans le Pays
F.1.2. Total	:	:	:	:	:	8	15	:	F.1.2. Total
F.1.3. Shares									F.1.3. Actions
F.1.3.1. Domestic Companies	:	1 295	:	:	2 411	26 101	4 670	7 346	F.1.3.1. Entreprises Nationales
F.1.3.2. (Foreign Controlled Companies)	:	:	:	:	:	:	2 099	3 996	F.1.3.2. (Entreprises Sous Contrôle Etranger)
F.1.3.3. Branches & Agencies of Foreign Cies	:	31	:	:	:	:	:	:	F.1.3.3. Succursales et Agences d'Ent. Etrangères
F.1.3.4. Domestic Investment	:	1 309	:	:	:	1 930	:	:	F.1.3.4. Placement dans le Pays
F.1.3.5. Foreign Investment	:	17	:	:	:	24 171	:	:	F.1.3.5. Placement à l'Etranger
F.1.3. Total	:	1 326	4 160	3 010	:	26 101	4 670	:	F.1.3. Total

LUXEMBOURG

Monetary Unit: million Luxembourg francs

Unité monétaire : million de Francs luxembourgeois

	1990	1991	1992	1993	1994	1995	1996	1997
F.1.4. Bonds with Fixed Revenue / F.1.4. Obligations								
F.1.4.1. Domestic Companies / F.1.4.1. Entreprises Nationales	...	13 147	...	...	12 762	141 374	181 035	243 575
F.1.4.2. (Foreign Controlled Companies) / F.1.4.2. (Entreprises Sous Contrôle Etranger)	...	...	...	...			164 175	212 309
F.1.4.3. Branches & Agencies of Foreign Cies / F.1.4.3. Succursales et Agences d'Ent. Etrangeres	...	2 939	...	...			...	...
F.1.4.4. Domestic Investment / F.1.4.4. Placement dans le Pays	...	15 095	...				...	...
F.1.4.5. Foreign Investment / F.1.4.5. Placement a l'Etranger	...	990	...				...	...
F.1.4. Total / F.1.4. Total	...	16 086	19 982	21 766		141 374	181 035	
F.1.5. Loans other than Mortgage Loans / F.1.5. Prêts Autres qu'Hypothécaires								
F.1.5.1. Domestic Companies / F.1.5.1. Entreprises Nationales	...	0	...			0	695	685
F.1.5.2. (Foreign Controlled Companies) / F.1.5.2. (Entreprises Sous Contrôle Etranger)	...	...	...				533	550
F.1.5. Total / F.1.5. Total	...	0	...			0	695	
F.1.6. Other Investments / F.1.6. Autres Placements								
F.1.6.1. Domestic Companies / F.1.6.1. Entreprises Nationales	...	2 145	...		4 041	24 882	15 444	19 272
F.1.6.2. (Foreign Controlled Companies) / F.1.6.2. (Entreprises Sous Contrôle Etranger)	...	...	...				12 694	1 972
F.1.6.3. Branches & Agencies of Foreign Cies / F.1.6.3. Succursales et Agences d'Ent. Etrangeres	...	266	...				...	...
F.1.6. Total / F.1.6. Total	...	2 410	3 806	3 949		24 882	15 444	
F.1.7. Total / F.1.7. Total								
F.1.7.1. Domestic Companies / F.1.7.1. Entreprises Nationales	...	17 528	...		20 155	193 474	202 640	272 208
F.1.7.2. (Foreign Controlled Companies) / F.1.7.2. (Entreprises Sous Contrôle Etranger)	...	...	...				179 844	219 686
F.1.7.3. Branches & Agencies of Foreign Cies / F.1.7.3. Succursales et Agences d'Ent. Etrangeres	...	3 377	...				...	...
F.1.7. Total of Life Investments / F.1.7. Total des Placements Vie	...	20 906	28 855	29 745		193 474	202 640	
F.2. Non-Life / **F.2. Non-Vie**								
F.2.1. Real Estate / F.2.1. Immobilier								
F.2.1.1. Domestic Companies / F.2.1.1. Entreprises Nationales	...	793	...		1 411	946	831	1 982
F.2.1.2. (Foreign Controlled Companies) / F.2.1.2. (Entreprises Sous Contrôle Etranger)	...	...	...				266	1 125
F.2.1.3. Branches & Agencies of Foreign Cies / F.2.1.3. Succursales et Agences d'Ent. Etrangeres	...	308	...				...	...
F.2.1.4. Domestic Investment / F.2.1.4. Placement dans le Pays	...	1 101	...			946		...
F.2.1. Total / F.2.1. Total	...	1 101	1 134	1 178		946	831	
F.2.2. Mortgage Loans / F.2.2. Prêts Hypothécaires								
F.2.2.1. Domestic Companies / F.2.2.1. Entreprises Nationales	...	32	...			30	41	31
F.2.2.2. (Foreign Controlled Companies) / F.2.2.2. (Entreprises Sous Contrôle Etranger)	...	...	...				11	
F.2.2.4. Domestic Investment / F.2.2.4. Placement dans le Pays	...	...	...			30		
F.2.2. Total / F.2.2. Total	...	32	...			30	41	
F.2.3. Shares / F.2.3. Actions								
F.2.3.1. Domestic Companies / F.2.3.1. Entreprises Nationales	...	1 331	...		3 802	5 352	7 944	9 852
F.2.3.2. (Foreign Controlled Companies) / F.2.3.2. (Entreprises Sous Contrôle Etranger)	...	...	...				5 531	4 210
F.2.3.3. Branches & Agencies of Foreign Cies / F.2.3.3. Succursales et Agences d'Ent. Etrangeres	...	46	...				...	...
F.2.3.4. Domestic Investment / F.2.3.4. Placement dans le Pays	...	1 345	...			2 558		...
F.2.3.5. Foreign Investment / F.2.3.5. Placement a l'Etranger	...	32	...			2 794		...
F.2.3. Total / F.2.3. Total	...	1 377	1 613	2 695		5 352	7 944	
F.2.4. Bonds with Fixed Revenue / F.2.4. Obligations								
F.2.4.1. Domestic Companies / F.2.4.1. Entreprises Nationales	...	8 349	...		26 732	21 069	30 467	34 375
F.2.4.2. (Foreign Controlled Companies) / F.2.4.2. (Entreprises Sous Contrôle Etranger)	...	...	...				18 639	15 609
F.2.4.3. Branches & Agencies of Foreign Cies / F.2.4.3. Succursales et Agences d'Ent. Etrangeres	...	1 812	...				...	...
F.2.4.4. Domestic Investment / F.2.4.4. Placement dans le Pays	...	9 351	...				...	...
F.2.4.5. Foreign Investment / F.2.4.5. Placement a l'Etranger	...	809	...				...	...
F.2.4. Total / F.2.4. Total	...	10 161	12 261	14 444		21 069	30 467	
F.2.5. Loans other than Mortgage Loans / F.2.5. Prêts Autres qu'Hypothécaires								
F.2.5.1. Domestic Companies / F.2.5.1. Entreprises Nationales	...	0	...			0	160	171
F.2.5.2. (Foreign Controlled Companies) / F.2.5.2. (Entreprises Sous Contrôle Etranger)	...	...	...				13	
F.2.5. Total / F.2.5. Total	...	0	...			0	160	
F.2.6. Other Investments / F.2.6. Autres Placements								
F.2.6.1. Domestic Companies / F.2.6.1. Entreprises Nationales	...	1 536	...		5 119	7 545	8 034	8 254
F.2.6.2. (Foreign Controlled Companies) / F.2.6.2. (Entreprises Sous Contrôle Etranger)	...	...	...				4 569	1 700
F.2.6.3. Branches & Agencies of Foreign Cies / F.2.6.3. Succursales et Agences d'Ent. Etrangeres	...	325	...				...	...
F.2.6.4. Domestic Investment / F.2.6.4. Placement dans le Pays	...	1 861	...					...
F.2.6. Total / F.2.6. Total	...	1 861	2 350	3 345		7 546	8 034	

LUXEMBOURG

Monetary Unit: million Luxembourg francs

Unité monétaire : million de Francs luxembourgeois

G. BREAKDOWN OF NON-LIFE PREMIUMS — G. VENTILATIONS DES PRIMES NON-VIE

	1990	1991	1992	1993	1994	1995	1996	1997
F.2.7. Total								
F.2.7.1. Domestic Companies — Entreprises Nationales	..	12 042	..	..	37 064	34 942	47 477	54 665
F.2.7.2. (Foreign Controlled Companies) — (Entreprises Sous Contrôle Etranger)	..	2 490	..	..	..	29 029	29 029	22 644
F.2.7.3. Branches & Agencies of Foreign Cies — Succursales et Agences d'Ent. Etrangères	..							
F.2.7. Total of Non-Life Investments — Total des Placements Non-Vie	..	14 532	17 360	21 662	..	34 943	47 477	..
G.1. Motor vehicle — G.1. Assurance Automobile								
G.1.1. Direct Business — G.1.1. Assurances Directes								
G.1.1.1. Gross Premiums — Primes Brutes	5 780	5 240	5 732	5 821	6 524	6 832	7 847	7 206
G.1.1.2. Ceded Premiums — Primes Cédées	..	..	..	..	..	1 264	746	845
G.1.1.3. Net Written Premiums — Primes Nettes Emises	..	..	..	..	..	5 568	7 101	6 361
G.2. Marine, Aviation — G.2. Marine, Aviation								
G.2.1. Direct Business — G.2.1. Assurances Directes								
G.2.1.1. Gross Premiums — Primes Brutes	28	7	43	83	81	10	9	69
G.2.1.2. Ceded Premiums — Primes Cédées	..	..	..	..	..	5	3	4
G.2.1.3. Net Written Premiums — Primes Nettes Emises	..	..	..	..	..	4	6	65
G.3. Freight — G.3. Fret								
G.3.1. Direct Business — G.3.1. Assurances Directes								
G.3.1.1. Gross Premiums — Primes Brutes	239	250	429	252	275	356	319	420
G.3.1.2. Ceded Premiums — Primes Cédées	..	..	..	..	..	263	227	326
G.3.1.3. Net Written Premiums — Primes Nettes Emises	..	..	..	..	..	93	92	94
G.4. Fire, Property Damages — G.4. Incendie, Dommages aux Biens								
G.4.1. Direct Business — G.4.1. Assurances Directes								
G.4.1.1. Gross Premiums — Primes Brutes	2 483	2 726	3 050	3 352	3 533	3 712	3 888	3 991
G.4.1.2. Ceded Premiums — Primes Cédées	..	..	..	..	..	1 590	1 109	1 217
G.4.1.3. Net Written Premiums — Primes Nettes Emises	..	..	..	..	..	2 121	2 779	2 774
G.5. Pecuniary Losses — G.5. Pertes Pécuniéres								
G.5.1. Direct Business — G.5.1. Assurances Directes								
G.5.1.1. Gross Premiums — Primes Brutes	1 024	1 383	944	716	807	1 292	1 805	1 755
G.5.1.2. Ceded Premiums — Primes Cédées	..	..	..	..	..	558	1 228	1 020
G.5.1.3. Net Written Premiums — Primes Nettes Emises	..	..	..	..	..	733	577	735
G.6. General Liability — G.6. Responsabilité Génèrae								
G.6.1. Direct Business — G.6.1. Assurances Directes								
G.6.1.1. Gross Premiums — Primes Brutes	860	880	1 030	1 270	1 630	1 580	1 666	1 843
G.6.1.2. Ceded Premiums — Primes Cédées	..	..	..	..	..	787	686	845
G.6.1.3. Net Written Premiums — Primes Nettes Emises	..	..	..	..	..	793	980	998
G.7. Accident, Health — G.7. Accident, Santé								
G.7.1. Direct Business — G.7.1. Assurances Directes								
G.7.1.1. Gross Premiums — Primes Brutes	539	607	682	665	783	845	901	887
G.7.1.2. Ceded Premiums — Primes Cédées	..	..	..	..	..	140	84	102
G.7.1.3. Net Written Premiums — Primes Nettes Emises	..	..	..	..	..	705	817	785
G.8. Others — G.8. Autres								
G.8.1. Direct Business — G.8.1. Assurances Directes								
G.8.1.1. Gross Premiums — Primes Erutes	177	192	346	239	280	307	495	343
G.8.1.2. Ceded Premiums — Primes Cédées	..	..	..	..	..	59	171	46
G.8.1.3. Net Written Premiums — Primes Nettes Emises	..	..	..	..	..	248	324	297
G.10. Total — G.10. Total								
G.10.1. Direct Business — G.10.1. Assurances Directes								
G.10.1.1. Gross Premiums — Primes Brutes	11 130	11 285	12 256	12 398	13 913	14 935	16 930	16 514
G.10.1.2. Ceded Premiums — Primes Cédées	..	..	..	..	..	4 666	4 254	4 405
G.10.1.3. Net Written Premiums — Primes Nettes Emises	..	..	..	..	..	10 265	12 676	12 109
G.10.2. Reinsurance Accepted — G.10.2. Réassurance Acceptée								
G.10.2.1. Gross Premiums — Primes Brutes	..	..	..	..	..	28	36	43
G.10.2.2. Ceded Premiums — Primes Cédées	..	..	..	..	..	1	3	6
G.10.2.3. Net Written Premiums — Primes Nettes Emises	..	..	..	..	..	27	33	37
G.10.3. Total — G.10.3. Total								
G.10.3.1. Gross Premiums — Primes Brutes	..	..	..	..	..	14 963	16 966	16 557
G.10.3.2. Ceded Premiums — Primes Cédées	..	..	..	..	..	4 667	4 257	4 411
G.10.3.3. Net Written Premiums — Primes Nettes Emises	..	..	..	..	..	10 292	12 709	12 146

Monetary Unit: million Luxembourg francs

H. GROSS CLAIMS PAYMENTS / H. PAIEMENTS BRUTS DES SINISTRES

H.1. Life / H.1. Vie

	1990	1991	1992	1993	1994	1995	1996	1997
H.1.1. Domestic Companies / H.1.1. Entreprises Nationales				4 069	5 601	8 167	17 741	27 582
H.1.2. (Foreign Controlled Companies) / H.1.2. (Entreprises Sous Contrôle Etranger)				1 830	3 957	6 053	14 811	24 475
H.1.3. Branches & Agencies of Foreign Cies / H.1.3. Succursales et Agences d'Ent. Etrangères				522	593	743	1 105	1 950
H.1. Total				4 591	6 194	8 910	18 846	29 532

H.2. Non-Life / H.2. Non-Vie

	1990	1991	1992	1993	1994	1995	1996	1997
H.2.1. Domestic Companies / H.2.1. Entreprises Nationales				5 922	5 492	6 940	7 889	6 592
H.2.2. (Foreign Controlled Companies) / H.2.2. (Entreprises Sous Contrôle Etranger)				1 305	965	1 968	2 349	1 215
H.2.3. Branches & Agencies of Foreign Cies / H.2.3. Succursales et Agences d'Ent. Etrangères				1 280	1 353	1 153	1 198	1 147
H.2. Total				7 202	6 845	8 093	9 087	7 739

I. GROSS OPERATING EXPENSES / I. DEPENSES BRUITES D'EXPLOITATION

I.1. Life / I.1. Vie

	1990	1991	1992	1993	1994	1995	1996	1997
I.1.1. Domestic Companies / I.1.1. Entreprises Nationales				2 057	2 852	3 573	1 253	5 748
I.1.2. (Foreign Controlled Companies) / I.1.2. (Entreprises Sous Contrôle Etranger)				1 429	2 114	2 840	893	4 629
I.1.3. Branches & Agencies of Foreign Cies / I.1.3. Succursales et Agences d'Ent. Etrangères				168	186	218	103	592
I.1. Total / I.1. Total des Primes Nettes Vie				2 225	3 038	3 791	1 356	6 340

I.2. Non-Life / I.2. Non-Vie

	1990	1991	1992	1993	1994	1995	1996	1997
I.2.1. Domestic Companies / I.2.1. Entreprises Nationales				3 147	3 344	2 694	738	3 127
I.2.2. (Foreign Controlled Companies) / I.2.2. (Entreprises Sous Contrôle Etranger)				837	702	585	237	709
I.2.3. Branches & Agencies of Foreign Cies / I.2.3. Succursales et Agences d'Ent. Etrangères				735	737	612	211	784
I.2. Total				3 882	4 081	3 306	949	3 911

J. COMMISSIONS

J.1. Life / J.1. Vie

J.1.1. Direct Business / J.1.1. Assurance directe

	1990	1991	1992	1993	1994	1995	1996	1997
J.1.1.1. Domestic Companies / J.1.1.1. Entreprises Nationales				818	1 202	2 546	2 826	3 964
J.1.1.2. (Foreign Controlled Companies) / J.1.1.2. (Entreprises Sous Contrôle Etranger)				620	968	2 130	2 366	3 321
J.1.1.3. Branches & Agencies of Foreign Cies / J.1.1.3. Succursales et Agences d'Ent. Etrangères				53	57	131	256	479
J.1.1. Total				871	1 259	2 677	3 082	4 443

J.1.2. Reinsurance Accepted / J.1.2. Réassurances acceptées

	1990	1991	1992	1993	1994	1995	1996	1997
J.1.2.1. Domestic Companies / J.1.2.1. Entreprises Nationales				0	14	0	2	2
J.1.2.3. Branches & Agencies of Foreign Cies / J.1.2.3. Succursales et Agences d'Ent. Etrangères				0	0	0	0	1
J.1.2. Total				0	14	0	2	3

J.1.3. Total

	1990	1991	1992	1993	1994	1995	1996	1997
J.1.3.1. Domestic Companies / J.1.3.1. Entreprises Nationales				818	1 216	2 546	2 828	3 966
J.1.3.2. (Foreign Controlled Companies) / J.1.3.2. (Entreprises Sous Contrôle Etranger)				620	968	2 130	2 366	3 321
J.1.3.3. Branches & Agencies of Foreign Cies / J.1.3.3. Succursales et Agences d'Ent. Etrangères				53	57	131	256	480
J.1.3. Total of Life Net Premiums / J.1.3. Total				871	1 273	2 677	3 084	4 446

LUXEMBOURG

Monetary Unit: million Luxembourg francs

Unité monétaire : million de Francs luxembourgeois

J.2. Non-Life / J.2. Non-Vie

	1990	1991	1992	1993	1994	1995	1996	1997	
J.2.1. Direct Business									J.2.1. Assurance directe
J.2.1.1. Domestic Companies				1 306	1 299	2 050	2 492	2 676	J.2.1.1. Entreprises Nationales
J.2.1.2. (Foreign Controlled Companies)				361	275	385	674	787	J.2.1.2. (Entreprises Sous Contrôle Etranger)
J.2.1.3. Branches & Agencies of Foreign Cies				316	284	419	470	544	J.2.1.3. Succursales et Agences d'Ent. Etrangères
J.2.1. Total				1 622	1 583	2 469	2 962	3 220	J.2.1. Total des Primes Nettes Vie
J.2.2. Reinsurance Accepted									J.2.2. Réassurances acceptées
J.2.2.1. Domestic Companies				0	24	7	7	9	J.2.2.1. Entreprises Nationales
J.2.2.3. Branches & Agencies of Foreign Cies				0	0	0	0	2	J.2.2.3. Succursales et Agences d'Ent. Etrangères
J.2.2. Total				0	24	7	7	11	J.2.2. Total
J.2.3. Total									J.2.3. Total
J.2.3.1. Domestic Companies				1 306	1 323	2 057	2 499	2 685	J.2.3.1. Entreprises Nationales
J.2.3.2. (Foreign Controlled Companies)				361	275	385	674	787	J.2.3.2. (Entreprises Sous Contrôle Etranger)
J.2.3.3. Branches & Agencies of Foreign Cies				316	284	419	470	546	J.2.3.3. Succursales et Agences d'Ent. Etrangères
J.2.3. Total				1 622	1 607	2 476	2 969	3 231	J.2.3. Total

167

Monetary Unit: million pesos   Unité monétaire : million de pesos

	1990	1991	1992	1993	1994	1995	1996	1997
A. NUMBER OF COMPANIES IN THE REPORTING COUNTRY — A. NOMBRE D'ENTREPRISES DANS LE PAYS DECLARANT								
A.1. Life — A.1. Vie								
A.1.1. Domestic Companies — A.1.1. Entreprises Nationales	..	..	1	4	3	5	3	3
A.1.2. (Foreign Controlled Companies) — A.1.2. (Entreprises Sous Contrôle Etranger)			0	0	0	3	2	1
A.1. All Companies — A.1. Ensemble des Entreprises	..	..	1	4	3	5	3	3
A.2. Non-Life — A.2. Non-Vie								
A.2.1. Domestic Companies — A.2.1. Entreprises Nationales	..	..	9	7	13	16	13	14
A.2.2. (Foreign Controlled Companies) — A.2.2. (Entreprises Sous Contrôle Etranger)			0	0	1	5	4	6
A.2. All Companies — A.2. Ensemble des Entreprises	..	..	9	7	13	16	13	14
A.3. Composite — A.3. Mixte								
A.3.1. Domestic Companies — A.3.1. Entreprises Nationales	..	..	31	33	29	33	43	44
A.3.2. (Foreign Controlled Companies) — A.3.2. (Entreprises Sous Contrôle Etranger)			0	0	0	5	12	15
A.3. All Companies — A.3. Ensemble des Entreprises	..	..	31	33	29	33	43	44
A.4. Reinsurance — A.4. Réassurance								
A.4.1. Domestic Companies — A.4.1. Entreprises Nationales	..	..	2	2	2	2	2	3
A.4. All Companies — A.4. Ensemble des Entreprises	..	..	2	2	2	2	2	3
A.5. Total								
A.5.1. Domestic Companies — A.5.1. Entreprises Nationales	..	..	43	45	47	56	61	64
A.5.2. (Foreign Controlled Companies) — A.5.2. (Entreprises Sous Contrôle Etranger)			0	0	1	13	18	22
A.5. All Insurance Companies — A.5. Ensemble des Entreprises d'Assurances	..	..	43	45	47	56	61	64
B. NUMBER OF EMPLOYEES — B. NOMBRE D'EMPLOYES								
B.1. Insurance Companies — B.1. Entreprises d'Assurances	..	..	20 687	20 067	20 348	19 398	19 661	20 539
B.2. Intermediaries — B.2. Intermediaires	..	..	..	28 418	27 827	30 587	25 163	29 466
B. Total	..	..	..	48 485	48 175	49 985	44 824	50 005
C. BUSINESS WRITTEN IN THE REPORTING COUNTRY — C. OPERATIONS CONCLUES DANS LE PAYS DECLARANT								
C.1. Life — C.1. Vie								
C.1.1. Gross Premiums — C.1.1. Primes Brutes								
C.1.1.1. Direct Business — C.1.1.1. Assurances Directes								
C.1.1.1.1. Domestic Companies — C.1.1.1.1. Entreprises Nationales	..	..	5 193	6 053	7 159	8 053	10 672	14 496
C.1.1.1.2. (Foreign Controlled Companies) — C.1.1.1.2. (Entreprises Sous Contrôle Etranger)	..	..	..	0	0	92	137	1 447
C.1.1.1. Total	..	..	5 193	6 053	7 159	8 053	10 672	14 496
C.1.1.2. Reinsurance Accepted — C.1.1.2. Réassurance Acceptée								
C.1.1.2.1. Domestic Companies — C.1.1.2.1. Entreprises Nationales	..	..	52	69	82	93	116	193
C.1.1.2.2. (Foreign Controlled Companies) — C.1.1.2.2. (Entreprises Sous Contrôle Etranger)	..	..	0	0	0	1	83	1
C.1.1.2. Total	..	..	52	69	82	93	116	193
C.1.1.3. Total								
C.1.1.3.1. Domestic Companies — C.1.1.3.1. Entreprises Nationales	..	..	5 246	6 122	7 241	8 146	10 787	14 689
C.1.1.3.2. (Foreign Controlled Companies) — C.1.1.3.2. (Entreprises Sous Contrôle Etranger)	..	..	..	0	0	92	220	1 447
C.1.1.3. Total Gross Premiums — C.1.1.3. Total des Primes Brutes	..	..	5 246	6 122	7 241	8 146	10 787	14 689
C.1.2. Ceded Premiums — C.1.2. Primes Cédées								
C.1.2.1. Domestic Companies — C.1.2.1. Entreprises Nationales	..	..	292	337	463	548	801	1 088
C.1.2.2. (Foreign Controlled Companies) — C.1.2.2. (Entreprises Sous Contrôle Etranger)	..	..	0	0	0	14	18	74
C.1.2. Total	..	..	292	337	463	548	801	1 088
C.1.3. Net Written Premiums — C.1.3. Primes Nettes Emises								
C.1.3.1. Domestic Companies — C.1.3.1. Entreprises Nationales	..	..	4 953	5 785	6 778	7 598	9 987	13 601
C.1.3.2. (Foreign Controlled Companies) — C.1.3.2. (Entreprises Sous Contrôle Etranger)	..	..	..	0	0	78	202	1 373
C.1.3. Total	..	..	4 953	5 785	6 778	7 598	9 987	13 601

Monetary Unit: million pesos

Unité monétaire : million de pesos

C.2. Non-Life / C.2. Non-Vie

	1990	1991	1992	1993	1994	1995	1996	1997
C.2.1. Gross premiums / C.2.1. Primes Brutes								
C.2.1.1. Direct Business / C.2.1.1. Assurances Directes								
C.2.1.1.1. Domestic Companies / C.2.1.1.1. Entreprises Nationales			10 018	11 934	13 367	15 755	20 197	25 318
C.2.1.1.2. (Foreign Controlled Companies) / C.2.1.1.2. (Entreprises Sous Contrôle Etranger)			0	0		635	1 444	2 771
C.2.1.1. Total			10 018	11 934	13 367	15 755	20 197	25 318
C.2.1.2. Reinsurance Accepted / C.2.1.2. Réassurance Acceptée								
C.2.1.2.1. Domestic Companies / C.2.1.2.1. Entreprises Nationales			603	719	762	1 030	1 065	1 160
C.2.1.2.2. (Foreign Controlled Companies) / C.2.1.2.2. (Entreprises Sous Contrôle Etranger)			0	0	0	15	42	136
C.2.1.2. Total			603	719	762	1 030	1 065	1 160
C.2.1.3. Total								
C.2.1.3.1. Domestic Companies / C.2.1.3.1. Entreprises Nationales			10 621	12 652	14 129	16 784	21 263	26 478
C.2.1.3.2. (Foreign Controlled Companies) / C.2.1.3.2. (Entreprises Sous Contrôle Etranger)			0	0	7	650	1 486	2 908
C.2.1.3. Total Gross Premiums / C.2.1.3. Tota des Primes Brutes			10 621	12 652	14 129	16 784	21 263	26 478
C.2.2. Ceded Premiums / C.2.2. Primes Cédées								
C.2.2.1. Domestic Companies / C.2.2.1. Entreprises Nationales			2 765	3 455	3 689	4 959	6 410	7 366
C.2.2.2. (Foreign Controlled Companies) / C.2.2.2. (Entreprises Sous Contrôle Etranger)			0	0	4	336	670	1 112
C.2.2. Total			2 765	3 455	3 689	4 959	6 410	7 366
C.2.3. Net Written Premiums / C.2.3. Primes Nettes Emises								
C.2.3.1. Domestic Companies / C.2.3.1. Entreprises Nationales			7 857	9 198	10 440	11 826	14 853	19 112
C.2.3.2. (Foreign Controlled Companies) / C.2.3.2. (Entreprises Sous Contrôle Etranger)			0	0	3	314	816	1 796
C.2.3. Total			7 857	9 198	10 440	11 826	14 853	19 112

C.3. Total / C.3. Total

	1990	1991	1992	1993	1994	1995	1996	1997
C.3.1. Gross Premiums / C.3.1. Primes Brutes								
C.3.1.1. Direct Business / C.3.1.1. Assurances Directes								
C.3.1.1.1. Domestic Companies / C.3.1.1.1. Entreprises Nationales			15 211	17 987	20 527	23 807	30 869	39 814
C.3.1.1.2. (Foreign Controlled Companies) / C.3.1.1.2. (Entreprises Sous Contrôle Etranger)						727	1 580	4 218
C.3.1.1. Total			15 211	17 987	20 527	23 807	30 869	39 814
C.3.1.2. Reinsurance Accepted / C.3.1.2. Réassurance Acceptée								
C.3.1.2.1. Domestic Companies / C.3.1.2.1. Entreprises Nationales			656	788	844	1 123	1 181	1 353
C.3.1.2.2. (Foreign Controlled Companies) / C.3.1.2.2. (Entreprises Sous Contrôle Etranger)			0	0	0	16	125	137
C.3.1.2. Total			656	788	844	1 123	1 181	1 353
C.3.1.3. Total								
C.3.1.3.1. Domestic Companies / C.3.1.3.1. Entreprises Nationales			15 867	18 774	21 371	24 930	32 050	41 167
C.3.1.3.2. (Foreign Controlled Companies) / C.3.1.3.2. (Entreprises Sous Contrôle Etranger)			0	0	0	742	1 705	4 355
C.3.1.3. Total Gross Premiums / C.3.1.3. Total des Primes Brutes			15 867	18 774	21 371	24 930	32 050	41 167
C.3.2. Ceded Premiums / C.3.2. Primes Cédées								
C.3.2.1. Domestic Companies / C.3.2.1. Entreprises Nationales			3 057	3 792	4 152	5 506	7 210	8 454
C.3.2.2. (Foreign Controlled Companies) / C.3.2.2. (Entreprises Sous Contrôle Etranger)			0	0	4	350	688	1 186
C.3.2. Total			3 057	3 792	4 152	5 506	7 210	8 454
C.3.3. Net Written Premiums / C.3.3. Primes Nettes Emises								
C.3.3.1. Domestic Companies / C.3.3.1. Entreprises Nationales			12 810	14 982	17 219	19 424	24 840	32 712
C.3.3.2. (Foreign Controlled Companies) / C.3.3.2. (Entreprises Sous Contrôle Etranger)			0	0	3	392	1 017	3 169
C.3.3. Total			12 810	14 982	17 219	19 424	24 840	32 712

Monetary Unit: million pesos

Unité monétaire : million de pesos

D. NET WRITTEN PREMIUMS IN THE REPORTING COUNTRY IN TERMS OF DOMESTIC AND FOREIGN RISKS
D. PRIMES NETTES EMISES DANS LE PAYS DECLARANT EN RISQUES NATIONAUX ET ETRANGERS

D.1. Life / D.1. Vie

	1990	1991	1992	1993	1994	1995	1996	1997	
D.1.1. Domestic Risks									D.1.1. Risques Nationaux
D.1.1.1. Domestic Companies	..	..	4 953	..	..	..	..	..	D.1.1.1. Entreprises Nationales
D.1.1. Total	..	..	4 953	..	..	..	..	..	D.1.1. Total des Primes Nettes Vie
D.1.3. Total									D.1.3. Total
D.1.3.1. Domestic Companies	..	..	4 953	5 785	6 778	7 598	9 987	13 601	D.1.3.1. Entreprises Nationales
D.1.3.2. (Foreign Controlled Companies)			0	0	0	78	202	1 373	D.1.3.2. (Entreprises Sous Contrôle Etranger)
D.1.3. Total of Life Net Premiums	..	..	4 953	5 785	6 778	7 598	9 987	13 601	D.1.3. Total des Primes Nettes Vie

D.2. Non-Life / D.2. Non-Vie

	1990	1991	1992	1993	1994	1995	1996	1997	
D.2.1. Domestic Risks									D.2.1. Risques Nationaux
D.2.1.1. Domestic Companies	..	..	7 857	..	..	..	..	..	D.2.1.1. Entreprises Nationales
D.2.1. Total	..	..	7 857	..	..	..	..	..	D.2.1. Total des Primes Nettes Vie
D.2.3. Total									D.2.3. Total
D.2.3.1. Domestic Companies	..	..	7 857	9 198	10 440	11 826	14 853	19 112	D.2.3.1. Entreprises Nationales
D.2.3.2. (Foreign Controlled Companies)			0	0	0	314	816	1 796	D.2.3.2. (Entreprises Sous Contrôle Etranger)
D.2.3. Total	..	..	7 857	9 198	10 440	11 826	14 853	19 112	D.2.3. Total des Primes Nettes Vie

G. BREAKDOWN OF NON-LIFE PREMIUMS / G. VENTILATIONS DES PRIMES NON-VIE

G.1. Motor vehicle / G.1. Assurance Automobile

	1990	1991	1992	1993	1994	1995	1996	1997	
G.1.1. Direct Business									G.1.1. Assurances Directes
G.1.1.1. Gross Premiums			5 018	5 695	6 070	6 300	7 825	10 612	G.1.1.1. Primes Brutes
G.1.1.2. Ceded Premiums			34	66	38	70	75	134	G.1.1.2. Primes Cédées
G.1.1.3. Net Written Premiums			4 983	5 629	6 032	6 231	7 750	10 478	G.1.1.3. Primes Nettes Emises
G.1.2. Reinsurance Accepted									G.1.2. Réassurance Acceptée
G.1.2.1. Gross Premiums			0	0	27	41	40	44	G.1.2.1. Primes Brutes
G.1.2.2. Ceded Premiums			0	2	2	0	3	7	G.1.2.2. Primes Cédées
G.1.2.3. Net Written Premiums			0	41	25	41	37	36	G.1.2.3. Primes Nettes Emises
G.1.3. Total									G.1.3. Total
G.1.3.1. Gross Premiums			5 018	5 738	6 096	6 342	7 866	10 655	G.1.3.1. Primes Brutes
G.1.3.2. Ceded Premiums			35	68	40	70	78	141	G.1.3.2. Primes Cédées
G.1.3.3. Net Written Premiums			44 983	5 670	6 057	6 272	7 787	10 514	G.1.3.3. Primes Nettes Emises

G.2. Marine, Aviation / G.2. Marine, Aviation

	1990	1991	1992	1993	1994	1995	1996	1997	
G.2.1. Direct Business									G.2.1. Assurances Directes
G.2.1.1. Gross Premiums			1 031	950	1 173	1 479	2 324	2 696	G.2.1.1. Primes Brutes
G.2.1.2. Ceded Premiums			667	710	733	918	1 462	1 601	G.2.1.2. Primes Cédées
G.2.1.3. Net Written Premiums			364	240	440	560	862	1 096	G.2.1.3. Primes Nettes Emises
G.2.2. Reinsurance Accepted									G.2.2. Réassurance Acceptée
G.2.2.1. Gross Premiums			0	183	212	354	355	401	G.2.2.1. Primes Brutes
G.2.2.2. Ceded Premiums			0	109	115	185	207	239	G.2.2.2. Primes Cédées
G.2.2.3. Net Written Premiums			0	73	97	168	148	162	G.2.2.3. Primes Nettes Emises
G.2.3. Total									G.2.3. Total
G.2.3.1. Gross Premiums			1 031	1 132	1 385	1 832	2 679	3 097	G.2.3.1. Primes Brutes
G.2.3.2. Ceded Premiums			667	819	848	1 104	1 669	1 840	G.2.3.2. Primes Cédées
G.2.3.3. Net Written Premiums			364	313	537	729	1 010	1 258	G.2.3.3. Primes Nettes Emises

MEXICO

Monetary Unit: million pesos

	1990	1991	1992	1993	1994	1995	1996	1997		(Français)
G.4. Fire, Property Damages										G.4. Incendie, Dommages aux Biens
G.4.1. Direct Business										G.4.1. Assurances Directes
G.4.1.1. Gross Premiums			1 808	2 029	2 292	2 898	3 408	3 866		G.4.1.1. Primes Brutes
G.4.1.2. Ceded Premiums			1 227	1 540	1 389	1 778	2 120	2 535		G.4.1.2. Primes Cédées
G.4.1.3. Net Written Premiums			581	489	902	1 121	1 288	1 331		G.4.1.3. Primes Nettes Emises
G.4.2. Reinsurance Accepted										G.4.2. Réassurance Acceptée
G.4.2.1. Gross Premiums			0	306	347	459	455	425		G.4.2.1. Primes Brutes
G.4.2.2. Ceded Premiums			0	114	60	107	160	156		G.4.2.2. Primes Cédées
G.4.2.3. Net Written Premiums			0	192	287	351	294	269		G.4.2.3. Primes Nettes Emises
G.4.3. Total										G.4.3. Total
G.4.3.1. Gross Premiums			1 808	2 335	2 638	3 357	3 863	4 291		G.4.3.1. Primes Brutes
G.4.3.2. Ceded Premiums			1 227	1 654	1 449	1 885	2 281	2 691		G.4.3.2. Primes Cédées
G.4.3.3. Net Written Premiums			581	681	1 189	1 472	1 582	1 600		G.4.3.3. Primes Nettes Emises
G.5. Pecuniary Losses										G.5. Pertes Pécunières
G.5.1. Direct Business										G.5.1 Assurances Directes
G.5.1.1. Gross Premiums			37	23	26	48	61	74		G.5.1.1. Primes Brutes
G.5.1.2. Ceded Premiums			19	19	22	40	51	63		G.5.1.2. Primes Cédées
G.5.1.3. Net Written Premiums			17	4	4	8	9	11		G.5.1.3. Primes Nettes Emises
G.5.2. Reinsurance Accepted										G.5.2. Réassurance Acceptée
G.5.2.1. Gross Premiums			0	21	17	14	14	21		G.5.2.1. Primes Brutes
G.5.2.2. Ceded Premiums			0	0	0	0	0	1		G.5.2.2. Primes Cédées
G.5.2.3. Net Written Premiums			0	21	17	14	14	21		G.5.2.3. Primes Nettes Emises
G.5.3. Total										G.5.3. Total
G.5.3.1. Gross Premiums			37	44	43	62	74	95		G.5.3.1. Primes Brutes
G.5.3.2. Ceded Premiums			19	19	22	40	51	63		G.5.3.2. Primes Cédées
G.5.3.3. Net Written Premiums			17	25	21	21	23	32		G.5.3.3. Primes Nettes Emises
G.6. General Liability										G.6. Responsabilité Générae
G.6.1. Direct Business										G.6.1. Assurances Directes
G.6.1.1. Gross Premiums			217	292	377	644	788	997		G.6.1.1. Primes Brutes
G.6.1.2. Ceded Premiums			125	176	226	393	543	742		G.6.1.2. Primes Cédées
G.6.1.3. Net Written Premiums			92	117	151	251	244	256		G.6.1.3. Primes Nettes Emises
G.6.2. Reinsurance Accepted										G.6.2. Réassurance Acceptée
G.6.2.1. Gross Premiums			0	12	11	18	24	34		G.6.2.1. Primes Brutes
G.6.2.2. Ceded Premiums			0	2	1	1	7	15		G.6.2.2. Primes Cédées
G.6.2.3. Net Written Premiums			0	10	10	18	17	20		G.6.2.3. Primes Nettes Emises
G.6.3. Total										G.6.3. Total
G.6.3.1. Gross Premiums			217	305	388	662	811	1 032		G.6.3.1. Primes Brutes
G.6.3.2. Ceded Premiums			125	178	227	393	550	756		G.6.3.2. Primes Cédées
G.6.3.3. Net Written Premiums			92	126	161	269	261	275		G.6.3.3. Primes Nettes Emises
G.7. Accident, Health										G.7. Accident, Santé
G.7.1. Direct Business										G.7.1. Assurances Directes
G.7.1.1. Gross Premiums			1 231	1 435	1 734	2 101	3 019	4 046		G.7.1.1. Primes Brutes
G.7.1.2. Ceded Premiums			71	79	80	65	85	137		G.7.1.2. Primes Cédées
G.7.1.3. Net Written Premiums			1 161	1 355	1 654	2 036	2 934	3 908		G.7.1.3. Primes Nettes Emises
G.7.2. Reinsurance Accepted										G.7.2. Réassurance Acceptée
G.7.2.1. Gross Premiums			0	47	40	30	10	17		G.7.2.1. Primes Brutes
G.7.2.2. Ceded Premiums			0	0	0	0	0	1		G.7.2.2. Primes Cédées
G.7.2.3. Net Written Premiums			0	46	40	30	10	16		G.7.2.3. Primes Nettes Emises
G.7.3. Total										G.7.3. Total
G.7.3.1. Gross Premiums			1 231	1 481	1 773	2 131	3 029	4 062		G.7.3.1. Primes Brutes
G.7.3.2. Ceded Premiums			71	80	80	66	85	139		G.7.3.2. Primes Cédées
G.7.3.3. Net Written Premiums			1 161	1 402	1 693	2 066	2 944	3 924		G.7.3.3. Primes Nettes Emises

Monetary Unit: million pesos

Unité monétaire : million de pesos

	1990	1991	1992	1993	1994	1995	1996	1997
G.8. Others / G.8. Autres								
G.8.1. Direct Business / G.8.1. Assurances Directes								
G.8.1.1. Gross Premiums / G.8.1.1. Primes Brutes			1 280	1 510	1 696	2 284	2 773	3 027
G.8.1.2. Ceded Premiums / G.8.1.2. Primes Cédées			621	865	1 001	1 386	1 664	1 691
G.8.1.3. Net Written Premiums / G.8.1.3. Primes Nettes Emises			658	645	696	898	1 109	1 336
G.8.2. Reinsurance Accepted / G.8.2. Réassurance Acceptée								
G.8.2.1. Gross Premiums / G.8.2.1. Primes Brutes			0	107	109	114	168	218
G.8.2.2. Ceded Premiums / G.8.2.2. Primes Cédées			0	26	23	15	31	45
G.8.2.3. Net Written Premiums / G.8.2.3. Primes Nettes Emises			0	81	87	99	137	173
G.8.3. Total								
G.8.3.1. Gross Premiums / G.8.3.1. Primes Brutes			1 280	1 617	1 806	2 399	2 941	3 245
G.8.3.2. Ceded Premiums / G.8.3.2. Primes Cédées			621	891	1 024	1 401	1 696	1 736
G.8.3.3. Net Written Premiums / G.8.3.3. Primes Nettes Emises			658	726	782	998	1 246	1 509
G.10. Total								
G.10.1. Direct Business / G.10.1. Assurances Directes								
G.10.1.1. Gross Premiums / G.10.1.1. Primes Brutes			10 621	11 934	13 367	15 755	20 197	25 318
G.10.1.2. Ceded Premiums / G.10.1.2. Primes Cédées			2 765	3 455	3 489	4 650	6 001	6 903
G.10.1.3. Net Written Premiums / G.10.1.3. Primes Nettes Emises			7 857	8 479	9 878	11 105	14 196	18 415
G.10.2. Reinsurance Accepted / G.10.2. Réassurance Acceptée								
G.10.2.1. Gross Premiums / G.10.2.1. Primes Brutes			0	719	762	1 030	1 065	1 160
G.10.2.2. Ceded Premiums / G.10.2.2. Primes Cédées			0	254	200	309	409	464
G.10.2.3. Net Written Premiums / G.10.2.3. Primes Nettes Emises			0	465	562	721	657	696
G.10.3. Total								
G.10.3.1. Gross Premiums / G.10.3.1. Primes Brutes			10 621	12 652	14 129	16 784	21 263	26 478
G.10.3.2. Ceded Premiums / G.10.3.2. Primes Cédées			2 765	3 709	3 689	4 959	6 410	7 366
G.10.3.3. Net Written Premiums / G.10.3.3. Primes Nettes Emises			7 857	8 943	10 440	11 826	14 853	19 112
H. GROSS CLAIMS PAYMENTS / H. PAIEMENTS BRUTS DES SINISTRES								
H.1. Life / H.1. Vie								
H.1.1. Domestic Companies / H.1.1. Entreprises Nationales				4 483	5 403	5 949	7 327	9 363
H.1.2. (Foreign Controlled Companies) / H.1.2. (Entreprises Sous Contrôle Etranger)				0	..	..	125	593
H.1. Total				4 483	5 403	5 949	7 327	9 363
H.2. Non-Life / H.2. Non-Vie								
H.2.1. Domestic Companies / H.2.1. Entreprises Nationales				6 736	7 755	11 615	14 564	16 209
H.2.2. (Foreign Controlled Companies) / H.2.2. (Entreprises Sous Contrôle Etranger)				0	..	..	526	1 286
H.2. Total				6 736	7 755	11 615	14 564	16 209
I. GROSS OPERATING EXPENSES / I. DEPENSES BRUTES D'EXPLOITATION								
I.1. Life / I.1. Vie								
I.1.1. Domestic Companies / I.1.1. Entreprises Nationales				863	1 063	1 169	1 516	2 058
I.1.2. (Foreign Controlled Companies) / I.1.2. (Entreprises Sous Contrôle Etranger)				0	..	..	..	248
I.1. Total / I.1. Total des Primes Nettes Vie				863	1 063	1 169	1 516	2 058
I.2. Non-Life / I.2. Non-Vie								
I.2.1. Domestic Companies / I.2.1. Entreprises Nationales				1 785	2 074	2 414	2 988	3 161
I.2.2. (Foreign Controlled Companies) / I.2.2. (Entreprises Sous Contrôle Etranger)				0	..	..	..	487
I.2. Total				1 785	2 074	2 414	2 988	3 161

Monetary Unit: million pesos   Unité monétaire : million de pesos

	1990	1991	1992	1993	1994	1995	1996	1997	
J. COMMISSIONS									**J. COMMISSIONS**
J.1. Life									**J.1. Vie**
J.1.1. Direct Business									J.1.1. Assurance directe
J.1.1.1. Domestic Companies				870	927	1 082	1 448	1 931	J.1.1.1. Entreprises Nationales
J.1.1.2. (Foreign Controlled Companies)				0	..	..	37	142	J.1.1.2. (Entreprises Sous Contrôle Etranger)
J.1.1. Total				870	927	1 082	1 448	1 931	J.1.1. Total
J.1.2. Reinsurance Accepted									J.1.2. Réassurances acceptées
J.1.2.1. Domestic Companies				18	29	37	53	84	J.1.2.1. Entreprises Nationales
J.1.2.2. (Foreign Controlled Companies)				0	..	..	0	0	J.1.2.2. (Entreprises Sous Contrôle Etranger)
J.1.2. Total				18	29	37	53	84	J.1.2. Total
J.1.3. Total									J.1.3. Total
J.1.3.1. Domestic Companies				888	956	1 118	1 501	2 014	J.1.3.1. Entreprises Nationales
J.1.3.2. (Foreign Controlled Companies)				0	..	..	37	142	J.1.3.2. (Entreprises Sous Contrôle Etranger)
J.1.3. Total of Life Net Premiums				888	956	1 118	1 501	2 014	J.1.3. Total
J.2. Non-Life									**J.2. Non-Vie**
J.2.1. Direct Business									J.2.1. Assurance directe
J.2.1.1. Domestic Companies				1 614	1 879	2 243	2 998	4 364	J.2.1.1. Entreprises Nationales
J.2.1.2. (Foreign Controlled Companies)				0	..	..	139	427	J.2.1.2. (Entreprises Sous Contrôle Etranger)
J.2.1. Total				1 614	1 879	2 243	2 998	4 364	J.2.1. Total des Prim res Nettes Vie
J.2.2. Reinsurance Accepted									J.2.2. Réassurances acceptées
J.2.2.1. Domestic Companies				203	209	280	237	301	J.2.2.1. Entreprises Nationales
J.2.2.2. (Foreign Controlled Companies)				0	..	..	0	1	J.2.2.2. (Entreprises Sous Contrôle Etranger)
J.2.2. Total				203	209	280	237	301	J.2.2. Total
J.2.3. Total									J.2.3. Total
J.2.3.1. Domestic Companies				1 816	2 089	2 523	3 234	4 665	J.2.3.1. Entreprises Nationales
J.2.3.2. (Foreign Controlled Companies)				0	..	..	139	428	J.2.3.2. (Entreprises Sous Contrôle Etranger)
J.2.3. Total				1 816	2 089	2 523	3 234	4 665	J.2.3. Total

NETHERLANDS

Monetary Unit: million guilders

	1990	1991	1992	1993	1994	1995	1996	1997		(FR)
A. NUMBER OF COMPANIES IN THE REPORTING COUNTRY										**A. NOMBRE D'ENTREPRISES DANS LE PAYS DECLARANT**
A.1. Life										**A.1. Vie**
A.1.1. Domestic Companies	85	86	87	89	90	92	96	104		A.1.1. Entreprises Nationales
A.1.2. (Foreign Controlled Companies)	16	16	17	16	17	20	17	19		A.1.2. (Entreprises Sous Contrôle Etranger)
A.1.3. Branches & Agencies of Foreign Cies	11	10	10	10	5	4	3	7		A.1.3. Succursales et Agences d'Ent. Etrangères
A.1. All Companies	96	96	97	99	95	96	99	111		A.1. Ensemble des Entreprises
A.2. Non-Life										**A.2. Non-Vie**
A.2.1. Domestic Companies	558	530	533	532	523	277	286	293		A.2.1. Entreprises Nationales
A.2.2. (Foreign Controlled Companies)	36	38	36	36	32	34	32	43		A.2.2. (Entreprises Sous Contrôle Etranger)
A.2.3. Branches & Agencies of Foreign Cies	139	139	140	136	131	23	22	18		A.2.3. Succursales et Agences d'Ent. Etrangères
A.2. All Companies	697	669	673	668	654	300	308	311		A.2. Ensemble des Entreprises
A.4. Reinsurance										**A.4. Réassurance**
A.4.1. Domestic Companies	18	18	15	15	8	..	..	0		A.4.1. Entreprises Nationales
A.4.2. (Foreign Controlled Companies)	1	1	2	2	0	..	..	0		A.4.2. (Entreprises Sous Contrôle Etranger)
A.4.3. Branches & Agencies of Foreign Cies	..	..	2	2	0	..	..	0		A.4.3. Succursales et Agences d'Ent. Etrangères
A.4. All Companies	18	18	17	17	8	..	..	0		A.4. Ensemble des Entreprises
A.5. Total										**A.5. Total**
A.5.1. Domestic Companies	661	634	634	636	621	369	382	397		A.5.1. Entreprises Nationales
A.5.2. (Foreign Controlled Companies)	53	34	54	54	49	54	49	62		A.5.2. (Entreprises Sous Contrôle Etranger)
A.5.3. Branches & Agencies of Foreign Cies	..	149	152	148	136	27	25	25		A.5.3. Succursales et Agences d'Ent. Etrangères
A.5. All Insurance Companies	811	783	786	784	757	396	407	422		A.5. Ensemble des Entreprises d'Assurances
B. NUMBER OF EMPLOYEES										**B. NOMBRE D'EMPLOYES**
B.1. Insurance Companies	54 700	56 100	58 500	..	..	47 900	..	49 500		B.1. Entreprises d'Assurances
B.2. Intermediaries	11 000	11 000	10 500	..	..	19 000	..	23 200		B.2. Intermediaires
B. Total	65 700	67 100	69 000	70 500	77 400	66 900	..	72 700		B. Total
C. BUSINESS WRITTEN IN THE REPORTING COUNTRY										**C. OPERATIONS CONCLUES DANS LE PAYS DECLARANT**
C.1. Life										**C.1. Vie**
C.1.1. Gross Premiums										C.1.1. Primes Brutes
C.1.1.1. Direct Business										C.1.1.1. Assurances Directes
C.1.1.1.1. Domestic Companies	..	..	..	..	..	28 370	31 325	35 159		C.1.1.1.1. Entreprises Nationales
C.1.1.1.2. (Foreign Controlled Companies)	..	..	..	..	..	4 894	4 877	5 915		C.1.1.1.2. (Entreprises Sous Contrôle Etranger)
C.1.1.1.3. Branches & Agencies of Foreign Cies	..	..	..	..	..	1 759	1 858	1 928		C.1.1.1.3. Succursales et Agences d'Ent. Etrangères
C.1.1.1. Total	..	..	..	..	..	30 129	33 183	37 087		C.1.1.1. Total
C.1.1.2. Reinsurance Accepted										C.1.1.2. Réassurance Acceptée
C.1.1.2.1. Domestic Companies	..	..	..	..	..	1 086	606	446		C.1.1.2.1. Entreprises Nationales
C.1.1.2.2. (Foreign Controlled Companies)	..	..	..	..	..	284	283	321		C.1.1.2.2. (Entreprises Sous Contrôle Etranger)
C.1.1.2. Total	..	..	..	..	..	1 086	606	446		C.1.1.2. Total
C.1.1.3. Total										C.1.1.3. Total
C.1.1.3.1. Domestic Companies	19 727	22 140	23 838	23 880	26 112	29 456	31 931	35 605		C.1.1.3.1. Entreprises Nationales
C.1.1.3.2. (Foreign Controlled Companies)	3 629	3 199	4 425	4 174	4 617	5 178	5 160	6 236		C.1.1.3.2. (Entreprises Sous Contrôle Etranger)
C.1.1.3.3. Branches & Agencies of Foreign Cies	1 707	1 503	1 472	1 664	1 572	1 759	1 858	1 928		C.1.1.3.3. Succursales et Agences d'Ent. Etrangères
C.1.1.3. Total Gross Premiums	21 434	23 643	25 310	25 544	27 684	31 215	33 789	37 533		C.1.1.3. Total des Primes Brutes
C.1.2. Ceded Premiums										C.1.2. Primes Cédées
C.1.2.1. Domestic Companies	921	987	1 192	2 374	2 553	2 193	1 859	2 063		C.1.2.1. Entreprises Nationales
C.1.2.2. (Foreign Controlled Companies)	218	184	303	234	209	274	196	277		C.1.2.2. (Entreprises Sous Contrôle Etranger)
C.1.2.3. Branches & Agencies of Foreign Cies	28	33	21	18	31	24	21	49		C.1.2.3. Succursales et Agences d'Ent. Etrangères
C.1.2. Total	949	1 020	1 213	2 392	2 584	2 216	1 880	2 113		C.1.2. Total
C.1.3. Net Written Premiums										C.1.3. Primes Nettes Emises
C.1.3.1. Domestic Companies	18 806	21 153	22 646	21 506	23 559	27 263	30 072	33 542		C.1.3.1. Entreprises Nationales
C.1.3.2. (Foreign Controlled Companies)	3 411	3 015	4 122	3 940	4 408	4 904	4 964	5 959		C.1.3.2. (Entreprises Sous Contrôle Etranger)
C.1.3.3. Branches & Agencies of Foreign Cies	1 679	1 470	1 451	1 646	1 541	1 735	1 837	1 879		C.1.3.3. Succursales et Agences d'Ent. Etrangères
C.1.3. Total	20 485	22 623	24 097	23 152	25 100	28 998	31 909	35 420		C.1.3. Total

NETHERLANDS

Monetary Unit: mill on guilders — Unité monétaire : million de florins

C.2. Non-Life — C.2. Non-Vie

English	Français	1990	1991	1992	1993	1994	1995	1996	1997
C.2.1. Gross premiums	**C.2.1. Primes Brutes**								
C.2.1.1. Direct Business	C.2.1.1. Assurance Directes								
C.2.1.1.1. Domestic Companies	C.2.1.1.1. Entreprises Nationales	17 733	16 830	19 629	21 813	24 570	25 715	27 145	28 430
C.2.1.1.2. (Foreign Controlled Companies)	C.2.1.1.2. (Entreprises Sous Contrôle Etranger)	3 964	2 539	4 747	4 589	4 705	4 998	5 006	6 093
C.2.1.1.3. Branches & Agencies of Foreign Cies	C.2.1.1.3. Succursales et Agences d'Ent. Etrangères	1 251	1 096	1 279	1 299	1 280	808	644	752
C.2.1.1. Total	C.2.1.1. Total	18 984	17 926	20 908	23 112	25 850	26 522	27 789	29 182
C.2.1.2. Reinsurance Accepted	C.2.1.2. Réassurance Acceptée								
C.2.1.2.1. Domestic Companies	C.2.1.2.1. Entreprises Nationales	920	759	804	744	809	827	916	889
C.2.1.2.2. (Foreign Controlled Companies)	C.2.1.2.2. (Entreprises Sous Contrôle Etranger)	230	106	219	212	217	267	296	376
C.2.1.2.3. Branches & Agencies of Foreign Cies	C.2.1.2.3. Succursales et Agences d'Ent. Etrangères	18	14	87	89	87	32	91	1
C.2.1.2. Total	C.2.1.2. Total	938	773	891	833	896	859	1 007	890
C.2.1.3. Total	C.2.1.3. Total								
C.2.1.3.1. Domestic Companies	C.2.1.3.1. Entreprises Nationales	18 653	17 589	20 433	22 557	25 379	26 541	28 061	29 319
C.2.1.3.2. (Foreign Controlled Companies)	C.2.1.3.2. (Entreprises Sous Contrôle Etranger)	4 194	2 645	4 966	4 801	4 922	5 265	5 302	6 469
C.2.1.3.3. Branches & Agencies of Foreign Cies	C.2.1.3.3. Succursales et Agences d'Ent. Etrangères	1 268	1 110	1 366	1 388	1 367	839	735	753
C.2.1.3. Total Gross Premiums	C.2.1.3. Tota des Primes Brutes	19 921	18 699	21 799	23 945	26 746	27 381	28 796	30 072
C.2.2. Ceded Premiums	**C.2.2. Primes Cédées**								
C.2.2.1. Domestic Companies	C.2.2.1. Entreprises Nationales	2 744	2 758	2 897	3 082	3 386	3 320	3 375	3 320
C.2.2.2. (Foreign Controlled Companies)	C.2.2.2. (Entreprises Sous Contrôle Etranger)	697	441	1 145	974	892	889	833	1 219
C.2.2.3. Branches & Agencies of Foreign Cies	C.2.2.3. Succursales et Agences d'Ent. Etrangères	258	243	289	332	360	158	126	120
C.2.2. Total	C.2.2. Total	3 002	3 001	3 186	3 414	3 746	3 478	3 501	3 440
C.2.3. Net Written Premiums	**C.2.3. Primes Nettes Emises**								
C.2.3.1. Domestic Companies	C.2.3.1. Entreprises Nationales	15 909	14 831	17 536	19 475	21 993	23 221	24 686	25 999
C.2.3.2. (Foreign Controlled Companies)	C.2.3.2. (Entreprises Sous Contrôle Etranger)	3 497	2 204	3 821	3 827	4 030	4 376	4 469	5 250
C.2.3.3. Branches & Agencies of Foreign Cies	C.2.3.3. Succursales et Agences d'Ent. Etrangères	1 010	867	1 077	1 056	1 007	681	609	633
C.2.3. Total	C.2.3. Total	16 919	15 698	18 613	20 531	23 000	23 902	25 295	26 632

C.3. Total — C.3. Total

English	Français	1990	1991	1992	1993	1994	1995	1996	1997
C.3.1. Gross Premiums	**C.3.1. Primes Brutes**								
C.3.1.1. Direct Business	C.3.1.1. Assurances Directes								
C.3.1.1.1. Domestic Companies	C.3.1.1.1. Entreprises Nationales	..	..	..	..	..	54 085	58 470	63 589
C.3.1.1.2. (Foreign Controlled Companies)	C.3.1.1.2. (Entreprises Sous Contrôle Etranger)	..	..	..	..	..	9 892	9 883	12 008
C.3.1.1.3. Branches & Agencies of Foreign Cies	C.3.1.1.3. Succursales et Agences d'Ent. Etrangères	..	..	..	..	..	2 567	2 502	2 680
C.3.1.1. Total	C.3.1.1. Total	..	..	..	..	..	56 651	60 972	66 269
C.3.1.2. Reinsurance Accepted	C.3.1.2. Réassurance Acceptée								
C.3.1.2.1. Domestic Companies	C.3.1.2.1. Entreprises Nationales	..	..	..	..	..	1 913	1 522	1 335
C.3.1.2.2. (Foreign Controlled Companies)	C.3.1.2.2. (Entreprises Sous Contrôle Etranger)	..	..	..	..	..	551	579	697
C.3.1.2.3. Branches & Agencies of Foreign Cies	C.3.1.2.3. Succursales et Agences d'Ent. Etrangères	..	..	..	..	..	32	91	..
C.3.1.2. Total	C.3.1.2. Total	..	..	..	..	..	1 945	1 613	1 336
C.3.1.3. Total	C.3.1.3. Total								
C.3.1.3.1. Domestic Companies	C.3.1.3.1. Entreprises Nationales	38 380	39 729	44 271	46 437	51 491	55 997	59 992	64 924
C.3.1.3.2. (Foreign Controlled Companies)	C.3.1.3.2. (Entreprises Sous Contrôle Etranger)	7 823	5 844	9 391	8 975	9 539	10 443	10 462	12 705
C.3.1.3.3. Branches & Agencies of Foreign Cies	C.3.1.3.3. Succursales et Agences d'Ent. Etrangères	2 975	2 613	2 838	3 052	2 939	2 598	2 593	2 681
C.3.1.3. Total Gross Premiums	C.3.1.3. Total des Primes Brutes	41 355	42 342	47 109	49 489	54 430	58 596	62 585	67 605
C.3.2. Ceded Premiums	**C.3.2. Primes Cédées**								
C.3.2.1. Domestic Companies	C.3.2.1. Entreprises Nationales	3 665	3 745	4 089	5 456	5 939	5 513	5 234	5 383
C.3.2.2. (Foreign Controlled Companies)	C.3.2.2. (Entreprises Sous Contrôle Etranger)	915	625	1 448	1 208	1 101	1 163	1 029	1 496
C.3.2.3. Branches & Agencies of Foreign Cies	C.3.2.3. Succursales et Agences d'Ent. Etrangères	286	276	310	350	391	182	147	169
C.3.2. Total	C.3.2. Total	3 951	4 021	4 399	5 806	6 330	5 694	5 381	5 553
C.3.3. Net Written Premiums	**C.3.3. Primes Nettes Emises**								
C.3.3.1. Domestic Companies	C.3.3.1. Entreprises Nationales	34 715	35 984	40 182	40 981	45 552	50 484	54 758	59 541
C.3.3.2. (Foreign Controlled Companies)	C.3.3.2. (Entreprises Sous Contrôle Etranger)	6 908	5 219	7 943	7 767	8 438	9 280	9 433	11 209
C.3.3.3. Branches & Agencies of Foreign Cies	C.3.3.3. Succursales et Agences d'Ent. Etrangères	2 689	2 337	2 528	2 702	2 548	2 416	2 446	2 512
C.3.3. Total	C.3.3. Total	37 404	38 321	42 710	43 683	48 100	52 900	57 204	62 052

NETHERLANDS

Monetary Unit: million guilders | Unité monétaire : million de florins

E. BUSINESS WRITTEN ABROAD / E. OPERATIONS A L'ETRANGER

	1990	1991	1992	1993	1994	1995	1996	1997
E.1. Life / E.1. Vie								
E.1.1. Gross Premiums / E.1.1. Primes Brutes								
E.1.1.1. Direct Business / E.1.1.1. Assurance Directe								
E.1.1.1.2. Subsidiaries / E.1.1.1.2. Filiales	..	..	..	128	..	..	..	..
E.1.1.3. Total / E.1.1.3. Total								
E.1.1.3.1. Branches & Agencies / E.1.1.3.1. Succursales & Agences	421	698	1 000	1 337	..	..	..	..
E.1.1.3.2. Subsidiaries / E.1.1.3.2. Filiales	6 944	7 560	8 069	13 022	..	..	..	..
E.1.1.3. Total Gross Premiums / E.1.1.3. Total des Primes Brutes	7 365	8 258	9 069	14 359	..	..	..	..
E.1.2. Ceded Premiums / E.1.2. Primes Cédées								
E.1.2.1. Branches & Agencies / E.1.2.1. Succursales & Agences	9	13	22	35	..	..	..	..
E.1.2.2. Subsidiaries / E.1.2.2. Filiales	470	532	529	649	..	..	..	..
E.1.2. Total / E.1.2. Total	479	545	551	684	..	..	..	..
E.1.3. Net Written Premiums / E.1.3. Primes Nettes Emises								
E.1.3.1. Branches & Agencies / E.1.3.1. Succursales & Agences	412	685	978	1 302	..	..	..	..
E.1.3.2. Subsidiaries / E.1.3.2. Filiales	6 474	7 028	7 540	12 373	..	..	..	..
E.1.3. Total / E.1.3. Total	6 886	7 713	8 518	13 675	..	..	..	..
E.2. Non-Life / E.2. Non-Vie								
E.2.1. Gross Premiums / E.2.1. Primes Brutes								
E.2.1.3. Total / E.2.1.3. Total								
E.2.1.3.1. Branches & Agencies / E.2.1.3.1. Succursales & Agences	105	130	133	155	..	..	..	..
E.2.1.3.2. Subsidiaries / E.2.1.3.2. Filiales	12 208	14 931	16 044	14 644	..	..	..	..
E.2.1.3. Total Gross Premiums / E.2.1.3. Total des Primes Brutes	12 313	15 061	16 177	14 799	..	..	..	..
E.2.2. Ceded Premiums / E.2.2. Primes Cédées								
E.2.2.1. Branches & Agencies / E.2.2.1. Succursales & Agences	20	26	24	27	..	..	..	..
E.2.2.2. Subsidiaries / E.2.2.2. Filiales	1 843	2 487	2 510	1 867	..	..	..	..
E.2.2. Total / E.2.2. Total	1 863	2 513	2 534	1 894	..	..	..	..
E.2.3. Net Written Premiums / E.2.3. Primes Nettes Emises								
E.2.3.1. Branches & Agencies / E.2.3.1. Succursales & Agences	85	104	109	128	..	..	..	..
E.2.3.2. Subsidiaries / E.2.3.2. Filiales	10 365	12 444	13 534	12 777	..	..	..	..
E.2.3. Total / E.2.3. Total	10 450	12 548	13 643	12 905	..	..	..	..

F. OUTSTANDING INVESTMENT BY DIRECT INSURANCE COMPANIES / F. ENCOURS DES PLACEMENTS DES ENTREPRISES D'ASSURANCES DIRECTES

	1990	1991	1992	1993	1994	1995	1996	1997
F.1. Life / F.1. Vie								
F.1.1. Real Estate / F.1.1. Immobilier								
F.1.1.1. Domestic Companies / F.1.1.1. Entreprises Nationales	14 097	14 817	15 396	15 430	14 459	16 981	16 147	19 325
F.1.1.2. (Foreign Controlled Companies) / F.1.1.2. (Entreprises Sous Contrôle Etranger)	2 080	2 329	2 420	2 454	2 495	2 641	2 524	212
F.1.1.3. Branches & Agencies of Foreign Cies / F.1.1.3. Succursales et Agences d'Ent. Etrangères	584	479	523	648	507	478	526	
F.1.1.4. Domestic Investment / F.1.1.4. Placement dans le Pays	14 211	14 455	15 018	15 199	14 155		16 270	19 334
F.1.1.5. Foreign Investment / F.1.1.5. Placement à l'Etranger	470	841	901	879	811		403	203
F.1.1. Total / F.1.1. Total	14 681	15 296	15 919	16 078	14 966		16 673	19 537
F.1.2. Mortgage Loans / F.1.2. Prêts Hypothécaires								
F.1.2.1. Domestic Companies / F.1.2.1. Entreprises Nationales	32 100	35 287	35 997	34 599	38 187	41 569	43 903	43 331
F.1.2.2. (Foreign Controlled Companies) / F.1.2.2. (Entreprises Sous Contrôle Etranger)	3 202	3 540	3 779	4 245	4 711	5 919	4 096	
F.1.2.3. Branches & Agencies of Foreign Cies / F.1.2.3. Succursales et Agences d'Ent. Etrangères	1 164	959	354	968	1 069	1 780	1 199	1 687
F.1.2.4. Domestic Investment / F.1.2.4. Placement dans le Pays	33 264	36 246	36 351	35 567	39 256		45 102	45 018
F.1.2. Total / F.1.2. Total	33 264	36 246	36 351	35 567	39 256		45 102	45 018
F.1.3. Shares / F.1.3. Actions								
F.1.3.1. Domestic Companies / F.1.3.1. Entreprises Nationales	14 895	19 376	21 668	33 640	35 404	56 913	60 826	86 093
F.1.3.2. (Foreign Controlled Companies) / F.1.3.2. (Entreprises Sous Contrôle Etranger)	1 040	1 507	2 163	2 994	3 883	4 627	5 062	
F.1.3.3. Branches & Agencies of Foreign Cies / F.1.3.3. Succursales et Agences d'Ent. Etrangères	444	210	340	618	860	1 227	2 065	4 248
F.1.3.4. Domestic Investment / F.1.3.4. Placement dans le Pays	11 639	15 499	18 941	29 238	31 507		56 968	82 964
F.1.3.5. Foreign Investment / F.1.3.5. Placement à l'Etranger	3 700	4 087	3 067	5 020	4 757		5 923	7 377
F.1.3. Total / F.1.3. Total	15 339	19 586	22 008	34 258	36 264		62 891	90 341

Monetary Unit: million guilders — Unité monétaire : million de florins

Code / Label (EN)	Label (FR)	1990	1991	1992	1993	1994	1995	1996	1997
F.1.4. Bonds with Fixed Revenue	F.1.4. Obligations								
F.1.4.1. Domestic Companies	F.1.4.1. Entreprises Nationales	17 455	30 873	34 864	47 059	62 431	64 657	81 951	107 791
F.1.4.2. (Foreign Controlled Companies)	F.1.4.2. (Entreprises Sous Contrôle Etranger)	3 515	4 816	7 968	9 931	10 571	13 822	17 595	
F.1.4.3. Branches & Agencies of Foreign Cies	F.1.4.3. Succursales et Agences d'Ent. Etrangères	3 566	2 564	3 602	4 745	5 108	7 629	9 562	10 511
F.1.4.4. Domestic Investment	F.1.4.4. Placement dans le Pays	15 521	22 115	30 540	37 877	58 938	..	69 217	91 369
F.1.4.5. Foreign Investment	F.1.4.5. Placement à l' Etranger	5 500	11 322	7 926	13 927	8 601	..	22 296	26 933
F.1.4. Total	F.1.4. Total	21 021	33 437	38 466	51 804	67 539	..	91 513	118 302
F.1.5. Loans other than Mortgage Loans	F.1.5. Prêts Autres qu'Hypothécaires								
F.1.5.1. Domestic Companies	F.1.5.1. Entreprises Nationales	70 750	79 661	80 919	87 358	90 111	85 203	82 829	78 629
F.1.5.2. (Foreign Controlled Companies)	F.1.5.2. (Entreprises Sous Contrôle Etranger)	10 316	10 011	10 942	11 664	12 565	12 689	10 830	
F.1.5.3. Branches & Agencies of Foreign Cies	F.1.5.3. Succursales et Agences d'Ent. Etrangères	3 570	3 669	3 180	3 773	3 784	1 809	1 969	1 464
F.1.5.4. Domestic Investment	F.1.5.4. Placement dans le Pays	71 620	80 657	81 431	88 050	91 105	..	80 981	77 941
F.1.5.5. Foreign Investment	F.1.5.5. Placement à l' Etranger	2 700	2 673	2 668	3 081	2 790	..	3 817	2 151
F.1.5. Total	F.1.5. Total	74 320	83 330	84 099	91 131	93 895	..	84 798	80 093
F.1.6. Other Investments	F.1.6. Autres Placements								
F.1.6.1. Domestic Companies	F.1.6.1. Entreprises Nationales	13 320	9 882	11 851	16 435	15 421	22 375	28 239	30 524
F.1.6.2. (Foreign Controlled Companies)	F.1.6.2. (Entreprises Sous Contrôle Etranger)	1 900	1 468	2 293	3 132	2 712	5 347	2 644	
F.1.6.3. Branches & Agencies of Foreign Cies	F.1.6.3. Succursales et Agences d'Ent. Etrangères	19	16	17	17	312	312	331	256
F.1.6. Total	F.1.6. Total	13 339	9 898	11 868	16 454	15 440	..	28 570	30 780
F.1.7. Total	F.1.7. Total								
F.1.7.1. Domestic Companies	F.1.7.1. Entreprises Nationales	162 617	189 896	200 695	234 521	256 013	287 698	313 895	365 693
F.1.7.2. (Foreign Controlled Companies)	F.1.7.2. (Entreprises Sous Contrôle Etranger)	22 053	23 671	29 565	34 420	36 937	45 045	42 751	
F.1.7.3. Branches & Agencies of Foreign Cies	F.1.7.3. Succursales et Agences d'Ent. Etrangères	9 347	7 897	8 016	10 771	11 347	13 235	15 652	18 378
F.1.7. Total of Life Investments	F.1.7. Total des Placements Vie	171 964	197 793	208 711	245 292	267 360	..	329 547	384 071
F.2. Non-Life	**F.2. Non-Vie**								
F.2.1. Real Estate	F.2.1. Immobilier								
F.2.1.1. Domestic Companies	F.2.1.1. Entreprises Nationales	988	965	1 024	1 115	692	979	923	973
F.2.1.2. (Foreign Controlled Companies)	F.2.1.2. (Entreprises Sous Contrôle Etranger)	338	262	433	349	301	308	295	
F.2.1.3. Branches & Agencies of Foreign Cies	F.2.1.3. Succursales et Agences d'Ent. Etrangères	88	113	95	113	45	50	54	37
F.2.1.4. Domestic Investment	F.2.1.4. Placement dans le Pays	1 056	1 060	1 103	1 205	737	..	967	966
F.2.1.5. Foreign Investment	F.2.1.5. Placement à l' Etranger	20	18	16	23	0	..	10	44
F.2.1. Total	F.2.1. Total	1 076	1 078	1 119	1 228	737	..	977	1 010
F.2.2. Mortgage Loans	F.2.2. Prêts Hypothécaires								
F.2.2.1. Domestic Companies	F.2.2.1. Entreprises Nationales	916	849	1 054	891	908	860	739	704
F.2.2.2. (Foreign Controlled Companies)	F.2.2.2. (Entreprises Sous Contrôle Etranger)	40	16	57	40	38	58	43	
F.2.2.3. Branches & Agencies of Foreign Cies	F.2.2.3. Succursales et Agences d'Ent. Etrangères	26	30	31	29	29	27	24	26
F.2.2.4. Domestic Investment	F.2.2.4. Placement dans le Pays	942	879	1 085	920	937	..	763	730
F.2.2. Total	F.2.2. Total	942	879	1 085	920	937	..	763	730
F.2.3. Shares	F.2.3. Actions								
F.2.3.1. Domestic Companies	F.2.3.1. Entreprises Nationales	2 520	2 704	3 276	4 578	5 049	5 794	8 489	11 908
F.2.3.2. (Foreign Controlled Companies)	F.2.3.2. (Entreprises Sous Contrôle Etranger)	592	279	725	999	905	1 033	1 335	
F.2.3.3. Branches & Agencies of Foreign Cies	F.2.3.3. Succursales et Agences d'Ent. Etrangères	185	146	249	344	292	188	221	319
F.2.3.4. Domestic Investment	F.2.3.4. Placement dans le Pays	2 415	2 456	3 122	4 320	4 826	..	7 965	9 873
F.2.3.5. Foreign Investment	F.2.3.5. Placement à l' Etranger	290	394	403	602	515	..	745	2 354
F.2.3. Total	F.2.3. Total	2 705	2 850	3 525	4 922	5 341	..	8 710	12 227
F.2.4. Bonds with Fixed Revenue	F.2.4. Obligations								
F.2.4.1. Domestic Companies	F.2.4.1. Entreprises Nationales	7 792	7 763	9 619	11 273	11 826	13 975	19 309	23 050
F.2.4.2. (Foreign Controlled Companies)	F.2.4.2. (Entreprises Sous Contrôle Etranger)	2 472	1 595	2 773	2 698	2 850	3 262	3 946	
F.2.4.3. Branches & Agencies of Foreign Cies	F.2.4.3. Succursales et Agences d'Ent. Etrangères	1 170	1 223	1 453	1 390	1 232	888	853	822
F.2.4.4. Domestic Investment	F.2.4.4. Placement dans le Pays	7 772	7 885	9 774	10 610	11 200	..	15 717	17 882
F.2.4.5. Foreign Investment	F.2.4.5. Placement à l' Etranger	1 190	1 101	1 298	2 053	1 858	..	4 445	5 990
F.2.4. Total	F.2.4. Total	8 962	8 986	11 072	12 663	13 058	..	20 162	23 872
F.2.5. Loans other than Mortgage Loans	F.2.5. Prêts Autres qu'Hypothécaires								
F.2.5.1. Domestic Companies	F.2.5.1. Entreprises Nationales	9 543	8 695	9 423	9 705	10 398	9 569	8 172	7 076
F.2.5.2. (Foreign Controlled Companies)	F.2.5.2. (Entreprises Sous Contrôle Etranger)	1 164	974	1 327	1 148	1 180	1 198	1 087	
F.2.5.3. Branches & Agencies of Foreign Cies	F.2.5.3. Succursales et Agences d'Ent. Etrangères	114	143	147	186	183	129	118	117
F.2.5.4. Domestic Investment	F.2.5.4. Placement dans le Pays	9 407	8 640	9 360	9 605	10 281	..	7 944	6 905
F.2.5.5. Foreign Investment	F.2.5.5. Placement à l' Etranger	250	198	210	286	300	..	346	288
F.2.5. Total	F.2.5. Total	9 657	8 838	9 570	9 891	10 581	..	8 290	7 193

NETHERLANDS

Monetary Unit: million guilders

Unité monétaire : million de florins

		1990	1991	1992	1993	1994	1995	1996	1997
F.2.6.	Other Investments / Autres Placements								
F.2.6.1.	Domestic Companies / Entreprises Nationales	92	79	88	208	164	6 281	5 942	6 504
F.2.6.2.	(Foreign Controlled Companies) / (Entreprises Sous Contrôle Etranger)	45	78	10	160	20	643	499	..
F.2.6.3.	Branches & Agencies of Foreign Cies / Succursales et Agences d'Ent. Etrangères	1	0	..	..	0	129	71	38
F.2.6.4.	Domestic Investment / Placement dans le Pays	..	..	..	89	..	..	..	6 441
F.2.6.5.	Foreign Investment / Placement à l' Etranger	..	..	..	119	..	..	..	101
F.2.6.	Total	93	79	88	208	164	..	6 013	6 542
F.2.7.	Total								
F.2.7.1.	Domestic Companies / Entreprises Nationales	21 851	21 055	24 484	27 770	29 037	37 458	43 574	50 215
F.2.7.2.	(Foreign Controlled Companies) / (Entreprises Sous Contrôle Etranger)	4 651	3 204	5 325	5 394	5 294	6 502	7 204	..
F.2.7.3.	Branches & Agencies of Foreign Cies / Succursales et Agences d'Ent. Etrangères	1 584	1 655	1 975	2 062	1 781	1 411	1 341	1 359
F.2.7.4.	Domestic Investment / Placement dans le Pays	..	..	..	..	..	..	..	42 797
F.2.7.5.	Foreign Investment / Placement à l' Etranger	..	..	..	..	..	..	..	8 777
F.2.7.	Total of Non-Life Investments / Total des Placements Non-Vie	23 435	22 710	26 459	29 832	30 818	..	44 915	51 574
G. BREAKDOWN OF NON-LIFE PREMIUMS	**G. VENTILATIONS DES PRIMES NON-VIE**								
G.1.	Motor vehicle / Assurance Automobile								
G.1.1.	Direct Business / Assurances Directes								
G.1.1.1.	Gross Premiums / Primes Brutes	4 916	4 943	5 215	5 073	6 415	6 414	6 825	7 023
G.1.1.2.	Ceded Premiums / Primes Cédées	279	291	328	257	312	273	260	242
G.1.1.3.	Net Written Premiums / Primes Nettes Emises	4 637	4 652	4 887	4 816	6 103	6 140	6 565	6 781
G.1.2.	Reinsurance Accepted / Réassurance Acceptée								
G.1.2.1.	Gross Premiums / Primes Brutes	69	74	88	70	83	73	70	44
G.1.2.2.	Ceded Premiums / Primes Cédées	2	3	30	3	6	3	2	3
G.1.2.3.	Net Written Premiums / Primes Nettes Emises	67	71	58	67	77	71	68	41
G.1.3.	Total								
G.1.3.1.	Gross Premiums / Primes Brutes	4 986	5 017	5 303	5 143	6 498	6 487	6 895	7 067
G.1.3.2.	Ceded Premiums / Primes Cédées	281	294	358	260	318	276	262	245
G.1.3.3.	Net Written Premiums / Primes Nettes Emises	4 705	4 723	4 945	4 883	6 180	6 211	6 633	6 822
G.2.	Marine, Aviation								
G.2.1.	Direct Business / Assurances Directes								
G.2.1.1.	Gross Premiums / Primes Brutes	832	802	1 010	818	1 205	1 024	1 039	1 055
G.2.1.2.	Ceded Premiums / Primes Cédées	184	198	271	246	326	320	302	308
G.2.1.3.	Net Written Premiums / Primes Nettes Emises	648	604	739	572	879	704	737	747
G.2.2.	Reinsurance Accepted / Réassurance Acceptée								
G.2.2.1.	Gross Premiums / Primes Brutes	55	60	70	70	78	92	109	109
G.2.2.2.	Ceded Premiums / Primes Cédées	17	20	24	19	19	25	38	35
G.2.2.3.	Net Written Premiums / Primes Nettes Emises	38	40	46	51	59	67	71	74
G.2.3.	Total								
G.2.3.1.	Gross Premiums / Primes Brutes	887	862	1 080	888	1 283	1 116	1 148	1 164
G.2.3.2.	Ceded Premiums / Primes Cédées	201	218	295	265	345	345	340	343
G.2.3.3.	Net Written Premiums / Primes Nettes Emises	686	644	785	623	938	771	808	821
G.4.	Fire, Property Damages / Incendie, Dommages aux Biens								
G.4.1.	Direct Business / Assurances Directes								
G.4.1.1.	Gross Premiums / Primes Brutes	3 827	3 887	4 190	4 289	5 004	4 969	5 057	5 252
G.4.1.2.	Ceded Premiums / Primes Cédées	1 120	1 134	1 253	1 316	1 426	1 431	1 389	1 337
G.4.1.3.	Net Written Premiums / Primes Nettes Emises	2 706	2 753	2 937	2 973	3 578	3 538	3 668	3 915
G.4.2.	Reinsurance Accepted / Réassurance Acceptée								
G.4.2.1.	Gross Premiums / Primes Brutes	261	164	218	190	301	237	284	203
G.4.2.2.	Ceded Premiums / Primes Cédées	67	35	68	61	144	106	144	84
G.4.2.3.	Net Written Premiums / Primes Nettes Emises	193	130	150	129	157	131	140	119
G.4.3.	Total								
G.4.3.1.	Gross Premiums / Primes Brutes	4 086	4 051	4 408	4 479	5 305	5 205	5 341	5 455
G.4.3.2.	Ceded Premiums / Primes Cédées	1 188	1 169	1 321	1 377	1 570	1 536	1 533	1 421
G.4.3.3.	Net Written Premiums / Primes Nettes Emises	2 900	2 882	3 087	3 102	3 735	3 669	3 808	4 034

Monetary Unit: million guilders

Unité monétaire : million de florins

	1990	1991	1992	1993	1994	1995	1996	1997
G.7. Accident, Health — G.7. Accident, Santé								
G.7.1. Direct Business — G.7.1. Assurances Directes								
G.7.1.1. Gross Premiums — G.7.1.1. Primes Brutes	2 704	5 971	7 997	9 413	10 154	11 289	12 043	12 795
G.7.1.2. Ceded Premiums — G.7.1.2. Primes Cédées	713	632	494	555	628	547	671	700
G.7.1.3. Net Written Premiums — G.7.1.3. Primes Nettes Emises	1 991	5 338	7 483	8 858	9 526	10 742	11 373	12 095
G.7.2. Reinsurance Accepted — G.7.2. Réassurance Acceptée								
G.7.2.1. Gross Premiums — G.7.2.1. Primes Brutes	354	281	309	231	216	225	294	315
G.7.2.2. Ceded Premiums — G.7.2.2. Primes Cédées	11	18	7	7	2	6	4	33
G.7.2.3. Net Written Premiums — G.7.2.3. Primes Nettes Emises	343	262	302	224	214	220	290	282
G.7.3. Total								
G.7.3.1. Gross Premiums — G.7.3.1. Primes Brutes	7 558	6 252	3 286	9 644	10 370	11 514	12 337	13 110
G.7.3.2. Ceded Premiums — G.7.3.2. Primes Cédées	724	650	501	562	630	553	675	733
G.7.3.3. Net Written Premiums — G.7.3.3. Primes Nettes Emises	6 834	5 602	7 765	9 082	9 740	10 962	11 662	12 377
G.8. Others — G.8. Autres								
G.8.1. Direct Business — G.8.1. Assurances Directes								
G.8.1.1. Gross Premiums — G.8.1.1. Primes Brutes	2 205	2 323	2 515	2 220	3 072	2 826	2 827	3 057
G.8.1.2. Ceded Premiums — G.8.1.2. Primes Cédées	566	632	672	578	837	736	647	672
G.8.1.3. Net Written Premiums — G.8.1.3. Primes Nettes Emises	1 639	1 691	1 843	1 642	2 235	2 090	2 180	2 385
G.8.2. Reinsurance Accepted — G.8.2 Réassurance Acceptée								
G.8.2.1. Gross Premiums — G.8.2.1. Primes Brutes	200	194	207	183	218	232	250	219
G.8.2.2. Ceded Premiums — G.8.2.2. Primes Cédées	42	38	39	40	46	32	46	26
G.8.2.3. Net Written Premiums — G.8.2.3. Primes Nettes Emises	158	156	168	143	172	200	204	193
G.8.3. Total								
G.8.3.1. Gross Premiums — G.8.3.1. Primes Brutes	2 405	2 517	2 722	2 403	3 290	3 058	3 077	3 276
G.8.3.2. Ceded Premiums — G.8.3.2. Primes Cédées	608	670	711	618	883	768	693	698
G.8.3.3. Net Written Premiums — G.8.3.3. Primes Nettes Emises	1 796	1 847	2 011	1 785	2 407	2 290	2 384	2 578
G.10. Total								
G.10.1. Direct Business — G.10.1. Assurances Directes								
G.10.1.1. Gross Premiums — G.10.1.1. Primes Brutes	18 984	17 926	20 908	21 813	25 850	26 522	27 791	29 182
G.10.1.2. Ceded Premiums — G.10.1.2. Primes Cédées	2 863	2 887	3 018	2 952	3 529	3 308	3 269	3 259
G.10.1.3. Net Written Premiums — G.10.1.3. Primes Nettes Emises	16 120	15 038	17 889	18 861	22 321	23 215	24 523	25 923
G.10.2. Reinsurance Accepted — G.10.2. Réassurance Acceptée								
G.10.2.1. Gross Premiums — G.10.2.1. Primes Brutes	938	773	891	744	896	859	1 007	890
G.10.2.2. Ceded Premiums — G.10.2.2. Primes Cédées	139	114	168	130	217	171	234	181
G.10.2.3. Net Written Premiums — G.10.2.3. Primes Nettes Emises	799	659	725	614	679	688	773	709
G.10.3. Total								
G.10.3.1. Gross Premiums — G.10.3.1. Primes Brutes	19 921	18 699	21 799	28 557	26 746	27 381	28 798	30 072
G.10.3.2. Ceded Premiums — G.10.3.2. Primes Cédées	3 002	3 001	3 186	3 082	3 746	3 478	3 503	3 440
G.10.3.3. Net Written Premiums — G.10.3.3. Primes Nettes Emises	16 919	15 698	18 613	19 475	23 000	23 902	25 295	26 632
H. GROSS CLAIMS PAYMENTS — H. PAIEMENTS BRUTS DES SINISTRES								
H.1. Life — H.1. Vie								
H.1.1. Domestic Companies — H.1.1. Entreprises Nationales				..	..	12 412	16 962	17 923
H.1.2. (Foreign Controlled Companies) — H.1.2. (Entreprises Sous Contrôle Etranger)				..	..	..	2 595	950
H.1.3. Branches & Agencies of Foreign Cies — H.1.3. Succursales et Agences d'Ent. Etrangères				..	..	632	759	
H.1. Total				..	..	13 044	17 721	18 873
H.2. Non-Life — H.2. Non-Vie								
H.2.1. Domestic Companies — H.2.1 Entreprises Nationales				..	..	17 485	18 195	20 028
H.2.2. (Foreign Controlled Companies) — H.2.2. (Entreprises Sous Contrôle Etranger)				..	..	..	3 329	
H.2.3. Branches & Agencies of Foreign Cies — H.2.3 Succursales et Agences d'Ent. Etrangères				..	..	487	416	543
H.2. Total				..	..	17 972	18 611	20 571

	1990	1991	1992	1993	1994	1995	1996	1997	
I. GROSS OPERATING EXPENSES									**I. DEPENSES BRUTES D'EXPLOITATION**
I.1. Life									**I.1. Vie**
I.1.1. Domestic Companies					:	3 709	4 032	4 649	I.1.1. Entreprises Nationales
I.1.2. (Foreign Controlled Companies)					:	:	777	..	I.1.2. (Entreprises Sous Contrôle Etranger)
I.1.3. Branches & Agencies of Foreign Cies					:	262	283	350	I.1.3. Succursales et Agences d'Ent. Etrangères
I.1. Total					:	3 971	4 315	4 999	I.1. Total des Primes Nettes Vie
I.2. Non-Life									**I.2. Non-Vie**
I.2.1. Domestic Companies					:	5 549	6 229	6 603	I.2.1. Entreprises Nationales
I.2.2. (Foreign Controlled Companies)					:	:	2 890	..	I.2.2. (Entreprises Sous Contrôle Etranger)
I.2.3. Branches & Agencies of Foreign Cies					:	207	285	262	I.2.3. Succursales et Agences d'Ent. Etrangères
I.2. Total					:	5 756	6 514	6 865	I.2. Total
J. COMMISSIONS									**J. COMMISSIONS**
J.1. Life									**J.1. Vie**
J.1.1. Direct Business									J.1.1. Assurance directe
J.1.1.1. Domestic Companies					:	:	:	1 973	J.1.1.1. Entreprises Nationales
J.1.1.3. Branches & Agencies of Foreign Cies					:	:	:	15	J.1.1.3. Succursales et Agences d'Ent. Etrangères
J.1.1. Total					:	:	:	1 988	J.1.1. Total
J.1.2. Reinsurance Accepted									J.1.2. Réassurances acceptées
J.1.3. Total									J.1.3. Total
J.2. Non-Life									**J.2. Non-Vie**
J.2.1. Direct Business									J.2.1. Assurance directe
J.2.1.1. Domestic Companies					:	:	:	2 090	J.2.1.1. Entreprises Nationales
J.2.1.3. Branches & Agencies of Foreign Cies					:	:	:	15	J.2.1.3. Succursales et Agences d'Ent. Etrangères
J.2.1. Total					:	:	:	2 100	J.2.1. Total des Primes Nettes Vie
J.2.2. Reinsurance Accepted									J.2.2. Réassurances acceptées
J.2.3. Total									J.2.3. Total

Monetary Unit: million New Zealand dollars

Unité monétaire : million de dollars de Nouvelle-Zélande

A. NUMBER OF COMPANIES IN THE REPORTING COUNTRY — A. NOMBRE D'ENTREPRISES DANS LE PAYS DECLARANT

	1990	1991	1992	1993	1994	1995	1996	1997	
A.1. Life									**A.1. Vie**
A.1.1. Domestic Companies	22	23	29	..	46	43	40	38	A.1.1. Entreprises Nationales
A.1.2. (Foreign Controlled Companies)	0	0	0	..	21	25	22	21	A.1.2. (Entreprises Sous Contrôle Etranger)
A.1.3. Branches & Agencies of Foreign Cies	18	18	10	..	..	..	0	0	A.1.3. Succursales et Agences d'Ent. Etrangères
A.1. All Companies	40	41	39	..	46	43	40	38	A.1. Ensemble des Entreprises
A.2. Non-Life									**A.2. Non-Vie**
A.2.1. Domestic Companies	113	105	104	..	186	182	182	156	A.2.1. Entreprises Nationales
A.2.2. (Foreign Controlled Companies)	0	0	0	..	37	32	36	39	A.2.2. (Entreprises Sous Contrôle Etranger)
A.2.3. Branches & Agencies of Foreign Cies	36	43	24	..	..	..	0	0	A.2.3. Succursales et Agences d'Ent. Etrangères
A.2. All Companies	149	148	128	..	186	182	182	156	A.2. Ensemble des Entreprises
A.5. Total									**A.5. Total**
A.5.1. Domestic Companies	135	128	133	..	232	225	222	194	A.5.1. Entreprises Nationales
A.5.2. (Foreign Controlled Companies)	0	0	0	..	58	57	58	60	A.5.2. (Entreprises Sous Contrôle Etranger)
A.5.3. Branches & Agencies of Foreign Cies	54	61	34	..	..	..	0	0	A.5.3. Succursales et Agences d'Ent. Etrangères
A.5. All Insurance Companies	189	189	167	..	232	225	222	194	A.5. Ensemble des Entreprises d'Assurances

B. NUMBER OF EMPLOYEES — B. NOMBRE D'EMPLOYES

	1990	1991	1992	1993	1994	1995	1996	1997	
B.1. Insurance Companies	10 226	9 278	9 045	8 823	8 926	9 280	9 362	9 801	B.1. Entreprises d'Assurances
B. Total	..	..	..	..	..	..	..	..	B. Total

C. BUSINESS WRITTEN IN THE REPORTING COUNTRY — C. OPERATIONS CONCLUES DANS LE PAYS DECLARANT

	1990	1991	1992	1993	1994	1995	1996	1997	
C.1. Life									**C.1. Vie**
C.1.1. Gross Premiums									**C.1.1. Primes Brutes**
C.1.1.1. Direct Business									C.1.1.1. Assurances Directes
C.1.1.1.1. Domestic Companies	769	1 139	1 168	1 182	1 240	1 004	..	..	C.1.1.1.1. Entreprises Nationales
C.1.1.1.3. Branches & Agencies of Foreign Cies	316	..	..	..	..	..	..	..	C.1.1.1.3. Succursales et Agences d'Ent. Etrangères
C.1.1.1. Total	1 084	1 139	1 168	1 182	1 240	1 004	..	..	C.1.1.1. Total
C.1.1.3. Total									C.1.1.3. Total
C.1.1.3.1. Domestic Companies	769	1 139	1 168	1 182	1 240	1 004	..	..	C.1.1.3.1. Entreprises Nationales
C.1.1.3.3. Branches & Agencies of Foreign Cies	316	..	..	..	..	..	..	..	C.1.1.3.3. Succursales et Agences d'Ent. Etrangères
C.1.1.3. Total Gross Premiums	1 084	1 139	1 168	1 182	1 240	1 004	1 263	1 365	C.1.1.3. Total des Primes Brutes
C.1.3. Net Written Premiums									C.1.3. Primes Nettes Emises
C.1.3.1. Domestic Companies	769	1 139	1 168	1 182	1 240	1 004	..	..	C.1.3.1. Entreprises Nationales
C.1.3.3. Branches & Agencies of Foreign Cies	316	..	..	..	..	..	..	..	C.1.3.3. Succursales et Agences d'Ent. Etrangères
C.1.3. Total	1 084	1 139	1 168	1 182	1 240	1 004	..	..	C.1.3. Total
C.2. Non-Life									**C.2. Non-Vie**
C.2.1. Gross premiums									**C.2.1. Primes Brutes**
C.2.1.1. Direct Business									C.2.1.1. Assurances Directes
C.2.1.1.1. Domestic Companies	1 309	1 540	..	..	..	..	..	..	C.2.1.1.1. Entreprises Nationales
C.2.1.1.3. Branches & Agencies of Foreign Cies	560	..	..	..	..	..	..	..	C.2.1.1.3. Succursales et Agences d'Ent. Etrangères
C.2.1.1. Total	1 869	1 540	1 813	1 574	1 608	1 822	2 374	2 486	C.2.1.1. Total
C.2.1.2. Reinsurance Accepted									C.2.1.2. Réassurance Acceptée
C.2.1.2.1. Domestic Companies	17	41	..	..	..	..	..	..	C.2.1.2.1. Entreprises Nationales
C.2.1.2.3. Branches & Agencies of Foreign Cies	33	17	..	..	..	..	..	..	C.2.1.2.3. Succursales et Agences d'Ent. Etrangères
C.2.1.2. Total	49	58	..	..	..	..	37	36	C.2.1.2. Total
C.2.1.3. Total									C.2.1.3. Total
C.2.1.3.1. Domestic Companies	1 326	1 581	..	..	..	..	..	..	C.2.1.3.1. Entreprises Nationales
C.2.1.3.3. Branches & Agencies of Foreign Cies	593	..	..	..	..	..	..	..	C.2.1.3.3. Succursales et Agences d'Ent. Etrangères
C.2.1.3. Total Gross Premiums	1 919	1 581	1 813	1 574	1 608	1 822	2 411	2 522	C.2.1.3. Total des Primes Brutes

Monetary Unit: million New Zealand dollars　　　　　　　　　　　　Unité monétaire : million de dollars de Nouvelle-Zélande

		1990	1991	1992	1993	1994	1995	1996	1997
C.2.2. Ceded Premiums	C.2.2. Primes Cédées								
C.2.2.1. Domestic Companies	C.2.2.1. Entreprises Nationales	52	54	64	:	:	:	:	:
C.2.2.3. Branches & Agencies of Foreign Cies	C.2.2.3. Succursales et Agences d'Ent. Etrangères	96	101	120	:	:	:	:	:
C.2.2. Total	C.2.2. Total	149	155	184	237	286	347	318	305
C.2.3. Net Written Premiums	C.2.3. Primes Nettes Emises								
C.2.3.1. Domestic Companies	C.2.3.1. Entreprises Nationales	1 274	1 527	1 750	1 336	1 322	1 475		
C.2.3.3. Branches & Agencies of Foreign Cies	C.2.3.3. Succursales et Agences d'Ent. Etrangères	497	:	:	:	:	:	:	:
C.2.3. Total	C.2.3. Total	1 770	1 527	1 750	1 336	1 322	1 475	2 093	2 217
C.3. Total	**C.3. Total**								
C.3.1. Gross Premiums	C.3.1. Primes Brutes								
C.3.1.1. Direct Business	C.3.1.1. Assurances Directes								
C.3.1.1.1. Domestic Companies	C.3.1.1.1. Entreprises Nationales	2 078	2 679	:	:	:	:	:	:
C.3.1.1.3. Branches & Agencies of Foreign Cies	C.3.1.1.3. Succursales et Agences d'Ent. Etrangères	876	:	:	:	:	:	:	:
C.3.1.1. Total	C.3.1.1. Total	2 954	2 679	:	:	:	:	:	:
C.3.1.3. Total	C.3.1.3. Total								
C.3.1.3.1. Domestic Companies	C.3.1.3.1. Entreprises Nationales	2 095	2 720	2 982	2 756	2 848	2 826	:	:
C.3.1.3.3. Branches & Agencies of Foreign Cies	C.3.1.3.3. Succursales et Agences d'Ent. Etrangères	908	:	:	:	:	:	:	:
C.3.1.3. Total Gross Premiums	C.3.1.3. Total des Primes Brutes	3 003	2 720	2 982	2 756	2 848	2 826	3 674	3 887
C.3.3. Net Written Premiums	C.3.3. Primes Nettes Emises								
C.3.3.1. Domestic Companies	C.3.3.1. Entreprises Nationales	2 042	2 666	2 918	2 518	2 562	2 479	:	:
C.3.3.3. Branches & Agencies of Foreign Cies	C.3.3.3. Succursales et Agences d'Ent. Etrangères	812	:	:	:	:	:	:	:
C.3.3. Total	C.3.3. Total	2 854	2 666	2 918	2 518	2 562	2 479	:	:
G. BREAKDOWN OF NON-LIFE PREMIUMS	**G. VENTILATIONS DES PRIMES NON-VIE**								
G.1. Motor vehicle	G.1. Assurance Automobile								
G.1.1. Direct Business	G.1.1. Assurances Directes								
G.1.1.1. Gross Premiums	G.1.1.1. Primes Brutes	:	477	517	535	524	549	:	:
G.1.3. Total	G.1.3. Total								
G.1.3.1. Gross Premiums	G.1.3.1. Primes Brutes	:	:	:	:	:	:	516	627
G.2. Marine, Aviation	G.2. Marine, Aviation								
G.2.1. Direct Business	G.2.1. Assurances Directes								
G.2.1.1. Gross Premiums	G.2.1.1. Primes Brutes	:	31	24	32	45	34	:	:
G.2.3. Total	G.2.3. Total								
G.2.3.1. Gross Premiums	G.2.3.1. Primes Brutes	:	:	:	:	:	:	22	32
G.3. Freight	G.3. Fret								
G.3.1. Direct Business	G.3.1. Assurances Directes								
G.3.1.1. Gross Premiums	G.3.1.1. Primes Brutes	:	35	39	33	28	27	:	:
G.3.3. Total	G.3.3. Total								
G.3.3.1. Gross Premiums	G.3.3.1. Primes Brutes	:	:	:	:	:	:	21	30
G.4. Fire, Property Damages	G.4. Incendie, Dommages aux Biens								
G.4.1. Direct Business	G.4.1. Assurances Directes								
G.4.1.1. Gross Premiums	G.4.1.1. Primes Brutes	:	497	571	628	644	729	:	:
G.4.3. Total	G.4.3. Total								
G.4.3.1. Gross Premiums	G.4.3.1. Primes Brutes	:	:	:	:	:	:	625	767
G.7. Accident, Health	G.7. Accident, Santé								
G.7.1. Direct Business	G.7.1. Assurances Directes								
G.7.1.1. Gross Premiums	G.7.1.1. Primes Brutes	:	388	:	:	:	:	:	:
G.7.3. Total	G.7.3. Total								
G.7.3.1. Gross Premiums	G.7.3.1. Primes Brutes	:	:	:	:	:	:	445	738

NEW ZEALAND

Monetary Unit: million New Zealand dollars

	1990	1991	1992	1993	1994	1995	1996	1997	
G.8. Others									G.8. Autres
G.8.1. Direct Business									G.8.1. Assurances Directes
G.8.1.1. Gross Premiums	:	112	122	132	172	142			G.8.1.1. Primes Brutes
G.8.3. Total									G.8.3. Total
G.8.3.1. Gross Premiums	:	:	:	:	:	:	129	136	G.8.3.1. Primes Brutes
G.10. Total									G.10. Total
G.10.1. Direct Business									G.10.1. Assurances Directes
G.10.1.1. Gross Premiums	:	1 540	:	1 509	1 413	1 481	:	:	G.10.1.1. Primes Brutes
G.10.1.2. Ceded Premiums	:	54	64	:	:	:	:	:	G.10.1.2. Primes Cédées
G.10.1.3. Net Written Premiums	:	1 486	:	:	:	:	:	:	G.10.1.3. Primes Nettes Emises
G.10.2. Reinsurance Accepted									G.10.2. Réassurance Acceptée
G.10.2.1. Gross Premiums	:	41	:	237	:	:	:	:	G.10.2.1. Primes Brutes
G.10.2.3. Net Written Premiums	:	41	:	:	:	:	:	:	G.10.2.3. Primes Nettes Emises
G.10.3. Total									G.10.3. Total
G.10.3.1. Gross Premiums	:	1 581	1 813	1 574	1 608	:	1 757	2 329	G.10.3.1. Primes Brutes
G.10.3.2. Ceded Premiums	:	54	64	237	286	:	:	:	G.10.3.2. Primes Cédées
G.10.3.3. Net Written Premiums	:	1 527	1 750	1 336	1 322	:	:	:	G.10.3.3. Primes Nettes Emises
H. GROSS CLAIMS/PAYMENTS									**H. PAIEMENTS BRUTS DES SINISTRES**
H.1. Life									**H.1. Vie**
H.1. Total				998	1 076	1 211	1 178	1 430	H.1. Total
H.2. Non-Life									**H.2. Non-Vie**
H.2. Total				866	1 150	1 348	1 435	1 592	H.2. Total
I. GROSS OPERATING EXPENSES									**I. DEPENSES BRUITES D EXPLOITATION**
I.1. Life									**I.1. Vie**
I.1. Total				1 213	1 292	1 131	1 113	1 614	I.1. Total des Primes Nettes Vie
I.2. Non-Life									**I.2. Non-Vie**
I.2. Total				642	542	542	629	636	I.2. Total
J. COMMISSIONS									**J. COMMISSIONS**
J.1. Life									**J.1. Vie**
J.1.3. Total of Life Net Premiums					:	:	49	214	J.1.3. Total
J.2. Non-Life									**J.2. Non-Vie**
J.2.3. Total				128	98	118	105	184	J.2.3. Total

Monetary Unit: million Norwegian kroner

Unité monétaire : million de couronnes norvégiennes

	1990	1991	1992	1993	1994	1995	1996	1997	
A. NUMBER OF COMPANIES IN THE REPORTING COUNTRY									**A. NOMBRE D'ENTREPRISES DANS LE PAYS DECLARANT**
A.1. Life									**A.1. Vie**
A.1.1. Domestic Companies	11	10	10	10	10	9	9	16	A.1.1. Entreprises Nationales
A.1.2. (Foreign Controlled Companies)	0	2	2	1	1	1	1	1	A.1.2. (Entreprises Sous Contrôle Etranger)
A.1.3. Branches & Agencies of Foreign Cies	0	0	0	0	0	0	1	1	A.1.3. Succursales et Agences d'Ent. Etrangères
A.1. All Companies	11	10	10	10	10	9	10	17	A.1. Ensemble des Entreprises
A.2. Non-Life									**A.2. Non-Vie**
A.2.1. Domestic Companies	118	55	111	113	104	107	106	110	A.2.1. Entreprises Nationales
A.2.2. (Foreign Controlled Companies)	4	1	2	2	2	1	5	7	A.2.2. (Entreprises Sous Contrôle Etranger)
A.2.3. Branches & Agencies of Foreign Cies	30	13	22	14	18	18	12	13	A.2.3. Succursales et Agences d'Ent. Etrangères
A.2. All Companies	148	68	133	127	122	125	118	123	A.2. Ensemble des Entreprises
A.4. Reinsurance									**A.4. Réassurance**
A.4.1. Domestic Companies	3	..	2	2	2	2	2	2	A.4.1. Entreprises Nationales
A.4.2. (Foreign Controlled Companies)	1	..	0	0	0	1	1	1	A.4.2. (Entreprises Sous Contrôle Etranger)
A.4. All Companies	3	..	2	2	2	2	2	2	A.4. Ensemble des Entreprises
A.5. Total									**A.5. Total**
A.5.1. Domestic Companies	132	65	123	125	116	118	117	128	A.5.1. Entreprises Nationales
A.5.2. (Foreign Controlled Companies)	5	..	4	3	3	3	3	9	A.5.2. (Entreprises Sous Contrôle Etranger)
A.5.3. Branches & Agencies of Foreign Cies	30	13	22	14	18	18	13	14	A.5.3. Succursales et Agences d'Ent. Etrangères
A.5. All Insurance Companies	162	78	145	139	134	136	130	142	A.5. Ensemble des Entreprises d'Assurances
B. NUMBER OF EMPLOYEES									**B. NOMBRE D'EMPLOYES**
B.1. Insurance Companies	11 000	12 000	12 000	11 640	8 083	7 817	9 319	9 132	B.1. Entreprises d'Assurances
B.2. Intermediaries	..	6 000	..	..	..	..	..	..	B.2. Intermediaires
B. Total	..	18 000	..	..	..	..	..	..	B. Total
C. BUSINESS WRITTEN IN THE REPORTING COUNTRY									**C. OPERATIONS CONCLUES DANS LE PAYS DECLARANT**
C.1. Life									**C.1. Vie**
C.1.1. Gross Premiums									C.1.1. Primes Brutes
C.1.1.1. Direct Business									C.1.1.1. Assurances Directes
C.1.1.1.1. Domestic Companies	11 864	15 144	..	15 862	19 255	18 893	19 787	25 211	C.1.1.1.1. Entreprises Nationales
C.1.1.1.2. (Foreign Controlled Companies)	0	262	..	281	434	468	551	707	C.1.1.1.2. (Entreprises Sous Contrôle Etranger)
C.1.1.1.3. Branches & Agencies of Foreign Cies	0	0	0	0	0	0	3	3	C.1.1.1.3. Succursales et Agences d'Ent. Etrangères
C.1.1.1. Total	11 864	15 144	..	15 862	19 255	18 893	19 790	25 214	C.1.1.1. Total
C.1.1.2. Reinsurance Accepted									C.1.1.2. Réassurance Acceptée
C.1.1.2.1. Domestic Companies	75	5	..	0	0	0	0	0	C.1.1.2.1. Entreprises Nationales
C.1.1.2. Total	75	5	..	0	0	0	0	0	C.1.1.2. Total
C.1.1.3. Total									C.1.1.3. Total
C.1.1.3.1. Domestic Companies	11 939	15 149	15 546	15 862	19 255	18 893	19 787	25 211	C.1.1.3.1. Entreprises Nationales
C.1.1.3.2. (Foreign Controlled Companies)	0	262	346	281	434	468	551	707	C.1.1.3.2. (Entreprises Sous Contrôle Etranger)
C.1.1.3.3. Branches & Agencies of Foreign Cies	0	0	0	0	0	0	3	3	C.1.1.3.3. Succursales et Agences d'Ent. Etrangères
C.1.1.3. Total Gross Premiums	11 939	15 149	15 892	15 862	19 255	18 893	19 790	25 214	C.1.1.3. Total des Primes Brutes

Monetary Unit: million Norwegian kroner — Unité monétaire : million de couronnes norvégiennes

Code	English	French	1990	1991	1992	1993	1994	1995	1996	1997
C.1.2.	Ceded Premiums	Primes Cédées								
C.1.2.1.	Domestic Companies	Entreprises Nationales	108	32	8	0	0	0	245	272
C.1.2.2.	(Foreign Controlled Companies)	(Entreprises Sous Contrôle Etranger)	0	9	7	0	0	0	1	2
C.1.2.	Total	Total	108	32	15	0	0	0	245	272
C.1.3.	Net Written Premiums	Primes Nettes Emises								
C.1.3.1.	Domestic Companies	Entreprises Nationales	11 831	15 117	15 538	15 862	19 255	18 893	19 542	24 939
C.1.3.2.	(Foreign Controlled Companies)	(Entreprises Sous Contrôle Etranger)	0	253	339	281	434	468	550	705
C.1.3.3.	Branches & Agencies of Foreign Cies	Succursales et Agences d'Ent. Etrangères	0	0	0	0	0	0	3	3
C.1.3.	Total	Total	11 831	15 117	15 877	15 862	19 255	18 893	19 545	24 942
C.2.	**Non-Life**	**Non-Vie**								
C.2.1.	Gross premiums	Primes Brutes								
C.2.1.1.	Direct Business	Assurances Directes								
C.2.1.1.1.	Domestic Companies	Entreprises Nationales	20 591	20 706	22 752	24 057	24 741	23 837	24 576	25 079
C.2.1.1.2.	(Foreign Controlled Companies)	(Entreprises Sous Contrôle Etranger)	2 890	3 088	3 418	3 807	3 825	3 766	4 418	4 684
C.2.1.1.3.	Branches & Agencies of Foreign Cies	Succursales et Agences d'Ent. Etrangères	322	369	345	386	...	...	444	742
C.2.1.1.	Total	Tota	20 913	21 075	23 097	24 443	...	...	25 020	25 821
C.2.1.2.	Reinsurance Accepted	Réassurance Acceptée								
C.2.1.2.1.	Domestic Companies	Entreprises Nationales	4 268	3 299	2 389	2 233	1 081	678	253	277
C.2.1.2.2.	(Foreign Controlled Companies)	(Entreprises Sous Contrôle Etranger)	604	780	239	236	165	207	2	61
C.2.1.2.3.	Branches & Agences of Foreign Cies	Succursales et Agences d'Ent. Etrangères	5	0	5	0	...	...	0	0
C.2.1.2.	Total	Total	4 273	3 299	2 394	2 233	...	...	253	277
C.2.1.3.	Total	Total								
C.2.1.3.	Domestic Companies	Entreprises Nationales	24 859	24 005	25 141	26 290	25 822	24 514	24 829	25 356
C.2.1.3.2.	(Foreign Controlled Companies)	(Entreprises Sous Contrôle Etranger)	3 494	3 868	3 657	4 043	3 990	3 973	4 420	4 745
C.2.1.3.3.	Branches & Agencies of Foreign Cies	Succursales et Agences d'Ent. Etrangères	327	369	349	386	...	...	444	742
C.2.1.3.	Total Gross Premiums	Total des Primes Brutes	25 186	24 374	25 490	26 676	...	...	25 273	26 098
C.2.2.	Ceded Premiums	Primes Cédées								
C.2.2.1.	Domestic Companies	Entreprises Nationales	6 308	5 605	5 767	6 529	6 169	5 141	3 954	4 226
C.2.2.2.	(Foreign Controlled Companies)	(Entreprises Sous Contrôle Etranger)	1 139	1 000	813	1 052	833	708	678	722
C.2.2.3.	Branches & Agencies of Foreign Cies	Succursales et Agences d'Ent. Etrangères	35	40	34	83	...	...	44	100
C.2.2.	Total	Total	6 343	5 645	5 801	6 612	...	...	3 998	4 326
C.2.3.	Net Written Premiums	Primes Nettes Emises								
C.2.3.1.	Domestic Companies	Entreprises Nationales	18 551	18 400	19 374	19 761	19 653	19 373	20 875	21 130
C.2.3.2.	(Foreign Controlled Companies)	(Entreprises Sous Contrôle Etranger)	2 355	2 868	2 844	2 991	3 157	3 265	3 742	4 023
C.2.3.3.	Branches & Agencies of Foreign Cies	Succursales et Agences d'Ent. Etrangères	292	329	315	303	...	...	400	642
C.2.3.	Total	Total	18 843	18 729	19 689	20 064	...	...	21 275	21 772
C.3.	**Total**	**Total**								
C.3.1.	Gross Premiums	Primes Brutes								
C.3.1.1.	Direct Business	Assurances Directes								
C.3.1.1.1.	Domestic Companies	Entreprises Nationales	32 455	35 850	...	39 919	43 996	42 730	44 363	50 290
C.3.1.1.2.	(Foreign Controlled Companies)	(En reprises Sous Contrôle Etranger)	2 890	3 350	...	4 088	4 259	4 234	4 969	5 391
C.3.1.1.3	Branches & Agencies of Foreign Cies	Succursales et Agences d'Ent. Etrangères	322	369	345	386	...	...	447	745
C.3.1.1.	Total	Total	32 777	36 219	...	40 305	...	...	44 810	51 035
C.3.1.2.	Reinsurance Accepted	Réassurance Acceptée								
C.3.1.2.1.	Domestic Companies	Entreprises Nationales	4 343	3 304	...	2 233	1 081	678	253	277
C.3.1.2.2.	(Foreign Controlled Companies)	(Entreprises Sous Contrôle Etranger)	604	780	...	236	165	207	2	61
C.3.1.2.3.	Branches & Agencies of Foreign Cies	Succursales et Agences d'Ent. Etrangères	5	0	5	0	...	...	0	0
C.3.1.2.	Total	Total	4 348	3 304	...	2 233	...	...	253	277
C.3.1.3.	Total	Total								
C.3.1.3.1.	Domestic Companies	Entreprises Nationales	36 798	39 154	40 687	42 152	45 077	43 407	44 616	50 567
C.3.1.3.2.	(Foreign Controlled Companies)	(Entreprises Sous Contrôle Etranger)	3 494	4 130	4 003	4 324	4 424	4 441	4 971	5 452
C.3.1.3.3.	Branches & Agencies of Foreign Cies	Succursales et Agences d'Ent. Etrangères	327	369	349	386	...	...	447	745
C.3.1.3.	Total Gross Premiums	Total des Primes Brutes	37 125	39 523	41 382	42 538	...	...	45 063	51 312

185

Monetary Unit: million Norwegian kroner — Unité monétaire : million de couronnes norvégiennes

	1990	1991	1992	1993	1994	1995	1996	1997	
C.3.2. Ceded Premiums									C.3.2. Primes Cédées
C.3.2.1. Domestic Companies	6 416	5 637	5 775	6 529	6 169	5 141	4 199	4 498	C.3.2.1. Entreprises Nationales
C.3.2.2. (Foreign Controlled Companies)	1 139	1 009	820	1 052	833	708	679	724	C.3.2.2. (Entreprises Sous Contrôle Etranger)
C.3.2.3. Branches & Agencies of Foreign Cies	35	40	34	83	..	..	..	100	C.3.2.3. Succursales et Agences d'Ent. Etrangères
C.3.2. Total	6 451	5 677	5 816	6 612	..	..	4 243	4 598	C.3.2. Total
C.3.3. Net Written Premiums									C.3.3. Primes Nettes Emises
C.3.3.1. Domestic Companies	30 382	33 517	34 912	35 623	38 908	38 266	40 417	46 069	C.3.3.1. Entreprises Nationales
C.3.3.2. (Foreign Controlled Companies)	2 355	3 121	3 183	3 272	3 591	3 733	4 292	4 728	C.3.3.2. (Entreprises Sous Contrôle Etranger)
C.3.3.3. Branches & Agencies of Foreign Cies	292	292	315	303	..	..	403	645	C.3.3.3. Succursales et Agences d'Ent. Etrangères
C.3.3. Total	30 674	33 846	35 566	35 926	..	..	40 820	46 714	C.3.3. Total

D. NET WRITTEN PREMIUMS IN THE REPORTING COUNTRY IN TERMS OF DOMESTIC AND FOREIGN RISKS — D. PRIMES NETTES EMISES DANS LE PAYS DECLARANT EN RISQUES NATIONAUX ET ETRANGERS

	1990	1991	1992	1993	1994	1995	1996	1997	
D.1. Life									**D.1. Vie**
D.1.1. Domestic Risks									D.1.1. Risques Nationaux
D.1.1.1. Domestic Companies	11 831	..	..	..	..	..	..	..	D.1.1.1. Entreprises Nationales
D.1.1.3. Branches & Agencies of Foreign Cies	0	..	0	..	..	..	..	3	D.1.1.3. Succursales et Agences d'Ent. Etrangères
D.1.1. Total	11 831	..	..	..	..	..	..	..	D.1.1. Total des Primes Nettes Vie
D.1.3. Total									D.1.3. Total
D.1.3.1. Domestic Companies	11 831	15 083	15 538	15 862	19 255	18 893	19 542	24 939	D.1.3.1. Entreprises Nationales
D.1.3.2. (Foreign Controlled Companies)	0	227	339	281	434	468	550	705	D.1.3.2. (Entreprises Sous Contrôle Etranger)
D.1.3.3. Branches & Agencies of Foreign Cies	0	0	0	0	0	0	3	3	D.1.3.3. Succursales et Agences d'Ent. Etrangères
D.1.3. Total of Life Net Premiums	11 831	15 083	15 877	15 862	19 255	18 893	19 545	24 942	D.1.3. Total des Primes Nettes Vie
D.2. Non-Life									**D.2. Non-Vie**
D.2.3. Total									D.2.3. Total
D.2.3.1. Domestic Companies	18 551	18 400	19 374	19 761	19 653	19 373	20 875	21 130	D.2.3.1. Entreprises Nationales
D.2.3.2. (Foreign Controlled Companies)	2 355	2 868	2 844	2 991	3 157	3 265	3 742	4 023	D.2.3.2. (Entreprises Sous Contrôle Etranger)
D.2.3.3. Branches & Agencies of Foreign Cies	292	329	315	303	..	..	400	642	D.2.3.3. Succursales et Agences d'Ent. Etrangères
D.2.3. Total	18 843	18 729	19 689	20 064	..	..	21 275	21 772	D.2.3. Total des Primes Nettes Vie

E. BUSINESS WRITTEN ABROAD — E. OPERATIONS A L'ETRANGER

	1990	1991	1992	1993	1994	1995	1996	1997	
E.2. Non-Life									**E.2. Non-Vie**
E.2.1. Gross Premiums									E.2.1. Primes Brutes
E.2.1.1. Direct Business									E.2.1.1. Assurance Directe
E.2.1.1.1. Branches & Agencies	..	..	..	..	..	..	441	496	E.2.1.1.1. Succursales & Agences
E.2.1.1.2. Subsidiaries	..	..	..	..	..	..	368	402	E.2.1.1.2. Filliales
E.2.1.1. Total	..	..	..	..	..	..	809	898	E.2.1.1. Total
E.2.1.3. Total									E.2.1.3. Total
E.2.1.3.1. Branches & Agencies	..	..	..	..	..	..	441	496	E.2.1.3.1. Succursales & Agences
E.2.1.3.2. Subsidiaries	..	..	..	..	..	..	368	402	E.2.1.3.2. Filliales
E.2.1.3. Total Gross Premiums	..	..	..	..	..	..	809	898	E.2.1.3. Total des Primes Brutes

Monetary Unit: million Norwegian kroner

Unité monétaire : million de couronnes norvégiennes

F. OUTSTANDING INVESTMENT BY DIRECT INSURANCE COMPANIES

F. ENCOURS DES PLACEMENTS DES ENTREPRISES D'ASSURANCES DIRECTES

F.1. Life / F.1. Vie

	1990	1991	1992	1993	1994	1995	1996	1997
F.1.1. Real Estate — F.1.1. Immobilier								
F.1.1.1. Domestic Companies — F.1.1.1. Entreprises Nationales	8 157	8 841	9 726	10 330	12 461	14 459	18 191	19 347
F.1.1.2. (Foreign Controlled Companies) — F.1.1.2. (Entreprises Sous Contrôle Etranger)	0	0	2	9	132	264	265	385
F.1.1.4. Domestic Investment — F.1.1.4. Placement dans le Pays	8 157	..	9 726	..	..	..	..	..
F.1.1.5. Foreign Investment — F.1.1.5. Placement à l'Etranger	0	..	2	..	..	..	..	..
F.1.1. Total — F.1.1. Total	8 157	8 841	9 728	10 330	12 461	14 459	18 919	19 347
F.1.2. Mortgage Loans — F.1.2. Prêts Hypothécaires								
F.1.2.1. Domestic Companies — F.1.2.1. Entreprises Nationales	45 847	68 401	37 683	67 773	51 960	39 091	37 285	31 593
F.1.2.2. (Foreign Controlled Companies) — F.1.2.2. (Entreprises Sous Contrôle Etranger)	0	7	0	343	529	484	..	..
F.1.2.4. Domestic Investment — F.1.2.4. Placement dans le Pays	45 847	..	37 683	..	..	..	..	31 336
F.1.2.5. Foreign Investment — F.1.2.5. Placement à l'Etranger	0	..	0	..	..	..	..	257
F.1.2. Total — F.1.2. Total	45 847	68 408	37 683	67 773	51 960	39 091	37 285	31 593
F.1.3. Shares — F.1.3. Actions								
F.1.3.1. Domestic Companies — F.1.3.1. Entreprises Nationales	17 051	17 459	14 357	22 021	20 460	26 080	35 174	56 596
F.1.3.2. (Foreign Controlled Companies) — F.1.3.2. (Entreprises Sous Contrôle Etranger)	0	13	51	182	348	458	803	1 084
F.1.3.4. Domestic Investment — F.1.3.4. Placement dans le Pays	14 051	14 357	14 357	..	..	..	22 602	32 739
F.1.3.5. Foreign Investment — F.1.3.5. Placement à l'Etranger	3 000	..	51	..	..	..	12 572	23 857
F.1.3. Total — F.1.3. Total	17 051	17 472	14 408	22 021	20 460	26 080	35 174	56 596
F.1.4. Bonds with Fixed Revenue — F.1.4. Obligations								
F.1.4.1. Domestic Companies — F.1.4.1. Entreprises Nationales	59 639	63 454	71 014	95 616	102 724	125 200	121 368	140 055
F.1.4.2. (Foreign Controlled Companies) — F.1.4.2. (Entreprises Sous Contrôle Etranger)	0	657	1 580	1 511	1 594	2 287	3 803	4 578
F.1.4.4. Domestic Investment — F.1.4.4. Placement dans le Pays	59 385	..	71 014	..	..	..	88 910	96 508
F.1.4.5. Foreign Investment — F.1.4.5. Placement à l'Etranger	254	..	1 580	..	..	..	32 458	43 547
F.1.4. Total — F.1.4. Total	59 639	64 111	72 594	95 616	102 724	125 200	121 368	140 055
F.1.5. Loans other than Mortgage Loans — F.1.5. Prêts Autres qu'Hypothécaires								
F.1.5.1. Domestic Companies — F.1.5.1. Entreprises Nationales	19 073	..	36 219	0	11 030	13 624	13 002	14 257
F.1.5.2. (Foreign Controlled Companies) — F.1.5.2. (Entreprises Sous Contrôle Etranger)	..	..	335	0	0	0	..	..
F.1.5.4. Domestic Investment — F.1.5.4. Placement dans le Pays	19 072	..	36 219	..	..	..	..	..
F.1.5.5. Foreign Investment — F.1.5.5. Placement à l'Etranger	1	..	335	..	..	..	..	..
F.1.5. Total — F.1.5. Total	19 073	..	36 554	0	11 030	13 624	13 002	14 257
F.1.6. Other Investments — F.1.6. Autres Placements								
F.1.6.1. Domestic Companies — F.1.6.1. Entreprises Nationales	15 690	19 617	17 193	13 548	20 496	18 324	26 381	21 326
F.1.6.2. (Foreign Controlled Companies) — F.1.6.2. (Entreprises Sous Contrôle Etranger)	0	229	368	127	366	312	831	..
F.1.6.4. Domestic Investment — F.1.6.4. Placement dans le Pays	15 690	..	17 193	..	..	..	..	..
F.1.6.5. Foreign Investment — F.1.6.5. Placement à l'Etranger	0	..	368	..	..	..	..	..
F.1.6. Total — F.1.6. Total	15 690	19 846	17 561	13 548	20 496	18 324	26 381	21 326
F.1.7. Total — F.1.7. Total								
F.1.7.1. Domestic Companies — F.1.7.1. Entreprises Nationales	165 457	177 772	186 192	209 288	219 131	236 778	251 401	283 174
F.1.7.2. (Foreign Controlled Companies) — F.1.7.2. (Entreprises Sous Contrôle Etranger)	0	906	2 336	2 172	2 969	3 805	4 871	6 878
F.1.7.4. Domestic Investment — F.1.7.4. Placement dans le Pays	162 202	..	186 192	..	..	..	..	..
F.1.7.5. Foreign Investment — F.1.7.5. Placement à l'Etranger	3 255	..	2 336	..	..	..	..	..
F.1.7. Total of Life Investments — F.1.7. Total des Placements Vie	165 457	178 678	188 528	209 288	219 131	236 778	251 401	283 174

F.2. Non-Life / F.2. Non-Vie

	1990	1991	1992	1993	1994	1995	1996	1997
F.2.1. Real Estate — F.2.1. Immobilier								
F.2.1.1. Domestic Companies — F.2.1.1. Entreprises Nationales	2 810	2 618	2 939	2 767	2 756	3 227	3 069	3 719
F.2.1.2. (Foreign Controlled Companies) — F.2.1.2. (Entreprises Sous Contrôle Etranger)	168	296	279	274	484	474	461	470
F.2.1.4. Domestic Investment — F.2.1.4. Placement dans le Pays	2 978	..	3 218	..	..	..	..	..
F.2.1. Total — F.2.1. Total	2 978	2 914	3 218	2 767	2 756	3 227	3 069	3 719
F.2.2. Mortgage Loans — F.2.2. Prêts Hypothécaires								
F.2.2.1. Domestic Companies — F.2.2.1. Entreprises Nationales	2 796	1 814	2 824	3 352	3 628	3 585	4 269	3 925
F.2.2.2. (Foreign Controlled Companies) — F.2.2.2. (Entreprises Sous Contrôle Etranger)	0	0	0	518	655	533	1 180	1 448
F.2.2.4. Domestic Investment — F.2.2.4. Placement dans le Pays	2 796	..	2 824	2 974	..	..	..	..
F.2.2.5. Foreign Investment — F.2.2.5. Placement à l'Etranger	0	..	0	378	..	..	..	..
F.2.2. Total — F.2.2. Total	2 796	1 814	2 824	3 352	3 628	3 585	4 269	3 925

Monetary Unit: million Norwegian kroner — Unité monétaire : million de couronnes norvégiennes

	1990	1991	1992	1993	1994	1995	1996	1997	
F.2.3. Shares									**F.2.3. Actions**
F.2.3.1. Domestic Companies	5348	7303	5620	8804	11211	12821	13224	19037	F.2.3.1. Entreprises Nationales
F.2.3.2. (Foreign Controlled Companies)	953	927	554	1600	2075	2319	2640	3211	F.2.3.2. (Entreprises Sous Contrôle Etranger)
F.2.3.4. Domestic Investment	5064	..	4507	5979	..	..	..	12604	F.2.3.4. Placement dans le Pays
F.2.3.5. Foreign Investment	1237	8230	1667	2825	..	..	..	6433	F.2.3.5. Placement à l' Etranger
F.2.3. Total	6301	8230	6174	8804	..	..	13224	19037	F.2.3. Total
F.2.4. Bonds with Fixed Revenue									**F.2.4. Obligations**
F.2.4.1. Domestic Companies	9033	12358	12347	20529	17712	30260	31269	33570	F.2.4.1. Entreprises Nationales
F.2.4.2. (Foreign Controlled Companies)	2223	1967	2546	3334	3100	3849	4321	4220	F.2.4.2. (Entreprises Sous Contrôle Etranger)
F.2.4.4. Domestic Investment	9107	..	11502	14616	..	..	..	..	F.2.4.4. Placement dans le Pays
F.2.4.5. Foreign Investment	2149	..	3391	5913	..	..	..	..	F.2.4.5. Placement à l' Etranger
F.2.4. Total	11256	14325	14893	20529	..	..	31269	33570	F.2.4. Total
F.2.5. Loans other than Mortgage Loans									**F.2.5. Prêts Autres qu'Hypothécaires**
F.2.5.1. Domestic Companies	1865	2203	4363	1379	2440	441	334	330	F.2.5.1. Entreprises Nationales
F.2.5.2. (Foreign Controlled Companies)	0	0	624	82	29	0	1	70	F.2.5.2. (Entreprises Sous Contrôle Etranger)
F.2.5.4. Domestic Investment	1865	2203	4987	1379	..	..	..	330	F.2.5.4. Placement dans le Pays
F.2.5. Total	1865	2203	4987	1379	..	..	334	330	F.2.5. Total
F.2.6. Other Investments									**F.2.6. Autres Placements**
F.2.6.1. Domestic Companies	15967	15226	13162	20393	19575	18319	16438	17378	F.2.6.1. Entreprises Nationales
F.2.6.2. (Foreign Controlled Companies)	1558	1721	1909	1482	1374	1444	1811	136	F.2.6.2. (Entreprises Sous Contrôle Etranger)
F.2.6.4. Domestic Investment	17525	16947	15071	20393	..	..	..	..	F.2.6.4. Placement dans le Pays
F.2.6. Total	17525	16947	15071	20393	..	..	16438	17378	F.2.6. Total
F.2.7. Total									**F.2.7. Total**
F.2.7.1. Domestic Companies	37819	41522	41255	57224	56722	68653	68603	77959	F.2.7.1. Entreprises Nationales
F.2.7.2. (Foreign Controlled Companies)	4902	4911	5912	7290	7717	8619	10414	9555	F.2.7.2. (Entreprises Sous Contrôle Etranger)
F.2.7.4. Domestic Investment	39335	..	..	..	..	..	..	..	F.2.7.4. Placement dans le Pays
F.2.7.5. Foreign Investment	3386	..	..	..	..	..	..	..	F.2.7.5. Placement à l' Etranger
F.2.7. Total of Non-Life Investments	42721	46433	47167	57224	..	..	68603	77959	F.2.7. Total des Placements Non-Vie

G. BREAKDOWN OF NON-LIFE PREMIUMS — **G. VENTILATIONS DES PRIMES NON-VIE**

	1990	1991	1992	1993	1994	1995	1996	1997	
G.1. Motor vehicle									**G.1. Assurance Automobile**
G.1.1. Direct Business									G.1.1. Assurances Directes
G.1.1.1. Gross Premiums	6543	6019	5929	6401	5725	7207	7506	7760	G.1.1.1. Primes Brutes
G.1.1.2. Ceded Premiums	188	162	173	223	76	145	149	128	G.1.1.2. Primes Cédées
G.1.1.3. Net Written Premiums	6355	5856	5756	6178	5649	7062	7357	7632	G.1.1.3. Primes Nettes Emises
G.1.2. Reinsurance Accepted									G.1.2. Réassurance Acceptée
G.1.2.1. Gross Premiums	77	79	..	..	..	..	..	..	G.1.2.1. Primes Brutes
G.1.2.2. Ceded Premiums	2	2	..	..	..	..	..	..	G.1.2.2. Primes Cédées
G.1.2.3. Net Written Premiums	75	77	..	..	..	..	..	..	G.1.2.3. Primes Nettes Emises
G.1.3. Total									G.1.3. Total
G.1.3.1. Gross Premiums	6620	6098	..	6401	..	..	7506	7760	G.1.3.1. Primes Brutes
G.1.3.2. Ceded Premiums	190	164	..	223	..	..	149	128	G.1.3.2. Primes Cédées
G.1.3.3. Net Written Premiums	6430	5933	..	6178	..	..	7357	7632	G.1.3.3. Primes Nettes Emises
G.2. Marine, Aviation									**G.2. Marine, Aviation**
G.2.1. Direct Business									G.2.1. Assurances Directes
G.2.1.1. Gross Premiums	4652	5644	4578	7503	7451	6110	6679	6451	G.2.1.1. Primes Brutes
G.2.1.2. Ceded Premiums	2238	2724	2109	3669	3894	3149	2374	2495	G.2.1.2. Primes Cédées
G.2.1.3. Net Written Premiums	2414	2920	2469	3834	3557	2961	4305	3956	G.2.1.3. Primes Nettes Emises
G.2.2. Reinsurance Accepted									G.2.2. Réassurance Acceptée
G.2.2.1. Gross Premiums	1676	1524	..	..	..	..	..	..	G.2.2.1. Primes Brutes
G.2.2.2. Ceded Premiums	1148	862	..	..	..	..	..	..	G.2.2.2. Primes Cédées
G.2.2.3. Net Written Premiums	528	662	..	..	..	..	..	..	G.2.2.3. Primes Nettes Emises
G.2.3. Total									G.2.3. Total
G.2.3.1. Gross Premiums	6327	7168	..	7503	..	..	6679	6451	G.2.3.1. Primes Brutes
G.2.3.2. Ceded Premiums	3387	3586	..	3669	..	..	2374	2495	G.2.3.2. Primes Cédées
G.2.3.3. Net Written Premiums	2940	3582	..	3834	..	..	4305	3956	G.2.3.3. Primes Nettes Emises

NORWAY

Monetary Unit: million Norwegian kroner

		1990	1991	1992	1993	1994	1995	1996	1997
G.3. Freight	**G.3. Fret**								
G.3.1. Direct Business	G.3.1. Assurances Directes								
G.3.1.1. Gross Premiums	G.3.1.1. Primes Brutes	..	..	278	285	312	335	..	1
G.3.1.2. Ceded Premiums	G.3.1.2. Primes Cédées	..	..	42	233	64	44	..	0
G.3.1.3. Net Written Premiums	G.3.1.3. Primes Nettes Emises	..	..	236	52	248	291	..	1
G.3.3. Total	G.3.3. Total								
G.3.3.1. Gross Premiums	G.3.3.1. Primes Brutes	..	..	..	285	..	..	..	1
G.3.3.2. Ceded Premiums	G.3.3.2. Primes Cédées	..	..	..	233	..	..	..	0
G.3.3.3. Net Written Premiums	G.3.3.3. Primes Nettes Emises	..	..	..	52	..	..	..	1
G.4. Fire, Property Damages	**G.4. Incendie, Dommages aux Biens**								
G.4.1. Direct Business	G.4.1. Assurances Directes								
G.4.1.1. Gross Premiums	G.4.1.1. Primes Brutes	7065	6052	6245	5963	5832	5766	6093	6199
G.4.1.2. Ceded Premiums	G.4.1.2. Primes Cédées	1419	1138	1102	1177	965	826	680	701
G.4.1.3. Net Written Premiums	G.4.1.3. Primes Nettes Emises	5646	4914	5143	4786	4867	4940	5413	5498
G.4.2. Reinsurance Accepted	G.4.2. Réassurance Acceptée								
G.4.2.1. Gross Premiums	G.4.2.1. Primes Brutes	1855	1157	..	..	..	..	..	..
G.4.2.2. Ceded Premiums	G.4.2.2. Primes Cédées	611	58	..	..	..	..	..	..
G.4.2.3. Net Written Premiums	G.4.2.3. Primes Nettes Emises	1244	1099	..	..	..	..	..	..
G.4.3. Total	G.4.3. Total								
G.4.3.1. Gross Premiums	G.4.3.1. Primes Brutes	8921	7209	..	5963	..	..	6093	5199
G.4.3.2. Ceded Premiums	G.4.3.2. Primes Cédées	2031	1196	..	1177	..	..	680	701
G.4.3.3. Net Written Premiums	G.4.3.3. Primes Nettes Emises	6890	6013	..	4786	..	..	5413	5498
G.5. Pecuniary Losses	**G.5. Pertes Pécuniaires**								
G.5.1. Direct Business	G.5.1. Assurances Directes								
G.5.1.1. Gross Premiums	G.5.1.1. Primes Brutes	202	175	139	115	94	91	70	80
G.5.1.2. Ceded Premiums	G.5.1.2. Primes Cédées	129	114	86	71	59	60	46	56
G.5.1.3. Net Written Premiums	G.5.1.3. Primes Nettes Emises	73	61	53	44	35	31	24	24
G.5.2. Reinsurance Accepted	G.5.2. Réassurance Acceptée								
G.5.2.1. Gross Premiums	G.5.2.1. Primes Brutes	81	39	..	..	..	..	..	..
G.5.2.2. Ceded Premiums	G.5.2.2. Primes Cédées	17	1	..	..	..	..	..	..
G.5.2.3. Net Written Premiums	G.5.2.3. Primes Nettes Emises	64	38	..	..	..	..	..	..
G.5.3. Total	G.5.3. Total								
G.5.3.1. Gross Premiums	G.5.3.1. Primes Brutes	283	214	..	115	..	..	70	80
G.5.3.2. Ceded Premiums	G.5.3.2. Primes Cédées	146	115	..	71	..	..	46	54
G.5.3.3. Net Written Premiums	G.5.3.3. Primes Nettes Emises	137	99	..	44	..	..	24	24
G.6. General Liability	**G.6. Responsabilité Générae**								
G.6.1. Direct Business	G.6.1. Assurances Directes								
G.6.1.1. Gross Premiums	G.6.1.1. Primes Brutes	736	834	691	672	613	647	694	737
G.6.1.2. Ceded Premiums	G.6.1.2. Primes Cédées	156	150	111	148	115	113	139	166
G.6.1.3. Net Written Premiums	G.6.1.3. Primes Nettes Emises	580	684	580	524	498	534	555	571
G.6.2. Reinsurance Accepted	G.6.2. Réassurance Acceptée								
G.6.2.1. Gross Premiums	G.6.2.1. Primes Brutes	116	113	..	..	..	..	..	..
G.6.2.2. Ceded Premiums	G.6.2.2. Primes Cédées	0	4	..	..	..	..	..	..
G.6.2.3. Net Written Premiums	G.6.2.3. Primes Nettes Emises	116	109	..	..	..	..	..	..
G.6.3. Total	G.6.3. Total								
G.6.3.1. Gross Premiums	G.6.3.1. Primes Brutes	852	947	..	672	..	..	694	737
G.6.3.2. Ceded Premiums	G.6.3.2. Primes Cédées	156	154	..	148	..	..	139	166
G.6.3.3. Net Written Premiums	G.6.3.3. Primes Nettes Emises	696	793	..	524	..	..	555	571
G.7. Accident, Health	**G.7. Accident, Santé**								
G.7.1. Direct Business	G.7.1. Assurances Directes								
G.7.1.1. Gross Premiums	G.7.1.1. Primes Brutes	918	1233	1919	1877	1827	1734	1837	2138
G.7.1.2. Ceded Premiums	G.7.1.2. Primes Cédées	102	136	246	313	227	165	139	176
G.7.1.3. Net Written Premiums	G.7.1.3. Primes Nettes Emises	816	1097	1673	1564	1600	1569	1698	1962
G.7.2. Reinsurance Accepted	G.7.2. Réassurance Acceptée								
G.7.2.1. Gross Premiums	G.7.2.1. Primes Brutes	59	76	..	..	..	..	..	..
G.7.2.2. Ceded Premiums	G.7.2.2. Primes Cédées	15	8	..	..	..	..	..	..
G.7.2.3. Net Written Premiums	G.7.2.3. Primes Nettes Emises	44	68	..	..	..	..	..	..
G.7.3. Total	G.7.3. Total								
G.7.3.1. Gross Premiums	G.7.3.1. Primes Brutes	977	1309	..	1877	..	..	1837	2138
G.7.3.2. Ceded Premiums	G.7.3.2. Primes Cédées	117	142	..	313	..	..	139	176
G.7.3.3. Net Written Premiums	G.7.3.3. Primes Nettes Emises	860	1167	..	1564	..	..	1698	1962

NORWAY

Monetary Unit: million Norwegian kroner
Unité monétaire : million de couronnes norvégiennes

	1990	1991	1992	1993	1994	1995	1996	1997
G.8. Others / G.8. Autres								
G.8.1. Direct Business / G.8.1. Assurances Directes								
G.8.1.1. Gross Premiums / Primes Brutes	832	1118	3318	1627	2887	1947	2141	2455
G.8.1.2. Ceded Premiums / Primes Cédées	153	177	1686	387	461	404	399	532
G.8.1.3. Net Written Premiums / Primes Nettes Emises	679	941	1632	1240	2426	1543	1742	1923
G.8.2. Reinsurance Accepted / G.8.2. Réassurance Acceptée								
G.8.2.1. Gross Premiums / Primes Brutes	375	311	:	:	:	:	:	:
G.8.2.2. Ceded Premiums / Primes Cédées	164	109	:	:	:	:	:	:
G.8.2.3. Net Written Premiums / Primes Nettes Emises	211	202	:	:	:	:	:	:
G.8.3. Total								
G.8.3.1. Gross Premiums / Primes Brutes	1206	1429		1627			2141	2455
G.8.3.2. Ceded Premiums / Primes Cédées	317	286		387			399	532
G.8.3.3. Net Written Premiums / Primes Nettes Emises	889	1143		1240			1742	1923
G.9. Treaty Reinsurance / G.9. Réassurance Obligatoire								
G.9.1. Direct Business / G.9.1. Assurances Directes								
G.9.1.1. Gross Premiums / Primes Brutes	:	:	2394	:	:	:	:	:
G.9.1.2. Ceded Premiums / Primes Cédées	:	:	246	:	:	:	:	:
G.9.1.3. Net Written Premiums / Primes Nettes Emises	:	:	2148	:	:	:	:	:
G.9.2. Reinsurance Accepted / G.9.2. Réassurance Acceptée								
G.9.2.1. Gross Premiums / Primes Brutes	:	:	:	2233	1081	678	253	277
G.9.2.2. Ceded Premiums / Primes Cédées	:	:	:	391	308	236	72	72
G.9.2.3. Net Written Premiums / Primes Nettes Emises	:	:	:	1842	773	442	181	205
G.9.3. Total								
G.9.3.1. Gross Premiums / Primes Brutes	:	:	:	2233			253	277
G.9.3.2. Ceded Premiums / Primes Cédées	:	:	:	391			72	72
G.9.3.3. Net Written Premiums / Primes Nettes Emises	:	:	:	1842			181	205
G.10. Total								
G.10.1. Direct Business / G.10.1. Assurances Directes								
G.10.1.1. Gross Premiums / Primes Brutes	20948	21075	25491	24443	24741	23837	25020	25821
G.10.1.2. Ceded Premiums / Primes Cédées	4385	4601	5801	6221	5861	4906	3926	4254
G.10.1.3. Net Written Premiums / Primes Nettes Emises	16563	16474	19690	18222	18880	18931	21094	21567
G.10.2. Reinsurance Accepted / G.10.2. Réassurance Acceptée								
G.10.2.1. Gross Premiums / Primes Brutes	4239	3299	:	2233	1081	678	253	277
G.10.2.2. Ceded Premiums / Primes Cédées	1957	1044	:	391	308	236	72	72
G.10.2.3. Net Written Premiums / Primes Nettes Emises	2282	2255	:	1842	773	442	181	205
G.10.3. Total								
G.10.3.1. Gross Premiums / Primes Brutes	25186	24374	25491	26676	25822	25273	26098	
G.10.3.2. Ceded Premiums / Primes Cédées	6344	5645	:	6612	6169	:	3998	4326
G.10.3.3. Net Written Premiums / Primes Nettes Emises	18842	18729	:	20064	19653	:	21275	21772
H. GROSS CLAIMS PAYMENTS / H. PAIEMENTS BRUTS DES SINISTRES								
H.1. Life / H.1. Vie								
H.1.1. Domestic Companies / Entreprises Nationales							12995	13947
H.1.2. (Foreign Controlled Companies) / (Entreprises Sous Contrôle Etranger)							152	136
H.1. Total							12995	13947
H.2. Non-Life / H.2. Non-Vie								
H.2.1. Domestic Companies / Entreprises Nationales							18214	20311
H.2.2. (Foreign Controlled Companies) / (Entreprises Sous Contrôle Etranger)							3120	3556
H.2.3. Branches & Agencies of Foreign Cies / Succursales et Agences d'Ent. Etrangères							304	664
H.2. Total							18518	20975

NORWAY

NORVEGE

Monetary Unit: million Norwegian kroner

Unité monétaire : million de couronnes norvégiennes

	1990	1991	1992	1993	1994	1995	1996	1997	
I. GROSS OPERATING EXPENSES									**I. DEPENSES BRUTES D'EXPLOITATION**
I.1. Life									**I.1. Vie**
I.1.1. Domestic Companies							2618	2631	I.1.1. Entreprises Nationales
I.1.2. (Foreign Controlled Companies)							53	69	I.1.2. (Entreprises Sous Contrôle Etranger)
I.2. Non-Life									**I.2. Non-Vie**
I.2.1. Domestic Companies							6021	5912	I.2.1. Entreprises Nationales
I.2.2. (Foreign Controlled Companies)							994	1151	I.2.2. (Entreprises Sous Contrôle Etranger)
J. COMMISSIONS									**J. COMMISSIONS**
J.2. Non-Life									**J.2. Non-Vie**
J.2.1. Direct Business									J.2.1. Assurance directe
J.2.1.1. Domestic Companies							563	474	J.2.1.1. Entreprises Nationales
J.2.1.2. (Foreign Controlled Companies)							99	119	J.2.1.2. (Entreprises Sous Contrôle Etranger)
J.2.1.3. Branches & Agencies of Foreign Cies							17	20	J.2.1.3. Succursales et Agences d'Ent. Etrangères
J.2.1. Total							580	494	J.2.1. Total des Primes Nettes Vie
J.2.3. Total									J.2.3. Total
J.2.3.1. Domestic Companies							563	474	J.2.3.1. Entreprises Nationales
J.2.3.2. (Foreign Controlled Companies)							99	119	J.2.3.2. (Entreprises Sous Contrôle Etranger)
J.2.3.3. Branches & Agencies of Foreign Cies							17	20	J.2.3.3. Succursales et Agences d'Ent. Etrangères
J.2.3. Total							580	494	J.2.3. Total

Monetary Unit: million zlotys   Unité monétaire : million de zlotys

	1990	1991	1992	1993	1994	1995	1996	1997	
A. NUMBER OF COMPANIES IN THE REPORTING COUNTRY									**A. NOMBRE D'ENTREPRISES DANS LE PAYS DECLARANT**
A.1. Life									**A.1. Vie**
A.1.1. Domestic Companies	..	..	..	6	9	13	15	21	A.1.1. Entreprises Nationales
A.1.2. (Foreign Controlled Companies)	..	..	..	5	5	6	6	11	A.1.2. (Entreprises Sous Contrôle Etranger)
A.1. All Companies	..	..	..	6	9	13	15	21	A.1. Ensemble des Entreprises
A.2. Non-Life									**A.2. Non-Vie**
A.2.1. Domestic Companies	..	..	..	22	21	27	29	29	A.2.1. Entreprises Nationales
A.2.2. (Foreign Controlled Companies)	..	..	..	4	4	5	9	10	A.2.2. (Entreprises Sous Contrôle Etranger)
A.2. All Companies	..	..	..	22	21	27	29	29	A.2. Ensemble des Entreprises
A.4. Reinsurance									**A.4. Réassurance**
A.4.1. Domestic Companies	..	..	..	0	0	0	1	1	A.4.1. Entreprises Nationales
A.4. All Companies	..	..	..	0	0	0	1	1	A.4. Ensemble des Entreprises
A.5. Total									**A.5. Total**
A.5.1. Domestic Companies	..	..	..	28	30	40	45	51	A.5.1. Entreprises Nationales
A.5.2. (Foreign Controlled Companies)	..	..	..	9	9	11	15	21	A.5.2. (Entreprises Sous Contrôle Etranger)
A.5. All Insurance Companies	..	..	..	28	30	40	45	51	A.5. Ensemble des Entreprises d'Assurances
B. NUMBER OF EMPLOYEES									**B. NOMBRE D'EMPLOYES**
B.1. Insurance Companies	..	..	..	..	..	26 211	25 762	25 902	B.1. Entreprises d'Assurances
B.2. Intermediaries	..	..	..	..	..	..	..	46 082	B.2. Intermediaires
B. Total	..	..	..	..	..	..	..	71 984	B. Total
C. BUSINESS WRITTEN IN THE REPORTING COUNTRY									**C. OPERATIONS CONCLUES DANS LE PAYS DECLARANT**
C.1. Life									**C.1. Vie**
C.1.1. Gross Premiums									C.1.1. Primes Brutes
C.1.1.1. Direct Business									C.1.1.1. Assurances Directes
C.1.1.1.1. Domestic Companies	..	..	..	887	887	1 538	2 342	3 407	C.1.1.1.1. Entreprises Nationales
C.1.1.1.2. (Foreign Controlled Companies)	..	..	..	..	10	216	559	1 127	C.1.1.1.2. (Entreprises Sous Contrôle Etranger)
C.1.1.1. Total	..	..	..	887	887	1 538	2 342	3 407	C.1.1.1. Total
C.1.1.3. Total									C.1.1.3. Total
C.1.1.3.1. Domestic Companies	..	..	..	887	887	1 538	2 342	3 407	C.1.1.3.1. Entreprises Nationales
C.1.1.3.2. (Foreign Controlled Companies)	..	..	..	10	68	216	559	1 127	C.1.1.3.2. (Entreprises Sous Contrôle Etranger)
C.1.1.3. Total Gross Premiums	..	..	..	887	887	1 538	2 342	3 407	C.1.1.3. Total des Primes Brutes
C.1.2. Ceded Premiums									C.1.2. Primes Cédées
C.1.2.1. Domestic Companies	..	..	..	..	1	2	7	39	C.1.2.1. Entreprises Nationales
C.1.2.2. (Foreign Controlled Companies)	..	..	..	..	1	2	7	39	C.1.2.2. (Entreprises Sous Contrôle Etranger)
C.1.2. Total	..	..	..	0	0	2	7	39	C.1.2. Total
C.1.3. Net Written Premiums									C.1.3. Primes Nettes Emises
C.1.3.1. Domestic Companies	..	..	..	887	887	1 536	2 335	3 368	C.1.3.1. Entreprises Nationales
C.1.3.2. (Foreign Controlled Companies)	..	..	..	10	67	214	553	1 088	C.1.3.2. (Entreprises Sous Contrôle Etranger)
C.1.3. Total	..	..	..	887	887	1 536	2 335	3 368	C.1.3. Total

Monetary Unit: million zlotys — Unité monétaire : million de zlotys

C.2. Non-Life / C.2. Non-Vie

	1990	1991	1992	1993	1994	1995	1996	1997
C.2.1. Gross premiums / Primes Brutes								
C.2.1.1. Direct Business / Assurances Directes								
C.2.1.1.1. Domestic Companies / Entreprises Nationales	..	..	..	..	..	4 020	5 811	8 756
C.2.1.1.2. (Foreign Controlled Companies) / (Entreprises Sous Contrôle Etranger)	..	..	..	..	..	..	174	699
C.2.1.1. Total	..	..	..	..	..	4 020	5 811	8 756
C.2.1.2. Reinsurance Accepted / Réassurance Acceptée								
C.2.1.2.1. Domestic Companies / Entreprises Nationales	..	..	..	..	..	25	36	147
C.2.1.2.2. (Foreign Controlled Companies) / (Entreprises Sous Contrôle Etranger)	..	..	..	..	..	..	2	4
C.2.1.2. Total	..	..	..	..	..	25	36	147
C.2.1.3. Total								
C.2.1.3.1. Domestic Companies / Entreprises Nationales	..	..	..	2 209	2 862	4 046	5 847	8 903
C.2.1.3.2. (Foreign Controlled Companies) / (Entreprises Sous Contrôle Etranger)	..	..	..	27	30	70	176	702
C.2.1.3. Total Gross Premiums / Total des Primes Brutes	..	..	..	2 209	2 862	4 046	5 847	8 903
C.2.2. Ceded Premiums / Primes Cédées								
C.2.2.1. Domestic Companies / Entreprises Nationales	..	..	..	834	1 132	1 381	2 022	3 022
C.2.2.2. (Foreign Controlled Companies) / (Entreprises Sous Contrôle Etranger)	..	..	..	15	18	33	67	211
C.2.2. Total	..	..	..	834	1 132	1 381	2 022	3 022
C.2.3. Net Written Premiums / Primes Nettes Emises								
C.2.3.1. Domestic Companies / Entreprises Nationales	..	..	..	1 375	1 730	2 664	3 825	5 881
C.2.3.2. (Foreign Controlled Companies) / (Entreprises Sous Contrôle Etranger)	..	..	..	12	13	37	108	491
C.2.3. Total	..	..	..	1 375	1 730	2 664	3 825	5 881

C.3. Total / C.3. Total

	1990	1991	1992	1993	1994	1995	1996	1997
C.3.1. Gross Premiums / Primes Brutes								
C.3.1.1. Direct Business / Assurances Directes								
C.3.1.1.1. Domestic Companies / Entreprises Nationales	..	..	..	..	..	..	8 154	12 163
C.3.1.1.2. (Foreign Controlled Companies) / (Entreprises Sous Contrôle Etranger)	..	..	..	..	..	..	733	1 825
C.3.1.1. Total	..	..	..	..	..	..	8 154	12 163
C.3.1.2. Reinsurance Accepted / Réassurance Acceptée								
C.3.1.2.1. Domestic Companies / Entreprises Nationales	..	..	..	..	..	..	36	147
C.3.1.2.2. (Foreign Controlled Companies) / (Entreprises Sous Contrôle Etranger)	..	..	..	..	..	..	2	4
C.3.1.2. Total	..	..	..	..	..	..	36	147
C.3.1.3. Total								
C.3.1.3.1. Domestic Companies / Entreprises Nationales	..	..	..	3 096	4 146	5 583	8 189	12 310
C.3.1.3.2. (Foreign Controlled Companies) / (Entreprises Sous Contrôle Etranger)	..	..	..	37	98	286	735	1 829
C.3.1.3. Total Gross Premiums / Total des Primes Brutes	..	..	..	3 096	4 146	5 583	8 189	12 310
C.3.2. Ceded Premiums / Primes Cédées								
C.3.2.1. Domestic Companies / Entreprises Nationales	..	..	..	..	1 133	1 383	2 029	3 061
C.3.2.2. (Foreign Controlled Companies) / (Entreprises Sous Contrôle Etranger)	..	..	..	..	19	35	74	250
C.3.2. Total	..	..	..	834	1 133	1 383	2 029	3 061
C.3.3. Net Written Premiums / Primes Nettes Emises								
C.3.3.1. Domestic Companies / Entreprises Nationales	..	..	..	2 262	3 013	4 200	6 160	9 249
C.3.3.2. (Foreign Controlled Companies) / (Entreprises Sous Contrôle Etranger)	..	..	..	22	80	251	661	1 579
C.3.3. Total	..	..	..	2 262	3 013	4 200	6 160	9 249

F. OUTSTANDING INVESTMENT BY DIRECT INSURANCE COMPANIES
F. ENCOURS DES PLACEMENTS DES ENTREPRISES D'ASSURANCES DIRECTES

F.1. Life / F.1. Vie

	1990	1991	1992	1993	1994	1995	1996	1997
F.1.1. Real Estate / Immobilier								
F.1.1.1. Domestic Companies / Entreprises Nationales	..	..	..	6	23	78	103	147
F.1.1.2. (Foreign Controlled Companies) / (Entreprises Sous Contrôle Etranger)	..	..	..	..	..	0	0	15
F.1.1.4. Domestic Investment / Placement dans le Pays	..	..	..	6	23	78	103	147
F.1.1. Total	..	..	..	6	23	78	103	147

	1990	1991	1992	1993	1994	1995	1996	1997
F.1.2. Mortgage Loans / Prêts Hypothécaires								
F.1.2.1. Domestic Companies / Entreprises Nationales			...	...	...	...	1	1
F.1.2.2. (Foreign Controlled Companies) / (Entreprises Sous Contrôle Etranger)			...	...	...	...	1	1
F.1.2.4. Domestic Investment / Placement dans le Pays			...	...	...	...	1	1
F.1.2. Total			...	...	...	...	1	1
F.1.3. Shares / Actions								
F.1.3.1. Domestic Companies / Entreprises Nationales			...	11	21	480	904	2 311
F.1.3.2. (Foreign Controlled Companies) / (Entreprises Sous Contrôle Etranger)			...	...	...	3	10	29
F.1.3.4. Domestic Investment / Placement dans le Pays			...	11	21	480	904	2 311
F.1.3. Total			...	11	21	480	904	2 311
F.1.4. Bonds with Fixed Revenue / Obligations								
F.1.4.1. Domestic Companies / Entreprises Nationales			...	249	900	1 355	2 245	2 975
F.1.4.2. (Foreign Controlled Companies) / (Entreprises Sous Contrôle Etranger)			...	2	29	119	431	1 062
F.1.4.4. Domestic Investment / Placement dans le Pays			...	249	900	1 355	2 245	2 971
F.1.4.5. Foreign Investment / Placement à l' Etranger						0	0	5
F.1.4. Total			...	249	900	1 355	2 245	2 975
F.1.5. Loans other than Mortgage Loans / Prêts Autres qu'Hypothécaires								
F.1.5.1. Domestic Companies / Entreprises Nationales			...	...	...	...	...	1
F.1.5.2. (Foreign Controlled Companies) / (Entreprises Sous Contrôle Etranger)			...	...	...	...	...	1
F.1.5.4. Domestic Investment / Placement dans le Pays			...	...	...	...	...	1
F.1.5. Total			...	...	...	...	...	1
F.1.6. Other Investments / Autres Placements								
F.1.6.1. Domestic Companies / Entreprises Nationales			...	324	231	189	372	573
F.1.6.2. (Foreign Controlled Companies) / (Entreprises Sous Contrôle Etranger)			...	14	23	29	71	169
F.1.6.4. Domestic Investment / Placement dans le Pays			...	324	231	189	372	573
F.1.6. Total			...	324	231	189	372	573
F.1.7. Total								
F.1.7.1. Domestic Companies / Entreprises Nationales			...	591	1 175	2 102	3 625	6 008
F.1.7.2. (Foreign Controlled Companies) / (Entreprises Sous Contrôle Etranger)			...	16	53	152	513	1 277
F.1.7.4. Domestic Investment / Placement dans le Pays			...	591	1 175	2 102	3 625	6 003
F.1.7.5. Foreign Investment / Placement à l' Etranger								5
F.1.7. Total of Life Investments / Total des Placements Vie			...	...	...	2 102	3 625	6 008
F.2. Non-Life / F.2. Non-Vie								
F.2.1. Real Estate / Immobilier								
F.2.1.1. Domestic Companies / Entreprises Nationales			...	50	78	140	180	221
F.2.1.2. (Foreign Controlled Companies) / (Entreprises Sous Contrôle Etranger)			...	...	...	...	1	12
F.2.1.4. Domestic Investment / Placement dans le Pays			...	50	78	140	180	221
F.2.1. Total			...	50	78	140	180	221
F.2.2. Mortgage Loans / Prêts Hypothécaires								
F.2.2.1. Domestic Companies / Entreprises Nationales			...	2	3	30	51	51
F.2.2.2. (Foreign Controlled Companies) / (Entreprises Sous Contrôle Etranger)			...	...	...	...	...	7
F.2.2.4. Domestic Investment / Placement dans le Pays			...	2	3	30	51	51
F.2.2. Total			...	2	3	30	51	51
F.2.3. Shares / Actions								
F.2.3.1. Domestic Companies / Entreprises Nationales			...	95	249	320	374	839
F.2.3.2. (Foreign Controlled Companies) / (Entreprises Sous Contrôle Etranger)			...	0	0	1	10	32
F.2.3.4. Domestic Investment / Placement dans le Pays			...	95	249	320	374	835
F.2.3.5. Foreign Investment / Placement à l' Etranger								4
F.2.3. Total			...	95	249	320	374	839
F.2.4. Bonds with Fixed Revenue / Obligations								
F.2.4.1. Domestic Companies / Entreprises Nationales			...	129	376	773	1 645	2 562
F.2.4.2. (Foreign Controlled Companies) / (Entreprises Sous Contrôle Etranger)			...	0	1	19	56	273
F.2.4.4. Domestic Investment / Placement dans le Pays			...	129	376	773	1 645	2 562
F.2.4. Total			...	129	376	773	1 645	2 562
F.2.5. Loans other than Mortgage Loans / Prêts Autres qu'Hypothécaires								
F.2.5.1. Domestic Companies / Entreprises Nationales			...	...	...	...	1	2
F.2.5.2. (Foreign Controlled Companies) / (Entreprises Sous Contrôle Etranger)			...	...	...	...	1	1
F.2.5.4. Domestic Investment / Placement dans le Pays			...	...	...	...	1	2
F.2.5. Total			...	...	...	...	1	2

Monetary Unit: million zlotys Unité monétaire : million de zlotys

	1990	1991	1992	1993	1994	1995	1996	1997	
F.2.6. Other Investments									F.2.6. Autres Placements
F.2.6.1. Domestic Companies				529	624	502	561	902	F.2.6.1. Entreprises Nationales
F.2.6.2. (Foreign Controlled Companies)				10	17	40	41	44	F.2.6.2. (Entreprises Sous Contrôle Etranger)
F.2.6.4. Domestic Investment				529	624	502	561	895	F.2.6.4. Placement dans le Pays
F.2.6.5. Foreign Investment				…	…	0	0	7	F.2.6.5. Placement à l' Etranger
F.2.6. Total				529	624	502	561	902	F.2.6. Total
F.2.7. Total									F.2.7. Total
F.2.7.1. Domestic Companies				804	1 331	1 765	2 813	4 577	F.2.7.1. Entreprises Nationales
F.2.7.2. (Foreign Controlled Companies)				11	18	61	109	370	F.2.7.2. (Entreprises Sous Contrôle Etranger)
F.2.7.4. Domestic Investment				804	1 331	1 765	2 813	4 566	F.2.7.4. Placement dans le Pays
F.2.7.5. Foreign Investment								11	F.2.7.5. Placement à l' Etranger
F.2.7. Total of Non-Life Investments				804	1 331	1 765	2 813	4 577	F.2.7. Total des Placements Non-Vie

G. BREAKDOWN OF NON-LIFE PREMIUMS / G. VENTILATIONS DES PRIMES NON-VIE

	1990	1991	1992	1993	1994	1995	1996	1997	
G.1. Motor vehicle									G.1. Assurance Automobile
G.1.1. Direct Business									G.1.1. Assurances Directes
G.1.1.1. Gross Premiums				…	…	2 225	3 464	5 714	G.1.1.1. Primes Brutes
G.1.1.2. Ceded Premiums				…	…	855	1 390	2 281	G.1.1.2. Primes Cédées
G.1.1.3. Net Written Premiums				…	…	1 369	2 074	3 433	G.1.1.3. Primes Nettes Emises
G.1.3. Total									G.1.3. Total
G.1.3.1. Gross Premiums				…	…	2 225	3 464	…	G.1.3.1. Primes Brutes
G.1.3.2. Ceded Premiums				…	…	855	1 390	…	G.1.3.2. Primes Cédées
G.1.3.3. Net Written Premiums				…	…	1 369	2 074	…	G.1.3.3. Primes Nettes Emises
G.2. Marine, Aviation									G.2. Marine, Aviation
G.2.1. Direct Business									G.2.1. Assurances Directes
G.2.1.1. Gross Premiums				…	…	130	123	124	G.2.1.1. Primes Brutes
G.2.1.2. Ceded Premiums				…	…	79	49	50	G.2.1.2. Primes Cédées
G.2.1.3. Net Written Premiums				…	…	51	74	74	G.2.1.3. Primes Nettes Emises
G.2.3. Total									G.2.3. Total
G.2.3.1. Gross Premiums				…	…	130	123	…	G.2.3.1. Primes Brutes
G.2.3.2. Ceded Premiums				…	…	79	49	…	G.2.3.2. Primes Cédées
G.2.3.3. Net Written Premiums				…	…	51	74	…	G.2.3.3. Primes Nettes Emises
G.3. Freight									G.3. Fret
G.3.1. Direct Business									G.3.1. Assurances Directes
G.3.1.1. Gross Premiums				…	…	55	75	91	G.3.1.1. Primes Brutes
G.3.1.2. Ceded Premiums				…	…	12	13	22	G.3.1.2. Primes Cédées
G.3.1.3. Net Written Premiums				…	…	43	62	69	G.3.1.3. Primes Nettes Emises
G.3.2. Reinsurance Accepted									G.3.2. Réassurance Acceptée
G.3.3.1. Gross Premiums				…	…	55	75	…	G.3.3.1. Primes Brutes
G.3.3.2. Ceded Premiums				…	…	12	13	…	G.3.3.2. Primes Cédées
G.3.3.3. Net Written Premiums				…	…	43	62	…	G.3.3.3. Primes Nettes Emises
G.4. Fire, Property Damage									G.4. Incendie, Dommages aux Biens
G.4.1. Direct Business									G.4.1. Assurances Directes
G.4.1.1. Gross Premiums				…	…	846	1 099	1 402	G.4.1.1. Primes Brutes
G.4.1.2. Ceded Premiums				…	…	345	440	481	G.4.1.2. Primes Cédées
G.4.1.3. Net Written Premiums				…	…	501	658	922	G.4.1.3. Primes Nettes Emises
G.4.3. Total									G.4.3. Total
G.4.3.1. Gross Premiums				…	…	846	1 099	…	G.4.3.1. Primes Brutes
G.4.3.2. Ceded Premiums				…	…	345	440	…	G.4.3.2. Primes Cédées
G.4.3.3. Net Written Premiums				…	…	501	658	…	G.4.3.3. Primes Nettes Emises
G.5. Pecuniary Losses									G.5. Pertes Pécunières
G.5.1. Direct Business									G.5.1. Assurances Directes
G.5.1.1. Gross Premiums				…	…	76	123	151	G.5.1.1. Primes Brutes
G.5.1.2. Ceded Premiums				…	…	6	11	30	G.5.1.2. Primes Cédées
G.5.1.3. Net Written Premiums				…	…	70	112	121	G.5.1.3. Primes Nettes Emises
G.5.3. Total									G.5.3. Total
G.5.3.1. Gross Premiums				…	…	76	123	…	G.5.3.1. Primes Brutes
G.5.3.2. Ceded Premiums				…	…	6	11	…	G.5.3.2. Primes Cédées
G.5.3.3. Net Written Premiums				…	…	70	112	…	G.5.3.3. Primes Nettes Emises

POLAND

Monetary Unit: million zlotys

	1990	1991	1992	1993	1994	1995	1996	1997	
G.6. General Liability									**G.6. Responsabilité Générale**
G.6.1. Direct Business									G.6.1. Assurances Directes
G.6.1.1. Gross Premiums				..	..	99	121	170	G.6.1.1. Primes Brutes
G.6.1.2. Ceded Premiums				..	..	11	15	26	G.6.1.2. Primes Cédées
G.6.1.3. Net Written Premiums				..	..	88	106	144	G.6.1.3. Primes Nettes Emises
G.6.3. Total									G.6.3. Total
G.6.3.1. Gross Premiums				..	..	99	121	..	G.6.3.1. Primes Brutes
G.6.3.2. Ceded Premiums				..	..	11	15	..	G.6.3.2. Primes Cédées
G.6.3.3. Net Written Premiums				..	..	88	106	..	G.6.3.3. Primes Nettes Emises
G.7. Accident, Health									**G.7. Accident, Santé**
G.7.1. Direct Business									G.7.1. Assurances Directes
G.7.1.1. Gross Premiums				..	..	550	756	1 058	G.7.1.1. Primes Brutes
G.7.1.2. Ceded Premiums				..	..	32	51	68	G.7.1.2. Primes Cédées
G.7.1.3. Net Written Premiums				..	..	518	704	990	G.7.1.3. Primes Nettes Emises
G.7.3. Total									G.7.3. Total
G.7.3.1. Gross Premiums				..	..	550	756	..	G.7.3.1. Primes Brutes
G.7.3.2. Ceded Premiums				..	..	32	51	..	G.7.3.2. Primes Cédées
G.7.3.3. Net Written Premiums				..	..	518	704	..	G.7.3.3. Primes Nettes Emises
G.8. Others									**G.8. Autres**
G.8.1. Direct Business									G.8.1. Assurances Directes
G.8.1.1. Gross Premiums				..	..	40	52	44	G.8.1.1. Primes Brutes
G.8.1.2. Ceded Premiums				..	..	40	50	43	G.8.1.2. Primes Cédées
G.8.1.3. Net Written Premiums				..	..	0	2	1	G.8.1.3. Primes Nettes Emises
G.8.3. Total									G.8.3. Total
G.8.3.1. Gross Premiums				..	..	40	52	..	G.8.3.1. Primes Brutes
G.8.3.2. Ceded Premiums				..	..	40	50	..	G.8.3.2. Primes Cédées
G.8.3.3. Net Written Premiums				..	..	0	2	..	G.8.3.3. Primes Nettes Emises
G.9. Treaty Reinsurance									**G.9. Réassurance Obligatoire**
G.9.2. Reinsurance Accepted									G.9.2. Réassurance Acceptée
G.9.2.1. Gross Premiums				..	..	25	36	147	G.9.2.1. Primes Brutes
G.9.2.2. Ceded Premiums				..	..	1	3	19	G.9.2.2. Primes Cédées
G.9.2.3. Net Written Premiums				..	..	25	33	128	G.9.2.3. Primes Nettes Emises
G.9.3. Total									G.9.3. Total
G.9.3.1. Gross Premiums				..	..	25	36	147	G.9.3.1. Primes Brutes
G.9.3.2. Ceded Premiums				..	..	1	3	19	G.9.3.2. Primes Cédées
G.9.3.3. Net Written Premiums				..	..	25	33	128	G.9.3.3. Primes Nettes Emises
G.10. Total									**G.10. Total**
G.10.1. Direct Business									G.10.1. Assurances Directes
G.10.1.1. Gross Premiums				..	..	4 020	5 811	8 756	G.10.1.1. Primes Brutes
G.10.1.2. Ceded Premiums				..	..	1 380	2 019	3 002	G.10.1.2. Primes Cédées
G.10.1.3. Net Written Premiums				..	..	2 640	3 792	5 754	G.10.1.3. Primes Nettes Emises
G.10.2. Reinsurance Accepted									G.10.2. Réassurance Acceptée
G.10.2.1. Gross Premiums				..	..	25	36	147	G.10.2.1. Primes Brutes
G.10.2.2. Ceded Premiums				..	..	1	3	19	G.10.2.2. Primes Cédées
G.10.2.3. Net Written Premiums				..	..	25	33	128	G.10.2.3. Primes Nettes Emises
G.10.3. Total									G.10.3. Total
G.10.3.1. Gross Premiums				..	..	4 046	5 847	8 903	G.10.3.1. Primes Brutes
G.10.3.2. Ceded Premiums				..	..	1 381	2 022	3 022	G.10.3.2. Primes Cédées
G.10.3.3. Net Written Premiums				..	..	2 664	3 825	5 881	G.10.3.3. Primes Nettes Emises

H. GROSS CLAIMS PAYMENTS
H. PAIEMENTS BRUTS DES SINISTRES

H.1. Life
H.1. Vie

	1990	1991	1992	1993	1994	1995	1996	1997	
H.1.1. Domestic Companies					695	750	963	1 176	H.1.1. Entreprises Nationales
H.1.2. (Foreign Controlled Companies)					..	8	13	33	H.1.2. (Entreprises Sous Contrôle Etranger)
H.1. Total					695	750	963	1 176	H.1. Total

Monetary Unit: million zlotys   Unité monétaire : million de zlotys

H.2. Non-Life — H.2. Non-Vie

	1990	1991	1992	1993	1994	1995	1996	1997
H.2.1. Domestic Companies — H.2.1. Entreprises Nationales				2	1 670	2 364	3 271	5 256
H.2.2. (Foreign Controlled Companies) — H.2.2. (Entreprises Sous Contrôle Etranger)				..	7	18	34	358
H.2. Total				2	1 670	2 364	3 271	5 256

I. GROSS OPERATING EXPENSES — I. DEPENSES BRUITES D'EXPLOITATION

I.1. Life — I.1. Vie

	1990	1991	1992	1993	1994	1995	1996	1997
I.1.1. Domestic Companies — I.1.1. Entreprises Nationales				133	216	349	606	905
I.1.2. (Foreign Controlled Companies) — I.1.2. (Entreprises Sous Contrôle Etranger)				..	44	136	274	492
I.1. Total — I.1. Total des Primes Nettes Vie				133	216	349	606	905

I.2. Non-Life — I.2. Non-Vie

	1990	1991	1992	1993	1994	1995	1996	1997
I.2.1. Domestic Companies — I.2.1. Entreprises Nationales				497	707	1 081	1 468	2 048
I.2.2. (Foreign Controlled Companies) — I.2.2. (Entreprises Sous Contrôle Etranger)				..	9	27	71	258
I.2. Total				497	707	1 081	1 468	2 048

J. COMMISSIONS

J.1. Life — J.1. Vie

J.1.1. Direct Business — J.1.1. Assurance directe

	1990	1991	1992	1993	1994	1995	1996	1997
J.1.1.1. Domestic Companies — J.1.1.1. Entreprises Nationales				..	..	..	368	556
J.1.1.2. (Foreign Controlled Companies) — J.1.1.2. (Entreprises Sous Contrôle Etranger)				..	..	..	204	344
J.1.1. Total				..	..	..	368	556
J.1.3. Total								
J.1.3.1. Domestic Companies — J.1.3.1. Entreprises Nationales				..	..	..	368	556
J.1.3.2. (Foreign Controlled Companies) — J.1.3.2. (Entreprises Sous Contrôle Etranger)				..	..	..	204	344
J.1.3. Total of Life Net Premiums — J.1.3. Total				..	..	..	368	556

J.2. Non-Life — J.2. Non-Vie

J.2.1. Direct Business — J.2.1. Assurance directe

	1990	1991	1992	1993	1994	1995	1996	1997
J.2.1.1. Domestic Companies — J.2.1.1. Entreprises Nationales				..	..	..	406	648
J.2.1.2. (Foreign Controlled Companies) — J.2.1.2. (Entreprises Sous Contrôle Etranger)				..	..	..	18	86
J.2.1. Total — J.2.1. Total des Primes Nettes Vie				..	..	..	406	648
J.2.2. Reinsurance Accepted — J.2.2. Réassurances acceptées								
J.2.2.1. Domestic Companies — J.2.2.1. Entreprises Nationales				..	..	..	10	18
J.2.2. Total				..	..	..	10	18
J.2.3. Total								
J.2.3.1. Domestic Companies — J.2.3.1. Entreprises Nationales				..	..	..	416	666
J.2.3.2. (Foreign Controlled Companies) — J.2.3.2. (Entreprises Sous Contrôle Etranger)				..	..	..	18	86
J.2.3. Total				..	..	..	416	666

PORTUGAL

Monetary Unit: million escudos

	1990	1991	1992	1993	1994	1995	1996	1997
A. NUMBER OF COMPANIES IN THE REPORTING COUNTRY — **A. NOMBRE D'ENTREPRISES DANS LE PAYS DECLARANT**								
A.1. Life — **A.1. Vie**								
A.1.1. Domestic Companies — A.1.1. Entreprises Nationales	7	10	11	12	15	15	16	16
A.1.2. (Foreign Controlled Companies) — A.1.2. (Entreprises Sous Contrôle Etranger)	2	3	3	5	5	5	6	6
A.1.3. Branches & Agencies of Foreign Cies — A.1.3. Succursales et Agences d'Ent. Etrangères	10	11	13	14	14	15	14	15
A.1. All Companies — A.1. Ensemble des Entreprises	17	21	24	26	29	30	30	31
A.2. Non-Life — **A.2. Non-Vie**								
A.2.1. Domestic Companies — A.2.1. Entreprises Nationales	15	17	22	22	21	24	27	26
A.2.2. (Foreign Controlled Companies) — A.2.2. (Entreprises Sous Contrôle Etranger)	4	4	3	5	6	6	6	7
A.2.3. Branches & Agencies of Foreign Cies — A.2.3. Succursales et Agences d'Ent. Etrangères	23	29	32	32	34	32	29	33
A.2. All Companies — A.2. Ensemble des Entreprises	38	46	54	54	55	56	56	59
A.3. Composite — **A.3. Mixte**								
A.3.1. Domestic Companies — A.3.1. Entreprises Nationales	13	11	8	9	9	8	8	7
A.3.2. (Foreign Controlled Companies) — A.3.2. (Entreprises Sous Contrôle Etranger)	4	4	4	4	4	4	4	3
A.3.3. Branches & Agencies of Foreign Cies — A.3.3. Succursales et Agences d'Ent. Etrangères	1	1	1	1	1	0	0	1
A.3. All Companies — A.3. Ensemble des Entreprises	14	12	9	10	10	8	8	8
A.4. Reinsurance — **A.4. Réassurance**								
A.4.1. Domestic Companies — A.4.1. Entreprises Nationales	1	1	1	1	1	1	1	1
A.4. All Companies — A.4. Ensemble des Entreprises	1	1	1	1	1	1	1	1
A.5. Total — **A.5. Total**								
A.5.1. Domestic Companies — A.5.1. Entreprises Nationales	36	39	42	44	46	48	52	50
A.5.2. (Foreign Controlled Companies) — A.5.2. (Entreprises Sous Contrôle Etranger)	10	11	10	14	15	15	16	16
A.5.3. Branches & Agencies of Foreign Cies — A.5.3. Succursales et Agences d'Ent. Etrangères	34	41	46	47	49	47	43	49
A.5. All Insurance Companies — A.5. Ensemble des Entreprises d'Assurances	70	80	88	91	95	95	95	99
B. NUMBER OF EMPLOYEES — **B. NOMBRE D'EMPLOYES**								
B.1. Insurance Companies — B.1. Entreprises d'Assurances	14 726	14 176	14 941	14 592	14 008	14 037	13 677	14 578
B.2. Intermediaries — B.2. Intermediaires	42 736	43 329	42 907	43 176	44 202	44 987	41 766	41 842
B. Total — B. Total	57 462	57 505	57 848	57 768	58 210	59 024	55 443	56 420
C. BUSINESS WRITTEN IN THE REPORTING COUNTRY — **C. OPERATIONS CONCLUES DANS LE PAYS DECLARANT**								
C.1. Life — **C.1. Vie**								
C.1.1. Gross Premiums — C.1.1. Primes Brutes								
C.1.1.1. Direct Business — C.1.1.1. Assurances Directes								
C.1.1.1.1. Domestic Companies — C.1.1.1.1. Entreprises Nationales	53 544	70 619	101 726	144 356	195 427	306 567	393 192	395 632
C.1.1.1.2. (Foreign Controlled Companies) — C.1.1.1.2. (Entreprises Sous Contrôle Etranger)	5 728	7 867	11 321	26 311	48 723	...	40 864	43 946
C.1.1.1.3. Branches & Agencies of Foreign Cies — C.1.1.1.3. Succursales et Agences d'Ent. Etrangères	15 682	23 426	23 472	21 306	12 232	6 955	7 752	9 447
C.1.1.1. Total — C.1.1.1. Total	69 226	94 045	125 198	165 662	207 659	313 522	400 944	405 079
C.1.1.2. Reinsurance Accepted — C.1.1.2. Réassurance Acceptée								
C.1.1.2.1. Domestic Companies — C.1.1.2.1. Entreprises Nationales	19	25	143	24	28	74	617	792
C.1.1.2.2. (Foreign Controlled Companies) — C.1.1.2.2. (Entreprises Sous Contrôle Etranger)	0	10	124	0	0	...	0	...
C.1.1.2.3. Branches & Agencies of Foreign Cies — C.1.1.2.3. Succursales et Agences d'Ent. Etrangères	0	0	0	105	0	0	0	...
C.1.1.2. Total — C.1.1.2. Total	19	25	143	129	28	74	617	792
C.1.1.3. Total — C.1.1.3. Total								
C.1.1.3.1. Domestic Companies — C.1.1.3.1. Entreprises Nationales	53 563	70 644	101 869	144 380	195 455	306 641	393 809	396 424
C.1.1.3.2. (Foreign Controlled Companies) — C.1.1.3.2. (Entreprises Sous Contrôle Etranger)	5 728	7 877	11 445	26 311	48 723	31 138	40 864	43 946
C.1.1.3.3. Branches & Agencies of Foreign Cies — C.1.1.3.3. Succursales et Agences d'Ent. Etrangères	15 682	23 426	23 472	21 411	12 232	6 955	7 752	9 447
C.1.1.3. Total Gross Premiums — C.1.1.3. Total des Primes Brutes	69 245	94 070	125 341	165 791	207 687	313 596	401 561	405 871
C.1.2. Ceded Premiums — C.1.2. Primes Cédées								
C.1.2.1. Domestic Companies — C.1.2.1. Entreprises Nationales	2 733	3 225	2 689	3 456	4 047	6 817	7 289	6 690
C.1.2.2. (Foreign Controlled Companies) — C.1.2.2. (Entreprises Sous Contrôle Etranger)	144	87	73	676	963	715	1 888	1 904
C.1.2.3. Branches & Agencies of Foreign Cies — C.1.2.3. Succursales et Agences d'Ent. Etrangères	628	609	586	417	291	276	293	352
C.1.2. Total — C.1.2. Total	3 361	3 834	3 275	3 873	4 338	7 093	7 582	7 042

PORTUGAL

Monetary Unit: million escudos

Unité monétaire : million de escudos

	1990	1991	1992	1993	1994	1995	1996	1997
C.1.3. Net Written Premiums / Primes Nettes Emises								
C.1.3.1. Domestic Companies / Entreprises Nationales	50 830	67 419	99 180	140 924	191 408	299 824	386 520	389 734
C.1.3.2. (Foreign Controlled Companies) / (Entreprises Sous Contrôle Etranger)	5 584	7 790	11 372	25 635	47 760	30 423	38 976	42 042
C.1.3.3. Branches & Agencies of Foreign Cies / Succursales et Agences d'Ent. Etrangères	15 054	22 817	22 886	20 994	11 941	6 679	7 459	9 095
C.1.3. Total / Tota	65 884	90 236	122 066	161 918	203 349	306 503	393 979	398 829
C.2. Non-Life / Non-Vie								
C.2.1. Gross premiums / Primes Brutes								
C.2.1.1. Direct Business / Assurances Directes								
C.2.1.1.1. Domestic Companies / Entreprises Nationales	204 632	241 631	284 908	334 744	374 679	403 429	445 040	469 684
C.2.1.1.2. (Foreign Controlled Companies) / (Entreprises Sous Contrôle Etranger)	12 032	51 957	57 116	18 318	20 911	..	64 007	68 099
C.2.1.1.3. Branches & Agencies of Foreign Cies / Succursales et Agences d'Ent. Etrangères	16 412	19 076	21 374	26 402	13 978	2 791	3 107	3 436
C.2.1.1. Total / Total	221 044	260 707	306 282	361 146	388 657	406 220	448 147	473 120
C.2.1.2. Reinsurance Accepted / Réassurance Acceptée								
C.2.1.2.1. Domestic Companies / Entreprises Nationales	4 598	3 534	3 833	5 072	6 130	8 138	11 422	14 210
C.2.1.2.2. (Foreign Controlled Companies) / (Entreprises Sous Contrôle Etranger)	146	106	80	505	650	..	1 405	1 583
C.2.1.2.3. Branches & Agences of Foreign Cies / Succursales et Agences d'Ent. Etrangères	1 010	1 391	1 603	1 728	511	128	144	152
C.2.1.2. Total / Tota	5 608	4 925	5 436	6 800	6 641	8 266	11 566	14 362
C.2.1.3. Total								
C.2.1.3.1. Domestic Companies / Entreprises Nationales	209 230	245 165	288 741	339 816	380 809	411 567	456 462	483 894
C.2.1.3.2. (Foreign Controlled Companies) / (Entreprises Sous Contrôle Etranger)	12 178	52 063	57 196	18 823	21 561	60 708	65 412	69 682
C.2.1.3.3. Branches & Agences of Foreign Cies / Succursales et Agences d'Ent. Etrangères	17 422	20 467	22 977	28 130	14 489	2 919	3 251	3 588
C.2.1.3. Total Gross Premiums / Total des Primes Brutes	226 652	265 632	311 718	367 946	395 298	414 486	459 713	487 482
C.2.2. Ceded Premiums / Primes Cédées								
C.2.2.1. Domestic Companies / Entreprises Nationales	30 519	34 861	38 752	44 690	47 745	53 221	67 159	74 206
C.2.2.2. (Foreign Controlled Companies) / (Entreprises Sous Contrôle Etranger)	1 659	9 024	7 389	2 630	2 788	6 952	8 221	8 486
C.2.2.3. Branches & Agencies of Foreign Cies / Succursales et Agences d'Ent. Etrangères	3 300	3 720	4 309	5 333	2 140	761	1 054	1 128
C.2.2. Total	33 819	38 581	43 061	50 023	49 885	53 982	68 213	75 334
C.2.3. Net Written Premiums / Primes Nettes Emises								
C.2.3.1. Domestic Companies / Entreprises Nationales	178 711	210 304	249 989	295 126	333 064	358 346	389 303	409 688
C.2.3.2. (Foreign Controlled Companies) / (Entreprises Sous Contrôle Etranger)	10 519	43 039	49 807	16 193	18 773	53 756	57 191	61 196
C.2.3.3. Branches & Agencies of Foreign Cies / Succursales et Agences d'Ent. Etrangères	14 122	16 747	18 668	22 797	12 349	2 158	2 197	2 460
C.2.3. Total	192 833	227 051	268 657	317 923	345 413	360 504	391 500	412 148
C.3. Total								
C.3.1. Gross Premiums / Primes Brutes								
C.3.1.1. Direct Business / Assurances Directes								
C.3.1.1.1. Domestic Companies / Entreprises Nationales	258 176	312 250	386 634	479 100	570 106	709 996	838 232	865 316
C.3.1.1.2. (Foreign Controlled Companies) / (Entreprises Sous Contrôle Etranger)	17 760	59 824	68 437	44 629	69 634	..	104 871	112 045
C.3.1.1.3 Branches & Agencies of Foreign Cies / Succursales et Agences d'Ent. Etrangères	32 094	42 502	44 846	47 708	26 210	9 746	10 859	12 883
C.3.1.1. Total	290 270	354 752	431 480	526 808	596 316	719 742	849 091	878 199
C.3.1.2. Reinsurance Accepted / Réassurance Acceptée								
C.3.1.2.1 Domestic Companies / Entreprises Nationales	4 617	3 559	3 976	5 096	6 158	8 212	12 039	15 002
C.3.1.22. (Foreign Controlled Companies) / (Entreprises Sous Contrôle Etranger)	146	116	204	505	650	..	1 405	1 583
C.3.1.2.3. Branches & Agencies of Foreign Cies / Succursales et Agences d'Ent. Etrangères	1 010	1 391	1 603	1 833	511	128	144	152
C.3.1.2. Total	5 627	4 950	5 579	6 929	6 669	8 340	12 183	15 154
C.3.1.3. Total								
C.3.1.3.1. Domestic Companies / Entreprises Nationales	262 793	315 809	390 610	484 196	576 264	718 208	850 271	880 318
C.3.1.3.2. (Foreign Controlled Companies) / (En reprises Sous Contrôle Etranger)	17 906	59 940	68 641	45 134	70 284	91 846	106 276	113 628
C.3.1.3.3. Branches & Agencies of Foreign Cies / Succursales et Agences d'Ent. Etrangères	33 104	43 893	46 449	49 541	26 721	9 874	11 003	13 035
C.3.1.3. Total Gross Premiums / Total des Primes Brutes	295 897	359 702	437 059	533 737	602 985	728 082	861 274	893 353
C.3.2. Ceded Premiums / Primes Cédées								
C.3.2.1. Domestic Companies / Entreprises Nationales	33 252	38 086	41 441	48 146	51 792	60 038	74 448	80 896
C.3.2.2. (Foreign Controlled Companies) / (Entreprises Sous Contrôle Etranger)	1 803	9 111	7 462	3 306	3 751	7 667	10 109	10 390
C.3.2.3. Branches & Agencies of Foreign Cies / Succursales et Agences d'Ent. Etrangères	3 928	4 329	4 895	5 750	2 431	1 037	1 347	1 480
C.3.2. Total	37 180	42 415	46 336	53 896	54 223	61 075	75 795	82 376

Monetary Unit: million escudos

Unité monétaire : million de escudos

	1990	1991	1992	1993	1994	1995	1996	1997	
C.3.3. Net Written Premiums									C.3.3. Primes Nettes Emises
C.3.3.1. Domestic Companies	229 541	277 723	349 169	436 050	524 472	658 170	775 823	799 422	C.3.3.1. Entreprises Nationales
C.3.3.2. (Foreign Controlled Companies)	16 103	50 829	61 179	41 828	66 533	84 179	96 167	103 238	C.3.3.2. (Entreprises Sous Contrôle Etranger)
C.3.3.3. Branches & Agencies of Foreign Cies	29 176	39 564	41 554	43 791	24 290	8 837	9 656	11 555	C.3.3.3. Succursales et Agences d'Ent. Etrangères
C.3.3. Total	258 717	317 287	390 723	479 841	548 762	667 007	785 479	810 977	C.3.3. Total
E. BUSINESS WRITTEN ABROAD									**E. OPERATIONS A L'ETRANGER**
E.1. Life									**E.1. Vie**
E.1.1. Gross Premiums									E.1.1. Primes Brutes
E.1.1.1. Direct Business									E.1.1.1. Assurance Directe
E.1.1.1.1. Branches & Agencies	2 534	0	0	0	0	:	:	:	E.1.1.1.1. Succursales & Agences
E.1.1.1. Total	2 534	0	0	0	:	:	:	:	E.1.1.1. Total
E.1.1.3. Total									E.1.1.3. Total
E.1.1.3.1. Branches & Agencies	2 534	0	0	0	0	7	1 897	992	E.1.1.3.1. Succursales & Agences
E.1.1.3. Total Gross Premiums	2 534	0	0	0	:	:	:	992	E.1.1.3. Total des Primes Brutes
E.1.2. Ceded Premiums									E.1.2. Primes Cédées
E.1.2.1. Branches & Agencies	17	0	0	0	0	:	:	:	E.1.2.1. Succursales & Agences
E.1.2. Total	17	0	0	0	:	:	:	:	E.1.2. Total
E.1.3. Net Written Premiums									E.1.3. Primes Nettes Emises
E.1.3.1. Branches & Agencies	2 517	0	0	0	0	:	:	:	E.1.3.1. Succursales & Agences
E.1.3. Total	2 517	0	0	0	:	:	:	:	E.1.3. Total
E.2. Non-Life									**E.2. Non-Vie**
E.2.1. Gross Premiums									E.2.1. Primes Brutes
E.2.1.1. Direct Business									E.2.1.1. Assurance Directe
E.2.1.1.1. Branches & Agencies	1 332	1 475	1 467	1 916	2 229	:	:	:	E.2.1.1.1. Succursales & Agences
E.2.1.1. Total	1 332	1 475	1 467	1 916	:	:	:	:	E.2.1.1. Total
E.2.1.2. Reinsurance Accepted									E.2.1.2. Réassurance Acceptée
E.2.1.2.1. Branches & Agencies	16	10	15	13	169	:	:	:	E.2.1.2.1. Succursales & Agences
E.2.1.2. Total	16	10	15	13	:	:	:	:	E.2.1.2. Total
E.2.1.3. Total									E.2.1.3. Total
E.2.1.3.1. Branches & Agencies	1 348	1 485	1 482	1 929	2 398	3 759	6 117	6 302	E.2.1.3.1. Succursales & Agences
E.2.1.3. Total Gross Premiums	1 348	1 485	1 482	1 929	:	:	:	6 302	E.2.1.3. Total des Primes Brutes
E.2.2. Ceded Premiums									E.2.2. Primes Cédées
E.2.2.1. Branches & Agencies	189	250	261	306	449	:	:	:	E.2.2.1. Succursales & Agences
E.2.2. Total	189	250	261	306	:	:	:	:	E.2.2. Total
E.2.3. Net Written Premiums									E.2.3. Primes Nettes Emises
E.2.3.1. Branches & Agencies	1 159	1 235	1 221	1 623	1 949	:	:	:	E.2.3.1. Succursales & Agences
E.2.3. Total	1 159	1 235	1 221	1 623	:	:	:	:	E.2.3. Total
F. OUTSTANDING INVESTMENT BY DIRECT INSURANCE COMPANIES									**F. ENCOURS DES PLACEMENTS DES ENTREPRISES D'ASSURANCES DIRECTES**
F.1. Life									**F.1. Vie**
F.1.1. Real Estate									F.1.1. Immobilier
F.1.1.1. Domestic Companies	9 131	1 946	4 078	17 408	16 879	23 183	25 817	28 428	F.1.1.1. Entreprises Nationales
F.1.1.2. (Foreign Controlled Companies)	581	581	581	1 096	2 173	11 293	13 048	17 695	F.1.1.2. (Entreprises Sous Contrôle Etranger)
F.1.1.3. Branches & Agencies of Foreign Cies	2 944	3 267	2 530	2 220	1 513	536	553	0	F.1.1.3. Succursales et Agences d'Ent. Etrangères
F.1.1.4. Domestic Investment									F.1.1.4. Placement dans le Pays
F.1.1. Total	12 075	5 213	6 608	19 628	18 392	23 719	26 370	28 428	F.1.1. Total
F.1.2. Mortgage Loans									F.1.2. Prêts Hypothécaires
F.1.2.1. Domestic Companies	41	50	167	1 031	1 065	776	775	757	F.1.2.1. Entreprises Nationales
F.1.2.2. (Foreign Controlled Companies)	0	16	71	988	1 015	250	296	323	F.1.2.2. (Entreprises Sous Contrôle Etranger)
F.1.2.3. Branches & Agencies of Foreign Cies	106	132	339	238	145	178	158	0	F.1.2.3. Succursales et Agences d'Ent. Etrangères
F.1.2.4. Domestic Investment									F.1.2.4. Placement dans le Pays
F.1.2. Total	147	182	506	1 269	1 210	954	933	757	F.1.2. Total

Monetary Unit: million escudos

Item	1990	1991	1992	1993	1994	1995	1996	1997
F.1.3. Shares / F.1.3. Actions								
F.1.3.1. Domestic Companies / F.1.3.1. Entreprises Nationales	86 037	37 704	74 539	322 291	481 772	30 884	94 938	163 457
F.1.3.2. (Foreign Controlled Companies) / F.1.3.2. (Entreprises Sous Contrôle Etranger)	11 687	16 731	27 505	61 573	120 166	6 222	7 870	16 749
F.1.3.3. Branches & Agencies of Foreign Cies / F.1.3.3. Succursales et Agences d'Ent. Etrangères	24 648	38 959	42 342	44 010	21 210	554	835	1 633
F.1.3.4. Domestic Investment / F.1.3.4. Placement dans le Pays	110 685	76 663	116 881	366 301	502 982	31 438	95 773	165 090
F.1.3. Total / F.1.3. Total	110 685	76 663	116 881	366 301	502 982	31 438	95 773	165 090
F.1.4. Bonds with Fixed Revenue / F.1.4. Obligations								
F.1.4.1. Domestic Companies / F.1.4.1. Entreprises Nationales	..	..	..	..	..	393 419	554 356	671 107
F.1.4.2. (Foreign Controlled Companies) / F.1.4.2. (Entreprises Sous Contrôle Etranger)	..	..	..	..	..	106 801	149 329	172 751
F.1.4.3. Branches & Agencies of Foreign Cies / F.1.4.3. Succursales et Agences d'Ent. Etrangères	..	..	..	..	..	19 925	26 148	6 502
F.1.4. Total / F.1.4. Total	..	..	..	..	..	413 344	580 504	677 609
F.1.5. Loans other than Mortgage Loans / F.1.5. Prêts Autres qu'Hypothécaires								
F.1.5.1. Domestic Companies / F.1.5.1. Entreprises Nationales	430	81	76	342	749	532	1 314	1 375
F.1.5.2. (Foreign Controlled Companies) / F.1.5.2. (Entreprises Sous Contrôle Etranger)	9	0	0	261	574	312	329	307
F.1.5.3. Branches & Agencies of Foreign Cies / F.1.5.3. Succursales et Agences d'Ent. Etrangères	2 563	2 648	1 395	60	105	32	49	0
F.1.5.4. Domestic Investment / F.1.5.4. Placement dans le Pays	2 729	2 729	1 471	402	854	564	1 363	1 375
F.1.5. Total / F.1.5. Total	2 993	2 729	1 471	402	854	564	1 363	1 375
F.1.6. Other Investments / F.1.6. Autres Placements								
F.1.6.1. Domestic Companies / F.1.6.1. Entreprises Nationales	847	1 433	3 968	25 231	49 818	78 726	132 925	186 476
F.1.6.2. (Foreign Controlled Companies) / F.1.6.2. (Entreprises Sous Contrôle Etranger)	0	0	0	1 898	11 150	6 374	9 527	3 087
F.1.6.3. Branches & Agencies of Foreign Cies / F.1.6.3. Succursales et Agences d'Ent. Etrangères	14	1 228	2 147	4 237	817	1 308	697	35
F.1.6.4. Domestic Investment / F.1.6.4. Placement dans le Pays	861	2 661	6 115	29 469	50 635	80 034	133 622	186 511
F.1.6. Total / F.1.6. Total	861	2 661	6 115	29 469	50 635	80 034	133 622	186 511
F.1.7. Total								
F.1.7.1. Domestic Companies / F.1.7.1. Entreprises Nationales	96 486	41 214	82 828	366 303	550 283	527 520	810 125	1 051 600
F.1.7.2. (Foreign Controlled Companies) / F.1.7.2. (Entreprises Sous Contrôle Etranger)	12 268	17 328	28 157	65 816	135 078	131 252	180 399	210 912
F.1.7.3. Branches & Agencies of Foreign Cies / F.1.7.3. Succursales et Agences d'Ent. Etrangères	30 275	46 234	48 753	50 765	23 790	22 533	28 440	8 170
F.1.7.4. Domestic Investment / F.1.7.4. Placement dans le Pays	126 761	87 448	131 581	417 069	574 073	550 053	838 565	1 059 770
F.1.7. Total of Life Investments / F.1.7. Total des Placements Vie	126 761	87 448	131 581	417 069	574 073	550 053	838 565	1 059 770
F.2. Non-Life / F.2. Non-Vie								
F.2.1. Real Estate / F.2.1. Immobilier								
F.2.1.1. Domestic Companies / F.2.1.1. Entreprises Nationales	88 623	130 156	157 310	152 781	165 823	203 904	217 708	223 387
F.2.1.2. (Foreign Controlled Companies) / F.2.1.2. (Entreprises Sous Contrôle Etranger)	3 234	14 929	17 659	5 216	7 161	34 312	38 905	34 319
F.2.1.3. Branches & Agencies of Foreign Cies / F.2.1.3. Succursales et Agences d'Ent. Etrangères	2 998	4 583	5 259	5 533	1 666	1 312	1 284	1 369
F.2.1.4. Domestic Investment / F.2.1.4. Placement dans le Pays	91 621	134 739	162 569	158 314	167 489	205 216	218 992	224 756
F.2.1. Total / F.2.1. Total	91 621	134 739	162 569	158 314	167 489	205 216	218 992	224 756
F.2.2. Mortgage Loans / F.2.2. Prêts Hypothécaires								
F.2.2.1. Domestic Companies / F.2.2.1. Entreprises Nationales	485	1 180	1 129	2 024	3 963	3 444	3 334	4 907
F.2.2.2. (Foreign Controlled Companies) / F.2.2.2. (Entreprises Sous Contrôle Etranger)	0	274	461	0	0	94	108	427
F.2.2.3. Branches & Agencies of Foreign Cies / F.2.2.3. Succursales et Agences d'Ent. Etrangères	0	56	56	0	0	0	0	183
F.2.2.4. Domestic Investment / F.2.2.4. Placement dans le Pays	485	1 180	1 185	2 024	3 963	3 444	3 334	5 090
F.2.2. Total / F.2.2. Total	485	1 180	1 185	2 024	3 963	3 444	3 334	5 090
F.2.3. Shares / F.2.3. Actions								
F.2.3.1. Domestic Companies / F.2.3.1. Entreprises Nationales	144 764	259 655	314 423	237 648	275 737	61 240	74 692	182 503
F.2.3.2. (Foreign Controlled Companies) / F.2.3.2. (Entreprises Sous Contrôle Etranger)	2 628	46 340	51 043	10 208	16 126	6 167	7 809	12 348
F.2.3.3. Branches & Agencies of Foreign Cies / F.2.3.3. Succursales et Agences d'Ent. Etrangères	9 349	11 222	12 228	15 774	4 335	776	116	130
F.2.3.4. Domestic Investment / F.2.3.4. Placement dans le Pays	154 113	270 877	326 651	253 422	280 072	62 016	74 808	182 633
F.2.3. Total / F.2.3. Total	154 113	270 877	326 651	253 422	280 072	62 016	74 808	182 633
F.2.4. Bonds with Fixed Revenue / F.2.4. Obligations								
F.2.4.1. Domestic Companies / F.2.4.1. Entreprises Nationales	..	..	..	..	..	458 185	583 167	696 156
F.2.4.2. (Foreign Controlled Companies) / F.2.4.2. (Entreprises Sous Contrôle Etranger)	..	..	..	..	..	52 122	60 963	63 852
F.2.4.3. Branches & Agencies of Foreign Cies / F.2.4.3. Succursales et Agences d'Ent. Etrangères	..	..	..	..	..	1 614	2 246	28 562
F.2.4. Total / F.2.4. Total	..	..	..	..	..	459 799	585 413	724 718
F.2.5. Loans other than Mortgage Loans / F.2.5. Prêts Autres qu'Hypothécaires								
F.2.5.1. Domestic Companies / F.2.5.1. Entreprises Nationales	0	0	288	0	0	9 864	865	943
F.2.5.2. (Foreign Controlled Companies) / F.2.5.2. (Entreprises Sous Contrôle Etranger)	0	0	0	0	0	0	0	88
F.2.5.3. Branches & Agencies of Foreign Cies / F.2.5.3. Succursales et Agences d'Ent. Etrangères	..	0	0	0	0	..	..	..
F.2.5.4. Domestic Investment / F.2.5.4. Placement dans le Pays	0	0	288	0	0	9 864	865	1 031
F.2.5. Total / F.2.5. Total	0	0	288	0	0	9 864	865	1 031

Monetary Unit: million escudos

Unité monétaire : million de escudos

		1990	1991	1992	1993	1994	1995	1996	1997
F.2.6. Other Investments	**Autres Placements**								
F.2.6.1. Domestic Companies	F.2.6.1. Entreprises Nationales	2 160	1 129	14 404	12 169	25 325	386 175	419 026	437 096
F.2.6.2. (Foreign Controlled Companies)	F.2.6.2. (Entreprises Sous Contrôle Etranger)	0	0	1 685	375	280	7 361	5 343	4 898
F.2.6.3. Branches & Agencies of Foreign Cies	F.2.6.3. Succursales et Agences d'Ent. Etrangères	42	190	853	1 033	405	0	0	478
F.2.6.4. Domestic Investment	F.2.6.4. Placement dans le Pays	..	1 319	15 257	13 201	25 730	386 175	419 026	..
F.2.6. Total	F.2.6. Total	2 202	1 319	15 257	13 201	25 730	386 175	419 026	437 574
F.2.7. Total	**F.2.7. Total**								
F.2.7.1. Domestic Companies	F.2.7.1. Entreprises Nationales	236 032	392 120	487 554	404 622	470 848	1 122 812	1 298 792	1 544 992
F.2.7.2. (Foreign Controlled Companies)	F.2.7.2. (Entreprises Sous Contrôle Etranger)	5 862	61 543	70 848	15 799	23 567	100 056	113 128	155 844
F.2.7.3. Branches & Agencies of Foreign Cies	F.2.7.3. Succursales et Agences d'Ent. Etrangères	12 389	15 995	18 396	22 340	6 406	3 702	3 646	30 810
F.2.7.4. Domestic Investment	F.2.7.4. Placement dans le Pays	248 421	408 115	505 950	426 961	477 254	1 126 514	1 302 438	1 575 802
F.2.7. Total of Non-Life Investments	F.2.7. Total des Placements Non-Vie	248 421	408 115	505 950	426 961	477 254	1 126 514	1 302 438	1 575 802

G. BREAKDOWN OF NON-LIFE PREMIUMS
G. VENTILATIONS DES PRIMES NON-VIE

		1990	1991	1992	1993	1994	1995	1996	1997
G.1. Motor vehicle	**G.1. Assurance Automobile**								
G.1.1. Direct Business	G.1.1. Assurances Directes								
G.1.1.1. Gross Premiums	G.1.1.1. Primes Brutes	100 953	119 710	150 098	190 287	210 418	220 494	240 542	249 062
G.1.2. Reinsurance Accepted	G.1.2. Réassurance Acceptée								
G.1.2.1. Gross Premiums	G.1.2.1. Primes Brutes	86	187	179	266	300	277	256	358
G.1.3. Total	G.1.3. Total								
G.1.3.1. Gross Premiums	G.1.3.1. Primes Brutes	101 039	119 897	150 277	190 553	210 718	220 771	240 798	249 420
G.1.3.2. Ceded Premiums	G.1.3.2. Primes Cédées	2 833	3 748	3 844	5 671	5 577	6 443	7 360	8 494
G.1.3.3. Net Written Premiums	G.1.3.3. Primes Nettes Emises	98 206	116 149	146 433	184 882	205 141	214 328	233 438	240 926
G.2. Marine, Aviation	**G.2. Marine, Aviation**								
G.2.1. Direct Business	G.2.1. Assurances Directes								
G.2.1.1. Gross Premiums	G.2.1.1. Primes Brutes	3 287	3 846	4 143	4 885	4 976	6 331	7 199	6 824
G.2.2. Reinsurance Accepted	G.2.2. Réassurance Acceptée								
G.2.2.1. Gross Premiums	G.2.2.1. Primes Brutes	677	519	575	729	838	1 685	1 472	2 137
G.2.3. Total	G.2.3. Total								
G.2.3.1. Gross Premiums	G.2.3.1. Primes Brutes	3 964	4 365	4 718	5 614	5 814	8 016	8 671	8 961
G.2.3.2. Ceded Premiums	G.2.3.2. Primes Cédées	2 807	3 339	3 554	3 991	4 232	5 507	5 981	6 320
G.2.3.3. Net Written Premiums	G.2.3.3. Primes Nettes Emises	1 157	1 026	1 164	1 623	1 582	2 509	2 690	2 641
G.3. Freight	**G.3. Fret**								
G.3.1. Direct Business	G.3.1. Assurances Directes								
G.3.1.1. Gross Premiums	G.3.1.1. Primes Brutes	6 020	6 271	6 360	6 042	5 271	3 130	3 781	4 269
G.3.2. Reinsurance Accepted	G.3.2. Réassurance Acceptée								
G.3.2.1. Gross Premiums	G.3.2.1. Primes Brutes	177	224	394	415	255	3	10	4
G.3.3. Total	G.3.3. Total								
G.3.3.1. Gross Premiums	G.3.3.1. Primes Brutes	6 197	6 495	6 754	6 457	5 526	3 133	3 791	4 273
G.3.3.2. Ceded Premiums	G.3.3.2. Primes Cédées	2 901	3 002	3 124	2 606	2 641	1 495	1 996	2 337
G.3.3.3. Net Written Premiums	G.3.3.3. Primes Nettes Emises	3 296	3 493	3 630	3 851	2 885	1 638	1 795	1 936
G.4. Fire, Property, Damages	**G.4. Incendie, Dommages aux Biens**								
G.4.1. Direct Business	G.4.1. Assurances Directes								
G.4.1.1. Gross Premiums	G.4.1.1. Primes Brutes	33 198	40 131	42 559	47 675	49 175	52 092	62 367	68 258
G.4.2. Reinsurance Accepted	G.4.2. Réassurance Acceptée								
G.4.2.1. Gross Premiums	G.4.2.1. Primes Brutes	2 872	1 640	1 544	1 462	1 914	2 866	4 384	4 410
G.4.3. Total	G.4.3. Total								
G.4.3.1. Gross Premiums	G.4.3.1. Primes Brutes	36 070	41 771	44 103	49 137	51 089	54 958	66 751	72 668
G.4.3.2. Ceded Premiums	G.4.3.2. Primes Cédées	14 877	16 339	19 073	23 000	24 974	26 312	32 711	34 563
G.4.3.3. Net Written Premiums	G.4.3.3. Primes Nettes Emises	21 193	25 432	25 030	26 137	26 115	28 646	34 040	38 105
G.5. Pecuniary Losses	**G.5. Pertes Pécunières**								
G.5.1. Direct Business	G.5.1. Assurances Directes								
G.5.1.1. Gross Premiums	G.5.1.1. Primes Brutes	7 735	8 325	8 027	8 033	7 384	6 836	7 653	8 236
G.5.2. Reinsurance Accepted	G.5.2. Réassurance Acceptée								
G.5.2.1. Gross Premiums	G.5.2.1. Primes Brutes	683	842	940	1 106	1 330	1 470	1 121	1 186
G.5.3. Total	G.5.3. Total								
G.5.3.1. Gross Premiums	G.5.3.1. Primes Brutes	8 418	9 167	8 967	9 139	8 714	8 306	8 774	9 422
G.5.3.2. Ceded Premiums	G.5.3.2. Primes Cédées	5 148	5 449	5 164	5 013	4 622	4 535	5 570	6 310
G.5.3.3. Net Written Premiums	G.5.3.3. Primes Nettes Emises	3 270	3 718	3 803	4 126	4 092	3 771	3 204	3 112

Monetary Unit: million escudos / Unité monétaire : million de escudos

	1990	1991	1992	1993	1994	1995	1996	1997	
G.6. General Liability									G.6. Responsabilité Générale
G.6.1. Direct Business									G.6.1. Assurances Directes
G.6.1.1. Gross Premiums	3 323	4 020	4 772	5 490	5 553	5 939	6 835	7 350	G.6.1.1. Primes Brutes
G.6.2. Reinsurance Accepted									G.6.2. Réassurance Acceptée
G.6.2.1. Gross Premiums	119	110	115	290	214	334	316	307	G.6.2.1. Primes Brutes
G.6.3. Total									G.6.3. Total
G.6.3.1. Gross Premiums	3 442	4 130	4 887	5 780	5 767	6 273	7 151	7 657	G.6.3.1. Primes Brutes
G.6.3.2. Ceded Premiums	1 220	1 554	1 864	2 279	2 053	1 921	2 419	2 418	G.6.3.2. Primes Cédées
G.6.3.3. Net Written Premiums	2 222	2 576	3 023	3 501	3 714	4 352	4 732	5 239	G.6.3.3. Primes Nettes Emises
G.7. Accident, Health									G.7. Accident, Santé
G.7.1. Direct Business									G.7.1. Assurances Directes
G.7.1.1. Gross Premiums	66 175	77 782	89 493	97 712	104 808	110 082	118 056	127 194	G.7.1.1. Primes Brutes
G.7.2. Reinsurance Accepted									G.7.2. Réassurance Acceptée
G.7.2.1. Gross Premiums	166	349	308	357	444	399	2 048	3 701	G.7.2.1. Primes Brutes
G.7.3. Total									G.7.3. Total
G.7.3.1. Gross Premiums	66 341	78 131	89 801	98 069	105 252	110 481	120 104	130 895	G.7.3.1. Primes Brutes
G.7.3.2. Ceded Premiums	3 829	4 941	6 060	6 866	5 140	6 943	11 189	13 750	G.7.3.2. Primes Cédées
G.7.3.3. Net Written Premiums	62 512	73 190	83 741	91 203	100 112	103 538	108 915	117 145	G.7.3.3. Primes Nettes Emises
G.8. Others									G.8. Autres
G.8.1. Direct Business									G.8.1. Assurances Directes
G.8.1.1. Gross Premiums	353	622	830	1 022	1 072	1 316	1 714	1 927	G.8.1.1. Primes Brutes
G.8.2. Reinsurance Accepted									G.8.2. Réassurance Acceptée
G.8.2.1. Gross Premiums	828	1 054	1 381	2 175	1 346	1 232	1 959	2 259	G.8.2.1. Primes Brutes
G.8.3. Total									G.8.3. Total
G.8.3.1. Gross Premiums	1 181	1 676	2 211	3 197	2 418	2 548	3 673	4 186	G.8.3.1. Primes Brutes
G.8.3.2. Ceded Premiums	204	209	378	597	646	826	987	1 142	G.8.3.2. Primes Cédées
G.8.3.3. Net Written Premiums	977	1 467	1 833	2 600	1 772	1 722	2 686	3 044	G.8.3.3. Primes Nettes Emises
G.10. Total									G.10. Total
G.10.1. Direct Business									G.10.1. Assurances Directes
G.10.1.1. Gross Premiums	221 044	260 707	306 282	361 146	388 657	406 220	448 147	473 120	G.10.1.1. Primes Brutes
G.10.2. Reinsurance Accepted									G.10.2. Réassurance Acceptée
G.10.2.1. Gross Premiums	5 608	4 925	5 436	6 800	6 641	8 266	11 566	14 362	G.10.2.1. Primes Brutes
G.10.3. Total									G.10.3. Total
G.10.3.1. Gross Premiums	226 652	265 632	311 718	367 946	395 298	414 486	459 713	487 482	G.10.3.1. Primes Brutes
G.10.3.2. Ceded Premiums	33 819	38 581	43 061	50 023	49 885	53 982	68 213	75 334	G.10.3.2. Primes Cédées
G.10.3.3. Net Written Premiums	192 833	227 051	268 657	317 923	345 413	360 504	391 500	412 148	G.10.3.3. Primes Nettes Emises
H. GROSS CLAIMS PAYMENTS									**H. PAIEMENTS BRUTS DES SINISTRES**
H.1. Life									H.1. Vie
H.1.1. Domestic Companies				42 968	57 113	78 819	104 988	120 204	H.1.1. Entreprises Nationales
H.1.2. (Foreign Controlled Companies)				9 747	19 156	13 405	19 493	20 368	H.1.2. (Entreprises Sous Contrôle Etranger)
H.1.3. Branches & Agencies of Foreign Cies				7 950	4 593	3 105	3 005	3 254	H.1.3. Succursales et Agences d'Ent. Etrangères
H.1. Total				50 918	61 706	81 924	107 993	123 458	H.1. Total
H.2. Non-Life									H.2. Non-Vie
H.2.1. Domestic Companies				229 218	255 172	283 511	313 591	361 425	H.2.1. Entreprises Nationales
H.2.2. (Foreign Controlled Companies)				40 049	41 154	41 668	45 975	48 728	H.2.2. (Entreprises Sous Contrôle Etranger)
H.2.3. Branches & Agencies of Foreign Cies				17 610	10 078	1 994	2 088	2 510	H.2.3. Succursales et Agences d'Ent. Etrangères
H.2. Total				246 828	265 250	285 505	315 679	363 935	H.2. Total

PORTUGAL

Monetary Unit: million escudos — Unité monétaire : million de escudos

	1990	1991	1992	1993	1994	1995	1996	1997	
I. GROSS OPERATING EXPENSES									**I. DEPENSES BRUTES D'EXPLOITATION**
I.1. Life									**I.1. Vie**
I.1.1. Domestic Companies				14 022	15 324	19 350	22 594	26 229	I.1.1. Entreprises Nationales
I.1.2. (Foreign Controlled Companies)				4 207	4 569	5 200	6 336	5 824	I.1.2. (Entreprises Sous Contrôle Etranger)
I.1.3. Branches & Agencies of Foreign Cies				3 778	2 556	1 208	1 303	1 265	I.1.3. Succursales et Agences d'Ent. Etrangères
I.1. Total				17 800	17 880	20 558	23 897	27 494	I.1. Total des Primes Nettes Vie
I.2. Non-Life									**I.2. Non-Vie**
I.2.1. Domestic Companies				87 142	87 760	109 727	119 313	126 565	I.2.1. Entreprises Nationales
I.2.2. (Foreign Controlled Companies)				4 160	4 799	19 206	20 189	19 029	I.2.2. (Entreprises Sous Contrôle Etranger)
I.2.3. Branches & Agencies of Foreign Cies				8 585	3 264	1 035	1 060	1 040	I.2.3. Succursales et Agences d'Ent. Etrangères
I.2. Total				95 727	91 024	110 762	120 373	127 605	I.2. Total
J. COMMISSIONS									**J. COMMISSIONS**
J.1. Life									**J.1. Vie**
J.1.1. Direct Business									J.1.1. Assurance directe
J.1.1.1. Domestic Companies				4 765	5 595	:	5 284	7 786	J.1.1.1. Entreprises Nationales
J.1.1.2. (Foreign Controlled Companies)				1 541	1 577	:	3 899	3 222	J.1.1.2. (Entreprises Sous Contrôle Etranger)
J.1.1.3. Branches & Agencies of Foreign Cies				1 201	661	:	439	468	J.1.1.3. Succursales et Agences d'Ent. Etrangères
J.1.1. Total				5 966	6 256	:	5 723	8 254	J.1.1. Total
J.1.2. Reinsurance Accepted									J.1.2. Réassurances acceptées
J.1.2.1. Domestic Companies				6	9	:	:	:	J.1.2.1. Entreprises Nationales
J.1.2. Total				6	9	:	:	:	J.1.2. Total
J.1.3. Total									J.1.3. Total
J.1.3.1. Domestic Companies				4 771	5 604	:	:	:	J.1.3.1. Entreprises Nationales
J.1.3.2. (Foreign Controlled Companies)				1 541	1 577	:	:	:	J.1.3.2. (Entreprises Sous Contrôle Etranger)
J.1.3.3. Branches & Agencies of Foreign Cies				1 201	661	:	:	:	J.1.3.3. Succursales et Agences d'Ent. Etrangères
J.1.3. Total of Life Net Premiums				5 972	6 265	:	:	:	J.1.3. Total
J.2. Non-Life									**J.2. Non-Vie**
J.2.1. Direct Business									J.2.1. Assurance directe
J.2.1.1. Domestic Companies				29 813	33 836	:	32 063	37 050	J.2.1.1. Entreprises Nationales
J.2.1.2. (Foreign Controlled Companies)				1 809	2 276	:	8 624	10 515	J.2.1.2. (Entreprises Sous Contrôle Etranger)
J.2.1.3. Branches & Agencies of Foreign Cies				2 906	1 279	:	276	344	J.2.1.3. Succursales et Agences d'Ent. Etrangères
J.2.1. Total				32 719	35 115	:	32 339	37 394	J.2.1. Total des Primes Nettes Vie
J.2.2. Reinsurance Accepted									J.2.2. Réassurances acceptées
J.2.2.1. Domestic Companies				1 039	1 191	:	:	:	J.2.2.1. Entreprises Nationales
J.2.2.2. (Foreign Controlled Companies)				17	8	:	:	:	J.2.2.2. (Entreprises Sous Contrôle Etranger)
J.2.2.3. Branches & Agencies of Foreign Cies				126	49	:	:	:	J.2.2.3. Succursales et Agences d'Ent. Etrangères
J.2.2. Total				1 165	1 240	:	:	:	J.2.2. Total
J.2.3. Total									J.2.3. Total
J.2.3.1. Domestic Companies				30 852	35 027	:	:	:	J.2.3.1. Entreprises Nationales
J.2.3.2. (Foreign Controlled Companies)				1 826	2 284	:	:	:	J.2.3.2. (Entreprises Sous Contrôle Etranger)
J.2.3.3. Branches & Agencies of Foreign Cies				3 032	1 328	:	:	:	J.2.3.3. Succursales et Agences d'Ent. Etrangères
J.2.3. Total				33 884	36 355	:	:	:	J.2.3. Total

Monetary Unit: million pesetas

Unité monétaire : million de pesetas

A. NUMBER OF COMPANIES IN THE REPORTING COUNTRY / A. NOMBRE D'ENTREPRISES DANS LE PAYS DECLARANT

Item / Poste	1990	1991	1992	1993	1994	1995	1996	1997
A.1. Life / A.1. Vie								
A.1.1. Domestic Companies / Entreprises Nationales	66	68	63	56	57	56	56	54
A.1.2. (Foreign Controlled Companies) / (Entreprises Sous Contrôle Etranger)	17	18	18	19	18	18	17	13
A.1.3. Branches & Agencies of Foreign Cies / Succursales et Agences d'Ent. Etrangères	6	7	5	5	5	5	2	3
A.1. All Companies / Ensemble des Entreprises	72	75	68	61	62	59	58	57
A.2. Non-Life / A.2. Non-Vie								
A.2.1. Domestic Companies / Entreprises Nationales	273	314	291	278	261	244	238	228
A.2.2. (Foreign Controlled Companies) / (Entreprises Sous Contrôle Etranger)	25	31	33	30	28	30	27	25
A.2.3. Branches & Agencies of Foreign Cies / Succursales et Agences d'Ent. Etrangères	21	24	24	21	17	10	8	8
A.2. All Companies / Ensemble des Entreprises	294	338	315	299	278	254	246	236
A.3. Composite / A.3. Mixte								
A.3.1. Domestic Companies / Entreprises Nationales	127	82	82	81	73	71	66	65
A.3.2. (Foreign Controlled Companies) / (Entreprises Sous Contrôle Etranger)	25	28	29	32	26	24	24	19
A.3.3. Branches & Agencies of Foreign Cies / Succursales et Agences d'Ent. Etrangères	4	2	2	2	2	2	2	2
A.3. All Companies / Ensemble des Entreprises	131	84	84	83	75	73	68	67
A.4. Reinsurance / A.4. Réassurance								
A.4.1. Domestic Companies / Entreprises Nationales	8	7	6	6	5	5	5	4
A.4.3. Branches & Agencies of Foreign Cies / Succursales et Agences d'Ent. Etrangères	1	1	1	1	1	1	0	..
A.4. All Companies / Ensemble des Entreprises	9	8	7	7	6	6	5	4
A.5. Total								
A.5.1. Domestic Companies / Entreprises Nationales	474	471	442	421	396	376	365	351
A.5.2. (Foreign Controlled Companies) / (Entreprises Sous Contrôle Etranger)	67	77	80	81	72	72	68	57
A.5.3. Branches & Agencies of Foreign Cies / Succursales et Agences d'Ent. Etrangères	32	34	32	29	25	16	12	13
A.5. All Insurance Companies / Ensemble des Entreprises d'Assurances	506	505	474	450	421	392	377	364

B. NUMBER OF EMPLOYEES / B. NOMBRE D'EMPLOYES

Item / Poste	1990	1991	1992	1993	1994	1995	1996	1997
B.1. Insurance Companies / Entreprises d'Assurances	42 895	46 292	46 803	44 570	45 851	47 773	48 269	40 852
B.2. Intermediaries / Intermediaires	27 176	..	..	21 132	19 173	17 603	16 296	..
B. Total	70 071	..	..	65 702	65 024	65 376	64 565	..

C. BUSINESS WRITTEN IN THE REPORTING COUNTRY / C. OPERATIONS CONCLUES DANS LE PAYS DECLARANT

Item / Poste	1990	1991	1992	1993	1994	1995	1996	1997
C.1. Life / C.1. Vie								
C.1.1. Gross Premiums / Primes Brutes								
C.1.1.1. Direct Business / Assurances Directes								
C.1.1.1.1 Domestic Companies / Entreprises Nationales	509 304	722 627	760 297	830 007	1 338 439	1 322 217	1 569 674	1 838 247
C.1.1.1.2. (Foreign Controlled Companies) / (En reprises Sous Contrôle Etranger)	50 775	86 667	...	188 973	177 865	317 388	289 012	322 055
C.1.1.1.3 Branches & Agencies of Foreign Cies / Succursales et Agences d'Ent. Etrangères	37 617	44 340	51 481	48 295	103 141	50 384	65 973	69 690
C.1.1.1. Total	546 921	766 967	811 778	878 302	1 441 580	1 372 601	1 635 647	1 907 937
C.1.1.2. Reinsurance Accepted / Réassurance Acceptée								
C.1.1.2.1. Domestic Companies / Entreprises Nationales	5 406	3 846	5 022	5 570	6 605	8 711	8 554	13 087
C.1.1.2.2. (Foreign Controlled Companies) / (Entreprises Sous Contrôle Etranger)	1 451	30	..	2 161	538	716	499	277
C.1.1.2.3. Branches & Agencies of Foreign Cies / Succursales et Agences d'Ent. Etrangères	546	587	- 57	452	- 228	259	- 1 320	0
C.1.1.2. Total	5 952	4 433	4 965	6 022	6 377	8 970	7 234	13 087
C.1.1.3. Total								
C.1.1.3.1. Domestic Companies / Entreprises Nationales	514 710	726 473	765 319	835 577	1 345 044	1 330 928	1 578 228	1 851 334
C.1.1.3.2. (Foreign Controlled Companies) / (Entreprises Sous Contrôle Etranger)	52 226	86 697	...	191 134	178 403	318 104	289 511	322 332
C.1.1.3.3. Branches & Agencies of Foreign Cies / Succursales et Agences d'Ent. Etrangères	38 163	44 927	51 424	48 747	102 913	50 643	64 653	69 690
C.1.1.3. Total Gross Premiums / Total des Primes Brutes	552 873	771 400	816 743	884 324	1 447 957	1 381 571	1 642 881	1 921 024
C.1.2. Ceded Premiums / Primes Cédées								
C.1.2.1. Domestic Companies / Entreprises Nationales	17 384	18 350	22 244	24 382	25 196	31 584	34 849	33 118
C.1.2.2. (Foreign Controlled Companies) / (Entreprises Sous Contrôle Etranger)	4 989	7 578		14 153	8 595	11 389	11 787	8 770
C.1.2.3. Branches & Agencies of Foreign Cies / Succursales et Agences d'Ent. Etrangères	1 415	1 600	2 955	4 256	5 780	4 854	3 236	588
C.1.2. Total	18 799	19 950	25 199	28 638	30 976	36 438	38 085	33 706

Monetary Unit: million pesetas — Unité monétaire : million de pesetas

Label (EN)	1990	1991	1992	1993	1994	1995	1996	1997	Label (FR)
C.1.3. Net Written Premiums									**C.1.3. Primes Nettes Emises**
C.1.3.1. Domestic Companies	497 326	708 123	743 075	811 195	1 319 848	1 299 344	1 543 379	1 818 216	C.1.3.1. Entreprises Nationales
C.1.3.2. (Foreign Controlled Companies)	47 237	79 119	..	176 981	169 808	306 715	277 724	313 562	C.1.3.2. (Entreprises Sous Contrôle Etranger)
C.1.3.3. Branches & Agencies of Foreign Cies	36 748	43 327	448 469	44 491	97 133	45 789	61 417	69 102	C.1.3.3. Succursales et Agences d'Ent. Etrangères
C.1.3. Total	534 074	751 450	791 544	855 686	1 416 981	1 345 133	1 604 796	1 887 318	C.1.3. Total
C.2. Non-Life									**C.2. Non-Vie**
C.2.1. Gross premiums									**C.2.1. Primes Brutes**
C.2.1.1. Direct Business									**C.2.1.1. Assurances Directes**
C.2.1.1.1. Domestic Companies	1 130 647	1 293 212	1 481 544	1 630 146	1 739 438	1 907 641	2 010 594	2 049 219	C.2.1.1.1. Entreprises Nationales
C.2.1.1.2. (Foreign Controlled Companies)	300 323	458 076	124 681	621 668	492 555	598 320	558 664	525 459	C.2.1.1.2. (Entreprises Sous Contrôle Etranger)
C.2.1.1.3. Branches & Agencies of Foreign Cies	94 458	105 386	..	111 977	125 554	73 067	69 966	73 725	C.2.1.1.3. Succursales et Agences d'Ent. Etrangères
C.2.1.1. Total	1 225 105	1 398 598	1 606 225	1 742 128	1 864 992	1 980 708	2 080 460	2 122 944	C.2.1.1. Total
C.2.1.2. Reinsurance Accepted									**C.2.1.2. Réassurance Acceptée**
C.2.1.2.1. Domestic Companies	65 102	77 249	96 617	120 944	122 829	119 005	124 647	130 252	C.2.1.2.1. Entreprises Nationales
C.2.1.2.2. (Foreign Controlled Companies)	7 630	9 473	..	32 112	14 930	19 259	17 578	13 953	C.2.1.2.2. (Entreprises Sous Contrôle Etranger)
C.2.1.2.3. Branches & Agencies of Foreign Cies	6 221	7 155	6 740	6 126	7 436	6 333	592	2 474	C.2.1.2.3. Succursales et Agences d'Ent. Etrangères
C.2.1.2. Total	71 323	84 404	103 357	127 070	130 265	125 338	125 239	132 726	C.2.1.2. Total
C.2.1.3.									**C.2.1.3. Total**
C.2.1.3.1. Domestic Companies	1 195 749	1 370 461	1 578 161	1 751 090	1 862 267	2 026 646	2 135 241	2 179 471	C.2.1.3.1. Entreprises Nationales
C.2.1.3.2. (Foreign Controlled Companies)	307 953	467 549	131 421	653 780	507 485	617 579	576 242	539 412	C.2.1.3.2. (Entreprises Sous Contrôle Etranger)
C.2.1.3.3. Branches & Agencies of Foreign Cies	100 679	112 541	..	118 103	132 990	79 400	70 458	76 199	C.2.1.3.3. Succursales et Agences d'Ent. Etrangères
C.2.1.3. Total Gross Premiums	1 296 428	1 483 002	1 709 582	1 869 200	1 995 257	2 106 046	2 205 699	2 255 670	C.2.1.3. Total des Primes Brutes
C.2.2. Ceded Premiums									**C.2.2. Primes Cédées**
C.2.2.1. Domestic Companies	220 181	238 774	281 278	304 794	307 521	292 105	308 994	305 114	C.2.2.1. Entreprises Nationales
C.2.2.2. (Foreign Controlled Companies)	48 484	88 933	..	118 866	90 618	91 228	90 773	82 897	C.2.2.2. (Entreprises Sous Contrôle Etranger)
C.2.2.3. Branches & Agencies of Foreign Cies	17 464	19 930	22 036	27 275	21 704	16 485	9 622	7 654	C.2.2.3. Succursales et Agences d'Ent. Etrangères
C.2.2. Total	237 645	258 704	303 314	332 070	329 225	308 590	318 616	312 768	C.2.2. Total
C.2.3. Net Written Premiums									**C.2.3. Primes Nettes Emises**
C.2.3.1. Domestic Companies	975 568	1 131 687	1 296 883	1 446 296	1 554 746	1 734 541	1 826 247	1 874 357	C.2.3.1. Entreprises Nationales
C.2.3.2. (Foreign Controlled Companies)	259 469	378 616	..	534 914	416 867	526 351	458 469	456 515	C.2.3.2. (Entreprises Sous Contrôle Etranger)
C.2.3.3. Branches & Agencies of Foreign Cies	83 215	92 611	109 385	90 828	111 286	62 915	60 836	68 545	C.2.3.3. Succursales et Agences d'Ent. Etrangères
C.2.3. Total	1 058 783	1 224 298	1 406 268	1 537 124	1 666 032	1 797 456	1 887 083	1 942 902	C.2.3. Total
C.3. Total									**C.3. Total**
C.3.1. Gross Premiums									**C.3.1. Primes Brutes**
C.3.1.1. Direct Business									**C.3.1.1. Assurances Directes**
C.3.1.1.1. Domestic Companies	1 639 951	2 015 839	2 241 841	2 460 153	3 077 877	3 229 858	3 580 268	3 887 466	C.3.1.1.1. Entreprises Nationales
C.3.1.1.2. (Foreign Controlled Companies)	351 098	544 743	176 162	810 641	670 420	915 708	847 676	847 514	C.3.1.1.2. (Entreprises Sous Contrôle Etranger)
C.3.1.1.3. Branches & Agencies of Foreign Cies	132 075	149 726	..	160 272	228 695	123 451	135 839	143 415	C.3.1.1.3. Succursales et Agences d'Ent. Etrangères
C.3.1.1. Total	1 772 026	2 165 565	2 418 003	2 620 430	3 306 572	3 353 309	3 716 107	4 030 881	C.3.1.1. Total
C.3.1.2. Reinsurance Accepted									**C.3.1.2. Réassurance Acceptée**
C.3.1.2.1. Domestic Companies	70 508	81 095	101 639	126 514	129 434	127 716	133 201	143 339	C.3.1.2.1. Entreprises Nationales
C.3.1.2.2. (Foreign Controlled Companies)	9 081	9 503	..	34 273	15 468	19 975	18 077	14 230	C.3.1.2.2. (Entreprises Sous Contrôle Etranger)
C.3.1.2.3. Branches & Agencies of Foreign Cies	6 767	7 742	6 683	6 578	7 208	6 592	- 728	2 474	C.3.1.2.3. Succursales et Agences d'Ent. Etrangères
C.3.1.2. Total	77 275	88 837	108 322	133 092	136 642	134 308	132 473	145 813	C.3.1.2. Total
C.3.1.3.									**C.3.1.3. Total**
C.3.1.3.1. Domestic Companies	1 710 459	2 096 934	2 343 480	2 586 667	3 207 311	3 357 574	3 713 469	4 030 805	C.3.1.3.1. Entreprises Nationales
C.3.1.3.2. (Foreign Controlled Companies)	360 179	554 246	182 845	844 914	685 888	935 683	865 753	861 744	C.3.1.3.2. (Entreprises Sous Contrôle Etranger)
C.3.1.3.3. Branches & Agencies of Foreign Cies	138 842	157 468	..	166 850	235 903	130 043	135 111	145 889	C.3.1.3.3. Succursales et Agences d'Ent. Etrangères
C.3.1.3. Total Gross Premiums	1 849 301	2 254 402	2 526 325	2 753 524	3 443 214	3 487 617	3 848 580	4 176 694	C.3.1.3. Total des Primes Brutes
C.3.2. Ceded Premiums									**C.3.2. Primes Cédées**
C.3.2.1. Domestic Companies	237 565	257 124	303 522	329 176	332 717	323 689	343 843	338 232	C.3.2.1. Entreprises Nationales
C.3.2.2. (Foreign Controlled Companies)	53 473	96 511	..	133 019	99 213	102 617	102 560	91 667	C.3.2.2. (Entreprises Sous Contrôle Etranger)
C.3.2.3. Branches & Agencies of Foreign Cies	18 879	21 530	24 991	31 531	27 484	21 339	12 858	8 242	C.3.2.3. Succursales et Agences d'Ent. Etrangères
C.3.2. Total	256 444	278 654	328 513	360 708	360 201	345 028	356 701	346 474	C.3.2. Total

Monetary Unit: million pesetas

Unité monétaire : million de pesetas

	1990	1991	1992	1993	1994	1995	1996	1997
C.3.3. Net Written Premiums								
C.3.3.1. Domestic Companies	1 472 894	1 839 810	2 039 958	2 257 491	2 874 594	3 033 885	3 369 626	3 692 573
C.3.3.2. (Foreign Controlled Companies)	306 706	457 735	...	711 895	586 675	833 066	736 193	770 077
C.3.3.3. Branches & Agencies of Foreign Cies	119 963	135 938	557 854	135 319	208 419	108 704	122 253	137 647
C.3.3. Total	1 592 857	1 975 748	2 197 812	2 392 810	3 083 013	3 142 589	3 491 879	3 830 220
E. BUSINESS WRITTEN ABROAD								
E.1. Life								
E.1.1. Gross Premiums								
E.1.1.1. Direct Business								
E.1.1.1.1. Branches & Agencies	933	1 314	1 992	3 153	4 585	14 306	29 071	41 488
E.1.1.1. Total	933	1 314	1 992	3 153	4 585	14 306	29 071	41 488
E.1.1.2. Reinsurance Accepted								
E.1.1.2.1. Branches & Agences	28	25	..	..	..	0	0	..
E.1.1.2. Total	28	25	..	..	..	0	0	..
E.1.1.3. Total								
E.1.1.3. Branches & Agencies	961	1 339	1 992	3 153	4 585	14 306	29 071	41 488
E.1.1.3. Total Gross Premiums	961	1 339	1 992	3 153	4 585	14 306	29 071	41 488
E.1.2. Ceded Premiums								
E.1.2.1. Branches & Agencies	35	42	60	71	86	1 534	109	105
E.1.2. Total	35	42	60	71	86	1 534	109	
E.1.3. Net Written Premiums								
E.1.3.1. Branches & Agencies	926	1 297	1 932	3 082	4 499	12 772	28 962	41 383
E.1.3. Total	926	1 297	1 932	3 082	4 499	12 772	28 962	41 383
E.2. Non-Life								
E.2.1. Gross Premiums								
E.2.1.1. Direct Business								
E.2.1.1.1. Branches & Agencies	4 870	5 549	3 309	5 648	11 587	13 731	12 925	14 640
E.2.1.1. Total	4 870	5 549	3 309	5 648	11 587	13 731	12 925	14 640
E.2.1.2. Reinsurance Accepted								
E.2.1.2.1. Branches & Agencies	374	272	168	342	473	2 603	5 331	6 819
E.2.1.2. Total	374	272	168	342	473	2 603	5 331	..
E.2.1.3. Total								
E.2.1.3.1. Branches & Agencies	5 244	5 821	3 447	5 990	12 060	16 334	18 256	21 459
E.2.1.3. Total Gross Premiums	5 244	5 821	3 477	5 990	12 060	16 334	18 256	21 459
E.2.2. Ceded Premiums								
E.2.2.1. Branches & Agencies	1 917	2 037	892	1 025	1 411	2 966	2 577	2 727
E.2.2. Total	1 917	2 037	892	1 025	1 411	2 966	2 577	2 727
E.2.3. Net Written Premiums								
E.2.3.1. Branches & Agencies	3 327	3 784	2 585	4 965	10 649	13 368	15 679	18 732
E.2.3. Total	3 327	3 784	2 585	4 965	10 649	13 368	15 679	18 732
G. BREAKDOWN OF NON-LIFE PREMIUMS								
G.1. Motor vehicle								
G.1.1. Direct Business								
G.1.1.1. Cross Premiums	600 398	675 395	747 024	800 071	831 523	859 081	864 618	846 551
G.1.1.2. Ceded Premiums	51 200	49 026	58 814	69 226	60 224	45 208	47 363	42 362
G.1.1.3. Net Written Premiums	549 198	508 369	688 210	730 845	771 299	813 873	817 255	804 189
G.1.2. Reinsurance Accepted								
G.1.2.1. Gross Premiums	16 331	19 095	21 468	29 184	29 303	24 803	25 510	22 444
G.1.2.2. Ceded Premiums	2 104	2 420	3 253	3 788	3 946	3 642	3 129	3 242
G.1.2.3. Net Written Premiums	14 227	16 675	18 215	25 396	25 357	21 161	22 381	19 201
G.1.3. Total								
G.1.3.1. Gross Premiums	616 729	676 490	768 492	829 255	860 826	883 884	890 128	868 995
G.1.3.2. Ceded Premiums	53 304	51 446	62 047	73 014	64 170	48 850	50 492	45 604
G.1.3.3. Net Written Premiums	563 425	625 044	706 425	756 241	796 656	835 034	839 636	823 390

Monetary Unit: million pesetas   Unité monétaire : million de pesetas

	1990	1991	1992	1993	1994	1995	1996	1997
G.2. Marine, Aviation / G.2. Marine, Aviation								
G.2.1. Direct Business / G.2.1. Assurances Directes								
G.2.1.1. Gross Premiums / G.2.1.1. Primes Brutes	41 042	20 250	22 585	24 242	24 476	23 362	23 908	23 864
G.2.1.2. Ceded Premiums / G.2.1.2. Primes Cédées	25 020	15 988	17 210	19 357	19 023	16 489	16 915	15 854
G.2.1.3. Net Written Premiums / G.2.1.3. Primes Nettes Emises	15 022	4 262	5 375	4 885	5 453	6 873	6 993	8 010
G.2.2. Reinsurance Accepted / G.2.2. Réassurance Acceptée								
G.2.2.1. Gross Premiums / G.2.2.1. Primes Brutes	4 518	3 947	5 521	9 371	9 373	10 178	8 819	7 285
G.2.2.2. Ceded Premiums / G.2.2.2. Primes Cédées	1 704	1 570	2 565	4 111	4 521	3 935	4 130	3 309
G.2.2.3. Net Written Premiums / G.2.2.3. Primes Nettes Emises	2 814	2 377	2 956	5 227	4 852	6 243	4 689	3 977
G.2.3. Total / G.2.3. Total								
G.2.3.1. Gross Premiums / G.2.3.1. Primes Brutes	45 560	24 197	28 106	33 613	33 849	33 540	32 727	31 149
G.2.3.2. Ceded Premiums / G.2.3.2. Primes Cédées	27 724	17 558	19 775	23 501	23 544	20 424	21 045	19 163
G.2.3.3. Net Written Premiums / G.2.3.3. Primes Nettes Emises	17 836	6 639	8 331	10 112	10 305	13 116	11 682	11 986
G.3. Freight / G.3. Fret								
G.3.1. Direct Business / G.3.1. Assurances Directes								
G.3.1.1. Gross Premiums / G.3.1.1. Primes Brutes	..	22 536	35 142	24 102	27 204	29 068	29 586	26 308
G.3.1.2. Ceded Premiums / G.3.1.2. Primes Cédées	..	10 979	12 510	12 038	13 412	13 719	13 409	11 555
G.3.1.3. Net Written Premiums / G.3.1.3. Primes Nettes Emises	..	11 557	12 632	12 064	13 792	15 349	16 177	14 753
G.3.2. Reinsurance Accepted / G.3.2. Réassurance Acceptée								
G.3.2.1. Gross Premiums / G.3.2.1. Primes Brutes	..	1 132	1 508	2 731	3 132	2 458	2 977	3 059
G.3.2.2. Ceded Premiums / G.3.2.2. Primes Cédées	..	345	477	713	696	607	586	787
G.3.2.3. Net Written Premiums / G.3.2.3. Primes Nettes Emises	..	787	1 031	2 018	2 436	1 851	2 391	2 272
G.3.3. Total / G.3.3. Total								
G.3.3.1. Gross Premiums / G.3.3.1. Primes Brutes	..	23 668	26 650	26 833	30 336	31 526	32 563	29 367
G.3.3.2. Ceded Premiums / G.3.3.2. Primes Cédées	..	11 324	12 987	12 751	14 108	14 326	13 995	12 342
G.3.3.3. Net Written Premiums / G.3.3.3. Primes Nettes Emises	..	12 344	13 663	14 082	16 228	17 200	18 568	17 025
G.4. Fire, Property Damages / G.4. Incendie, Dommages aux Biens								
G.4.1. Direct Business / G.4.1. Assurances Directes								
G.4.1.1. Gross Premiums / G.4.1.1. Primes Brutes	215 088	88 407	87 527	87 180	85 598	86 195	94 238	89 859
G.4.1.2. Ceded Premiums / G.4.1.2. Primes Cédées	88 753	43 460	45 696	44 316	41 471	38 325	40 943	36 707
G.4.1.3. Net Written Premiums / G.4.1.3. Primes Nettes Emises	126 355	44 947	41 831	42 864	44 127	47 870	53 295	53 151
G.4.2. Reinsurance Accepted / G.4.2. Réassurance Acceptée								
G.4.2.1. Gross Premiums / G.4.2.1. Primes Brutes	30 148	24 433	31 151	35 343	34 020	30 782	35 269	37 305
G.4.2.2. Ceded Premiums / G.4.2.2. Primes Cédées	10 059	8 938	11 353	12 384	13 153	11 470	11 747	12 685
G.4.2.3. Net Written Premiums / G.4.2.3. Primes Nettes Emises	20 089	15 495	19 798	22 959	20 867	19 312	23 522	24 620
G.4.3. Total / G.4.3. Total								
G.4.3.1. Gross Premiums / G.4.3.1. Primes Brutes	245 236	112 840	118 678	122 523	119 618	116 977	129 507	127 167
G.4.3.2. Ceded Premiums / G.4.3.2. Primes Cédées	98 812	52 398	57 049	56 700	54 624	49 795	52 690	49 393
G.4.3.3. Net Written Premiums / G.4.3.3. Primes Nettes Emises	146 424	60 442	61 629	65 823	64 994	67 182	76 817	77 771
G.5. Pecuniary Losses / G.5. Pertes Pécunières								
G.5.1. Direct Business / G.5.1. Assurances Directes								
G.5.1.1. Gross Premiums / G.5.1.1. Primes Brutes	34 541	40 578	43 805	45 861	47 412	46 940	50 934	7 749
G.5.1.2. Ceded Premiums / G.5.1.2. Primes Cédées	24 493	28 257	31 345	31 148	32 974	34 036	34 822	3 718
G.5.1.3. Net Written Premiums / G.5.1.3. Primes Nettes Emises	10 048	12 321	12 460	14 713	14 438	12 904	16 112	4 032
G.5.2. Reinsurance Accepted / G.5.2. Réassurance Acceptée								
G.5.2.1. Gross Premiums / G.5.2.1. Primes Brutes	4 233	4 629	6 035	5 847	4 883	5 264	6 245	41
G.5.2.2. Ceded Premiums / G.5.2.2. Primes Cédées	1 061	2 084	2 041	2 400	2 077	2 791	3 644	22
G.5.2.3. Net Written Premiums / G.5.2.3. Primes Nettes Emises	3 172	2 545	3 994	3 447	2 806	2 473	2 601	18
G.5.3. Total / G.5.3. Total								
G.5.3.1. Gross Premiums / G.5.3.1. Primes Brutes	38 774	45 207	49 840	51 708	52 295	52 204	57 179	7 790
G.5.3.2. Ceded Premiums / G.5.3.2. Primes Cédées	25 554	30 241	33 386	33 548	35 051	36 827	38 466	3 740
G.5.3.3. Net Written Premiums / G.5.3.3. Primes Nettes Emises	13 220	14 866	16 454	18 160	17 244	15 377	18 713	4 050
G.6. General Liability / G.6. Responsabilité Générale								
G.6.1. Direct Business / G.6.1. Assurances Directes								
G.6.1.1. Gross Premiums / G.6.1.1. Primes Brutes	36 425	41 156	51 111	60 469	72 746	81 214	87 413	68 275
G.6.1.2. Ceded Premiums / G.6.1.2. Primes Cédées	15 262	17 783	22 324	24 595	25 831	35 355	26 767	21 450
G.6.1.3. Net Written Premiums / G.6.1.3. Primes Nettes Emises	21 163	23 373	28 787	35 874	46 915	55 859	60 646	46 825
G.6.2. Reinsurance Accepted / G.6.2. Réassurance Acceptée								
G.6.2.1. Gross Premiums / G.6.2.1. Primes Brutes	4 428	5 104	6 166	7 134	5 063	6 091	5 024	1 913
G.6.2.2. Ceded Premiums / G.6.2.2. Primes Cédées	1 970	2 176	2 904	3 725	2 840	2 302	1 322	549
G.6.2.3. Net Written Premiums / G.6.2.3. Primes Nettes Emises	2 458	2 928	3 262	3 409	2 223	3 789	3 702	1 364

SPAIN / ESPAGNE

Monetary Unit: mil on pesetas — Unité monétaire : million de pesetas

	1990	1991	1992	1993	1994	1995	1996	1997	
G.6.3. Total									G.6.3. Total
G.6.3.1. Gross Premiums	40 853	46 260	57 277	67 603	77 809	87 305	92 437	70 188	G.6.3.1. Primes Brutes
G.6.3.2 Ceded Premiums	17 232	19 959	25 228	28 320	28 671	27 657	28 089	21 999	G.6.3.2. Primes Cédées
G.6.3.3. Net Written Premiums	23 621	26 301	32 049	39 283	49 138	59 648	64 348	48 189	G.6.3.3. Primes Nettes Emises
G.7. Accident, Health									G.7. Accident, Santé
G.7.1. Direct Business									G.7.1. Assurances Directes
G.7.1.1. Gross Premiums	213 662	270 264	316 539	349 898	385 479	422 441	454 246	480 861	G.7.1.1. Primes Brutes
G.7.1.2. Ceded Premiums	10 262	11 834	13 741	14 202	15 892	15 340	18 124	18 349	G.7.1.2. Primes Cédées
G.7.1.3. Net Written Premiums	203 400	258 430	302 798	335 696	369 587	407 101	436 122	462 512	G.7.1.3. Primes Nettes Emises
G.7.2. Reinsurance Accepted									G.7.2. Réassurance Acceptée
G.7.2.1. Gross Premiums	3 485	5 238	6 023	6 846	8 083	7 834	5 243	7 769	G.7.2.1. Primes Brutes
G.7.2.2. Ceded Premiums	436	444	909	1 132	1 140	1 079	710	933	G.7.2.2. Primes Cédées
G.7.2.3. Net Written Premiums	3 049	4 794	5 114	5 714	6 943	6 755	4 533	6 837	G.7.2.3. Primes Nettes Emises
G.7.3. Total									G.7.3. Total
G.7.3.1. Gross Premiums	217 147	275 502	322 562	356 744	393 562	430 275	459 489	488 630	G.7.3.1. Primes Brutes
G.7.3.2. Ceded Premiums	10 698	12 278	14 650	15 334	17 032	16 419	18 834	19 281	G.7.3.2. Primes Cédées
G.7.3.3. Net Written Premiums	206 449	263 224	307 912	341 410	376 530	413 856	440 655	469 349	G.7.3.3. Primes Nettes Emises
G.8. Others									G.8. Autres
G.8.1. Direct Business									G.8.1. Assurances Directes
G.8.1.1. Gross Premiums	83 949	258 012	312 492	350 300	390 554	432 407	475 517	579 478	G.8.1.1. Primes Brutes
G.8.1.2. Ceded Premiums	2 671	58 340	73 048	80 578	84 840	84 753	88 198	129 959	G.8.1.2. Primes Cédées
G.8.1.3. Net Written Premiums	81 278	199 672	239 444	269 722	305 714	347 654	387 319	449 519	G.8.1.3. Primes Nettes Emises
G.8.2. Reinsurance Accepted									G.8.2. Réassurance Acceptée
G.8.2.1. Gross Premiums	8 180	20 826	25 485	30 614	36 408	37 928	36 152	52 910	G.8.2.1. Primes Brutes
G.8.2.2. Ceded Premiums	1 650	5 060	5 124	5 737	7 185	9 539	6 807	11 285	G.8.2.2. Primes Cédées
G.8.2.3. Net Written Premiums	6 530	15 766	20 361	24 877	29 223	28 389	29 345	41 624	G.8.2.3. Primes Nettes Emises
G.8.3. Total									G.8.3. Total
G.8.3.1. Gross Premiums	92 129	278 838	337 977	380 914	426 962	470 335	511 669	632 388	G.8.3.1. Primes Brutes
G.8.3.2. Ceded Premiums	4 321	63 400	78 172	86 315	92 025	94 292	95 005	141 245	G.8.3.2. Primes Cédées
G.8.3.3. Net Written Premiums	87 808	215 438	259 805	294 599	334 937	376 043	416 664	491 144	G.8.3.3. Primes Nettes Emises
G.10. Total									G.10. Total
G.10.1. Direct Business									G.10.1. Assurances Directes
G.10.1.1. Gross Premiums	1 225 105	1 398 598	1 606 225	1 742 128	1 864 992	1 980 708	2 080 460	..	G.10.1.1. Primes Brutes
G.10.1.2. Ceded Premiums	218 661	235 667	274 688	295 450	293 667	273 225	286 541	..	G.10.1.2. Primes Cédées
G.10.1.3. Net Written Premiums	1 066 444	1 162 931	1 331 537	1 446 673	1 571 325	1 707 483	1 793 919	..	G.10.1.3. Primes Nettes Emises
G.10.2. Reinsurance Accepted									G.10.2. Réassurance Acceptée
G.10.2.1. Gross Premiums	71 323	84 404	103 357	127 070	130 265	125 338	125 239	..	G.10.2.1. Primes Brutes
G.10.2.2. Ceded Premiums	18 984	23 037	28 626	34 023	35 559	35 365	32 075	..	G.10.2.2. Primes Cédées
G.10.2.3. Net Written Premiums	52 339	61 367	74 731	93 047	94 707	89 973	93 164	..	G.10.2.3. Primes Nettes Emises
G.10.3. Total									G.10.3. Total
G.10.3.1. Gross Premiums	1 296 428	1 483 002	1 709 582	1 869 193	1 995 257	2 106 046	2 205 699	..	G.10.3.1. Primes Brutes
G.10.3.2. Ceded Premiums	237 645	258 704	303 314	329 483	329 225	308 590	318 616	..	G.10.3.2. Primes Cédées
G.10.3.3. Net Written Premiums	1 058 783	1 224 298	1 406 268	1 539 710	1 666 032	1 797 456	1 887 083	..	G.10.3.3. Primes Nettes Emises

H. GROSS CLAIMS PAYMENTS — H. PAIEMENTS BRUTS DES SINISTRES

H.1. Life — H.1. Vie

	1990	1991	1992	1993	1994	1995	1996	1997	
H.1.1. Domestic Companies				533 722	591 826	765 976	836 372	993 337	H.1.1. Entreprises Nationales
H.1.2. (Foreign Controlled Companies)							147 238	152 532	H.1.2. (Entreprises Sous Contrôle Etranger)
H.1.3. Branches & Agencies of Foreign Cies				25 473	28 841	19 000	23 826	29 045	H.1.3. Succursales et Agences d'Ent. Etrangères
H.1. Total				559 195	620 667	784 976	860 198	1 022 382	H.1. Total

H.2. Non-Life — H.2. Non-Vie

	1990	1991	1992	1993	1994	1995	1996	1997	
H.2.1. Domestic Companies				1 266 582	1 303 217	1 413 739	1 464 696	1 523 414	H.2.1. Entreprises Nationales
H.2.2. (Foreign Controlled Companies)							395 774	379 651	H.2.2. (Entreprises Sous Contrôle Etranger)
H.2.3. Branches & Agencies of Foreign Cies				77 719	85 745	50 648	46 044	52 673	H.2.3. Succursales et Agences d'Ent. Etrangères
H.2. Total				1 344 301	1 388 962	1 464 387	1 510 740	1 576 087	H.2. Total

SPAIN

ESPAGNE

Monetary Unit: million pesetas

Unité monétaire : million de pesetas

	1990	1991	1992	1993	1994	1995	1996	1997
I. GROSS OPERATING EXPENSES / **I. DEPENSES BRUTES D'EXPLOITATION**								
I.1. Life / **I.1. Vie**								
I.1.1. Domestic Companies / I.1.1. Entreprises Nationales				99 261	107 238	124 955	133 252	149 736
I.1.2. (Foreign Controlled Companies) / I.1.2. (Entreprises Sous Contrôle Etranger)							47 308	43 115
I.1.3. Branches & Agencies of Foreign Cies / I.1.3. Succursales et Agences d'Ent. Etrangères				16 288	18 686	16 043	17 769	17 998
I.1. Total / I.1. Total des Primes Nettes Vie				115 549	125 924	140 998	151 021	167 734
I.2. Non-Life / **I.2. Non-Vie**								
I.2.1. Domestic Companies / I.2.1. Entreprises Nationales				549 047	577 991	625 402	662 150	686 410
I.2.2. (Foreign Controlled Companies) / I.2.2. (Entreprises Sous Contrôle Etranger)							235 814	192 878
I.2.3. Branches & Agencies of Foreign Cies / I.2.3. Succursales et Agences d'Ent. Etrangères				42 400	47 484	27 300	23 992	25 546
I.2. Total / I.2. Total				591 447	625 475	652 702	686 142	711 956
J. COMMISSIONS / **J. COMMISSIONS**								
J.1. Life / **J.1. Vie**								
J.1.1. Direct Business / J.1.1. Assurance directe								
J.1.1.1. Domestic Companies / J.1.1.1. Entreprises Nationales				29 719	33 855	42 762	49 685	57 708
J.1.1.2. (Foreign Controlled Companies) / J.1.1.2. (Entreprises Sous Contrôle Etranger)							16 791	15 671
J.1.1.3. Branches & Agencies of Foreign Cies / J.1.1.3. Succursales et Agences d'Ent. Etrangères				6 876	8 388	7 038	7 718	7 745
J.1.1. Total / J.1.1. Total				36 595	42 243	49 800	57 403	65 453
J.1.2. Reinsurance Accepted / J.1.2. Réassurances acceptées								
J.1.2.1. Domestic Companies / J.1.2.1. Entreprises Nationales				795	835	1 253	1 259	1 153
J.1.2.2. (Foreign Controlled Companies) / J.1.2.2. (Entreprises Sous Contrôle Etranger)							166	97
J.1.2.3. Branches & Agencies of Foreign Cies / J.1.2.3. Succursales et Agences d'Ent. Etrangères				99	- 40	69	68	
J.1.2. Total / J.1.2. Total				894	795	1 322	1 327	1 153
J.1.3. Total / J.1.3. Total								
J.1.3.1. Domestic Companies / J.1.3.1. Entreprises Nationales				30 514	34 690	44 015	50 944	58 861
J.1.3.2. (Foreign Controlled Companies) / J.1.3.2. (Entreprises Sous Contrôle Etranger)							16 957	15 768
J.1.3.3. Branches & Agencies of Foreign Cies / J.1.3.3. Succursales et Agences d'Ent. Etrangères				6 975	8 348	7 107	7 786	7 745
J.1.3. Total of Life Net Premiums / J.1.3. Total				37 489	43 038	51 122	58 730	66 606
J.2. Non-Life / **J.2. Non-Vie**								
J.2.1. Direct Business / J.2.1. Assurance directe								
J.2.1.1. Domestic Companies / J.2.1.1. Entreprises Nationales				226 503	240 098	263 795	281 276	285 559
J.2.1.2. (Foreign Controlled Companies) / J.2.1.2. (Entreprises Sous Contrôle Etranger)							90 799	81 974
J.2.1.3. Branches & Agencies of Foreign Cies / J.2.1.3. Succursales et Agences d'Ent. Etrangères				18 959	21 391	12 002	11 457	12 279
J.2.1. Total / J.2.1. Total				245 462	261 489	275 797	292 733	297 838
J.2.2. Reinsurance Accepted / J.2.2. Réassurances acceptées								
J.2.2.1. Domestic Companies / J.2.2.1. Entreprises Nationales				26 051	26 222	23 899	23 695	26 628
J.2.2.2. (Foreign Controlled Companies) / J.2.2.2. (Entreprises Sous Contrôle Etranger)							1 056	1 380
J.2.2.3. Branches & Agencies of Foreign Cies / J.2.2.3. Succursales et Agences d'Ent. Etrangères				764	1 269	1 404	137	486
J.2.2. Total / J.2.2. Total				26 815	27 491	25 303	23 832	27 114
J.2.3. Total / J.2.3. Total								
J.2.3.1. Domestic Companies / J.2.3.1. Entreprises Nationales				252 554	266 320	287 694	304 971	312 187
J.2.3.2. (Foreign Controlled Companies) / J.2.3.2. (Entreprises Sous Contrôle Etranger)							91 855	83 354
J.2.3.3. Branches & Agencies of Foreign Cies / J.2.3.3. Succursales et Agences d'Ent. Etrangères				19 723	22 660	13 406	11 594	12 765
J.2.3. Total / J.2.3. Total				272 277	288 980	301 100	316 565	324 952

Monetary Unit: million Swedish kroner — Unité monétaire : million de couronnes suédoises

		1990	1991	1992	1993	1994	1995	1996	1997
A. NUMBER OF COMPANIES IN THE REPORTING COUNTRY	**A. NOMBRE D'ENTREPRISES DANS LE PAYS DECLARANT**								
A.1. Life	**A.1. Vie**								
A.1.1. Domestic Companies	A.1.1. Entreprises Nationales	22	29	29	31	29	28	29	30
A.1. All Companies	A.1. Ensemble des Entreprises	22	29	29	31	29	28	29	30
A.2. Non-Life	**A.2. Non-Vie**								
A.2.1. Domestic Companies	A.2.1. Entreprises Nationales	228	95	93	100	107	110	98	100
A.2.2. (Foreign Controlled Companies)	A.2.2. (Entreprises Sous Contrôle Etranger)	2	2	2	2	2	3	3	4
A.2.3. Branches & Agencies of Foreign Cies	A.2.3. Succursales et Agences d'Ent. Etrangères	12	12	12	13	2	1	1	0
A.2. All Companies	A.2. Ensemble des Entreprises	240	107	105	113	109	111	99	100
A.4. Reinsurance	**A.4. Réassurance**								
A.4.1. Domestic Companies	A.4.1. Entreprises Nationales	7	5	6	5	6	6	8	8
A.4. All Companies	A.4. Ensemble des Entreprises	7	:	:	:	:	:	:	8
A.5. Total	**A.5. Total**								
A.5.1. Domestic Companies	A.5.1. Entreprises Nationales	257	129	128	136	142	144	135	138
A.5.2. (Foreign Controlled Companies)	A.5.2. (Entreprises Sous Contrôle Etranger)	2	2	2	2	2	3	3	4
A.5.3. Branches & Agencies of Foreign Cies	A.5.3. Succursales et Agences d'Ent. Etrangères	12	:	:	:	:	:	:	:
A.5. All Insurance Companies	A.5. Ensemble des Entreprises d'Assurances	269	:	:	:	:	:	:	138
B. NUMBER OF EMPLOYEES	**B. NOMBRE D'EMPLOYES**								
B.1. Insurance Companies	B.1. Entreprises d'Assurances	49 600	52 000	40 100	40 000	19 000	18 750	18 500	16 520
B.2. Intermediaries	B.2. Intermediaires	400	400	500	600	900	1 094	1 102	1 180
B. Total	B. Total	50 000	52 400	40 600	40 600	19 900	19 844	19 602	17 700
C. BUSINESS WRITTEN IN THE REPORTING COUNTRY	**C. OPERATIONS CONCLUES DANS LE PAYS DECLARANT**								
C.1. Life	**C.1. Vie**								
C.1.1. Gross Premiums	C.1.1. Primes Brutes								
C.1.1.1. Direct Business	C.1.1.1. Assurances Directes								
C.1.1.1.1 Domestic Companies	C.1.1.1.1. Entreprises Nationales	39 695	44 833	42 030	42 414	52 794	53 947	60 038	64 709
C.1.1.1. Total	C.1.1.1. Total	39 695	44 833	42 030	42 414	52 794	53 947	60 038	64 709
C.1.1.2. Reinsurance Accepted	C.1.1.2. Réassurance Acceptée								
C.1.1.2.1. Domestic Companies	C.1.1.2.1. Entreprises Nationales	2 212	2 302	2 882	2 415	1 579	2 398	79	200
C.1.1.2. Total	C.1.1.2. Total	:	2 302	2 882	2 416	1 579	2 398	79	200
C.1.1.3. Total	C.1.1.3. Total								
C.1.1.3.1. Domestic Companies	C.1.1.3.1. Entreprises Nationales	41 907	47 135	44 912	44 829	54 373	56 345	60 117	64 909
C.1.1.3. Total Gross Premiums	C.1.1.3. Total des Primes Brutes	:	47 135	44 912	44 829	54 373	56 345	60 117	64 909
C.1.2. Ceded Premiums	C.1.2. Primes Cédées								
C.1.2.1. Domestic Companies	C.1.2.1. Entreprises Nationales	384	619	426	1 381	725	1 242	613	726
C.1.2. Total	C.1.2. Total	:	619	426	1 381	725	1 242	613	726
C.1.3. Net Written Premiums	C.1.3. Primes Nettes Emises								
C.1.3.1. Domestic Companies	C.1.3.1. Entreprises Nationales	41 523	46 516	44 486	43 448	53 648	55 103	59 504	64 183
C.1.3. Total	C.1.3. Total	:	46 516	44 486	43 448	53 648	55 103	59 504	64 183

Monetary Unit: million Swedish kroner

Unité monétaire : million de couronnes suédoises

C.2. Non-Life — C.2. Non-Vie

		1990	1991	1992	1993	1994	1995	1996	1997
C.2.1. Gross premiums	C.2.1. Primes Brutes								
C.2.1.1. Direct Business	C.2.1.1. Assurances Directes								
C.2.1.1.1. Domestic Companies	C.2.1.1.1. Entreprises Nationales	31 002	36 478	36 422	45 606	35 611	36 103	34 994	36 368
C.2.1.1.2. (Foreign Controlled Companies)	C.2.1.1.2. (Entreprises Sous Contrôle Etranger)	481	606	659	766	656	1 048	1 124	1 152
C.2.1.1.3. Branches & Agencies of Foreign Cies	C.2.1.1.3. Succursales et Agences d'Ent. Etrangères	492	628	750	791	198	205	205	
C.2.1.1. Total	C.2.1.1. Total	31 494	37 106	37 172	46 397	35 809	36 308	35 199	36 368
C.2.1.2. Reinsurance Accepted	C.2.1.2. Réassurance Acceptée								
C.2.1.2.1. Domestic Companies	C.2.1.2.1. Entreprises Nationales	11 120	12 371	14 189	5 553	10 816	10 176	9 971	10 479
C.2.1.2.2. (Foreign Controlled Companies)	C.2.1.2.2. (Entreprises Sous Contrôle Etranger)	40	40	41	46	43	51	57	109
C.2.1.2. Total	C.2.1.2. Total	:	:	:	:	:	:	:	10 479
C.2.1.3. Total	C.2.1.3. Total								
C.2.1.3.1. Domestic Companies	C.2.1.3.1. Entreprises Nationales	42 122	48 849	50 611	51 159	46 427	46 279	44 965	46 847
C.2.1.3.2. (Foreign Controlled Companies)	C.2.1.3.2. (Entreprises Sous Contrôle Etranger)	521	646	700	812	699	1 099	1 181	1 261
C.2.1.3. Total Gross Premiums	C.2.1.3. Total des Primes Brutes	:	:	:	:	:	:	:	46 847
C.2.2. Ceded Premiums	C.2.2. Primes Cédées								
C.2.2.1. Domestic Companies	C.2.2.1. Entreprises Nationales	7 535	8 802	9 027	8 724	9 624	9 900	9 884	9 601
C.2.2.2. (Foreign Controlled Companies)	C.2.2.2. (Entreprises Sous Contrôle Etranger)	300	375	376	458	300	273	241	284
C.2.2. Total	C.2.2. Total	:	:	:	:	:	:	:	9 601
C.2.3. Net Written Premiums	C.2.3. Primes Nettes Emises								
C.2.3.1. Domestic Companies	C.2.3.1. Entreprises Nationales	34 587	40 047	41 584	42 435	36 803	36 379	35 081	37 246
C.2.3.2. (Foreign Controlled Companies)	C.2.3.2. (Entreprises Sous Contrôle Etranger)	221	271	324	354	399	826	940	977
C.2.3. Total	C.2.3. Total	:	:	:	:	:	:	:	37 246

C.3. Total — C.3. Total

		1990	1991	1992	1993	1994	1995	1996	1997
C.3.1. Gross Premiums	C.3.1. Primes Brutes								
C.3.1.1. Direct Business	C.3.1.1. Assurances Directes								
C.3.1.1.1. Domestic Companies	C.3.1.1.1. Entreprises Nationales	70 697	81 311	78 452	88 020	88 405	90 050	95 032	101 077
C.3.1.1.2. (Foreign Controlled Companies)	C.3.1.1.2. (Entreprises Sous Contrôle Etranger)	481	606	659	766	656	1 048	1 124	1 152
C.3.1.1.3. Branches & Agencies of Foreign Cies	C.3.1.1.3. Succursales et Agences d'Ent. Etrangères	492	628	750	791	198	205	205	0
C.3.1.1. Total	C.3.1.1. Total	71 189	81 939	79 202	88 811	88 603	90 255	95 237	101 077
C.3.1.2. Reinsurance Accepted	C.3.1.2. Réassurance Acceptée								
C.3.1.2.1. Domestic Companies	C.3.1.2.1. Entreprises Nationales	13 332	14 673	17 071	7 968	12 395	12 574	10 050	10 679
C.3.1.2.2. (Foreign Controlled Companies)	C.3.1.2.2. (Entreprises Sous Contrôle Etranger)	40	40	41	46	43	51	57	109
C.3.1.2. Total	C.3.1.2. Total	:	:	:	:	:	:	:	10 679
C.3.1.3. Total	C.3.1.3. Total								
C.3.1.3.1. Domestic Companies	C.3.1.3.1. Entreprises Nationales	84 029	95 984	95 523	95 988	100 800	102 624	105 082	111 756
C.3.1.3.2. (Foreign Controlled Companies)	C.3.1.3.2. (Entreprises Sous Contrôle Etranger)	521	646	700	812	699	1 099	1 181	1 261
C.3.1.3. Total Gross Premiums	C.3.1.3. Total des Primes Brutes	:	:	:	:	:	:	:	111 756
C.3.2. Ceded Premiums	C.3.2. Primes Cédées								
C.3.2.1. Domestic Companies	C.3.2.1. Entreprises Nationales	7 919	9 421	9 453	10 105	10 349	11 142	10 497	10 327
C.3.2.2. (Foreign Controlled Companies)	C.3.2.2. (Entreprises Sous Contrôle Etranger)	300	375	376	458	300	273	241	284
C.3.2. Total	C.3.2. Total	:	:	:	:	:	:	:	10 327
C.3.3. Net Written Premiums	C.3.3. Primes Nettes Emises								
C.3.3.1. Domestic Companies	C.3.3.1. Entreprises Nationales	76 110	86 563	86 070	85 883	90 451	91 482	94 585	101 429
C.3.3.2. (Foreign Controlled Companies)	C.3.3.2. (Entreprises Sous Contrôle Etranger)	221	271	324	354	399	826	940	977
C.3.3. Total	C.3.3. Total	:	:	:	:	:	:	:	101 429

Monetary Unit: million Swedish kroner

Unité monétaire : million de couronnes suédoises

D. NET WRITTEN PREMIUMS IN THE REPORTING COUNTRY IN TERMS OF DOMESTIC AND FOREIGN RISKS
D. PRIMES NETTES EMISES DANS LE PAYS DECLARANT EN RISQUES NATIONAUX ET ETRANGERS

	1990	1991	1992	1993	1994	1995	1996	1997
D.1. Life / **D.1. Vie**								
D.1.1. Domestic Risks / D.1.1. Risques Nationaux								
D.1.1.1. Domestic Companies / D.1.1.1. Entreprises Nationales	..	..	..	..	..	..	59 504	64 183
D.1.1. Total / D.1.1. Total des Primes Nettes Vie							59 504	64 183
D.1.3. Total / D.1.3. Total								
D.1.3.1. Domestic Companies / D.1.3.1. Entreprises Nationales	41 523	46 516	44 486	43 448	53 648	55 103	59 504	64 183
D.1.3. Total of Life Net Premiums / D.1.3. Total des Primes Nettes Vie	..	46 516	44 486	43 448	53 648	55 103	59 504	64 183
E. BUSINESS WRITTEN ABROAD / **E. OPERATIONS A L'ETRANGER**								
E.2. Non-Life / **E.2. Non-Vie**								
E.2.1. Gross Premiums / E.2.1. Primes Brutes								
E.2.1.1. Direct Business / E.2.1.1. Assurance Directe								
E.2.1.1.1. Branches & Agencies / E.2.1.1.1. Succursales & Agences	476	585	690	833	1 096	928	..	..
E.2.2. Ceded Premiums / E.2.2. Primes Cédées								
E.2.2.1. Branches & Agencies / E.2.2.1. Succursales & Agences	126	111	230	231	331	386	..	..
F. OUTSTANDING INVESTMENT BY DIRECT INSURANCE COMPANIES / **F. ENCOURS DES PLACEMENTS DES ENTREPRISES D'ASSURANCES DIRECTES**								
F.1. Life / **F.1. Vie**								
F.1.1. Real Estate / F.1.1. Immobilier								
F.1.1.1. Domestic Companies / F.1.1.1. Entreprises Nationales	35 992	35 530	34 864	34 887	36 486	37 629	51 130	51 566
F.1.1.4. Domestic Investment / F.1.1.4. Placement dans le Pays	35 992							
F.1.1. Total / F.1.1. Total	35 992	35 530	34 864	34 887	36 486	37 629	51 130	51 566
F.1.2. Mortgage Loans / F.1.2. Prêts Hypothécaires								
F.1.2.1. Domestic Companies / F.1.2.1. Entreprises Nationales	11 993	..	..	..	..	..	10 064	8 217
F.1.2. Total / F.1.2. Total	11 993	..	..	..	..	..	10 064	8 217
F.1.3. Shares / F.1.3. Actions								
F.1.3.1. Domestic Companies / F.1.3.1. Entreprises Nationales	70 069	85 852	83 697	103 284	116 284	148 993	308 918	393 967
F.1.3.4. Domestic Investment / F.1.3.4. Placement dans le Pays	47 249	..	..	..	..	..	..	..
F.1.3.5. Foreign Investment / F.1.3.5. Placement à l'Etranger	22 820	..	..	..	..	..	..	..
F.1.3. Total / F.1.3. Total	70 069	85 852	83 697	103 289	116 284	148 993	308 918	393 967
F.1.4. Bonds with Fixed Revenue / F.1.4. Obligations								
F.1.4.1. Domestic Companies / F.1.4.1. Entreprises Nationales	175 065	206 469	248 621	292 285	268 988	300 504	398 321	445 279
F.1.4.2. (Foreign Controlled Companies) / F.1.4.2. (Entreprises Sous Contrôle Etranger)	0	0	0	0	0	0	0	19
F.1.4.4. Domestic Investment / F.1.4.4. Placement dans le Pays	175 008	..	..	..	..	..	..	..
F.1.4.5. Foreign Investment / F.1.4.5. Placement à l'Etranger	57	..	..	..	..	..	..	..
F.1.4. Total / F.1.4. Total	175 065	206 469	248 621	292 285	268 988	300 504	398 321	445 279
F.1.5. Loans other than Mortgage Loans / F.1.5. Prêts Autres qu'Hypothécaires								
F.1.5.1. Domestic Companies / F.1.5.1. Entreprises Nationales	40 763	43 668	41 919	38 151	35 177	32 577	8 498	17 530
F.1.5.4. Domestic Investment / F.1.5.4. Placement dans le Pays	40 490	..	..	..	..	..	..	..
F.1.5.5. Foreign Investment / F.1.5.5. Placement à l'Etranger	273	..	..	..	..	..	..	..
F.1.5. Total / F.1.5. Total	40 763	43 668	41 919	38 151	35 177	32 577	8 498	17 530
F.1.6. Other Investments / F.1.6. Autres Placements								
F.1.6.1. Domestic Companies / F.1.6.1. Entreprises Nationales	43 300	53 494	39 883	41 793	46 121	40 503	39 453	52 623
F.1.6.4. Domestic Investment / F.1.6.4. Placement dans le Pays	43 275	..	..	..	..	..	..	..
F.1.6.5. Foreign Investment / F.1.6.5. Placement à l'Etranger	25	..	..	..	..	..	..	..
F.1.6. Total / F.1.6. Total	43 300	53 494	39 883	41 793	46 121	40 503	39 453	52 623

SWEDEN

Monetary Unit: million Swedish kroner | Unité monétaire : million de couronnes suédoises

	1990	1991	1992	1993	1994	1995	1996	1997	
F.1.7. Total									F.1.7. Total
F.1.7.1. Domestic Companies	365 189	425 013	448 984	510 400	503 056	560 206	816 384	969 182	F.1.7.1. Entreprises Nationales
F.1.7.2. (Foreign Controlled Companies)	0	0	0	0	0	0	0	19	F.1.7.2. (Entreprises Sous Contrôle Etranger)
F.1.7.4. Domestic Investment	342 014	:	:	:	:	:	:	:	F.1.7.4. Placement dans le Pays
F.1.7.5. Foreign Investment	23 175	:	:	:	:	:	:	:	F.1.7.5. Placement à l' Etranger
F.1.7. Total of Life Investments	365 189	425 013	448 984	510 400	503 056	560 206	816 384	969 182	F.1.7. Total des Placements Vie
F.2. Non-Life									**F.2. Non-Vie**
F.2.1. Real Estate									F.2.1. Immobilier
F.2.1.1. Domestic Companies	6 238	7 676	8 126	8 205	8 235	7 345	10 593	8 518	F.2.1.1. Entreprises Nationales
F.2.1.4. Domestic Investment	6 232	:	:	:	:	:	:	:	F.2.1.4. Placement dans le Pays
F.2.1.5. Foreign Investment	6	:	:	:	:	:	:	:	F.2.1.5. Placement à l' Etranger
F.2.1. Total	6 238	7 676	8 126	8 205	8 235	7 345	10 593	8 518	F.2.1. Total
F.2.2. Mortgage Loans									F.2.2. Prêts Hypothécaires
F.2.2.1. Domestic Companies	4 337	:	:	:	:	:	2 900	2 912	F.2.2.1. Entreprises Nationales
F.2.2.2. (Foreign Controlled Companies)	:	:	:	:	:	:	4	118	F.2.2.2.(Entreprises Sous Contrôle Etranger)
F.2.2. Total	:	:	:	:	:	:	2 900	2 912	F.2.2. Total
F.2.3. Shares									F.2.3. Actions
F.2.3.1. Domestic Companies	37 549	41 196	31 210	40 863	55 757	57 487	96 207	113 504	F.2.3.1. Entreprises Nationales
F.2.3.2. (Foreign Controlled Companies)	27	118	48	107	165	140	324	473	F.2.3.2. (Entreprises Sous Contrôle Etranger)
F.2.3.4. Domestic Investment	19 711	:	:	:	:	:	:	:	F.2.3.4. Placement dans le Pays
F.2.3.5. Foreign Investment	17 865	:	:	:	:	:	:	:	F.2.3.5. Placement à l' Etranger
F.2.3. Total	37 576	41 314	31 258	40 970	55 757	57 487	96 207	113 504	F.2.3. Total
F.2.4. Bonds with Fixed Revenue									F.2.4. Obligations
F.2.4.1. Domestic Companies	25 968	27 591	26 474	37 867	79 767	91 057	128 604	136 830	F.2.4.1. Entreprises Nationales
F.2.4.2. (Foreign Controlled Companies)	206	119	339	846	855	1 073	1 667	1 891	F.2.4.2. (Entreprises Sous Contrôle Etranger)
F.2.4.4. Domestic Investment	22 669	:	:	:	:	:	:	:	F.2.4.4. Placement dans le Pays
F.2.4.5. Foreign Investment	3 505	:	:	:	:	:	:	:	F.2.4.5. Placement à l' Etranger
F.2.4. Total	26 174	27 710	26 813	38 713	79 767	91 057	128 604	136 830	F.2.4. Total
F.2.5. Loans other than Mortgage Loans									F.2.5. Prêts Autres qu'Hypothécaires
F.2.5.1. Domestic Companies	10 542	7 852	7 680	6 884	7 051	5 042	1 342	5 467	F.2.5.1. Entreprises Nationales
F.2.5.2. (Foreign Controlled Companies)	20	151	156	163	162	142	240	8	F.2.5.2. (Entreprises Sous Contrôle Etranger)
F.2.5.4. Domestic Investment	10 482	:	:	:	:	:	:	:	F.2.5.4. Placement dans le Pays
F.2.5.5. Foreign Investment	80	:	:	:	:	:	:	:	F.2.5.5. Placement à l' Etranger
F.2.5. Total	10 562	8 003	7 836	7 047	7 051	5 042	1 342	5 467	F.2.5. Total
F.2.6. Other Investments									F.2.6. Autres Placements
F.2.6.1. Domestic Companies	16 641	9 209	8 654	9 328	13 823	14 376	5 314	6 003	F.2.6.1. Entreprises Nationales
F.2.6.2. (Foreign Controlled Companies)	506	560	575	166	126	339	0	0	F.2.6.2. (Entreprises Sous Contrôle Etranger)
F.2.6.3. Branches & Agencies of Foreign Cies	490	628	746	791	198	205	205	:	F.2.6.3. Succursales et Agences d'Ent. Etrangères
F.2.6.4. Domestic Investment	17 246	:	:	:	:	:	:	:	F.2.6.4. Placement dans le Pays
F.2.6.5. Foreign Investment	391	:	:	:	:	:	:	:	F.2.6.5. Placement à l' Etranger
F.2.6. Total	17 637	9 769	9 229	9 494	14 021	14 581	5 519	6 003	F.2.6. Total
F.2.7. Total									F.2.7. Total
F.2.7.1. Domestic Companies	96 938	93 524	82 144	103 147	164 633	175 307	244 960	273 234	F.2.7.1. Entreprises Nationales
F.2.7.2. (Foreign Controlled Companies)	759	948	1 118	1 282	1 308	1 694	2 235	2 490	F.2.7.2. (Entreprises Sous Contrôle Etranger)
F.2.7.3. Branches & Agencies of Foreign Cies	490	628	746	791	198	205	205	:	F.2.7.3. Succursales et Agences d'Ent. Etrangères
F.2.7.4. Domestic Investment	76 340	:	:	:	:	:	:	:	F.2.7.4. Placement dans le Pays
F.2.7.5. Foreign Investment	21 847	:	:	:	:	:	:	:	F.2.7.5. Placement à l' Etranger
F.2.7. Total of Non-Life Investments	98 187	94 472	83 262	104 429	164 831	175 512	245 165	273 234	F.2.7. Total des Placements Non-Vie

Monetary Unit: million Swedish kroner

Unité monétaire : million de couronnes suédoises

G. BREAKDOWN OF NON-LIFE PREMIUMS
G. VENTILATIONS DES PRIMES NON-VIE

	1990	1991	1992	1993	1994	1995	1996	1997	
G.1. Motor vehicle									**G.1. Assurance Automobile**
G.1.1. Direct Business									G.1.1. Assurances Directes
G.1.1.1. Gross Premiums	9 200	9 684	10 910	11 019	10 056	10 252	10 386	10 263	G.1.1.1. Primes Brutes
G.1.1.2. Ceded Premiums	603	..	870	886	839	669	734	676	G.1.1.2. Primes Cédées
G.1.1.3. Net Written Premiums	8 597	..	9 320	9 223	9 217	9 583	9 652	9 587	G.1.1.3. Primes Nettes Emises
G.2. Marine, Aviation									**G.2. Marine, Aviation**
G.2.1. Direct Business									G.2.1. Assurances Directes
G.2.1.1. Gross Premiums	653	811	912	1 178	1 314	1 193	1 003	935	G.2.1.1. Primes Brutes
G.2.1.2. Ceded Premiums	322	..	523	613	725	607	499	442	G.2.1.2. Primes Cédées
G.2.1.3. Net Written Premiums	331	..	389	665	589	586	504	493	G.2.1.3. Primes Nettes Emises
G.3. Freight									**G.3. Fret**
G.3.1. Direct Business									G.3.1. Assurances Directes
G.3.1.1. Gross Premiums	887	746	752	687	763	834	810	747	G.3.1.1. Primes Brutes
G.3.1.2. Ceded Premiums	321	..	258	209	308	303	317	260	G.3.1.2. Primes Cédées
G.3.1.3. Net Written Premiums	566	..	493	478	455	531	493	487	G.3.1.3. Primes Nettes Emises
G.4. Fire, Property Damages									**G.4. Incendie, Dommages aux Biens**
G.4.1. Direct Business									G.4.1. Assurances Directes
G.4.1.1. Gross Premiums	13 919	14 990	15 715	16 539	15 903	15 843	15 462	14 978	G.4.1.1. Primes Brutes
G.4.1.2. Ceded Premiums	2 987	..	3 519	3 645	4 127	4 388	3 972	3 399	G.4.1.2. Primes Cédées
G.4.1.3. Net Written Premiums	10 932	..	12 196	11 894	11 776	11 455	11 490	11 579	G.4.1.3. Primes Nettes Emises
G.5. Pecuniary Losses									**G.5. Pertes Pécunières**
G.5.1. Direct Business									G.5.1. Assurances Diractes
G.5.1.1. Gross Premiums	400	564	384	660	528	489	570	603	G.5.1.1. Primes Brutes
G.5.1.2. Ceded Premiums	139	..	- 169	61	79	177	159	75	G.5.1.2. Primes Cédées
G.5.1.3. Net Written Premiums	261	..	553	599	449	312	411	528	G.5.1.3. Primes Nettes Emises
G.7. Accident, Health									**G.7. Accident, Santé**
G.7.1. Direct Business									G.7.1. Assurances Directes
G.7.1.1. Gross Premiums	5 863	9 678	8 576	17 514	6 274	6 613	6 421	7 089	G.7.1.1. Primes Brutes
G.7.1.2. Ceded Premiums	109	..	101	168	141	167	1 402	137	G.7.1.2. Primes Cédées
G.7.1.3. Net Written Premiums	5 754	..	8 475	17 346	6 133	6 446	5 019	6 952	G.7.1.3. Primes Nettes Emises
G.8. Others									**G.8. Autres**
G.8.1. Direct Business									G.8.1. Assurances Directes
G.8.1.1. Gross Premiums	571	633	643	710	970	1 084	547	1 753	G.8.1.1. Primes Brutes
G.8.1.2. Ceded Premiums	12	..	11	10	5	5	6	6	G.8.1.2. Primes Cédées
G.8.1.3. Net Written Premiums	559	..	632	700	965	1 079	541	1 747	G.8.1.3. Primes Nettes Emises
G.9. Treaty Reinsurance									**G.9. Réassurance Obligatoire**
G.9.2. Reinsurance Accepted									G.9.2. Réassurance Acceptée
G.9.2.1. Gross Premiums	11 120	12 371	14 174	5 553	10 816	10 176	9 971	10 479	G.9.2.1. Primes Brutes
G.9.2.2. Ceded Premiums	3 042	3 482	3 917	3 132	3 400	3 584	2 795	4 606	G.9.2.2. Primes Cédées
G.9.2.3. Net Written Premiums	8 078	8 889	10 257	2 421	7 416	6 592	7 176	5 873	G.9.2.3. Primes Nettes Emises
G.9.3. Total									G.9.3. Total
G.9.3.1. Gross Premiums	..	12 371	14 174	5 553	10 816	10 176	9 971	:	G.9.3.1. Primes Brutes
G.9.3.2. Ceded Premiums	..	3 482	3 917	3 132	3 400	3 584	2 795	:	G.9.3.2. Primes Cédées
G.9.3.3. Net Written Premiums	..	8 889	10 257	2 421	7 416	6 592	7 176	:	G.9.3.3. Primes Nettes Emises
G.10. Total									**G.10. Total**
G.10.1. Direct Business									G.10.1. Assurances Directes
G.10.1.1. Gross Premiums	31 493	37 106	37 172	46 397	35 809	36 308	35 199	36 368	G.10.1.1. Primes Brutes
G.10.1.2. Ceded Premiums	4 493	5 320	5 113	5 592	6 224	6 316	7 089	4 995	G.10.1.2. Primes Cédées
G.10.1.3. Net Written Premiums	27 000	31 786	32 059	40 805	29 584	29 992	28 110	31 373	G.10.1.3. Primes Nettes Emises
G.10.2. Reinsurance Accepted									G.10.2. Réassurance Acceptée
G.10.2.1. Gross Premiums	11 120	12 371	..	..	..	..	9 971	10 479	G.10.2.1. Primes Brutes
G.10.2.2. Ceded Premiums	3 042	3 482	..	..	..	..	2 795	4 606	G.10.2.2. Primes Cédées
G.10.2.3. Net Written Premiums	8 078	8 889	..	..	..	..	7 176	5 873	G.10.2.3. Primes Nettes Emises
G.10.3. Total									G.10.3. Total
G.10.3.1. Gross Premiums	..	49 477	..	..	..	..	45 170	46 847	G.10.3.1. Primes Brutes
G.10.3.2. Ceded Premiums	..	8 802	..	..	..	..	9 884	9 601	G.10.3.2. Primes Cédées
G.10.3.3. Net Written Premiums	..	40 675	..	..	..	..	35 286	37 246	G.10.3.3. Primes Nettes Emises

Monetary Unit: million Swedish kroner — Unité monétaire : million de couronnes suédoises

H. GROSS CLAIMS PAYMENTS — H. PAIEMENTS BRUTS DES SINISTRES

		1990	1991	1992	1993	1994	1995	1996	1997
H.1. Life	**H.1. Vie**								
H.1.1. Domestic Companies	H.1.1. Entreprises Nationales							22 961	24 035
H.1. Total	H.1. Total							22 961	24 035
H.2. Non-Life	**H.2. Non-Vie**								
H.2.1. Domestic Companies	H.2.1. Entreprises Nationales							38 089	37 502
H.2.2. (Foreign Controlled Companies)	H.2.2. (Entreprises Sous Contrôle Etranger)							704	835
H.2.3. Branches & Agencies of Foreign Cies	H.2.3. Succursales et Agences d'Ent. Etrangères							67	0
H.2. Total	H.2. Total							38 156	37 502

I. GROSS OPERATING EXPENSES — I. DEPENSES BRUTES D'EXPLOITATION

		1990	1991	1992	1993	1994	1995	1996	1997
I.1. Life	**I.1. Vie**								
I.1.1. Domestic Companies	I.1.1. Entreprises Nationales							5 305	5 656
I.1. Total	I.1. Total des Primes Nettes Vie							5 305	5 656
I.2. Non-Life	**I.2. Non-Vie**								
I.2.1. Domestic Companies	I.2.1. Entreprises Nationales							8 430	8 406
I.2.2. (Foreign Controlled Companies)	I.2.2. (Entreprises Sous Contrôle Etranger)							292	312
I.2.3. Branches & Agencies of Foreign Cies	I.2.3. Succursales et Agences d'Ent. Etrangères							55	0
I.2. Total	I.2. Total							8 485	8 406

J. COMMISSIONS — J. COMMISSIONS

		1990	1991	1992	1993	1994	1995	1996	1997
J.1. Life	**J.1. Vie**								
J.1.1. Direct Business	J.1.1. Assurance directe								
J.1.1.1. Domestic Companies	J.1.1.1. Entreprises Nationales							1 906	2 249
J.1.1. Total	J.1.1. Total							1 906	2 249
J.1.2. Reinsurance Accepted	J.1.2. Réassurances acceptées								
J.1.2.1. Domestic Companies	J.1.2.1. Entreprises Nationales							5	4
J.1.2. Total	J.1.2. Total							5	4
J.1.3. Total	J.1.3. Total								
J.1.3.1. Domestic Companies	J.1.3.1. Entreprises Nationales							1 911	2 253
J.1.3. Total	J.1.3. Total							1 911	2 253
J.2. Non-Life	**J.2. Non-Vie**								
J.2.1. Direct Business	J.2.1. Assurance directe								
J.2.1.1. Domestic Companies	J.2.1.1. Entreprises Nationales							1 324	1 545
J.2.1.2. (Foreign Controlled Companies)	J.2.1.2. (Entreprises Sous Contrôle Etranger)							92	94
J.2.1. Total	J.2.1. Total des Primes Nettes Vie							1 324	1 545
J.2.2. Reinsurance Accepted	J.2.2. Réassurances acceptées								
J.2.2.1. Domestic Companies	J.2.2.1. Entreprises Nationales							2 362	2 125
J.2.2.2. (Foreign Controlled Companies)	J.2.2.2. (Entreprises Sous Contrôle Etranger)							11	4
J.2.2. Total	J.2.2. Total							2 362	2 125
J.2.3. Total	J.2.3. Total								
J.2.3.1. Domestic Companies	J.2.3.1. Entreprises Nationales							3 686	3 670
J.2.3.2. (Foreign Controlled Companies)	J.2.3.2. (Entreprises Sous Contrôle Etranger)							103	98
J.2.3. Total	J.2.3. Total							3 686	3 670

Monetary Unit: million Swiss francs

Unité monétaire : million de francs suisses

A. NUMBER OF COMPANIES IN THE REPORTING COUNTRY
A. NOMBRE D'ENTREPRISES DANS LE PAYS DECLARANT

		1990	1991	1992	1993	1994	1995	1996	1997
A.1. Life	**A.1. Vie**								
A.1.1. Domestic Companies	A.1.1. Entreprises Nationales	29	29	30	30	30	31	31	31
A.1.2. (Foreign Controlled Companies)	A.1.2. (Entreprises Sous Contrôle Etranger)	5	5	6	7	8	8	8	..
A.1.3. Branches & Agencies of Foreign Cies	A.1.3. Succursales et Agences d'Ent. Etrangères	0	0	0	0	..	0	0	1
A.1. All Companies	A.1. Ensemble des Entreprises	29	29	30	30	30	31	31	32
A.2. Non-Life	**A.2. Non-Vie**								
A.2.1. Domestic Companies	A.2.1. Entreprises Nationales	65	69	67	70	71	71	71	73
A.2.2. (Foreign Controlled Companies)	A.2.2. (Entreprises Sous Contrôle Etranger)	8	6	9	12	17	15	..	..
A.2.3. Branches & Agencies of Foreign Cies	A.2.3. Succursales et Agences d'Ent. Etrangères	24	24	26	25	27	25	25	27
A.2. All Companies	A.2. Ensemble des Entreprises	89	93	93	95	98	96	96	100
A.4. Reinsurance	**A.4. Réassurance**								
A.4.1. Domestic Companies	A.4.1. Entreprises Nationales	14	15	19	19	21	23	26	26
A.4.2. (Foreign Controlled Companies)	A.4.2. (Entreprises Sous Contrôle Etranger)	8	8	12	13	15	13	13	..
A.4. All Companies	A.4. Ensemble des Entreprises	14	15	19	21	23	26	26	27
A.5. Total	**A.5. Total**								
A.5.1. Domestic Companies	A.5.1. Entreprises Nationales	108	113	116	121	124	128	128	131
A.5.2. (Foreign Controlled Companies)	A.5.2. (Entreprises Sous Contrôle Etranger)	21	19	27	32	40	36	..	..
A.5.3. Branches & Agencies of Foreign Cies	A.5.3. Succursales et Agences d'Ent. Etrangères	24	24	26	25	27	25	25	28
A.5. All Insurance Companies	A.5. Ensemble des Entreprises d'Assurances	132	137	142	146	151	153	153	159

B. NUMBER OF EMPLOYEES
B. NOMBRE D'EMPLOYES

		1990	1991	1992	1993	1994	1995	1996	1997
B.1. Insurance Companies	B.1. Entreprises d'Assurances	35 811	37 313	37 313	37 241	36 510	36 619	..	..
B.2. Intermediaries	B.2. Intermédiaires	12 209	11 990	11 756	11 078	11 144	10 654	..	..
B. Total	B. Total	48 020	49 303	49 069	48 319	47 654	47 273	43 511	43 512

C. BUSINESS WRITTEN IN THE REPORTING COUNTRY
C. OPERATIONS CONCLUES DANS LE PAYS DECLARANT

		1990	1991	1992	1993	1994	1995	1996	1997
C.1. Life	**C.1. Vie**								
C.1.1. Gross Premiums	C.1.1. Primes Brutes								
C.1.1.1. Direct Business	C.1.1.1. Assurances Directes								
C.1.1.1.1. Domestic Companies	C.1.1.1.1. Entreprises Nationales	14 214	15 858	17 002	18 938	21 088	24 102	27 158	30 869
C.1.1.1.2. (Foreign Controlled Companies)	C.1.1.1.2. (Entreprises Sous Contrôle Etranger)	373	325	348	479	978	946	..	..
C.1.1.1. Total	C.1.1.1. Total	14 214	15 858	17 002	18 938	21 088	24 102	27 158	30 869
C.1.1.2. Reinsurance Accepted	C.1.1.2. Réassurance Acceptée								
C.1.1.2.1 Domestic Companies	C.1.1.2.1. Entreprises Nationales	1 569	1 651	1 734	1 890	1 661	1 881	1 058	555
C.1.1.2.2. (Foreign Controlled Companies)	C.1.1.2.2. (Entreprises Sous Contrôle Etranger)	88	100	92	100	69	965	..	..
C.1.1.2. Total	C.1.1.2. Total	1 569	1 651	1 734	1 890	1 661	1 881	1 058	555
C.1.1.3. Total	C.1.1.3. Total								
C.1.1.3.1 Domestic Companies	C.1.1.3.1. Entreprises Nationales	15 783	17 509	18 736	20 828	22 749	25 983	28 216	31 424
C.1.1.3.2. (Foreign Controlled Companies)	C.1.1.3.2. (Entreprises Sous Contrôle Etranger)	461	425	440	579	1 047	1 911	..	..
C.1.1.3. Total Gross Premiums	C.1.1.3. Total des Primes Brutes	15 783	17 509	18 736	20 828	22 749	25 983	28 216	31 424
C.1.2. Ceded Premiums	C.1.2. Primes Cédées								
C.1.2.1. Domestic Companies	C.1.2.1. Entreprises Nationales	585	581	616	679	748	740	525	425
C.1.2.2. (Foreign Controlled Companies)	C.1.2.2. (Entreprises Sous Contrôle Etranger)	91	57	90	74	72	82	..	..
C.1.2. Total	C.1.2. Total	585	581	616	679	748	740	525	425
C.1.3. Net Written Premiums	C.1.3. Primes Nettes Emises								
C.1.3.1. Domestic Companies	C.1.3.1. Entreprises Nationales	15 198	16 928	18 120	20 149	22 001	25 243	27 691	30 999
C.1.3. Total	C.1.3. Total	15 198	16 928	18 120	20 149	22 001	25 243	27 691	30 999

Monetary Unit: million Swiss francs

Unité monétaire : million de francs suisses

C.2. Non-Life — C.2. Non-Vie

	1990	1991	1992	1993	1994	1995	1996	1997
C.2.1. Gross premiums — C.2.1. Primes Brutes								
C.2.1.1. Direct Business — C.2.1.1. Assurances Directes								
C.2.1.1.1. Domestic Companies — Entreprises Nationales	10 972	11 510	12 100	12 542	12 932	13 200	13 301	13 039
C.2.1.1.2. (Foreign Controlled Companies) — (Entreprises Sous Contrôle Etranger)	414	432	554	581	637	1 072	..	..
C.2.1.1.3. Branches & Agencies of Foreign Cies — Succursales et Agences d'Ent. Etrangères	254	258	264	273	268	236	319	333
C.2.1.1. Total	11 226	11 768	12 364	12 815	13 200	13 436	13 620	13 372
C.2.1.2. Reinsurance Accepted — C.2.1.2. Réassurance Acceptée								
C.2.1.2.1. Domestic Companies — Entreprises Nationales	10 824	12 276	14 776	16 141	15 936	14 266	6 327	5 528
C.2.1.2.2. (Foreign Controlled Companies) — (Entreprises Sous Contrôle Etranger)	1 406	1 582	1 860	2 652	2 231	825	..	..
C.2.1.2.3. Branches & Agencies of Foreign Cies — Succursales et Agences d'Ent. Etrangères	104	30	33	37	43	33	..	10
C.2.1.2. Total	10 928	12 306	14 809	16 178	15 979	14 299	6 327	5 538
C.2.1.3. Total								
C.2.1.3.1. Domestic Companies — Entreprises Nationales	21 796	23 786	26 876	28 683	28 868	27 466	19 628	18 567
C.2.1.3.2. (Foreign Controlled Companies) — (Entreprises Sous Contrôle Etranger)	1 820	2 014	2 364	3 233	2 868	1 897	..	..
C.2.1.3.3. Branches & Agencies of Foreign Cies — Succursales et Agences d'Ent. Etrangères	358	288	297	310	311	269	319	343
C.2.1.3. Total Gross Premiums — Total des Primes Brutes	22 154	24 074	27 173	28 993	29 179	27 735	19 947	18 910
C.2.2. Ceded Premiums — C.2.2. Primes Cédées								
C.2.2.1. Domestic Companies — Entreprises Nationales	4 372	4 457	5 376	5 983	5 324	5 297	5 666	4 094
C.2.2.2. (Foreign Controlled Companies) — (Entreprises Sous Contrôle Etranger)	571	626	794	1 329	841	1 583	..	..
C.2.2. Total	4 372	4 457	5 376	5 983	..	..	5 666	4 094
C.2.3. Net Written Premiums — C.2.3. Primes Nettes Emises								
C.2.3.1. Domestic Companies — Entreprises Nationales	17 424	19 329	21 500	22 700	23 544	22 169	13 962	14 473
C.2.3.2. (Foreign Controlled Companies) — (Entreprises Sous Contrôle Etranger)	1 249	1 388	1 570	1 904	2 027	314	..	..
C.2.3.3. Branches & Agencies of Foreign Cies — Succursales et Agences d'Ent. Etrangères	358	288	297	310	..	..	319	343
C.2.3. Total	17 782	19 617	21 797	23 010	..	..	14 281	14 816

C.3. Total

	1990	1991	1992	1993	1994	1995	1996	1997
C.3.1. Gross Premiums — C.3.1. Primes Brutes								
C.3.1.1. Direct Business — C.3.1.1. Assurances Directes								
C.3.1.1.1. Domestic Companies — Entreprises Nationales	25 186	27 368	29 102	31 480	34 020	37 302	40 459	43 908
C.3.1.1.2. (Foreign Controlled Companies) — (Entreprises Sous Contrôle Etranger)	787	757	902	1 060	1 615	2 018	..	..
C.3.1.1.3. Branches & Agencies of Foreign Cies — Succursales et Agences d'Ent. Etrangères	254	258	264	273	273	236	319	..
C.3.1.1. Total	25 440	27 626	29 366	31 753	34 288	37 538	40 778	44 241
C.3.1.2. Reinsurance Accepted — C.3.1.2. Réassurance Acceptée								
C.3.1.2.1. Domestic Companies — Entreprises Nationales	12 393	13 927	16 510	18 031	17 597	16 147	7 385	6 083
C.3.1.2.2. (Foreign Controlled Companies) — (Entreprises Sous Contrôle Etranger)	1 494	1 682	1 952	2 752	2 300	1 790	..	..
C.3.1.2.3. Branches & Agencies of Foreign Cies — Succursales et Agences d'Ent. Etrangères	104	30	33	37	37	33	..	..
C.3.1.2. Total	12 497	13 957	16 543	18 068	17 640	16 180	7 385	6 093
C.3.1.3. Total								
C.3.1.3.1. Domestic Companies — Entreprises Nationales	37 579	41 295	45 612	49 511	51 617	53 449	47 844	49 991
C.3.1.3.2. (Foreign Controlled Companies) — (Entreprises Sous Contrôle Etranger)	2 281	2 439	2 804	3 812	3 915	3 808	..	..
C.3.1.3.3. Branches & Agencies of Foreign Cies — Succursales et Agences d'Ent. Etrangères	358	288	297	310	310	269	319	343
C.3.1.3. Total Gross Premiums — Total des Primes Brutes	37 937	41 583	45 909	49 821	51 928	53 718	48 163	50 334
C.3.2. Ceded Premiums — C.3.2. Primes Cédées								
C.3.2.1. Domestic Companies — Entreprises Nationales	4 957	5 038	5 992	6 662	6 072	6 037	6 191	4 519
C.3.2.2. (Foreign Controlled Companies) — (Entreprises Sous Contrôle Etranger)	662	683	884	1 403	913	1 665	..	..
C.3.2. Total	4 957	5 038	5 992	6 662	..	..	6 191	4 519
C.3.3. Net Written Premiums — C.3.3. Primes Nettes Emises								
C.3.3.1. Domestic Companies — Entreprises Nationales	32 622	36 257	39 620	42 849	45 545	47 412	41 653	45 472
C.3.3.2. (Foreign Controlled Companies) — (Entreprises Sous Contrôle Etranger)	1 249	1 388	1 570	1 904	2 027	314	..	..
C.3.3.3. Branches & Agencies of Foreign Cies — Succursales et Agences d'Ent. Etrangères	358	288	297	310	..	..	319	343
C.3.3. Total	32 980	36 545	39 917	43 159	..	..	41 972	45 815

Monetary Unit: million Swiss francs · Unité monétaire : million de francs suisses

E. BUSINESS WRITTEN ABROAD — E. OPERATIONS A L'ETRANGER

E.1. Life — E.1. Vie

	1990	1991	1992	1993	1994	1995	1996	1997
E.1.1. Gross Premiums / E.1.1. Primes Brutes								
E.1.1.1. Direct Business / E.1.1.1. Assurance Directe								
E.1.1.1.1. Branches & Agencies / Succursales & Agences	4 700	5 600	6 100	6 450	7 100	5 800		
E.1.1.1.2. Subsidiaries / Filliales	3 100	4 000	4 800	5 300	6 500	6 800		
E.1.1.1. Total / Total	7 800	9 600	10 900	11 750	13 600	12 600	...	...
E.1.1.2. Reinsurance Accepted / Réassurance Acceptée								
E.1.1.2.1. Branches & Agencies / Succursales & Agences	1 000	1 200	1 500	1 700	1 750	1 200		
E.1.1.2.2. Subsidiaries / Filliales	200	250	350	400	450	1 200		
E.1.1.2. Total / Total	1 200	1 450	1 850	2 100	2 200	2 400	...	...
E.1.1.3. Total / E.1.1.3. Total								
E.1.1.3.1. Branches & Agencies / Succursales & Agences	5 700	6 800	7 600	8 150	8 850	7 000		
E.1.1.3.2. Subsidiaries / Filliales	3 300	4 250	5 150	5 700	6 950	8 000	...	
E.1.1.3. Total Gross Premiums / Total des Primes Brutes	9 000	11 050	12 750	13 850	15 800	15 000	6 183	5 963
E.1.2. Ceded Premiums / E.1.2. Primes Cédées								
E.1.2.1. Branches & Agencies / Succursales & Agences	300	350	380	400	1 800	300		
E.1.2.2. Subsidiaries / Filliales	200	200	250	280	350	1 200		
E.1.2. Total / Total	500	550	630	680	2 150	1 500	...	...
E.1.3. Net Written Premiums / E.1.3. Primes Nettes Emises								
E.1.3.1. Branches & Agencies / Succursales & Agences	5 400	6 450	7 220	7 750	7 050	6 700		
E.1.3.2. Subsidiaries / Filliales	3 100	4 050	4 900	5 420	6 600	6 800		
E.1.3. Total / Total	8 500	10 500	12 120	13 170	13 650	13 500	...	...

E.2. Non-Life — E.2. Non-Vie

	1990	1991	1992	1993	1994	1995	1996	1997
E.2.1. Gross Premiums / E.2.1. Primes Brutes								
E.2.1.1. Direct Business / E.2.1.1. Assurance Directe								
E.2.1.1.1. Branches & Agencies / Succursales & Agences	8 200	9 100	8 700	9 300	9 200	8 300		
E.2.1.1.2. Subsidiaries / Filliales	15 200	18 000	20 500	22 000	25 100	18 300		
E.2.1.1. Total / Total	23 400	27 100	29 200	31 300	34 300	26 600	...	...
E.2.1.2. Reinsurance Accepted / Réassurance Acceptée								
E.2.1.2.1. Branches & Agencies / Succursales & Agences	10 000	11 800	13 700	15 000	16 500	8 900		
E.2.1.2.2. Subsidiaries / Filliales	2 000	2 350	3 050	3 300	3 700	11 100		
E.2.1.2. Total / Total	12 000	14 150	16 750	18 300	20 200	20 000	...	...
E.2.1.3. Total / E.2.1.3. Total								
E.2.1.3.1. Branches & Agencies / Succursales & Agences	18 200	20 900	22 400	24 300	25 700	17 200		
E.2.1.3.2. Subsidiaries / Filliales	17 200	20 350	23 550	25 300	28 800	29 400	...	
E.2.1.3. Total Gross Premiums / Total des Primes Brutes	35 400	41 250	45 950	49 600	54 500	46 600	8 695	8 618
E.2.2. Ceded Premiums / E.2.2. Primes Cédées								
E.2.2.1. Branches & Agencies / Succursales & Agences	2 400	2 700	2 900	3 200	3 300	2 200		
E.2.2.2. Subsidiaries / Filliales	2 300	2 600	3 050	3 300	3 700	3 800		
E.2.2. Total / Total	4 700	5 300	5 950	6 500	7 000	6 000	...	...
E.2.3. Net Written Premiums / E.2.3. Primes Nettes Emises								
E.2.3.1. Branches & Agencies / Succursales & Agences	15 800	18 200	19 500	21 100	22 400	15 000		
E.2.3.2. Subsidiaries / Filliales	14 900	17 750	20 500	22 000	25 100	25 600		
E.2.3. Total / Total	30 700	35 950	40 000	43 100	47 500	40 600	...	...

219

Monetary Unit: million Swiss francs

Unité monétaire : million de francs suisses

F. OUTSTANDING INVESTMENT BY DIRECT INSURANCE COMPANIES
F. ENCOURS DES PLACEMENTS DES ENTREPRISES D'ASSURANCES DIRECTES

F.1. Life / F.1. Vie

Label	1990	1991	1992	1993	1994	1995	1996	1997	Label (FR)
F.1.1. Real Estate									F.1.1. Immobilier
F.1.1.1. Domestic Companies	17 639	18 646	19 754	20 818	21 789	22 502	23 493	24 311	F.1.1.1. (Entreprises Nationales)
F.1.1.2. (Foreign Controlled Companies)	225	244	273	398	1 027	899	:	:	F.1.1.2. (Entreprises Sous Controle Etranger)
F.1.2. Mortgage Loans									F.1.2. Prêts Hypothécaires
F.1.2.1. Domestic Companies	24 672	26 306	27 477	27 183	27 134	26 683	26 407	26 568	F.1.2.1. (Entreprises Nationales)
F.1.2.2. (Foreign Controlled Companies)	353	374	358	481	798	609	:	:	F.1.2.2. (Entreprises Sous Controle Etranger)
F.1.3. Shares									F.1.3. Actions
F.1.3.1. Domestic Companies	6 939	8 334	11 154	16 284	20 330	24 965	32 885	33 973	F.1.3.1. (Entreprises Nationales)
F.1.3.2. (Foreign Controlled Companies)	46	47	52	369	498	616	:	:	F.1.3.2. (Entreprises Sous Controle Etranger)
F.1.4. Bonds with Fixed Revenue									F.1.4. Obligations
F.1.4.1. Domestic Companies	42 569	47 351	52 990	58 585	64 843	72 125	83 187	94 680	F.1.4.1. (Entreprises Nationales)
F.1.4.2. (Foreign Controlled Companies)	737	762	813	1 259	1 889	1 707	:	:	F.1.4.2. (Entreprises Sous Controle Etranger)
F.1.5. Loans other than Mortgage Loans									F.1.5. Prêts Autres qu'Hypothécaires
F.1.5.1. Domestic Companies	17 726	19 730	20 878	22 477	23 647	25 917	34 344	27 547	F.1.5.1. (Entreprises Nationales)
F.1.5.2. (Foreign Controlled Companies)	78	73	92	213	342	562	:	:	F.1.5.2. (Entreprises Sous Controle Etranger)
F.1.6. Other Investments									F.1.6. Autres Placements
F.1.6.1. Domestic Companies	3 364	4 411	4 709	4 723	5 612	14 302	2 434	1 629	F.1.6.1. (Entreprises Nationales)
F.1.6.2. (Foreign Controlled Companies)	198	285	314	391	487	442	:	:	F.1.6.2. (Entreprises Sous Controle Etranger)
F.1.7. Total									F.1.7. Total
F.1.7.1. Domestic Companies	112 909	124 778	136 962	150 070	163 355	186 494	202 750	208 708	F.1.7.1. (Entreprises Nationales)
F.1.7.2. (Foreign Controlled Companies)	1 637	1 785	1 905	3 727	5 041	4 835	:	:	F.1.7.2. (Entreprises Sous Controle Etranger)

F.2. Non-Life / F.2. Non-Vie

Label	1990	1991	1992	1993	1994	1995	1996	1997	Label (FR)
F.2.1. Real Estate									F.2.1. Immobilier
F.2.1.1. Domestic Companies	6 379	7 068	7 620	7 904	8 420	8 158	7 880	7 703	F.2.1.1. (Entreprises Nationales)
F.2.1.2. (Foreign Controlled Companies)	139	151	179	180	182	191	:	:	F.2.1.2. (Entreprises Sous Controle Etranger)
F.2.2. Mortgage Loans									F.2.2. Prêts Hypothécaires
F.2.2.1. Domestic Companies	3 431	3 698	3 829	3 715	3 602	3 590	3 492	3 537	F.2.2.1. (Entreprises Nationales)
F.2.2.2. (Foreign Controlled Companies)	29	31	28	25	23	20	:	:	F.2.2.2. (Entreprises Sous Controle Etranger)
F.2.3. Shares									F.2.3. Actions
F.2.3.1. Domestic Companies	10 399	11 559	12 385	13 906	15 381	17 071	23 777	9 908	F.2.3.1. (Entreprises Nationales)
F.2.3.2. (Foreign Controlled Companies)	100	138	141	296	423	412	:	:	F.2.3.2. (Entreprises Sous Controle Etranger)
F.2.4. Bonds with Fixed Revenue									F.2.4. Obligations
F.2.4.1. Domestic Companies	19 462	19 775	20 415	21 037	21 561	21 935	23 021	25 472	F.2.4.1. (Entreprises Nationales)
F.2.4.2. (Foreign Controlled Companies)	437	443	514	564	641	750	:	:	F.2.4.2. (Entreprises Sous Controle Etranger)
F.2.5. Loans other than Mortgage Loans									F.2.5. Prêts Autres qu'Hypothécaires
F.2.5.1. Domestic Companies	4 373	5 259	5 171	5 565	6 225	5 736	8 479	5 820	F.2.5.1. (Entreprises Nationales)
F.2.5.2. (Foreign Controlled Companies)	110	86	59	59	985	1 119	:	:	F.2.5.2. (Entreprises Sous Controle Etranger)
F.2.6. Other Investments									F.2.6. Autres Placements
F.2.6.1. Domestic Companies	0	0	0	0	:	10 238	1 629	6 723	F.2.6.1. (Entreprises Nationales)
F.2.6.2. (Foreign Controlled Companies)	0	0	0	0	:	592	:	:	F.2.6.2. (Entreprises Sous Controle Etranger)
F.2.7. Total									F.2.7. Total
F.2.7.1. Domestic Companies	44 044	47 359	49 420	52 127	55 189	66 728	68 278	59 163	F.2.7.1. (Entreprises Nationales)
F.2.7.2. (Foreign Controlled Companies)	815	849	921	1 007	2 254	3 084	:	:	F.2.7.2. (Entreprises Sous Controle Etranger)

G. BREAKDOWN OF NON-LIFE PREMIUMS
G. VENTILATIONS DES PRIMES NON-VIE

Label	1990	1991	1992	1993	1994	1995	1996	1997	Label (FR)
G.1. Motor vehicle									G.1. Assurance Automobile
G.1.1. Direct Business									G.1.1. Assurances Directes
G.1.1.1. Gross Premiums	3 472	3 637	3 871	4 025	4 127	4 206	3 990	3 878	G.1.1.1. Primes Brutes
G.2. Marine, Aviation									G.2. Marine, Aviation
G.2.1. Direct Business									G.2.1. Assurances Directes
G.2.1.1. Gross Premiums	41	41	41	50	43	59	390	372	G.2.1.1. Primes Brutes

SWITZERLAND

Monetary Unit: million Swiss francs

	1990	1991	1992	1993	1994	1995	1996	1997	
G.3. Freight									G.3. Fret
G.3.1. Direct Business									G.3.1. Assurances Directes
G.3.1.1. Gross Premiums	275	285	298	306	308	602	..	..	G.3.1.1. Primes Brutes
G.4. Fire, Property Damages									G.4. Incendie, Dommages aux Biens
G.4.1. Direct Business									G.4.1. Assurances Directes
G.4.1.1. Gross Premiums	2 357	2 475	2 600	2 693	2 745	2 804	3 135	3 069	G.4.1.1. Primes Brutes
G.5. Pecuniary Losses									G.5. Pertes Pécunières
G.5.1. Direct Business									G.5.1. Assurances Directes
G.5.1.1. Gross Premiums	76	89	75	63	66	101	222	260	G.5.1.1. Primes Brutes
G.6. General Liability									G.6. Responsabilité Générale
G.6.1. Direct Business									G.6.1. Assurances Directes
G.6.1.1. Gross Premiums	1 164	1 198	1 224	1 295	1 319	1 387	1 384	1 383	G.6.1.1. Primes Brutes
G.7. Accident, Health									G.7. Accident, Santé
G.7.1. Direct Business									G.7.1. Assurances Directes
G.7.1.1. Gross Premiums	3 236	3 423	3 630	3 749	3 904	3 867	4 230	4 125	G.7.1.1. Primes Brutes
G.8. Others									G.8. Autres
G.8.1. Direct Business									G.8.1. Assurances Directes
G.8.1.1. Gross Premiums	605	620	625	634	688	410	269	285	G.8.1.1. Primes Brutes
G.10. Total									G.10. Total
G.10.1. Direct Business									G.10.1. Assurances Directes
G.10.1.1. Gross Premiums	11 226	11 768	12 364	12 815	13 200	13 436	13 620	13 372	G.10.1.1. Primes Brutes
G.10.2. Reinsurance Accepted									G.10.2. Réassurance Acceptée
G.10.2.1. Gross Premiums	10 928	12 306	14 809	16 178	15 979	14 299	6 327	5 538	G.10.2.1. Primes Brutes
G.10.2.2. Ceded Premiums	..	..	..	..	..	..	3 419	4 094	G.10.2.2. Primes Cédées
G.10.2.3. Net Written Premiums	..	..	..	..	..	..	2 908	1 444	G.10.2.3. Primes Nettes Emises
G.10.3. Total									G.10.3. Total
G.10.3.1. Gross Premiums	22 154	24 074	27 173	28 993	29 179	27 735	19 947	18 910	G.10.3.1. Primes Brutes
G.10.3.2. Ceded Premiums	..	..	..	..	..	..	5 666	4 094	G.10.3.2. Primes Cédées
G.10.3.3. Net Written Premiums	..	..	..	..	..	..	14 281	14 816	G.10.3.3. Primes Nettes Emises

H. GROSS CLAIMS PAYMENTS

H. PAIEMENTS BRUTS DES SINISTRES

	1990	1991	1992	1993	1994	1995	1996	1997	
H.1. Life									**H.1. Vie**
H.1.1. Domestic Companies							19 718	20 707	H.1.1. Entreprises Nationales
H.1. Total							19 718	20 707	H.1. Total
H.2. Non-Life									**H.2. Non-Vie**
H.2.1. Domestic Companies							16 126	17 218	H.2.1. Entreprises Nationales
H.2.3. Branches & Agencies of Foreign Cies							169		H.2.3. Succursales et Agences d'Ent. Etrangères
H.2. Total							16 295	17 218	H.2. Total

I. GROSS OPERATING EXPENSES

I. DEPENSES BRUTES D'EXPLOITATION

	1990	1991	1992	1993	1994	1995	1996	1997	
I.1. Life									**I.1. Vie**
I.1.1. Domestic Companies							1 899	..	I.1.1. Entreprises Nationales
I.1. Total							1 899	..	I.1. Total des Primes Nettes Vie

Monetary Unit : million Turkish liras

Unité monétaire : million de livres turques

	1990	1991	1992	1993	1994	1995	1996	1997
A. NUMBER OF COMPANIES IN THE REPORTING COUNTRY / **A. NOMBRE D'ENTREPRISES DANS LE PAYS DECLARANT**								
A.1. Life / **A.1. Vie**								
A.1.1. Domestic Companies / A.1.1. Entreprises Nationales	4	8	9	12	12	17	17	14
A.1.2. (Foreign Controlled Companies) / A.1.2. (Entreprises Sous Contrôle Etranger)	2	2	3	4	3	4	4	4
A.1. All Companies / A.1. Ensemble des Entreprises	4	8	9	12	12	17	17	14
A.2. Non-Life / **A.2. Non-Vie**								
A.2.1. Domestic Companies / A.2.1. Entreprises Nationales	15	18	21	20	24	19	22	19
A.2.2. (Foreign Controlled Companies) / A.2.2. (Entreprises Sous Contrôle Etranger)	11	12	10	6	7	6	6	5
A.2.3. Branches & Agencies of Foreign Cies / A.2.3. Succursales et Agences d'Ent. Etrangères	3	3	1	2	1	2	2	0
A.2. All Companies / A.2. Ensemble des Entreprises	18	21	22	22	25	21	24	19
A.3. Composite / **A.3. Mixte**								
A.3.1. Domestic Companies / A.3.1. Entreprises Nationales	20	20	19	19	15	17	17	16
A.3.2. (Foreign Controlled Companies) / A.3.2. (Entreprises Sous Contrôle Etranger)	0	3	3	3	1	1	1	1
A.3. All Companies / A.3. Ensemble des Entreprises	20	20	19	19	15	17	17	16
A.4. Reinsurance / **A.4. Réassurance**								
A.4.1. Domestic Companies / A.4.1. Entreprises Nationales	4	4	4	4	4	4	4	4
A.4. All Companies / A.4. Ensemble des Entreprises	4	4	4	4	4	4	4	4
A.5. Total								
A.5.1. Domestic Companies / A.5.1. Entreprises Nationales	43	50	53	55	55	57	60	53
A.5.2. (Foreign Controlled Companies) / A.5.2. (Entreprises Sous Contrôle Etranger)	13	17	16	13	11	11	11	10
A.5.3. Branches & Agencies of Foreign Cies / A.5.3. Succursales et Agences d'Ent. Etrangères	3	3	1	2	1	2	2	0
A.5. All Insurance Companies / A.5. Ensemble des Entreprises d'Assurances	46	53	54	57	56	59	62	53
B. NUMBER OF EMPLOYEES / **B. NOMBRE D'EMPLOYES**								
B.1. Insurance Companies / B.1. Entreprises d'Assurances	4 668	5 186	5 215	5 932	5 598	6 578	7 453	8 076
B.2. Intermediaries / B.2. Intermediaires	13 105	8 324	:	9 948	10 995	10 723	12 191	13 862
B. Total	:	:	:	:	16 593	:	19 644	21 938
C. BUSINESS WRITTEN IN THE REPORTING COUNTRY / **C. OPERATIONS CONCLUES DANS LE PAYS DECLARANT**								
C.1. Life / **C.1. Vie**								
C.1.1. Gross Premiums / C.1.1. Primes Brutes								
C.1.1.1. Direct Business / C.1.1.1. Assurances Directes								
C.1.1.1.1. Domestic Companies / C.1.1.1.1. Entreprises Nationales	451 861	847 524	1 533 808	2 478 185	3 862 596	8 108 208	18 793 268	44 701 566
C.1.1.1.2. (Foreign Controlled Companies) / C.1.1.1.2. (Entreprises Sous Contrôle Etranger)	2 581	9 894	37 611	120 962	223 739	496 977	1 596 764	3 039 653
C.1.1.1. Total / C.1.1.1. Total	451 861	847 524	1 571 419	2 478 185	3 862 596	8 108 208	18 793 268	44 701 566
C.1.1.2. Reinsurance Accepted / C.1.1.2. Réassurance Acceptée								
C.1.1.2.1. Domestic Companies / C.1.1.2.1. Entreprises Nationales	192	384	288	446	1 332	46 751	102 227	248 807
C.1.1.2.2. (Foreign Controlled Companies) / C.1.1.2.2. (Entreprises Sous Contrôle Etranger)	0	0	0	0	244	41 533	95 741	0
C.1.1.2. Total / C.1.1.2. Total	192	384	288	446	1 332	46 751	102 227	248 807
C.1.1.3. Total / C.1.1.3. Total								
C.1.1.3.1. Domestic Companies / C.1.1.3.1. Entreprises Nationales	452 053	847 908	1 534 096	2 478 631	3 863 928	8 154 959	18 895 495	44 950 373
C.1.1.3.2. (Foreign Controlled Companies) / C.1.1.3.2. (Entreprises Sous Contrôle Etranger)	2 581	9 894	37 611	120 962	223 983	538 510	1 692 505	3 039 653
C.1.1.3. Total Gross Premiums / C.1.1.3. Total des Primes Brutes	452 053	847 908	1 571 707	2 478 631	3 863 928	8 154 959	18 895 495	44 950 373
C.1.2. Ceded Premiums / C.1.2. Primes Cédées								
C.1.2.1. Domestic Companies / C.1.2.1. Entreprises Nationales	19 614	36 455	54 956	35 058	62 153	205 715	468 374	1 005 923
C.1.2.2. (Foreign Controlled Companies) / C.1.2.2. (Entreprises Sous Contrôle Etranger)	834	956	4 663	2 175	1 429	24 031	88 408	33 741
C.1.2. Total / C.1.2. Total	19 614	36 455	59 619	35 058	62 153	205 715	468 374	1 005 923
C.1.3. Net Written Premiums / C.1.3. Primes Nettes Emises								
C.1.3.1. Domestic Companies / C.1.3.1. Entreprises Nationales	432 439	811 453	1 479 140	2 443 573	3 801 775	7 949 244	18 427 121	43 944 450
C.1.3.2. (Foreign Controlled Companies) / C.1.3.2. (Entreprises Sous Contrôle Etranger)	1 747	8 938	32 948	118 787	222 554	514 479	1 604 097	3 005 912
C.1.3. Total / C.1.3. Total	432 439	811 453	1 512 088	2 443 543	3 801 775	7 949 244	18 427 121	43 944 450

Monetary Unit: million Turkish liras   Unité monétaire : million de livres turques

	1990	1991	1992	1993	1994	1995	1996	1997
C.2. Non-Life / C.2. Non-Vie								
C.2.1. Gross premiums / C.2.1. Primes Brutes								
C.2.1.1. Direct Business / C.2.1.1. Assurances Directes								
C.2.1.1.1. Domestic Companies / C.2.1.1.1. Entreprises Nationales	1 764 016	3 183 196	5 776 740	14 377 303	27 904 903	54 842 768	109 012 293	237 841 036
C.2.1.1.2. (Foreign Controlled Companies) / C.2.1.1.2. (Entreprises Sous Contrôle Etranger)	224 348	409 779	815 436	1 626 184	2 761 653	5 352 774	11 170 228	20 715 654
C.2.1.1.3. Branches & Agencies of Foreign Cies / C.2.1.1.3. Succursales et Agences d'Ent. Etrangères	7 755	22 481	8 258	44 464	57 640	57 985	- 1 172	0
C.2.1.1. Total / C.2.1.1. Total	1 771 771	3 205 677	6 600 434	14 421 767	27 962 543	54 900 753	109 011 121	237 841 036
C.2.1.2. Reinsurance Accepted / C.2.1.2. Réassurance Acceptée								
C.2.1.2.1. Domestic Companies / C.2.1.2.1. Entreprises Nationales	109 575	148 227	161 085	251 422	447 730	724 448	1 383 443	2 595 257
C.2.1.2.2. (Foreign Controlled Companies) / C.2.1.2.2. (Entreprises Sous Contrôle Etranger)	3 579	15 547	9 233	12 283	25 789	51 587	70 142	290 669
C.2.1.2.3. Branches & Agencies of Foreign Cies / C.2.1.2.3. Succursales et Agences d'Ent. Etrangères	265	112	16	0	0	0	0	0
C.2.1.2. Total / C.2.1.2. Total	109 875	148 339	170 334	251 422	447 730	724 448	1 383 443	2 595 257
C.2.1.3. Total / C.2.1.3. Total								
C.2.1.3.1. Domestic Companies / C.2.1.3.1. Entreprises Nationales	1 873 591	3 331 423	5 937 825	14 628 725	28 352 633	55 567 216	110 395 735	240 436 293
C.2.1.3.2. (Foreign Controlled Companies) / C.2.1.3.2. (Entreprises Sous Contrôle Etranger)	227 927	425 326	824 669	1 638 467	2 787 442	5 404 361	11 240 370	21 006 323
C.2.1.3.3. Branches & Agencies of Foreign Cies / C.2.1.3.3. Succursales et Agences d'Ent. Etrangères	7 985	22 593	8 274	44 464	57 640	57 985	- 1 172	0
C.2.1.3. Total Gross Premiums / C.2.1.3. Tota des Primes Brutes	1 881 576	3 354 016	6 770 768	14 673 189	28 410 273	55 625 201	110 394 563	240 436 293
C.2.2. Ceded Premiums / C.2.2. Primes Cédées								
C.2.2.1. Domestic Companies / C.2.2.1. Entreprises Nationales	964 552	1 561 383	2 785 063	2 387 800	6 402 240	12 249 783	23 627 767	53 222 246
C.2.2.2. (Foreign Controlled Companies) / C.2.2.2. (Entreprises Sous Contrôle Etranger)	126 315	203 711	379 232	216 286	723 951	1 338 494	2 999 246	5 491 231
C.2.2.3. Branches & Agencies of Foreign Cies / C.2.2.3. Succursales et Agences d'Ent. Etrangères	6 819	9 218	6 802	15 594	32 319	25 909	542	0
C.2.2. Total / C.2.2. Total	971 371	1 570 601	3 171 097	2 403 394	6 434 559	12 275 692	23 627 225	53 222 246
C.2.3. Net Written Premiums / C.2.3. Primes Nettes Emises								
C.2.3.1. Domestic Companies / C.2.3.1. Entreprises Nationales	909 039	1 770 040	3 152 762	12 240 925	21 950 393	43 317 433	86 767 969	187 214 047
C.2.3.2. (Foreign Controlled Companies) / C.2.3.2. (Entreprises Sous Contrôle Etranger)	101 612	221 615	445 437	1 422 181	2 063 491	4 065 867	8 241 124	15 515 092
C.2.3.3. Branches & Agencies of Foreign Cies / C.2.3.3. Succursales et Agences d'Ent. Etrangères	1 166	13 375	1 472	28 870	25 321	32 076	630	0
C.2.3. Total / C.2.3. Total	910 205	1 783 415	3 599 671	12 269 795	21 975 714	43 349 509	86 767 339	187 214 047
C.3. Total / C.3. Total								
C.3.1. Gross Premiums / C.3.1. Primes Brutes								
C.3.1.1. Direct Business / C.3.1.1. Assurances Directes								
C.3.1.1.1. Domestic Companies / C.3.1.1.1. Entreprises Nationales	2 215 877	4 030 720	7 310 548	16 855 488	31 767 499	62 950 976	127 805 561	282 542 602
C.3.1.1.2. (Foreign Controlled Companies) / C.3.1.1.2. (Entreprises Sous Contrôle Etranger)	226 929	419 673	853 047	1 747 146	2 985 392	5 849 751	12 766 992	23 755 307
C.3.1.1.3. Branches & Agencies of Foreign Cies / C.3.1.1.3. Succursales et Agences d'Ent. Etrangères	7 755	22 481		44 464	57 640	57 985	- 1 172	0
C.3.1.1. Total / C.3.1.1. Total	2 223 632	4 053 201	8 171 853	16 899 952	31 825 139	63 008 961	127 804 389	282 542 602
C.3.1.2. Reinsurance Accepted / C.3.1.2. Réassurance Acceptée								
C.3.1.2.1. Domestic Companies / C.3.1.2.1. Entreprises Nationales	109 767	148 611	161 373	251 868	449 062	771 199	1 485 670	2 844 064
C.3.1.2.2. (Foreign Controlled Companies) / C.3.1.2.2. (Entreprises Sous Contrôle Etranger)	3 579	15 547	9 233	12 283	26 033	93 120	165 883	290 669
C.3.1.2.3. Branches & Agencies of Foreign Cies / C.3.1.2.3. Succursales et Agences d'Ent. Etrangères	265	112		0	0	0	0	0
C.3.1.2. Total / C.3.1.2. Total	110 067	148 723	170 622	251 868	449 062	771 199	1 485 670	2 844 064
C.3.1.3. Total / C.3.1.3. Total								
C.3.1.3.1. Domestic Companies / C.3.1.3.1. Entreprises Nationales	2 325 644	4 179 331	7 471 921	17 107 356	32 216 561	63 722 175	129 291 230	285 386 666
C.3.1.3.2. (Foreign Controlled Companies) / C.3.1.3.2. (Entreprises Sous Contrôle Etranger)	230 508	435 220	862 280	1 759 429	3 011 425	5 942 871	12 932 875	24 045 976
C.3.1.3.3 Branches & Agencies of Foreign Cies / C.3.1.3.3. Succursales et Agences d'Ent. Etrangères	7 985	22 593		44 464	57 640	57 985	- 1 172	0
C.3.1.3. Total Gross Premiums / C.3.1.3. Total des Primes Brutes	2 333 629	4 201 924	8 342 475	17 151 820	32 274 201	63 780 160	129 290 058	285 386 666
C.3.2. Ceded Premiums / C.3.2. Primes Cédées								
C.3.2.1. Domestic Companies / C.3.2.1. Entreprises Nationales	984 166	1 597 838	2 840 019	2 422 858	6 464 393	12 455 498	24 096 141	54 228 169
C.3.2.2. (Foreign Controlled Companies) / C.3.2.2. (Entreprises Sous Contrôle Etranger)	127 149	204 667	383 895	218 461	725 380	1 362 525	3 087 654	5 524 972
C.3.2.3. Branches & Agencies of Foreign Cies / C.3.2.3. Succursales et Agences d'Ent. Etrangères	6 819	9 218		15 594	32 319	25 909	542	0
C.3.2. Total / C.3.2. Total	990 985	1 607 056	3 230 716	2 438 452	6 496 712	12 481 407	24 095 599	54 228 169
C.3.3. Net Written Premiums / C.3.3. Primes Nettes Emises								
C.3.3.1. Domestic Companies / C.3.3.1. Entreprises Nationales	1 341 478	2 581 493	4 631 902	14 684 498	25 752 168	51 266 677	105 195 090	231 158 497
C.3.3.2. (Foreign Controlled Companies) / C.3.3.2. (Entreprises Sous Contrôle Etranger)	103 359	230 553	478 385	1 540 968	2 286 045	4 580 346	9 845 221	18 521 004
C.3.3.3. Branches & Agencies of Foreign Cies / C.3.3.3. Succursales et Agences d'Ent. Etrangères	1 166	13 375		28 870	25 321	32 076	630	0
C.3.3. Total / C.3.3. Total	1 342 644	2 594 868	5 111 759	14 713 338	25 777 489	51 298 753	105 194 460	231 158 497

TURKEY

Monetary Unit: million Turkish liras

**D. NET WRITTEN PREMIUMS IN THE REPORTING COUN-
TRY IN TERMS OF DOMESTIC AND FOREIGN RISKS**

**D. PRIMES NETTES EMISES DANS LE PAYS DECLARANT
EN RISQUES NATIONAUX ET ETRANGERS**

	1990	1991	1992	1993	1994	1995	1996	1997		
D.1. Life									**D.1. Vie**	
D.1.1. Domestic Risks									D.1.1. Risques Nationaux	
D.1.1.1. Domestic Companies	..	..	1 479 140	..	..	..	..	..	D.1.1.1. Entreprises Nationales	
D.1.1.2. (Foreign Controlled Companies)	..	..	32 948	..	..	..	..	..	D.1.1.2. (Entreprises Sous Contrôle Etranger)	
D.1.1. Total	..	..	1 512 088	..	..	..	..	..	D.1.1. Total des Primes Nettes Vie	
D.1.3. Total									D.1.3. Total	
D.1.3.1. Domestic Companies	..	..	1 479 140	2 443 573	3 801 775	7 949 244	18 427 121	43 944 450	D.1.3.1. Entreprises Nationales	
D.1.3.2. (Foreign Controlled Companies)	..	..	32 948	118 787	222 554	514 479	1 604 097	3 005 912	D.1.3.2. (Entreprises Sous Contrôle Etranger)	
D.1.3. Total of Life Net Premiums	..	..	1 512 088	2 443 543	3 801 775	7 949 244	18 427 121	43 944 450	D.1.3. Total des Primes Nettes Vie	
D.2. Non-Life									**D.2. Non-Vie**	
D.2.1. Domestic Risks									D.2.1. Risques Nationaux	
D.2.1.1. Domestic Companies	..	..	3 220 660	..	..	..	..	..	D.2.1.1. Entreprises Nationales	
D.2.1.2. (Foreign Controlled Companies)	..	..	448 737	..	..	..	..	..	D.2.1.2. (Entreprises Sous Contrôle Etranger)	
D.2.1.3. Branches & Agencies of Foreign Cies	..	..	1 472	..	..	..	..	..	D.2.1.3. Succursales et Agences d'Ent. Etrangères	
D.2.1. Total	..	..	3 670 869	..	..	..	..	..	D.2.1. Total des Primes Nettes Vie	
D.2.3. Total									D.2.3. Total	
D.2.3.1. Domestic Companies	..	..	3 220 660	12 240 925	21 950 393	43 317 433	86 767 969	187 214 047	D.2.3.1. Entreprises Nationales	
D.2.3.2. (Foreign Controlled Companies)	..	..	1 422 181	1 422 181	2 063 491	4 065 867	8 241 124	15 515 092	D.2.3.2. (Entreprises Sous Contrôle Etranger)	
D.2.3.3. Branches & Agencies of Foreign Cies	..	..	1 472	28 870	25 321	32 076	- 630		D.2.3.3. Succursales et Agences d'Ent. Etrangères	
D.2.3. Total	..	..	3 670 869	12 269 795	21 975 714	43 349 509	86 767 339	187 214 047	D.2.3. Total des Primes Nettes Vie	
E. BUSINESS WRITTEN ABROAD									**E. OPERATIONS A L'ETRANGER**	
E.2. Non-Life									**E.2. Non-Vie**	
E.2.1. Gross Premiums									E.2.1. Primes Brutes	
E.2.1.1.1. Branches & Agencies	..	..	..	..	55 640	..	..	..	E.2.1.1.1. Succursales & Agences	
E.2.1.3. Total	..	..	..	..	55 640	..	..	..	E.2.1.3. Total	
E.2.1.3.1. Branches & Agencies									E.2.1.3.1. Succursales & Agences	
E.2.3. Net Written Premiums									E.2.3. Primes Nettes Emises	
E.2.3.1. Branches & Agencies	..	..	..	..	55 640	..	..	..	E.2.3.1. Succursales & Agences	
**F. OUTSTANDING INVESTMENT BY
DIRECT INSURANCE COMPANIES**									**F. ENCOURS DES PLACEMENTS DES
ENTREPRISES D'ASSURANCES DIRECTES**	
F.1. Life									**F.1. Vie**	
F.1.1. Real Estate									F.1.1. Immobilier	
F.1.1.1. Domestic Companies	119 739	44 572	224 504	333 331	561 670	1 317 825	2 474 726	5 010 910	F.1.1.1. Entreprises Nationales	
F.1.1.2. (Foreign Controlled Companies)	0	5 386	7 439	0	0	57 874	99 089	178 557	F.1.1.2. (Entreprises Sous Contrôle Etranger)	
F.1.1.4. Domestic Investment	119 739	44 572	224 504	333 331	..	..	..	..	F.1.1.4. Placement dans le Pays	
F.1.1.5. Foreign Investment	0	0	0	0	..	..	..	..	F.1.1.5. Placement à l' Etranger	
F.1.1. Total	119 739	44 572	231 943	333 331	561 670	1 317 825	2 474 726	5 010 910	F.1.1. Total	
F.1.2. Mortgage Loans									F.1.2. Prêts Hypothécaires	
F.1.2.1. Domestic Companies	0	0	0	58 604	0	0	0	484 779	F.1.2.1. Entreprises Nationales	
F.1.2.2. (Foreign Controlled Companies)	..	0	0	0	0	0	0	2 258	F.1.2.2. (Entreprises Sous Contrôle Etranger)	
F.1.2.4. Domestic Investment	0	0	0	58 578	0	0	0	0	F.1.2.4. Placement dans le Pays	
F.1.2.5. Foreign Investment	0	0	..	26	0	0	0	0	F.1.2.5. Placement à l' Etranger	
F.1.2. Total	0	0	..	58 604	0	0	0	484 779	F.1.2. Total	

Monetary Unit: million Turkish liras — Unité monétaire : million de livres turques

English	1990	1991	1992	1993	1994	1995	1996	1997	Français
F.1.3. Shares									**F.1.3. Actions**
F.1.3.1. Domestic Companies	5 782	3 584	56 199	262 218	723 774	1 088 633	1 312 105	803 057	F.1.3.1. Entreprises Nationales
F.1.3.2. (Foreign Controlled Companies)	28	141	790	9 833	20 327	6 831	9 848	0	F.1.3.2. (Entreprises Sous Contrôle Etranger)
F.1.3.4. Domestic Investment	5 782	3 584	56 199	252 385	723 774	1 088 633	1 312 105	803 057	F.1.3.4. Placement dans le Pays
F.1.3.5. Foreign Investment	0	0	790	24 728	..	..	..	..	F.1.3.5. Placement à l' Etranger
F.1.3. Total	5 789	3 584	56 989	277 113	723 774	1 088 633	1 312 105	803 057	F.1.3. Total
F.1.4. Bonds with Fixed Revenue									**F.1.4. Obligations**
F.1.4.1. Domestic Companies	238 104	350 790	1 574 911	3 641 539	9 047 607	20 825 388	53 210 966	124 252 658	F.1.4.1. Entreprises Nationales
F.1.4.2. (Foreign Controlled Companies)	414	5 308	26 682	70 083	1 820	449 076	1 727 703	3 100 875	F.1.4.2. (Entreprises Sous Contrôle Etranger)
F.1.4.4. Domestic Investment	238 104	350 790	1 574 911	3 571 456	9 047 607	20 825 388	53 210 966	124 252 658	F.1.4.4. Placement dans le Pays
F.1.4.5. Foreign Investment	0	0	26 682	70 083	..	..	..	..	F.1.4.5. Placement à l' Etranger
F.1.4. Total	238 104	350 790	1 601 593	3 641 539	9 047 607	20 825 388	53 210 966	124 252 658	F.1.4. Total
F.1.5. Loans other than Mortgage Loans									**F.1.5. Prêts Autres qu'Hypothécaires**
F.1.5.1. Domestic Companies	10 564	18 429	34 947	58 347	91 169	154 387	85 420	794	F.1.5.1. Entreprises Nationales
F.1.5.2. (Foreign Controlled Companies)	4	..	2	26	0	7	66	..	F.1.5.2. (Entreprises Sous Contrôle Etranger)
F.1.5.4. Domestic Investment	10 564	18 429	34 947	58 321	91 169	154 387	85 420	794	F.1.5.4. Placement dans le Pays
F.1.5.5. Foreign Investment	0	0	2	26	..	..	..	..	F.1.5.5. Placement à l' Etranger
F.1.5. Total	10 564	18 429	34 949	58 347	91 169	154 387	85 420	794	F.1.5. Total
F.1.6. Other Investments									**F.1.6. Autres Placements**
F.1.6.1. Domestic Companies	..	0	0	0	0	1 151 375	2 645 701	2 729 069	F.1.6.1. Entreprises Nationales
F.1.6.2. (Foreign Controlled Companies)	..	0	0	0	0	62 915	244 675	..	F.1.6.2. (Entreprises Sous Contrôle Etranger)
F.1.6. Total	0	0	..	0	0	1 151 375	2 645 701	2 729 069	F.1.6. Total
F.1.7. Total									**F.1.7. Total**
F.1.7.1. Domestic Companies	374 189	417 375	1 890 561	4 354 039	10 424 220	24 537 608	59 728 918	133 281 267	F.1.7.1. Entreprises Nationales
F.1.7.2. (Foreign Controlled Companies)	446	10 839	34 913	79 968	22 147	576 703	2 081 381	3 281 690	F.1.7.2. (Entreprises Sous Contrôle Etranger)
F.1.7.4. Domestic Investment	374 189	417 375	1 890 561	4 274 071	10 424 220	24 537 608	59 728 918	133 281 267	F.1.7.4. Placement dans le Pays
F.1.7.5. Foreign Investment	0	0	34 913	94 863	..	..	..	..	F.1.7.5. Placement à ' Etranger
F.1.7. Total of Life Investments	374 189	417 375	1 925 474	4 368 934	10 424 220	24 537 608	59 728 918	133 281 267	F.1.7. Total des Placements Vie
F.2. Non-Life									**F.2. Non-Vie**
F.2.1. Real Estate									**F.2.1. Immobilier**
F.2.1.1. Domestic Companies	259 729	490 927	534 165	1 051 882	3 635 879	4 783 632	9 562 351	20 734 970	F.2.1.1. Entreprises Nationales
F.2.1.2. (Foreign Controlled Companies)	24 096	64 364	75 135	147 142	335 407	450 267	988 377	1 646 499	F.2.1.2. (Entreprises Sous Contrôle Etranger)
F.2.1.3. Branches & Agencies of Foreign Cies	0	16	16	16	0	0	0	..	F.2.1.3. Succursales et Agences d'Ent. Etrangères
F.2.1.4. Domestic Investment	259 729	490 927	534 165	904 740	..	4 783 632	9 562 351	20 734 970	F.2.1.4. Placement dans le Pays
F.2.1.5. Foreign Investment	..	16	75 151	147 158	..	9	..	..	F.2.1.5. Placement à l' Etranger
F.2.1. Total	259 729	490 943	609 316	1 051 898	3 635 879	4 783 641	9 562 351	20 734 970	F.2.1. Total
F.2.2. Mortgage Loans									**F.2.2. Prêts Hypothécaires**
F.2.2.1. Domestic Companies	2 075	2 389	2 236	1 401	2 573	1 148	1 285	6 689 768	F.2.2.1. Entreprises Nationales
F.2.2.2. (Foreign Controlled Companies)	..	62	1 246	147 142	150	0	- 210	470 854	F.2.2.2. (Entreprises Sous Contrôle Etranger)
F.2.2.4. Domestic Investment	2 075	2 389	2 236	1 401	..	..	..	..	F.2.2.4. Placement dans le Pays
F.2.2.5. Foreign Investment	0	0	1 246	0	..	..	..	..	F.2.2.5. Placement à l' Etranger
F.2.2. Total	2 075	2 389	3 482	1 401	2 573	1 148	1 285	6 689 768	F.2.2. Total
F.2.3. Shares									**F.2.3. Actions**
F.2.3.1. Domestic Companies	300 141	477 255	498 518	1 095 404	2 932 468	2 629 248	9 311 723	12 937 083	F.2.3.1. Entreprises Nationales
F.2.3.2. (Foreign Controlled Companies)	8 305	12 058	30 761	24 485	4 721	12 133	25 460	5 144	F.2.3.2. (Entreprises Sous Contrôle Etranger)
F.2.3.3. Branches & Agencies of Foreign Cies	6 550	10 570	10 077	10 076	..	..	0	..	F.2.3.3. Succursales et Agences d'Ent. Etrangères
F.2.3.4. Domestic Investment	300 141	477 255	498 518	818 534	2 932 468	2 629 248	9 311 723	12 937 083	F.2.3.4. Placement dans le Pays
F.2.3.5. Foreign Investment	6 550	10 570	40 838	9 833	..	..	..	..	F.2.3.5. Placement à l' Etranger
F.2.3. Total	306 691	487 825	539 356	828 367	2 932 468	2 629 248	9 311 723	12 937 083	F.2.3. Total
F.2.4. Bonds with Fixed Revenue									**F.2.4. Obligations**
F.2.4.1. Domestic Companies	593 873	857 412	863 379	3 126 035	15 894 949	14 127 804	39 076 358	71 692 979	F.2.4.1. Entreprises Nationales
F.2.4.2. (Foreign Controlled Companies)	61 880	104 075	195 443	402 035	622 635	1 437 508	2 175 287	3 516 038	F.2.4.2. (Entreprises Sous Contrôle Etranger)
F.2.4.3. Branches & Agencies of Foreign Cies	14 089	11 263	1 946	19 899	21 256	93 012	122 601	..	F.2.4.3. Succursales et Agences d'Ent. Etrangères
F.2.4.4. Domestic Investment	593 873	857 412	863 379	2 724 000	..	..	..	..	F.2.4.4. Placement dans le Pays
F.2.4.5. Foreign Investment	14 089	11 263	197 389	421 934	..	..	..	..	F.2.4.5. Placement à l' Etranger
F.2.4. Total	607 962	868 675	1 060 768	3 145 934	15 916 205	14 220 816	39 198 959	71 692 979	F.2.4. Total
F.2.5. Loans other then Mortgage Loans									**F.2.5. Prêts Autres qu'Hypothécaires**
F.2.5.1. Domestic Companies	0	0	0	0	0	0	0	2 652	F.2.5.1. Entreprises Nationales
F.2.5. Total	0	0	..	0	0	0	0	2 652	F.2.5. Total

TURKEY

Monetary Unit: million Turkish liras
Unité monétaire : million de livres turques

Item	1990	1991	1992	1993	1994	1995	1996	1997	Item (FR)
F.2.6. Other Investments									F.2.6. Autres Placements
F.2.6.1. Domestic Companies	..	0	0	0	0	1 353 002	2 677 492	4 776 894	F.2.6.1. Entreprises Nationales
F.2.6.2. (Foreign Controlled Companies)	0	0	0	0	0	6 926	202 794	347 152	F.2.6.2. (Entreprises Sous Contrôle Etranger)
F.2.6.3. Branches & Agencies of Foreign Cies	0	0	0	0	0	237	2 335	..	F.2.6.3. Succursales et Agences d'Ent. Etrangères
F.2.6. Total	0	0	0	0	0	1 353 239	2 679 827	4 776 894	F.2.6. Total
F.2.7. Total									F.2.7. Total
F.2.7.1. Domestic Companies	1 155 818	1 827 983	1 898 298	5 274 722	22 465 869	22 894 834	60 629 208	116 834 346	F.2.7.1. Entreprises Nationales
F.2.7.2. (Foreign Controlled Companies)	70 194	180 559	4 091 442	5 848 384	962 913	1 906 834	3 391 708	5 985 687	F.2.7.2. (Entreprises Sous Contrôle Etranger)
F.2.7.3. Branches & Agencies of Foreign Cies	20 639	21 849	12 039	29 975	21 256	93 258	124 936	..	F.2.7.3. Succursales et Agences d'Ent. Etrangères
F.2.7.4. Domestic Investment	1 155 818	1 827 983	1 898 298	4 448 675	..	..	..	..	F.2.7.4. Placement dans le Pays
F.2.7.5. Foreign Investment	20 639	21 849	314 624	578 925	..	..	..	..	F.2.7.5. Placement à l' Etranger
F.2.7. Total of Non-Life Investments	1 176 457	1 849 832	2 212 922	5 027 600	22 487 125	22 988 092	60 754 144	116 834 346	F.2.7. Total des Placements Non-Vie

G. BREAKDOWN OF NON-LIFE PREMIUMS / G. VENTILATIONS DES PRIMES NON-VIE

Item	1990	1991	1992	1993	1994	1995	1996	1997	Item (FR)
G.1. Motor vehicle									G.1. Assurance Automobile
G.1.1. Direct Business									G.1.1. Assurances Directes
G.1.1.1. Gross Premiums	968 768	1 927 328	3 564 840	676 554	16 058 939	30 966 343	58 505 007	133 019 709	G.1.1.1. Primes Brutes
G.1.1.2. Ceded Premiums	402 217	669 931	..	109 391	..	6 652 476	11 808 885	26 468 671	G.1.1.2. Primes Cédées
G.1.1.3. Net Written Premiums	566 521	1 257 397	..	567 163	..	24 313 867	46 696 122	106 551 038	G.1.1.3. Primes Nettes Emises
G.1.2. Reinsurance Accepted									G.1.2. Réassurance Acceptée
G.1.2.1. Gross Premiums	46 191	66 730	..	25 514	305 698	491 740	902 888	1 196 335	G.1.2.1. Primes Brutes
G.1.2.2. Ceded Premiums	32 464	46 421	..	47 533	..	20 083	96 129	378 074	G.1.2.2. Primes Cédées
G.1.2.3. Net Written Premiums	13 727	20 309	..	20 761	..	471 657	806 759	818 281	G.1.2.3. Primes Nettes Emises
G.1.3. Total									G.1.3. Total
G.1.3.1. Gross Premiums	1 014 929	1 994 058	..	702 068	16 364 637	31 458 083	59 407 895	134 216 064	G.1.3.1. Primes Brutes
G.1.3.2. Ceded Premiums	434 681	716 352	..	114 144	..	6 672 559	11 905 014	26 846 745	G.1.3.2. Primes Cédées
G.1.3.3. Net Written Premiums	580 248	1 277 706	..	587 924	..	24 785 524	47 502 881	107 369 319	G.1.3.3. Primes Nettes Emises
G.2. Marine, Aviation									G.2. Marine, Aviation
G.2.1. Direct Business									G.2.1. Assurances Directes
G.2.1.1. Gross Premiums	271 597	410 912	553 617	1 517 006	3 360 400	6 903 263	12 915 147	21 935 836	G.2.1.1. Primes Brutes
G.2.1.2. Ceded Premiums	150 949	246 484	..	346 079	..	1 493 555	2 591 451	4 865 270	G.2.1.2. Primes Cédées
G.2.1.3. Net Written Premiums	120 648	164 428	..	1 170 927	..	5 409 708	10 323 696	17 070 566	G.2.1.3. Primes Nettes Emises
G.2.2. Reinsurance Accepted									G.2.2. Réassurance Acceptée
G.2.2.1. Gross Premiums	11 592	18 921	..	22 336	27 481	57 606	122 440	481 870	G.2.2.1. Primes Brutes
G.2.2.2. Ceded Premiums	7 174	11 517	..	12 606	..	602	5 956	19 165	G.2.2.2. Primes Cédées
G.2.2.3. Net Written Premiums	4 418	7 404	..	9 730	..	57 004	116 484	462 705	G.2.2.3. Primes Nettes Emises
G.2.3. Total									G.2.3. Total
G.2.3.1. Gross Premiums	283 189	429 833	..	1 539 342	3 587 881	6 960 869	13 037 587	22 417 706	G.2.3.1. Primes Brutes
G.2.3.2. Ceded Premiums	158 123	258 001	..	358 685	..	1 494 157	2 597 407	4 884 435	G.2.3.2. Primes Cédées
G.2.3.3. Net Written Premiums	125 066	171 832	..	1 180 657	..	5 466 712	10 440 180	17 533 271	G.2.3.3. Primes Nettes Emises
G.3. Freight									G.3. Fret
G.3.1. Direct Business									G.3.1. Assurances Directes
G.3.1.1. Gross Premiums	..	..	253 823	..	0	..	..	..	G.3.1.1. Primes Brutes
G.4. Fire, Property Damages									G.4. Incendie, Dommages aux Biens
G.4.1. Direct Business									G.4.1. Assurances Directes
G.4.1.1. Gross Premiums	440 133	635 759	1 216 068	2 713 231	5 847 291	10 876 987	21 429 179	42 464 160	G.4.1.1. Primes Brutes
G.4.1.2. Ceded Premiums	273 637	396 154	..	426 564	..	2 750 789	5 169 588	12 483 718	G.4.1.2. Primes Cédées
G.4.1.3. Net Written Premiums	166 496	239 605	..	2 286 667	..	8 126 198	16 259 591	29 980 442	G.4.1.3. Primes Nettes Emises
G.4.2. Reinsurance Accepted									G.4.2. Réassurance Acceptée
G.4.2.1. Gross Premiums	45 525	49 617	..	71 542	81 225	130 647	271 462	620 722	G.4.2.1. Primes Brutes
G.4.2.2. Ceded Premiums	23 948	23 053	..	15 571	..	9 926	17 545	138 572	G.4.2.2. Primes Cédées
G.4.2.3. Net Written Premiums	21 577	26 564	..	55 971	..	120 721	253 917	482 150	G.4.2.3. Primes Nettes Emises
G.4.3. Total									G.4.3. Total
G.4.3.1. Gross Premiums	485 658	685 376	..	2 784 773	5 928 516	11 007 634	21 700 641	43 084 882	G.4.3.1. Primes Brutes
G.4.3.2. Ceded Premiums	297 585	419 207	..	442 135	..	2 760 715	5 187 133	12 622 290	G.4.3.2. Primes Cédées
G.4.3.3. Net Written Premiums	188 073	266 169	..	2 342 638	..	8 246 919	16 513 508	30 462 592	G.4.3.3. Primes Nettes Emises
G.6. General Liability									G.6. Responsabilité Générale
G.6.1. Direct Business									G.6.1. Assurances Directes
G.6.1.1. Gross Premiums	..	..	96 774	..	..	..	..	..	G.6.1.1. Primes Brutes

TURKEY

Monetary Unit: million Turkish liras

	1990	1991	1992	1993	1994	1995	1996	1997
G.7. Accident, Health — G.7. Accident, Santé								
G.7.1. Direct Business — G.7.1. Assurances Directes								
G.7.1.1. Gross Premiums — Primes Brutes	0	48 070	394 476	9 514 976	941 660	3 021 806	8 358 317	24 197 625
G.7.1.2. Ceded Premiums — Primes Cédées	0	12 411	:	1 456 737	:	494 985	1 442 730	3 491 499
G.7.1.3. Net Written Premiums — Primes Nettes Emises	0	35 659	:	8 058 239	:	2 526 821	6 915 587	20 706 126
G.7.2. Reinsurance Accepted — G.7.2. Réassurance Acceptée								
G.7.2.1. Gross Premiums — Primes Brutes	0	0	0	132 030	672	1 899	4 358	27 943
G.7.2.2. Ceded Premiums — Primes Cédées	0	0	:	31 693	:	0	1 060	3 093
G.7.2.3. Net Written Premiums — Primes Nettes Emises	0	0	:	100 337	:	1 899	3 298	24 850
G.7.3. Total — G.7.3 Total								
G.7.3.1. Gross Premiums — Primes Brutes	0	48 070	:	9 647 006	942 332	3 023 705	8 362 675	24 225 568
G.7.3.2. Ceded Premiums — Primes Cédées	0	12 411	:	14 884 300	:	494 985	1 443 790	3 494 592
G.7.3.3. Net Written Premiums — Primes Nettes Emises	0	35 659	:	8 158 576	:	2 528 720	6 918 885	20 730 976
G.8. Others — G.8. Autres								
G.8.1. Direct Business — G.8.1. Assurances Directes								
G.8.1.1. Gross Premiums — Primes Brutes	91 303	183 608	557 164	:	1 554 253	3 132 354	7 803 470	16 223 707
G.8.1.2. Ceded Premiums — Primes Cédées	74 753	154 746	:	:	:	850 830	2 489 769	5 495 214
G.8.1.3. Net Written Premiums — Primes Nettes Emises	16 550	28 862	:	:	:	2 281 524	5 313 700	10 728 493
G.8.2. Reinsurance Accepted — G.8.2. Réassurance Acceptée								
G.8.2.1. Gross Premiums — Primes Brutes	6 497	13 071	:	:	32 654	42 555	82 295	268 367
G.8.2.2. Ceded Premiums — Primes Cédées	6 229	9 884	:	:	:	2 445	4 111	2 228
G.8.2.3. Net Written Premiums — Primes Nettes Emises	268	3 187	:	:	:	40 110	78 184	266 139
G.8.3. Total — G.8.3. Total								
G.8.3.1. Gross Premiums — Primes Brutes	97 800	196 679	:	:	1 586 907	3 174 910	7 885 765	16 492 074
G.8.3.2. Ceded Premiums — Primes Cédées	80 982	164 630	:	:	:	853 276	2 493 880	5 497 442
G.8.3.3. Net Written Premiums — Primes Nettes Emises	16 818	32 049	:	:	:	2 321 634	5 391 885	10 994 632
G.10. Total — G.10. Total								
G.10.1. Direct Business — G.10.1. Assurances Directes								
G.10.1.1. Gross Premiums — Primes Brutes	1 771 771	3 205 677	6 636 762	14 421 767	27 962 543	54 900 753	109 011 121	:
G.10.1.2. Ceded Premiums — Primes Cédées	901 556	1 479 726	2 997 312	2 338 771	:	12 242 635	23 502 424	:
G.10.1.3. Net Written Premiums — Primes Nettes Emises	870 215	1 725 951	363 450	12 082 995	:	42 658 118	85 508 697	:
G.10.2. Reinsurance Accepted — G.10.2. Réassurance Acceptée								
G.10.2.1. Gross Premiums — Primes Brutes	109 805	148 339	205 204	251 422	447 730	724 448	1 383 443	:
G.10.2.2. Ceded Premiums — Primes Cédées	69 815	90 875	173 785	64 623	:	33 056	124 801	:
G.10.2.3. Net Written Premiums — Primes Nettes Emises	39 990	57 464	31 419	186 799	:	691 391	1 258 642	:
G.10.3. Total — G.10.3. Total								
G.10.3.1. Gross Premiums — Primes Brutes	1 881 576	3 354 016	6 841 965	14 673 189	28 410 273	55 625 201	110 394 563	:
G.10.3.2. Ceded Premiums — Primes Cédées	971 371	1 570 601	3 171 097	2 403 394	6 434 559	12 275 692	23 627 225	:
G.10.3.3. Net Written Premiums — Primes Nettes Emises	910 205	1 783 415	3 670 868	12 269 795	21 975 714	43 349 509	86 767 339	:

H. GROSS CLAIMS PAYMENTS — H. PAIEMENTS BRUTS DES SINISTRES

H.1. Life — H.1. Vie

	1990	1991	1992	1993	1994	1995	1996	1997
H.1.1. Domestic Companies — H.1.1. Entreprises Nationales				288 168	288 168	1 201 227	3 786 216	8 153 946
H.1.2. (Foreign Controlled Companies) — H.1.2. (Entreprises Sous Contrôle Etranger)				4 319	4 319	56 909	143 017	321 625
H.1. Total — H.1. Total				288 168	288 168	1 201 227	3 786 216	8 153 946

H.2. Non-Life — H.2. Non-Vie

	1990	1991	1992	1993	1994	1995	1996	1997
H.2.1. Domestic Companies — H.2.1. Entreprises Nationales				5 304 585	5 304 585	23 915 750	49 649 218	119 528 287
H.2.2. (Foreign Controlled Companies) — H.2.2. (Entreprises Sous Contrôle Etranger)				516 801	516 801	2 806 011	4 783 296	14 123 791
H.2.3. Branches & Agencies of Foreign Cies — H.2.3. Succursales et Agences d'Ent. Etrangères				22 113	22113	80780	8564	0
H.2. Total — H.2. Total				5326698	5326698	23996530	49657782	119528287

227

TURKEY

Monetary Unit: million Turkish liras

	1990	1991	1992	1993	1994	1995	1996	1997	
I. GROSS OPERATING EXPENSES									**I. DEPENSES BRUTES D'EXPLOITATION**
I.1. Life									**I.1. Vie**
I.1.1. Domestic Companies				668312	1331610	1540379	5462770	7926090	I.1.1. Entreprises Nationales
I.1.2. (Foreign Controlled Companies)				67726	157354	152384	632622	1177499	I.1.2. (Entreprises Sous Contrôle Etranger)
I.1. Total				668312	1331610	1540379	5462770	7926090	I.1. Total des Primes Nettes Vie
I.2. Non-Life									**I.2. Non-Vie**
I.2.1. Domestic Companies				2944862	5311156	5516003	20517098	25140851	I.2.1. Entreprises Nationales
I.2.2. (Foreign Controlled Companies)				402854	648470	708022	2370638	2660007	I.2.2. (Entreprises Sous Contrôle Etranger)
I.2.3. Branches & Agencies of Foreign Cies				21350	36440	33362	20864	0	I.2.3. Succursales et Agences d'Ent. Etrangères
I.2. Total				2966212	5347596	5549365	20537962	25140851	I.2. Total
J. COMMISSIONS									**J. COMMISSIONS**
J.1. Life									**J.1. Vie**
J.1.1. Direct Business									J.1.1. Assurance directe
J.1.1.1. Domestic Companies				30249	57181	137188	2009854	722482	J.1.1.1. Entreprises Nationales
J.1.1.2. (Foreign Controlled Companies)				18519	19582	47182	294649	185185	J.1.1.2. (Entreprises Sous Contrôle Etranger)
J.1.1. Total				30249	57181	137188	2009854	722482	J.1.1. Total
J.1.2. Reinsurance Accepted									J.1.2. Réassurances acceptées
J.1.2.1. Domestic Companies				0	727	289	9108	63865	J.1.2.1. Entreprises Nationales
J.1.2.2. (Foreign Controlled Companies)				0	288	5208	5365	0	J.1.2.2. (Entreprises Sous Contrôle Etranger)
J.1.2. Total				0	727	289	9108	63865	J.1.2. Total
J.1.3. Total									J.1.3. Total
J.1.3.1. Domestic Companies				30249	57908	137477	2018962	786347	J.1.3.1. Entreprises Nationales
J.1.3.2. (Foreign Controlled Companies)				18519	19870	52390	300014	185185	J.1.3.2. (Entreprises Sous Contrôle Etranger)
J.1.3. Total of Life Net Premiums				30249	57908	137477	2018962	786347	J.1.3. Total
J.2. Non-Life									**J.2. Non-Vie**
J.2.1. Direct Business									J.2.1. Assurance directe
J.2.1.1. Domestic Companies				1718328	3033042	5746114	8889525	24449467	J.2.1.1. Entreprises Nationales
J.2.1.2. (Foreign Controlled Companies)				207625	374340	638670	855135	2021584	J.2.1.2. (Entreprises Sous Contrôle Etranger)
J.2.1.3. Branches & Agencies of Foreign Cies				9075	0	9806	-3	0	J.2.1.3. Succursales et Agences d'Ent. Etrangères
J.2.1. Total				1727403	3033042	5755920	8889522	24449467	J.2.1. Total des Primes Nettes Vie
J.2.2. Reinsurance Accepted									J.2.2. Réassurances acceptées
J.2.2.1. Domestic Companies				20106	172373	28405	343793	118107	J.2.2.1. Entreprises Nationales
J.2.2.2. (Foreign Controlled Companies)				3769	9645	18541	11577	25472	J.2.2.2. (Entreprises Sous Contrôle Etranger)
J.2.2.3. Branches & Agencies of Foreign Cies				0	1	0	0	0	J.2.2.3. Succursales et Agences d'Ent. Etrangères
J.2.2. Total				20106	172374	28405	343793	118107	J.2.2. Total
J.2.3. Total									J.2.3. Total
J.2.3.1. Domestic Companies				1738434	3205415	5774519	9233319	24567574	J.2.3.1. Entreprises Nationales
J.2.3.2. (Foreign Controlled Companies)				211394	383985	657211	866712	2047056	J.2.3.2. (Entreprises Sous Contrôle Etranger)
J.2.3.3. Branches & Agencies of Foreign Cies				9075	1	9806	-3	0	J.2.3.3. Succursales et Agences d'Ent. Etrangères
J.2.3. Total				1747509	3205416	5784325	9233316	24567574	J.2.3. Total

Monetary Unit: million pounds sterling   Unité monétaire : million de livres sterling

A. NUMBER OF COMPANIES IN THE REPORTING COUNTRY — A. NOMBRE D'ENTREPRISES DANS LE PAYS DECLARANT

	1990	1991	1992	1993	1994	1995	1996	1997	
A.1. Life									**A.1. Vie**
A.1.1. Domestic Companies	193	190	182	180	173	160	163	162	A.1.1. Entreprises Nationales
A.1.2. (Foreign Controlled Companies)	..	..	..	3	4	3	..	..	A.1.2. (Entreprises Sous Contrôle Etranger)
A.1.3. Branches & Agencies of Foreign Cies	12	12	14	11	14	11	14	15	A.1.3. Succursales et Agences d'Ent. Etrangères
A.1. All Companies	205	202	196	194	191	174	177	177	A.1. Ensemble des Entreprises
A.2. Non-Life									**A.2. Non-Vie**
A.2.1. Domestic Companies	505	507	449	453	449	457	443	452	A.2.1. Entreprises Nationales
A.2.2. (Foreign Controlled Companies)	..	..	..	60	63	73	..	..	A.2.2. (Entreprises Sous Contrôle Etranger)
A.2.3. Branches & Agencies of Foreign Cies	65	64	117	63	62	64	135	147	A.2.3. Succursales et Agences d'Ent. Etrangères
A.2. All Companies	570	571	566	576	574	594	578	599	A.2. Ensemble des Entreprises
A.3. Composite									**A.3. Mixte**
A.3.1. Domestic Companies	57	57	52	50	50	51	52	58	A.3.1. Entreprises Nationales
A.3.2. (Foreign Controlled Companies)	..	..	..	3	4	4	..	..	A.3.2. (Entreprises Sous Contrôle Etranger)
A.3.3. Branches & Agencies of Foreign Cies	7	7	10	6	3	3	7	7	A.3.3. Succursales et Agences d'Ent. Etrangères
A.3. All Companies	64	64	62	59	57	58	59	65	A.3. Ensemble des Entreprises
A.5. Total									**A.5. Total**
A.5.1. Domestic Companies	755	754	683	683	672	668	658	672	A.5.1. Entreprises Nationales
A.5.2. (Foreign Controlled Companies)	..	..	..	66	71	80	..	..	A.5.2. (Entreprises Sous Contrôle Etranger)
A.5.3. Branches & Agencies of Foreign Cies	84	83	141	80	79	78	156	169	A.5.3. Succursales et Agences d'Ent. Etrangères
A.5. All Insurance Companies	839	837	824	829	822	826	814	841	A.5. Ensemble des Entreprises d'Assurances

B. NUMBER OF EMPLOYEES — B. NOMBRE D'EMPLOYES

	1990	1991	1992	1993	1994	1995	1996	1997	
B.1. Insurance Companies	263 300	242 900	260 000	267 800	221 031	203 500	200 400	228 500	B.1. Entreprises d'Assurances
B.2. Intermediaries	106 600	110 200	102 000	100 900	101 700	134 300	133 500	124 500	B.2. Intermédiaires
B. Total	369 900	353 100	362 000	368 700	322 731	337 800	333 900	353 000	B. Total

C. BUSINESS WRITTEN IN THE REPORTING COUNTRY — C. OPERATIONS CONCLUES DANS LE PAYS DECLARANT

	1990	1991	1992	1993	1994	1995	1996	1997	
C.1. Life									**C.1. Vie**
C.1.1. Gross Premiums									C.1.1. Primes Brutes
C. .1.1. Direct Business									C.1.1.1. Assurances Directes
C.1.1.1.1. Domestic Companies	..	..	..	..	..	..	53 652	59 908	C.1.1.1.1. Entreprises Nationales
C.1.1.1.2. (Foreign Controlled Companies)	..	..	..	..	..	..	10 131	10 406	C.1.1.1.2. (Entreprises Sous Contrôle Etranger)
C.1.1.1.3. Branches & Agencies of Foreign Cies	..	..	..	..	..	..	1 615	1 485	C.1.1.1.3. Succursales et Agences d'Ent. Etrangères
C.1.1.1. Total	..	..	..	..	..	..	55 267	61 393	C.1.1.1. Total
C. .1.2. Reinsurance Accepted									C.1.1.2. Réassurance Acceptée
C.1.1.2.1. Domestic Companies	..	..	..	..	..	..	335	370	C.1.1.2.1. Entreprises Nationales
C.1.1.2.2. (Foreign Controlled Companies)	..	..	..	..	..	..	140	370	C.1.1.2.2. (Entreprises Sous Contrôle Etranger)
C.1.1.2.3. Branches & Agencies of Foreign Cies	..	..	..	..	..	..	90	68	C.1.1.2.3. Succursales et Agences d'Ent. Etrangères
C.1.1.2. Total	..	..	..	..	..	..	425	438	C.1.1.2. Total
C.1.1.3. Total									C.1.1.3. Total
C.1.1.3.1. Domestic Companies	..	..	..	48 706	47 653	46 706	53 987	60 278	C.1.1.3.1. Entreprises Nationales
C.1.1.3.2. (Foreign Controlled Companies)	..	..	..	..	..	..	10 271	10 776	C.1.1.3.2. (Entreprises Sous Contrôle Etranger)
C.1.1.3.3. Branches & Agencies of Foreign Cies	..	..	..	1 129	1 033	1 288	1 705	1 553	C.1.1.3.3. Succursales et Agences d'Ent. Etrangères
C.1.1.3. Total Gross Premiums	..	..	..	49 835	48 686	47 994	55 692	61 831	C.1.1.3. Total des Primes Brutes

Monetary Unit: million pounds sterling — Unité monétaire : million de livres sterling

	1990	1991	1992	1993	1994	1995	1996	1997	
C.1.2. Ceded Premiums									**C.1.2. Primes Cédées**
C.1.2.1. Domestic Companies	..	..	..	2 232	4 480	1 896	1 595	1 363	C.1.2.1. Entreprises Nationales
C.1.2.2. (Foreign Controlled Companies)							290	403	C.1.2.2. (Entreprises Sous Contrôle Etranger)
C.1.2.3. Branches & Agencies of Foreign Cies	..	..	..	85	21	23	98	57	C.1.2.3. Succursales et Agences d'Ent. Etrangères
C.1.2. Total	..	..	..	2 317	4 501	1 919	1 693	1 420	C.1.2. Total
C.1.3. Net Written Premiums									**C.1.3. Primes Nettes Emises**
C.1.3.1. Domestic Companies	32 407	38 511	41 751	46 474	43 173	44 810	52 392	58 915	C.1.3.1. Entreprises Nationales
C.1.3.2. (Foreign Controlled Companies)							9 981	10 373	C.1.3.2. (Entreprises Sous Contrôle Etranger)
C.1.3.3. Branches & Agencies of Foreign Cies	1 774	1 902	1 959	1 044	1 012	1 265	1 607	1 496	C.1.3.3. Succursales et Agences d'Ent. Etrangères
C.1.3. Total	34 181	40 413	43 710	47 518	44 185	46 075	53 999	60 411	C.1.3. Total
C.2. Non-Life									**C.2. Non-Vie**
C.2.1. Gross premiums									**C.2.1. Primes Brutes**
C.2.1.1. Direct Business									**C.2.1.1. Assurances Directes**
C.2.1.1.1. Domestic Companies	23 281	26 402	30 819	32 751	33 296	32 750	31 650	32 053	C.2.1.1.1. Entreprises Nationales
C.2.1.1.2. (Foreign Controlled Companies)								9 662	C.2.1.1.2. (Entreprises Sous Contrôle Etranger)
C.2.1.1.3. Branches & Agencies of Foreign Cies	1 222	1 276	1 760	2358	2 351	2 266	2 218	2 426	C.2.1.1.3. Succursales et Agences d'Ent. Etrangères
C.2.1.1. Total	24 503	27 678	32 579	35 109	35 647	35 016	33 868	34 479	C.2.1.1. Total
C.2.1.2. Reinsurance Accepted									**C.2.1.2. Réassurance Acceptée**
C.2.1.2.1. Domestic Companies	5 953	6 751	7 799	7 074	5 595	5 587	5 282	4 516	C.2.1.2.1. Entreprises Nationales
C.2.1.2.2. (Foreign Controlled Companies)								2 161	C.2.1.2.2. (Entreprises Sous Contrôle Etranger)
C.2.1.2.3. Branches & Agencies of Foreign Cies	266	252	377	298	288	290	390	498	C.2.1.2.3. Succursales et Agences d'Ent. Etrangères
C.2.1.2. Total	6 219	7 003	8 176	7 372	5 883	5 877	5 672	5 014	C.2.1.2. Total
C.2.1.3. Total									**C.2.1.3. Total**
C.2.1.3.1. Domestic Companies	29 234	33 158	38 618	39 825	38 891	38 337	36 932	36 569	C.2.1.3.1. Entreprises Nationales
C.2.1.3.2. (Foreign Controlled Companies)								11 823	C.2.1.3.2. (Entreprises Sous Contrôle Etranger)
C.2.1.3.3. Branches & Agencies of Foreign Cies	1 488	1 528	2 137	2 656	2 639	2 556	2 608	2 924	C.2.1.3.3. Succursales et Agences d'Ent. Etrangères
C.2.1.3. Total Gross Premiums	30 722	34 681	40 755	42 481	41 530	40 893	39 540	39 493	C.2.1.3. Total des Primes Brutes
C.2.2. Ceded Premiums									**C.2.2. Primes Cédées**
C.2.2.1. Domestic Companies	7 130	8 466	8 413	7 943	8 026	8 099	7 378	7 054	C.2.2.1. Entreprises Nationales
C.2.2.2. (Foreign Controlled Companies)								3 606	C.2.2.2. (Entreprises Sous Contrôle Etranger)
C.2.2.3. Branches & Agencies of Foreign Cies	574	516	874	1 045	1 048	971	1 120	1 321	C.2.2.3. Succursales et Agences d'Ent. Etrangères
C.2.2. Total	7 704	8 982	9 287	8 988	9 074	9 070	8 498	8 375	C.2.2. Total
C.2.3. Net Written Premiums									**C.2.3. Primes Nettes Emises**
C.2.3.1. Domestic Companies	22 104	24 687	30 205	31 882	30 865	30 238	29 554	29 515	C.2.3.1. Entreprises Nationales
C.2.3.2. (Foreign Controlled Companies)								8 217	C.2.3.2. (Entreprises Sous Contrôle Etranger)
C.2.3.3. Branches & Agencies of Foreign Cies	914	1 012	1 263	1 611	1 591	1 585	1 488	1 603	C.2.3.3. Succursales et Agences d'Ent. Etrangères
C.2.3. Total	23 018	25 699	31 468	33 493	32 456	31 823	31 042	31 118	C.2.3. Total
C.3. Total									**C.3. Total**
C.3.1. Gross Premiums									**C.3.1. Primes Brutes**
C.3.1.1. Direct Business									**C.3.1.1. Assurances Directes**
C.3.1.1.1. Domestic Companies	..	..	..	88 531	86 544	85 043	85 302	91 961	C.3.1.1.1. Entreprises Nationales
C.3.1.1.2. (Foreign Controlled Companies)								20 068	C.3.1.1.2. (Entreprises Sous Contrôle Etranger)
C.3.1.1.3. Branches & Agencies of Foreign Cies	..	..	..	3 785	3 672	3 844	3 833	3 911	C.3.1.1.3. Succursales et Agences d'Ent. Etrangères
C.3.1.1. Total	..	..	..	92 316	90 216	88 887	89 135	95 872	C.3.1.1. Total
C.3.1.2. Reinsurance Accepted									**C.3.1.2. Réassurance Acceptée**
C.3.1.2.1. Domestic Companies							5 617	4 886	C.3.1.2.1. Entreprises Nationales
C.3.1.2.2. (Foreign Controlled Companies)								2 531	C.3.1.2.2. (Entreprises Sous Contrôle Etranger)
C.3.1.2.3. Branches & Agencies of Foreign Cies							480	566	C.3.1.2.3. Succursales et Agences d'Ent. Etrangères
C.3.1.2. Total							6 097	5 452	C.3.1.2. Total
C.3.1.3. Total									**C.3.1.3. Total**
C.3.1.3.1. Domestic Companies							90 919	96 847	C.3.1.3.1. Entreprises Nationales
C.3.1.3.2. (Foreign Controlled Companies)								22 599	C.3.1.3.2. (Entreprises Sous Contrôle Etranger)
C.3.1.3.3. Branches & Agencies of Foreign Cies							4 313	4 477	C.3.1.3.3. Succursales et Agences d'Ent. Etrangères
C.3.1.3. Total Gross Premiums							95 232	101 324	C.3.1.3. Total des Primes Brutes

Monetary Unit: million pounds sterling · Unité monétaire : million de livres sterling

	1990	1991	1992	1993	1994	1995	1996	1997
C.3.2. Ceded Premiums / Primes Cédées								
C.3.2.1. Domestic Companies / Entreprises Nationales	..	..	..	10 175	12 506	9 995	8 973	8 417
C.3.2.2. (Foreign Controlled Companies) / (Entreprises Sous Contrôle Etranger)								4 009
C.3.2.3. Branches & Agencies of Foreign Cies / Succursales et Agences d'Ent. Etrangères	..	..	..	1 130	1 069	994	1 218	1 378
C.3.2. Total	..	..	..	11 305	13 575	10 989	10 191	9 795
C.3.3. Net Written Premiums / Primes Nettes Emises								
C.3.3.1. Domestic Companies / Entreprises Nationales	54 511	63 198	71 956	78 356	74 038	75 048	81 946	88 430
C.3.3.2. (Foreign Controlled Companies) / (Entreprises Sous Contrôle Etranger)								18 590
C.3.3.3. Branches & Agencies of Foreign Cies / Succursales et Agences d'Ent. Etrangères	2 688	2 914	3 222	2 655	2 603	2 850	3 095	3 099
C.3.3. Total	57 199	66 112	75 178	81 011	76 641	77 898	85 041	91 529

D. NET WRITTEN PREMIUMS IN THE REPORTING COUNTRY IN TERMS OF DOMESTIC AND FOREIGN RISKS
D. PRIMES NETTES EMISES DANS LE PAYS DECLARANT EN RISQUES NATIONAUX ET ETRANGERS

D.2. Non-Life / D.2. Non-Vie

	1990	1991	1992	1993	1994	1995	1996	1997
D.2.1. Domestic Risks / Risques Nationaux								
D.2.1.1. Domestic Companies / Entreprises Nationales	16 433	17 808	20 524	22 015	22 406	21 785	21 443	22 042
D.2.1.3. Branches & Agencies of Foreign Cies / Succursales et Agences d'Ent. Etrangères	678	750	923	1 250	1 260	1 241	1 076	1 120
D.2.1. Total des Primes Nettes Vie	17 111	18 558	21 447	23 265	23 666	23 026	22 519	23 162
D.2.2. Foreign Risks / Risques Etrangers								
D.2.2.1. Domestic Companies / Entreprises Nationales	5 671	6 879	9 681	9 867	8 459	8 453	8 111	7 473
D.2.2.3. Branches & Agencies of Foreign Cies / Succursales et Agences d'Ent. Etrangères	236	262	340	361	331	344	412	483
D.2.2. Total des Primes Nettes Vie	5 907	7 141	10 021	10 228	8 790	8 797	8 523	7 956
D.2.3. Total								
D.2.3.1. Domestic Companies / Entreprises Nationales	22 104	24 687	30 205	31 882	30 865	30 238	29 554	29 515
D.2.3.3. Branches & Agencies of Foreign Cies / Succursales et Agences d'Ent. Etrangères	914	1 012	1 263	1 611	1 591	1 585	1 488	1 603
D.2.3. Total des Primes Nettes Vie	23 018	25 699	31 468	33 493	32 456	31 823	31 042	31 118

E. BUSINESS WRITTEN ABROAD
E. OPERATIONS A L'ETRANGER

E.1. Life / E.1. Vie

	1990	1991	1992	1993	1994	1995	1996	1997
E.1.1. Gross Premiums / Primes Brutes								
E.1.1.1. Direct Business / Assurance Directe — Total						..	12 744	14 326
E.1.1.2. Reinsurance Accepted / Réassurance Acceptée — Total						..	1 206	826
E.1.1.3. Total Gross Premiums / Total des Primes Brutes	..	..	..	10 397	11 537	12 808	13 950	15 152
E.1.2. Ceded Premiums / Primes Cédées — Total				994	715	1 494	241	714
E.1.3. Net Written Premiums / Primes Nettes Emises — Total	6 625	7 498	9 224	9 403	10 822	11 314	13 709	14 438

E.2. Non-life / E.2. Non-Vie

	1990	1991	1992	1993	1994	1995	1996	1997
E.2.1. Gross Premiums / Primes Brutes								
E.2.1.1. Direct Business / Assurance Directe — Total						15 039	14 406	13 333
E.2.1.2. Reinsurance Accepted / Réassurance Acceptée — Total						1 472	702	792
E.2.1.3. Total Gross Premiums / Total des Primes Brutes						16 511	15 108	14 125
E.2.2. Ceded Premiums / Primes Cédées — Total						2 285	2 155	1 964
E.2.3. Net Written Premiums / Primes Nettes Emises								
E.2.3.1. Branches & Agencies / Succursales & Agences							2 244	..
E.2.3.2. Subsidiaries / Filiales							10 709	..
E.2.3. Total	8 582	8 912	10 421	11 918	11 705	14 226	12 953	12 161

231

Monetary Unit: million pounds sterling

Unité monétaire : million de livres sterling

F. OUTSTANDING INVESTMENT BY DIRECT INSURANCE COMPANIES
F. ENCOURS DES PLACEMENTS DES ENTREPRISES D'ASSURANCES DIRECTES

F.1. Life — F.1. Vie

	1990	1991	1992	1993	1994	1995	1996	1997
F.1.1. Real Estate — F.1.1. Immobilier								
F.1.1.4. Domestic Investment — F.1.1.4. Placement dans le Pays	34 828	32 185	30 074	33 939	35 914	35 596	36 209	42 275
F.1.1.5. Foreign Investment — F.1.1.5. Placement à l'Etranger	236	3 034	2 299	144	151	118	114	98
F.1.1. Total	35 064	35 219	32 373	34 083	36 065	35 714	36 323	42 373
F.1.2. Mortgage Loans — F.1.2. Prêts Hypothécaires								
F.1.2.4. Domestic Investment — F.1.2.4. Placement dans le Pays	3 072	2 780	2 733	2 113	1 441	1 184	1 089	1 000
F.1.2.5. Foreign Investment — F.1.2.5. Placement à l'Etranger	..	595	651				0	0
F.1.2. Total	3 072	3 383	3 384	2 113	1 441	1 184	1 089	1 000
F.1.3. Shares — F.1.3. Actions								
F.1.3.4. Domestic Investment — F.1.3.4. Placement dans le Pays	102 088	128 412	149 962	204 035	189 019	237 345	266 320	333 354
F.1.3.5. Foreign Investment — F.1.3.5. Placement à l'Etranger	19 155	7 532	7 502	46 359	45 127	57 141	59 371	68 763
F.1.3. Total	121 243	135 944	157 464	250 394	234 146	294 486	325 691	402 117
F.1.4. Bonds with Fixed Revenue — F.1.4. Obligations								
F.1.4.4. Domestic Investment — F.1.4.4. Placement dans le Pays	40 588	50 557	68 518	97 441	86 630	107 976	119 282	149 349
F.1.4.5. Foreign Investment — F.1.4.5. Placement à l'Etranger	5 847	8 595	11 050	11 602	9 939	11 602	10 561	13 136
F.1.4. Total	46 435	59 152	79 568	109 043	96 569	119 578	129 843	162 485
F.1.5. Loans other than Mortgage Loans — F.1.5. Prêts Autres qu'Hypothécaires								
F.1.5.4. Domestic Investment — F.1.5.4. Placement dans le Pays	3 811	4 932	5 552	6 463	5 340	6 053	5 318	7 035
F.1.5.5. Foreign Investment — F.1.5.5. Placement à l'Etranger	420	568	561	55	52	68	246	236
F.1.5. Total	4 231	5 500	6 123	6 518	5 392	6 121	5 564	7 271
F.1.6. Other Investments — F.1.6. Autres Placements								
F.1.6.4. Domestic Investment — F.1.6.4. Placement dans le Pays	4 606	5 186	7 699	11 456	10 723	10 630	14 803	15 964
F.1.6.5. Foreign Investment — F.1.6.5. Placement à l'Etranger	1	803	965	528	1 042	355	152	244
F.1.6. Total	4 607	5 989	8 664	11 984	11 765	10 985	14 955	16 208
F.1.7. Total								
F.1.7.4. Domestic Investment — F.1.7.4. Placement dans le Pays	188 993	224 060	264 548	355 447	329 067	398 784	443 021	548 977
F.1.7.5. Foreign Investment — F.1.7.5. Placement à l'Etranger	25 659	21 127	23 028	58 688	56 311	69 284	70 444	82 477
F.1.7. Total of Life Investments — F.1.7. Total des Placements Vie	214 652	245 187	287 576	414 135	385 378	468 068	513 465	631 454

F.2. Non-Life — F.2. Non-Vie

	1990	1991	1992	1993	1994	1995	1996	1997
F.2.1. Real Estate — F.2.1. Immobilier								
F.2.1.4. Domestic Investment — F.2.1.4. Placement dans le Pays	3 288	160	124	2 375	2 121	2 100	2 077	2 842
F.2.1.5. Foreign Investment — F.2.1.5. Placement à l'Etranger	79	91	185	80	89	128	120	149
F.2.1. Total	3 367	251	309	2 455	2 210	2 228	2 197	2 991
F.2.2. Mortgage Loans — F.2.2. Prêts Hypothécaires								
F.2.2.4. Domestic Investment — F.2.2.4. Placement dans le Pays	1 334	..	..	815	808	691	620	653
F.2.2. Total	1 334	..	..	815	808	691	620	653
F.2.3. Shares — F.2.3. Actions								
F.2.3.4. Domestic Investment — F.2.3.4. Placement dans le Pays	8112	26094	29900	10587	10439	13182	13691	15464
F.2.3.5. Foreign Investment — F.2.3.5. Placement à l'Etranger	2139	2267	1890	2154	2158	2714	2636	3508
F.2.3. Total	10251	28361	31790	12741	12597	15896	16327	18972
F.2.4. Bonds with Fixed Revenue — F.2.4. Obligations								
F.2.4.4. Domestic Investment — F.2.4.4. Placement dans le Pays	7383	8022	10994	15197	15947	18293	20564	18885
F.2.4.5. Foreign Investment — F.2.4.5. Placement à l'Etranger	3806	5043	6517	7333	6484	8219	11982	11301
F.2.4. Total	11189	13065	17511	22530	22431	26512	32546	30186
F.2.5. Loans other than Mortgage Loans — F.2.5. Prêts Autres qu'Hypothécaires								
F.2.5.4. Domestic Investment — F.2.5.4. Placement dans le Pays	520	50	55	415	510	549	963	634
F.2.5.5. Foreign Investment — F.2.5.5. Placement à l'Etranger	16	3	4	3	3	97	7	98
F.2.5. Total	536	53	59	418	513	646	970	732
F.2.6. Other Investments — F.2.6. Autres Placements								
F.2.6.4. Domestic Investment — F.2.6.4. Placement dans le Pays	726	43	325	672	800	870	1133	2598
F.2.6.5. Foreign Investment — F.2.6.5. Placement à l'Etranger	6	12	23	28	32	164	88	45
F.2.6. Total	732	55	348	700	832	1034	1221	2643

Monetary Unit: million pounds sterling

Unité monétaire : million de livres sterling

	1990	1991	1992	1993	1994	1995	1996	1997	
F.2.7. Total									**F.2.7. Total**
F.2.7.4. Domestic Investment	21363	34369	41398	30061	30625	35685	39048	41076	F.2.7.4. Placement dans le Pays
F.2.7.5. Foreign Investment	6046	7416	8619	9598	8766	11322	14833	15101	F.2.7.5. Placement à l' Etranger
F.2.7. Total of Non-Life Investments	27409	41785	50017	39659	39391	47007	53881	56177	F.2.7. Total des Placemens Non-Vie
G. BREAKDOWN OF NON-LIFE PREMIUMS									**G. VENTILATIONS DES PRIMES NON-VIE**
G.1. Motor vehicle									**G.1. Assurance Automobile**
G.1.1. Direct Business									G.1.1. Assurances Directes
G.1.1.1. Gross Premiums	5893	6612	7713	8518	8432	8155	7912	8091	G.1.1.1. Primes Brutes
G.1.1.2. Ceded Premiums	234	365	506	528	660	914	674	751	G.1.1.2. Primes Cédées
G.1.1.3. Net Written Premiums	5659	6247	7207	7990	7772	7241	7238	7340	G.1.1.3. Primes Nettes Emises
G.1.3. Total									G.1.3. Total
G.1.3.1. Gross Premiums	5893	6612	7713	8518	8432	8155	7912	8091	G.1.3.1. Primes Brutes
G.1.3.2. Ceded Premiums	234	365	506	528	660	914	674	751	G.1.3.2. Primes Cédées
G.1.3.3. Net Written Premiums	5659	6247	7207	7990	7772	7241	7238	7340	G.1.3.3. Primes Nettes Emises
G.2. Marine, Aviation									**G.2. Marine, Aviation**
G.2.1. Direct Business									G.2.1. Assurances Directes
G.2.1.1. Gross Premiums	3826	4469	5695	5713	5489	4931	4199	3933	G.2.1.1. Primes Brutes
G.2.1.2. Ceded Premiums	2693	3337	3230	2642	2314	1844	1276	1066	G.2.1.2. Primes Cédées
G.2.1.3. Net Written Premiums	1133	1132	2465	3071	3175	3087	2923	2867	G.2.1.3. Primes Nettes Emises
G.2.2. Reinsurance Accepted									G.2.2. Réassurance Acceptée
G.2.2.1. Gross Premiums	1972	2542	2769	2114	1455	1443	1183	1093	G.2.2.1. Primes Brutes
G.2.2.2. Ceded Premiums	0	0	0	0	..	0	380	285	G.2.2.2. Primes Cédées
G.2.2.3. Net Written Premiums	1972	2542	2769	2114	1455	1443	803	808	G.2.2.3. Primes Nettes Emises
G.2.3. Total									G.2.3. Total
G.2.3.1. Gross Premiums	5798	7011	8464	7827	6944	6374	5382	5026	G.2.3.1. Primes Brutes
G.2.3.2. Ceded Premiums	2693	3337	3230	2642	2314	1844	1656	1351	G.2.3.2. Primes Cédées
G.2.3.3. Net Written Premiums	3105	3674	5234	5185	4630	4530	3726	3675	G.2.3.3. Primes Nettes Emises
G.4. Fire, Property Damages									**G.4. Incendie, Dommages aux Biens**
G.4.1. Direct Business									G.4.1. Assurances Directes
G.4.1.1. Gross Premiums	7558	8320	9709	10647	10833	10453	10048	10614	G.4.1.1. Primes Brutes
G.4.1.2. Ceded Premiums	1600	1955	2175	2638	2546	2338	2278	2581	G.4.1.2. Primes Cédées
G.4.1.3. Net Written Premiums	5958	6365	7534	8009	8287	8115	7770	8033	G.4.1.3. Primes Nettes Emises
G.4.3. Total									G.4.3. Total
G.4.3.1. Gross Premiums	7558	8320	9709	10647	10833	10453	10048	10614	G.4.3.1. Primes Brutes
G.4.3.2. Ceded Premiums	1600	1955	2175	2638	2546	2338	2278	2581	G.4.3.2. Primes Cédées
G.4.3.3. Net Written Premiums	5958	6365	7534	8009	8287	8115	7770	8033	G.4.3.3. Primes Nettes Emises
G.5. Pecuniary Losses									**G.5. Pertes Pécuniéres**
G.5.1. Direct Business									G.5.1. Assurances Directes
G.5.1.1. Gross Premiums	1864	2225	2471	2699	3323	3419	3687	3629	G.5.1.1. Primes Brutes
G.5.1.2. Ceded Premiums	569	692	747	871	996	1100	1258	1126	G.5.1.2. Primes Cédées
G.5.1.3. Net Written Premiums	1295	1533	1724	1828	2327	2319	2429	2503	G.5.1.3. Primes Nettes Emises
G.5.3. Total									G.5.3. Total
G.5.3.1. Gross Premiums	1864	2225	2471	2699	3323	3419	3687	3629	G.5.3.1. Primes Brutes
G.5.3.2. Ceded Premiums	569	692	747	871	996	1100	1258	1126	G.5.3.2. Primes Cédées
G.5.3.3. Net Written Premiums	1295	1533	1724	1828	2327	2319	2429	2503	G.5.3.3. Primes Nettes Emises
G.6. General Liability									**G.6. Responsabilité Générale**
G.6.1. Direct Business									G.6.1. Assurances Directes
G.6.1.1. Gross Premiums	2880	3156	3693	4048	3976	4034	3981	3923	G.6.1.1. Primes Brutes
G.6.1.2. Ceded Premiums	886	972	901	952	980	971	1088	1070	G.6.1.2. Primes Cédées
G.6.1.3. Net Written Premiums	1994	2184	2792	3096	2996	3063	2893	2853	G.6.1.3. Primes Nettes Emises
G.6.3. Total									G.6.3. Total
G.6.3.1. Gross Premiums	2880	3156	3693	4048	3976	4034	3981	3923	G.6.3.1. Primes Brutes
G.6.3.2. Ceded Premiums	886	972	901	952	980	971	1088	1070	G.6.3.2. Primes Cédées
G.6.3.3. Net Written Premiums	1994	2184	2792	3096	2996	3063	2893	2853	G.6.3.3. Primes Nettes Emises
G.7. Accident, Health									**G.7. Accident, Santé**
G.7.1. Direct Business									G.7.1. Assurances Directes
G.7.1.1. Gross Premiums	2482	2895	3299	3484	3594	4024	4041	4289	G.7.1.1. Primes Brutes
G.7.1.2. Ceded Premiums	206	266	246	274	539	848	756	734	G.7.1.2. Primes Cédées
G.7.1.3. Net Written Premiums	2276	2629	3053	3210	3055	3176	3285	3555	G.7.1.3. Primes Nettes Emises

Monetary Unit: million pounds sterling

Unité monétaire : million de livres sterling

	1990	1991	1992	1993	1994	1995	1996	1997
G.7.3. Total — G.7.3. Total								
G.7.3.1. Gross Premiums — G.7.3.1. Primes Brutes	2482	2895	3299	3484	3594	4024	4041	4289
G.7.3.2. Ceded Premiums — G.7.3.2. Primes Cédées	206	266	246	274	539	848	756	734
G.7.3.3. Net Written Premiums — G.7.3.3. Primes Nettes Emises	2276	2629	3053	3210	3055	3176	3285	3555
G.9. Treaty Reinsurance — G.9. Réassurance Obligatoire								
G.9.2. Reinsurance Accepted — G.9.2. Réassurance Acceptée								
G.9.2.1. Gross Premiums — G.9.2.1. Primes Brutes	4246	4461	5407	5258	4428	4434	4489	3921
G.9.2.2. Ceded Premiums — G.9.2.2. Primes Cédées	1515	1393	1483	1083	1039	1055	788	762
G.9.2.3. Net Written Premiums — G.9.2.3. Primes Nettes Emises	2731	3068	3924	4175	3389	3379	3701	3159
G.9.3. Total — G.9.3. Total								
G.9.3.1. Gross Premiums — G.9.3.1. Primes Brutes	4246	4461	5407	5258	4428	4434	4489	3921
G.9.3.2. Ceded Premiums — G.9.3.2. Primes Cédées	1515	1393	1483	1083	1039	1055	788	762
G.9.3.3. Net Written Premiums — G.9.3.3. Primes Nettes Emises	2731	3068	3924	4175	3389	3379	3701	3159
G.10. Total — G.10. Total								
G.10.1. Direct Business — G.10.1. Assurances Directes								
G.10.1.1. Gross Premiums — G.10.1.1. Primes Brutes	24503	27677	32580	35109	35647	35016	33868	34479
G.10.1.2. Ceded Premiums — G.10.1.2. Primes Cédées	6188	7587	7805	7905	8035	8015	7330	7328
G.10.1.3. Net Written Premiums — G.10.1.3. Primes Nettes Emises	18315	20090	24775	27204	27612	27001	26538	27151
G.10.2. Reinsurance Accepted — G.10.2. Réassurance Acceptée								
G.10.2.1. Gross Premiums — G.10.2.1. Primes Brutes	6218	7003	8176	7372	5883	5877	5672	5014
G.10.2.2. Ceded Premiums — G.10.2.2. Primes Cédées	1515	1393	1483	1083	1055	1055	1168	1047
G.10.2.3. Net Written Premiums — G.10.2.3. Primes Nettes Emises	4703	5610	6693	6289	4844	4822	4504	3967
G.10.3. Total — G.10.3. Total								
G.10.3.1. Gross Premiums — G.10.3.1. Primes Brutes	30721	34680	40756	42481	41530	40893	39540	39493
G.10.3.2. Ceded Premiums — G.10.3.2. Primes Cédées	7703	8980	9288	8988	9074	9070	8498	8375
G.10.3.3. Net Written Premiums — G.10.3.3. Primes Nettes Emises	23018	25700	31468	33493	32456	31823	31042	31118
H. GROSS CLAIMS PAYMENTS — H. PAIEMENTS BRUTS DES SINISTRES								
H.1. Life — H.1. Vie								
H.1.1. Domestic Companies — H.1.1. Entreprises Nationales							41136	45504
H.1.2. (Foreign Controlled Companies) — H.1.2. (Entreprises Sous Contrôle Etranger)							8375	6794
H.1.3. Branches & Agencies of Foreign Cies — H.1.3. Succursales et Agences d'Ent. Etrangères							452	1170
H.1. Total — H.1. Total							41588	46674
I. GROSS OPERATING EXPENSES — I. DEPENSES BRUTES D'EXPLOITATION								
I.1. Life — I.1. Vie								
I.1.1. Domestic Companies — I.1.1. Entreprises Nationales							5926	6120
I.1.2. (Foreign Controlled Companies) — I.1.2. (Entreprises Sous Contrôle Etranger)							1259	977
I.1.3. Branches & Agencies of Foreign Cies — I.1.3. Succursales et Agences d'Ent. Etrangères							17	4
I.1. Total — I.1. Total des Primes Nettes Vie							5943	6124
J. COMMISSIONS — J. COMMISSIONS								
J.1. Life — J.1. Vie								
J.1.1. Direct Business — J.1.1. Assurance directe								
J.1.1.1. Domestic Companies — J.1.1.1. Entreprises Nationales							2740	3077
J.1.1.2. (Foreign Controlled Companies) — J.1.1.2. (Entreprises Sous Contrôle Etranger)							636	729
J.1.1.3. Branches & Agencies of Foreign Cies — J.1.1.3. Succursales et Agences d'Ent. Etrangères							9	23
J.1.1. Total — J.1.1. Total							2749	3100
J.1.2. Reinsurance Accepted — J.1.2. Réassurances acceptées								
J.1.2.1. Domestic Companies — J.1.2.1. Entreprises Nationales							56	63
J.1.2.2. (Foreign Controlled Companies) — J.1.2.2. (Entreprises Sous Contrôle Etranger)							29	63
J.1.2.3. Branches & Agencies of Foreign Cies — J.1.2.3. Succursales et Agences d'Ent. Etrangères							6	5
J.1.2. Total — J.1.2. Total							62	68
J.1.3. Total — J.1.3. Total								
J.1.3.1. Domestic Companies — J.1.3.1. Entreprises Nationales							2796	3140
J.1.3.2. (Foreign Controlled Companies) — J.1.3.2. (Entreprises Sous Contrôle Etranger)							665	792
J.1.3.3. Branches & Agencies of Foreign Cies — J.1.3.3. Succursales et Agences d'Ent. Etrangères							15	28
J.1.3. Total — J.1.3. Total							2811	3168

Monetary Unit: million US dollars — Unité monétaire : million de dollars des EU

	1990	1991	1992	1993	1994	1995	1996	1997	
A. NUMBER OF COMPANIES IN THE REPORTING COUNTRY									**A. NOMBRE D'ENTREPRISES DANS LE PAYS DECLARANT**
A.1. Life									**A.1. Vie**
A.1.1. Domestic Companies	1 730	1 703	1 667	1 608	1 556	1 515	1 488	1 442	A.1.1. Entreprises Nationales
A.1.2. (Foreign Controlled Companies)	109	89	109	113	105	93	87	76	A.1.2. (Entreprises Sous Contrôle Etranger)
A.1.3. Branches & Agencies of Foreign Cies	11	9	11	11	10	9	8	6	A.1.3. Succursales e' Agences d'Ent. Etrangères
A.1. All Companies	1 741	1 712	1 678	1 619	1 566	1 524	1 496	1 448	A.1. Ensemble des Entreprises
A.2. Non-Life									**A.2. Non-Vie**
A.2.1. Domestic Companies	2 453	2 503	2 675	2 686	2 724	2 745	3 255	3 342	A.2.1. Entreprises Nationales
A.2.2. (Foreign Controlled Companies)	211	235	270	270	244	243	260	249	A.2.2. (Entreprises Sous Contrôle Etranger)
A.2.3. Branches & Agencies of Foreign Cies	17	14	19	19	21	20	21	21	A.2.3. Succursales et Agences d'Ent. Etrangères
A.2. All Companies	2 470	2 517	2 694	2 705	2 745	2 765	3 276	3 363	A.2. Ensemble des Entreprises
A.4. Reinsurance									**A.4. Réassurance**
A.4.1. Domestic Companies	628	656	450	470	419	400	381	297	A.4.1. Entreprises Nationales
A.4.2. (Foreign Controlled Companies)	89	62	51	55	48	44	44	39	A.4.2. (Entreprises Sous Contrôle Etranger)
A.4.3. Branches & Agencies of Foreign Cies	16	20	15	15	11	11	9	6	A.4.3. Succursales et Agences d'Ent. Etrangères
A.4. All Companies	644	676	465	485	430	411	390	303	A.4. Ensemble des Entreprises
A.5. Total									**A.5. Total**
A.5.1. Domestic Companies	4 811	4 862	4 792	4 764	4 699	4 660	5 124	5 081	A.5.1. Entreprises Nationales
A.5.2. (Foreign Controlled Companies)	409	386	430	438	397	380	391	364	A.5.2. (Entreprises Sous Contrôle Etranger)
A.5.3. Branches & Agencies of Foreign Cies	44	43	45	45	42	40	38	33	A.5.3. Succursales et Agences d'Ent. Etrangères
A.5. All Insurance Companies	4 855	4 905	4 837	4 809	4 741	4 700	5 162	5 114	A.5. Ensemble des Entreprises d'Assurances
B. NUMBER OF EMPLOYEES									**B. NOMBRE D'EMPLOYES**
B.1. Insurance Companies	1 463 100	1 494 600	1 480 000	1 518 400	1 550 700	1 541 200	..	..	B.1. Entreprises d'Assurances
B.2. Intermediaries	666 100	666 300	652 200	662 100	686 400	696 800	..	..	B.2. Intermediaires
B. Total	2 129 200	2 160 900	2 132 200	2 180 500	2 237 100	2 238 000	..	..	B. Total
C. BUSINESS WRITTEN IN THE REPORTING COUNTRY									**C. OPERATIONS CONCLUES DANS LE PAYS DECLARANT**
C.1. Life									**C.1. Vie**
C.1.1. Gross Premiums									C.1.1. Primes Brutes
C.1.1.1. Direct Business									C.1.1.1. Assurances Directes
C.1.1.1.1. Domestic Companies	209 874	205 328	218 372	241 566	262 276	270 315	291 646	319 434	C.1.1.1.1. Entreprises Nationales
C.1.1.1.2. (Foreign Controlled Companies)	13 865	12 066	22 008	28 940	32 294	31 269	36 625	37 665	C.1.1.1.2. (Entreprises Sous Contrôle Etranger)
C.1.1.1.3. Branches & Agencies of Foreign Cies	3 426	3 321	4 701	4 571	2 533	2 534	2 455	1 573	C.1.1.1.3. Succursales et Agences d'Ent. Etrangères
C.1.1.1. Total	213 300	208 649	223 073	246 137	264 809	272 849	294 101	321 007	C.1.1.1. Total
C.1.1.2. Reinsurance Accepted									C.1.1.2. Réassurance Acceptée
C.1.1.2.1. Domestic Companies	12 405	12 103	16 659	19 709	12 293	20 521	20 607	16 928	C.1.1.2.1. Entreprises Nationales
C.1.1.2.2. (Foreign Controlled Companies)	1 649	1 035	1 353	5 752	1 780	2 445	5 335	4 236	C.1.1.2.2. (Entreprises Sous Contrôle Etranger)
C.1.1.2.3. Branches & Agences of Foreign Cies	1 963	1 800	1 172	1 180	642	983	830	408	C.1.1.2.3. Succursales et Agences d'Ent. Etrangères
C.1.1.2. Total	14 368	13 903	17 831	20 889	12 935	21 504	21 437	17 336	C.1.1.2. Total
C.1.1.3. Total									C.1.1.3. Total
C.1.1.3. . Domestic Companies	222 279	217 431	235 031	261 275	274 569	290 836	312 253	336 362	C.1.1.3.1. Entreprises Nationales
C.1.1.3.2. (Foreign Controlled Companies)	15 514	13 101	23 361	34 692	34 074	33 714	41 960	41 901	C.1.1.3.2. (Entreprises Sous Contrôle Etranger)
C.1.1.3. Branches & Agencies of Foreign Cies	5 389	5 121	5 873	5 751	3 175	3 517	3 285	1 981	C.1.1.3.3. Succursales et Agences d'Ent. Etrangères
C.1.1.3. Total Gross Premiums	227 668	222 552	240 904	267 026	277 744	294 353	315 538	338 343	C.1.1.3. Total des Primes Brutes
C.1.2. Ceded Premiums									C.1.2. Primes Cédées
C.1.2.1. Domestic Companies	12 931	12 673	16 654	19 985	14 286	25 485	23 319	14 914	C.1.2.1. Entreprises Nationales
C.1.2.2. (Foreign Controlled Companies)	1 037	2 159	3 544	5 353	3 762	2 572	2 159	1 768	C.1.2.2. (Entreprises Sous Contrôle Etranger)
C.1.2.3. Branches & Agencies of Foreign Cies	194	319	500	558	225	226	188	103	C.1.2.3. Succursales et Agences d'Ent. Etrangères
C.1.2. Total	13 125	12 992	17 154	20 543	14 491	25 711	23 507	15 017	C.1.2. Total
C.1.3. Net Written Premiums									C.1.3. Primes Nettes Emises
C.1.3.1. Domestic Companies	209 348	204 758	218 377	241 290	260 303	265 351	288 934	321 448	C.1.3.1. Entreprises Nationales
C.1.3.2. (Foreign Controlled Companies)	14 477	10 942	19 817	29 339	30 312	31 142	39 801	40 133	C.1.3.2. (Entreprises Sous Contrôle Etranger)
C.1.3.3. Branches & Agencies of Foreign Cies	5 195	4 802	5 373	5 193	2 950	3 291	3 097	1 878	C.1.3.3. Succursales et Agences d'Ent. Etrangères
C.1.3. Total	214 543	209 560	223 750	246 483	263 253	268 642	292 031	323 326	C.1.3. Total

UNITED STATES

Monetary Unit: million US dollars

C.2. Non-Life / C.2. Non-Vie

	1990	1991	1992	1993	1994	1995	1996	1997
C.2.1. Gross premiums / C.2.1. Primes Brutes								
C.2.1.1. Direct Business / C.2.1.1. Assurances Directes								
C.2.1.1.1. Domestic Companies / C.2.1.1.1. Entreprises Nationales	343 964	362 343	375 017	395 702	409 146	419 913	430 809	506 719
C.2.1.1.2. (Foreign Controlled Companies) / C.2.1.1.2. (Entreprises Sous Contrôle Etranger)	18 619	29 236	31 667	34 268	33 189	33 440	36 324	34 355
C.2.1.1.3. Branches & Agencies of Foreign Cies / C.2.1.1.3. Succursales et Agences d'Ent. Etrangères	1 854	2 119	1 658	1 934	1 971	2 726	2 538	2 376
C.2.1.1. Total	345 818	364 462	376 675	397 636	411 117	422 639	433 347	509 095
C.2.1.2. Reinsurance Accepted / C.2.1.2. Réassurance Acceptée								
C.2.1.2.1. Domestic Companies / C.2.1.2.1. Entreprises Nationales	31 849	32 570	34 536	37 900	40 949	44 407	44 219	43 028
C.2.1.2.2. (Foreign Controlled Companies) / C.2.1.2.2. (Entreprises Sous Contrôle Etranger)	4 858	4 421	6 192	6 873	7 485	8 525	10 580	10 439
C.2.1.2.3. Branches & Agencies of Foreign Cies / C.2.1.2.3. Succursales et Agences d'Ent. Etrangères	1 590	1 829	1 956	2 446	1 863	2 240	2 011	1 228
C.2.1.2. Total	33 439	34 399	36 492	40 346	42 812	46 647	46 230	44 256
C.2.1.3. Total								
C.2.1.3.1. Domestic Companies / C.2.1.3.1. Entreprises Nationales	375 813	394 913	409 553	433 602	450 095	464 320	475 028	549 747
C.2.1.3.2. (Foreign Controlled Companies) / C.2.1.3.2. (Entreprises Sous Contrôle Etranger)	23 477	33 657	37 859	41 141	40 674	41 965	46 904	44 794
C.2.1.3.3. Branches & Agencies of Foreign Cies / C.2.1.3.3. Succursales et Agences d'Ent. Etrangères	3 444	3 948	3 614	4 380	3 834	4 966	4 549	3 604
C.2.1.3. Total Gross Premiums / C.2.1.3. Total des Primes Brutes	379 257	398 861	413 167	437 982	453 929	469 286	479 577	553 351
C.2.2. Ceded Premiums / C.2.2. Primes Cédées								
C.2.2.1. Domestic Companies / C.2.2.1. Entreprises Nationales	43 802	44 999	46 873	49 228	53 782	56 537	55 594	54 226
C.2.2.2. (Foreign Controlled Companies) / C.2.2.2. (Entreprises Sous Contrôle Etranger)	3 899	4 990	6 213	6 763	7 270	7 963	7 515	7 560
C.2.2.3. Branches & Agencies of Foreign Cies / C.2.2.3. Succursales et Agences d'Ent. Etrangères	826	1 183	1 220	1 430	1 492	2 130	1 615	1 174
C.2.2. Total	44 628	46 182	48 093	50 658	55 274	58 667	57 209	55 400
C.2.3. Net Written Premiums / C.2.3. Primes Nettes Emises								
C.2.3.1. Domestic Companies / C.2.3.1. Entreprises Nationales	332 011	349 914	362 680	384 374	396 313	407 783	419 434	495 521
C.2.3.2. (Foreign Controlled Companies) / C.2.3.2. (Entreprises Sous Contrôle Etranger)	19 578	28 667	31 646	34 378	33 404	34 002	39 389	37 234
C.2.3.3. Branches & Agencies of Foreign Cies / C.2.3.3. Succursales et Agences d'Ent. Etrangères	2 618	2 765	2 394	2 950	2 342	2 836	2 934	2 430
C.2.3. Total	334 629	352 679	365 074	387 324	398 655	410 619	422 368	497 951

C.3. Total / C.3. Total

	1990	1991	1992	1993	1994	1995	1996	1997
C.3.1. Gross Premiums / C.3.1. Primes Brutes								
C.3.1.1. Direct Business / C.3.1.1. Assurances Directes								
C.3.1.1.1. Domestic Companies / C.3.1.1.1. Entreprises Nationales	553 838	567 671	593 389	637 268	671 422	690 228	722 455	826 153
C.3.1.1.2. (Foreign Controlled Companies) / C.3.1.1.2. (Entreprises Sous Contrôle Etranger)	32 484	41 302	53 675	63 208	65 483	64 709	72 949	72 020
C.3.1.1.3. Branches & Agencies of Foreign Cies / C.3.1.1.3. Succursales et Agences d'Ent. Etrangères	5 280	5 440	6 359	6 505	4 504	5 260	4 993	3 949
C.3.1.1. Total	559 118	573 111	599 748	643 773	675 926	695 488	727 448	830 102
C.3.1.2. Reinsurance Accepted / C.3.1.2. Réassurance Acceptée								
C.3.1.2.1. Domestic Companies / C.3.1.2.1. Entreprises Nationales	44 254	44 673	51 195	57 609	53 242	64 928	64 826	59 956
C.3.1.2.2. (Foreign Controlled Companies) / C.3.1.2.2. (Entreprises Sous Contrôle Etranger)	6 507	5 456	7 545	12 625	9 265	10 970	15 915	14 675
C.3.1.2.3. Branches & Agencies of Foreign Cies / C.3.1.2.3. Succursales et Agences d'Ent. Etrangères	3 553	3 629	3 128	3 626	2 505	3 223	2 841	1 636
C.3.1.2. Total	47 807	48 302	54 323	61 235	55 747	68 151	67 667	61 592
C.3.1.3. Total								
C.3.1.3.1. Domestic Companies / C.3.1.3.1. Entreprises Nationales	598 092	612 344	644 584	694 877	724 664	755 156	787 281	886 109
C.3.1.3.2. (Foreign Controlled Companies) / C.3.1.3.2. (Entreprises Sous Contrôle Etranger)	38 991	46 758	61 220	75 833	74 748	75 679	88 864	86 695
C.3.1.3.3. Branches & Agencies of Foreign Cies / C.3.1.3.3. Succursales et Agences d'Ent. Etrangères	8 833	9 069	9 487	10 131	7 009	8 483	7 834	5 585
C.3.1.3. Total Gross Premiums / C.3.1.3. Total des Primes Brutes	606 925	621 413	654 071	705 008	731 673	763 639	795 115	891 694
C.3.2. Ceded Premiums / C.3.2. Primes Cédées								
C.3.2.1. Domestic Companies / C.3.2.1. Entreprises Nationales	56 733	57 672	63 527	69 213	68 048	82 022	78 913	69 140
C.3.2.2. (Foreign Controlled Companies) / C.3.2.2. (Entreprises Sous Contrôle Etranger)	4 936	7 149	9 757	12 116	11 032	10 535	9 674	9 328
C.3.2.3. Branches & Agencies of Foreign Cies / C.3.2.3. Succursales et Agences d'Ent. Etrangères	1 020	1 502	1 720	1 988	1 717	2 356	1 803	1 277
C.3.2. Total	57 753	59 174	65 247	71 201	69 765	84 378	80 716	70 417
C.3.3. Net Written Premiums / C.3.3. Primes Nettes Emises								
C.3.3.1. Domestic Companies / C.3.3.1. Entreprises Nationales	541 359	554 672	581 057	625 664	656 616	673 134	708 368	816 969
C.3.3.2. (Foreign Controlled Companies) / C.3.3.2. (Entreprises Sous Contrôle Etranger)	34 055	39 609	51 463	63 717	63 716	65 144	79 190	77 367
C.3.3.3. Branches & Agencies of Foreign Cies / C.3.3.3. Succursales et Agences d'Ent. Etrangères	7 813	7 567	7 767	8 143	5 292	6 127	6 031	4 308
C.3.3. Total	549 172	562 239	588 824	633 807	661 908	679 261	714 399	821 277

Monetary Unit: million US dollars   Unité monétaire : million de dollars des EU

F. OUTSTANDING INVESTMENT BY DIRECT INSURANCE COMPANIES
F. ENCOURS DES PLACEMENTS DES ENTREPRISES D'ASSURANCES DIRECTES

F.1. Life — F.1. Vie

Code (EN / FR)	1990	1991	1992	1993	1994	1995	1996	1997
F.1.1. Real Estate / F.1.1. Immobilier								
F.1.1.1. Domestic Companies / F.1.1.1. Entreprises Nationales	33 034	35 800	40 232	43 856	43 087	41 632	38 452	33 850
F.1.1.2. Foreign Controlled Companies / F.1.1.2. (Entreprises Sous Contrôle Etranger)	1 013	590	3 100	4 321	4 386	3 739	3 815	1 403
F.1.1.3. Branches & Agencies of Foreign Cies / F.1.1.3. Succursales et Agences d'Ent. Etrangères	517	359	1 515	1 122	890	360	375	416
F.1.1. Total / F.1.1. Total	..	..	..	44 978	43 977	41 992	38 827	34 266
F.1.2. Mortgage Loans / F.1.2. Prêts Hypothécaires								
F.1.2.1. Domestic Companies / F.1.2.1. Entreprises Nationales	272 634	261 649	244 172	226 859	218 797	216 614	212 680	210 102
F.1.2.2. Foreign Controlled Companies / F.1.2.2. (Entreprises Sous Contrôle Etranger)	11 849	4 532	19 526	22 136	20 282	19 418	19 602	17 953
F.1.2.3. Branches & Agencies of Foreign Cies / F.1.2.3. Succursales et Agences d'Ent. Etrangères	8 607	8 626	10 574	8 023	4 120	3 708	3 283	2 865
F.1.2. Total / F.1.2. Total	..	..	..	234 882	222 917	220 322	215 964	212 967
F.1.3. Shares / F.1.3. Actions								
F.1.3.1. Domestic Companies / F.1.3.1. Entreprises Nationales	63 425	70 433	73 664	80 885	81 920	91 250	101 954	118 922
F.1.3.2. Foreign Controlled Companies / F.1.3.2. (Entreprises Sous Contrôle Etranger)	3 271	3 275	6 944	8 858	8 232	8 942	10 724	10 088
F.1.3.3. Branches & Agencies of Foreign Cies / F.1.3.3. Succursales et Agences d'Ent. Etrangères	1 044	958	2 083	3 193	2 500	2 926	1 010	1 434
F.1.3.4. Domestic Investment / F.1.3.4. Placement dans le Pays	..	..	..	..	..	90 309	98 138	114 004
F.1.3.5. Foreign Investment / F.1.3.5. Placement à l' Etranger	..	..	..	..	..	3 867	4 826	6 352
F.1.3. Total / F.1.3. Total	..	..	..	84 078	84 420	94 176	102 964	120 356
F.1.4. Bonds with Fixed Revenue / F.1.4. Obligations								
F.1.4.1. Domestic Companies / F.1.4.1. Entreprises Nationales	726 433	794 096	892 553	1 010 262	1 086 740	1 171 598	1 238 683	1 300 704
F.1.4.2. Foreign Controlled Companies / F.1.4.2. (Entreprises Sous Contrôle Etranger)	46 884	44 903	76 702	99 813	107 060	116 806	133 523	122 291
F.1.4.3. Branches & Agencies of Foreign Cies / F.1.4.3. Succursales et Agences d'Ent. Etrangères	5 142	5 886	13 875	9 596	7 588	8 684	5 755	5 647
F.1.4.4. Domestic Investment / F.1.4.4. Placement dans le Pays	..	..	..	..	..	1 080 481	1 109 981	1 138 809
F.1.4.5. Foreign Investment / F.1.4.5. Placement à l' Etranger	..	..	..	..	..	99 801	134 457	167 542
F.1.4. Total / F.1.4. Total	..	..	..	1 019 858	1 094 328	1 180 282	1 244 438	1 306 351
F.1.5. Loans other than Mortgage Loans / F.1.5. Prêts Autres qu'Hypothécaires								
F.1.5.1. Domestic Companies / F.1.5.1. Entreprises Nationales	65 418	64 082	70 059	76 376	87 824	96 685	101 085	103 954
F.1.5.2. Foreign Controlled Companies / F.1.5.2. (Entreprises Sous Contrôle Etranger)	3 519	2 306	7 112	8 521	8 997	9 605	11 776	9 114
F.1.5.3. Branches & Agencies of Foreign Cies / F.1.5.3. Succursales et Agences d'Ent. Etrangères	1 491	1 708	1 853	2 174	1 623	1 741	614	628
F.1.5. Total / F.1.5. Total	..	..	..	78 550	89 447	98 426	101 699	104 582
F.1.6. Other Investments / F.1.6. Autres Placements								
F.1.6.1. Domestic Companies / F.1.6.1. Entreprises Nationales	76 054	77 697	73 054	69 860	75 092	70 713	67 963	90 383
F.1.6.2. Foreign Controlled Companies / F.1.6.2. (Entreprises Sous Contrôle Etranger)	2 648	1 916	7 611	8 523	7 643	6 810	7 492	7 969
F.1.6.3. Branches & Agencies of Foreign Cies / F.1.6.3. Succursales et Agences d'Ent. Etrangères	221	1 129	1 711	1 727	1 129	1 214	621	484
F.1.6. Total / F.1.6. Total	..	..	..	71 587	76 221	71 927	68 584	90 867
F.1.7. Total / F.1.7. Total								
F.1.7.1. Domestic Companies / F.1.7.1. Entreprises Nationales	1 237 473	1 303 757	1 393 734	1 508 098	1 593 460	1 688 491	1 760 818	1 857 915
F.1.7.2. Foreign Controlled Companies / F.1.7.2. (Entreprises Sous Contrôle Etranger)	69 184	57 522	120 994	152 172	156 599	165 319	186 932	168 818
F.1.7.3. Branches & Agencies of Foreign Cies / F.1.7.3. Succursales et Agences d'Ent. Etrangères	17 022	18 664	31 611	25 835	17 850	18 633	11 658	11 474
F.1.7. Total of Life Investments / F.1.7. Total des Placements Vie	..	..	..	1 533 933	1 611 310	1 707 125	1 772 476	1 869 389

ETATS-UNIS

Monetary Unit: million US dollars — Unité monétaire : million de dollars des EU

F.2. Non-Life / F.2. Non-Vie

	1990	1991	1992	1993	1994	1995	1996	1997
F.2.1. Real Estate / Immobilier								
F.2.1.1. Domestic Companies / Entreprises Nationales	7 693	8 774	9 576	10 213	10 723	10 411	10 918	10 710
F.2.1.2. (Foreign Controlled Companies) / (Entreprises Sous Contrôle Etranger)	240	397	473	482	481	495	579	498
F.2.1.3. Branches & Agencies of Foreign Cies / Succursales et Agences d'Ent. Etrangères	99	98	96	93	91	89	87	85
F.2.1. Total	:	:	:	10 306	10 814	10 500	11 005	10 795
F.2.2. Mortgage Loans / Prêts Hypothécaires								
F.2.2.1. Domestic Companies / Entreprises Nationales	6 944	6 656	5 848	4 704	3 921	2 962	2 615	2 368
F.2.2.2. (Foreign Controlled Companies) / (Entreprises Sous Contrôle Etranger)	69	53	64	70	68	138	182	246
F.2.2. Total	:	:	:	4 704	3 921	2 962	2 615	2 368
F.2.3. Shares / Actions								
F.2.3.1. Domestic Companies / Entreprises Nationales	88 311	102 289	105 093	112 483	116 069	137 576	164 476	198 482
F.2.3.2. (Foreign Controlled Companies) / (Entreprises Sous Contrôle Etranger)	4 850	11 350	10 739	12 825	12 008	14 467	16 733	22 477
F.2.3.3. Branches & Agencies of Foreign Cies / Succursales et Agences d'Ent. Etrangères	941	1 584	1 003	1 151	1 020	943	901	1 069
F.2.3.4. Domestic Investment / Placement dans le Pays	:	:	:	:	:	133 994	159 749	192 217
F.2.3.5. Foreign Investment / Placement à l'Etranger	:	:	:	:	:	4 525	5 628	7 334
F.2.3. Total	:	:	:	113 634	117 089	138 519	165 377	199 551
F.2.4. Bonds with Fixed Revenue / Obligations								
F.2.4.1. Domestic Companies / Entreprises Nationales	347 227	394 283	411 961	449 001	471 081	495 560	516 841	553 867
F.2.4.2. (Foreign Controlled Companies) / (Entreprises Sous Contrôle Etranger)	13 077	40 804	66 136	48 756	44 620	46 118	54 911	56 202
F.2.4.3. Branches & Agencies of Foreign Cies / Succursales et Agences d'Ent. Etrangères	2 862	5 332	5 098	5 606	5 724	5 980	5 980	4 867
F.2.4.4. Domestic Investment / Placement dans le Pays	:	:	:	:	:	481 776	501 534	534 921
F.2.4.5. Foreign Investment / Placement à l'Etranger	:	:	:	:	:	19 744	21 287	23 813
F.2.4. Total	:	:	:	454 607	476 805	501 520	522 821	558 734
F.2.5. Loans other than Mortgage Loans / Prêts Autres qu'Hypothécaires								
F.2.5.1. Domestic Companies / Entreprises Nationales	422	521	218	109	434	984	182	154
F.2.5.2. (Foreign Controlled Companies) / (Entreprises Sous Contrôle Etranger)	3	3	4	8	13	7	8	9
F.2.5. Total	:	:	:	109	434	984	182	154
F.2.6. Other Investments / Autres Placements								
F.2.6.1. Domestic Companies / Entreprises Nationales	46 463	42 850	51 979	50 188	47 315	56 775	57 079	67 798
F.2.6.2. (Foreign Controlled Companies) / (Entreprises Sous Contrôle Etranger)	1 529	3 532	4 293	4 505	5 115	5 641	6 825	6 437
F.2.6.3. Branches & Agencies of Foreign Cies / Succursales et Agences d'Ent. Etrangères	372	545	610	453	486	441	967	1 001
F.2.6. Total	:	:	:	50 641	47 801	57 216	58 046	68 799
F.2.7. Total								
F.2.7.1. Domestic Companies / Entreprises Nationales	485 620	555 373	584 675	626 698	649 543	704 268	752 111	833 379
F.2.7.2. (Foreign Controlled Companies) / (Entreprises Sous Contrôle Etranger)	19 754	56 138	59 709	66 646	62 306	66 867	79 238	85 839
F.2.7.3. Branches & Agencies of Foreign Cies / Succursales et Agences d'Ent. Etrangères	4 274	7 559	6 806	7 303	7 321	7 433	7 935	7 022
F.2.7. Total of Non-Life Investments / Total des Placements Non-Vie	:	:	:	634 001	656 864	711 701	760 046	840 401

G. BREAKDOWN OF NON-LIFE PREMIUMS / G. VENTILATIONS DES PRIMES NON-VIE

	1990	1991	1992	1993	1994	1995	1996	1997
G.1. Motor vehicle / Assurance Automobile								
G.1.1. Direct Business / Assurances Directes								
G.1.1.1. Gross Premiums / Primes Brutes	102 846	106 702	112 155	118 012	123 112	129 563	130 039	135 916
G.1.1.2. Ceded Premiums / Primes Cédées	7 476	7 714	7 670	8 055	9 738	10 595	:	:
G.1.1.3. Net Written Premiums / Primes Nettes Emises	95 370	98 988	104 485	109 957	113 374	118 968	130 039	:
G.1.2. Reinsurance Accepted / Réassurance Acceptée								
G.1.2.1. Gross Premiums / Primes Brutes	1 118	1 442	1 019	931	1 150	1 200	6 495	6 575
G.1.2.2. Ceded Premiums / Primes Cédées	190	218	117	94	133	131	:	:
G.1.2.3. Net Written Premiums / Primes Nettes Emises	928	1 224	902	837	1 017	1 069	6 495	:
G.1.3. Total								
G.1.3.1. Gross Premiums / Primes Brutes	103 964	108 144	113 174	118 943	124 262	130 763	136 534	142 491
G.1.3.2. Ceded Premiums / Primes Cédées	7 666	7 932	7 787	8 149	9 871	10 726	10 217	9 887
G.1.3.3. Net Written Premiums / Primes Nettes Emises	96 298	100 212	105 387	110 794	114 391	120 037	126 317	132 604

Monetary Unit: million US dollars   Unité monétaire : million de dollars des EU

	1990	1991	1992	1993	1994	1995	1996	1997
G.2. Marine, Aviation / G.2. Marine, Aviation								
G.2.1. Direct Business / G.2.1. Assurances Directes								
G.2.1.1. Gross Premiums / Primes Brutes	2 878	2 962	3 402	4 115	4 644	4 858	3 660	3 611
G.2.1.2. Ceded Premiums / Primes Cédées	1 254	1 404	1 623	1 873	1 958	2 025	..	..
G.2.1.3. Net Written Premiums / Primes Nettes Emises	1 624	1 558	1 779	2 242	2 686	2 833	3 660	..
G.2.2. Reinsurance Accepted / G.2.2. Réassurance Acceptée								
G.2.2.1. Gross Premiums / Primes Brutes	180	160	116	104	149	150	1 479	1 325
G.2.2.2. Ceded Premiums / Primes Cédées	48	25	15	14	13	14	..	..
G.2.2.3. Net Written Premiums / Primes Nettes Emises	132	135	101	90	136	136	1 479	..
G.2.3. Total / G.2.3. Total								
G.2.3.1. Gross Premiums / Primes Brutes	3 058	3 122	3 518	4 219	4 793	5 008	5 139	4 936
G.2.3.2. Ceded Premiums / Primes Cédées	1 302	1 429	1 638	1 887	1 971	2 039	2 092	2 000
G.2.3.3. Net Written Premiums / Primes Nettes Emises	1 756	1 693	1 880	2 332	2 822	2 969	3 047	2 936
G.3. Freight / G.3. Fret								
G.3.1. Direct Business / G.3.1. Assurances Directes								
G.3.1.1. Gross Premiums / Primes Brutes	6 327	5 962	6 317	6 834	7 496	7 988	7 297	7 317
G.3.1.2. Ceded Premiums / Primes Cédées	2 102	1 914	2 016	2 219	2 475	2 724	..	..
G.3.1.3. Net Written Premiums / Primes Nettes Emises	4 225	4 048	4 301	4 615	5 021	5 264	7 297	..
G.3.2. Reinsurance Accepted / G.3.2. Réassurance Acceptée								
G.3.2.1. Gross Premiums / Primes Brutes	363	427	174	146	118	124	877	788
G.3.2.2. Ceded Premiums / Primes Cédées	59	66	26	16	11	15	..	..
G.3.2.3. Net Written Premiums / Primes Nettes Emises	304	361	148	130	107	109	877	..
G.3.3. Total / G.3.3. Total								
G.3.3.1. Gross Premiums / Primes Brutes	6 690	6 389	6 491	6 980	7 614	8 112	8 174	8 105
G.3.3.2. Ceded Premiums / Primes Cédées	2 161	1 980	2 042	2 235	2 486	2 739	2 384	2 273
G.3.3.3. Net Written Premiums / Primes Nettes Emises	4 529	4 409	4 449	4 745	5 128	5 373	5 790	5 832
G.4. Fire, Property Damages / G.4. Incendie, Dommages aux Biens								
G.4.1. Direct Business / G.4.1. Assurances Directes								
G.4.1.1. Gross Premiums / Primes Brutes	30 034	31 118	33 742	36 523	40 374	42 966	41 292	43 031
G.4.1.2. Ceded Premiums / Primes Cédées	4 092	4 519	5 613	6 664	7 854	8 757	..	..
G.4.1.3. Net Written Premiums / Primes Nettes Emises	25 942	26 599	28 129	29 859	32 520	34 209	41 292	..
G.4.2. Reinsurance Accepted / G.4.2. Réassurance Acceptée								
G.4.2.1. Gross Premiums / Primes Brutes	1 325	1 472	1 046	1 271	1 359	1 282	4 819	4 362
G.4.2.2. Ceded Premiums / Primes Cédées	321	357	327	297	386	464	..	..
G.4.2.3. Net Written Premiums / Primes Nettes Emises	1 004	1 115	719	974	973	818	4 819	..
G.4.3. Total / G.4.3. Total								
G.4.3.1. Gross Premiums / Primes Brutes	31 359	32 590	34 788	37 794	41 733	44 248	46 111	47 393
G.4.3.2. Ceded Premiums / Primes Cédées	4 413	4 876	5 940	6 961	8 240	9 221	8 764	9 244
G.4.3.3. Net Written Premiums / Primes Nettes Emises	26 946	27 714	28 848	30 833	33 493	35 027	37 347	38 149
G.5. Pecuniary Losses / G.5. Pertes Pécunières								
G.5.1. Direct Business / G.5.1. Assurances Directes								
G.5.1.1. Gross Premiums / Primes Brutes	4 728	4 782	6 391	7 264	7 448	7 969	8 104	8 707
G.5.1.2. Ceded Premiums / Primes Cédées	1 103	1 038	1 154	1 289	1 253	1 303	..	..
G.5.1.3. Net Written Premiums / Primes Nettes Emises	3 625	3 744	5 237	5 975	6 195	6 666	8 104	..
G.5.2. Reinsurance Accepted / G.5.2. Réassurance Acceptée								
G.5.2.1. Gross Premiums / Primes Brutes	268	434	274	280	299	336	1 057	1 054
G.5.2.2. Ceded Premiums / Primes Cédées	25	60	44	29	26	76	..	..
G.5.2.3. Net Written Premiums / Primes Nettes Emises	243	374	230	251	273	260	1 057	..
G.5.3. Total / G.5.3. Total								
G.5.3.1. Gross Premiums / Primes Brutes	4 996	5 216	6 665	7 544	7 747	8 305	9 161	9 761
G.5.3.2. Ceded Premiums / Primes Cédées	1 128	1 098	1 198	1 318	1 279	1 379	1 378	1 522
G.5.3.3. Net Written Premiums / Primes Nettes Emises	3 868	4 118	5 467	6 226	6 468	6 926	7 783	8 239
G.6. General Liability / G.6. Responsabilité Générale								
G.6.1. Direct Business / G.6.1. Assurances Directes								
G.6.1.1. Gross Premiums / Primes Brutes	20 694	19 959	19 899	21 384	22 257	23 307	22 010	21 893
G.6.1.2. Ceded Premiums / Primes Cédées	2 731	2 777	3 190	3 496	3 760	3 665	..	..
G.6.1.3. Net Written Premiums / Primes Nettes Emises	17 963	17 182	16 709	17 888	18 497	19 642	22 010	..
G.6.2. Reinsurance Accepted / G.6.2. Réassurance Acceptée								
G.6.2.1. Gross Premiums / Primes Brutes	619	716	517	464	489	451	1 510	1 367
G.6.2.2. Ceded Premiums / Primes Cédées	128	105	103	60	68	77	..	..
G.6.2.3. Net Written Premiums / Primes Nettes Emises	491	611	414	404	421	374	1 510	..

Monetary Unit: million US dollars   Unité monétaire : million de dollars des EU

	1990	1991	1992	1993	1994	1995	1996	1997	
G.6.3. Total									
G.6.3.1. Gross Premiums	21 313	20 675	20 416	21 848	22 746	23 758	23 520	23 260	G.6.3.1. Primes Brutes
G.6.3.2. Ceded Premiums	2 859	2 882	3 293	3 556	3 828	3 742	3 562	3 270	G.6.3.2. Primes Cédées
G.6.3.3. Net Written Premiums	18 454	17 793	17 123	18 292	18 918	20 016	19 958	19 990	G.6.3.3. Primes Nettes Emises
G.7. Accident, Health									**G.7. Accident, Santé**
G.7.1. Direct Business									**G.7.1. Assurances Directes**
G.7.1.1. Gross Premiums	126 360	129 911	136 025	143 340	148 969	155 222	150 002	224 648	G.7.1.1. Primes Brutes
G.7.1.2. Ceded Premiums	7 501	6 867	7 474	8 116	9 412	11 437	..	..	G.7.1.2. Primes Cédées
G.7.1.3. Net Written Premiums	118 859	123 044	128 551	135 224	139 557	143 785	150 002	..	G.7.1.3. Primes Nettes Emises
G.7.2. Reinsurance Accepted									**G.7.2. Réassurance Acceptée**
G.7.2.1. Gross Premiums	765	943	1 406	1 763	2 128	2 089	11 547	11 566	G.7.2.1. Primes Brutes
G.7.2.2. Ceded Premiums	90	236	536	619	892	806	..	..	G.7.2.2. Primes Cédées
G.7.2.3. Net Written Premiums	675	707	870	1 144	1 236	1 283	11 547	..	G.7.2.3. Primes Nettes Emises
G.7.3. Total									**G.7.3. Total**
G.7.3.1. Gross Premiums	127 125	130 854	137 431	145 103	151 097	157 311	161 549	236 214	G.7.3.1. Primes Brutes
G.7.3.2. Ceded Premiums	7 591	7 103	8 010	8 735	10 304	12 243	13 999	14 893	G.7.3.2. Primes Cédées
G.7.3.3. Net Written Premiums	119 534	123 751	129 421	136 368	140 793	145 068	147 550	221 321	G.7.3.3. Primes Nettes Emises
G.8. Others									**G.8. Autres**
G.8.1. Direct Business									**G.8.1. Assurances Directes**
G.8.1.1. Gross Premiums	72 543	82 345	85 916	91 747	89 744	86 894	70 943	63 972	G.8.1.1. Primes Brutes
G.8.1.2. Ceded Premiums	16 197	17 575	17 296	17 221	16 717	15 855	..	..	G.8.1.2. Primes Cédées
G.8.1.3. Net Written Premiums	56 346	64 770	68 620	74 526	73 027	71 039	70 943	..	G.8.1.3. Primes Nettes Emises
G.8.2. Reinsurance Accepted									**G.8.2. Réassurance Acceptée**
G.8.2.1. Gross Premiums	8 209	9 526	4 768	3 804	4 193	4 887	18 446	17 219	G.8.2.1. Primes Brutes
G.8.2.2. Ceded Premiums	1 311	1 307	889	596	578	723	..	..	G.8.2.2. Primes Cédées
G.8.2.3. Net Written Premiums	6 898	8 219	3 879	3 208	3 615	4 164	18 446	..	G.8.2.3. Primes Nettes Emises
G.8.3. Total									**G.8.3. Total**
G.8.3.1. Gross Premiums	80 752	91 871	90 684	95 551	93 937	91 781	89 389	81 191	G.8.3.1. Primes Brutes
G.8.3.2. Ceded Premiums	17 508	18 882	18 185	17 817	17 295	16 578	14 813	12 311	G.8.3.2. Primes Cédées
G.8.3.3. Net Written Premiums	63 244	72 989	72 499	77 734	76 642	75 203	74 576	68 880	G.8.3.3. Primes Nettes Emises
G.10. Total									**G.10. Total**
G.10.1. Direct Business									**G.10.1. Assurances Directes**
G.10.1.1. Gross Premiums	366 410	383 741	403 847	429 219	..	458 767	433 347	509 095	G.10.1.1. Primes Brutes
G.10.1.2. Ceded Premiums	42 481	43 808	46 036	48 933	..	56 361	..	..	G.10.1.2. Primes Cédées
G.10.1.3. Net Written Premiums	323 954	339 933	357 811	380 286	..	402 406	433 347	..	G.10.1.3. Primes Nettes Emises
G.10.2. Reinsurance Accepted									**G.10.2. Réassurance Acceptée**
G.10.2.1. Gross Premiums	12 845	15 120	9 320	8 763	..	10 519	46 230	44 256	G.10.2.1. Primes Brutes
G.10.2.2. Ceded Premiums	2 172	2 374	2 057	1 725	..	2 306	..	..	G.10.2.2. Primes Cédées
G.10.2.3. Net Written Premiums	10 675	12 746	7 263	7 038	..	8 213	46 230	..	G.10.2.3. Primes Nettes Emises
G.10.3. Total									**G.10.3. Total**
G.10.3.1. Gross Premiums	379 257	398 861	413 167	437 982	453 929	469 286	479 577	553 351	G.10.3.1. Primes Brutes
G.10.3.2. Ceded Premiums	44 628	46 182	48 093	50 658	55 274	58 667	57 209	55 400	G.10.3.2. Primes Cédées
G.10.3.3. Net Written Premiums	334 629	352 679	365 074	387 324	398 655	410 619	422 368	497 951	G.10.3.3. Primes Nettes Emises

SLOVAK REPUBLIC

Monetary Unit: million Slovak koruna

REPUBLIQUE SLOVAQUE

Unité monétaire : million de couronnes slovaques

A. NUMBER OF COMPANIES IN THE REPORTING COUNTRY
A. NOMBRE D'ENTREPRISES DANS LE PAYS DECLARANT

	1990	1991	1992	1993	1994	1995	1996	1997	
A.1. Life									**A.1. Vie**
A.1.1. Domestic Companies								2	A.1.1. Entreprises Nationales
A.1.2. (Foreign Controlled Companies)								1	A.1.2. (Entreprises Sous Contrôle Etranger)
A.1. All Companies								2	A.1. Ensemble des Entreprises
A.2. Non-Life									**A.2. Non-Vie**
A.2.1. Domestic Companies								5	A.2.1. Entreprises Nationales
A.2.2. (Foreign Controlled Companies)								3	A.2.2. (Entreprises Sous Contrôle Etranger)
A.2. All Companies								5	A.2. Ensemble des Entreprises
A.3. Composite									**A.3. Mixte**
A.3.1. Domestic Companies								16	A.3.1. Entreprises Nationales
A.3.2. (Foreign Controlled Companies)								7	A.3.2. (Entreprises Sous Contrôle Etranger)
A.3. All Companies								16	A.3. Ensemble des Entreprises
A.5. Total									**A.5. Total**
A.5.1. Domestic Companies								23	A.5.1. Entreprises Nationales
A.5.2. (Foreign Controlled Companies)								11	A.5.2. (Entreprises Sous Contrôle Etranger)
A.5. All Insurance Companies								23	A.5. Ensemble des Entreprises d'Assurances

B. NUMBER OF EMPLOYEES
B. NOMBRE D'EMPLOYES

	1990	1991	1992	1993	1994	1995	1996	1997	
B.1. Insurance Companies								6 412	B.1. Entreprises d'Assurances
B.2. Intermediaries								19 789	B.2. Intermediaires
B. Total								26 201	B. Total

C. BUSINESS WRITTEN IN THE REPORTING COUNTRY
C. OPERATIONS CONCLUES DANS LE PAYS DECLARANT

	1990	1991	1992	1993	1994	1995	1996	1997	
C.1. Life									**C.1. Vie**
C.1.1. Gross Premiums									C.1.1. Primes Brutes
C.1.1.1. Direct Business									C.1.1.1. Assurances Directes
C.1.1.1.1 Domestic Companies								4 603	C.1.1.1.1. Entreprises Nationales
C.1.1.1.2. (Foreign Controlled Companies)								1 157	C.1.1.1.2. (Entreprises Sous Contrôle Etranger)
C.1.1.1. Total								4 603	C.1.1.1. Total
C.1.1.3.1 Domestic Companies								4 603	C.1.1.3.1. Entreprises Nationales
C.1.1.3.2. (Foreign Controlled Companies)								1 157	C.1.1.3.2. (Entreprises Sous Contrôle Etranger)
C.1.1.3. Total Gross Premiums								4 603	C.1.1.3. Total des Primes Brutes
C.1.2. Ceded Premiums									C.1.2. Primes Cédées
C.1.2.1. Domestic Companies								40	C.1.2.1. Entreprises Nationales
C.1.2.2. (Foreign Controlled Companies)								39	C.1.2.2. (Entreprises Sous Contrôle Etranger)
C.1.2. Total								40	C.1.2. Total
C.1.3. Net Written Premiums									C.1.3. Primes Nettes Emises
C.1.3.1. Domestic Companies								4 564	C.1.3.1. Entreprises Nationales
C.1.3.2. (Foreign Controlled Companies)								1 119	C.1.3.2. (Entreprises Sous Contrôle Etranger)
C.1.3. Total								4 564	C.1.3. Total

SLOVAK REPUBLIC

REPUBLIQUE SLOVAQUE

Monetary Unit: million Slovak koruna

Unité monétaire : million de couronnes slovaques

	1990	1991	1992	1993	1994	1995	1996	1997
C.2. Non-Life / **C.2. Non-Vie**								
C.2.1. Gross premiums / C.2.1. Primes Brutes								
C.2.1.1. Direct Business / C.2.1.1. Assurances Directes								
C.2.1.1.1. Domestic Companies / C.2.1.1.1. Entreprises Nationales								12 389
C.2.1.1.2. (Foreign Controlled Companies) / C.2.1.1.2. (Entreprises Sous Contrôle Etranger)								3 866
C.2.1.1. Total / C.2.1.1. Total								12 389
C.2.1.2. Reinsurance Accepted / C.2.1.2. Réassurance Acceptée								
C.2.1.2.1. Domestic Companies / C.2.1.2.1. Entreprises Nationales								95
C.2.1.2.2. (Foreign Controlled Companies) / C.2.1.2.2. (Entreprises Sous Contrôle Etranger)								49
C.2.1.2. Total / C.2.1.2. Total								95
C.2.1.3. Total / C.2.1.3. Total								
C.2.1.3.1. Domestic Companies / C.2.1.3.1. Entreprises Nationales								12 484
C.2.1.3.2. (Foreign Controlled Companies) / C.2.1.3.2. (Entreprises Sous Contrôle Etranger)								3 915
C.2.1.3. Total Gross Premiums / C.2.1.3. Total des Primes Brutes								12 484
C.2.2. Ceded Premiums / C.2.2. Primes Cédées								
C.2.2.1. Domestic Companies / C.2.2.1. Entreprises Nationales								3 107
C.2.2.2. (Foreign Controlled Companies) / C.2.2.2. (Entreprises Sous Contrôle Etranger)								1 707
C.2.2. Total / C.2.2. Total								3 107
C.2.3. Net Written Premiums / C.2.3. Primes Nettes Emises								
C.2.3.1. Domestic Companies / C.2.3.1. Entreprises Nationales								9 377
C.2.3.2. (Foreign Controlled Companies) / C.2.3.2. (Entreprises Sous Contrôle Etranger)								2 208
C.2.3. Total / C.2.3. Total								9 377
C.3. Total / **C.3. Total**								
C.3.1. Gross Premiums / C.3.1. Primes Brutes								
C.3.1.1. Direct Business / C.3.1.1. Assurances Directes								
C.3.1.1.1. Domestic Companies / C.3.1.1.1. Entreprises Nationales								16 992
C.3.1.1.2. (Foreign Controlled Companies) / C.3.1.1.2. (Entreprises Sous Contrôle Etranger)								5 023
C.3.1.1. Total / C.3.1.1. Total								16 992
C.3.1.2. Reinsurance Accepted / C.3.1.2. Réassurance Acceptée								
C.3.1.2.1. Domestic Companies / C.3.1.2.1. Entreprises Nationales								95
C.3.1.2.2. (Foreign Controlled Companies) / C.3.1.2.2. (Entreprises Sous Contrôle Etranger)								49
C.3.1.2. Total / C.3.1.2. Total								95
C.3.1.3. Total / C.3.1.3. Total								
C.3.1.3.1. Domestic Companies / C.3.1.3.1. Entreprises Nationales								17 087
C.3.1.3.2. (Foreign Controlled Companies) / C.3.1.3.2. (Entreprises Sous Contrôle Etranger)								5 073
C.3.1.3. Total Gross Premiums / C.3.1.3. Total des Primes Brutes								17 087
C.3.2. Ceded Premiums / C.3.2. Primes Cédées								
C.3.2.1. Domestic Companies / C.3.2.1. Entreprises Nationales								3 147
C.3.2.2. (Foreign Controlled Companies) / C.3.2.2. (Entreprises Sous Contrôle Etranger)								1 746
C.3.2. Total / C.3.2. Total								3 147
C.3.3. Net Written Premiums / C.3.3. Primes Nettes Emises								
C.3.3.1. Domestic Companies / C.3.3.1. Entreprises Nationales								13 941
C.3.3.2. (Foreign Controlled Companies) / C.3.3.2. (Entreprises Sous Contrôle Etranger)								3 326
C.3.3. Total / C.3.3. Total								13 941
D. NET WRITTEN PREMIUMS IN THE REPORTING COUNTRY IN TERMS OF DOMESTIC AND FOREIGN RISKS / **D. PRIMES NETTES EMISES DANS LE PAYS DECLARANT EN RISQUES NATIONAUX ET ETRANGERS**								
D.1. Life / **D.1. Vie**								
D.1.1. Domestic Risks / D.1.1. Risques Nationaux								
D.1.1.1. Domestic Companies / D.1.1.1. Entreprises Nationales								4 564
D.1.1.2. (Foreign Controlled Companies) / D.1.1.2. (Entreprises Sous Contrôle Etranger)								1 119
D.1.1. Total / D.1.1. Total des Primes Nettes Vie								4 564
D.1.3. Total / D.1.3. Total								
D.1.3.1. Domestic Companies / D.1.3.1. Entreprises Nationales								4 564
D.1.3.2. (Foreign Controlled Companies) / D.1.3.2. (Entreprises Sous Contrôle Etranger)								1 119
D.1.3. Total of Life Net Premiums / D.1.3. Total des Primes Nettes Vie								4 564

SLOVAK REPUBLIC   REPUBLIQUE SLOVAQUE

Monetary Unit: million Slovak koruna   Unité monétaire : million de couronnes slovaques

	1990	1991	1992	1993	1994	1995	1996	1997
D.2. Non-Life / D.2. Non-Vie								
D.2.1. Domestic Risks / Risques Nationaux								
D.2.1.1. Domestic Companies / Entreprises Nationales								9 377
D.2.1.2. (Foreign Controlled Companies) / (Entreprises Sous Contrôle Etranger)								2 208
D.2.1. Total / Total des P'imes Nettes Vie								9 377
D.2.3. Total								
D.2.3.1. Domestic Companies / Entreprises Nationales								9 377
D.2.3.2. (Foreign Controlled Companies) / (Entreprises Sous Contrôle Etranger)								2 208
D.2.3. Total / Total des Primes Nettes Vie								9 377
F. OUTSTANDING INVESTMENT BY DIRECT INSURANCE COMPANIES / ENCOURS DES PLACEMENTS DES ENTREPRISES D'ASSURANCES DIRECTES								
F.1. Life / F.1. Vie								
F.1.7. Total								
F.1.7.1. Domestic Companies / Entreprises Nationales								24 114
F.1.7.2. (Foreign Controlled Companies) / (Entreprises Sous Contrôle Etranger)								1 562
F.2. Non-Life / F.2. Non-Vie								
F.2.7. Total								
F.2.7.1. Domestic Companies / Entreprises Nationales								6 384
F.2.7.2. (Foreign Controlled Companies) / (Entreprises Sous Contrôle Etranger)								2 572
G. BREAKDOWN OF NON-LIFE PREMIUMS / VENTILATIONS DES PRIMES NON-VIE								
G.1. Motor vehicle / Assurance Automobile								
G.1.3. Total								
G.1.3.1. Gross Premiums / Primes Brutes								5 427
G.2. Marine, Aviation / Marine, Aviation								
G.2.3. Total								
G.2.3.1. Gross Premiums / Primes Brutes								26
G.3. Freight / Fret								
G.3.3. Total								
G.3.3.1. Gross Premiums / Primes Brutes								151
G.4. Fire, Property Damages / Incendie, Dommages aux Biens								
G.4.3. Total								
G.4.3.1. Gross Premiums / Primes Brutes								2 132
G.5. Pecuniary Losses / Pertes Pécunières								
G.5.3. Total								
G.5.3.1. Gross Premiums / Primes Brutes								77
G.6. General Liability / Responsabilité Générale								
G.6.3. Total								
G.6.3.1. Gross Premiums / Primes Brutes								1 520
G.7. Accident, Health / Accident, Santé								
G.7.3. Total								
G.7.3.1. Gross Premiums / Primes Brutes								949
G.8. Others / Autres								
G.8.3. Total								
G.8.3.1. Gross Premiums / Primes Brutes								2 203
G.10. Total								
G.10.3. Total								
G.10.3.1. Gross Premiums / Primes Brutes								12 484

SLOVAK REPUBLIC / REPUBLIQUE SLOVAQUE

Monetary Unit: million Slovak koruna / Unité monétaire : million de couronnes slovaques

	1990	1991	1992	1993	1994	1995	1996	1997	
H. GROSS CLAIMS PAYMENTS									**H. PAIEMENTS BRUTS DES SINISTRES**
H.1. Life									**H.1. Vie**
H.1.1. Domestic Companies				1 950	2 059	2 116	..	2 618	H.1.1. Entreprises Nationales
H.1.2. (Foreign Controlled Companies)				..	537	..	..	32	H.1.2. (Entreprises Sous Contrôle Etranger)
H.1. Total				1 950	2 059	2 116	..	2 618	H.1. Total
H.2. Non-Life									**H.2. Non-Vie**
H.2.1. Domestic Companies				4 816	4 522	4 388	..	7 032	H.2.1. Entreprises Nationales
H.2.2. (Foreign Controlled Companies)				..	0	..	..	1 542	H.2.2. (Entreprises Sous Contrôle Etranger)
H.2. Total				4 816	4 522	4 388	..	7 032	H.2. Total
I. GROSS OPERATING EXPENSES									**I. DEPENSES BRUITES D'EXPLOITATION**
I.1. Life									**I.1. Vie**
I.1.1. Domestic Companies				8	638	771	2 014	2 713	I.1.1. Entreprises Nationales
I.1.2. (Foreign Controlled Companies)				0	20	39	141	833	I.1.2. (Entreprises Sous Contrôle Etranger)
I.1. Total				8	638	771	2 014	2 713	I.1. Total des Primes Nettes Vie
I.2. Non-Life									**I.2. Non-Vie**
I.2.1. Domestic Companies				128	1 413	1 747	2 283	3 330	I.2.1. Entreprises Nationales
I.2.2. (Foreign Controlled Companies)				5	23	97	637	1 356	I.2.2. (Entreprises Sous Contrôle Etranger)
I.2. Total				128	1 413	1 747	2 283	3 330	I.2. Total

244

PART III

PARTIE III

DEFINITIONS AND NOTES

DÉFINITIONS ET NOTES

I. COMMON DEFINITIONS AND NOTES

GENERAL

a)   Life and Non-life categories follow the definitions used in national law. However, the premiums for accident and sickness insurances underwritten by Life companies should be included in Non-life figures;

b)   Figures provided for the number of companies and for insurance premiums should include all insurance companies licensed or authorised in the reporting country, *including* professional reinsurers, whether or not these are controlled, but *excluding* any statutory system of social security administered by the State;

c)   *Domestic companies* means those companies incorporated under national law, together with those companies in the reporting country which are unincorporated, but excluding the branches and agencies of foreign companies;

d)   *Foreign-controlled companies* means those domestic companies controlled by foreign interests, such "control" being defined according to national law (see the definition of foreign controlled companies in notes by country).   The data of *foreign-controlled companies* are part of those of *Domestic companies*;

e)   *Foreign companies* means companies incorporated outside the reporting country.

A.   NUMBER OF COMPANIES IN THE REPORTING COUNTRIES

a)   *Composite*: Company which deals with both life and non-life business.

B.   NUMBER OF EMPLOYEES

a)   *Insurance companies*: Staff (full-time or part-time) employed in the insurance industry.

b)   *Intermediaries*;   Number of persons (brokers or agents and their staffs), excluding intermediaries who may sell insurance but are not directly involved in the insurance industry (e.g. bank managers, solicitors, garage owners) or those included under a) above.

C.   BUSINESS WRITTEN IN THE REPORTING COUNTRY

a)   *Business written in the reporting country* should include all business written in the reporting country, whether in respect of domestic or foreign (world-wide) risks, and analysed according to the guidelines in "General" above.

b)   "*Net written premiums*" are total retention in the reporting country.   There should be no double-counting in these figures, even though double-counting may exist in the gross figures.

c)   "*Gross premiums*" are total premiums written, excluding any premium taxes or other charges, but before deduction of commission or reinsurance outwards. It is acknowledged that the inclusion of reinsurance will mean that there is some element of double-counting in the figures provided.

"*Gross premiums*" are the sum of "*premiums of direct business*" and "*premiums of reinsurance accepted*".

d)   Facultative reinsurance may be included under "Direct business" or "Reinsurance accepted" according to practice in the reporting country.

e)   *Premiums ceded* include all premiums (reinsurance and retrocessions) ceded.

f)   Normally "*Net written premiums*" should equal total "*Gross premiums*" less "*Premiums ceded*". If there are special problems in the reporting country which prevent this relationship an appropriate compensatory element should be then included under "Premiums ceded".

D.   NET WRITTEN PREMIUMS IN THE REPORTING COUNTRY IN TERMS OF DOMESTIC AND FOREIGN RISKS

Same notes as a) and b) of Section C above.

a)   This part breaks down business between domestic and foreign risks and is an amplification of the "Net written premiums" lines of Section C ("Business Written in the Reporting Country").

b)   "*Domestic risks*" include all business in the reporting country on domestic risks.

c)   "*Foreign risks*" include all business written in the reporting country on risks situated outside the reporting country (it does not include business written outside the reporting country by national companies).

E.   BUSINESS WRITTEN ABROAD

Same notes as c), d), e) and f) of Section C above.

a)   *Business written abroad* should include all business written outside the reporting country (in both OECD and non-OECD countries) by subsidiaries, branches and agencies established abroad of domestic companies.

F.   OUTSTANDING INVESTMENT BY DIRECT INSURANCE COMPANIES

a)   These data include only outstanding investment by all direct insurance companies in the reporting country; investments by reinsurance companies are not included.

b)   The evaluation method for investment is defined by each country; some of them are mentioned in the notes by country.

c)   Investment has been classified by category, by companies' nationality (domestic companies, foreign controlled companies or branches and agencies of foreign companies) and by destination (inside or outside of the country).

G.   BREAKDOWN OF NON-LIFE PREMIUMS

Same notes as c), d), e) and f) of Section C above,

a)   This part shows *premiums written by classes of non-life insurance* for the business written in the reporting country and breaks down figures shown on the non-life "Net written premiums" of Section C ("Business Written in the Reporting Country").

b)   For the precise definitions used for the classification, see in part III". Definitions of classes of non-life insurance".

c)   The line "Treaty Reinsurance" is used by countries having difficulty in breaking down "Reinsurance Accepted" by classes.

H.   GROSS CLAIMS PAYMENTS

a)   "*Gross claims payments*", covering all gross payments on claims made during the financial year, are to be used in the calculation of gross claims incurred.

I. GROSS OPERATING EXPENSES

a) *"Gross operating expenses"* should normally mean the sum of acquisition costs, change in deferred acquisition costs and administrative expenses.

J. COMMISSIONS

a) This part shows the total of commissions and breaks down commissions for direct business and those for reinsurance accepted.

II. DEFINITIONS AND NOTES BY COUNTRY

General remarks for the EU/EEA member countries: Following regulatory changes introduced by the EU Third Insurance Directives, since 1995, data of EU/EEA countries do not include data on branches and agencies of foreign companies whose head offices are situated in other EU/EEA countries. The Working Group on insurance statistics is currently considering the way to solve this issue, in co-operation with EUROSTAT. It is hoped that at least some of these data could be added at a later stage (see section V of Part III, which provides preliminary information on this issue).

AUSTRALIA

General remarks: For 1994, all figures on life insurance data are based on the fiscal year (July 1993 to June 1994).

Definition of foreign-controlled companies: Predominant control exercised from abroad (either through share ownership or control of votes).

C. *Business written in the reporting country*: In non-life direct business, figures include inward facultative reinsurance premiums but exclude statutory charges. The figures include private sector data only.

F. *Outstanding investment by direct insurance companies:* Investment figures are mostly recorded at their market value.

G. *Breakdown of non-life premiums*:
   a) Freight Insurance is included in Marine and Aviation Insurance;
   b) Pecuniary Loss Insurance and Accident and Sickness Insurances are included in "Others".
   c) Premiums for accident and sickness insurance underwritten by life companies are not included. They are included in life figures.

AUSTRIA

General remarks: For technical reasons, the data of small mutuals are not included in the statistics. However, the premium income of those mutuals amounts to a total of 145 mio ATS only in 1996.

Definition of foreign-controlled companies: Participation of foreign companies exceeding 50 per cent of the share capital.

G.   *Breakdown of non-life premiums*: Premiums ceded recorded in the category "Others" include retrocession premiums (other than those related to Marine and Freight Insurance) which cannot be broken down.

BELGIUM

General remarks: Concerning the number of companies and premiums, data do not include branches of foreign companies whose head offices are situated in the EEA, since 1994. Concerning the number of companies and premiums, data do not include professional reinsurers which do not need a license and are not supervised, so that no information on them is available.

B.   *Number of employees:* The figures for intermediaries represent the approximate number of brokers and non-salaried agents, including agents who occasionally write insurance contracts although this is not their main activity.

C.   *Business written in the reporting country:* Since 1996, the data on direct insurance include domestic risks only. "Reinsurance accepted" includes business written abroad through branches.

D.   *Net written premiums in the reporting country in terms of domestic and foreign risks*: No distinction can be made between domestic and foreign business, since the item "Reinsurance Accepted" cannot be broken down into these two categories of operations.

E.   *Business written abroad:*
        a) No figures on Belgian subsidiaries abroad are available;
        b) No breakdown of gross premiums into direct business and reinsurance accepted is available for the activities abroad of branches and agencies of Belgian companies.

G.   *Breakdown of non-life premiums:*
        a) Figures refer to business written on domestic risks only;
        b) Freight insurance is included in Marine and Aviation Insurance;
        c) Accident and Health Insurance includes Workmen's Compensation Insurance.

CANADA

General remarks: Provincially-regulated companies are not included. Life companies include fraternal benefit societies.

Definition of foreign-controlled companies: Insurer incorporated under the laws of Canada (Federal) where majority control of the voting stock of the insurer is held directly or indirectly by an entity or entities incorporated or established outside Canada.

A.   *Number of companies in the reporting country:* Before 1994 the number of composite reinsurance companies, which transact both life reinsurance business and property and casualty reinsurance business, is included in Composite. Since 1994, the number of these companies (7, 1994 and 1995 data) is included in Reinsurance.

C.   *Business written in the reporting country:* In principle, the accident and sickness business of life companies is shown under non-life business. However, for 1994 and 1995 the accident and sickness business of life companies is exceptionally shown under life business.

F.   *Outstanding investment by direct insurance companies*: Investment of domestic enterprises and of foreign-controlled companies refers to assets invested world-wide. Investment of branches and agencies of foreign companies, however, refers only to assets invested in Canada. Figures for life business exclude asset in segregated funds. Assets are valued in accordance with Canadian generally accepted accounting principles (GAAP) as outlined in the Canadian Institute of Chartered Accountants (CICA) Handbook. Very generally, for property and casualty insurance companies: real estate is valued at depreciated cost, mortgage loans are valued at amortised cost, shares are valued at cost unless there is a permanent decline in the market in which case market is used, and bonds are valued at amortised cost. Very generally, for life insurance companies: real estate is valued according to the moving average market method (cost amortised toward market at 10 per cent), mortgage loans are valued at amortised cost, shares are valued according to the moving average market method (cost amortised toward market at 15 per cent), and bonds are valued at amortised cost. Insurance companies and fraternals are required to adhere to investment and lending policies, standards and procedures that a reasonable and prudent person would apply in respect of a portfolio of investments and loans to avoid undue risk of loss and obtain a reasonable return. In addition, each insurance company and fraternal must comply with a few statutory investment limits as set out in the legislation.

CZECH REPUBLIC

Definition of foreign-controlled companies: Company incorporated under the law of the Czech Republic with more than 50 per cent of the share capital foreign-owned.

F.   *Outstanding investment by direct insurance companies:* Due to the change of the legislative framework in 1994, returns of insurance companies for 1993 are not comparable in many items with those on investments received in the later years.

DENMARK

General remarks: Since 1994, figures for pension funds under the Danish Insurance Business Act are included in life figures.

Definition of foreign-controlled companies: Companies of which more than 50 per cent of the share capital is foreign-owned.

B.   *Number of employees:* Numbers of employees are estimates for full-time employees.

D.   *Net written premiums in the reporting country in terms of domestic and foreign risks:* Non-life figures in this part are earned premiums, whereas the figures in Section C are written premiums.

F.   *Outstanding investment by direct insurance companies:* Domestic shares includes shares in subsidiaries established abroad and shares in foreign associated companies.

FINLAND

General remarks: Since 1993, public pension is not included in data on life insurance.

Definition of foreign-controlled companies: Company in which a foreigner owns at least 50 per cent of the shares or can use at least 50 per cent of the voting rights.

A.   *Number of companies in the reporting country:* Since 1994, non-life figures include small insurance associations which mainly operate in rural districts.

B.   *Number of Employees:* Since 1995, the number of intermediaries include brokers only.

F.   *Outstanding investment by direct insurance companies*: Investment figures are valued at book values. Since 1994, "Bonds" are included in "Loans other than Mortgage Loans".

G.   *Breakdown of non-life premiums*: "Others" includes compulsory motor third party insurance.

FRANCE

Definition of foreign-controlled companies: Companies of which more than 20 per cent of the capital is held by a non-resident (legal or physical person) or by a French company under foreign control.

A.   *Number of companies in the reporting country:* Composite insurers can write only life insurance and the accident and sickness classes of non-life insurance.

F.   *Outstanding investment by direct insurance companies*: Generally-speaking, assets are valued at historical cost. Investment of domestic companies and of branches and agencies of foreign companies refers only to domestic investment.

G.   *Breakdown of non-life premiums:* All categories of Freight Insurance are included in Marine and Aviation Insurance. Treaty Reinsurance concerns companies operating in direct insurance and specialised professional reinsurers. Since 1994, Pecuniary Losses Insurance is included in "Others".

GERMANY

Definition of foreign-controlled companies: Foreign direct or indirect majority interests over 50 per cent.

A.   *Number of companies in the reporting country:*
          a) The figures of the small mutual societies supervised by the Länder are excluded. Number of the small mutual societies supervised by the Länder: 1424 (1995),

1401(1996), 1358 (1997). The market share of these small mutual societies is about 0.04 per cent;

    b) In life companies, pension and death benefit schemes are included;

    c) In non-life companies, specialised health insurance companies are included. Number of health insurance companies: 58 (1995), 57 (1996), 56 (1997).

C.   *Business written in the reporting country:* Figures for 1992 for the first time include data from professional reinsurers. Between 1992 and 1994, for premiums ceded, a distinction between business written in the reporting country and business written abroad is not available. Therefore figures in Section C and Section G show total business (domestic and abroad) for these years.

E.   *Business written abroad:* Same note as Section C above. Between 1992 and 1994, for reinsurance accepted, a distinction between life and non-life is not available, e.g. non-life includes life reinsurance. For reinsurance accepted, business written abroad is business accepted from an insurance enterprise located abroad. The location of the insured risk is not available.

F.   *Outstanding investment by direct insurance companies:* The evaluation method for investment is historic valuation. Since 1995, a distinction between domestic companies and branches and agencies of foreign undertakings is not available, neither are separate figures for foreign controlled companies. No distinction for domestic and foreign investment is available.

G.   *Breakdown of non-life premiums:* Same note as Section C above.

    a) Freight Insurance is included in Marine and Aviation Insurance;

    b) "Others" is the data of insurance for legal protections.

GREECE

Definition of foreign-controlled companies: In accordance with articles 1 and 41 of the Seventh Directive 349/83/EEC and articles 9 and 25 of the Fourth Directive 660/78/EEC.

A.   *Number of companies in the reporting country*: Lloyd's brokers [number of Lloyd's brokers; 38 (1990, 1991)] are not included in "branches and agencies of foreign companies".

G.   *Breakdown of non-life premiums*: "Others" refers only to judicial protection insurance.

HUNGARY

General remarks: Since 1996, the data of insurance associations are included. Because there are 23 insurance associations, 1996 data on the number of insurance companies are no longer comparable with previous data. As far as the data of premium income, investments, costs are concerned, however, this inclusion does not have obvious effect, because their turnover is modest.

Definition of foreign-controlled companies: More than half of shares are owned by foreign shareholders.

E.   *Business written abroad:* Insurance companies do not have subsidiaries or branches abroad.

F.   *Outstanding investment by direct insurance companies:*
a) Only the investments of the insurance technical reserves are included. Investments of subscribed capital, capital reserve and provisions for the general operation of the company are not shown.
b) Evaluation of investments is based on cost price. After minimum one year permanent loss of value, investments are revaluated. In Hungary only depreciation is possible.

G.   *Breakdown of non-life premiums:*
a) Marine, aviation and other transport insurance are included in "Others".
b) Before 1994, flat insurance was classified into "Fire and other property". Since 1995, flat insurance belongs to "Others".

ICELAND

Definition of foreign-controlled companies : Company in which foreigners hold majority of interests.

B.   *Number of employees:* The figure is full-time equivalent, i.e., one person working 50 per cent is counted as a half employee.

F.   *Outstanding investment by direct insurance companies :* Investment figures are mostly valued at market values. There is no authorised limits of investment by categories but the safety of the technical reserves must be secured.

IRELAND

General remarks: Health insurance premiums are not included. Concerning the number of companies and premiums, data do not include professional reinsurers which do not need a license and are not supervised, so that no information on them is available.

D.   *Net written premiums in the reporting country in terms of domestic and foreign risks:* Life-business, of which risks are situated outside the reporting country, is not reported but understood to be minuscule.

E.   *Business written abroad:* Reinsurance figures are included in direct business.

F.   *Outstanding investment by direct insurance companies:* As no breakdown of linked assets (assets representing investments in linked funds/unit trusts) was available, they are included in "other investments". Foreign investment in life insurance refers only to the non-linked assets representing the life insurance business amount which are not localised in Ireland. Non-life investment comprise of cash with building societies, banks and other financial institutions. Investment figures are evaluated at market value. Due to technical reasons, since 1995, non-life figures are based on historic valuation. Other investments of life insurance include the following items; Variable Interest Securities, Deposit and Current Accounts, Unit Trusts, Cash, Mortgage Loans (on land) etc. Since 1994, the data on branches and agencies of foreign undertakings only include third country branches established in Ireland. Investments of EU branches are no longer available.

G.   *Breakdown of non-life premiums*:
        a) Freight insurance is included in Marine and Aviation insurance;
        b) Since 1996, Pecuniary losses insurance is included in Others.

ITALY

Definition of foreign-controlled companies: A company, over 50 per cent of whose capital is held by one or more companies whose head offices are located abroad.

B.   *Number of employees:* The number of intermediaries is an estimation and includes independent agents.

F.   *Outstanding investment by direct insurance companies:* Investment figures are valued at historic value.

JAPAN

General remarks: Apart from section E, figures are for the fiscal year (1 April of the corresponding year to 31 March of the following year).

Definition of foreign-controlled companies: Companies owned for 50 per cent or more by foreign shareholders.

B.   *Number of employees*:
        a) Employees of insurance companies do not include part-time employees;
        b) Intermediaries include agents whose main activities are not insurance.

C.   *Business written in the reporting country*:
        a) The statistics for life insurance companies are before deduction of refund premiums;
        b) Gross premiums for non-life insurance are before deduction of the savings-portion of maturity-refund-type insurance. This is not the case with net written premiums. Therefore, non-life net written premiums do not correspond to "gross premiums less premiums ceded".

E.   *Business written abroad*: In the non-life category, some subsidiaries are unable to supply separate figures for "Direct Business" and "Reinsurance Premiums Accepted".

F.   *Outstanding investment by direct insurance companies*:
        a) Acquisition cost valuation method is applied in general. Depreciation of real estate other than land for investment is done by fixed percentage based on the reducing balance method. Listed securities are valued on a cost or market basis, whichever is lower;
        b) Since 1996, "Mortgage Loans" is included in "Loans other than Mortgage Loans";
        c) "Bonds" includes foreign securities, other securities and securities loaned;
        d) "Other Investments" include deposits, call loans, monetary receivables bought, commodity securities, money, trusts, etc.

G.   *Breakdown of non-life premiums*: Premiums for fire and property damage insurance and for accident and health insurance are before deduction of the savings-portion of maturity-refund-type insurance.

The following services and entities are not included in statistical data:

1.   Postal Life Insurance

This non-profit service operated by the government provides life insurance which is made available to the people nation-wide, thereby ensuring the economic stability of the people and promoting their well-being. It is operated by the Ministry of Posts and Telecommunications under the provisions of the Postal Life Insurance Law. Its budget and accounts are subject to deliberation by the Diet.

Insurance premiums	13,638,813 million yen	of FY 1996
Total assets	100,772,008 million yen	as of the end of FY 1996

2.   Environmental Sanitation Trade Association Mutual Aid

The environmental sanitation associations are entities whose purposes are to improve the sanitation standard through ensuring the soundness of the businesses related to environmental sanitation, thereby securing the interests of the consumers as well. They are established in accordance with the relevant law. The associations provide, as part of their operations, non-profit services similar to life and fire insurance to their members.

Premium income in direct business	NOT AVAILABLE
Total assets	NOT AVAILABLE

3.   Shopping District Promotion Association Mutual Aid

Non-profit services similar to fire insurance are provided by shopping district promotion associations to their members, based on the unique nature of the shopping districts in which many shops are clustered close together in a relatively small area. Most of the associations are small, of which minimal or very small number actually conduct mutual aid services.

Premium income in direct business	NOT AVAILABLE
Total assets	NOT AVAILABLE

4.   Consumers' Co-operation Association Mutual Aid

The consumer's co-operative associations are entities established in accordance with the relevant law whose purpose is to promote the spontaneous developments of the people's communal associations, thereby securing the stability of the people's life and promoting their living culture. Consumers' co-operative associations and their federation provide non-profit mutual aid services including life and automobile mutual aid to their members.

Premium income in direct business	669,011 million yen	according to a survey for FY 1995
Total assets	NOT AVAILABLE	

5.   Forest Co-operative Association Mutual Aid for Forest Disaster

This system is established in accordance with the relevant law which aims at improving the economic and social status of forest owners and securing sustained yield from the forests as well as increasing its potential output, thereby contributing to the development of the national economy. The National Federation of Forest Owners' Co-operative Associations operates this system for forest owners, which is similar to the non-life insurance for forests, on non-profits basis.

Premium income in	2,625 million yen	FY 1996
Total assets	NOT AVAILABLE	

6.   Fishery Co-operative Association Mutual Aid

This system is established in accordance with the relevant law whose purpose is to promote the development of the fishermen's and fishery processors' communal associations, thereby promoting their economic and social status and improving the potential output of fishery, as well as developing the national economy. Fishery co-operative associations provide non-profit services similar to life and non-life insurance to their members.

Premium income in direct business	79,031 million yen	FY 1996
Total assets	404,455 million yen	as of the end of FY 1996

7.   Small and Medium Enterprise Co-operative Association Mutual Aid

Co-operative association composed of small and medium enterprises in a certain area provide non-profit services similar to life and non-life insurance to their members. The total number of such co-operative associations amounts to approximately 49,000 throughout Japan. While there is no detailed statistics, the typical types of services are as follow :

i)   Fire mutual aid provided by Fire Insurance Co-operative

These associations composed of small and medium enterprises provide, on the principle of mutual aid, non-profit services similar to fire insurance to insure their members against loss caused by fire.

Premium income in direct business	20,041 million yen	FY 1996
Total assets	66,087 million yen	as of the end of FY 1996

ii) Automobile mutual aid provided by Motor Insurance Co-operative

These associations composed of small and medium enterprises provide, on the principle of mutual aid, non-profit services similar to automobile insurance to insure their members against accidents associated with the possession, use and control of privately-owned cars.

Premium income in direct business	24,575 million yen	FY 1996
Total assets	16,900 million yen	as of the end of FY 1996

8. Agricultural co-operative Association Mutual Aid

This system is established in accordance with the relevant law whose purpose is to promote the development of the farmer's communal associations, thereby improving the potential output of agriculture and promoting their economic and social status, as well as developing the national economy. Agricultural co-operative associations and their federation provide, as one body, non-profit services similar to life and non-life insurance to their members.

Premium income in direct business	4,713,500 million yen	FY 1996, approximate figure
Total assets	30,141,400 million yen	as of the end of FY 1996, approximate figure

9. Labour's mutual aid

Labour unions and the national federation of labour union mutual aid, which are voluntarily organised by labour with the main purpose of promoting their economic status, maintaining and providing the labour standard in particular, provide non-profit services similar to life and non-life insurance to their members.

Premium income in direct business	NOT AVAILABLE
Total assets	NOT AVAILABLE

KOREA

Definition of foreign-controlled companies: Foreign subsidiary.

F. *Outstanding investment by direct insurance companies:* The investment is evaluated on the historical cost basis other than listed stocks. The listed stocks are evaluated on the average market value (ref. Article 18-2 of the Enforcement Decree of the Insurance Business Law).

LUXEMBOURG

Definition of foreign-controlled companies: Principal shareholders are not of Luxembourg's nationality.

C. *Business written in the reporting country:* Data concern insurance products commercialised (flow).

F. *Outstanding investment by direct insurance companies:* Only data on investments in flow are available.

G. *Breakdown of non-life premiums:* Same note as Section C above.

MEXICO

Definition of foreign-controlled companies: Those undertakings which capital is mostly contributed by foreigners, that is 51 per cent and above.

G.   *Breakdown of non-life premiums:*
       a) "Marine, aviation and other transport insurance" includes "Freight Insurance";
       b) "Other non-life insurance" includes agricultural and miscellaneous insurances.

NETHERLANDS

General remarks:

a) Before 1995, the number and the premium income of professional reinsurance companies are estimated since these companies are exempt from governmental control. Since 1995, they are no longer included. In 1995, there are 9 professional reinsures which generate premium income of about 751 millions guilders (517 millions in non-life, 234 millions in life);

b) The number and the premium income of foreign-controlled companies are estimated since the figures provided refer to supervised companies only;

Definition of foreign-controlled companies: Locally-incorporated domestic insurance companies with a share-capital of which over 50 per cent belongs to one or more companies with (a) head office(s) located o outside the Netherlands.

A.   *Number of companies in the reporting country*:
       a) Before 1995, the number of non-life companies includes the so-called exempted small local mutuals (1995, 239). Their market share is no more than 0.2 per cent (1995).
       b) Since 1995, the number of branches of foreign insurers with a head office within the EU/EEA is no longer included. The number of these branches is 115 (1995, life= 3, non-life= 112).

B.   *Number of employees*: Numbers of insurance employees and intermediaries (carrying out business on a professional basis) are estimated.

C.   *Business written in the reporting country*: Since there is no obligation for life insurance companies in the Netherlands to disclose reinsurance business, it is to be noted that the separation of gross premiums into direct business and reinsurance accepted is not possible.

E.   *Business written abroad*: Before 1994, the figures provided are estimates related to the three major Netherlands insurance companies carrying insurance business on an international scale. Since 1994, no estimation is available.

F.   *Outstanding investment by direct insurance companies :* The following valuation methods are commonly applied :
       - real estate : market value/estimated value

- (mortgage) loans :
  - life: amortisation value or face value
  - non-life: face value
- shares:
  - quoted: market value
  - unquoted estimated value
- bonds:
  - life: amortisation value or market value
  - non-life: market value

Before the implementation of the third EU Directives, there were no rules limiting the percentage of the investments of the total assets to be invested by an insurance company.

G. *Breakdown of non-life premiums*:
   a) Freight Insurance is included in Marine and Aviation Insurance;
   b) Pecuniary Loss Insurance and General Liability Insurance are included in other non-life insurance.

NEW ZEALAND

Definition of foreign-controlled companies: 50 per cent or more overseas ownership.

C. *Business written in the reporting country*: Gross premiums of direct life insurance by domestic companies include net premiums of life reinsurance.

G. *Breakdown of non-life premiums:* "Other" means medical insurance.

NORWAY

General remarks: For 1994 and 1995, without data on branches and agencies of foreign undertakings for non-life insurance.

Definition of foreign-controlled companies: Companies where the voting majority is held by foreign interests. Since 1997, all undertakings belonging to the same insurance group are classified in an identical manner.

C. *Business written in the reporting country*: As reinsurance accepted are residually calculated, i.e. total gross premiums minus direct Norwegian business, reinsurance accepted might include direct foreign business.

F. *Outstanding investment by direct insurance companies:*
   Total amount of investment placed by non-life insurance companies do not include branches and agencies of foreign companies.

POLAND

General remarks: The establishment of branches and agencies of foreign undertakings has been allowed since 1 January 1999.

Definition of foreign-controlled companies: At least 51 per cent share of foreign capital

A.   *Number of companies in the reporting country:* The total number of insurance companies includes 5 mutual insurance societies and 46 stock companies (2 public insurance companies and 49 private insurers).

B.   *Number of employees:* The number of insurance employees is estimated. In 1996 and 1997, the State Office for Insurance Supervision issued ca. 85 440 permissions for conducting insurance intermediary (together permissions for agents and brokers).

F.   *Outstanding investment by direct insurance companies:* Investment figures are generally valued at historic value.

I.   *Gross operating expenses:* This item includes acquisition costs, administrative expenses and other technical expenses.

PORTUGAL

Definition of foreign-controlled companies: Proportion of foreign capital is more than 50 per cent.

C.   *Business written in the reporting country*: Total gross premiums represents total premiums and accessory charges.

F.   *Outstanding investment by direct insurance companies*:
        a) Before 1995, only assets representing technical provisions are taken into consideration.
           Since 1995, non-engaged investments are also included;
        b) Government securities, government bonds, credits to the public investment, bonds, shares, shares and units of shares to the investment funds are included in data on shares.
        c) "Loans other than Mortgage Loans" includes loans against policies and loans against securities;
        d) "Other Investments" includes deposits and certificates of deposits.

G.   *Breakdown of non-life premiums*: "Accident and Health Insurance" includes workmen's compensation insurance.

SPAIN

Definition of foreign-controlled companies: Participation in social capital equal to or more than 50 per cent.

F.   *Outstanding investment by direct insurance companies:* Acquisition cost valuation method is applied in general.

G.   *Breakdown of non-life premiums*:
        a) Medical insurance is included in " Accident and Health insurance";
        b) In 1990, "Freight insurance" is included in "Marine and Aviation insurance".

SWEDEN

Definition of foreign-controlled companies: At least 50 per cent of the shares are under foreign control.

A.   *Number of companies in the reporting country*: The non-life figures exclude approximately 340 small local mutual insurers, whose estimated share of the non-life market is below 0.5 per cent (1997 data). Since 1994, there are no statistics available concerning branches of insurance undertakings with their head office in another EEA Member State. There are 12 such branches and their share of the direct insurance premiums written is estimated to be about 2 per cent of the non-life premiums (1997 data).

B.   *Number of employees*:
        The number of employees of insurance undertakings includes employed agents, of which approximately 20,000 are working on a part-time basis (1993 data). Since 1994, the number of employees of insurance undertakings excludes agents working on part-time or franchise basis. The corresponding number for 1993 should be approximately the same as the number for 1994, i.e. 19,000. The number of intermediaries includes insurance brokers only, which include some 200 juridical persons.

C.   *Business written in the reporting country*: No reliable information is available as regards branches and agencies of foreign <u>reinsurance</u> undertakings. They are, however, believed to concentrate on non-life reinsurance, so their life reinsurance premiums written have been approximated by 0.

D.   *Net written premiums in the reporting country in terms of domestic and foreign risks:* No reliable information is available on the breakdown between domestic and foreign risks. It is probable, however, that only a minor share of the non-life direct business is written on foreign risks and that almost no direct life business is written on such risks.

E.   *Business written abroad:* There is only some information on direct business and premiums ceded for non-life branches and agencies of domestic insurers. There is no corresponding information on the subsidiaries.

F.   *Outstanding investment by direct insurance companies*:
        a) Before 1996, Investments are valued, in general, at purchase price or market value, whichever is lower. Since 1996, the market value method is used.
        b) Fixed income assets corresponding to technical provisions of life insurance may be valued at cost, even if it exceeds the market value.
        c) From 1991 to 1995, mortgage loans cannot be separated from loans other than mortgage loans. The latter has been taken to include all loans.
        d) There were no authorised limits of investments by categories, although there were restrictions on the choice of assets corresponding to technical provisions. At least 80 per

cent of the technical provisions for life insurance (other than unit-linked) must be covered by certain types of assets. The remaining 20 per cent may not be invested in shares. The holding of shares is indirectly restricted in that the voting power of shares in a single company may not in general exceed 5 per cent. On 1 July 1995 the EU rules on investments were implemented. In particular, none of the categories "shares" or "property" may exceed 25 per cent of the technical provisions net of reinsurance.

e) As regards agencies of non-EEA undertakings, only legal deposits are included. Deposits are reported under the heading of "Other investments". Since 1994, branches and agencies of EEA undertakings are no longer covered.

f) Although no reliable information is available on distribution on investment on domestic and foreign placements, foreign real estate, shares and bonds do indeed play a certain role.

G. *Breakdown of non-life premiums*:

a) As regards treaty reinsurance accepted, premiums written by branches or agencies of foreign reinsurers have not been included;

b) General liability cannot be reported as a separate class, since it is in general a component of several mixed products such as house-owner's and house-owner's comprehensive insurance;

c) Accident and health insurance includes employers' no-fault insurance.

SWITZERLAND

Definition of foreign-controlled companies: Companies with more than 50 per cent of foreign participation. Since 1993, companies with directly or indirectly more than 50 per cent of foreign participation.

B. *Number of employees*: The concept "Intermediary" means the insurance agents linked to an insurance company by a contract, excluding brokers and general independent agents whose number in Switzerland is around 200 (in 1990), 400 (in 1991 and 1992) and 400-500 (in 1993 and 1994).

D. *Net written premiums in the reporting country in terms of domestic and foreign risks :* Premiums from Foreign reinsurance are included.

E. *Business written abroad:* The figures of reinsurance accepted in this section are also included in the column corresponding to Section C.

F. *Outstanding investment by direct insurance companies*: Mortgages: total mortgages, since those granted for the acquisition of private accommodation are not mentioned separately. Other investments: - Life: including term deposits and money market claims, loans and advances on policies; - Life and non-life: liquid and other assets are included. These are among others the assets with agents, insurance proposers, insurers and reinsurers and deposits for reinsurance accepted.

G. *Breakdown of non-life premiums*: Gross premiums of reinsurance accepted and gross premiums of Total are estimates.

Insurance entities not included in statistical data
(activities on Swiss market only, in 1996)

Insurance entities	Number	Direct gross premiums (million SF)
Recognised Health Funds subject to the supervisory authority of the Federal Social Insurance Office	159	16,420
Swiss National Accident Insurance Organisation (SUVA)	1	3,281
Swiss Public Fire Insurances (SPFI)	19	818
Total	**179**	**20,519**

TURKEY

Definition of foreign-controlled companies: Companies, in which a foreign shareholder owns more than 50 per cent share of the capital.

B.   *Number of employees*: Number of employees for intermediaries covers only that of agents excluding banks operating as an agent.

F.   *Outstanding investment by direct insurance companies*: Real estate is re-evaluated to take inflation into account. Real estate, shares and other investments are evaluated by purchase value.

G.   *Others : Breakdown of non-life premiums:* Data by reinsurance companies are excluded in the premiums written by classes of non-life insurance. Marine and Aviation insurance includes Freight insurance.

UNITED KINGDOM

A.   *Number of companies in the reporting country:*
        a) For 1993, the number of "Domestic Companies" should be read as that of "EU companies with head office in UK", the number of "Foreign Controlled Companies" should be read as that of "EU companies with head office outside UK", and the number of "Branches and Agencies of Foreign Companies" should be read as that of "External companies". The number of "EU companies with head office outside UK" is not included in that of "EU companies with head office in UK". For 1994 and 1995, the number of "Domestic Companies" should be read as that of "EEA companies with head

office in UK", the number of "Foreign Controlled Companies" should be read as that of "EEA companies with head office outside UK", and the number of "Branches and Agencies of Foreign Companies" should be read as that of "External companies". The number of "EEA companies with head office outside UK" is not included in that of "EEA companies with head office in UK";

b) Lloyd's is counted as one domestic non-life company although, strictly speaking, it is not a corporate body. The number of companies does not include Friendly Societies; there are thousands of these but their income (included in the premium data) is very small;

c) Reinsurance companies are included in the numbers for non-life companies.

B. *Number of employees:* Since 1994, the data on the number of employees in insurance companies are based on the Standard Industrial Classification (SIC) 1992. The previous figures are based on the SIC 1980. The following figures indicate updated estimates for previous years: June 1990 - 243,143 June 1991 - 249,809 June 1992 - 237,280 June 1993 - 225,066.

G. *Breakdown of non-life premiums:* Marine and Aviation Insurance includes freight insurance.

UNITED STATES

General remarks: US data are based upon information provided by the National Association of Insurance Commissioners (NAIC).

Definition of foreign-controlled companies: Since 1990, foreign (non-US) person or entity owning directly or indirectly through a holding company system 10 per cent or more of the company. Farmers group, a foreign owned insurance exchange, is also defined as a foreign controlled company. Since 1994, foreign (non-US) person or entity owns directly or indirectly through a holding company system 50 per cent or more of the company.

A. *Number of companies in the reporting country:*
a) "Number of companies" refers to companies filing annual reports with the NAIC. There are several hundreds of small companies that do not file with the NAIC. The premiums of these companies are estimated at less than two per cent of all premiums;

b) The number of life insurance companies includes those whose predominant business is accident and health insurance. Insurers licensed only for accident and health are in non-life companies.

B. *Number of employees:* The number of employees is those on payroll only, which are compiled by the Bureau of Labour Statistics, US Department of Labour.

C. *Business written in the reporting country:*
Reinsurance accepted and ceded premiums reflect only business with unaffiliated companies. In general, unaffiliated business represents the market for reinsurance in the United States, while affiliated business represents reinsurance retained within an insurance group to take advantage of available surplus.

E.   *Business written abroad:* Data are sales of foreign insurance affiliates of the United States entities. Sales equal premium plus investment income plus other income. These data are compiled by the United States Department of Commerce.

F.   *Outstanding investment by direct insurance companies:*
      a) The NAIC recommends the method of assets valuation; it is followed in every state. Bonds are reported at amortised cost or, when not amortizable, at market value. Common stocks are reported at market value. Preferred stocks are reported at cost by life insurers and at market value by property/casualty insurers. Mortgage loans are reported at unpaid principal balance. All other invested assets are reported at cost or market value, whichever is less;
      b) Some double counting of assets is expected.

G.   *Breakdown of non-life premiums:* Reinsurance accepted and ceded includes unaffiliated business only. Accident/Health insurance includes life insurance companies activities.

III. DEFINITIONS OF CLASSES OF NON-LIFE INSURANCE

(Definitions are based on OECD common classification of the classes of insurance)

CLASSES	*DEFINITIONS*
1. MOTOR VEHICLE	3. LAND VEHICLES (other than railway rolling stock) All damage to or loss of: -- Land motor vehicles, -- Land vehicles other than motor vehicles.
	10. MOTOR VEHICLE LIABILITY All liability arising out of the use of motor vehicles operating on land (including carrier's liability).
2. TRANSPORT (including MARINE, AVIATION	4. RAILWAY ROLLING STOCK AND OTHERTRANSPORT All damage to or loss of railway rolling stock.
	5. AIRCRAFT All damage to or loss of aircraft.
	6. SHIPS (sea, lake, and river and canal vessels) All damage to or loss of: -- River and canal vessels, -- Lake vessels, -- Sea vessels.
	11. AIRCRAFT LIABILITY All liability arising out of the use of aircraft (including carrier's liability).
	12. LIABILITY FOR SHIPS (sea, lake, and river and canal vessels) All liability arising out of the use of ships, vessels or boats on the sea, lakes, rivers or canals (including carrier's liability).

3. FREIGHT

4. FIRE AND OTHER PROPERTY DAMAGE

5. PECUNIARY LOSS

7. GOODS IN TRANSIT (including merchandise, baggage and all other goods). All damage to or loss of goods in transit or baggage, irrespective of the form of transport.

8. FIRE AND NATURAL FORCES All damage or loss of property (other than property included in classes 3, 4, 5, 6 and 7) due to:
-- Fire
-- Explosion
-- Storm
-- Natural forces other than storm
-- Nuclear energy
-- Land subsidence

9. OTHER DAMAGE TO PROPERTY
All damage to or loss of property (other than property included in classes 3, 4, 5, 6 and 7) due to hail or frost, and any event such as theft, other than those mentioned under 8.

14. CREDIT
-- Insolvency (general)
-- Export credit
-- Instalment credit
-- Mortgages
-- Agricultural credit

15. SURETYSHIP
-- Suretyship (direct)
-- Suretyship (indirect)

16. MISCELLANEOUS FINANCIAL LOSS
-- Employment risks
-- Insufficiency of income (general)
-- Bad weather
-- Loss of benefits
-- Continuing general expenses
-- Unforeseen trading expenses
-- Loss of market value
-- Loss of rent or revenue
-- Indirect trading losses other than those mentioned above
-- Other financial loss (non-trading)
-- Other forms of financial loss

6. GENERAL LIABILITY

13. GENERAL LIABILITY
All liability other than those forms mentioned under 10, 11 and 12.

7. ACCIDENT AND SICKNESS

1. ACCIDENT (including industrial injury and occupational diseases)
-- Fixed pecuniary benefits
-- Benefits in the nature of indemnity
-- Combinations of the two
-- Injury to passengers

2. SICKNESS
-- Fixed pecuniary benefits
-- Benefits in the nature of indemnity
-- Combinations of the two

8. OTHER NON-LIFE INSURANCE

17. LEGAL EXPENSES
Legal expenses and costs of litigation.

18. ASSISTANCE

19. MISCELLANEOUS

9. TREATY REINSURANCE

I. DEFINITIONS ET NOTES COMMUNES

REMARQUES GENERALES

a) Les définitions des opérations "vie" et "non-vie" sont celles dc la législation nationale. Les primes d'assurances-accident et maladie souscrites par des compagnies vie doivent cependant être incluses dans les chiffres d'assurances non-vie.

b) Les chiffres fournis sur le nombre d'entreprises et le montant des primes d'assurance incluent toutes les entreprises d'assurances agréées dans le pays déclarant, *y compris* les réassureurs professionnels, qu'ils fassent ou non l'objet d'un contrôle, mais *à l'exclusion* de tout régime légal de sécurité sociale administré par l'État.

c) Par "*entreprises nationales*" il faut entendre les entreprises constituées selon la législation nationale ainsi que les entreprises du pays déclarant qui ne sont pas constituées en sociétés; les succursales et agences d'entreprises étrangères sont exclues.

d) Par "*entreprises sous contrôle étranger*" il faut entendre les entreprises nationales (selon la définition) qui sont contrôlées par des intérêts étrangers, le "contrôle" étant défini conformément à la législation nationale (voir la définition des entreprises sous contrôle étranger). Les données sur les "*Entreprises sous contrôle étranger*" sont incluses dans les données sur les "*Entreprises nationales*".

e) Par "*entreprises étrangères*", il faut entendre les entreprises constituées dans un pays autre que le pays déclarant.

A. NOMBRE D'ENTREPRISES DANS LE PAYS DECLARANT

a) *Mixtes* : Les entreprises opérant dans le secteur de l'assurance-vie et non-vie.

B. NOMBRE D'EMPLOYES

a) *Entreprises d'assurances* : Effectifs employés (à plein temps ou à temps partiel) dans les entreprises d'assurances.

b) *Intermédiaires* : Nombre des personnes se livrant à ce type d'activité (courtiers ou agents et leur personnel), à l'exclusion des intermédiaires qui peuvent vendre des contrats d'assurance mais ne se rattachent pas directement à la branche des assurances (par exemple, gestionnaires de banques, notaires, garagistes) ou de ceux qui ont été inclus en a) ci-dessus.

C. OPERATIONS CONCLUES DANS LE PAYS DECLARANT

a) Les *opérations conclues dans le pays déclarant* incluent toutes les opérations conclues dans le pays déclarant, qu'il s'agisse de risques nationaux ou situés à l'étranger (dans le monde entier), analysés comme indiqué dans les Remarques générales ci-dessus.

b) Le montant des "*primes nettes émises*" représente les primes retenues dans le pays déclarant. Ces doubles comptabilisations, parfois rencontrées dans les chiffres bruts, devraient être évitées ici.

c) Le montant des *"primes brutes"* représente le total des primes émises, sans les taxes sur les primes ou autres charges, et avant déduction des commissions ou frais de réassurances cédées. L'inclusion de la réassurance peut entraîner des doubles comptabilisations dans les chiffres fournis.

Le montant des *"primes brutes"* est la somme des *"assurances directes"* et des *"réassurances acceptées"*.

d) La réassurance facultative peut être incluse soit sous la rubrique "assurance directe", soit sous la rubrique "réassurances acceptées", selon la pratique du pays déclarant.

e) Les *primes cédées* incluent toutes les primes cédées (réassurances et rétrocession).

f) En principe, le montant des *"primes nettes émises"* doit être égal au total des *"primes brutes"*, déduction faite des *"primes cédées"*. En cas d'inadéquation, un élément compensateur approprié peut être ajouté dans la rubrique "primes cédées".

D. PRIMES NETTES EMISES DANS LE PAYS DECLARANT : RISQUES NATIONAUX ET ETRANGERS

Mêmes notes que a) et b) de la section C ci-dessus.

a) Cette partie traite, en les distinguant, des opérations portant sur des risques intérieurs et sur des risques situés à l'étranger, et détaille la ligne "primes nettes émises" de C "opérations conclues dans le pays déclarant".

b) Les *"risques dans le pays"* incluent toutes les opérations conclues dans le pays déclarant qui portent sur des risques intérieurs.

c) Les *"risques à l'étranger"* incluent toutes les opérations conclues dans le pays déclarant qui portent sur des risques situés en dehors du pays déclarant. (Ne sont pas incluses les opérations conclues en dehors du pays déclarant par des entreprises nationales.)

E. OPERATIONS CONCLUES À L'ETRANGER

Mêmes notes que c), d), e) et f) de la Section C ci-dessus.

a) Les *opérations à l'étranger* incluent tous les contrats conclus en dehors du pays déclarant (à la fois dans les pays Membres) de l'OCDE et dans les pays non Membres, ventilés par filiales, succursales et agences d'établir à l'étranger d'entreprises nationales.

F. ENCOURS DES PLACEMENTS DES ENTREPRISES D'ASSURANCES DIRECTES

a) Ces données incluent seulement les encours des placements de toutes les entreprises d'assurances directes dans le pays déclarant, mais non les placements par les entreprises de réassurance.

b) La méthode d'évaluation des placements est définie par chaque pays ; elle est parfois mentionnée dans les notes sur ces pays.

c) Les placements sont classés par catégorie, par nationalité des entreprises (entreprises nationales, entreprises sous contrôle étranger ou succursales et agences d'entreprises étrangères), aussi que par destination (dans le pays ou à l'étranger).

G. VENTILATIONS DES PRIMES NON-VIE

Mêmes notes que c), d), e) et f) de la Section C ci-dessus.

a) Cette Partie recense les *Primes émises par catégories d'assurances non-vie* pour les opérations conclues dans le pays déclarant, et donne une ventilation des "primes nettes émises" de C "Opérations conclues dans le pays déclarant".

b) Concernant les définitions précises de la classification, voir dans la partie III : "III. Définitions relatives aux branches des assurances non-vie".

c) La ligne "Réassurance obligatoire" est utilisée par les pays Membres ayant des difficultés à ventiler le poste "Réassurances acceptées" par branches.

H. PAIEMENTS BRUTS DES SINISTRES

a) *"Les paiements bruts des sinistres"* qui couvrent tous les paiements bruts pour les sinistres au titre de l'exercice financier, doivent être utilisés dans le calcul des paiements bruts des sinistres survenus.

I. DÉPENSES BRUTES D'EXPLOITATION

a) *"Les Dépenses brutes d'exploitation"*, correspondent normalement à la somme des frais d'acquisition, de la variation du montant des frais d'acquisition reportés et des frais d'administration.

J. COMMISSIONS

a) Cette partie correspond au total des commissions et ventile également celles-ci entre les commissions relatives à l'assurance directe et celles relatives à la réassurance acceptée.

II. DEFINITIONS ET NOTES PAR PAYS

Remarques générales pour les pays membres de l'Union Européenne/Espace Economique Européen (UE/EEE) : Suite aux changements réglementaires introduits par les Troisièmes Directives d'assurance de l'UE, depuis 1995, les données pour les pays de l'UE/EEE n'incluent pas les succursales et agences d'entreprises étrangères dont le siège social est situé dans un autre pays de l'UE/EEE. Le Groupe de travail sur les statistiques d'assurance est actuellement en train de considérer la façon de résoudre cette question, en coopération avec EUROSTAT. Il est espéré qu'au moins certaines de ces données pourront être ajoutées dans un stade ultérieur (voir la section V de la partie III, qui fournit des informations préliminaires sur cette question).

AUSTRALIE

Remarques générales : Pour l'année 1994 toutes les données relatives à l'assurance vie sont fondées sur l'année fiscale (juillet 1993 à juin 1994).

Définition des entreprises sous contrôle étranger : Contrôle prédominant exercé de l'étranger (via la propriété de titres ou le contrôle des votes)

C.   *Opérations conclues dans le pays déclarant :* Les opérations directes non-vie incluent les primes de réassurance facultative interne, mais excluent les charges légales. Les chiffres ne prennent en compte que les données du secteur privé.

F.   *Encours des placements des entreprises d'assurances directes* : La plupart des chiffres concernant l'investissement sont établis sur base de la valeur du marché.

G.   *Ventilation des primes non-vie* :
a) L'assurance frets est comprise dans l'assurance maritime/aviation ;
b) L'assurance pertes pécuniaires, l'assurance-accident et l'assurance-maladie sont comptabilisées dans "Autres".
c) Les primes pour l'assurance accident et l'assurance maladie souscrites par des compagnies d'assurance-vie ne sont pas incluses. Elles figurent dans les chiffres "vie".

AUTRICHE

Remarques générales : Pour des raisons techniques, les données relatives aux petites Mutuelles ne sont pas incluses. Cependant, les primes de ces Mutuelles se chiffraient à un total de 145 millions d'ATS seulement en 1996.

Définition des entreprises sous contrôle étranger : Participation des compagnies étrangères à hauteur de plus de 50 pour cent des actions.

G.   *Ventilation des primes non-vie* : Les primes cédées comptabilisées dans "Autres" incluent les primes de rétrocession (indépendantes de l'assurance maritime et aviation) qui ne peuvent pas être ventilées.

BELGIQUE

Remarques générales : Depuis 1994, les données relatives au nombre d'entreprises et aux primes ne comprennent pas les succursales d'entreprises étrangères dont le siège social est situé dans l'EEE. Les données relatives au nombre d'entreprises et aux primes ne comprennent pas les réassureurs professionnels qui ne sont ni soumis à l'agrément ni contrôlés, et pour lesquels il n'existe donc pas de données disponibles.

B.   *Nombre d'employés* : Le nombre d'intermédiaires représente le nombre approximatif de courtiers et d'agents non salariés, y compris les agents qui vendent occasionnellement des contrats d'assurance mais dont ce n'est pas l'activité principale.

C.   *Opérations conclues dans le pays déclarant:* Depuis 1996, les données relatives à "l'assurance directe" incluent seulement les risques dans le pays. Les données relatives à la réassurance acceptée concernent toutes les opérations en Belgique et à l'étranger, par succursale ou en libre prestation de services.

D.   *Primes nettes émises dans le pays déclarant : risques nationaux et étrangers :* Il n'est pas possible d'opérer une distinction entre les risques dans le pays et les risques à l'étranger, étant donné que le poste "Réassurances acceptées" ne peut être ventilé entre ces deux catégories d'opérations.

E.   *Opérations conclues à l'étranger* :
   a) On ne dispose pas de données relatives aux filiales d'entreprises belges établies à l'étranger ;
   b) La ventilation des primes brutes entre assurances directes et réassurances acceptées n'est pas disponible en ce qui concerne l'activité à l'étranger des succursales et agences d'entreprises belges.

G.   *Ventilation des primes non-vie* :
   a) Les chiffres reflètent exclusivement les opérations conclues quant aux risques nationaux ;
   b) L'assurance fret est incluse dans l'assurance maritime et aviation ;
   c) L'assurance-accident et maladie inclut l'assurance-accident du travail.

CANADA

Remarques générales : Les données sur des compagnies d'assurances à charte provinciale ne sont pas incluses. Les compagnies vie incluent les "fraternal benefit societies".

Définition des entreprises sous contrôle étranger : Assureur agréé selon les lois (fédérales) du Canada et dont la majorité des actions donnant le droit de vote est contrôlée directement ou indirectement par une/des entité(s) incorporée(s) ou établie(s) hors du Canada.

A.   *Nombre d'entreprises dans le pays déclarant :* Avant 1994, les données sur les entreprises de réassurance mixtes (entreprises exerçant à la fois dans le domaine de la réassurance vie et non vie étaient répertoriées sous la rubrique "mixte". Depuis 1994, le nombre de ces compagnies (7 en 1994 et 1995) est inclus sous la rubrique "Réassurance".

C   *Primes nettes émises dans le pays déclarant :* En principe les activités accident et maladie des compagnies d'assurance vie sont intégrées dans les chiffres d'assurance non vie. Cependant, en 1994 et 1995, ces activités sont exceptionnellement incluses dans les chiffres d'assurance vie.

F.   *Encours des placements des entreprises d'assurances directes* : Les investissements des entreprises domestiques et ceux des entreprises sous contrôle étranger correspondent à des actifs placés dans le monde entier. En revanche, ne sont comptabilisés parmi les investissements des succursales et agences d'entreprises étrangères que ceux réalisés au Canada. Les données sur l'assurance vie excluent les actifs des fonds cantonnés. Au Canada, les actifs sont évalués en fonction des principes comptables généralement reconnus (PCGR), comme il l'est indiqué dans le Manuel de l'Institut Canadien des Comptables Agréés (ICCA). En résumé, pour les compagnies d'assurance non-vie, l'immobilier est évalué au prix déprécié, les prêts hypothécaires : sur la base du coût d'amortissement, les actions : au prix d'achat sauf si le marché est en baisse permanente, auquel cas on retient le prix du marché et les obligations : en fonction du coût d'amortissement. Pour les compagnies d'assurance-vie, l'immobilier est évalué en fonction de la méthode du cours moyen du marché (le coût d'amortissement par rapport au marché étant de 10 pour cent), les prêts hypothécaires : en fonction du coût d'amortissement, les actions : en fonction de la méthode du cours moyen du marché (le coût d'amortissement par rapport au marché étant de 15 pour cent), et les obligations : en fonction du coût d'amortissement. Les compagnies d'assurance et les sociétés de secours mutuel doivent se plier aux politiques de prêts et d'investissements, aux normes et procédures qu'une personne sensée et prudente appliquerait vis-à-vis d'un portefeuille d'investissements et de prêts, et ce, afin d'éviter des risques et pertes injustifiables et d'obtenir le meilleur rendement. De plus, chaque compagnie d'assurance et société de secours mutuel doit se conformer à quelques limites statutaires sur les investissements, comme l'indique la législation.

REPUBLIQUE TCHEQUE

Définition des entreprises sous contrôle étranger : Compagnies agréées selon la loi Tchèque et qui ont plus de 50 pour cent de leur capital détenu par des étrangers.

F.   *Encours des placements des entreprises d'assurance directes:* Suite au changement législatif de 1994, les rapports relatifs aux investissements des compagnies d'assurance en 1993, ne sont pas comparables à plusieurs égards à ceux transmis les années précédentes.

DANEMARK

Remarques générales : Depuis 1994, les chiffres sur les fonds de pensions couverts par la loi danoise sur les activités d'assurances sont compris dans la rubrique "Vie".

Définition des entreprises sous contrôle étranger : Entreprises dont plus de 50 pour cent du capital est détenu par des étrangers.

B.   *Nombre d'employés* : L'estimation du nombre d'employés ne se rapporte qu'aux employés à plein temps.

D.   *Primes nettes émises dans le pays déclarant : risques nationaux et étrangers* : Les chiffres de la branche non-vie de cette Section sont des primes acquises, tandis que les chiffres de la Section C sont des primes émises.

F.   *Encours des placements des entreprises d'assurances directes :* Les actions dans le pays incluent les actions détenues dans les filiales établies à l'étranger et les actions détenues dans des entreprises liées étrangères.

FINLANDE

Remarques générales : Depuis 1993, les fonds de pension publics ne sont pas inclus dans les données sur l'assurance-vie.

Définition des entreprises sous contrôle étranger : Entreprises dans lesquelles un étranger détient au moins 50 pour cent des actions ou peut disposer d'au moins 50 pour cent des droits de vote.

A.   *Nombre d'entreprises dans le pays déclarant :* Depuis 1994, les données "non-vie" comprennent les petites associations d'assurance opérant principalement dans les zones rurales.

B.   *Nombre d'employés :* Depuis 1995, le nombre des intermédiaires n'inclut que les courtiers.

F.   *Encours des placements des entreprises d'assurances directes* : Les investissements sont comptabilisés à leur coût d'acquisition. Depuis 1994, les "obligations" sont incluses dans "prêts autres qu'hypothécaires".

G.   *Ventilation des primes non-vie* : "Autres" inclut l'assurance RC automobile obligatoire.

FRANCE

Définition des entreprises sous contrôle étranger : Entreprises dont 20 pour cent au moins du capital est détenu par un non-résident (personne physique ou morale) ou par une société française elle-même sous contrôle étranger.

A.   *Nombre d'entreprises dans le pays déclarant:* Les sociétés "mixtes" ne peuvent pratiquer que l'assurance vie et les branches d'assurance non-vie "accidents" et "maladie".

F. *Encours des placements des entreprises d'assurances directes* : D'une manière générale, les actifs sont évalués à leur valeur historique. Les investissements des entreprises nationales et des succursales et agences d'entreprises étrangères correspondent seulement aux placements dans le pays.

G. *Ventilation des primes non-vie :* Toutes les catégories d'assurance fret sont incluses dans l'assurance maritime et aviation. La réassurance obligatoire concerne les sociétés opérant en assurance directe et les réassureurs professionnels spécialisés. Depuis 1994, les données sur l'assurance des pertes pécuniaires sont répertoriées sous l'intitulé "Autres".

ALLEMAGNE

Définition des entreprises sous contrôle étranger : Intérêts étrangers, directs ou indirects, supérieurs à 50 pour cent.

A. *Nombre d'entreprises dans le pays déclarant* :
a) Les données relatives aux petites sociétés mutuelles soumises au contrôle des Länder sont exclues. Nombre des petites sociétés mutuelles soumises au contrôle des Länder ; 1424 (1995), 1401 (1996), 1358 (1997). La part de marché de ces sociétés est de plus ou moins 0,04 pour cent;
b) S'agissant des entreprises d'assurance-vie, les régimes de pension et d'indemnités en cas de décès sont inclus ;
c) Dans le cas des entreprises d'assurance non-vie, les entreprises d'assurance-maladie spécialisées sont incluses [nombre des entreprises d'assurance-maladie : 58 (1995), 57 (1996), 56 (1997)].

C. *Opérations conclues dans le pays déclarant:* Les chiffres pour 1992 incluent pour la première fois ceux concernant les réassureurs professionnels. Entre 1992-1994, pour les primes cédées, on ne dispose pas de ventilation entre les opérations souscrites dans le pays déclarant et celles souscrites à l'étranger. Par conséquent, les chiffres de la section C et la section G concernent les opérations totales (nationales et étrangères) pour ces années .

E. *Opérations conclues à l'étranger* : Même remarque que sous le point C. Entre 1992-1994, pour les opérations de réassurance acceptées, on ne dispose pas de ventilation entre les branches vie et non-vie ; par conséquent la réassurance vie comprend la réassurance non-vie. Les opérations de réassurance acceptées souscrites à l'étranger sont celles acceptées d'une entreprise d'assurance située à l'étranger. On ne dispose pas de données concernant la localisation du risque assuré.

F. *Encours des placements des entreprises d'assurances directes* : La méthode d'évaluation des placements est la méthode du coût historique. Depuis 1995, une distinction entre entreprises nationales et succursales et agences d'entreprises étrangères n'est pas disponible; Il n'y a de même pas de données séparées pour les entreprises sous contrôle étranger. Les placements nationaux et étrangers ne sont pas ventilés.

G. *Ventilations des primes non-vie :* Même note que la Section C ci-dessus.
a) L'assurance fret est incluse dans l'assurance maritime et aviation.
b) La rubrique "Divers " correspond aux données sur l'assurance "protection juridique".

GRECE

Définition des entreprises sous contrôle étranger : Définitions conformes aux articles 1 et 41 de la Septième Directive 349/83 de la CEE et aux articles 9 et 25 de la Quatrième Directive 660/78 de la CEE.

A.   *Nombre d'entreprises dans le pays déclarant :* Les représentants des courtiers d'assurance Lloyds [nombre des courtiers d'assurance Lloyds : 38 (1990, 1991)] ne sont pas inclus dans "les succursales et agences d'entreprises étrangères".

G.   *Ventilation des primes non-vie :* "Autres" renvoie uniquement à l'assurance protection juridique.

HONGRIE

Remarques générales : Depuis 1996, les données des associations d'assurance sont incluses. Comme il y a 23 associations d'assurance, les données de 1996 sur le nombre des compagnies d'assurance ne sont plus comparables avec les données antérieures. En ce qui concerne les données sur les primes, les investissements, les coûts, cette addition n'a pas d'effet évident parce que le chiffre d'affaires de ces associations est modeste.

Définition des entreprises sous contrôle étranger : Plus de la moitié du capital est détenu par des actionnaires étrangers.

E.   *Opérations conclues à l'étranger :* Aucune compagnie d'assurance n'a de filiale ou de succursale à l'étranger.

F.   *Encours des placements des entreprises d'assurances directes :*
a) Seuls les investissements relatifs aux provisions techniques sont inclus. Les investissements du capital souscrit, du capital réservé et des provisions pour les opérations générales de la compagnie ne sont pas indiqués.
b) L'évaluation des placements se fait au prix coûtant. Après un minimum d'un an de perte de valeurs, les investissements sont réévalués. En Hongrie, seule la dépréciation est admise.

G.   *Ventilation des primes non-vie.*
a) Les données sur "marine, aviation et autres transports" sont répertoriés sous l'intitulé "Autres";
b) Avant 1994, l'assurance habitation était classée dans la rubrique "incendie et autres". Depuis 1995, elle est classée dans la rubrique "Autres".

ISLANDE

Définition des entreprises sous contrôle étranger : Entreprises dans lesquelles les intérêts étrangers sont majoritaires.

B.   *Nombre d'employés :* Le chiffre correspond à des emplois à plein temps. Ainsi, une personne travaillant à mi-temps est considérée comme représentant la moitié d'un employé.

F.   *Encours des placements des entreprises d'assurances directes :* L'évaluation s'effectue essentiellement sur base de la valeur de marché. Il n'existe aucune limite autorisée de placement par catégorie, mais la sécurité des réserves techniques doit être assurée.

IRLANDE

Remarques générales : Les primes d'assurance-maladie sont exclues. Les données sur le nombre d'entreprises et les primes excluent les réassureurs professionnels qui ne sont pas soumis à agrément, et qui ne sont pas supervisés. Aucune information n'est donc disponible à leur sujet.

D.   *Primes nettes émises dans le pays déclarant :* risques nationaux et étrangers : Les chiffres concernant l'assurance-vie de risques situés à l'étranger, ne sont pas disponibles. Cependant, ils sont estimés négligeables.

E.   *Opérations conclues à l'étranger :* Les chiffres concernant la réassurance sont compris dans les assurances directes.

F.   *Encours des placements des entreprises d'assurances directes :* Comme la ventilation des actifs liés (actifs représentant des placements dans des fonds d'investissements ou des OPCVM) n'est pas disponible, ils sont comptabilisés dans "autres placements". L'investissement à l'étranger dans la branche assurance vie correspond seulement aux actifs non liés représentant l'activité de l'assurance vie qui n'est pas localisée en Irlande. L'investissement dans la branche non-vie inclut les liquidités placées dans des sociétés immobilières, banques et autres institutions financières. Les chiffres sur les placements sont évalués à leur valeur de marché. Suite à des raisons techniques, depuis 1995, les données non-vie sont basées sur la valeur historique. Autres placements de l'assurance-vie incluant les postes ci-après ; Titres à intérêt variable, Comptes de dépôt et comptes ordinaires, Fonds de placement, Espèces et Prêts hypothécaires (immobilier), etc. Depuis 1994, les données sur les succursales et agences d'entreprises étrangères comprennent seulement les succursales d'un pays tiers (hors Union Européenne) établies en Irlande. Les investissements de succursales d'entreprises UE ne sont plus disponibles.

G.   *Ventilation des primes non-vie :*
          a) L'assurance fret est incluse dans l'assurance maritime et aviation ;
          b) Depuis 1996, l'assurance des pertes pécuniaires est incluse dans la rubrique "Autres".

ITALIE

Définition des entreprises sous contrôle étranger : Toute entreprise dont plus de 50 pour cent du capital social appartient à une ou plusieurs sociétés ayant leur siège social à l'étranger.

B.   *Nombre d'employés :* Le chiffre des intermédiaires est une estimation et comprend les producteurs indépendants.

F.   *Encours des placements des entreprises d'assurances directes* : Les chiffres sur les placements sont enregistrés à leur valeur de historique.

JAPON

Remarques générales (sauf pour la section E): Les chiffres sont ceux de l'année fiscale (1 avril de l'année examinée au 31 mars de l'année suivante).

Définition des entreprises sous contrôle étranger : Compagnies détenues par des actionnaires étrangers à hauteur de 50 pour cent au moins du capital.

B.   *Nombre d'employés :*
a) Les effectifs employés à temps partiel ne sont pas inclus dans "Effectifs employés" ;
b) Les agents dont l'assurance n'est pas l'activité principale figurent dans les "intermédiaires"

C.   *Opérations conclues dans le pays déclarant :*
a) Les chiffres concernant les entreprises d'assurance-vie s'entendent avant déduction des primes de remboursement ;
b) Les primes brutes pour l'assurance non-vie comprennent l'élément épargne des "assurances avec remboursement à l'échéance". Ce n'est pas le cas des primes nettes émises. Dès lors, les primes nettes émises de l'assurance non-vie ne correspondent pas aux "primes brutes moins primes cédées".

E.   *Opérations conclues à l'étranger :* Dans la partie non-vie, certaines filiales ne sont pas en mesure de fournir des chiffres distincts pour les "assurance directes" et les "réassurances acceptées".

F.   *Encours des placements des entreprises d'assurances directes :*
a) La méthode de l'évaluation au coût d'acquisition est généralement appliquée. L'amortissement de l'immobilier (autre que les terrains) à des fins de placement s'effectue par application d'un pourcentage fixe sur la base de la méthode de l'amortissement dégressif. L'évaluation des valeurs cotées s'effectue sur la base du coût d'acquisition ou du prix du marché (en choisissant le chiffre le plus bas) ;
b) Depuis 1996, les prêts hypothécaires sont inclus dans les "Prêts autres qu'hypothécaires".
c) Les "obligations" incluent les titres étrangers, les autres titres et les titres prêtés;
d) Autres investissements : inclut les dépôts, prêts au jour le jour, "Monetary Receivables Bought", "Commodity Securities", fonds de gestion de patrimoine, etc.

G.   *Ventilation des primes non-vie :* Les primes d'assurance incendie et dommages aux biens, ainsi que celles d'assurance-accident et maladie, sont calculées avant déduction de la composante épargne des "assurances avec remboursement à l'échéance".

Les services et entités suivants ne sont pas inclus dans les données statistiques :

1.   Assurance vie de la Poste

Ce service à but non lucratif administré par l'Etat distribue des assurances vie auprès de la population dans tout le pays, ce qui contribue à la stabilité économique de la population et à son bien-être. Il est administré par le ministère de la Poste et des Télécommunications conformément aux dispositions de la Loi sur l'assurance vie de la poste. Son budget et sa comptabilité font l'objet de délibérations à la Diète.

Revenu de primes d'assurance directe	13 638.813 milliards de yen	Exercice 1996
Total des actifs	100 772.008 milliards de yen	fin de l'exercice 1996

2.   Assistance mutuelle des associations d'entreprises soumises aux normes d'hygiène et de conditions sanitaires

Les associations d'entreprises soumises aux normes d'hygiène et de conditions sanitaires sont des entités dont le but est d'améliorer les normes d'hygiène et de conditions sanitaires en veillant au bon état sanitaire des entreprises concernées, ce qui va dans le sens des intérêts des consommateurs. Ces associations sont établies conformément à la loi correspondante. Les associations fournissent, dans le cadre de leur exploitation, des services sans but lucratif assimilables à des assurances vie ou assurance incendie à leurs adhérents.

Revenu de primes d'assurance directe	NON DISPONIBLE
Total des actifs	NON DISPONIBLE

3.   Assistance mutuelle des associations de promotion des centres commerciaux

Ces services sans but lucratif assimilables à des assurances incendie sont fournis par les associations de promotion des centres commerciaux à leurs adhérents, en raison des caractéristiques spécifiques des centres commerciaux dans lesquels de nombreuses boutiques sont concentrées sur une surface relativement petite. La plupart des associations sont petites et elles sont très peu nombreuses à fournir effectivement des services d'assistance mutuelle.

Revenu de primes d'assurance directe	NON DISPONIBLE
Total des actifs	NON DISPONIBLE

4. Assistance mutuelle des coopératives de consommateurs

Les coopératives de consommateurs sont des associations établies conformément à la Loi et dont l'objet est de promouvoir le développement spontané des associations locales, ce qui contribue à la stabilité économique de la population et à la mise en valeur de son mode de vie. Les coopératives de consommateurs et leur fédération fournissent à leurs adhérents des services sans but lucratif d'assistance mutuelle, notamment dans le domaine de l'assurance vie ou de l'assurance automobile.

Revenu de primes d'assurance directe   669.011 milliards de yen   d'après une enquête pour
                                                                    l'exercice 1995
Total des actifs   NON DISPONIBLE

5. Assistance mutuelle des coopératives sylvicoles au titre des calamités

Ce dispositif a été mis en place conformément à la Loi et vise à améliorer le statut économique et social des propriétaires d'exploitations sylvicoles, à garantir un rendement durable des forêts ainsi qu'à accroître leur production potentielle, ce qui contribue au développement de l'économie nationale. La Fédération nationale des coopératives de propriétaires d'exploitations sylvicoles administre ce dispositif sans but lucratif qui est analogue à une assurance non-vie pour les exploitations sylvicoles.

Revenu de primes d'assurance   2.625 milliards de yen   exercice 1996
directe
Total des actifs   NON DISPONIBLE

6. Assistance mutuelle des coopératives de pêche

Ce dispositif a été mis en place conformément à la Loi et vise à promouvoir le développement des associations locales de pêcheurs et d'intervenants de la transformation du produit de la pêche, ce qui favorise leur statut économique et social, améliore la production potentielle des pêcheries et contribue par là-même au développement de l'économie nationale. Les coopératives de pêche fournissent à leurs adhérents des services sans but lucratif assimilables à des assurances vie et non-vie.

Revenu de primes d'assurance   79.031 milliards de yen   exercice 1996
directe
Total des actifs   404.455 milliards de yen   fin de l'exercice 1996

7. Assistance mutuelle des coopératives de PME

Ces associations composées de petites et moyennes entreprises de certaines zones fournissent à leurs adhérents des services sans but lucratif assimilables à des assurances vie et non-vie. Le nombre total de ces coopératives s'élève approximativement à 49 000 dans tout le Japon. Même si l'on ne dispose pas de statistiques précises, leurs services habituels sont les suivants :

i)   Assistance mutuelle incendie des coopératives d'assurance incendie

Ces coopératives composées de PME fournissent, selon le principe de l'assistance mutuelle, des services sans but lucratif assimilables à des assurances incendie afin de couvrir les adhérents contre les sinistres provoqués par le feu.

Revenu de primes d'assurance directe	20.041 milliards de yen	exercice 1996
Total des actifs	66.087 milliards de yen	fin de l'exercice 1996

ii) Assistance mutuelle automobile des coopératives d'assurance des véhicules à moteur

Ces coopératives composées de PME fournissent, selon le principe de l'assistance mutuelle, des services sans but lucratif assimilables à des assurances automobile afin de couvrir les adhérents contre les accidents liés à la possession, à l'utilisation et au contrôle de véhicules personnels.

Revenu de primes d'assurance directe	24.575 milliards de yen	exercice 1996
Total des actifs	16.900 milliards de yen	fin de l'exercice 1996

8.   Assistance mutuelle des coopératives agricoles

Ce dispositif a été mis en place conformément à la Loi et vise à promouvoir le développement des associations collectives d'agriculteurs, ce qui améliore la production potentielle de l'agriculture, favorise leur statut économique et social et contribue au développement de l'économie nationale. Les coopératives agricoles et leur fédération fournissent à leurs adhérents, en tant qu'organisme unique, des services sans but lucratif assimilables à des assurances vie et non-vie.

Revenu de primes d'assurance directe	4 713.500 milliards de yen	chiffre approximatif en fin d'exercice 1996
Total des actifs	30 141.400 milliards de yen	chiffre approximatif en fin d'exercice 1996

9.   Assistance mutuelle des syndicats de salariés

Les syndicats de salariés et la fédération nationale d'assistance mutuelle des syndicats, qui sont organisées volontairement par les salariés avec pour principal objectif de promouvoir leur statut économique, et plus particulièrement de maintenir et améliorer les normes du travail, fournissent à leurs adhérents des services sans but lucratif assimilables à des assurances vie et non-vie.

Revenu de primes d'assurance directe	NON DISPONIBLE
Total des actifs	NON DISPONIBLE

COREE

Définition des entreprises sous contrôle étranger : filiale d'une entreprise étrangère.

F.   *Encours des placements des entreprises d'assurances directes :* Les investissements se mesurent sur la base du coût historique, à l'exception des titres cotés, pour lesquels on retient le cours moyen du marché (cf. Article 18-2 du décret mettant en oeuvre la loi sur les activités d'assurance.

LUXEMBOURG

Définition des entreprises sous contrôle étranger : L'actionnaire principal n'est pas de nationalité luxembourgeoise.

C.   *Opérations conclues dans le pays déclarant:* Les chiffres concernent les produits d'assurance commercialisés (flux).

F.   *Encours des placements des entreprises d'assurances directes :* Seuls les données sur les placements en flux sont disponibles.

G.   *Ventilation des primes non-vie :* Même note que la Section C ci-dessus.

MEXIQUE

Définition des entreprises sous contrôle étranger : Entreprises dont 51 pour cent ou plus du capital est détenu par des étrangers.

G.   *Ventilation des primes non-vie :*
        a) "Assurances transport maritime, aviation et autres transports" inclut l'assurance fret.
        b) Les autres assurances non-vie incluent l'assurance des risques agricoles et divers.

PAYS-BAS

Remarques générales :

        a) Avant 1995, le nombre, ainsi que les primes encaissées par les réassureurs professionnels, sont des estimations puisque ces entreprises sont exemptées du contrôle gouvernemental ; Depuis 1995, ces entreprises ne sont plus incluses. En 1995, il y avait 9 réassureurs professionnels qui ont généré des primes de près de 751 millions de florins (517 millions en non-vie et 234 millions en vie).
        b) Le nombre, ainsi que les primes encaissées par les entreprises sous contrôle étranger, sont des estimations, les chiffres fournis ne concernant que les entreprises soumises au contrôle ;

Définition des entreprises sous contrôle étranger : Compagnies d'assurance agréées dans le pays, dont au moins 50 pour cent du capital est détenu par une ou plusieurs compagnies, dont les sièges sociaux sont situés hors des Pays-Bas.

A.   *Nombre d'entreprises dans le pays déclarant* :
      a) Avant 1995, le nombre des entreprises d'assurance non-vie inclut de petites compagnies mutuelles qui ne sont pas soumises au contrôle (1995, 239). Leur part du marché n'a pas excédé 0,2 pour cent(1995).
      b) Depuis 1995, le nombre de succursales d'entreprises étrangères avec un siège social au sein de l'UE/EEE n'est plus inclus. Le nombre de ces succursales est de 115 (en 1995, soit 3 en vie et 112 en non-vie).

B.   *Nombre d'employés :* Les chiffres sur les effectifs employés et les intermédiaires (réalisant des affaires sur une base professionnelle) sont des estimations ;

C.   *Opérations conclues dans le pays déclarant* : Les compagnies d'assurance-vie aux Pays-Bas n'étant pas tenues de déclarer leurs activités de réassurance, on ne peut distinguer, dans les primes brutes, les assurances directes des réassurances acceptées.

E.   *Opérations conclues à l'étranger :* Avant 1995 les données disponibles sont des approximations relatives aux trois plus grandes compagnies d'assurances hollandaises opérant à l'échelle internationale. Depuis 1994, aucune estimation n'est disponible.

F.   *Encours des placements des entreprises d'assurances directes* : Les techniques d'évaluation en vigueur sont généralement les suivantes :
      - immobilier : valeur du marché/valeur estimée
      - prêts (hypothécaires) :
          vie: valeur d'amortissement ou valeur nominale
          non-vie: valeur nominale
      - actions :
           côtées :   valeur du marché
           non-côtées :   valeur estimée
      - obligations
          vie :   valeur d'amortissement ou valeur du marché
          non-vie :   valeur du marché
      Avant la mise en oeuvre des Troisièmes Directives de L'UE, il n'y avait aucune limite réglementaire quant au pourcentage des placements des actifs totaux par une entreprise d'assurance.

G.   *Ventilation des primes non-vie :*
      a) L'assurance fret est incluse dans l'assurance maritime/aviation ;
      b) Les assurances pertes pécuniaires et responsabilité générale sont incluses dans les autres assurances non-vie.

NOUVELLE-ZELANDE

Définition des entreprises sous contrôle étranger : 50 pour cent ou plus d'intérêts étrangers.

C.   *Opérations conclues dans le pays déclarant* : Les primes brutes d'assurance-vie directe par les entreprises nationales incluent les primes nettes de réassurance-vie.

G.   *Ventilation des primes non-vie :* "Autres" correspond à l'assurance médicale.

NORVEGE

Remarques générales : Pour 1994 et 1995, sans les données concernant les succursales et agences d'entreprises étrangères de l'assurance non-vie.

Définition des entreprises sous contrôle étranger : Entreprises où la majorité des droits de vote est détenue par des étrangers. Depuis 1997, toutes les compagnies appartenant au même groupe d'assurance sont classées de façon identique.

C.   *Opérations conclues dans le pays déclarant :* Les réassurances acceptées sont calculées par soustraction, c'est-à-dire le montant total des primes brutes diminué des primes correspondant à des assurances directes en Norvège. Cela signifie que les réassurances acceptées peuvent englober des assurances directes souscrites à l'étranger.

F.   *Encours des placements des entreprises d'assurances directes* : Le total des placements effectués par les sociétés de la branche non-vie ne comprend pas les placements des succursales et agences de sociétés étrangères.

POLOGNE

Remarques générales : L'établissement des succursales et agences d'entreprises étrangères est autorisé depuis 1er janvier 1999.

Définition des entreprises sous contrôle étranger : 51 pour cent au moins du capital sous contrôle étranger.

A.   *Nombre d'entreprises dans le pays déclarant :* Le nombre total d'entreprises d'assurance inclut 5 mutuelles d'assurance et 46 sociétés par action (2 entreprises publiques et 49 entreprises privées).

B.   *Nombre d'employés :* Le nombre d'employés d'assurance est estimé. En 1996 et 1997, l'organe étatique en charge du contrôle de l'assurance a donné approximativement 85.440 autorisations de mener une activité d'intermédiation (les autorisations concernaient tant des agents que des courtiers).

F.   *Encours des placements des entreprises d'assurances directes* : Les chiffres sur les placements sont généralement enregistrés à leur valeur historique.

I.   *Dépenses brutes d'exploitation* : Cette rubrique inclut les coûts d'acquisition, les dépenses administratives et les autres dépenses techniques.

PORTUGAL

Définition des entreprises sous contrôle étranger : Proportion du capital détenu par des étrangers supérieure à 50 pour cent.

C.   *Opérations conclues dans le pays déclarant* : Le montant des primes brutes représente le total des primes et accessoires.

F.   *Encours des placements des entreprises d'assurances directes* :
- *a)* Avant 1995, seuls les actifs représentatifs des provisions techniques sont considérés ; Depuis 1995, les actifs libres sont aussi inclus.
- *b)* Parmi les valeurs mobilières sont inclus : titres du trésor, bons du trésor, titres de créance pour l'investissement public, obligations, actions, titres de participation et parts de fonds communs de placement.
- *c)* "Prêts autres qu'hypothécaires" comprennent les emprunts sur les polices et les emprunts sur les titres ;
- *d)* "Autres placements" incluent les dépôts et les certificats de dépôts.

G.   *Ventilation des primes non-vie* : Les assurances-maladie et accident incluent l'assurance contre les accidents du travail.

ESPAGNE

Définition des entreprises sous contrôle étranger : Participation dans le capital social égale ou supérieure à 50 pour cent.

F.   *Encours des placements des entreprises d'assurances directes* : En général, la méthode d'estimation du coût d'acquisition est appliquée.

G.   *Ventilation des primes non-vie* :
- *a)* L'assurance médicale est incluse dans l'assurance-accident et santé ;
- *b)* Pour l'année 1990, toutes les opérations d'assurance transport sont comptabilisées dans l'assurance maritime/aviation.

SUEDE

Définition des entreprises sous contrôle étranger : 50 pour cent des titres au moins est sous contrôle étranger.

A.   *Nombre d'entreprises dans le pays déclarant* : Les données "non-vie" excluent environ 340 petites mutuelles d'assurance locales dont la part estimée de marché "non-vie" est inférieure à 0,5 pour cent (données 1997). Depuis 1994, il n'existe aucun chiffre pour les succursales d'assurances dont le siège social est situé dans un pays membre de l'EEE. Il en existe 12 ; et le chiffre de leurs primes directes est estimée à 2 pour cent des primes non-vie (données 1997).

B. *Nombre d'employés :*
Le nombre d'employés de compagnies d'assurance inclut les agents employés, dont approximativement 20 000 travaillent à temps partiel (données de 1993). Depuis 1994, les données des employés des compagnies d'assurance excluent les agents à temps partiel ou travaillant en franchise. Les données de 1993 correspondantes devraient être du même ordre de grandeur qu'en 1994 soit, 19 000. Le nombre des intermédiaires inclut seulement les courtiers d'assurance (qui comprennent 200 entités légales);

C. *Opérations conclues dans le pays déclarant* : Aucune information fiable n'est disponible concernant les succursales et les agences des entreprises de réassurance étrangères. Cependant, comme on considère qu'elles se concentrent sur la réassurance non-vie, leurs primes de réassurance vie sont estimées à 0 (zéro).

D. *Primes nettes émises dans le pays déclarant : risques nationaux et étrangers* : Aucune information fiable n'est disponible sur la ventilation entre les risques nationaux et les risques étrangers. Cependant, il est probable que seulement une part de marché mineure de l'assurance non-vie directe est émise sur les risques étrangers et qu'il n'y a pratiquement aucune activité d'assurance vie directe sur cette catégorie de risques.

E. *Opérations conclues à l'étranger :* On ne dispose que de certaines informations pour les assurances directes et les primes cédées dans le cas des succursales et agences non-vie des assureurs nationaux. Il n'existe pas d'information correspondante sur les filiales.

F. *Encours des placements des entreprises d'assurances directes* :
a) Avant 1996, l'évaluation s'effectue, en général, sur la base de la valeur d'achat ou de la valeur du marché (en choisissant le chiffre le plus bas). Depuis 1996, la méthode de la valeur du marché est utilisée ;
b) L'évaluation des actifs à revenu fixe correspondant aux provisions techniques de l'assurance vie peut être faite en fonction du coût, même si la valeur obtenue est supérieure à la valeur du marché.
c) De 1991 à 1995, les prêts hypothécaires ne peuvent être séparés des prêts autres qu'hypothécaires ; ces derniers incluent donc tous les prêts.
d) Il n'y avait aucune limite autorisée du placement par catégorie, cependant il y avait des restrictions sur le choix des actifs correspondant aux provisions techniques. Au moins 80 pour cent des provisions techniques en assurance-vie (autre qu'à capital variable) doit être couverts par certains types d'actifs. Les 80 pour cent restant ne peuvent être investis en actions. La détention d'actions est limitée indirectement du fait que les droits de vote détenus dans une même société ne peuvent en général dépasser 5 pour cent. Le 1er juillet 1995, les règles de l'UE sur les investissements ont été mises ne vigueur. En particulier, aucune des catégories "actions" ou "immobilier" ne peuvent excéder 25 pour cent des provisions techniques nets de réassurance.
e) Les données sur les agences d'entreprises non EEE n'incluent que les dépôts juridiquement reconnus. Les dépôts sont comptabilisés sous la rubrique "Autres Placements". Depuis 1994, les données ne couvrent plus celles des pays membres de l'EEE.

f) Quoi qu'aucune information fiable ne soit disponible concernant la distribution des placements dans le pays et à l'étranger, les placements en immobilier, actions et obligations à l'étranger ont certainement une influence.

G.   *Ventilation des primes non-vie* :

a) En ce qui concerne les réassurances obligatoires acceptées, les primes émises par les succursales ou agences de réassureurs étrangers n'ont pas été prises en compte ;

b) L'assurance de responsabilité générale ne peut être comptabilisée comme une catégorie séparée puisque, en général, elle fait partie d'un ensemble de produits variés tels que l'assurance risques habitation et "tous risques" habitation ;

c) L'assurance-accident et santé inclut l'assurance sans faute des employeurs ;

SUISSE

Définition des entreprises sous contrôle étranger : Entreprises avec une participation étrangère de plus de 50 pour cent. Depuis 1993, entreprises dont plus de 50 pour cent du capital est détenu pas des étrangers, directement ou en cascade.

B.   *Nombre d'employés* : La notion d'"'intermédiaire" signifie les agents d'assurance liés à une société d'assurances par un contrat de travail, à l'exclusion des courtiers et des agents généraux indépendants dont le nombre s'élève à 200 en 1990 et 400 en 1991 et 1992 et 400-500 en 1993 et 1994.

D.   *Primes nettes émises dans le pays déclarant : risques nationaux et étrangers :* Les primes de réassurance étrangères sont incluses.

E.   *Opérations conclues à l'étranger* : Les chiffres des réassurances acceptées dans cette Section sont également inclus dans les colonnes correspondantes des tableaux de la Section C.

F.   *Encours des placements des entreprises d'assurances directes* : Hypothèques : ensemble des hypothèques, celles accordées pour l'acquisition d'un logement privé n'étant pas mentionnées séparément. Autres placements : - Vie : ils incluent les dépôts à terme et créances sur le marché monétaire, prêts et avances sur polices. - Vie et non-vie : les avoirs liquides et autres actifs sont inclus, il s'agit entre autres d'avoirs auprès d'agents, de preneurs d'assurances, d'assureurs et réassureurs, et de dépôts pour réassurances acceptées.

G.   *Ventilation des primes non-vie :* Les primes brutes de réassurances acceptées ainsi que le total des primes brutes sont des estimations.

Entités d'assurance ne figurant pas dans les statistiques
(Activités sur le marché suisse seulement, en 1996)

Entités d'assurance	Nombre des entités	Primes brutes assurances directe en million de CHF
Caisses maladie reconnues soumises à la surveillance de l'Office fédéral des assurances sociales	159	16,420
Caisse nationale suisse d'assurance en cas d'accidents (CNA)	1	3,281
Etablissements cantonaux d'assurance incendie	19	818
Total	**179**	**20,519**

TURQUIE

Définition des entreprises sous contrôle étranger : Entreprises dont plus de 50 pour cent du capital sont détenus par un actionnaire étranger.

B.   *Nombre d'employés :* Le nombre d'employés des intermédiaires ne représente que celui des agents, et exclut les banques agissant en tant qu'agents.

D.   *Primes nettes émises dans le pays déclarant :* risques nationaux et étrangers : Tous les chiffres sont établis sur la base des primes brutes avant 1990.

F.   *Encours des placements des entreprises d'assurances directes :* Les immeubles sont réévalués pour tenir compte de l'inflation. Les immeubles, actions et autres placements sont évalués sur base de la valeur d'acquisition.

G   *Ventilation des primes non-vie :* Les données relatives aux sociétés de réassurance ne sont pas comprises dans les primes ventilées par catégories d'assurance non vie. L'assurance maritime et aviation inclut l'assurance fret.

ROYAUME-UNI

A.   *Nombre d'entreprises dans le pays déclarant :*
        a) Pour l'année 1993, les données concernant l'intitulé "Entreprises Nationales" se réfèrent
             aux "Entreprises UE dont le siège social est au Royaume-Uni". L'intitulé "Entreprises

Sous Contrôle Etranger" porte sur les "Entreprises UE dont le siège social est situé en dehors du Royaume-Uni" et l'intitulé "Succursales et Agences d'Entreprises Etrangères" correspond aux "Entreprises Externes". Le nombre d'"Entreprise UE dont le siège social est situé en dehors du Royaume-Uni" ne tient pas compte des "Entreprises UE dont le siège est au Royaume-Uni". Pour les années 1994 et 1995, les données pour les "Entreprises Nationales" se réfèrent aux "Entreprises de l'EEE dont le siège est au Royaume-Uni", "Entreprises Sous Contrôle Etranger" aux "Entreprises de l'EEE dont le siège est situé en dehors du Royaume-Uni" et Succursales et Agences d'Entreprises Etrangères" aux "Entreprises Externes". Le nombre d'"Entreprises EEE dont le siège est au Royaume-Uni" exclut les "Entreprises EEE dont le siège social est situé en dehors du Royaume-Uni".

b) Le Lloyds est comptabilisé comme une seule entreprise nationale non-vie même si ce n'est pas, à proprement parler, une personne morale. Le nombre d'entreprises ne comprend pas les sociétés de secours mutuel ; il en existe des milliers mais leurs recettes (qui figurent dans les données relatives aux primes) sont très faibles.

c) Les entreprises de réassurance sont comprises dans le nombre d'entreprises non-vie.

B. *Nombre d'employés :* Depuis 1994, les informations sur le nombre d'employés dans les entreprises d'assurance est basé sur la CITI de 1992. Les données pour les années antérieures sont basées sur celles de 1980. Les chiffres suivants mettent à jour ceux publiés pour les années précédentes : juin 1990 - 243 143, juin 1991 - 249 809, juin 1992 - 237 280, juin 1993 - 225 066.

G. *Ventilation des primes non-vie :* Les assurances maritimes/aviation comprennent l'assurance fret.

ETATS-UNIS

Remarques générales : Les données sont fondées sur les informations fournies par "the National Association of Insurance Commissioners" (NAIC).

Définition des entreprises sous contrôle étranger : Depuis 1990, personne ou entité étrangère détenant directement ou indirectement par le biais d'un holding, au moins 10 pour cent du capital de la société. Le "Farmers group", bourses d'assurance détenues par des intérêts étrangers, est également considéré comme une société étrangère. Depuis 1994, une personne ou entité étrangère détenant directement ou indirectement par le biais d'un holding, au moins 50 pour cent du capital de la compagnie. Le "Farmer's Group" est également considéré comme une entité étrangère.

A. *Nombre d'entreprises dans le pays déclarant :*
a) Les entreprises dénombrées sont celles dont les rapports annuels sont enregistrés auprès de la NAIC. Il existe cependant plusieurs centaines de petites entreprises qui ne sont pas enregistrées à la NAIC. Les primes de ces compagnies sont estimées à moins de 2 pour cent du total des primes de la profession ;
b) Les chiffres concernant l'assurance-vie incluent les compagnies d'assurance-vie dont l'activité principale est l'assurance-accident et maladie. Les assureurs agréés seulement pour les accidents et la maladie sont classés parmi les entreprises d'assurance non-vie.

B.   *Nombre d'employés :* Le nombre d'employés comprend les salariés seulement. Chiffres recueillis par le "Bureau of Labour Statistics, US Department of Labour".

C.   *Opérations conclues dans le pays déclarant :*
Les primes de réassurances acceptées et cédées ne reflètent que des affaires avec des entreprises non liées. En général, aux Etats-Unis, les affaires avec des entreprises non liées représentent le marché de la réassurance, tandis que les affaires avec des entreprises liées représentent, en fait, la réassurance retenue à l'intérieur d'un groupe d'assurances pour mieux utiliser les excédents ;

E.   *Opérations conclues à l'étranger :* Les données correspondent aux ventes des filiales étrangères des compagnies américaines. Ces ventes sont égales à la somme des primes, des revenus d'investissement et d'autres revenus. Ces données sont fournies par le "Department of Commerce" des Etats-Unis.

F.   *Encours des placements des entreprises d'assurances directes :*
a) La NAIC recommande la méthode d'évaluation des actifs qui est employée dans tous les états. Les obligations sont déclarées à leur coût après amortissement ou, lorsqu'elles ne sont pas amortissables, au prix du marché. Les actions ordinaires sont comptabilisées à leur cours sur le marché. Pour les actions à droit de vote préférentiel, les assureurs-vie indiquent le coût d'acquisition et les assureurs-dommages le prix du marché. Les prêts hypothécaires figurent pour le capital restant dû. Tous les autres actifs de placement figurent à leur prix le plus bas (coût ou prix du marché) ;
b) Il faut s'attendre à ce que certains actifs soient comptabilisés deux fois.

G.   *Ventilation des primes non-vie :* Les réassurances acceptées et cédées incluent seulement les affaires non affiliées. L'assurance "Accident et maladie" inclut les activités des compagnies d'assurance-vie.

III. DEFINITIONS RELATIVES AUX BRANCHES DES ASSURANCES NON-VIE

(Les définitions sont fondées sur la classification des branches d'assurances
commune aux pays Membres de l'OCDE)

BRANCHES

DÉFINITIONS

1. AUTOMOBILE

3. CORPS DE VÉHICULES
TERRESTRES (autres que
ferroviaires)Tout dommage subi par :
-- véhicules terrestres automoteurs,
-- véhicules terrestres non automoteurs.

10. RC VÉHICULES TERRESTRES
AUTOMOTEURS
Toute responsabilité résultant de
l'emploi de véhicules terrestres
automoteurs (y compris la
responsabilité du transporteur).

2. TRANSPORTS (y compris
MARITIME ET AVIATION

4. CORPS DE VÉHICULES
FERROVIAIRES
Tout dommage subi par les véhicules
ferroviaires.

5. CORPS DE VÉHICULES AÉRIENS
Tout dommage subi par les véhicules
aériens.

6. CORPS DE VÉHICULES
MARITIMES, LACUSTRES ET
FLUVIAUX
Tout dommage subi par :
-- véhicules fluviaux,
-- véhicules lacustres,
-- véhicules maritimes.

11. RC VÉHICULES AÉRIENS
Toute responsabilité résultant de
l'emploi de véhicules aériens (y compris
la responsabilité transporteur).

3. FRET

4. INCENDIE ET DOMMAGES AUX BIENS

5. PERTES PÉCUNIAIRES

12. RC VÉHICULES MARITIMES, LACUSTRES ET FLUVIAUX
Toute responsabilité résultant de l'emploi de véhicules fluviaux, lacustres et maritimes (y compris la responsabilité du transporteur).

7. MARCHANDISES TRANSPORTÉES
(y compris les marchandises, bagages et tous autres biens)
Tout dommage subi par les marchandises transportées ou bagages, quel que soit le moyen de transport.

8. INCENDIE ET ÉLÉMENTS NATURELS
Tout dommage subi par les biens (autres que les biens compris dans les branches 3, 4, 5, 6 et 7) lorsqu'il est causé par :
-- incendie,
-- explosion,
-- tempête,
-- éléments naturels autres que la tempête,
-- énergie nucléaire,
-- affaissement de terrain.

9. AUTRES DOMMAGES AUX BIENS
Tout dommage subi par les biens (autres que les biens compris dans les branches 3, 4, 5, 6 et 7) lorsque ce dommage est causé par la grêle ou la gelée, ainsi que par tout événement, tel le vol, autre que ceux compris sous 8.

14. CRÉDIT
-- insolvabilité générale
-- crédit à l'exportation
-- vente à tempérament
-- crédit hypothécaire
-- crédit agricole

15. CAUTION
-- caution directe
-- caution indirecte

16. PERTES PÉCUNIAIRES DIVERSES
    -- risques liés à l'emploi
    -- insuffisance de recettes (générale)
    -- mauvais temps
    -- perte de bénéfices
    -- persistance de frais généraux
    -- dépenses commerciales imprévues
    -- perte de la valeur vénale
    -- pertes de loyers ou de revenus
    -- pertes commerciales indirectes autres que celles mentionnées précédemment
    -- pertes pécuniaires non commerciales
    -- autres pertes pécuniaires

6. RESPONSABILITÉ CIVILE GÉNÉRALE

13. RC GÉNÉRALE
    Toute responsabilité autre que celles mentionnées sous les numéros 10, 11 et 12.

7. ACCIDENTS ET MALADIE

1. ACCIDENTS (y compris les accidents du travail et les maladies professionnelles)
    -- prestations forfaitaires
    -- prestations indemnitaires
    -- personnes transportées

2. MALADIE
    -- prestations forfaitaires
    -- prestations indemnitaires
    -- combinaisons

8. AUTRES ASSURANCES NON-VIE

17. PROTECTION JURIDIQUE
    Protection juridique et coûts des litiges

18. ASSISTANCE

19. ASSURANCES DIVERSES

9. RÉASSURANCES OBLIGATOIRES

A. NUMBER OF COMPANIES IN THE REPORTING COUNTRY

A.1. Life
  A.1.1. Domestic Companies
    A.1.2. (Foreign Controlled Companies)
  A.1.3. Branches & Agencies of Foreign Cies
  A.1.   All Companies
A.2. Non-Life
  A.2.1. Domestic Companies
    A.2.2. (Foreign Controlled Companies)
  A.2.3. Branches & Agencies of Foreign Cies
  A.2.   All Companies
A.3. Composite
  A.3.1. Domestic Companies
    A.3.2. (Foreign Controlled Companies)
  A.3.3. Branches & Agencies of Foreign Cies
  A.3.   All Companies
A.4. Reinsurance
  A.4.1. Domestic Companies
    A.4.2. (Foreign Controlled Companies)
  A.4.3. Branches & Agencies of Foreign Cies
  A.4.   All Companies
A.5. Total
  A.5.1. Domestic Companies
    A.5.2. (Foreign Controlled Companies)
  A.5.3. Branches & Agencies of Foreign Cies
  A.5.   All Insurance Companies

B. NUMBER OF EMPLOYEES

B.1. Insurance Companies
B.2. Intermediaries
B.   Total

C. BUSINESS WRITTEN IN THE REPORTING COUNTRY

C.1. Life

C.1.1. Gross Premiums
  C.1.1.1. Direct Business
    C.1.1.1.1. Domestic Companies
      C.1.1.1.2. (Foreign Controlled Companies)
    C.1.1.1.3. Branches & Agencies of Foreign Cies
    C.1.1.1.   Total
  C.1.1.2. Reinsurance Accepted
    C.1.1.2.1. Domestic Companies
      C.1.1.2.2. (Foreign Controlled Companies)
    C.1.1.2.3. Branches & Agencies of Foreign Cies
    C.1.1.2.   Total
  C.1.1.3. Total
    C.1.1.3.1. Domestic Companies
      C.1.1.3.2. (Foreign Controlled Companies)
    C.1.1.3.3. Branches & Agencies of Foreign Cies
    C.1.1.3.   Total Gross Premiums
C.1.2. Ceded Premiums
    C.1.2.1. Domestic Companies
      C.1.2.2. (Foreign Controlled Companies)
    C.1.2.3. Branches & Agencies of Foreign Cies
    C.1.2.   Total
C.1.3. Net Written Premiums
    C.1.3.1. Domestic Companies
      C.1.3.2. (Foreign Controlled Companies)
    C.1.3.3. Branches & Agencies of Foreign Cies
    C.1.3.   Total

C.2. Non-Life

C.2.1. Gross premiums
  C.2.1.1. Direct Business
    C.2.1.1.1. Domestic Companies
      C.2.1.1.2. (Foreign Controlled Companies)
    C.2.1.1.3. Branches & Agencies of Foreign Cies
    C.2.1.1.   Total

A. NOMBRE D'ENTREPRISES DANS LE PAYS DECLARANT

A.1. Vie
  A.1.1. Entreprises nationales
    A.1.2. (Entreprises sous contrôle étranger)
  A.1.3. Succursales et agences d'ent. étrangères
  A.1.   Ensemble des entreprises
A.2. Non-vie
  A.2.1. Entreprises nationales
    A.2.2. (Entreprises sous contrôle étranger)
  A.2.3. Succursales et agences d'ent. étrangères
  A.2.   Ensemble des entreprises
A.3. Mixte
  A.3.1. Entreprises nationales
    A.3.2. (Entreprises sous contrôle étranger)
  A.3.3. Succursales et agences d'ent. étrangères
  A.3.   Ensemble des entreprises
A.4. Réassurance
  A.4.1. Entreprises nationales
    A.4.2. (Entreprises sous contrôle étranger)
  A.4.3. Succursales et agences d'ent. étrangères
  A.4.   Ensemble des entreprises
A.5. Total
  A.5.1. Entreprises nationales
    A.5.2. (Entreprises sous contrôle étranger)
  A.5.3. Succursales et agences d'ent. étrangères
  A.5.   Ensemble des entreprises d'assurances

B. NOMBRE D'EMPLOYES

B.1. Entreprises d'assurances
B.2. Intermédiaires
B.   Total

C. OPERATIONS CONCLUES DANS LE PAYS DECLARANT

C.1. Vie

C.1.1. Primes brutes
  C.1.1.1. Assurances directes
    C.1.1.1.1. Entreprises nationales
      C.1.1.1.2. (Entreprises sous contrôle étranger)
    C.1.1.1.3. Succursales et agences d'ent. étrangères
    C.1.1.1.   Total
  C.1.1.2. Réassurance acceptée
    C.1.1.2.1. Entreprises nationales
      C.1.1.2.2. (Entreprises sous contrôle étranger)
    C.1.1.2.3. Succursales et agences d'ent. étrangères
    C.1.1.2.   Total
  C.1.1.3. Total
    C.1.1.3.1. Entreprises nationales
      C.1.1.3.2. (Entreprises sous contrôle étranger)
    C.1.1.3.3. Succursales et agences d'ent. étrangères
    C.1.1.3.   Total des primes brutes
C.1.2. Primes cédées
    C.1.2.1. Entreprises nationales
      C.1.2.2. (Entreprises sous contrôle étranger)
    C.1.2.3. Succursales et agences d'ent. étrangères
    C.1.2.   Total
C.1.3. Primes nettes émises
    C.1.3.1. Entreprises nationales
      C.1.3.2. (Entreprises sous contrôle étranger)
    C.1.3.3. Succursales et agences d'ent. étrangères
    C.1.3.   Total

C.2. Non-vie

C.2.1. Primes brutes
  C.2.1.1. Assurances directes
    C.2.1.1.1. Entreprises nationales
      C.2.1.1.2. (Entreprises sous contrôle étranger)
    C.2.1.1.3. Succursales et agences d'ent. étrangères
    C.2.1.1.   Total

C.2.1.2. *Reinsurance Accepted*
  C.2.1.2.1. Domestic Companies
   C.2.1.2.2. (Foreign Controlled Companies)
  C.2.1.2.3. Branches & Agencies of Foreign Cies
  C.2.1.2. Total
 C.2.1.3. *Total*
  C.2.1.3.1. Domestic Companies
   C.2.1.3.2. (Foreign Controlled Companies)
  C.2.1.3.3. Branches & Agencies of Foreign Cies
  C.2.1.3. Total Gross Premiums
C.2.2. Ceded Premiums
  C.2.2.1. Domestic Companies
   C.2.2.2. (Foreign Controlled Companies)
  C.2.2.3. Branches & Agencies of Foreign Cies
  C.2.2. Total
C.2.3. Net Written Premiums
  C.2.3.1. Domestic Companies
   C.2.3.2. (Foreign Controlled Companies)
  C.2.3.3. Branches & Agencies of Foreign Cies
  C.2.3. Total

C.3. Total

C.3.1. Gross Premiums
 C.3.1.1. *Direct Business*
  C.3.1.1.1. Domestic Companies
   C.3.1.1.2. (Foreign Controlled Companies)
  C.3.1.1.3. Branches & Agencies of Foreign Cies
  C.3.1.1. Total
 C.3.1.2. *Reinsurance Accepted*
  C.3.1.2.1. Domestic Companies
   C.3.1.2.2. (Foreign Controlled Companies)
  C.3.1.2.3. Branches & Agencies of Foreign Cies
  C.3.1.2. Total
 C.3.1.3. *Total*
  C.3.1.3.1. Domestic Companies
   C.3.1.3.2. (Foreign Controlled Companies)
  C.3.1.3.3. Branches & Agencies of Foreign Cies
  C.3.1.3. Total Gross Premiums
C.3.2. Ceded Premiums
  C.3.2.1. Domestic Companies
   C.3.2.2. (Foreign Controlled Companies)
  C.3.2.3. Branches & Agencies of Foreign Cies
  C.3.2. Total
C.3.3. Net Written Premiums
  C.3.3.1. Domestic Companies
   C.3.3.2. (Foreign Controlled Companies)
  C.3.3.3. Branches & Agencies of Foreign Cies
  C.3.3. Total

**D. NET WRITTEN PREMIUMS IN THE REPORTING COUN-
TRY IN TERMS OF DOMESTIC AND FOREIGN RISKS**

D.1. Life

D.1.1. Domestic Risks
  D.1.1.1. Domestic Companies
   D.1.1.2. (Foreign Controlled Companies)
  D.1.1.3. Branches & Agencies of Foreign Cies
  D.1.1. Total
D.1.2. Foreign Risks
  D.1.2.1. Domestic Companies
   D.1.2.2. (Foreign Controlled Companies)
  D.1.2.3. Branches & Agencies of Foreign Cies
  D.1.2. Total
D.1.3. Total
  D.1.3.1. Domestic Companies
   D.1.3.2. (Foreign Controlled Companies)
  D.1.3.3. Branches & Agencies of Foreign Cies
  D.1.3. Total of Life Net Premiums

D.2. Non-Life

D.2.1. Domestic Risks
  D.2.1.1. Domestic Companies
   D.2.1.2. (Foreign Controlled Companies)
  D.2.1.3. Branches & Agencies of Foreign Cies
  D.2.1. Total

C.2.1.2. *Réassurance acceptée*
  C.2.1.2.1. Entreprises nationales
   C.2.1.2.2. (Entreprises sous contrôle étranger)
  C.2.1.2.3. Succursales et agences d'ent. étrangères
  C.2.1.2. Total
 C.2.1.3. *Total*
  C.2.1.3.1. Entreprises nationales
   C.2.1.3.2. (Entreprises sous contrôle étranger)
  C.2.1.3.3. Succursales et agences d'ent. étrangères
  C.2.1.3. Total des primes brutes
C.2.2. Primes cédées
  C.2.2.1. Entreprises nationales
   C.2.2.2. (Entreprises sous contrôle étranger)
  C.2.2.3. Succursales et agences d'ent. étrangères
  C.2.2. Total
C.2.3. Primes nettes émises
  C.2.3.1. Entreprises nationales
   C.2.3.2. (Entreprises sous contrôle étranger)
  C.2.3.3. Succursales et agences d'ent. étrangères
  C.2.3. Total

C.3. Total

C.3.1. Primes brutes
 C.3.1.1. *Assurances directes*
  C.3.1.1.1. Entreprises nationales
   C.3.1.1.2. (Entreprises sous contrôle étranger)
  C.3.1.1.3. Succursales et agences d'ent. étrangères
  C.3.1.1. Total
 C.3.1.2. *Réassurance acceptée*
  C.3.1.2.1. Entreprises nationales
   C.3.1.2.2. (Entreprises sous contrôle étranger)
  C.3.1.2.3. Succursales et agences d'ent. étrangères
  C.3.1.2. Total
 C.3.1.3. *Total*
  C.3.1.3.1. Entreprises nationales
   C.3.1.3.2. (Entreprises sous contrôle étranger)
  C.3.1.3.3. Succursales et agences d'ent. étrangères
  C.3.1.3. Total des primes brutes
C.3.2. Primes cédées
  C.3.2.1. Entreprises nationales
   C.3.2.2. (Entreprises sous contrôle étranger)
  C.3.2.3. Succursales et agences d'ent. étrangères
  C.3.2. Total
C.3.3. Primes nettes émises
  C.3.3.1. Entreprises nationales
   C.3.3.2. (Entreprises sous contrôle étranger)
  C.3.3.3. Succursales et agences d'ent. étrangères
  C.3.3. Total

**D. Primes nettes émises DANS LE PAYS DECLARANT :
RISQUES NATIONAUX ET ETRANGERS**

D.1. Vie

D.1.1. Risques nationaux
  D.1.1.1. Entreprises nationales
   D.1.1.2. (Entreprises sous contrôle étranger)
  D.1.1.3. Succursales et agences d'ent. étrangères
  D.1.1. Total
D.1.2. Risques étrangers
  D.1.2.1. Entreprises nationales
   D.1.2.2. (Entreprises sous contrôle étranger)
  D.1.2.3. Succursales et agences d'ent. étrangères
  D.1.2. Total
D.1.3. Total
  D.1.3.1. Entreprises nationales
   D.1.3.2. (Entreprises sous contrôle étranger)
  D.1.3.3. Succursales et agences d'ent. étrangères
  D.1.3. Total des primes nettes vie

D.2. Non-vie

D.2.1. Risques nationaux
  D.2.1.1. Entreprises nationales
   D.2.1.2. (Entreprises sous contrôle étranger)
  D.2.1.3. Succursales et agences d'ent. étrangères
  D.2.1. Total

D.2.2. Foreign Risks
    D.2.2.1. Domestic Companies
      D.2.2.2. (Foreign Controlled Companies)
    D.2.2.3. Branches & Agencies of Foreign Cies
    D.2.2.   Total
D.2.3. Total
    D.2.3.1. Domestic Companies
      D.2.3.2. (Foreign Controlled Companies)
    D.2.3.3. Branches & Agencies of Foreign Cies
    D.2.3.   Total of Non-Life Net Premiums

E. BUSINESS WRITTEN ABROAD

E.1. Life

E.1.1. Gross Premiums
    E.1.1.1. Direct Business
      E.1.1.1.1. Branches & Agencies
      E.1.1.1.2. Subsidiaries
      E.1.1.1.   Total
    E.1.1.2. Reinsurance Accepted
      E.1.1.2.1. Branches & Agencies
      E.1.1.2.2. Subsidiaries
      E.1.1.2.   Total
    E.1.1.3. Total
      E.1.1.3.1. Branches & Agencies
      E.1.1.3.2. Subsidiaries
      E.1.1.3.   Total Gross Premiums
E.1.2. Ceded Premiums
    E.1.2.1. Branches & Agencies
    E.1.2.2. Subsidiaries
    E.1.2.   Total
E.1.3. Net Written Premiums
    E.1.3.1. Branches & Agencies
    E.1.3.2. Subsidiaries
    E.1.3.   Total

E.2. Non-Life

E.2.1. Gross Premiums
    E.2.1.1. Direct Business
      E.2.1.1.1. Branches & Agencies
      E.2.1.1.2. Subsidiaries
      E.2.1.1.   Total
    E.2.1.2. Reinsurance Accepted
      E.2.1.2.1. Branches & Agencies
      E.2.1.2.2. Subsidiaries
      E.2.1.2.   Total
    E.2.1.3. Total
      E.2.1.3.1. Branches & Agencies
      E.2.1.3.2. Subsidiaries
      E.2.1.3.   Total Gross Premiums
E.2.2. Ceded Premiums
    E.2.2.1. Branches & Agencies
    E.2.2.2. Subsidiaries
    E.2.2.   Total
E.2.3. Net Written Premiums
    E.2.3.1. Branches & Agencies
    E.2.3.2. Subsidiaries
    E.2.3.   Total

F. OUTSTANDING INVESTMENT BY DIRECT INSURANCE COMPANIES

F.1. Life

F.1.1. Real Estate
    F.1.1.1. Domestic Companies
      F.1.1.2. (Foreign Controlled Companies)
    F.1.1.3. Branches & Agencies of Foreign Cies
    F.1.1.4. Domestic Investment
    F.1.1.5. Foreign Investment
    F.1.1.   Total
F.1.2. Mortgage Loans
    F.1.2.1. Domestic Companies
      F.1.2.2. (Foreign Controlled Companies)
    F.1.2.3. Branches & Agencies of Foreign Cies
    F.1.2.4. Domestic Investment
    F.1.2.5. Foreign Investment
    F.1.2.   Total

D.2.2. Risques étrangers
    D.2.2.1. Entreprises nationales
      D.2.2.2. (Entreprises sous contrôle étranger)
    D.2.2.3. Succursales et agences d'ent. étrangères
    D.2.2.   Total
D.2.3. Total
    D.2.3.1. Entreprises nationales
      D.2.3.2. (Entreprises sous contrôle étranger)
    D.2.3.3. Succursales et agences d'ent. étrangères
    D.2.3.   Total des primes nettes non-vie

E. OPERATIONS A L'ETRANGER

E.1. Vie

E.1.1. Primes brutes
    E.1.1.1. Assurance directe
      E.1.1.1.1. Succursales & agences
      E.1.1.1.2. Filiales
      E.1.1.1.   Total
    E.1.1.2. Réassurance acceptée
      E.1.1.2.1. Succursales & agences
      E.1.1.2.2. Filiales
      E.1.1.2.   Total
    E.1.1.3. Total
      E.1.1.3.1. Succursales & agences
      E.1.1.3.2. Filiales
      E.1.1.3.   Total des primes brutes
E.1.2. Primes cédées
    E.1.2.1. Succursales & agences
    E.1.2.2. Filiales
    E.1.2.   Total
E.1.3. Primes nettes émises
    E.1.3.1. Succursales & agences
    E.1.3.2. Filiales
    E.1.3.   Total

E.2. Non-vie

E.2.1. Primes brutes
    E.2.1.1. Assurance directe
      E.2.1.1.1. Succursales & agences
      E.2.1.1.2. Filiales
      E.2.1.1.   Total
    E.2.1.2. Réassurance acceptée
      E.2.1.2.1. Succursales & agences
      E.2.1.2.2. Filiales
      E.2.1.2.   Total
    E.2.1.3. Total
      E.2.1.3.1. Succursales & agences
      E.2.1.3.2. Filiales
      E.2.1.3.   Total des primes brutes
E.2.2. Primes cédées
    E.2.2.1. Succursales & agences
    E.2.2.2. Filiales
    E.2.2.   Total
E.2.3. Primes nettes émises
    E.2.3.1. Succursales & agences
    E.2.3.2. Filiales
    E.2.3.   Total

F. ENCOURS DES PLACEMENTS DES ENTREPRISES D'Assurances directes

F.1. Vie

F.1.1. Immobilier
    F.1.1.1. Entreprises nationales
      F.1.1.2. (Entreprises sous contrôle étranger)
    F.1.1.3. Succursales et agences d'ent. étrangères
    F.1.1.4. Placement dans le pays
    F.1.1.5. Placement à l'étranger
    F.1.1.   Total
F.1.2. Prêts hypothécaires
    F.1.2.1. Entreprises nationales
      F.1.2.2. (Entreprises sous contrôle étranger)
    F.1.2.3. Succursales et agences d'ent. étrangères
    F.1.2.4. Placement dans le pays
    F.1.2.5. Placement à l'étranger
    F.1.2.   Total

F.1.3. Shares
    F.1.3.1. Domestic Companies
     F.1.3.2. (Foreign Controlled Companies)
    F.1.3.3. Branches & Agencies of Foreign Cies
    F.1.3.4. Domestic Investment
    F.1.3.5. Foreign Investment
    F.1.3.   Total
F.1.4. Bonds with Fixed Revenue
    F.1.4.1. Domestic Companies
     F.1.4.2. (Foreign Controlled Companies)
    F.1.4.3. Branches & Agencies of Foreign Cies
    F.1.4.4. Domestic Investment
    F.1.4.5. Foreign Investment
    F.1.4.   Total
F.1.5. Loans other than Mortgage Loans
    F.1.5.1. Domestic Companies
     F.1.5.2. (Foreign Controlled Companies)
    F.1.5.3. Branches & Agencies of Foreign Cies
    F.1.5.4. Domestic Investment
    F.1.5.5. Foreign Investment
    F.1.5.   Total
F.1.6. Other Investments
    F.1.6.1. Domestic Companies
     F.1.6.2. (Foreign Controlled Companies)
    F.1.6.3. Branches & Agencies of Foreign Cies
    F.1.6.4. Domestic Investment
    F.1.6.5. Foreign Investment
    F.1.6.   Total
F.1.7. Total
    F.1.7.1. Domestic Companies
     F.1.7.2. (Foreign Controlled Companies)
    F.1.7.3. Branches & Agencies of Foreign Cies
    F.1.7.4. Domestic Investment
    F.1.7.5. Foreign Investment
    F.1.7.   Total of Life Investments

F.2. Non-Life

F.2.1. Real Estate
    F.2.1.1. Domestic Companies
     F.2.1.2. (Foreign Controlled Companies)
    F.2.1.3. Branches & Agencies of Foreign Cies
    F.2.1.4. Domestic Investment
    F.2.1.5. Foreign Investment
    F.2.1.   Total
F.2.2. Mortgage Loans
    F.2.2.1. Domestic Companies
     F.2.2.2. (Foreign Controlled Companies)
    F.2.2.3. Branches & Agencies of Foreign Cies
    F.2.2.4. Domestic Investment
    F.2.2.5. Foreign Investment
    F.2.2.   Total
F.2.3. Shares
    F.2.3.1. Domestic Companies
     F.2.3.2. (Foreign Controlled Companies)
    F.2.3.3. Branches & Agencies of Foreign Cies
    F.2.3.4. Domestic Investment
    F.2.3.5. Foreign Investment
    F.2.3.   Total
F.2.4. Bonds with Fixed Revenue
    F.2.4.1. Domestic Companies
     F.2.4.2. (Foreign Controlled Companies)
    F.2.4.3. Branches & Agencies of Foreign Cies
    F.2.4.4. Domestic Investment
    F.2.4.5. Foreign Investment
    F.2.4.   Total
F.2.5. Loans other than Mortgage Loans
    F.2.5.1. Domestic Companies
     F.2.5.2. (Foreign Controlled Companies)
    F.2.5.3. Branches & Agencies of Foreign Cies
    F.2.5.4. Domestic Investment
    F.2.5.5. Foreign Investment
    F.2.5.   Total
F.2.6. Other Investments
    F.2.6.1. Domestic Companies
     F.2.6.2. (Foreign Controlled Companies)
    F.2.6.3. Branches & Agencies of Foreign Cies
    F.2.6.4. Domestic Investment
    F.2.6.5. Foreign Investment
    F.2.6.   Total

F.1.3. Actions
    F.1.3.1. Entreprises nationales
     F.1.3.2. (Entreprises sous contrôle étranger)
    F.1.3.3. Succursales et agences d'ent. étrangères
    F.1.3.4. Placement dans le pays
    F.1.3.5. Placement à l'étranger
    F.1.3.   Total
F.1.4. Obligations
    F.1.4.1. Entreprises nationales
     F.1.4.2. (Entreprises sous contrôle étranger)
    F.1.4.3. Succursales et agences d'ent. étrangères
    F.1.4.4. Placement dans le pays
    F.1.4.5. Placement à l'étranger
    F.1.4.   Total
F.1.5. Prêts autres qu'hypothécaires
    F.1.5.1. Entreprises nationales
     F.1.5.2. (Entreprises sous contrôle étranger)
    F.1.5.3. Succursales et agences d'ent. étrangères
    F.1.5.4. Placement dans le pays
    F.1.5.5. Placement à l'étranger
    F.1.5.   Total
F.1.6. Autres Placements
    F.1.6.1. Entreprises nationales
     F.1.6.2. (Entreprises sous contrôle étranger)
    F.1.6.3. Succursales et agences d'ent. étrangères
    F.1.6.4. Placement dans le pays
    F.1.6.5. Placement à l'étranger
    F.1.6.   Total
F.1.7. Total
    F.1.7.1. Entreprises nationales
     F.1.7.2. (Entreprises sous contrôle étranger)
    F.1.7.3. Succursales et agences d'ent. étrangères
    F.1.7.4. Placement dans le pays
    F.1.7.5. Placement à l'étranger
    F.1.7.   Total des placements vie

F.2. Non-vie

F.2.1. Immobilier
    F.2.1.1. Entreprises nationales
     F.2.1.2. (Entreprises sous contrôle étranger)
    F.2.1.3. Succursales et agences d'ent. étrangères
    F.2.1.4. Placement dans le pays
    F.2.1.5. Placement à l'étranger
    F.2.1.   Total
F.2.2. Prêts hypothécaires
    F.2.2.1. Entreprises nationales
     F.2.2.2. (Entreprises sous contrôle étranger)
    F.2.2.3. Succursales et agences d'ent. étrangères
    F.2.2.4. Placement dans le pays
    F.2.2.5. Placement à l'étranger
    F.2.2.   Total
F.2.3. Actions
    F.2.3.1. Entreprises nationales
     F.2.3.2. (Entreprises sous contrôle étranger)
    F.2.3.3. Succursales et agences d'ent. étrangères
    F.2.3.4. Placement dans le pays
    F.2.3.5. Placement à l'étranger
    F.2.3.   Total
F.2.4. Obligations
    F.2.4.1. Entreprises nationales
     F.2.4.2. (Entreprises sous contrôle étranger)
    F.2.4.3. Succursales et agences d'ent. étrangères
    F.2.4.4. Placement dans le pays
    F.2.4.5. Placement à l'étranger
    F.2.4.   Total
F.2.5. Prêts Autres qu'hypothécaires
    F.2.5.1. Entreprises nationales
     F.2.5.2. (Entreprises sous contrôle étranger)
    F.2.5.3. Succursales et agences d'ent. étrangères
    F.2.5.4. Placement dans le pays
    F.2.5.5. Placement à l'étranger
    F.2.5.   Total
F.2.6. Autres Placements
    F.2.6.1. Entreprises nationales
     F.2.6.2. (Entreprises sous contrôle étranger)
    F.2.6.3. Succursales et agences d'ent. étrangères
    F.2.6.4. Placement dans le pays
    F.2.6.5. Placement à l'étranger
    F.2.6.   Total

F.2.7. Total	F.2.7. Total
F.2.7.1. Domestic Companies	F.2.7.1. Entreprises nationales
F.2.7.2. (Foreign Controlled Companies)	F.2.7.2. (Entreprises sous contrôle étranger)
F.2.7.3. Branches & Agencies of Foreign Cies	F.2.7.3. Succursales et agences d'ent. étrangères
F.2.7.4. Domestic Investment	F.2.7.4. Placement dans le pays
F.2.7.5. Foreign Investment	F.2.7.5. Placement à l'étranger
F.2.7. Total of Non-Life Investments	F.2.7. Total des placements non-vie

G. BREAKDOWN OF NON-LIFE PREMIUMS   **G. VENTILATIONS DES PRIMES Non-vie**

G.1. Motor vehicle	G.1. Assurance automobile
G.1.1. Direct Business	G.1.1. Assurances directes
G.1.1.1. Gross Premiums	G.1.1.1. Primes brutes
G.1.1.2. Ceded Premiums	G.1.1.2. Primes cédées
G.1.1.3. Net Written Premiums	G.1.1.3. Primes nettes émises
G.1.2. Reinsurance Accepted	G.1.2. Réassurance acceptée
G.1.2.1. Gross Premiums	G.1.2.1. Primes brutes
G.1.2.2. Ceded Premiums	G.1.2.2. Primes cédées
G.1.2.3. Net Written Premiums	G.1.2.3. Primes nettes émises
G.1.3. Total	G.1.3. Total
G.1.3.1. Gross Premiums	G.1.3.1. Primes brutes
G.1.3.2. Ceded Premiums	G.1.3.2. Primes cédées
G.1.3.3. Net Written Premiums	G.1.3.3. Primes nettes émises
G.2. Marine, Aviation	G.2. Marine, aviation
G.2.1. Direct Business	G.2.1. Assurances directes
G.2.1.1. Gross Premiums	G.2.1.1. Primes brutes
G.2.1.2. Ceded Premiums	G.2.1.2. Primes cédées
G.2.1.3. Net Written Premiums	G.2.1.3. Primes nettes émises
G.2.2. Reinsurance Accepted	G.2.2. Réassurance acceptée
G.2.2.1. Gross Premiums	G.2.2.1. Primes brutes
G.2.2.2. Ceded Premiums	G.2.2.2. Primes cédées
G.2.2.3. Net Written Premiums	G.2.2.3. Primes nettes émises
G.2.3. Total	G.2.3. Total
G.2.3.1. Gross Premiums	G.2.3.1. Primes brutes
G.2.3.2. Ceded Premiums	G.2.3.2. Primes cédées
G.2.3.3. Net Written Premiums	G.2.3.3. Primes nettes émises
G.3. Freight	G.3. Fret
G.3.1. Direct Business	G.3.1. Assurances directes
G.3.1.1. Gross Premiums	G.3.1.1. Primes brutes
G.3.1.2. Ceded Premiums	G.3.1.2. Primes cédées
G.3.1.3. Net Written Premiums	G.3.1.3. Primes nettes émises
G.3.2. Reinsurance Accepted	G.3.2. Réassurance acceptée
G.3.2.1. Gross Premiums	G.3.2.1. Primes brutes
G.3.2.2. Ceded Premiums	G.3.2.2. Primes cédées
G.3.2.3. Net Written Premiums	G.3.2.3. Primes nettes émises
G.3.3. Total	G.3.3. Total
G.3.3.1. Gross Premiums	G.3.3.1. Primes brutes
G.3.3.2. Ceded Premiums	G.3.3.2. Primes cédées
G.3.3.3. Net Written Premiums	G.3.3.3. Primes nettes émises
G.4. Fire, Property Damages	G.4. Incendie, dommages aux biens
G.4.1. Direct Business	G.4.1. Assurances directes
G.4.1.1. Gross Premiums	G.4.1.1. Primes brutes
G.4.1.2. Ceded Premiums	G.4.1.2. Primes cédées
G.4.1.3. Net Written Premiums	G.4.1.3. Primes nettes émises
G.4.2. Reinsurance Accepted	G.4.2. Réassurance acceptée
G.4.2.1. Gross Premiums	G.4.2.1. Primes brutes
G.4.2.2. Ceded Premiums	G.4.2.2. Primes cédées
G.4.2.3. Net Written Premiums	G.4.2.3. Primes nettes émises
G.4.3. Total	G.4.3. Total
G.4.3.1. Gross Premiums	G.4.3.1. Primes brutes
G.4.3.2. Ceded Premiums	G.4.3.2. Primes cédées
G.4.3.3. Net Written Premiums	G.4.3.3. Primes nettes émises
G.5. Pecuniary Losses	G.5. Pertes pécunières
G.5.1. Direct Business	G.5.1. Assurances directes
G.5.1.1. Gross Premiums	G.5.1.1. Primes brutes
G.5.1.2. Ceded Premiums	G.5.1.2. Primes cédées
G.5.1.3. Net Written Premiums	G.5.1.3. Primes nettes émises
G.5.2. Reinsurance Accepted	G.5.2. Réassurance acceptée
G.5.2.1. Gross Premiums	G.5.2.1. Primes brutes
G.5.2.2. Ceded Premiums	G.5.2.2. Primes cédées
G.5.2.3. Net Written Premiums	G.5.2.3. Primes nettes émises
G.5.3.1. Gross Premiums	G.5.3.1. Primes brutes
G.5.3.2. Ceded Premiums	G.5.3.2. Primes cédées
G.5.3.3. Net Written Premiums	G.5.3.3. Primes nettes émises
G.6. General Liability	G.6. Responsabilité générale
G.6.1. Direct Business	G.6.1. Assurances directes
G.6.1.1. Gross Premiums	G.6.1.1. Primes brutes
G.6.1.2. Ceded Premiums	G.6.1.2. Primes cédées
G.6.1.3. Net Written Premiums	G.6.1.3. Primes nettes émises

G.6.2. Reinsurance Accepted
    G.6.2.1. Gross Premiums
    G.6.2.2. Ceded Premiums
    G.6.2.3. Net Written Premiums
G.6.3. Total
    G.6.3.1. Gross Premiums
    G.6.3.2. Ceded Premiums
    G.6.3.3. Net Written Premiums

G.7. Accident, Health
G.7.1. Direct Business
    G.7.1.1. Gross Premiums
    G.7.1.2. Ceded Premiums
    G.7.1.3. Net Written Premiums
G.7.2. Reinsurance Accepted
    G.7.2.1. Gross Premiums
    G.7.2.2. Ceded Premiums
    G.7.2.3. Net Written Premiums
G.7.3. Total
    G.7.3.1. Gross Premiums
    G.7.3.2. Ceded Premiums
    G.7.3.3. Net Written Premiums

G.8. Others
G.8.1. Direct Business
    G.8.1.1. Gross Premiums
    G.8.1.2. Ceded Premiums
    G.8.1.3. Net Written Premiums
G.8.2. Reinsurance Accepted
    G.8.2.1. Gross Premiums
    G.8.2.2. Ceded Premiums
    G.8.2.3. Net Written Premiums
G.8.3. Total
    G.8.3.1. Gross Premiums
    G.8.3.2. Ceded Premiums
    G.8.3.3. Net Written Premiums

G.9. Treaty Reinsurance
G.9.1. Direct Business
    G.9.1.1. Gross Premiums
    G.9.1.2. Ceded Premiums
    G.9.1.3. Net Written Premiums
G.9.2. Reinsurance Accepted
    G.9.2.1. Gross Premiums
    G.9.2.2. Ceded Premiums
    G.9.2.3. Net Written Premiums
G.9.3. Total
    G.9.3.1. Gross Premiums
    G.9.3.2. Ceded Premiums
    G.9.3.3. Net Written Premiums

G.10. Total
G.10.1. Direct Business
    G.10.1.1. Gross Premiums
    G.10.1.2. Ceded Premiums
    G.10.1.3. Net Written Premiums
G.10.2. Reinsurance Accepted
    G.10.2.1. Gross Premiums
    G.10.2.2. Ceded Premiums
    G.10.2.3. Net Written Premiums
G.10.3. Total
    G.10.3.1. Gross Premiums
    G.10.3.2. Ceded Premiums
    G.10.3.3. Net Written Premiums

H.GROSS CLAIMS PAYMENTS

H.1. Life
    H.1.1. Domestic Companies
    H.1.2. (Foreign Controlled Companies)
    H.1.3. Branches & Agencies of Foreign Cies
    H.1.   Total
H.2. Non-Life
    H.2.1. Domestic Companies
    H.2.2. (Foreign Controlled Companies)
    H.2.3. Branches & Agencies Cies
    H.2.   Total

G.6.2. Réassurance acceptée
    G.6.2.1. Primes brutes
    G.6.2.2. Primes cédées
    G.6.2.3. Primes nettes émises
G.6.3. Total
    G.6.3.1. Primes brutes
    G.6.3.2. Primes cédées
    G.6.3.3. Primes nettes émises

G.7. Accident, santé
G.7.1. Assurances directes
    G.7.1.1. Primes brutes
    G.7.1.2. Primes cédées
    G.7.1.3. Primes nettes émises
G.7.2. Réassurance acceptée
    G.7.2.1. Primes brutes
    G.7.2.2. Primes cédées
    G.7.2.3. Primes nettes émises
G.7.3. Total
    G.7.3.1. Primes brutes
    G.7.3.2. Primes cédées
    G.7.3.3. Primes nettes émises

G.8. Autres
G.8.1. Assurances directes
    G.8.1.1. Primes brutes
    G.8.1.2. Primes cédées
    G.8.1.3. Primes nettes émises
G.8.2. Réassurance acceptée
    G.8.2.1. Primes brutes
    G.8.2.2. Primes cédées
    G.8.2.3. Primes nettes émises
G.8.3. Total
    G.8.3.1. Primes brutes
    G.8.3.2. Primes cédées
    G.8.3.3. Primes nettes émises

G.9. Réassurance obligatoire
G.9.1. Assurances directes
    G.9.1.1. Primes brutes
    G.9.1.2. Primes cédées
    G.9.1.3. Primes nettes émises
G.9.2. Réassurance acceptée
    G.9.2.1. Primes brutes
    G.9.2.2. Primes cédées
    G.9.2.3. Primes nettes émises
G.9.3. Total
    G.9.3.1. Primes brutes
    G.9.3.2. Primes cédées
    G.9.3.3. Primes nettes émises

G.10. Total
G.10.1. Assurances directes
    G.10.1.1. Primes brutes
    G.10.1.2. Primes cédées
    G.10.1.3. Primes nettes émises
G.10.2. Réassurance acceptée
    G.10.2.1. Primes brutes
    G.10.2.2. Primes cédées
    G.10.2.3. Primes nettes émises
G.10.3. Total
    G.10.3.1. Primes brutes
    G.10.3.2. Primes cédées
    G.10.3.3. Primes nettes émises

H. SINISTRES BRUTS

H.1. Vie
    H.1.1. Entreprises nationales
    H.1.2. (Entreprises sous contrôle étranger)
    H.1.3. Succursales et agences d'ent. étrangère
    H.1.   Total
H.2. Non-vie
    H.2.1. Entreprises nationales
    H.2.2. (Entreprises sous contrôle étranger)
    H.2.3. Succursales et agences d'ent. étrangère
    H.2.   Total

I. GROSS OPERATING EXPENSES	I. DEPENSES BRUTES
I.1. Life	**I.1. Vie**
I.1.1. Domestic Companies	I.1.1. Entreprises nationales
I.1.2. (Foreign Controlled Companies)	I.1.2. (Entreprises sous contrôle étranger)
I.1.3. Branches & Agencies of Foreign Cies	I.1.3. Succursales et agences d'ent. étrangère
I.1. Total	I.1. Total
I.2. Non-Life	**I.2. Non-vie**
I.2.1. Domestic Companies	I.2.1. Entreprises nationales
I.2.2. (Foreign Controlled Companies)	I.2.2. (Entreprises sous contrôle étranger)
I.2.3. Branches & Agencies of Foreign Cies	I.2.3. Succursales et agences d'ent. étrangère
I.2. Total	I.2. Total
J. COMMISSIONS	**J. COMMISSIONS**
J.1. Life	**J.1. Vie**
J.1.1. Direct Business	J.1.1. Assurance directe
J.1.1.1. Domestic Companies	J.1.1.1. Entreprises nationales
J.1.1.2. (Foreign Controlled Companies)	J.1.1.2. (Entreprises sous contrôle étranger)
J.1.1.3. Branches & Agencies of Foreign Cies	J.1.1.3. Succursales et agences d'ent. étrangère
J.1.1. Total	J.1.1. Total
J.1.2. Reinsurance Accepted	J.1.2. Réassurances acceptées
J.1.2.1. Domestic Companies	J.1.2.1. Entreprises nationales
J.1.2.2. (Foreign Controlled Companies)	J.1.2.2. (Entreprises sous contrôle étranger)
J.1.2.3. Branches & Agencies of Foreign Cies	J.1.2.3. Succursales et agences d'ent. étrangère
J.1.2. Total	J.1.2. Total
J.1.3. Total	J.1.3. Total
J.1.3.1. Domestic Companies	J.1.3.1. Entreprises nationales
J.1.3.2. (Foreign Controlled Companies)	J.1.3.2. (Entreprises sous contrôle étranger)
J.1.3.3. Branches & Agencies of Foreign Cies	J.1.3.3. Succursales et agences d'ent. étrangère
J.1.3. Total	J.1.3. Total
J.2. Non-Life	**J.2. Non-Life**
J.2.1. Direct Business	J.2.1. Assurance directe
J.2.1.1. Domestic Companies	J.2.1.1. Entreprises nationales
J.2.1.2. (Foreign Controlled Companies)	J.2.1.2. (Entreprises sous contrôle étranger)
J.2.1.3. Branches & Agencies of Foreign Cies	J.2.1.3. Succursales et agences d'ent. étrangère
J.2.1. Total	J.2.1. Total
J.2.2. Reinsurance Accepted	J.2.2. Réassurances acceptées
J.2.2.1. Domestic Companies	J.2.2.1. Entreprises nationales
J.2.2.2. (Foreign Controlled Companies)	J.2.2.2. (Entreprises sous contrôle étranger)
J.2.2.3. Branches & Agencies of Foreign Cies	J.2.2.3. Succursales et agences d'ent. étrangère
J.2.2. Total	J.2.2. Total
J.2.3. Total	J.2.3. Total
J.2.3.1. Domestic Companies	J.2.3.1. Entreprises nationales
J.2.3.2. (Foreign Controlled Companies)	J.2.3.2. (Entreprises sous contrôle étranger)
J.2.3.3. Branches & Agencies of Foreign Cies	J.2.3.3. Succursales et agences d'ent. étrangère
J.2.3. Total	J.2.3. Total

V. BUSINESS WRITTEN ABROAD BY EU/EEA INSURERS THROUGH BRANCHES AND AGENCIES
V. OPERATIONS DES ASSUREURS DE L'UE/EEE A L'ETRANGER PAR DES AGENCES ET SUCCURSALES

LIFE INSURANCE / ASSURANCE VIE (1997)

Direct Gross Premiums / Primes brutes directes

Monetary Unit = million of the local currency of each home country / Unité monétaire: en millions de monnaie nationale

HOME COUNTRY / PAYS D'ORIGINE → HOST COUNTRY / PAYS D'ACCUEIL ↓	Austria / Autriche (S)	Belgium / Belgique (BFr)	Denmark / Danemark (DKr)	Finland / Finlande (Fmk)	France / France (FF)	Germany / Allemagne (DM)	Greece / Grèce (Dr)	Iceland / Islande (ISK)	Ireland / Irlande (£)	Italy / Italie (Lit)	Luxembourg / Luxembourg (LuxF)	Netherlands / Pays-Bas (Fl)	Norway / Norvège (NKr)	Portugal / Portugal[1] (Esc)	Spain / Espagne (Ptas)	Sweden / Suède (SKr)	United Kingdom / Royaume-Uni (£)
Austria / Autriche																	..
Belgium / Belgique					3	8	..		..			..					..
Denmark / Danemark																	..
Finland / Finlande							..		..			..					..
France / France		64							0.1					101			..
Germany / Allemagne		2 069												6			..
Greece / Grèce		111					..		..			..					..
Iceland / Islande																	
Ireland / Irlande		1					..		..			..					..
Italy / Italie					254		..		3.5			..		522			..
Luxembourg / Luxembourg		470			22	1	..		..			..					..
Netherlands / Pays-Bas					8												..
Norway / Norvège							..		..			..					..
Portugal / Portugal					83										41 013	27	..
Spain / Espagne										163 200				363			..
Sweden / Suède																	..
United Kingdom / Royaume-Uni							..		6.6	140 200		..				1	..
EU 15 + EEA Total / Total de l'UE 15 + EEE (1)	0	2 715	0	0	370	10	..	0	10.2	303 400	0	0	0	99	41 013	29	..
Total Other OECD countries / Total autres pays OCDE	1	..	..	..	..	..		..	..		..	..	..	0	..	..	..
Total Outside OECD countries / Total des pays hors de l'OCDE	0	..	..	..	..	..		..	..	25 900	..	..	..	0	475	..	..
TOTAL	1	2 715	0	0	445	10	..	0	10.2	329 300	0	0	0	99	41 488	29	..

[1] Total gross premiums / Primes brutes totales

NON-LIFE INSURANCE / ASSURANCE NON-VIE (1997)

Direct Gross Premiums / Primes brutes directes

Monetary Unit = million of the local currency of each home country / Unité monétaire: en millions de monnaie nationale

HOST COUNTRY / PAYS D'ACCUEIL \ PAYS D'ORIGINE / HOME COUNTRY	Austria / Autriche (S)	Belgium / Belgique (BFr)	Denmark / Danemark (DKr)	Finland / Finlande (Fmk)	France / France (FF)	Germany / Allemagne (DM)	Greece / Grèce (Dr)	Iceland / Islande (ISK)	Ireland / Irlande (£)	Italy / Italie (Lit)	Luxembourg / Luxembourg (LuxF)	Netherlands / Pays-Bas (Fl)	Norway / Norvège (NKr)	Portugal / Portugal (Esc)	Spain / Espagne (Ptas)	Sweden / Suède (SKr)	United Kingdom / Royaume-Uni (£)
Austria / Autriche		86			11	75	..				24	..					..
Belgium / Belgique					567	111	..		2.0	13 000	19	..			16	279	..
Denmark / Danemark		933			89	14	..			2 200	30	..	359				..
Finland / Finlande		63			35	1	..				1	..				1	..
France / France		10 827	2	- 2		225	..			10 600	255	..		440		80	..
Germany / Allemagne		3 989	3	3	845		..		0.3	23 400	1 452	..		917		140	..
Greece / Grèce		34			19	25					774	..		3 241			..
Iceland / Islande							..					..					..
Ireland / Irlande		1 147				5	..				34	..			54		..
Italy / Italie		3 019			577	78	..				16	..					..
Luxembourg / Luxembourg		863			23	2	..					..		9			..
Netherlands / Pays-Bas		3 796			57	127	..		3.4	6 700	278			113		47	..
Norway / Norvège		209	13		45	8	..				11	..				277	..
Portugal / Portugal		12			58	5	..			82 000	48	..			11 777		..
Spain / Espagne		1 531			263	49	..			329 300	1	..		1 498			..
Sweden / Suède		1 119	55	12	93	13	..				4	..	130				..
United Kingdom / Royaume-Uni		21 389	4		1 897	415	..		122.4	328 400	298	..		84	618	161	
EU 15 + EEA Total / Total de l'UE 15 + EEE (1)	0	49 017	75	13	4 579	1 150	..	..	128.1	831 700	3 245	..	489	6 302	12 465	984	..
Total Other OECD countries / Total autres pays OCDE	1	319	10	..		217	..	..	..	300 400	7 368	..	7	0	125	..	..
Total Outside OECD countries / Total des pays hors de l'OCDE	0	2	..	..		0	..	..	..	80 300	0	..	0	0	2 050	..	..
TOTAL	1	49 338	85	..	5 880	1 367	..	0	128.1	1 212 400	10 613	..	496	6 302	14 640	..	..

[1] Total gross premiums / Primes brutes totales

Did you Know?

This publication is available in electronic form

Many OECD publications and data sets are now available in electronic form to suit your needs at affordable prices.

For our statistical publications we use powerful software platforms (Ivation's Beyond 20/20 or STATWISE) that allow you to get the maximum value from the data. Other publications are available using the simple Acrobat/PDF presentation. **Delivery platforms** range from magnetic tape through CD-Rom and diskettes to online via internet. **Stand alone and network** versions are offered for many titles.

For more information about electronic editions of this publication, or to ask for a catalogue of all our electronic publications, contact your nearest OECD Centre (see overleaf).

Le saviez-vous ?

La version électronique de cette publication est disponible !

Désormais, afin de mieux répondre à vos besoins, un grand nombre de publications et de données de l'OCDE sont disponibles sous forme électronique à des prix très abordables.

Nos études statistiques sont présentées sur des logiciels puissants (Beyond 20/20 ou Statwise) permettant d'optimiser les données au maximum. Certaines publications sont également disponibles sur Acrobat/PDF.

Par ailleurs, **un éventail très large de supports** vous est proposé : bande magnétique, Cédérom, disquette et interrogation en ligne via Internet. De nombreux titres sont également proposés en **versions monoposte et réseau.**

Pour de plus amples informations sur les versions électroniques de cette publication ou pour obtenir le catalogue de nos éditions électroniques, n'hésitez pas à contacter le Centre OCDE le plus proche (voir verso).

OECD-OCDE

A POTENT INSTRUMENT OF GLOBAL CHANGE

UN INSTRUMENT PUISSANT DE CHANGEMENT ET DE REFORME DANS LE MONDE

Where to send your request:

Où envoyer votre demande:

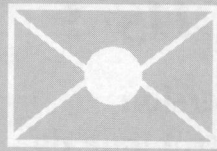

In Austria, Germany and Switzerland / En Allemagne, en Autriche et en Suisse

OECD CENTRE BONN / CENTRE OCDE DE BONN
August-Bebel-Allee 6,
D-53175 Bonn
Tel.: (49-228) 959 1215
Fax: (49-228) 959 1218
E-mail: bonn.contact@oecd.org
Internet: www.oecd.org/bonn

In Latin America / En Amérique latine

OECD CENTRE MEXICO / CENTRE OCDE DE MEXICO
Edificio INFOTEC
Av. San Fernando No. 37
Col. Toriello Guerra
Tlalpan C.P. 14050,
Mexico D.F.
Tel.: (525) 528 10 38
Fax: (525) 606 13 07
E-mail: mexico.contact@oecd.org
Internet: rtn.net.mx/ocde/

In the United States / Aux États-Unis

OECD CENTER WASHINGTON / CENTRE OCDE DE WASHINGTON
2001 L Street N.W., Suite 650
Washington, DC 20036-4922
Tel.: (202) 785 6323
Toll free / Numéro vert : (800) 456-6323
Fax: (202) 785 0350
E-mail: washington.contact@oecd.org
Internet: www.oecdwash.org

In Asia / En Asie

OECD CENTRE TOKYO / CENTRE OCDE DE TOKYO
Landic Akasaka Bldg.
2-3-4 Akasaka, Minato-ku,
Tokyo 107-0052
Tel.: (81-3) 3586 2016
Fax: (81-3) 3584 7929
E-mail : center@oecdtokyo.org
Internet: www.oecdtokyo.org

In the rest of the world / Dans le reste du monde
OECD PARIS CENTRE / CENTRE OCDE DE PARIS
2 rue André-Pascal, 75775 Paris Cedex 16, France
Orders / Commandes : Fax: 33 (0)1 49 10 42 76

Enquiries / Renseignements : Tel: 33 (0)1 45 24 81 22 Fax: 33 (0) 1 45 24 19 50
E-mail : sales@oecd.org

Online Ordering: www.oecd.org/publications *(secure payment with credit card)*
Commande en ligne : www.oecd.org/publications *(paiement sécurisé par carte de crédit)*

OECD Main Switchboard / Standard OCDE : 33 (0) 1 45 24 82 00

Internet: www.oecd.org

LES ÉDITIONS DE L'OCDE, 2, rue André-Pascal, 75775 PARIS CEDEX 16
IMPRIMÉ EN FRANCE
(21 1999 05 3 P) ISBN 92-64-05858-3 – n° 50666 1999